W9-BND-094

BREWER STATE JR. COLLEGE
LIBRARY
TUSCALOOSA CAMPUS

DISCARDED

BR
515
.R435 Religion in American
history

DATE			
JUL 31 '79			
OCT 24 '80			
FEB 27 '83			
JUL 15 1987			
JUL 16 '91			
JUN 05 '92			
NOV 02 1999			

© THE BAKER & TAYLOR CO.

RELIGION
IN
AMERICAN HISTORY

3541

RELIGION IN AMERICAN HISTORY

Interpretive Essays

JOHN M. MULDER
Princeton Theological Seminary

JOHN F. WILSON
Princeton University

EDITORS

PRENTICE-HALL, INC., *Englewood Cliffs, New Jersey 07632*

Library of Congress Cataloging in Publication Data

Main entry under title:

Religion in American history.

    Bibliography: p.
    1. United States—Religion—Addresses, essays,
lectures. I. Mulder, John M., (date). II. Wilson,
John Frederick.
BR515.R435   200'.973   77-2883
ISBN 0-13-771998-1
ISBN 0-13-771980-9 pbk.

© 1978 by Prentice-Hall, Inc.
Englewood Cliffs, N.J. 07632

All rights reserved. No part of this book
may be reproduced in any form
or by any means
without permission in writing
from the publisher.

Printed in the United States of America

10 9 8 7 6 5 4 3 2

Prentice-Hall International, Inc., *London*
Prentice-Hall of Australia Pty. Limited, *Sydney*
Prentice-Hall of Canada, Ltd., *Toronto*
Prentice-Hall of India Private Limited, *New Delhi*
Prentice-Hall of Japan, Inc., *Tokyo*
Prentice-Hall of Southeast Asia Pte. Ltd., *Singapore*
Whitehall Books Limited, *Wellington, New Zealand*

Contents

16

17

18

19

20

21

22

23

24

25

Introduction

In 1964, Henry F. May proposed to his fellow historians in the *American Historical Review* that "for the study and understanding of American culture, the recovery of American religious history may well be the most important achievement of the last thirty years."[1] This volume of interpretive essays is testimony to the recovery of America's religious past that May heralded and to the continued flourishing of the study of American religious history that has proceeded unabated throughout the intervening period. Often ignored and even ridiculed in the 1920s as an important subject for intellectual inquiry, religious subjects were revived initially by secular historians in the 1930s and were made an integral part of American historical scholarship. Among the pioneers were Herbert Schneider, Ralph Henry Gabriel, Arthur M. Schlesinger, Sr., and above all, Perry Miller, whose studies of Puritanism delineated its vital characteristics and explored its tenacious influence on American thought and culture. As the articles reproduced in this volume make clear, the study of American religious history continues to be enriched by secular historians, although historians who specialize in religious topics have made substantial contributions to the "renaissance" of interest in this subject.

Scholarly interest in American religion has contributed both directly and indirectly to the development of religion departments in academic settings. Once found almost exclusively in church-related colleges, they are now commonplace in state colleges and universities, as well as in most private institutions. Nevertheless, the study of Amerian religious history has not become the exclusive domain of professional students of religion, and

[1]Henry F. May, "The Recovery of American Religious History," *American Historical Review*, LXX (1964), pp. 79-92.

the enterprise continues to be invigorated by the insights of many other disciplines. The essays which follow demonstrate how the historical understanding of American religion has been broadened by work in psychology, sociology, anthropology, political science, literary criticism, and other fields.

Perhaps most significant, historians have recently begun to interpret religion as a part of the larger history of American life and culture. William A. Clebsch has gone so far as to identify this as a new synthesis of American religious history.[2] Although it was once studied as the story of different denominations or different faiths in different regions, historians now treat American religion as a whole. While distinctions between groups remain, and changes over time are critical, what emerges from many of the recent studies is perception of the similarities in religious life that transcend traditional denominational or ecclesiastical divisions.

This synthetic approach to American religious history has characterized a number of narrative histories published in the last two decades. The most comprehensive and inclusive of these works has been Sydney E. Ahlstrom's prize-winning *A Religious History of the American People* (1972), a superb chronicling of the variety of American religion from the earliest Spanish settlements to the 1960s. Ahlstrom's volume is one of several recent attempts to provide a synoptic treatment of American religion. These include Clifton E. Olmstead, *History of Religion in the United States* (1960); Winthrop S. Hudson, *Relgion in America* (1965, 1973); and Edwin S. Gaustad, *A Religious History of America* (1966). Other secondary resources are listed in the back of this volume.

The essays in this book do not pose a single interpretation, but by design they are characterized by their varying points of view. Neither are they intended to be, in some abstract sense, "the best" pieces which have appeared on broadly religious subjects in American history in the course of the last several decades. Some articles have been excluded which have been highly influential; others have been included which may seem to be problematic. Thus the Contents listing should not be thought of as an honor roll of shorter publications in the field in recent years. Rather, the selections in this volume are intended as a set especially useful in conjunction with interpretive study of American religious history and in the context of a course of lectures.

The selection of articles for this book has proceeded in terms of two goals.

First, the attempt to identify shorter studies concerned with central aspects of religion in the three-and-one-half centuries since the colonization of the east coast of North America. This settlement laid the basis for the development of the United States as a new nation which, although derived from European sources, was from the outset stubbornly independent in self-understanding and in patterns of behavior.

[2]William A. Clebsch, "A New Historiography of American Religion," *Historical Magazine of the Protestant Episcopal Church,* XXXII (1963), pp. 226-57.

Second, the concern to make readily available a set of readings which would introduce students to vital and inherently interesting topics in the interpretation of religion in American history.

If this reader is intended to be a supplement to existing narrative studies, it is also developed in relationship to collections of primary materials, which are available in comparatively great number and variety. Several of these collections are listed in the bibliography at the back of this volume. What has not been available for use within general courses, in the experience of the editors, is the kind of material to which Henry May called attention—the studies of specific periods and problems which have explored, often imaginatively, particular religious subjects in the American past.

The selection of essays is made, self-consciously, with the serious survey course in mind. In the context of such an offering the range of articles should provide ample materials for discussions and also provide help with research papers. In different combinations the selections should foster intensive discussion of particular issues and suggest historical orientations toward primary traits of the American culture and character. In addition, many of the articles provide links to the study of American history, literature, and politics.

Each selection is introduced by a headnote to facilitate its use. Editing has been held to a minimum given constraints of space and, insofar as possible, notes have been retained as a means of rendering the volume a starting point for research projects or as a guide to supplementary reading.

JOHN M. MULDER
JOHN F. WILSON

RELIGION
IN
AMERICAN HISTORY

1

Understanding the Puritans

David D. Hall

In recent decades, wide-ranging scholarly discussions have been concerned with the question: Does seventeenth century Puritanism define American experience from the outset? In turn, that question raises the issue of how Puritanism is to be understood. Professor David D. Hall of the Department of History at Boston University offers a thoughtful and suggestive review of the nature of Puritanism in the article printed here.

"How does one define Puritanism?" This question, the first sentence of Alan Simpson's *Puritanism in Old and New England,* is one to which the answers in recent years have grown increasingly complex and contradictory.[1] Thirty years ago there was no doubt about the answer; the scholarship of Morison and Haller, and, towering over both, the massive symmetry of Perry Miller's *The New England Mind,* gave compelling definition to the subject.[2] But climates of opinion change, and with them the historian's angle of perception. What Perry Miller had to say now has the ring of the 1930's, for the period in which he wrote saw the old myth that the Puritan hated life still strong upon us. If Miller's great achievement was to free us from that myth, the question remains as to the proper understanding of Puritanism. To describe the differences of opinion between Miller and his critics is one purpose of this essay.[3] But its deeper task is to identify the problems that every student of the Puritans must inevitably confront, the problems of in-

First published in Herbert J. Bass, ed., *The State of American History* (Chicago: Quadrangle), pp. 330-349 (notes abridged). Copyright © 1970 by David D. Hall.

1

terpretation and methodology that always seem to turn up in dealing with this subject.[4]

Abraham Lincoln once said that slavery was "somehow" the cause of the Civil War. Historians of Puritanism know likewise that the history of the movement was somehow related to the contemporary culture and social structure. Puritanism had social sources and social consequences; were historians to define precisely which groups supported (and dissented from) the Puritan program, as well as the movement's consequences for the broader culture, they would move closer to an understanding of its nature. One of their tasks, then, is to determine how Puritanism was socially functional.

A second problem arises out of the close relationship between Puritanism and two other religious movements, the Reformed tradition and Pietism. Heir of the first and parent of the second, Puritanism at the onset of its history depended for ideas on Reformed Protestantism, and at the close faded into Pietism. John Eusden has suggested that Puritanism may be understood as an "evangelical Calvinism," a term that links it both to the sixteenth-century world of Calvin and to the eighteenth-century world of the Pietists.[5] If Eusden's suggestion is correct, historians must also be able to distinguish between Puritanism and these other movements. At the same time their task is to fix the time span within which Puritanism played out its course; to give dates to a movement is, perforce, to make a statement about its origins and legacy. A periodization of Puritanism and an inventory of its distinctive (or shared) religious ideas are two sides of the same problem: to mark off the historical and intellectual boundaries of the movement.

A third problem is to construct a definition that includes the range of Puritan types. Here I agree with Alan Simpson, who insists on viewing the broad spectrum from Presbyterians to Quakers as one continuous whole. He is right in criticizing historians who legitimize too narrow a slice of this spectrum, and he is right also in asking if there is not something fundamental in the nature of Puritanism that made it dynamic and expansive.[6] The history of the movement offers innumerable examples of the Puritan as a man in motion, a man possessed by a peculiar restlessness, a man who may attack the idea of a gathered church while still a minister in England, yet form such a group within his English parish and publicly defend the practice once he reached America. These inconsistencies, and more besides, mark the career of John Cotton, and the life histories of countless other Puritans were fashioned in the same erratic manner.

We need a definition of Puritanism which takes account of this restlessness, and if dissatisfaction with the scholarship of the 1930's is on the rise, the reason is largely its failure to meet such a test. It fails this test in one obvious way. Together with the denominational historians, Perry Miller assumed that denominational categories could be imposed upon Puritan conceptions of the church.[7] But can we call the New England Puritans "congregationalists" with a capital C when the actual working-out of their church order was so confused and contradictory? Or can we call Thomas Cartwright a "presbyterian" with a capital P when his conception of the church involved recognizably "congregational" elements? More recent studies, in recognition of these ambiguities, have moved away from the categories of denominational history, substituting in their place an emphasis upon the "continuity of experience" which united all Puritans.[8] The result may be a certain loss of clarity, but the new scholarship at least has the virtue of restoring the dynamic quality of Puritanism to the center of any definition.

The scholarship of the 1930's minimized the restlessness within Puritanism because of another assumption. In Perry Miller's view, "Puritanism was not only a religious creed, it was a philosophy and a metaphysic; it was an organization of man's whole life, emotional and intellectual." The structure of *The New England Mind* imposed a coherence upon Puritanism which Miller described as the reconciliation of "piety" and "intellect." To define the movement in these terms was explicitly to rule out any spiritualists as un-Puritan; it was to cut off the spectrum short of the Quakers and Antinomians. Here again, recent scholarship points toward a more inclusive definition. In place of the intellectual commitments Miller saw as crucial, Alan Simpson would put the terms "experience" and "thrust," intending by them a particular type of religious experience which unleashed the zeal of the Puritan saint.[9] The value of these terms must not obscure their weaknesses; though they permit the Quakers to reenter the fold as authentic Puritans, their meaning seems inherently subjective,[10] and they may act to exclude the array of distinctions that Miller so successfully identified as woven into the texture of Puritanism.

An adequate definition of the Puritan movement must therefore seek to unite the experiential dimension with the formal structure of the Puritan intellect. It must locate the movement within a particular time period, and with reference to the Reformed tradition and Pietism. It must identify the bond between the social sources of the movement and its history, between its rhetoric and its social consequences.

How close do we stand to such a definition? The literature that deals with the relationship between John Calvin and the Puritans is both extensive and contradictory, and for these reasons affords an opportunity to begin the task of evaluation. All historians agree that Puritanism belongs within the family of Reformed churches.[11] Yet the family resemblance has not prevented many historians from detecting differences between the two—differences, broadly speaking, of two kinds, philosophical and theological. The philosophical loom especially large in Perry Miller's account. "In defining the intellectual character of the New England Puritans," he declared in 1938, "we must always exercise caution about calling them Calvinists. John Calvin's metaphysics were still Aristotelian and scholastic; New Englanders had thrown aside much of the philosophy which is implied at every point in Calvin's theology, and had taken up a system of which the implications were quite different." These differences were due largely to the Puritans' acceptance of Peter Ramus, a French educator and logician; because the New Englanders were Ramists, Miller argued, they had emancipated themselves from Aristotle and scholasticism. More profoundly, Calvin was a nominalist who asserted the doctrine of an "arbitrary" God wholly unconditioned and deterministic in His actions; Puritans (at least those in New England) imposed limitations on the will of God and order upon the universe.[12]

More recent scholarship suggests, on the other hand, that the philosophical differences between Calvin and the Puritans were not very great. The essential continuity between the two was partly a matter of their common reliance upon the nominalistic distinction between *potentia absoluta* and *potentia ordinata*. Sharing the same confidence in the order of the world, they shared also the scholastic definition of man as a rational animal. Both agreed that God respected the nature of man in the process of redemption. Both agreed that in the "order of nature" (another concept taken over from scholasticism) man's will was free in such a way that he voluntarily obeyed the laws of God. And if the comparison stand between the Puritans and the continental theologians commonly known as Reformed scholastics, the continuities in philosophy and metaphysics are still more striking.[13]

But what of Peter Ramus? The road to an understanding of his significance for the Puritans is littered with obstacles, some of them placed there by Perry Miller. *The New England Mind* contains the suggestion that Ramus, a victim of the St. Bartholomew's Day massacre, "died equally for the cause of logic" and for the cause of Protestantism. In a manner characteristic of his approach to intellectual history, Miller framed the difference between Ramus and Aristotle as one between mortal enemies: those who murdered Ramus must have been disciples of Aristotle. For the New England Puritans to read Ramist texts thus amounted to a declaration of war; it was a decision, declared Miller, that entailed enormous consequences.[14] But no war between Aristotelians and Ramists was ever fought in New England, or even on the continent. The curriculum at Harvard College depended on textbooks written by a group of continental Reformed scholastics—Alsted, Keckermann, Heereboord, Burgersdicius—who blended Ramist and scholastic elements into an eclectic whole.[15] The second president of Harvard, Charles Chauncy, was hostile to Ramus, but he was never martyred on this account. To drain the ferocity from the mortal combat between Aristotelian and Ramist is, admittedly, to lessen the drama of the Puritan mind. But the truth seems to be that Ramist method, though practiced in New England, did not serve in any major way to divide the Puritans from the Reformed tradition. Nor did their reading in Ramus provide the New England Puritans with a metaphysic, the congregational church order, and a "plain style" of preaching, as Miller argued; all of these have other sources that far outweigh Ramus in importance.[16]

As for the second category of difference, there is general agreement among many historians that Puritanism has a different theological outlook from Calvinism. Comparison of the Puritans with John Calvin easily turns up some divergences: Calvin retained a sense of the real presence in his understanding of the Lord's Supper, while most Puritans followed Zwingli in adopting a memorialist view; Calvin's doctrine of assurance excluded the evidence of "works," evidence which many Puritans thought legitimate.[17]

In broader terms, Thomas Torrance has contrasted Calvin's Christocentric focus to the anthropocentric orientation of the Puritans. And Perry Miller declared that the New England Puritans fashioned the covenant theology in order to escape from the rigors of "strict Calvinism."[18]

No idea of Miller's has gained greater currency, or been more widely attacked. Counter-interpretations of the covenant theology have generally succeeded in establishing two points. One is that the covenantal idiom figured in the Reformed tradition long before it appeared among the Puritans whom Miller cited. Certain of these studies suggest, in other words, that the Puritans in resorting to the idiom were not particularly novel or illegitimate by Reformed standards. The second point is that the idea of a covenant, though apparently implying a voluntary, contractual relationship between God and man, was not intended by the Puritans as a means of bringing God more within man's reach, but rather to accomplish other ends—to provide a rationale for the sacraments, or a basis for their doctrine of assurance.[19]

In spite of all this scholarship we still lack a clear understanding of the covenant theology, and on the larger question of the theological differences between Calvin and the Puritans the confusion is just as great. The time has come, I believe, to reconsider the terms of the question, for we seem to be dealing with a question *mal posée,* so posed as to lead to answers which are never satisfactory. The essential error has been to postulate a "strict" orthodoxy, a "pure" Calvinism, defined in terms of John Calvin and the *Institutes of the Christian Religion.* Once the name of Calvin becomes synonymous with "orthodoxy," certain deadly consequences ensue: the concept presumes a static system of ideas, so that change of any kind—any variation, no matter how slight—is taken as evidence of declining rigor and faith. Perry Miller fell into this trap, and so have many others.[20] But we have been warned against it by the post-Millerian scholarship on the covenant theology: on the one hand this scholarship suggests that the strict orthodoxy of the pure Calvin must not be interpreted so narrowly as to exclude the idiom of the covenant, and on the other, that the Puritans who invoked the idiom did not thereby fall from the heights of orthodoxy. These warnings must be extended. In particular, the differences between Puritans and continental Reformed theology must not be measured solely in terms of Calvin. Reformed theology[21] was a system of thought elaborated and defended in varying ways by many persons in the sixteenth century. Several of these Reformed theologians—Beza, Piscator, Zanchy, Bullinger, Pareus—figure more often than Calvin in the religious thought of seventeenth-century New England.[22] To overlook these intermediary figures, in any case, is to risk overlooking the complexities of the Reformed tradition, and consequently the materials for proving the continuity between this tradition and the Puritans. In fact, once these Calvinists, and not Calvin, are brought into the comparison, the continuities far outweigh the differences.

Let me cite some recent scholarship in support of this assertion. One of the more notable contributions of the past decade to our understanding of Puritanism is Norman Pettit's *The Heart Prepared,* a history of the doctrine of "preparation for salvation" as invoked (or rejected) by Reformed theologians from Calvin to Stoddard. Pettit's approach is significantly different from that of Miller, who argued that the Puritans in New England developed the idea as a means of extending social control over the entire population. Miller set the doctrine within a functional context, Pettit within a scriptural one, for he begins by showing how Scripture itself establishes the problem of reconciling man's initiative with God's. Thereafter the focus is upon a continuity of speculation which begins with Calvin and moves on through English to American Puritanism. In this fashion Pettit locates the New England appropriation of the doctrine firmly within the broad context of Reformed theology.[23]

Recent scholarship on William Perkins provides further evidence of continuity between Puritanism and the Reformed tradition on the continent. Perkins was a key link between Reformed scholasticism and English Puritanism. He drew freely on the writings of continental theologians for ideas and even actual texts; included in his collected works were translations (or adaptations) of treatises by Beza and Zanchy. At the same time his own writings were widely reprinted on the continent, where his reputation was nearly as considerable as in England. It is not surprising, therefore, that Jacobus Arminius should have challenged Perkins on the doctrine of predestination, thereby precipitating the debate that led eventually to the synod of Dort.[24] Such evidence of connections between Puritanism and Reformed theology could be multiplied many times over, and all of it goes to suggest that the two were essentially congruent, if not identical.[25]

Yet we need not rely on external evidence to demonstrate the congruence. Calvin, his successors on the continent, and the Puritans all shared a theological outlook founded on a common understanding of God. The God they defined was the sovereign creator of the world, a creator who stood aloof from His handiwork. Calvinist and Puritan alike asserted the radical separation of grace and nature, declaring that an ever-free and independent God stood over and above "the created world of man and nature." Both went on to describe God in terms of His will, and for both the action of the Holy Spirit in restoring fallen man to the state of grace was the focus of "divinity." Both Calvinist and Puritan saw God as ceaselessly at work bending the course of human history toward the goal of the kingdom.[26]

It was this eschatological understanding of God which gave the Reformed tradition (including Puritanism) its special cast. To put the matter broadly, all Calvinists were imbued with a certain kind of historical consciousness. All of them understood reality as dynamic, not static. All of them looked forward to the coming of the new order, and the urge to hasten on the kingdom was what lay behind their programs of communal discipline. The same historical consciousness may account for the prominence of the decree of election in their thought. As they interpreted the doctrine of predestination, it was a statement of God's promise to enter into and renew a fallen world. The doctrine offered men the assurance that "God has willed and is acting in his power to restore and justify them through his love."

Restated in this fashion, the doctrine took on an eschatological significance, for it linked the election of the saints with the coming of the kingdom.[27]

Elsewhere the activist, historical orientation of Reformed divinity was reflected in the great interest Calvin and the Puritans expressed in the Holy Spirit and in the Atonement, rather than the Incarnation; in their use of the covenant theology,[28] and in their fascination with "method." William Perkins provided readers of his works with a fold-out chart marking off the stages of salvation. This chart was actually a form of history, for when the Puritan wrote his spiritual autobiography, he ordered his life according to the spatial and dynamic plan that Perkins had outlined. The methodizing of the *ordo salutis,* the elaboration of the "morphology of conversion," the development of a "plain style" of preaching that was deliberately "practical"—these aspects of seventeenth-century Puritanism emerged from an eschatological consciousness which the Puritans shared with the Reformed tradition.[29]

If it is important in understanding the Puritans to recognize their alliance with the international Reformed tradition, certain differences between the two must also be noted. Like members of a family, the national churches within the Reformed tradition resembled one another but also varied in detail, for each adapted a common idiom to particular circumstances. The special character of Puritanism arose from the refusal of Elizabeth I to allow certain changes in the structure and worship of the Church of England, changes favored by many English Protestants but especially by a group which gained the name of "Puritans." Denied a hearing by the Queen, these Puritans turned to Parliament and to the population at large for support, at the same time sharpening their indictment of the Church beyond what Calvin would have said. By the 1570's they were declaring that the bishops of the Church—the persons charged with suppressing them—were unlawful, which was to say that their office had no warrant in the word of God. Calvin had never been so explicit, nor did he make the validity of the Church depend on the exercise of discipline, as many Puritans maintained. It was Calvin, to be sure, who taught the Puritans their legalism, but the political situation in which they found themselves encouraged the development of this legalism beyond the point where he had stopped. Similarly, the Puritans inherited a bias against Catholic sacerdotalism, a bias intensified in England in the heat of struggle against the "popish remnants" in the Church. And because the Puritans could not rely on bishops or civil magistrates to enforce the moral code they taught, the preachers in the movement directed their attention increasingly to the individual conscience, encouraging the practice of pietistic self-scrutiny.[30]

This final tendency is one to which many historians have pointed as the crucial difference between the Reformed tradition (or Calvin) and the Puritans. When more is known of the Reformed scholastics from whom the Puritans borrowed so deeply, this "piety" may not seem so original.[31] Nor was it taught in the same way by every preacher.[32] Throughout the history of the movement, Puritans debated a wide range of religious issues, many of

them arising out of the tension between this pietistic bias and Reformed
sacramentalism, others out of the complexities of methodizing the *ordo
salutis*. What was the normative experience of conversion, an awakening by
degrees or some compressed reaction?[33] How was man's striving for grace
and his cleansing under the Law to be accommodated with the gospel
promise of grace without conditions? What was the role and nature of the
means of grace—the ministry and the sacraments—in a system in which the
elect were predestinated to salvation? These questions arose in part because
most Puritans, as heirs of the Reformed tradition, held on to the sacraments
and an objective understanding of the ministry. To be sure, they held on to
both in an attenuated form; their heightened interest in the workings of the
Holy Spirit left little room for a high doctrine of the sacraments or a sacer-
dotal view of the ministry. The logic of their spiritism was such, moreover,
that amidst the turmoil of the seventeenth century some Puritans would
overthrow the sacraments and ministry altogether.[34] Perhaps it could be said
that Puritans finally divided on these issues according to their view of
history and the world. Millenarian Puritans saw the world as in process of
renewal, and discounted all existing structures; others saw it in legalistic and
static terms as composed of ordained institutions and fixed forms, and
spoke of the millennium as far off.

The political situation of the Puritans had one further consequence.
Resentful of the Church's imperfection, yet believing that schism was a sin,
Puritans found themselves caught in a dilemma from which flowed much of
their restlessness.[35] The same dilemma was a cause of the fragmentation of
the movement into sects, a process that began in the late sixteenth century
with the emergence of the separatists. By one set of Reformed standards the
separatists were perfectly legitimate in demanding freedom for the church to
cleanse itself; by another they were schismatics who carried their legalism
too far. The emergence of the separatists is thus a perfect measure of how
the English situation acted to confuse the meaning and application of
Reformed ideas.[36]

It is in this context, moreover, that denominational categories become
inadequate; too abstract and rigid, they sever the Puritan sects from their
dynamic and fluid relationship with the Reformed tradition.
Denominational categories conceal the fact that all Puritans, whether
"presbyterian" or "congregationalist" or some other group, held four
propositions in common: the revitalization of the laymen's role, including
greater privileges in the government of the church; the purification of church
membership; the assignment of the power of the keys to each parish or congregation; and the separation of church and state so as to give the church
effective responsibility for discipline. Many historians would add a fifth
proposition to this list: the assertion that the nature of the church must conform to the will of God.[37] But the Biblicism of the Puritans is less important
in explaining their ecclesiology than the emphasis they placed upon the Holy
Spirit. The essential impulse within the movement was to relate the church
to the intervention of the Spirit, to understand the community of the saints
as a type of the kingdom. In this they were not unique. Calvin himself

looked upon the church in two ways, as an institution ordained by God to exist upon earth, and as the realm of the Spirit, a realm in which "the original order of creation" had been restored.[38] Inheriting both views, the Puritans were driven to identify the first with the Church of England, and so to emphasize the second. But the issue of keeping the two in balance was inherent within the Reformed tradition.

There is another reason for discarding denominational categories. Puritanism began as a movement within the Church of England at the time of the Elizabethan religious settlement of 1559. From that time until the accession of William III, most Puritans thought of themselves as members of the Church, not as founders of new churches. It was only when the religious settlement under William denied the legitimacy of this claim that the connections between English Puritans and the Church were finally severed. On this side of the Atlantic, the new charter of 1691 and the events associated with it mark a similar end to the affiliation. Thereafter, any colonist who claimed membership or ministerial orders within the Church would have to renounce his current status and formally rejoin the mother body.[39]

The historic association of Puritanism with the Church of England is a means of giving dates to the movement, a periodization which other evidence sustains. The decade of the 1690's saw Reformed scholasticism giving way under the impact of the Enlightenment, leaving eighteenth-century Reformed theologians to work out a new alliance between philosophy and religion.[40] On the whole, however, Pietists were content to abandon philosophy and science, just as they abandoned the theocratic vision of a holy commonwealth which inspired Calvin and the Puritans. What passed from Puritanism to Pietism was the assertion that religion fundamentally involved the affective self, the heart, rather than the reason.[41]

An adequate definition of Puritanism must incorporate this periodization of the movement, and go on from there to recognize the essential continuity between Calvinists and Puritans. An adequate definition must allow for the adaptation of Reformed ideas to England, a process that eventually resulted in the splintering of the movement into many sects. Despite this splintering, an adequate definition must recognize the wholeness to Puritan history. What gave substance to the movement was a certain inventory of ideas—the separation of grace and nature, an understanding of God and man as active forces, an eschatology. And what linked the Puritan program for reform of the church to Puritan descriptions of the spiritual life was the common motif of renewal. Edmund S. Morgan has seen the Puritan as caught in the dilemma of remaining pure while living in the world. Such a posture was forced upon the Puritan by the dynamic relationship between this world and the next. He knew himself to be a mid-point between these worlds, and his striving for self-discipline, his endless self-scrutiny were directed toward the end of winning freedom from the world and entrance to the kingdom.[42]

There still remains to be answered, finally, the problem of the relationship between Puritanism and culture. What we know for sure is very little. The extensive scholarship of Christopher Hill has shown that class, status, and occupation have something to do with Puritanism, but Hill himself would surely agree that they are not sufficient as analytical categories.[43] It seems likely that the social sources of Puritanism will eventually be described in terms of personality structure (and thus of family structure), life style, generations, and negative reference groups, but exact information is wanting on all of these for both England and America. It is possible to declare with more certainty that the dynamics of Puritanism in England bear a direct relationship to its status as an outgroup remote from the center of power; the greater this distance, the more intense became the urge to free the church from the world and hasten on the coming kingdom.[44]

The millenarian fervor which runs through Puritanism may provide the best clue to the social function of the movement. Puritanism, it seems, furnished certain Englishmen with a new identity as members of a special group. All English Protestants believed that the history of the Christian church revealed God's favoring providence toward England. And Christian history also taught that God's people must fight a cruel and bloody war against Anti-Christ and all his minions.[45] The Puritans were able to appropriate this rhetoric and apply it to their cause for two reasons: they were most outspoken in attacking Catholicism, and their outgroup status lent itself to a sense of persecution. The identity of the Puritan as saint in covenant with God was reinforced by the idea that history was moving rapidly toward the coming of the kingdom. The prophetic stance of the Puritan teachers grew out of an historical perspective which saw the task of reformation as increasingly urgent, lest the final day prove a day of judgment. Those who responded to this preaching, those Englishmen who in life style withdrew from the "world" and set their hearts upon the kingdom, established a new identity for themselves as the Lord's free people.

From this identity flowed the Puritan understanding of the church as a voluntary, gathered congregation. From it came also the Puritan theory of community, the vision of a social order (to quote John Winthrop) "knit together" in a "bond of love." The immigration to New England can equally be counted as a consequence of this millenarianism. In the late 1620's events in England and abroad convinced many Puritans that the final day was close at hand. New England loomed before them both as refuge and as paradise, the wilderness which they could make into the kingdom. Not only did the chiliastic zeal of certain Puritans precipitate their immigration; it also inspired the congregationalism that emerged in New England in the 1630's—the strict limits on church membership, the more democratic church structure.[46]

Whether the colonists were exceptional in their chiliasm is not clear. In their general vision of the kingdom, and in their activist drive, they stood as one with the entire Puritan movement, sharing in a historical consciousness that originated with Calvin and Bucer. Any understanding of Puritanism in America must ignore artificial boundaries and distinctions and build instead upon the continuities that linked England and America. On this matter of continuities, American scholarship has far to go in working out the relationships between institutional forms, and even ideas.[47]

Does this mean there is nothing distinctive about American Puritanism, nothing American historians can study without going back to Perkins or Calvin? There is not as much as many would assert, but there is something. We can speak of the Americanizing of Puritan ideas just as historians of the Revolutionary period speak of the Americanizing of Whig ideas. The analogy is nearly exact; the colonists imported the radical Whig ideology from abroad, and we can only understand what they are saying by reference to the English sources. Yet there is a difference, for although the ideas seem the same on both sides of the Atlantic, the pattern of culture in America had departed from the English model in ways that affected the meaning and consequences of these ideas.[48] So also in the seventeenth century, the Reformed tradition took on a new significance in the "free air of a new world." Here Puritanism became the majority point of view, and preachers who had whetted their fiery preaching on targets that the Church of England had to offer underwent an agonizing adjustment to a new life style. Here the ideal of a gathered church had strange consequences, and here the alliance between church and state gave the "New England Way" its notoriety.[49] The future of Puritan studies in America, a future that seems without limit, lies in articulating these differences, as well as the continuities, between Old World and New.

NOTES

[1] I am indebted to John Eusden of Williams College and Sacvan Bercovitch for comments that enlarged my view of the subject.

[2] Samuel Eliot Morison, *The Puritan Pronaos* (New York, 1936); William Haller, *The Rise of Puritanism* (New York, 1938); Perry Miller, *The New England Mind: The Seventeenth Century* (Cambridge, Mass., 1939). Miller's contributions in the 1930's also included many of the essays in *Errand into the Wilderness* (Cambridge, Mass., 1956), as well as the anthology *The Puritans* (New York, 1938), co-edited with Thomas Johnson.

[3] It falls beyond the limits of this essay to describe the intersection of Puritan scholarship in America with the search for a "usable past" in which Americans have engaged in the twentieth century. A good beginning on the history of this search, including information on changing views of the Puritans, is Richard Ruland, *The Reinterpretation of American Literature* (Cambridge, Mass., 1967).

[4] There have been several other published essays of a similar nature: Edmund S. Morgan, "The Historians of Early New England," in Ray Billington, ed., *The Reinterpretation of Early American History* (San Marino, Calif., 1966); Richard Schlatter, "The Puritan Strain," in John Higham, ed., *The Reconstruction of American History* (New York, 1962); Sidney James, introduction, *The New England Puritans* (New York, 1968).

[5] William Ames, *The Marrow of Theology*, translated and edited by John Eusden (Boston, 1968), p. 19.

[6] Alan Simpson, *Puritanism in Old and New England,* paperback ed. (Chicago, 1961), pp. 1-2.

[7]Though Miller distinguished between "separating" and "nonseparating" Congregationalists, thereby departing from earlier explanations of the genesis of Massachusetts Congregationalism, he left unchallenged the premise of denominational scholarship (as represented by Williston Walker and Henry Martyn Dexter) that the thread of Congregationalism could be unraveled from the tapestry of Puritanism. The most important critique of Miller, careful to distinguish true Congregationalism from its "prehistory," is Geoffrey Nuttall, *Visible Saints, The Congregational Way, 1640-1660* (Oxford, 1957), though I would press Nuttall's critique of denominational history further than he does. See also Robert Paul, ed., *An Apologeticall Narration* (Philadelphia, 1963), pp. 57-66, and the scholarship cited therein.

[8]Simpson, *Puritanism in Old and New England,* p. 2. In a footnote, Simpson cites A. S. P. Woodhouse, *Puritanism and Liberty* (London, 1938), p. xxxvii: "It is unnecessary to posit a unity in all Puritan thought; it is sufficient to recognize a continuity."

[9]Simpson, *Puritanism in Old and New England,* chap. I. Earlier, William Haller had criticized denominational historians for their "historical piety," and called for an inclusive definition of Puritanism structured around the figure of the preacher: "The disagreements that rendered Puritans into presbyterians, independents, separatists, and baptists were in the long run not so significant as the qualities of character, of mind and imagination, which kept them all alike Puritans." *The Rise of Puritanism,* paperpack ed. (New York, 1957), p. 17. Earlier still, William York Tindall had insisted upon "the essential identity of the radical sects in both nature and purpose." *John Bunyan, Mechanick Preacher* (New York, 1934), p. 5. See also James F. Maclear, " 'The Heart of New England Rent': The Mystical Element in Early Puritan History," *Mississippi Valley Historical Review,* XLII (1956), 621-656.

[10]Cf. the remark by Richard T. Vann—"This 'thrust'—whatever that means"— in his review essay of Michael Walzer, *Revolution of the Saints,* in *History and Theory,* VII (1968), 108.

[11]Much can be learned about Puritanism from general histories of the Reformed tradition, among which are John T. McNeill, *The History and Character of Calvinism* (New York, 1954); James L. Ainslie, *The Doctrine of Ministerial Order in the Reformed Churches of the Sixteenth and Seventeenth Centuries* (Edinburgh, 1940); Geddes MacGregor, *Corpus Christi: The Nature of the Church According to the Reformed Tradition* (London, 1959).

[12]Miller, *The Puritans,* pp. 24, 32-33; Miller, *The New England Mind,* pp. 92-97, 157, 194-195. One of the problems with his argument is to agree on a meaning of "scholasticism." The Puritans frequently denounced the "School-men," as Miller pointed out; but he also warned against taking their denunciations at "face value." On the one hand he thus asserted that the Puritans "revolted" against scholasticism, while on the other he perceived that they accepted "scholastic premises in physics and astronomy, the scholastic theory of the four elements or the four causes," and much else besides. Miller, *The Puritans,* pp. 25-26; *The New England Mind,* pp. 100-102.

[13]Francois Wendel, *Calvin: The Origins and Development of His Religious Thought* (New York, 1963), pp. 127ff, 179; Eusden, ed., *The Marrow of Theology,* pp. 51-52; Heinrich Heppe, *Reformed Dogmatics* (London, 1950), pp. 144, 155, 159, 167; David D. Hall, ed., *The Antinomian Controversy,1636-1638: A Documentary History* (Middletown, Conn., 1968), see "Cause" and "Order" under index. More precise study is needed of the place such scholastic terms had in the Puritan mind.

[14]Miller, *The New England Mind,* pp. 117-120.

[15]Samuel Eliot Morison, *Harvard College in the Seventeenth Century* (Cambridge, Mass., 1936), I, 157-159, 191-192. Miller drew heavily upon these same writers in reconstructing the Puritan mind—the statements and extended quotation on page 264 are from Zanchy and Ursinus, and the quotation bridging pages 287-288 is from Zanchy—to an extent that the text does not reveal, though he also was explicit in recognizing the importance of these Protestant scholastics. *The New England Mind,* pp. 102-105; the citations above are drawn from the annotated copy in the Harvard Library. The fullest study of Keckermann, Heereboord, and Burgersdicius in the educational setting of the late sixteenth and early seventeenth centuries is Paul Dibon, *L'Enseignement Philosophique dans les Universités Néerlandaises à l'Epoque Pré-Cartésienne (1575-1650)* (Paris, 1954). Dibon argues (pp. 10, 133, and throughout) against reading the philosophical instruction of the period as a battle between Aristotelianism and Ramism; instead he perceives "une tendence *conciliatrice*" in the logic teaching: "Il ne s'agit pas tant d'opposer Ramus à Aristotle que de completer celui-ci par ceui-là" (p. 133).

[16]Miller, *The New England Mind,* chaps. 5, 6, 11, and 12. On the rhetoric of the Puritans, cf. J. W. Blench, *Preaching in England in the Late Fifteenth and Sixteenth Centuries* (New York, 1964), and Wilbur S. Howell, *Logic and Rhetoric in England, 1500-1700* (Princeton, 1961).

[17]Wilhelm Niesel, *The Theology of Calvin* (London, 1956), pp. 170-171, cites Calvin's disapproval of the "practical syllogism" and his carefully hedged exegesis of 2 Peter 1.10, a text William Perkins placed on the title page of a treatise dealing with assurance, and which the "legal" preachers in New England invoked repeatedly during the Antinomian controversy, together with the "practical syllogism." Perkins, *Works* (London, 1608-1631), I, 419; Hall, *The Antinomian Controversy,* pp. 58, 237.

[18]Thomas Torrance, *The School of Faith* (New York, 1959); Torrance, "Justification: Its Radical Nature and Place in Reformed Doctrine and Life," *Scottish Journal of Theology,* XIII (1960), 225-246; Miller, *Errand into the Wilderness,* pp. 51-53, an argument repeated in *The New England Mind.*

[19]Leonard J. Trinterud, "The Origins of Puritanism," *Church History,* XX (1951), 37-57; Jens G. Moller, "The Beginnings of Puritan Covenant Theology," *Journal of Ecclesiastical History,* XIV (1963), 46-67; Everett H. Emerson, "Calvin and the Covenant Theology," *Church History,* XXV (1956), 136-144; Emerson, "Thomas Hooker: The Puritan as Theologian," *Anglican Theological Review,* XLIX (1967), 190-203; John von Rohr, "Covenant and Assurance in Early English Puritanism," *Church History,* XXXIV (1965), 195-203; C. J. Sommerville, "Conversion *versus* the Early Puritan Covenant of Grace," *Journal of Presbyterian History,* XLIV (1966), 178-197; J. A. Ross MacKenzie, "The Covenant Theology—A Review Article," *Journal of Presbyterian History,* XLIV (1966), 198-204.

[20]In describing Calvin's theology, Miller relied as much upon tone as upon specific doctrines. Both the tone and content of his "Calvin" are suggested by the following citations: Calvinism was "the relatively simple dogmatism of its founder"; "pure Calvinism"; "the absolute dogmatism of original Calvinism"; "primitive Calvinism"; "the doctrine of divine determinism"; "the inexorable logic of Calvin"; "Calvinism pictured man as lifeless clay in the potter's hand." Miller, *Errand into the Wilderness* (Cambridge, Mass., 1956), pp. 53, 69, 84; Miller, *Nature's Nation* (Cambridge, Mass., 1967), pp. 50, 53-54.

[21]"Reformed" is a better term than "Calvinist," precisely for the reason that it avoids the unnecessary connotations of direct discipleship. "Calvinist" is, in any

event, an overused and much abused term. Cf. Basil Hall, "Calvin Against the Calvinists," *Proceedings* of the Huguenot Society of London, XX (1958-1964), 284-301.

[22]Miller himself called attention to these theologians: *The New England Mind,* pp. 92-93. John Norton's annotations in *The Orthodox Evangelist* (London, 1657), and John Cotton's references in the debates during the Antinomian controversy (cf. Hall, *The Antinomian Controversy, 1636-1638)* provide other leads to the colonists' indebtedness to Reformed scholasticism.

[23]Norman Pettit, *The Heart Prepared;* Miller, " 'Preparation for Salvation' in Seventeenth-Century New England," in *Nature's Nation.*

[24]I. Breward, "The Significance of William Perkins," *Journal of Religious History,* IV (1966-1967), 113-128.

[25]The career of William Ames is a case in point: cf. Eusden, introduction to Ames, *Marrow of Theology,* and Karl Reuter, *William Ames: The Leading Theologian in the Awakening of Reformed Pietism,* trans. D. Horton (Cambridge, Mass., 1965).

[26]David Little, "Max Weber Revisited: The 'Protestant Ethic' and the Puritan Experience of Order," *Harvard Theological Review,* LIX (1966), 422; Eusden, ed., Ames, *Marrow of Theology,* pp. 21-23, 77-78.

[27]A major work spelling out in detail the "relation of eschatology to the life of the Church" in the theology of Calvin and Bucer is Thomas Torrance, *Kingdom and Church* (Edinburgh, 1956). There is a growing literature on millenarian thought among the Puritans, much of it originating in studies of typology and aesthetics. Cf. Bercovitch, "Typology in Puritan New England: The Williams-Cotton Controversy Reassessed," *American Quarterly,* XIX (1967), 166-190; Jesper Rosenmeier, "Veritas: The Sealing of the Promise," *Harvard Library Bulletin,* XVI (1968), 26-37; Joy B. Gilsdorf, "The Puritan Apocalypse: New England Eschatology in the Seventeenth Century," Unpublished Ph.D. Dissertation (Yale University, 1964); Le Roy Edwin Froom, *The Prophetic Faith of Our Fathers* (Washington, D.C., 1946), III.

[28]Charles S. McCoy, "Johannes Cocceius: Federal Theologian," *Scottish Journal of Theology,* XVI (1963), 352-370; and Eusden, introduction, Ames, *Marrow of Theology.*

[29]The chart precedes page 11 in Perkins, *Works,* I. The fullest study of how Puritans methodized the spiritual life remains Haller, *The Rise of Puritanism;* the phrase "morphology of conversion" is taken from Edmund S. Morgan, *Visible Saints: The History of a Puritan Idea* (New York, 1963). On Puritan rhetoric as eschatological, see Larzer Ziff, *The Career of John Cotton* (Princeton, 1962), chap. 5.

[30]George Yule, "Theological Developments in Elizabethan Puritanism," *Journal of Ecclesiastical History,* I (1960-1961), 21-23; Patrick Collinson, *The Elizabethan Puritan Movement* (London, 1967).

[31]Pettit, *The Heart Prepared,* p. 6. In his comments on this paper John Eusden sketched a number of sub-traditions within Reformed theology, one of which included William Ames and the Puritans in New England. These "covenant of grace" theologians, as Eusden calls them, are the subject of an extended study he is making.

[32]Charles H. and Katherine George, *The Protestant Mind of the English Reformation* (Princeton, 1961), argue that Puritan and Anglican shared the same faith. Although this is disputed by John New, *Anglican and Puritan* (Stanford, 1964), the argument reminds us that the meaning of the terms Puritan and Anglican was

relative and changing. Just as the line between the two in England was a fluid one, so the relationship of the Puritans to Calvin varied from one period to another, from William Perkins, say, to John Bunyan. Methodologically the problem is to abstract an ideal type while doing justice to variety.

[33]The tendency among modern historians has been to single out the most tormented accounts of the conversion experience and make of them the normative pattern.

[34]The logic of spiritism is explained in Maclear, " 'The Heart of New England Rent': The Mystical Element in Early Puritan History," and in Geoffrey Nuttall, *The Holy Spirit in Puritan Faith and Experience* (Oxford, 1946). The contradictions within Puritanism have been variously described by Nuttall, Maclear, Morgan, Miller, Sommerville, Pettit, and others, but agreement would be general on the proposition that Puritan sacramentalism, together with a "preparationist" approach to the spiritual life, clashed with Puritan spiritism, together with a "conversionist" mentality. Pettit has noted the connections between the doctrine of preparation and sacramental views, *The Heart Prepared,* pp. 117-124, 134-136. The problem is a legacy from the Reformed tradition, as John Baillie indicates in *Baptism and Conversion* (London, 1964).

[35]Collinson, *The Elizabethan Puritan Movement,* p. 132.

[36]Morgan, *Visible Saints,* cites the separatist Henry Barrow's explicit denunciation of Calvin, an action forced upon Barrow by the contradictions in which he was enmeshed.

[37]Paul, *An Apologeticall Narration,* pp. 123-125; Miller, *The Puritans,* pp. 41-55. Sacvan Bercovitch writes, ". . . the connection between eschatology and historiography—one which relies heavily on scriptural exegesis and prediction—should make us hesitate to render tribute to the things of the Spirit *at the expense* of giving due emphasis to the settlers' profound 'Biblicism.' "

[38]Benjamin C. Milner, Jr., "Calvin's Doctrine of the Church," *Harvard Theological Review,* LVIII (1965), 458; Little, "Max Weber Revisited: The 'Protestant Ethic' and the Puritan Experience of Order," p. 423. The problem that Calvin passed on to the Puritans was described by Ernst Troeltsch in these terms: ". . . how could a 'holy community' composed of sterling Christians, whose faith was a matter of profound personal conviction, and whose lives were controlled by an exalted and austere ideal, be at the same time a Church which would provide a spiritual home for the masses of the population?" *The Social Teachings of the Christian Churches* (Glencoe, Ill., 1949), II, 659. See also Geoffrey Nuttall, "The Early Congregational Conception of the Church," *Transactions of the Congregational Historical Society,* XIV, 197-204, and George H. Williams, *The Radical Reformation* (Philadelphia, 1962), pp. 581n, 787-788.

[39]It could, of course, be argued that the significant break came in 1640 or 1662, the date of the act excluding nonconformists from the Church and declaring their orders illegitimate. The most important studies that seek to transcend denominational categories are Collinson, *The Elizabethan Puritan Movement,* and Morgan, *Visible Saints,* a carefully measured reply to Perry Miller, *Orthodoxy in Massachusetts* (Cambridge, Mass., 1933).

[40]Perry Miller, *Jonathan Edwards* (New York, 1949), describes Edwards' labors in this regard. The collapse of scholasticism occurred more rapidly in England than in America; rational theology was making inroads among English presbyterians in the 1690's, and the dissenting academies were ahead of their time in teaching the new logic and the new sciences. The situation in New England with respect to the

academic curriculum is described in Edmund S. Morgan, *The Gentle Puritan* (New Haven, 1962), chap.3, and in Perry Miller, *The New England Mind: From Colony to Province* (Cambridge, Mass., 1953). On the English side, Olive M. Griffiths, *Religion and Learning: A Study in English Presbyterian Thought from the Bartholomew Ejections (1662) to the Foundation of the Unitarian Movement* (Cambridge, 1935) is valuable.

[41] The emergence of Pietism is described in Reuter, *William Ames,* and in F. Ernest Stoeffler, *The Rise of Evangelical Pietism* (Leyden, 1965).

[42] Morgan, *The Puritan Dilemma* (Boston, 1958).

[43] Perhaps the best of Hill's many surveys is *Society and Puritanism in Pre-Revolutionary England* (New York, 1964).

[44] "The fertilized ground [for the word as preached by Puritans] was the ground which for one reason or another was out of sympathy with official policy." A list of outgroups, together with a brief critique of Hill's position, is in Simpson, *Puritanism in Old and New England,* pp. 11-12. In the 1930's there were attempts to link left-wing Puritanism (measured theologically) with lower social and economic groups; cf. Tindall, *John Bunyan, Mechanick Preacher.*

As for the social consequences of Puritanism, recent studies suggest that the movement worked to create a new kind of personality—Michael Walzer's radical saint, or, more correctly, David Little's self-disciplining activist. Walzer, *Revolution of the Saints: A Study in the Origins of Radical Politics* (Cambridge, Mass., 1965); Little, *Religion, Order and Law,* paperback ed. (New York, 1970). Walzer's study should be read in the light of two extended reviews, both indicating difficulties with his interpretation: Little, "Max Weber Revisited," and Richard T. Vann, *History and Theory,* VII (1968), 102-114.

[45] William Haller, *Foxe's Book of Martyrs and the Elect Nation* (London, 1967).

[46] Cf. Gilsdorf, "The Puritan Apocalypse."

[47] Harvard College, which Morison located within the broad context of Western humanism, needs to be studied in the context of Reformed educational practices; one of the major characteristics of Reformed Protestantism in the sixteenth century was the founding of schools for training ministers. New England political history needs to be studied in light of the "holy commonwealth" literature, both continental and English.

[48] Oscar and Mary Handlin, "James Burgh and American Revolutionary Theory," *Proceedings* of the Massachusetts Historical Society, LXXIII, 38-57; Bernard Bailyn, *The Ideological Origins of the American Revolution* (Cambridge, Mass., 1967).

[49] The bibliography of relevant studies is too immense to be listed here. An interesting overview is Darrett B. Rutman, "The Mirror of Puritan Authority," in G. A. Billias, ed., *Law and Authority in Colonial America* (Barre, Mass., 1965). The accommodation of Puritanism to the "wilderness" is the theme of *From Colony to Province,* the second volume of Miller's *The New England Mind.* The first describes a static system of ideas (hedging on whether they were held only in New England or also abroad), the second the meaning and consequence of these ideas in America. *From Colony to Province* is open to many criticisms. Still, it offers an amazing number of insights into the nature of New England history. A fair estimate of Miller is not easy to achieve, and although I have joined in the "ritual patricidal totem feast" (to borrow Bercovitch's phrase), I share his feeling that *The New England Mind* continues to supply "the best overview we have of American Puritanism."

2

The Covenanted Community

Alan Simpson

Perry Miller's major studies of New England Puritanism established the point that, despite its complexity, the Puritan movement was dedicated to building a society attuned to divine will, a project that was frustrated in the Old World. Professor Alan Simpson, more recently President of Vassar College, offers this analysis of the "New England Way" which was developed in the northern American colonies.

The first chance to see what the Puritan saint would make of life, if he had the freedom to experiment, came in America. The early history of Massachusetts (together with that of Plymouth, Connecticut, and New Haven, for the differences are unimportant from our point of view) is the story of men who shared an ideal, left the Old World to realize it in the New, only to discover when the work of planting was done that the spirit had evaporated. Frustration was the fate which awaited every Puritan. In England, where the defeat came in war, it has all the features of tragedy; here, where there was no defeat but apparent success, it becomes a kind of ironic tale.

The Puritans who came to America continued to have much in common with those who stayed at home. Take, for instance, that apocalyptic view of their place in history which all Puritans shared and which can hardly be overemphasized if we want to understand the quality of their enthusiasm.

First published as Chapter II of *Puritanism in Old and New England* by Alan Simpson. (Chicago: University of Chicago Press), pp. 19-38 (notes abridged). Copyright © 1955 The University of Chicago Press.

We are all familiar today with the Communist's conviction that he is moving toward a preordained victory. His science tells him that the historical process is obeying a determinate logic, and, so far from the inevitability of this process slowing down his efforts, it acts as an enormous spur to them. The Puritan has a similar theory of history and the same sort of compulsion to cooperate with destiny. Admittedly, Divine Providence is a good deal more mysterious than dialectical materialism. But this unpredictability, if an argument in some situations for more patience than a Communist could admit in his timetable, always offers the possibility of a miraculous delivery. The winters of the church may be cruelly long; but when that frozen world thaws, as in the springtime of the Reformation, the whole earth seems to rush toward its harvest.

The Puritan thought of human history as the field in which God gathered his saints, saving the few from the fate which all had deserved and imparting to that few some knowledge of his Will. For reasons known only to himself, God had permitted ignorance of his Will to envelop the visible church between the age of the apostles and the age of the Reformation. These thirteen or fourteen centuries had seen a downward swing to the lowest depths of depravity; then a slow ascent had begun as God chose to reveal more and more of himself. Wave after wave of witnesses had been summoned to testify; country after country seemed likely to be the scene in which the destiny of the age would be fulfilled. On the crest of that movement stood the Puritan, with his "panting, longing, eager" desire to find the revelation completed in himself.[1] These adjectives are not mine, nor are they those of some simple enthusiast. They might be Oliver Cromwell's or John Milton's. They are, in fact, the words of John Cotton, the leading intellectual among the founders of the New England Way.

Incidentally, the intellectual quality in the Puritan's piety can easily be overstated. When every compliment has been paid to Professor Miller's studies of Puritanism[2] —and I yield to no one in my admiration for those ingenious works—at least one gentle criticism may be made. He has told us too much about the Puritan mind and not enough about the Puritan's feelings. If the seventeenth-century Puritan, with his formal training in scholasticism, usually tries to give a rational account of his faith, it is the stretched passion which makes him what he is. They are people who suffered and yearned and strived with an unbelievable intensity; and no superstructure of logic ought to be allowed to mask that turmoil of feeling.

It may be said, of course, that the Puritan was better prepared for disappointment than most men and therefore less disposed to commit himself to a utopian dream. It was some such thought as this that led Professor Miller to say that a disillusioned Puritan is impossible to conceive.[3] Was it not the Puritan who had preached the arbitrariness of God and the depravity of man? Who was he to falter if the age missed what in his foolish pride he had allowed himself to believe was its destiny? I can only say this was not the mood of 1630, when the Pilgrims left England to build their Zion in the wilderness. It was not the mood of Oliver Cromwell when he told a Parliament of Puritan saints that they stood on the edge of the promises and the prophecies.[4] It was the Puritan's compromise with defeat, and when he finally made it—either in the despairing cry of the English Puritan, "God has spit in our faces,"[5] or in the melancholy dirge of the American Puritan at the end of the century—the crusade was finished.

The founders of New England not only shared the apocalyptic view of history with the Puritans whom they left behind. Their confession of faith, their search for regeneration and sanctification, their techniques of self-trial and self-denial, all spring from the same community of experience. A series of New England sermons explaining how God calls, justifies, and sanctifies his elect; a New England diary recording an agonizing search for the evidence of this work in the diarist's soul; New England's advice to educators on the education of a saint or to businessmen on the duty of combining "diligence in business with deadness to the world";[6] New England's conviction that every man is his brother's keeper; New England's persuasion that a good joke ought to be balanced with some savory morsel to keep merriment in its proper bounds; New England's cultivation of the Puritan art forms: the biography of the saint, the record of divine judgments, the history which weaves both into a narrative of God's blessings and punishments—all this, and much else, can be matched on both sides of the water. Behind it shines that vision which a tinker living on the ecstatic fringe of the movement described for all Puritans in the *Pilgrim's Progress.*

The specialty of the New England Way only emerged as its founders came to grips with the problems of embodying the vision in institutions. It is suggested by that analogy which was not confined to them but which acquired a more concrete and durable form in their experience than elsewhere: the analogy between themselves and the first people who were admitted into a covenant of grace with God. New England was to be a New Israel—a covenanted community. Its founders, who had already experienced in their own lives the sensation of being offered, and of accepting, the covenant of grace, were to form themselves into a community of saints for the enjoyment of God's ordinances and the elevation of their colony into the status of a chosen people. Such seemed to be the opportunity which God, working through the secondary causes which made colonization possible at this juncture of history, was offering to the regenerate. The labor of explorers, the greed of merchants, the ambition of kings, the pressure of persecution, the incidence of economic hardship, every motive and every capacity for colonization was but a web of contrivance designed by invisible hands for ends which only the elect could fathom. The interpretation of those ends in terms of a covenanted community begins with the famous sermon by Governor Winthrop in mid-ocean and only ends among the disenchantments of the late seventeenth century after desperate efforts to recall the wandering pilgrims to a proper sense of their destiny.

Let me quote Governor Winthrop's own words. They are taken from the sermon called "A Modell of Christian Charity," which was delivered on board the *Arabella:*

> Thus stands the cause between God and us; we are entered into Covenant with him for this work; we have taken out a Commission; the Lord hath given us leave to draw our own Articles; we have professed to enterprise these actions

upon these and these ends; we have hereupon besought him of favor and blessing. Now if the Lord shall please to hear us, and bring us in peace to the place
we desire, then hath he ratified this Covenant and sealed our Commission, and
will expect a strict performance of the Articles contained in it, but if we shall
neglect the observation of these Articles which are the ends we have
propounded, and dissembling with our God, shall fall to embrace this present
world and prosecute our carnal intentions, seeking great things for ourselves
and our posterity, the Lord will surely break out in wrath against us, be
revenged of such a perjured people, and make us know the price of the breach
of such a Covenant.[7]

What this decision came to mean was the tribalization of the Puritan
spirit. The goals of regeneration and sanctification, common to Puritans
everywhere, were to be sought within a tribal community. Let me sketch
some of the implications of this conception as it appeared to its authors.

First, no diversity of opinion in fundamentals would be permitted
within the tribe. Regenerate men, using that faculty of reason which grace
had restored, and applying it to the Word of God as revealed in Scripture,
could come to only one conclusion. Rightly informed consciences do not
judge differently; they concur. What they perceive is that regenerate men
must form their lives within an external discipline and cooperate in enforcing that discipline on the unregenerate. The mission of the elect is to uphold
an orthodoxy.

The external discipline of the tribe would involve, in Winthrop's
words, "a due form of ecclesiastical and civil government."[8] So far as the
first was concerned, all Puritans believed that the true form of ecclesiastical
government had been prescribed in Scripture, and what these Puritans
found in Scripture was authority for confining church membership to "visible saints." Churches would be composed of groups of converted souls who
formed a covenant among themselves to create a church and who looked
forward to a perpetual succession of saints who would enter the church
covenant as the work of conversion continued. The orthodox idea of a
church, whether in Anglican England or Presbyterian Scotland, was a body
coextensive with the community, admission to which depended on baptism,
subsequently confirmed by a profession of faith. But this New England
church is going to be built out of the conversion experience, and it is assumed that a subjective experience can be detected by objective tests.
However, there is one other class of members attached to the church besides
the converted. God's covenant with Abraham had included not only
Abraham but his seed. The children of the converted will be admitted to
baptism, in the expectation that they will eventually be able to attest the
conversion experience and qualify for full membership.

These churches, around which the New England towns will be built,
are autonomous congregations. The powers of church government were not
given by God to bishops, or to Presbyterian assemblies, but to them.
However, no anarchic consequences need be feared from their autonomy.
Rightly informed consciences reach the same conclusions; that is the essence
of the promise. Congregations are expected to consult if they encounter

difficulties, and erroneous consciences, persisting in their errors, will find themselves opposed by the massed forces of orthodoxy.

So much for the ecclesiastical discipline. But in a covenanted community the discipline of the state must also be directed by saints. It is true that all Puritans talk about the separation of church and state, and this is one of the things that distinguish them from all Anglicans. But nine out of ten Puritans only want to separate church and state in order to bind them together again. In other words, they have to break the indissoluble unity of church and state in Anglican England so as to get the church on its scriptural basis, Presbyterian or Congregational, as the case may be; but, once on that basis, they expect the state to uphold it, to be "the nursing father" of the church. Separation of church and state, in such a context, meant simply a division of functions between two partners with a tendency to reduce the state to a junior partner where the clergy claimed a superior insight into the Divine Will. In New England it was expected to be a partnership in unison, for church and state alike were to be dominated by saints.

The same compact among saints would underlie the civil government as it underlay the ecclesiastical government. The idea that political authority, while authorized by God, derives from the consent of the people was a familiar one in the English tradition, and Puritans invoked it to suit their purposes. The founders of Massachusetts were prepared to interpret their charter as a social covenant, and the communities which hived off from Massachusetts used the covenant device to launch their plantations. But the consent which is expressed in these compacts is not to be confused with any notion of popular sovereignty. Popular sovereignty is the grossest atheism in a Puritan universe governed by God. It is a consent to be governed according to the ordinances of God: an acceptance by saints of the political obligations of a chosen people.

These compacts do not commit them to any particular form of government. Forms of civil government, unlike forms of ecclesiastical government, are not prescribed in Scripture, and there is no reason why English representative institutions and English common-law principles should not be admitted into the holy community provided they do not prevent saints from governing that community, from protecting its church, and from making such changes as are necessary to bring English legal custom in line with the laws of God. However, this is some proviso. It means that in a remote corner of His Majesty's realm there will be a group of one-party states, where access to power depends on evidence of conversion. Party politicians will uphold the party preacher; laws will be modified to suit the party ethic; the administration of law will not be embarrassed by procedural safeguards; and all deviationists will either repent or suffer expulsion.

So much for "the due form of ecclesiastical and civil government." One further decision will be necessary to underpin the stability of the whole enterprise: a crucial decision about the qualifications of the prophet in the chosen community. The Puritan way of life had been worked out by a learned clergy, and learning—the learning of the schools—had been regarded as an indispensable means for the discovery and the application of the Divine Will in the lives of the regenerate. However, Puritanism had preached that without grace reason was helpless, that the pilgrim must await the miracle which no merit on his part could produce, and that, once this miracle had been bestowed, Christ was "ingrafted" in his heart. Could these regenerate spirits be held within any bounds? Could reason, which had begun by abdicating its authority, reassert itself so as to insure that one true discipline which was God's design for men—or even to insure any society at all? The whole history of Puritanism is a commentary on its failure to satisfy the cravings which its preaching had aroused. It was forever producing rebellions against its own teachers: rebellions within the learned camp and rebellions from outside that camp against the assertion that learned reason had anything to teach the illuminated spirit.

How much of this the founders of the covenanted community foresaw is open to question. The history of the Reformation had been full of it, and they were always being reminded by their enemies of the risks they ran; but in the nature of things these risks would not be fully revealed until the opportunity came for the saint to claim his privileges—the opportunity so delightfully expressed by that admirer of Anne Hutchinson who said to Edward Johnson: "I'll bring you to a woman that preaches better gospel than any of your black-coats that have been at the Ninneversity."[9] However, whether they foresaw it or not, it is certain that they carried with them the ideal of a learned clergy, and everyone knows of their determination to reproduce on the frontier the basic intellectual institutions of the Old World: the school, the college, the library, and the press. What is less clear, perhaps, since Professor Morison wrote his history of Harvard, is the purpose of these institutions. The merits of that great work speak for themselves, but it has one small flaw. The author has tried, in devious ways, to redeem his alma mater from the suspicion of being too much troubled by sin.[10] But the founders of Harvard College would hardly have thanked him for this carnal enterprise. What they aimed at producing was not Christian gentlemen with a liberal education but saints with a saving knowledge. The college was to be a school of prophets—learned prophets, certainly, but emphatically prophets. What else would a chosen people expect from its educational institutions?

I have tried to sketch the lines along which the vision would be embodied in these communities. Between 1630 and the mid-forties the work of planting and consolidating went on, until at last one species of Puritanism had been stabilized. Viewed simply as an achievement of order in the wilderness, out of human beings as potentially explosive as Puritans, this was certainly impressive. But it is no slight to the leadership to suggest that the problem of welding communities out of Puritan material was somewhat simplified for them.

The most obvious simplification was the opportunity to create a new community without having to tear an old one to pieces and to go on creating new communities if the first proved disappointing. These Puritans leave all their opponents behind them. They pass straight from settled life to the tasks of creating a new life without any disorderly interlude. When they reach the wilderness, work crowds in and danger binds them. If the worse comes to the worst, there is always the frontier. The deviationists can take their chances in Rhode Island. Thomas Hooker, who is no deviationist, but who may have felt that Massachusetts was too small for two such redoubtable saints as himself and Mr. Cotton, can become the founder of Connecticut. The saints in England must often have sighed for some such *Lebensraum*.

The other great advantage might seem to be the preagreement about ecclesiastical policy. Puritans had little difficulty in agreeing about doctrine. What they usually disagreed about was the form of church government within which the elect should fulfil their mission. When the Puritans came into power in England, they were prepared to fight a civil war over the rival merits of Presbyterianism, Nonseparating Congregationalism, and Separatism. New England, although it shares part of this experience in its contests with separatists like Roger Williams, rallies with surprising ease around the principle of Nonseparating Congregationalism and has relatively little difficulty with Presbyterianism. How did this happen?

It used to be thought that the adoption of Congregationalism was suggested by the example of Plymouth which the main body of the colonists found when they got there. It is now assumed that Professor Miller has conclusively demonstrated a pre-engagement among the majority of the clergymen which can be traced back through their Dutch experience to the original advocates of Nonseparating Congregationalism as a middle way between Presbyterianism and Separatism. However, Professor Miller has to admit that some ministers were Presbyterians; that others, who had not gone through the Dutch experience, might have been uncommitted, and that the views of the secular leaders, at the time of their arrival, are largely unknown.[11]

Doubtless the Congregationalists were in a position to take the initiative. But the acquiescence in that initiative must certainly have been helped by the composition of the Puritan population that came over here and by the frontier situation. Congregationalism aroused objections in England as an unsuitable organization for a community which was both hierarchical and centralized. It deprived the great Puritan magnate of his power to appoint ministers. It seemed to place hereditary influence at the mercy of the conversion experience, for, unless his children could attest it, they would presumably find themselves deprived of both church membership and political power.[12] Worst of all, it looked like a dangerous loosening of the social bonds to substitute a church of autonomous congregations for the corporate and centrally controlled church of tradition. Just how dangerous was to become clear enough in the Civil Wars when Congregationalism, in its separatist form, became the medium through which every kind of radicalism found expression. But few of these fears were realistic in New England. Puritan peers and very rich Puritans, the backbone of English Presbyterianism, were conspicuous by their absence. The lesser leaders who came over were reasonably insured against social, as distinct from theological, unrest by their monopoly of talent and by the frontier opportunities which took the sting out of class bitterness. And the communities to be administered were, after all, a handful of decentralized settlements as compared with a highly integrated England. Congregationalism commended itself to clerical specialists like Cotton and Hooker as the one form of church government prescribed by God for his saints; but, if the local situation had not made it a safe enough proposition, the Word would doubtless have seemed less clear.

So much for the New England Way viewed simply as an achievement of order. But how far did it fulfil the expectations of its founders: that this covenanted people would represent the ideal toward which all history was converging; that there would be a succession of saints with the same intense piety as themselves; and that under the rule of these saints the whole community would be held to the obligations of the covenant and sanctified by its blessings?

Much of the frustration which follows is common to Puritans everywhere. They had dreamed of themselves as a united army forming the vanguard of history; but the army splinters into columns, battalions, and platoons, while history seems to be marching on. They had thought that conversion could become an institution, but they find themselves with church members where they had hoped for saints. They had devised one of the most formidable disciplines ever seen for keeping sin within bounds, but there seemed to be as much of it inside the covenant as outside. They had demanded an impossible tension from the elect and an impossible submission from the mass. Everywhere the taut springs relax, the mass rebels, and compromises eat away at the distinction on which the whole system was based.

The history of the New England Way is the history of a losing struggle to preserve the intensity of the experience of the saint and his authority over society. On the one hand, a church of visible saints, each of whom could attest the miracle of conversion, is gradually transformed into a church where membership depends on a profession of faith and a standard of Puritan morality. On the other hand, the church, thus formalized, is deprived of its organic control of political power and forced to depend for its control over society on the opportunity its clergy have had to make themselves a ruling class and the allies of ruling families.

The decay of spiritual intensity is the theme of almost all the founders as they survey the tribal community in their declining years. Few things are more moving than the comparisons drawn by a Bradford, a Winthrop, or a Shephard between the spirit that sustained them and the spirit they find around them.

Let me quote from Bradford—that simple hero who never forgot, in all the labor of planting a colony, that his true home was elsewhere. He had copied into his journal the claim which the leaders of their little church had made when they applied in 1617 for permission to settle in the New World:

> We are knit together as a body in a most strict and sacred bond and covenant of the Lord, of the violation whereof we make great conscience, and by virtue

whereof we do hold ourselves straightly tied to all care of each other's good, and of the whole by every one, and so mutually.[13]

When he read that entry in his old age, he wrote this confession on the back of the page:

O sacred bond, whilst inviolably preserved! How sweet and precious were the fruits that flowed from the same, but when this fidelity decayed, then their ruin approached. O that these ancient members had not died or been dissipated (if it had been the will of God) or else that this holy care and constant faithfulness had still lived, and remained with those that survived, and were in times afterward added unto them. But (alas) that subtle serpent hath slyly wound in himself under fair pretenses of necessity and the like to untwist these sacred bonds and ties, and as it were insensibly, by degrees, to dissolve or in a great measure to weaken, the same. I have been happy, in my first times, to see, and with much comfort to enjoy, the blessed fruits of this sweet communion, but it is now a part of my misery in old age, to find and feel the decay and want thereof (in a great measure), and with grief and sorrow of heart to lament and bewail the same. And for others warning and admonition, and my own humiliation, do I here note the same.[14]

What had happened to them is part of the common experience of all creative revivals, when the first generation hands over to the second, when the organizer follows the visionary, and habit replaces direct experience as the source of guidance. But, of course, it is colored by their own circumstances. There is little to keep alive their memories of persecution. There is less and less to sustain their sense of the New World as a beacon for the Old when the progress of events in England reduces the New England Way first to a backwater of the Puritan spirit and later to a provincial anachronism. There is plenty of evidence that, in spite of all their precautions, worldliness is still with them and that saints who struggle to rule the world may find themselves ruled by it—especially the Puritan, who develops for religious purposes a type of character which can hardly fail to be a worldly success.

All this they see. What they fail to see is that the very work to which they have set their hands with so much resolution—the tribalization of the Puritan experience—is stifling its free spirit. Every repression of dissent, every insistence on the subordination of subjective experience to the judgment of the church, makes the work of enlisting zeal so much harder. They were probably right in thinking that order was possible on no other terms; but so was Anne Hutchinson when she accused them of substituting a covenant of works for a covenant of grace. Obedience to an external order, rather than immediate confrontation of God, was becoming, in spite of its formal theology, the criterion of New England Puritanism.

Before this first generation had passed away, it was obvious that the second generation would not be able to attest the conversion experience in sufficient numbers to perpetuate the succession of saints. It is some testimony to the severity of their standards that the fact was faced: that the second generation was held to be, and admitted itself to be, deficient in grace, though it was willing to support the church and to conform itself to its discipline. However, the sincerity of all parties only heightens the irony of a situation in which a chosen people cannot find enough chosen people to prolong its existence. Everything depended on saints. They composed the church and ruled the state. What would happen if the supply ran out? The escape was found through the famous halfway covenant, a device whereby the second generation was admitted to church membership, after making a profession of obedience, and so enabled to have its children baptized. The return to tradition had begun.[15] Of course the effort to produce conversions among the children and grandchildren was not abandoned. The preachers kept reminding themselves, and the clans, that the covenant had included Abraham's seed. But somehow, in spite of all their struggles, the religious experiences of the first generation refused to become a hereditary endowment. "Doth not a careless, remiss, flat, dry, cold, dead frame of spirit, grow in upon us secretly, strangely, prodigiously?"[16] We are hardly surprised to learn that the halfway covenant was in most cases just a halfway house between a church from which all but the saint had been excluded and one in which all but the flagrant sinner was admitted.

It was inevitable that this subsidence of the saints into a company of conformists should be reflected in the deterioration of Puritan piety. The congregations are not, of course, to be judged by the condemnations which the preachers heaped on them as part of the Puritan ritual during that prolonged jeremiad known to history as "God's controversy with New England." The deterioration is not a matter of crimes or misdemeanors. It is entirely compatible with the most persevering virtues. But it means contracted sensibility; gestures replacing feelings; taste subduing zeal; pride elbowing out humility; intellect playing a game; divided souls acting a part their ancestors have forced on them. It is the well-meant mimicries of Samuel Sewall which produce such farcical effects when compared with the old, high seriousness. The diarist who finds it "an awful yet pleasing treat" to review the coffins in his family vault has traveled a long way from Bradford or Winthrop.[17] Equally far is the distance between the Puritan who knew the difference between spiritual and financial success and his descendant who sometimes confused them. The old Puritans had a grim description for his comprise with the covenant: they called it "the forms of godliness without the power."

Meanwhile, as a utopian church subsides into an established church, its grip over political power also relaxes. An early symptom was that pressure for a rule of law as opposed to a rule of discretion which distinguished the politics of Englishmen everywhere in the seventeenth century. Saints in power were always tempted to demand as free a hand for themselves as possible. A life-tenure for the trusted saint seemed to Cotton, as it later seemed to Milton, the best security for the holy commonwealth, and Winthrop's effort to keep a wide discretion in the hands of a chosen few has its counterpart in Cromwell's practice. But on both sides of the water the parliamentary tradition refused to be ousted by the theocrats. In Old England it was temporarily swept aside and then vindicated at the expense of the saints. In

New England the saints discovered early that they would have to compromise with it if they hoped to control it. They were not even able to establish the system in Massachusetts without concessions to the principles of limited government which were extracted by the freemen in their struggles with the magistrates.

The intention, notwithstanding these concessions, was to maintain a theocracy within the forms of representative government, and the essence of the system was the restriction of political power to church members. In Massachusetts and New Haven this was achieved by confining the franchise to the elite. In Connecticut the same result could be expected without a formal restriction. But in the long run this monopoly of power was bound to be weakened by combined pressure from inside and outside: the pressure of expanding communities for a relaxation of religious tests and the pressure of imperial authority on a colonial theocracy. New Haven, the purest theocracy of the original settlements, had already suffered from its restrictive practices before its enforced absorption in Connecticut in 1662. Massachusetts, under pressure from England, went through the motions of liberalizing its religious tests at the same time. Finally, with the loss of the old charter in 1684, and the issue of a new one in 1691, the custodians of the Puritan ideal in Massachusetts were obliged to defend it under increasingly difficult conditions.

The power to choose their governor had passed to the Crown. Synods no longer advised legislatures. Boston flaunted the corruptions of a colonial court, the heresies of enforced toleration, and the sins of a thriving seaport before the eyes of the faithful, while the secularized culture of western Europe seeped in through a hundred different channels. No doubt all was far from lost. Preachers might keep their hold on rural communities by the combined force of personality and tradition. Conversions would certainly come back again; and the notion of a chosen people, still maintained in the pulpit, was only beginning its career in the world. But none of this should obscure the fact that an effort to escape from history into a utopia ruled by saints had suffered its usual failure.

NOTES

[1]John Cotton, *Christ the Fountaine of Life; or, Sundry Choyce Sermons on Part of the Fifth Chapter of the First Epistle of St. John* (London, 1651), p. 148.

[2]E.g., Perry Miller, *Orthodoxy in Massachusetts, 1630-1650* (Cambridge, Mass.: Harvard University Press, 1933); *The New England Mind: The Seventeenth Century* (New York: Macmillan Co., 1939); and *The New England Mind: From Colony to Province* (Cambridge, Mass.: Harvard University Press, 1953).

[3]"It is impossible to conceive of a disillusioned Puritan; no matter what misfortune befell him, no matter how often or how tragically his fellowmen failed him, he would have been prepared for the worst, and would have expected no better" (Perry Miller and T. H. Johnson, *The Puritans* [New York: American Book Co., 1938], p. 60).

[4]*The Letters and Speeches of Oliver Cromwell with Elucidations by Thomas Carlyle,* ed. S. C. Lomas (London: Methuen & Co., 1904), II, 299.

[5]This remark was the reaction of Charles Fleetwood, commander-in-chief, to the discovery that the last gamble of the military saints, in the autumn of 1659, had failed (quoted by M. Guizot, *History of Richard Cromwell and the Restoration of Charles II* [London, 1856], II, 64).

[6]The phrase is John Cotton's (quoted by Miller and Johnson, *op. cit.,* p. 61).

[7]Winthrop Papers, II (Boston: Massachusetts Historical Society, 1931), 294. The spelling in the quotation has been modernized.

[8]*Ibid.,* p. 293.

[9]Edward Johnson, *Wonder-working Providence of Sions Saviour in New England* (Andover, Mass.: Warren F. Draper, 1867), pp. 95-96.

[10]Professor Morison's determination to make humanists out of his Puritan ancestors appears in *Harvard College in the Seventeenth Century* (Cambridge, Mass.: Harvard University Press, 1936), p. 165; *Three Centuries of Harvard, 1636-1936* (Cambridge, Mass.: Harvard University Press, 1936), pp. 22-25; and *Puritan Pronaos* (New York: New York University Press, 1936), pp. 29-30, 39, 45, 52-53.

[11]See Miller, *Orthodoxy in Massachusetts.*

[12]The correspondence between John Cotton and Lord Say and Seal, who was contemplating emigration in 1636, reflects the latter's anxiety on this point (Thomas Hutchinson, *History of Massachusetts Bay* [1764], I, Appendix III, 496-501).

[13]*Bradford's History of Plymouth Plantation, 1606-1646,* ed. William T. Davis (New York: Charles Scribner's Sons, 1908), pp. 54-55.

[14]*Ibid.,* p. 55.

[15]Perry Miller, "The Half-Way Covenant," *New England Quarterly,* VI (1933), 703.

[16]Samuel Danforth, *A Briefe Recognition of New Englands Errand into the Wilderness* (Cambridge, Mass., 1671), pp. 12-13.

[17]*Diary of Samuel Sewall* ("Collections of the Massachusetts Historical Society: Fifth Series," Vol. V [Boston, 1878]), I, 444.

3
The Halfway Covenant
Edmund S. Morgan

Recent scholarship has made it clear that the church "way" was fostered with great care by the first generation of New Englanders to insure that members would be, insofar as humanly ascertainable, manifestly pious. Increasingly however, the intensity of the religious life expected of the "saint" seemed beyond the reach of the next generation. Professor Edmund S. Morgan, Department of History, Yale University, explores the ramifications of this development which issued in the so-called "halfway covenant."

The English emigrants to New England were the first Puritans to restrict membership in the church to visible saints, to persons, that is, who had felt the stirrings of grace in their souls, and who could demonstrate this fact to the satisfaction of other saints. The early Separatists had demanded the exclusion from the church of the visibly wicked; the later Separatists, and especially Henry Ainsworth, had implied that the exclusion of the wicked meant the inclusion only of saints; and at the same time the non-separating English Puritan divines had been teaching their readers and listeners how to recognize the movements of grace within the soul and thus to determine whether one was a saint or not. It had remained for the New Englanders to combine and carry these ideas to fruition by constructing their churches entirely of persons who had demonstrated their sainthood to one another.

Reprinted by permission of New York University Press from *Visible Saints: The History of a Puritan Idea*, by Edmund S. Morgan, © 1963 by New York University.

The impulse that produced this development was not novel. It had moved Donatists, Montanists, Albigensians, and many other Christians over the centuries. In the sixteenth and seventeenth centuries it carried the Baptists and the Quakers even farther than the Puritans. It was nothing more than man's yearning for holiness. The church has always been man's way of approaching divinity, and those who have joined the church have often sought to carry it with them in their progress from the wickedness of the world toward the goodness of God. The danger in such a move is seldom apparent to those who make it, the danger of deserting the world in search of a perfection that belongs only to heaven.

Those Puritans who believed in Congregationalism, that is, in churches gathered from the world by free consent, were especially prone to the danger. Although they prided themselves on not seeking perfection, the very act of gathering a church implied a departure from the world and a closer approach to perfection than others had attained. In New England the requirement that members have saving faith moved the churches farther from the world than the Separatist ones in England and Holland, which had required only good behavior and orthodox belief. To be sure, the New England Puritans admitted that their churches inevitably contained bad men as well as good, hypocrites who deceived their brethren and perhaps themselves by false assurance. But no such persons were knowingly tolerated. As Thomas Shepard, the pastor of the church at Cambridge, said, "if we could be so Eagle-eyed, as to discern them now that are Hypocrites, we should exclude them now," for "one man or woman secretly vile, which the Church hath not used all means to discover, may defile a whole Church."[1]

In moving their churches so close to God and so far from the world, the New England Puritans were doing what they believed that God required. But the move created a special difficulty for them, which was closely related to the problem that I have elsewhere called the Puritan dilemma, the problem of doing right in a world that does wrong. In a study of John Winthrop I have tried to show how an individual Puritan met this dilemma and how it affected his conduct of the civil government of Massachusetts. John Winthrop, while trying to live as God required, learned that he must live *in* the world, face its temptations, and share its guilt; and Winthrop helped to prevent the government of Massachusetts from seeking a greater perfection in this world than God required or allowed.[2]

Winthrop had less control, and less understanding, of the church than of the state. And the church, by any standards, had to be more pure than the state. But the New England churches, by the mid-1630's, were committed to a degree of purity that left their relationship with the world highly uncertain and untried by any previous experience in England or Europe. If the church could have been truly gathered from the world into eternity, there would have been no problem, for in eternity the visible and invisible churches would have become one. Freed from the world, and from their own corruptions, the members could have adored God in perpetual glory. But the visible church, like man himself, must remain *in* the world and must not only bring its members closer to God but must also help to redeem the rest of the world.

It was the church's task, acknowledged by Christians in all ages, to spread the gospel, to offer to all men the means of salvation. Though Puritans and other Calvinists thought the means would be effective only with God's predestined elect, not even the New England churches could hope to identify God's elect *before* God made that election manifest in saving faith. Though the New England churches might accept for membership only those who already had saving faith, they must offer the means of faith indiscriminately to all, serving as God's instrument for begetting faith in those who were predestined to receive it but had not yet done so. How to discharge this basic responsibility of the church became an increasingly difficult problem for the New England Puritans as they developed their idea of restricted church membership: their churches must not only be gathered out of the world but must continually gather *in* the world, continually search for new saints.

To the Anglican as to the Roman Catholic Church, this was no problem. With all but the most notorious sinners included, indeed compelled, within the visible church, each man could gain from it whatever God wished him to gain: the saint could grow in grace; the as-yet-unconverted saint could gain the understanding he needed for conversion; and all others could learn the justice of God in damning them. Everyone in the community was perforce exposed to all the means of grace, and there was no need to distinguish one man's eternal condition from another's. But how could a church serve God as an instrument for converting sinners if it consisted only of those who had been converted already?

This problem had faced the first gathered churches of Separatists. Even though they did not pretend to discern saving faith in the religious experiences of their members, they did appear to turn their backs on the mass of sinners around them. The Anglicans and the nonseparating Puritans accused them of neglecting the task of converting sinners and of plucking the fruit of other men's labors, of gathering men and women who had been taught Christianity in the very churches they complained of. How many persons, it was asked, had the Separatists "brought from grosse ignorance, unto true knowledge, from infidelitie, to holy Faith, from profanesse of life, to a conscionable walking with God?" Whatever understanding or faith the Separatists could lay claim to, they had "received by the ministerie of those men, and in the bosome of those Churches, which now they condemne."[3] In 1618 Thomas Drakes pointed out that "The Apostles, Evangelists, and ther holy successors, converted all sorts unto God, but these refined reformers, onely seduce the sound, and pervert and estrange from us, those, that are otherwise well affected."[4] And in Plymouth in 1624, the Pilgrims were accused of withholding the means of grace from all but the members of the church on the ground that "the Lord hath not appointed any ordinary ministrie for the conversion of those that are without."[5]

To such charges the Separatists could return only the feeblest of answers. They dodged the question of their own guilt by insisting that the business of the ministry was not to convert souls "but to fede and edifie" and discipline those already converted.[6] On this basis they could defend their own churches as true churches in spite of their failure to minister to sinners; and they could simultaneously attack the Anglican church as no church in spite of its conversions of sinners. In this argument and others the Separatists virtually denied the evangelistic function of the church. They even suggested that the government hire talented laymen to convert sinners, not as ministers but simply as preachers or speakers who would instruct the people in parish assemblies. Any who profited by the instruction could then join a church and come under the care of a true minister.[7] But such a suggestion implied that someone other than a minister could preach the gospel, and if so why not the vicars and curates and priests whom the Separatists denounced? The Separatists were indeed caught with the old riddle of the chicken and the egg. One nonseparating Puritan put the question to John Robinson, as to how on Separatist principles true churches could ever have been gathered in England after their alleged destruction by popery:

> Nowe, yf egge and bird be distroyed, I meane Church and ministerye, as you imagine, and the one cannott be without the other, riddle and tell me which shall be first, and where we shall beginne, whether at the bird or att the egg, whether at the ministerye or at the Church? Not at the Church, for that must be gathered by a ministerye of God's appoyntment, not at the ministerye, for there can be none but pastors and teachers, and these cannot exercise a ministerye without a calling, nor have a calling but from a true Church, which must not be compelled by the majestrate, but gathered by doctrine of the word into a voluntarye covenant with God. If you saie that till the Churches be gathered, there maie be another ministerye then that of Appostles, prophets, evangelistes, pastors, or teachers, then you confes Christ hath not taken order for all those kinds of ministeryes which should be needfull for the gathering together of all the saintes, contrarye to Ephe. 4, by your selues alleadged, and that there maie be some other ministery lawfullye and profitablie used, then he hath ordeyned, which you denye.
>
> Looke about you well and see that you are wrapped up in your owne cobweb, and eyther must breake it and lett the flie goe, or be swept awaie with it and her. Nowe God give you a wise hearte to consider this well. . . .[8]

The riddle was more than a technical difficulty, for it exposed a fatal arrogance at the heart of Separatism. The Separatist churches had no way of redeeming the world, no way of gathering new members except through the labors of other ministers whose mission they refused to recognize. The nonseparating Puritans in England escaped this dilemma and embraced the world of sinners in order to clasp the saints contained within it. They recognized the churches of England as true churches in need of reform but not without hope, and they charged the Separatists with arrogating to themselves an absurd self-righteousness, "as yf," one of them told John Robinson, "God had sent Mr. Johnson and you as the fire from heaven and had on earth no true visible Church rightlie gathered and constituted in his worship but yours at Leyden and his at Amsterdam."[9]

While the nonseparating Puritans remained in England, it must be remembered, they had not yet developed the idea of a church composed exclusively of saints. When they proposed to reform the churches of England, they thought of expelling the visibly wicked, not of regathering the church from persons demonstrating saving faith. (Even in New England, once they admitted a man to church membership, they would expel him only for open wickedness.) Doubtless they would have limited the Lord's Supper to a smaller group within each church, but they would have encompassed the majority of the population as church members and would have excluded or expelled only that part of the world which was in open rebellion against God. It came as a distinct shock to the English Puritans when rumors began to drift across the Atlantic in the late 1630's that their New England brethren, who in England had condemned the exclusiveness of the Separatists, were now practicing an even more invidious exclusiveness themselves.

When they left England in the 1630's, many Puritans assumed that they could and would leave the bad part of the world behind. They soon found that they could not. The fifteen or twenty thousand men and women who disembarked in New England between 1630 and 1640 included large numbers who had to be classified as visibly wicked, so many indeed that some of the founders contemplated a further withdrawal to an isolated area from which this "mixed multitude" should be excluded. The wisest recognized that the world neither could nor should be left behind, and no further exodus occurred. But in the 1630's, by adopting the new strict view of church membership, the New England Puritans executed a spiritual withdrawal from the mixed multitude that amounted almost to an ecclesiastical abdication from the world. They failed to consider, before adopting the new standards of membership, what relation their churches should bear to the mass of men excluded by those standards, and their failure exposed them to even more serious charges of neglect and arrogance than they themselves had formerly made against the Separatists.

Outside the church in New England stood not only the mixed multitude of wicked Englishmen and heathen natives, but also the visibly good, who understood and believed the doctrines of Christianity and lived accordingly but who lacked the final experience of grace. The New England churches made no differentiation among these seemingly different men. Indeed the New England ministers devoted a good deal of time to showing that there was no difference in the eyes of God between the vilest sinner and the "civil" man, who obeyed God's commands outwardly but did not love God in his heart.[10] The only distinction among men in the eyes of God was between those who had saving faith and those who lacked it. Therefore the civil and the uncivil alike were kept outside God's church.

Outside the church in New England, moreover, a man was much farther removed from most of the means of grace than he would have been in the Old World. In England and Holland the establishment of Separatist churches had deprived no one of church membership, for the Separatists were surrounded by other, more comprehensive churches open to all. In

New England the Puritans, certain that their way was the only one, forbade the erection of other churches. If a man could not qualify as a visible saint, he was wholly outside any church. He could not be baptized. He could not have his children baptized. He could not take communion. In England both these ordinances were available to everyone and were widely believed to be means of conversion through which God acted on the individual just as He did through preaching of the Gospel. But the New England Puritans did not share this belief and therefore felt obliged to deny baptism and communion to the unconverted. In their view both ordinances were seals of the covenant of grace which God extended to his elect. To permit an unbeliever to participate in them would be blasphemous. By this exclusion, however, the church deprived itself of two traditional means of bringing unregenerate men closer to God.

Church discipline, which might also have served this purpose, was similarly confined to those who least needed it. It was used only for recovering or expelling backsliding members. In England, though church discipline was lax, everyone in the community was subject to it. But the New England Puritans assigned to the state the task of disciplining those whom they excluded from their churches.

The absence of ties between the unregenerate part of the community and the church gave the latter an unprecedented purity, but it also placed the very life of the church in jeopardy. The members of the New England churches had themselves come from imperfect churches, in which they had learned the doctrines of Christianity, had taken the sacraments, and received the experience of grace that qualified them for membership in the proper churches of New England. But how would the mass of men who had come to New England unqualified for membership ever become qualified? How would civil men be encouraged to persevere in their outward obedience in the hope of eventual faith? How would the wicked be shown their wickedness? How would the gospel be spread to the heathen? Before leaving for America, many Puritan spokesmen had affirmed a desire to convert the natives. How would they do it with a church designed only for the saved? Without a surrounding of imperfect, unreformed churches, where would the reformed ones obtain a supply of members? How would God's elect be plucked from the mixed multitude?

New Englanders had failed to consider these questions, and when English Puritans asked them, the New Englanders, like the Separatists before them, replied in terms that exposed their failure to recognize the church's mission in the world. John Cotton, for example, the principal spokesman for the New England Way, could only ask of his critics: "May there not fall out to be Hypocrites in our Flock? and must wee not preach for their conversion? And are not the children of the Members of our Church, many of them such, as when they grow up stand in need of converting grace? . . . Besides when an Indian or unbeleever commeth into the Church, doe not all the prophets that preach the Word . . . apply their speech to his conviction and conversion?"[11]

The honest answer to the last of these questions was probably no. Nevertheless the New England Puritans did take one measure to fulfill the church's evangelical mission. Instead of waiting for unbelievers to wander into the meetinghouse, the civil government of Massachusetts in 1646 passed a law requiring everyone within a town to attend the preaching of the word.[12] Such laws were also passed in the New Haven and Connecticut colonies.[13] The government undoubtedly hoped that compulsory church attendance would improve the colonists not only in godliness but in behavior. Whether the result matched the hope is questionable, for those who attended from compulsion were unlikely to derive from the experience any feeling of kinship to the church. New England preaching, from the point of view of the unregenerate, left much to be desired. Although the Puritans acknowledged preaching to be the principal means through which God converted men, ministers addressed themselves more to saints than to sinners, in sermons designed less to plant the seed of faith than to nourish it where it already grew.[14]

To be sure, not all ministers neglected the unregenerate. Some preachers undoubtedly tried to make new converts from their captive audiences. The surviving sermons of Thomas Hooker, for example, are often addressed to perishing sinners. A few ministers like John Eliot even devoted their spare time to converting the Indians. But for the most part the New England churches, in striving for purity of membership, neglected sinners and heathen and civil men to concentrate on the advancement in grace of those who had already demonstrated saving faith.

If a New Englander did pause to consider the sinners outside the church, he was likely to compromise his insistence on purity of membership. John Eliot, for example, in corresponding with English Puritans about the church's evangelical mission, found himself proposing measures that were inconsistent with New England practice. At one point he advocated admitting everyone in a congregation to the privileges of the church "so as to keep the whole heape of chaff and corne together, only excluding the ignorant and prophane and scandalous." From this undifferentiated mass, there might be simultaneously gathered a special group of "the holy Saints, who are called higher by the grace of Christ," and who might "injoy together a more strickt and select communion" without deserting the regular parochial communion.[15] At another time Eliot proposed transplanting the holiest members of outstanding congregations into other congregations which needed some shining examples to leaven the wicked in their midst.[16]

Eliot never attempted to carry out these novel proposals which he made to Richard Baxter as suggestions for the churches of England. In New England, he and other Puritan ministers continued to exclude from the sacraments all but the proven regenerate. In spite of prodding from English Presbyterians and Anglicans, the New Englanders refused to reverse their withdrawal from the world, and refused any accommodation within the church to the well meaning and well behaved. But the world has its own ways of controlling those who propel themselves too far from it; and the

New England churches were eventually brought back to earth, not by the corruptions of the flesh, but by its biology.

The way of the world even in Massachusetts was to be born, grow old, and die. In the process each generation had to beget the next; and children did not spring fullgrown and fully educated from their mothers' wombs. They had to be nursed and nurtured mentally and spiritually as well as physically until they were fit to stand by themselves. Somehow the organization of the church had to be accommodated to these facts of life. As the saints died and their children grew up, there had to be a way of getting the new generation into the church.

The Baptists, with a yearning for purity similar to that of the Puritans, solved the problem, or succeeded in ignoring it, by recruiting all new members from adult Christians who had been awakened by Baptist preaching or the preaching of other ministers. As old believers died, newly converted ones would take their places; children were incapable of any kind of membership. The Puritans, both Separatist and non-Separatist, had disclaimed "Anabaptism." Although the most ardent sometimes succumbed to its attractions, the great majority believed that God required the church to baptize not only converted saints previously unbaptized but also the children of saints. Such children became members of the church, but not in the same sense as their parents.

In what sense was a question that troubled the Separatists in England and Holland very little. The younger children of Separatist church members there did not participate in the Lord's Supper, but as they grew to maturity, they could easily qualify for all the privileges of the church, if they wished to, simply by behaving themselves and learning what they were taught. But the Separatist experience could offer no assistance to New Englanders in this matter. New England had prescribed not merely understanding and good behavior but an experience of conversion, an experience beyond the range of human volition, as a qualification for adult membership. Yet New England still admitted children to this church by baptism, apparently expecting that they would pass from child membership to adult membership when they grew up, just as they had done in the Separatist churches and in the Church of England.[17] It was an arrogant and inconsistent expectation, for it implied a presumption that every child of a saint was destined for salvation and such a presumption was obviously wrong. No Christian could believe that grace was really hereditary.

The Puritans tried to overcome this inconsistency by demanding that when the child of a saint grew up he must demonstrate to the church that he was indeed saved. Until he did so, by the same kind of examination that adults seeking membership were subjected to, he should not be admitted to the Lord's Supper. So said John Cotton, Richard Mather, and the synod of divines who between 1646 and 1648 drafted the exposition of Puritan beliefs and practices which is usually referred to as the Cambridge Platform.[18] But the men who framed the Cambridge Platform did not say what happened to the membership of a child if he grew up and did not experience faith.

Before two decades had passed, the fact was plain that most children of saints did not receive saving faith by the time they were physically mature.

To judge from surviving records, it was uncommon for a man or woman to have the requisite religious experience before he was in his twenties. Often it came much later, and many otherwise good men and women never received it.

But if the holy spirit reached these men and women late or not at all, biological urges reached them early. They married young and had large families. When an unconverted child of a church member produced a child of his own, the minister of his church was presented with a problem, the complexity of which had not been foreseen by the architects of the New England system. The new father (or mother) had been in some sense a member of the church. Was he still? If so, was he a member in a different sense than before? What about the child? Was the child a member? Should the child be baptized?

The questions were difficult to answer, because every answer generated several more questions. If a child who grew to physical maturity without receiving faith was to be considered no longer a member of the church, how and when should his expulsion take place? The fact that he had acquired a child before he acquired faith was no sign that he would not eventually attain faith. Should the church meanwhile cast him out? If so, upon what grounds could it be done? The New Englanders, in adopting the new standard of membership, had not correspondingly altered their conception of church discipline. Admonitions and excommunications were still applied only for misconduct or for openly expressed heretical ideas; no one suggested that anyone be excommunicated for failure to display signs of saving faith. When, therefore, a child of a member grew to maturity without faith but without misconduct, it was impossible to find grounds for expelling him. To excommunicate him for having a child in lawful wedlock was palpably absurd. On the other hand, if he remained a member, his child must be entitled to baptism, and if so, why not that child's child too, and so on until the church should cease to be a company of the faithful and should become a genealogical society of the descendants of the faithful.

The Puritans had in fact moved the church so far from the world that it would no longer fit the biological facts of life. Had they been willing to move it a little farther still, by forming monasteries instead of churches, they might have concentrated on their own purity and left to others the task of supplying the church with new members. Had they been willing to abandon infant baptism, they might at least have avoided the embarrassment of trying to adjust spiritual growth to physical. As it was, they had chosen to apply in time and space a conception of the church that could never fit those dimensions. Given both infant baptism and restriction of church membership to visible saints, it was impossible for the Puritans either to evade the questions just posed or to answer them without an elaborate casuistry that bred dissatisfaction and disagreement. The history of the New England churches during the seventeenth and eighteenth centuries was in large measure a history of these dissatisfactions and disagreements.

In the first decade after the establishment of the more rigorous standard of membership, the questions were not yet urgent. The older children of church members in the new churches had been baptized in England and were perhaps not considered as sharing in their parents' membership. By the late 1640's, however, an increasing number of children who had been baptized in New England churches were coming of age without a religious experience and starting families of their own. The synod which met at Cambridge in 1646-1648 had been asked to decide the status of these persons. Since it failed to do so, every church during the 1650's had to face the question for itself, and most of them seem to have adopted a do-nothing policy by neither expelling the second-generation adults nor baptizing their third-generation children.[19]

By the late 1650's, the preaching of the word was generating few conversions, and with the end of the Great Migration, the overseas supply of saints had been cut off. As the first generation of Puritans died, the churches declined rapidly in membership, and it appeared that a majority of the population would soon be unbaptized.[20] This was an alarming situation for a community which had been founded for religious purposes. It was one thing to create a church of saints; it was another to let those saints carry the church out of the world with them entirely when they died. A meeting of ministers in 1657 and a full-scale synod in 1662 considered the problem and tried to find a solution that would retain a pure membership without destroying the church.

The synod did not address itself to the fundamental problem of the church's relation to the world at large, the problem of how to convert the unconverted. Instead, it confined itself to the more limited question posed by the birth of children to baptized persons who had not or not yet received saving faith. The synod adopted seven propositions, most of which simply affirmed the prevailing New England ideas about infant baptism and the construction of churches from visible saints. But the third, fourth, and fifth propositions settled the problem of the unconverted members and their children, as follows:

> Proposition 3d. The Infant-seed of confederate visible Believers, are members of the same Church with their parents, and when grown up, are personally under the Watch, Discipline and Government of that Church.
>
> Proposition 4th. These Adult persons are not therefore to be admitted to full Communion, meerly because they are and continue members, without such further qualifications, as the Word of God requireth thereunto.
>
> Proposition 5th. Church-members who were admitted in minority, understanding the Doctrine of Faith, and publickly professing their assent thereto; not scandalous in life, and solemnly owning the Covenant before the Church, wherein they give up themselves and their Children to the Lord, and subject themselves to the Government of Christ in the Church, their Children are to be Baptized.[21]

The fifth proposition was the crucial one. It meant that if a person born and baptized in the church did not receive faith he could still continue his membership and have his own children baptized, by leading a life free of scandal, by learning and professing the doctrines of Christianity, and by making a voluntary submission to God and His church. This submission, which proposition five calls "owning" the covenant, involved acknowledging the covenant with Christ and the church that had been made for one in infancy by one's parents, acknowledging, that is, so far as it lay within human power to do so. Although Puritan theology made such an acknowledgment meaningless unless it was the product of saving faith, owning the covenant was not intended to imply the genuine participation in the covenant of grace that came from saving faith. Nor was "understanding the Doctrine of Faith" supposed to imply the actual possession of faith. All the actions prescribed by the fifth proposition could be performed without saving faith. All were designed for the well-meaning, well-behaved but faithless offspring of the faithful. By the fifth proposition, these persons could retain their membership in the pure churches of New England simply by fulfilling the conditions which had formerly been required for membership in the Separatist churches of England and Holland.

The membership they retained, however, was not the full membership that had been granted in the Separatist churches. Rather it was the continuation of the membership they had had as children: they could not vote in church affairs, and they could not participate in the Lord's Supper (they were not members in "full communion"). What they gained was two privileges which had probably been hitherto denied them in most New England churches: the application of church discipline (they could be admonished or excommunicated for bad conduct) and baptism for their children. They were "half-way" members, and the synod's whole solution to the question of their status was dubbed the "half-way covenant."

The term was one of derision, invented by those who thought the synod's solution constituted a lowering of standards. But these opponents of the synod, who were numerous, proposed an absurd alternative to the concept of halfway membership. Faced with the problem of deciding on the status of the adults whom the synod made halfway members, the opponents admitted that the persons whom the synod placed in this category had been members of the church in their minority and also that they were subject to censure and admonition (but not excommunication) when they became adult. Yet, the opponents held, these persons at some undefined point, without action either by themselves or by the church, ceased to be members. They were *"felos de se,"* who cast themselves out of the church. Although the New England churches had never admitted the right of a church member to leave a church unless excommunicated or formally dismissed to another church, grown children were now held to have departed from the church without either themselves or the church knowing it.[22]

Such a view carried the church even farther from the world than the position it had taken in the 1630's. To be sure, the development of restricted membership, from the first Separatists onward, had steadily proceeded toward a greater withdrawal of the church from the world, and this had been accomplished by a continual refinement of doctrine. But the extreme position taken by the opponents of the synod was neither refined nor rational; and most of those who took it must eventually have either retreated to the halfway covenant or moved on to repudiate infant baptism.

The halfway covenant, while wholly insufficient as a recognition of the church's relationship to the world, was probably the most satisfactory way of reconciling the Puritans' conflicting commitments to infant baptism and to a church composed exclusively of saints. Its advocates argued persuasively against their opponents that the establishment of halfway membership was the only way in the long run to preserve the purity of full membership. Unless there was such a category the prospect of declining membership and the desire of parents to have their children baptized might tempt churches to admit persons to membership who were unworthy of the Lord's Supper. Men and women would be encouraged to play the hypocrite or to imagine themselves converted, by a process of wishful thinking, in order to gain baptism for their children. Only by distinguishing between those worthy of baptism and those worthy of the Lord's Supper, could the latter be preserved for the truly faithful.[23]

Baptism, it was pointed out, had never been considered as exclusive a sacrament as the Lord's Supper, for Puritans had always recognized baptism in any church, even the Roman Catholic, as valid, and did not repeat the rite for persons converted from that or any other Christian denomination. The drive toward exclusive membership had always aimed primarily at excluding the unworthy from the Lord's Supper. By establishing a category of halfway members, worthy of baptism, the synod hoped to preserve the sanctity of the Lord's Supper.

The supporters of the synod were able to collect a large number of testimonies from the books and manuscripts of the founding fathers, to show that insofar as the fathers considered the problem they had felt the same way about it as the synod. Thomas Shepard, Jr., unearthed and published a manuscript by his father, written three months before the latter's death in 1649. In it the elder Shepard, engaging in the familiar Puritan art of making distinctions, differentiated between the "inward reall holyness" of true saints and "federal holyness, whether externally professed as in grown persons, or graciously promised unto their seed." Only federal holiness was necessary for church membership. The children of saints must be presumed to have this and must be considered as church members until cast out by formal act of the church. Moreover, they must be cast out only if they committed open, outward offenses serious enough to bring the same judgment on any other member who committed them. Shepard, who had once warned against tolerating any known hypocrite in the church, was not dismayed in 1649 by a church in which the majority of members were unregenerate or as yet unregenerate children and children's children. Such a church, he acknowledged, would contain "many chaffy hypocrites and oft times prophane persons." But the same, he said, was true of a church freshly gathered of visible saints: you could never keep out hypocrites.[24]

Increase Mather, who liked to remind people that he was the son of Richard Mather and the son-in-law of John Cotton, at first opposed the halfway covenant. But when he swung round to support it, he produced an abundance of manuscripts from the desks of his father and father-in-law to show that they and their colleagues would have supported it too. Some of the statements adduced by Increase Mather may have antedated the full development of the New England system, but there were plenty of later ones to show that when the problem arose, the founders were disposed toward the solution adopted by the synod. Richard Mather, for example, in a letter dated in 1651, had stated his opinion "that the Children of *Church members* submitting themselves to the *Discipline of Christ in the Church,* by an act of their own, when they are grown up to mens and womens Estate, ought to be *watched* over as other *members,* and to have their Infants baptized, but themselves not to be received to the *Lords Table,* nor to *voting* in the *Church,* till by the manifestation of *Faith* and *Repentance,* they shall approve themselves to be fit for the same." Mather had admitted, however, in the same letter, that his church had "not yet thus practiced."[25]

The opponents of the synod did have one founding father on their side: John Davenport of New Haven was still alive and could speak for himself. He was the most articulate and strenuous enemy of the halfway covenant, but his opposition was not as damaging as it might have been because there was published proof that during New England's founding years he had held different views. As a candidate for the ministry in the English church at Amsterdam, Davenport had insisted that he would not baptize all infants presented to him but only those presented by their parents, and then only if the parents submitted to an examination about their beliefs or status. In a lengthy defense of this position printed in 1636 he had explained what he demanded of a parent, and that was simply membership in a Christian church (the Anglican church would do) or profession of the Christian faith. Thus in 1636 he had himself demanded much less than the synod demanded in 1662, and as a result he was not in a strong position to accuse the synod of betraying the standards of the founders.[26]

Although the theological battles of the 1660's were frequently waged with ammunition from the writings of the founding fathers, actually neither Davenport nor the other founders of New England had fully considered the problem of the next generation when in the 1630's they had adopted the test of saving faith for membership. And though historians have followed the opponents of the halfway covenant in hailing it as a betrayal of earlier standards and hence a symptom of the decline of piety, it was no such thing— unless John Calvin, Henry Barrow, Henry Ainsworth, John Robinson, William Perkins, William Ames, and William Bradshaw were all inferior in piety to the minority of New England divines in the 1660's who opposed the measure, unless John Davenport in 1636 was inferior in piety to John Davenport in 1664, unless indeed the founders of New England showed more piety by not facing the problem than their successors did by facing and answering it in 1662.

New England piety may have been declining, but the halfway covenant was *not* a symptom of decline. Rather it was an attempt to answer questions which neither English Puritans nor Separatists had had to face, questions which were created by New England's rigorous new conception of church membership but which the originators of that concept, during their brief experience, had generally been able to evade. By the 1660's the questions could no longer be evaded, but if the clergy and members of the New England churches had really been less pious than their predecessors, those questions might never have arisen. If, for example, they had succumbed to Arminianism, it would have been possible for anyone who wished to do so to join the church, simply by affirming his possession of a faith that lay within the reach of human volition. The halfway covenant became necessary, because New England churches of the second generation did hold to the standards of the first, because they did retain the belief in infant baptism, and because they did insist on the pattern of conversion outlined by Perkins and Hildersam and Ames.

Whether there was a decline of piety in the population at large is another question entirely, for the halfway covenant had nothing to do with the population at large. It is not a question I am prepared to settle, but it may be worth pointing out that though the rate of conversions during the second and third decades of New England's history was probably much lower than the founders had anticipated, this was not necessarily a sign of a decline in piety. The bulk of the population had arrived during the Great Migration of the 1630's and probably a large number of the first church members became so before the new admissions system was completely set up. How many would have become members if they had had to pass the new test we cannot tell. Since the second generation of New Englanders was thus actually the first generation in which every church member did have to pass the new test, a comparison of membership statistics in the first few decades, if they were available, would not solve our problem.

The halfway covenant, I would maintain then, was neither a sign of decline in piety nor a betrayal of the standards of the founding fathers, but an honest attempt to rescue the concept of a church of visible saints from the tangle of problems created in time by human reproduction. Nevertheless, the halfway covenant does mark the end of a phase in Puritan church history during which ministers and church members were so dazzled by the pure new institution they had succeeded in creating that they were for the moment blinded to their obligations to the rest of New England and to the world. The halfway covenant, taken by itself, was a narrow tribal way of recruiting saints, for it wholly neglected the church's evangelical mission to perishing sinners outside the families of its members. But it did turn attention, in however limited a manner, to the problem of propagating the church. As Jonathan Mitchel said, in defending the synod of 1662, "The Lord hath not set up Churches onely that *a few old Christians* may keep one another warm while they live, and then carry away the Church into the cold grave with them when they dye: no, but that they might, with all the care, and with all the Obligations, and Advantages to that care that may be, *nurse up* still successively *another Generation* of Subjects to Christ that may stand up in his *Kingdome* when they are gone, that so he might have a People and

Kingdome *successively* continued to him from one Generation to another."[27] With the New England churches' recognition of this obligation, the Puritans' single-minded march toward purity came to rest.

The halfway covenant brought into the open the difficulties that had been lurking in the Puritan conception of church membership from the beginning. From the time when the first Separatists left the Church of England until the establishment in Massachusetts of tests for saving faith, that conception had developed toward making the visible church a closer and closer approximation of the invisible. With the halfway covenant the Puritans recognized that they had pushed their churches to the outer limits of visibility; and the history of the idea we have been tracing reached, if not a stop, at least a turning point.

NOTES

[1]*Parable of the Ten Virgins,* II, 197, 198.

[2]*The Puritan Dilemma.*

[3]William Rathband, *A Most Grave and Modest Confutation of the Sect, commonly called Brownists or Separatists* (London, 1644), Preface. Though printed in 1644, this tract was written "many yeares since."

[4]Burrage, *Early English Dissenters,* II, 141. Cf. Robinson, *Works,* II, 54-55.

[5]Bradford, *History,* I, 399. Cf. the Pilgrims' answer to this accusation, *ibid.,* 401-402.

[6]Robinson, *Works,* II, 9-10, 401; Smyth, *Paralleles,* p. 140; Ainsworth, *Counterpoyson,* pp. 11, 69.

[7]Smyth, *Paralleles,* p. 111; Barrow, *A Collection of Certain Letters,* p. 59.

[8]Burrage, *Answer to John Robinson,* p. 76. Cf. Barrow, *A Collection of Certain Letters,* pp. 58-59; R. Alison, *A Plaine Confutation of Brownisme* (London, 1590), p. 125.

[9]Burrage, *Answer to John Robinson,* p. 79.

[10]See, for example, Thomas Hooker, *The Christians Two Chiefe Lessons* (London, 1640), p. 213; Thomas Shepard, *Works,* ed. John Albro (3 vols.; Boston, 1853), I, 29.

[11]*The Way of the Congregational Churches Cleared,* p. 74.

[12]*Records of the Massachusetts Bay Company,* III, 99.

[13]*Records of the Colony or Jurisdiction of New Haven, from May, 1653, to the Union,* ed. C. J. Hoadly (Hartford, 1858), p. 588; *The Public Records of the Colony of Connecticut, Prior to the Union with New Haven Colony,* ed. J. Hammond Trumbull (Hartford, 1850), p. 524.

[14]E. S. Morgan, *The Puritan Family* (Boston, 1944, 1956), pp. 90-104.

[15]*Correspondence of Baxter and Eliot,* p. 25. Cf. John Eliot, *Communion of Churches* (Cambridge, Mass., 1665).

[16]*Correspondence of Baxter and Eliot,* p. 40.

[17]The founders of the Salem church evidently shared the Separatists' expectation that the ensuing generations would enter the church as they acquired an adult understanding of the principles of religion. See Morton, *New Englands Memoriall,* p. 77.

[18]Cotton, *The Way of the Congregational Churches Cleared,* pp. 5, 79-80, 111-13; Mather, *Church Government and Church Covenant Discussed,* pp. 20-22; Walker, *Creeds and Platforms,* p. 224.

[19]The surviving records are not clear on this matter, but the controversial literature following the synod of 1662 seems to support this statement. Jonathan Mitchel charged the opponents of the synod with holding principles that would require the expulsion of "all the adult Children of our Churches that are not come up to full Communion." The implication is that such expulsions had not taken place and would be shocking if they did. (*A Defence of the Answer,* pp. 4-16.) Richard Mather implies that the churches had not generally exercised discipline toward adult children of members: ". . . we know but little of the exercise of Church-discipline towards such." (*Ibid.,* p. 60.) Increase Mather in *A Discourse Concerning the Subject of Baptisme* (Cambridge, Mass., 1675) states (p. 29) that churches in Plymouth colony exercised discipline toward children of the church, but (pp. 30-32) that elsewhere it was neglected. But perhaps these statements all refer to excommunication rather than lesser forms of discipline, for Henry Dunster in a letter written about 1652, stated concerning unconverted children of members: ". . . such there be amongst us with whom the Church bears patiently, using means for their Conviction and Conversion. And in case they break out into any unchristian courses, admonish them, and if they continue in them, wholy withdraw from them. But I have not knowne any of these formally excommunicated because they neither cared for nor sought Communion." Jeremiah Chaplin, *Life of Henry Dunster* (Boston, 1872), p. 288.

[20]"It is easie to see that in the way your self and some others go, *the bigger half of the people in this Country will in a little Time be unbaptized.*" Jonathan Mitchel to Increase Mather, appended to Increase Mather, *The First Principles of New England* (Cambridge, Mass., 1675).

[21]Walker, *Creeds and Platforms,* pp. 325-28.

[22]Charles Chauncy, *Anti-Synodalia Scripta Americana* ([London], 1662); John Davenport, *Another Essay for Investigation of the Truth* (Cambridge, Mass., 1663).

[23]Jonathan Mitchel and Richard Mather, *A Defence of the Answer,* pp. 45-46; Increase Mather, *Discourse Concerning Baptisme,* p. 52.

[24]Thomas Shepard, *The Church Membership of Children, and their Right to Baptisme* (Cambridge, Mass., 1663) pp. 13-14.

[25]Increase Mather, *The First Principles of New England,* pp. 10-11.

[26]John Davenport, *An Apologeticall Reply to a booke Called An Answer to the unjust complaint of W. B.* (Rotterdam, 1636); *Another Essay for Investigation of the Truth* (Cambridge, Mass., 1663).

[27]*Defence of the Answer,* p. 45.

4

The Myth of Declension

Robert G. Pope

*The course of Puritan fortune in the New World has generally been interpreted, begin-
ning with the Puritans themselves, as one of decline—from colonists to provincials,
Puritans to Yankees, and finally from visible saints to indifferent (if successful) farmers
and merchants. Professor Robert G. Pope, Department of History, the State University
of New York at Buffalo, challenges interpretations based on this premise in the following article.*

If any single concept pervades the historiography of seventeenth-
century New England, it is clearly the idea of "declension." Regardless of
their intellectual predispositions or their overall assessment of Puritan
society, historians have agreed on one thing—New England Puritanism had
fallen on bad days by the time Increase Mather brought home the new
charter of 1691. Some historians have cheered the change; others have
lamented it; but all have accepted it as fact.

The religious filiopietists like Leonard Bacon and Henry Martyn Dexter bemoaned the loss of purity and pointed accusing fingers at their
forebears' willingness to sacrifice principle to expediency. Both men singled
out the adoption of the half-way covenant in 1662 as a turning point for
New England, the beginning of the innovations which had continued unto
their own day.[1] More hostile secular historians, and one thinks here of the

First published as "New England versus the New England Mind: The Myth of Declension,"
The Journal of Social History, III, (1969-70), pp. 95-108. Reprinted by permission of *The Journal of Social History* and the author. Copyright Peter N. Stearns.

triumvirate of Adamses—Brooks, Charles Francis, and James Truslow—
applauded the transformation. If their attitude toward the first generation
oligarchy was ambivalent, they were openly contemptuous of the second
and third generation elite and in its fall they saw the opening of a brighter
new day.[2] In recent decades a far more sophisticated analysis of declension
has supplanted the views of these men. In the monumental work of
America's finest intellectual historian, the late Perry Miller, and that of his
disciples, the dissection of the New England mind has revealed a far more
subtle and complex alteration than any of their predecessors imagined.[3]
Since the 1930s the history of seventeenth-century New England has been
almost exclusively the province of the intellectual historian. When others in-
truded, they found their problems already defined and their vocabulary
delimited. That in many instances the intellectual historians were
remarkably gifted and perceptive men has, ironically, compounded the
problem. Our wholesale devotion to the intricate process of the New
England mind—something that earlier generations rarely acknowledged
even existed—has given us a distorted view of New England's transformation from the world of John Winthrop into the world of Cotton Mather. We
have, in effect, made New England over in the image of its literature.
Swayed by the Puritans' rhetoric we have lost track of New England's
realities.

Probably no other generation of Americans has had its writing
scrutinized more carefully or taken more seriously. The enormous scholarly
exegesis of Miller in particular has noted, explained, and amplified almost
the entire corpus of Puritan literature. All other aspects of cultural and institutional change are made intelligible through this key. Unfortunately the
attempt to extrapolate social history from intellectual sources has created
some misconceptions about New England. For example, Solomon Stoddard
is regularly enshrined in New England's pantheon for his supposed role in
revitalizing Congregationalism with a daring innovation which discarded
the regenerative experience and opened the church to all godly inhabitants.[4]
But several Congregational ministers in Connecticut anticipated "Stoddardeanism" by at least a decade and they applied the practice far more successfully than Stoddard himself had in Northampton. A generation before
Stoddard and Mather filled the Boston presses with tracts on church
membership and sacraments, Connecticut churches faced and resolved the
same issues.[5] But Connecticut's innovators have been relegated to historical
limbo because they failed to leave behind the theological literature upon
which historians have reconstructed New England.

Obviously history cannot be divorced from the realm of ideas without
rendering it as sterile as an accountant's ledger. But when intellectual
history attempts to interpret social change it must occasionally look to the
external realities. When these are ignored the basis for the critical judgment
of ideas is lost. The interpretation of New England Puritanism that has
emerged in the last two decades reveals the dangers of extrapolation and
suggests that historians need to reread the literature of Puritanism in a new
light.

The traditional portrait of New England's declension depicts a period of increasing religious apathy—a spiritual deadness and loss of piety which was manifested in steadily declining church membership. That stream of new saints envisioned by the founding generation simply failed to materialize in the free air of the new world. The ministers, in order to cope with the threat this represented to the continued institutional life of the churches and their own influence in the community, supposedly devised a succession of innovations which made church membership more easily attainable. These innovations not only compromised the original toughness and intellectual integrity of the first generation, but also contributed to further attenuation of religious zeal.[6]

Foremost on the list of innovations is the half-way covenant, the change in polity which permitted baptized but unconverted children of the saints to retain partial membership and have their own children baptized.[7] Virtually everyone accepts the thesis that the churches immediately filled with half-way members who found their limited status completely satisfactory and would have been incapable of attaining full church membership had they desired it. Two decades later, in the face of continuing decline, the ministers compromised again with the mass covenant renewal, first for church members and then for the entire community, hoping vainly to achieve through a communal rite what apparently lay beyond the power of individuals.[8] To fill their churches ministers cheapened the covenant beyond recognition and it was left to Solomon Stoddard to tell the emperor he had no clothes. Once the historian has absorbed the contemporary Puritan literature, with Miller's aid, he finds all around him obvious examples which reinforce the impression of declension. The half-way covenant, the mass covenant renewals, the admission of strangers into the covenant, all become indices of a weakened religious life. That John Cotton would have scorned them and that later generations were uncomfortable in their apostasy are ample proofs that they are, de facto, declension.

Three basic objections can be raised to this portrait of declension: first, it assumes that at some point the Puritans achieved an ideal intellectual and social system; secondly, the term itself is value laden; and finally, it misrepresents the realities of Massachusetts history.

In *The New England Mind* Miller first recreates the Puritan's all-encompassing world view, and then he details the demise of that view and the creation of a New England provincial mentality. For Miller, the transformation began in the late 1640's, accelerated with the Half-Way Synod (in fact, he calls 1662 the end of the medieval mind in America),[9] and then hurtled toward its nadir in the first decades of the eighteenth century. More recently, in a detailed study of Boston, Darrett Rutman has suggested that the process of declension began very early and was almost fully accomplished by Winthrop's death in 1649.[10] As we gradually push the beginnings of declension back toward the founding of the colony, we reveal the inadequacy of the concept. If decline began when John Winthrop and his fellow travellers stepped ashore from the *Arabella* and transformed the idea into reality (and this seems the logical conclusion), then all we are saying is that from the very start Puritans adapted and changed to fit the environment. The only absolute from which they declined was a theoretical one and that may exist only in that twentieth-century imaginative construct called "the New England mind."

The term itself suggests the imposition of a set of values on the historical context. Declension implies a retrogression or fall from a higher state to a lower. But clearly the concept cannot apply to decline from what an individual historian perceives as "ideal" religion; if it is to have meaning it must apply to the nature of change itself. But who decides when change is progress or decline à la Spengler and Henry Adams? Declension has become a shorthand device that perpetuates misunderstanding; it categorizes the quality of change without analyzing the substance of it.

The most serious shortcoming, however, is that the concept conflicts with social and institutional realities. It totally misconstrues what was going on in Massachusetts churches in the seventeenth century. The half-way covenant, on which so much of the "proof" of declension has depended, simply did not produce the results that historians have attributed to it. Despite the stamp of approval from the ministers and from the General Court, neither churches nor individuals flocked to take advantage of more generous baptism. By 1675, only two-fifths of the churches in Massachusetts had adopted even the *principle* of the innovation. Only a few churches used the half-way covenant extensively or had fully integrated it into their polity as the synod had envisioned. A large number of those that had endorsed the principle had never had a member "own the covenant."[11] The remarkable element after 1662 is not the way in which members took advantage of the easier way into the church, but rather their intransigence. In a majority of Massachusetts churches the members simply refused to give their assent to the innovation, despite the pleas of the clergy. Even where the principle was accepted it often came out of deference to the minister, and the congregation refused to use it within their own families, thus effectively nullifying the innovation. Most Massachusetts Congregationalists apparently remained convinced that only one right way existed to qualify their children for baptism and that was through full communion and the required regenerative experience—even if that meant that their own children remained unbaptized. This is the quality of religious scrupulosity that most historians have lost sight of.[12]

A good example of this occurred in Dorchester where Richard Mather had fruitlessly devoted twenty years to convincing his congregation to accept the half-way covenant. In 1668 he told the members of the desire of one woman, baptized in the Dorchester church, to own the covenant and have her children baptized. After considerable debate the congregation asked Mather to speak with her to see if she would join in full communion instead (which would, of course, also have qualified her children for baptism). Mrs. Taylor refused: "She did not judge her self as yet fitt for ye Lords Supp & therefore durst not adventure ther uppon, but yet did desier baptizme for her Children." The church reluctantly refused.[13] Had she been less scrupulous, had she wanted baptism for her children above all, Mrs. Taylor could easily have joined in full communion.

Those who mark the half-way covenant as certain proof of declension might well consider this second dimension of scrupulosity. In Mrs. Taylor it appeared as reluctance to come to communion when asked, although she qualified by all external evidence. More frequently scrupulosity appeared as the unwillingness to use the half-way covenant even when it became available. Testified regenerate membership had become so ingrained that parents would rather stay out than take the proffered shortcut. Nor was this simply a matter of waiting a few years until lay resistance dissipated; at the rate Massachusetts churches were proceeding it would have taken two generations or more before the half-way covenant became an integral part of the New England Way. The general reaction was particularly dismaying to the clergy; as John Woodbridge described it, "the churches are such a heavy stone at the ministers' legs that they cannot fly their own course."[14] In other words, after almost three decades of agitation and thirteen years as part of the official "orthodoxy" the half-way covenant had had almost no measurable effect on church membership in Massachusetts.

Only after 1675 did the half-way covenant come into its own as part of the new orthodoxy. In 1675 the colony stood on the brink of a traumatic social upheaval. In the decade and half of crisis which began with King Philip's War, church after church adopted and utilized the half-way principle until by 1690 probably less than one church in five still followed the older practice. The half-way covenant no longer generated controversy; in fact, the propositions of the Half-Way Synod represented a moderate position. A large number of churches, as they confronted a radically altered religious context, introduced innovations which broadened the covenant beyond anything conceived in 1662 or for the thirteen years thereafter.

In 1675 God's judgment fell on New England and the jeremiads seemed fulfilled in ample measure. But no one could have prophesied the terror of King Philip's War. Half the towns in Massachusetts and Plymouth suffered Indian attacks and at least ten towns were abandoned. The war decimated the militia and left the colony reeling. No sooner had this scourge passed than new signs of God's wrath appeared: two great fires in Boston; a smallpox epidemic; an outbreak of the fever; and threats to the charter and the economy in the person of Edward Randolph. The 1680s proved even more disastrous to the existing order. The political confusion which followed the revocation of the charter and culminated in the Andros regime threatened every element of stability in the colony; land tenure, self-government, Congregationalism, all appeared marked for major revision. The broad implementation of the half-way covenant can only be understood as response to crisis. Insecurity and anxiety convinced church members, as the ministers had never been able to do, that they must re-interpret their relation to the church.

In fact, what happened in Massachusetts in these fifteen years can only be described as a major revival in church membership—a turning to religion and the churches on a scale that had not been experienced since the first decade of settlement. The assumption that church membership steadily declined in the last three decades of the century is totally inaccurate. Data from research on all the churches in Massachusetts and Connecticut for which material is still available lead to one firm conclusion—the middle of the century, not the end, marks the lowest ebb in church membership. In three Boston area churches—Charlestown, Roxbury, and Dorchester—the average increments of new communicants in the fifteen years of crisis almost doubled the levels of the 1660s, and they are higher than at any time since the churches were founded. All three of these churches almost certainly had a higher percentage of the inhabitants in full communion in 1690 than they had had twenty years earlier.[15]

A second aspect of church membership that supports this thesis of revival in response to crisis or social disruption is the religious involvement of the men. Traditionally in stable Western societies religious activity becomes the province of the woman; she handles that part of the socializing process. In every Massachusetts church examined, the women consistently became a numerical majority of the church within the first five years of its foundation. By 1640 women constituted a majority of church members and the ratio of women to men progressively increased until 1675. When the crisis began there is evidence of a shift. Two of the three churches mentioned above noted quite radical changes. In Roxbury the percentage of men joining in full communion increased from 19 percent between 1670 and 1676 to 46 percent between 1680 and 1689; in Dorchester it went from 38 percent to 49 percent and in this church 56 percent of the half-way members were men. Although some improvement also occurred in Charlestown, it was less dramatic (an increase from 25 percent to 30 percent).[16] Men were most likely to suffer from the social dysfunction of the period and they came into the churches in numbers unequalled since the 1630s.

Religion is in part the human response to contingency and powerlessness; as these factors increase in any given era, the overt religious response is almost certain to increase. From 1675 on, and particularly after 1684, the churches of Massachusetts offered to men a solace and stability that had disappeared in their normal context. The implementation of the half-way covenant after 1675 must be understood in the same light—as a religious response to crisis. Massachusetts was uniquely prepared psychologically for internal and external disaster. The jeremiads had conditioned the Puritan mind to the logic of the covenant: sin, affliction, confession, restoration.[17] When the calamities, even more fearful than the ministers had dared predict, befell Massachusetts, the people recognized them for what they were— judgments of God. The response of the churches and the people could not have come out of an apathetic society; it was not a sign of declension, as we are frequently told, but of piety.

But we cannot simply jettison the misleading concept of declension, for that only renews the conceptual void that Miller was striving to fill and makes the processes of change as mysterious as ever. Two concepts from the sociology of religion, when they are used in conjunction, offer new possibilities for understanding what happened in seventeenth-century Massachusetts. One is the "church-sect" typology developed by Ernst Troeltsch and elaborated upon by Weber, Wach, Wilson, and Niebuhr,[18] and the other is functional analysis. The remainder of this essay will explore church membership in the role of the churches and their relationship with society at large. Here it seems the evolution of the "church-sect" typology is most apparent.

The original Puritan vision of their holy commonwealth contained a dual mission: first, they wanted to create in the new Israel a moral, covenanted society where men abided by God's laws; second, they wanted to erect truly reformed churches containing only visible saints. At the time of their migration the Puritans embodied the Calvinistic union of both church and sect, with some functions tending to be more sectarian and others more churchly. The churches themselves were both national *and* free—a holy community and an institution—and the society itself had a concrete mission which gave it a cultural unity that was enforced by the state. Thus from the outset there existed an inherent tension and conflict between the goal of a covenanted community and that of the covenanted churches, since they were not coextensive as they had been in Geneva or in medieval Christianity. In the first few years in Massachusetts the Congregational churches appear to have followed the Separatist example to determine church membership, for after all few of them had known the opportunity in England to determine who was and who was not a visible saint. The tests imposed in the Massachusetts churches—decent civil behavior, knowledge of the principles of the faith, and a desire to join the church—minimized the tension by leaving the doors of the churches open to most men of good-will thereby reducing the gap between the religious and the civil communities. But the Puritan zeal for a purer church brought an innovation that tightened the requirements. By 1640 almost every church required a candidate for admission to relate to the assembled congregation the process of his conversion. Good behavior, knowledge, and desire no longer sufficed.[19]

The morphology of conversion, initially developed by English Puritan divines as a guide for the individual soul, was transformed into a yardstick to measure the faithful. Testified regenerate membership put beyond the grasp of all but a few what had once been within the reach of most men. The strictness of the new test—and, of course, it quite rapidly became routinized and even more difficult to experience—made entry into the church so limited that few persons qualified. But Congregational policy, devised in a simpler era, limited baptism and church discipline to members and their children. Here was Congregationalism's quandary: it had predicated the continuing life of the church and the religious mission of the community upon a hereditary growth of faith, but the new test put a barrier between the children and the church. The primacy which Puritans placed on visible conversion as the basis for church membership destroyed the initial equilibrium between church and sect and turned New England toward sectarianism.

The emphasis on the doctrine of preparation[20] which underlies the entire antinomian controversy may represent an attempt to ameliorate the rigidity of the new test and preserve the essentially communal aspects of striving for sanctification. But preparation by itself was inadequate in the new environment. The religious history of seventeenth-century Massachusetts is the story of the struggle to live with a concept of purity within the context of a covenanted community.

In part the clergy devised the half-way covenant to restore the equilibrium, although they were not completely conscious of this function. By creating a dual membership—the first for baptized believers who would be subject to church discipline and given a reason to strive for holiness, and the second for the core of regenerate believers—they preserved what they considered a real advance in reformation and they also closed the broadening gulf between the churches and the community. They achieved this revolution only by compromising the original concept of the covenant of grace and by attributing to the unregenerate capabilities they had previously denied existed. The chief opponents of the half-way covenant, John Davenport and Charles Chauncy, did not lack theological sophistication, nor were they short-sighted purists. They understood the issues clearly, but preferred marching the churches out of the world to compromising purity for the sake of the city on a hill.[21]

Perhaps the only reason New England was able to maintain its ideals as long as it did—compare it to England where the same idealism was shattered by the Civil Wars and the idea of free churches became a reality—was because of the state. For Massachusetts the state served as church and the churches served as sects within it. The state made it possible for the churches to behave as sectarians by keeping the entire community in line with God's laws and by serving many of the roles normally fulfilled by the church. The greatest catastrophe of the century for the colony's mission was the revocation of the charter in 1684.[22] For a half-century the state had bound the whole community in covenant with God. When Massachusetts lost the charter and with it the "due forme of government" that Winthrop and his friends had established, only the churches remained to fulfill the mission of the covenanted community.

Revocation of the charter destroyed the protective shield of a sympathetic state which had permitted the churches to retain their sectarian practices. The loss thrust new burdens on the churches and forced them to redefine their relationship to society. The old tribalism that had contented itself with familial Christianity could not preserve the covenanted community. The Congregational churches faced an unpleasant dilemma: they could either bring themselves more fully into the community, or they ran the risk of losing control completely. If Massachusetts was to meet the internal and external threats to the Puritan way, the churches had to speak to and effectively influence a segment of the population they had previously ignored. This meant developing a new evangelism, taking a different attitude toward the unchurched, and further revising the standards for church membership.

The churches met the challenge fairly successfully. The expansion of church membership which had begun after 1675 with "crisis" conversions and implementation of the half-way convenant continued and even expanded. Some New Englanders who had tenuous church connections but who had hitherto hung back from church membership because of religious scruples, doubts, or disinterest now came forward to strengthen by their membership the principal institution that remained for the expression of the Puritan way. It became an act of fealty.[23] Prior to revocation most new members were the descendants of the saints and the easing of requirements was directed primarily at those who had "holy roots." After 1684 the appeal was directed to the people with or without church connections. Mass covenant renewals and a broader half-way covenant meant that almost every adult in the community had a way into the church.[24] It is probably quite true that the "quality" or rigor of the conversion experience required for admission to communion declined with this new outreach, although that does not signify that people were less religious. In 1635 the Puritans feared the pollution of the sanctuary; in 1690 their survival depended on filling the sanctuary. A share in the covenant had become a political, social, and religious obligation by the end of the century and the evolution of Massachusetts from sect to church was complete. The man who most fully recognized the implications of the previous eighty years was not Cotton Mather but Solomon Stoddard.

The Puritans confronted in Massachusetts what every sect has faced in its children, and it should not surprise us that they, like others, failed to understand what was happening. H. Richard Niebuhr has suggested that it may be impossible for a sect to survive beyond the first generation[25] and the Massachusetts experience tends to support that thesis. Revision was inescapable, yet revision created the anxiety and guilt that permeated the rhetoric of the age.

The majority of the men and women who settled Massachusetts in the first decade represented an extraordinary religious experience. They were "twice-winnowed": first they had dared or had felt inwardly compelled to advocate Puritanism in the hostile English environment, and second they had risked lives and estates to create a new Israel in the wilderness. It appears from Michael Walzer's superb study[26] that Puritanism appealed most directly to those who sensed in early Stuart England a profound disorder verging on chaos and turned to Puritanism for meaning or an internal gyroscope. (Witness, for example, John Winthrop's increasing anxiety in the 1620s.) As a group or party the Puritans anticipated their rise to power as an opportunity to restore order and stability—in private lives and public lives—through what Walzer calls repression. Although in old England the attempt to bring order out of chaos failed dramatically, in New England it was a triumphant success.

For their success in establishing order however the Puritans paid an unexpected price. The second generation, the children of the saints, grew to maturity in the stable religious environment of New England. For them there were no counterparts to Laud's pursuivants, the Tower, or the exodus, and their parents may well have thanked God for that. But where elders and magistrates enforced God's laws with the general approbation of the people, it became less and less likely that the rising generation would experience the "soul-shattering" conversion. That wrenching out of the world's sin so common to their parents in religiously contentious England appeared all too rarely in the holy commonwealth. The challenge to the children of the saints lay in conquering the physical wilderness in accordance with God's laws.

The introduction of testified regenerate membership thus placed an added burden on the children; it demanded what they were least capable of realizing. Further the testimony of regeneration became an obstacle to conversion as the churches quickly routinized it: guidelines became hard lines. Not that churches denied membership to those that applied, for this happened very rarely, but the children had a model before them, a normative experience. When their own religious experiences failed to conform, they questioned their validity and waited. The conversion experience established by the first generation was a "patterning" based on an English environment which bore little resemblance to the "mature" faith that came from stability and habit.

A second aspect of the dilemma facing the second and third generation Puritans came from their distorted historical perspective. They engaged in an oppressive filiopietism that transformed the founding generation into paragons of social virtue, wisdom, and saintliness. Although this is a common tradition, for Massachusetts it was nearly disastrous. It not only established difficult standards to live up to, but it also reflected a failure to understand what the founders had, in fact, done in Massachusetts. Later generations never seemed to realize that in the first two decades of the colony's history the founders had more or less continuously experimented, adapted, and changed their politics and their polity to fit the new environment. Only in 1648 had they set down their "final" thoughts in the Cambridge Platform, outlining and justifying the New England Way. Subsequent generations saw only this construct, achieved at one point in time, and read it back into the colony's history. They saw themselves as stewards of that "truth" and judged themselves by how far they strayed from the straight and narrow orthodoxy. They never understood that change was normative; it had been for the founders, it was for them, and it would be for those that followed.

Thus the jeremiads are not only a rhetorical plea to the covenanted people, they are also the sounds of confusion. "All is flux," they seem to say. By invoking the past, they found some balm for living in the present but at a heavy psychological price. They are not unlike Marvin Meyers' Jacksonians sanctifying the Jeffersonian past while scrambling for the entrepreneurial gains of a new world.[27]

The process which historians have labelled declension is nothing more than the maturation of a sectarian movement. The churches of Massachusetts developed new functions which fulfilled the changing needs of a community they wished to preserve—a process as old as Christendom itself. The difference between the Massachusetts of 1630 and that of 1690 is the difference between Paul preaching conversion in Christ and II Peter pondering the problems of electing a bishop. It is important for us to recognize that the Massachusetts clergy who lived through this transformation understood it as declension, but it is even more important for us to stop letting the seventeenth-century mind define the processes of change which it only dimly perceived.

NOTES

Bacon, *Thirteen Historical Discourses* (New Haven, 1839); Dexter, "Two Hundred Years Ago in New England," *Congregational Quarterly* 4 (1862).

[2]Brooks Adams, *The Emancipation of Massachusetts,* Sentry Ed. (Cambridge, Mass., 1962); Charles Francis Adams, *Three Episodes of Massachusetts History,* 2 vols. (Boston, 1892); James Truslow Adams, *The Founding of New England* (Boston, 1921).

[3]The best examples of Miller's exploration of Puritanism are *The New England Mind: The Seventeenth Century* (Cambridge, Mass., 1939) and *The New England Mind, From Colony to Province* (Cambridge, Mass., 1953).

[4]Miller, "Solomon Stoddard, 1643-1729," *Harvard Theological Review* 34 (1941): 277-320; Thomas Schafer, "Solomon Stoddard and the Theology of the Revival," in *A Miscellany of American Christianity,* ed. Stuart Henry (Durham, 1963), pp.328-361, and "Stoddardeanism," *The New Englander* 4 (1846): 350-355.

[5]See my *The Half-Way Covenant* (Princeton, 1969), chap 4; also, "Correspondence of John Woodbridge, Jr., and Richard Baxter," ed. Raymond Stearns, *New England Quarterly* 10 (1937): 557-583; Northampton Church Records, microfilm (Forbes Library, Northampton).

[6]The case is most thoroughly and carefully developed in Miller, *From Colony to Province,* pp. 3-118. Quite often readers of Miller's volumes are guilty of a simplification that he warily avoided with his knowledge of New England's complexity.

[7]The full text of this revision in Congregational polity can be found in Williston Walker, *The Creeds and Platforms of Congregationalism,* Pilgrim Ed. (Boston, 1960), pp. 301-339. Prior to adoption of the half-way covenant only those children whose parents were full communicants could be baptized; thus the baptized child of a saint could reach maturity, marry, and, if he failed to experience conversion, find his children excluded from the church. The Half-Way Synod provided for the continuation of baptism for generations as long as the recipients descended from regenerate stock.

[8]Mass covenant renewals usually brought together the entire community to reaffirm its covenant with God and pledge itself to moral reform. Originally only church members participated in the ceremony, but as time passed and dangers increased all the inhabitants were invited to participate. Frequently it became the occasion for children to own the half-way covenant. See Miller, *From Colony to Province,* pp. 105-118; Pope, *Half-Way Covenant,* chap. 9.

[9]"Solomon Stoddard," p. 318.

[10]*Winthrop's Boston* (Chapel Hill, 1965).

[11]Pope, *Half-Way Covenant,* chaps. 5 and 8.

[12]Edmund S. Morgan, "New England Puritanism: Another Approach," *William and Mary Quarterly* 18 (1961): 241, raises this issue and points out a number of new directions that need exploration.

[13]*Records of the First Church at Dorchester; 1636-1734*, ed. Charles Pope (Boston, 1891), p. 55.

[14]"Woodbridge-Baxter Correspondence," p. 574; Cotton Mather, *Magnalia Christi Americana* (Hartford, 1855), 2 bk. 5: 266; William Hubbard, *A General History of New England* (Boston, 1840), p. 570. Among the churches which had serious reservations about the half-way covenant were Dorchester, Charlestown, Roxbury, and First Church Boston; Pope, *Half-Way Covenant*, chaps. 5-7.

[15]Pope, *Half-Way Covenant,* chap. 8, appendix.

[16]Pope, *Half-Way Covenant,* chap. 8, appendix.

[17]Miller, *From Colony to Province,* p. 192.

[18]Troeltsch, *Social Teachings of the Christian Churches*, trans. Olive Wyon, 2 vols. (New York, 1931); Joachim Wach, *Sociology of Religion* (Chicago, 1944); *From Max Weber: Essays in Sociology,* trans. Hans Gerth and Don Martindale (Glencoe, 1952); H. Richard Niebuhr, *Social Sources of Denominationalism,* Meridian Ed. (New York, 1963); Bryan Wilson, *Sects and Society* (Berkeley, 1961).

[19]Edmund S. Morgan, *Visible Saints* (New York, 1963), pp. 36-47, 77-93.

[20]On preparation and its place in New England theology see Norman Pettit, *The Heart Prepared* (New Haven, 1966), which revises the views of Miller, "Preparation for Salvation," *Journal of the History of Ideas* 3 (1943): 253-286.

[21]Pope, *Half-Way Covenant,* chap. 2; Walker, *Creeds and Platforms,* pp. 244-280.

[22]The loss of the corporate charter of 1629 meant the transfer of political power from the hands of the saints to the rising merchants and imperial administrators who had far less interest in religion than in their own pocket-books. It meant Congregationalism faced new restraints both from Boston and London.

[23]An example of this delayed religious affiliation is Wait Winthrop, grandson of John Winthrop: he joined Third Church Boston in 1689 after nearly a decade of involvement in politics (Richard Dunn, *Puritans and Yankees* [Princeton, 1962], p. 257.)

[24]Miller, *From Colony to Province,* pp. 105-118, 209-225; Pope, *Half-Way Covenant,* chap. 9; Morgan, *Visible Saints,* pp. 142-150.

[25]Pp. 17-19.

[26]"Puritanism as a Revolutionary Ideology," *History and Theory* 3 (1961): 59-90.

[27]*The Jacksonian Persuasion,* Vintage Ed. (New York, 1960); Meyer's restoration theme is strikingly similar to rhetoric of the jeremiads and suggests a profitable area for analysis.

5

The Election Sermons

A. W. Plumstead

*Much of our fascination with Puritanism stems not from simply observing the develop-
ment of American culture, but rather from the great variety of materials which are
available for the study of this subject. Among the most useful are social and political
records, personal remains, and literary materials of various types which suggest the
almost remarkable stability of that society. Professor A. W. Plumstead, Department of
English, University of Minnesota, introduces a group of "election sermons"—a special
tradition—and provides a literary analysis of that institution. Readers may wish to consult the unabridged version and literature cited there for details about the tradition of
such sermons.*

I

The custom of opening the annual General Court in May with an election sermon is unique to New England. Sermons were given in Connecticut
from 1674 to 1830, in New Hampshire from 1784 to 1831, and in Vermont
from 1777 to 1834; but it is to the Colony of Massachusetts Bay that we
turn, as the home of the tradition. Here it began and ended.[1] The first
sermon was given in Boston in 1634 and the tradition continued for two
hundred and fifty years, until 1884—one of the longest in American political
history. . . .

First published in A. W. Plumstead, *The Wall and the Garden: Selected Massachusetts Election
Sermons 1670-1775*. University of Minnesota Press, Minneapolis. Copyright © 1968 by the
University of Minnesota.

II

To preach the election sermon in the seventeenth century was a challenge. . . . The audience was both a geographical and political cross-section of Governor, Deputy-Governor, clergy, outgoing Magistrates (who hoped to be re-elected), and voting Deputies, here was the only annual opportunity to speak to the "people" of New England in that special sense of the word as a specific community, with clear lines of identity and cohesion—God's chosen people in New England. The election sermon was destined from the beginning to become an occasion for assessment and prophecy of New England's "errand into the wilderness." Any sermon is important because it "awakens the sparks of light that are in the consciences of men" and "stirs up a principle of grace where it is, and a principle of natural conscience where there is no grace."[2] But the election sermon was more than an address to the individual conscience; it was the center of a ritual in which a community gave thanks and took stock, held at the traditional time of festival, in late May, "when the heads of our tribes are met together in a solemn assembly to give thanks to the God of heaven for the many great and distinguishing privileges, both civil and religious, which we are favored with; and to ask direction and a blessing from on high, upon all the administrations of government in the land. . . ."[3]

If the election preachers were to offer thanks for greatness received, they were also to be "watchmen upon Jerusalem's wall, whose proper business is to descry dangers, and give seasonable notice thereof; to observe the sins of the times, and the awful symptoms of God's departure."[4] The colonial preachers had a deep and nervous sense of their role as prophets and "watchmen," and the election sermon was the high point of this responsibility. Perry Miller distinguishes between two mainstreams in Puritanism. There is an "Augustinian Piety," a mystical concern with the inner, psychological status of one's direct relationship with God, a sense of one's tremulous progress in gaining and keeping God's grace. This is the inner battle so remarkably recorded in Cotton Mather's *Diary* and Jonathan Edwards' *Personal Narrative*. But colonial Puritanism was also a concern with the cold facts of building God's city on a hill here and now in the sun and cold of Massachusetts. It was "a program for society," a rigid system "of law and order, of regulation and control."[5] The election sermon, first in the pulpit and then in print, was the most important occasion to define this civil strain of New England Puritanism; it was an annual trumpet call to review the essential laws which God had put into the Bible for all to see pertaining to how Christians in covenant should govern themselves as God required. It was a special occasion because each year it was a challenge to defend the great paradox of the "New England Way." The Congregational Church of early Massachusetts was based on democratic election of ministers and it cooperated in the election of civil magistrates. But this democratic potential for fresh ideas was restricted by a rigid tradition of ideas. It was a church dedicated to only one view of civil government, the permitted view of God's intentions; "heretics" like Roger Williams, Anne Hutchinson, and the Quakers were banished; law was not susceptible to various interpretations; change was not the way of the world; the church did not accumulate its wisdom from man's traditions nor should it grow like a plant; its nature was immutable; it was like a rock and it was based on commandments etched in stone. It progressed numerically by breaking off pieces of itself to be carried farther into the hinterland and by trying diligently to mold itself more accurately to God's law. It had little conception of evolving (until 1700-1730 at least); the laws of one generation should not be rewritten by the next. The Father of all had spoken once; that was enough. To understand the *raison d'être* of the election sermon tradition in the seventeenth and early eighteenth centuries, turn to Samuel Willard's *Only Sure Way* of 1682 for an apologia of the indispensable necessity of exhortation, definition, and chastisement.

There is perhaps another reason for the election sermon tradition. New England recognized from the beginning that it was being watched by Europe and by other American colonies. The "New England Way" was on trial. Much seventeenth-century Puritan writing—history, sermon, treatise—has an element of propaganda to it. The writers intended their work for a European audience as evidence that the New World experiment was thriving, indeed that it was preparing itself to lead the Protestant world in reform. The election sermon was theoretically an ideal form of public relations—the first Voice of America—as long as the apostasy theme did not outweigh the evidence that the errand into the wilderness was worthwhile. "We are outcasts indeed, and reproached," says John Norton in his election sermon of 1661, referring to those in England who still looked on the New Englanders as separatists from king and church; "but let us be such outcasts as are caring for the truth, and therefore not to neglect an apology."[6] Norton means "apology" here in the sense of a defense or explanation. One of the motives in the Court's decision to undertake the expense of printing these sermons, and their distribution to every minister in the Colony, was its sense of the sermons' value as an annual apologia. . . . The sermons would show everyone how fortunate the Colony was in its civil liberties, and that it took this liberty seriously. They would also show that the Colony was well educated in political theory and that the New Englanders were earnest in their errand to achieve, at last, a solution to the old dilemma of rendering unto Caesar the things that are Caesar's and unto God the things that are his.

III

It is natural that a few motifs should emerge as the special concern of the election sermons. Of course there is a great range in their length and scope; few are confined to one topic. An occasion which called for an exegesis on the history of Israel, a survey of Biblical ideas on government and the good ruler, a look at the good old days, a catalog of what's wrong with New England, a plea to do better, and a look at what might lie ahead—this hardly lends itself to a narrow scope. Still, in all the extant sermons up to 1775, several related motifs emerge continually.

One of the basic concepts in Puritan thought is the covenant, or meaning of the word "chosen." It is the nature of God to choose or elect both individuals and nations for his kingdom on earth as well as for eternity. The election sermon up to about 1730 was a presidential address to the annual convention of God's Chosen People in New England, Inc.—and it was precisely the "incorporated" that mattered. God incorporates a special group and while it is not a closed club, neither is it an open community with a loose sense of identity and fuzzy boundary lines.

> The taking down the partition wall between Jews and Gentiles whereby the vine of the church was made to spread its branches over the wall did not take in the whole world into the Lord's vineyard at once; but there is still a distinction to be made between the church and the rest of the world which lies in wickedness; between a religious people by a visible profession and the rest of the world that are perishing for want of vision.[7]

"The churches of Christ in this land," says Peter Clark in 1739, "are founded on a sacred covenant, transacted between God and them, in a more solemn and explicit manner than perhaps in most churches in the world."[8] The clergy seized upon the election sermon from its beginnings to define the boundaries of God's vineyard wherein lived his New England people, and an interesting feature of reading the sermons chronologically is to see the changes in the definition as a unique American community finds itself surrounded by other faiths in the "wilderness" outside, and challenged by the Charter requirement of toleration (after 1691) and the growth of liberal views from within.

The concept of covenant was not only religious and Biblical, however, but a matter of practical politics. God's covenants in the Bible must be extended by man into patents, charters, and compacts, created on paper as legal documents, defended and referred to by courts, enacted by godly men for their own well-being as well as in response to their desire to do things as God would have them. Thus another strong theme in the election sermons is the divine source of government and God's sanction of the study of political science.[9] Government is ordained of God: "that there must be government is not from the bare will of men, but from the most High who ruleth in the kingdoms of men and giveth it to whomsoever he will; he has put his sovereign sanction upon it and made it a fixed ordinance of heaven that there be a rule over men; the God of Israel has say'd it and the rock of Israel has spoken it."[10] Without government, Ebenezer Pemberton continues in his fine sermon, "there could be nothing of beauty, proportion, strength, unity, order in societies; liberty and property would be exposed to fatal invasions. The flood-gates of lusts would be open and a deluge of sin and woe would sweep away all that is pleasant and desirable in the world. Men would be like fishes in the sea and as beasts in the wilderness, the greater devour the less."[11] One of the differences between the enclosed garden and the wilderness without is that the wall or hedge of protection separates order from disorder, harmony of parts from confusion of parts, government from anarchy. In his election sermon of 1676, William Hubbard puts it this way:

> "Where order prevails, beauty shines forth." It was order that gave beauty to this goodly fabric of the world, which before was but a confused chaos, without form and void. . . . It suited the wisdom of the infinite and omnipotent Creator to make the world of differing parts, which necessarily supposes that there must be differing places for those differing things to be disposed into, which is order. The like is necessary to be observed in the rational and political world where persons of differing endowments and qualifications need a differing station to be disposed into, the keeping of which is both the beauty and strength of such a society. Naturalists tell us that beauty in the body arises from an exact symmetry or proportion of contrary humors equally mixed one with another; so doth an orderly and artificial distribution of diverse materials make a comely building, while homogeneous bodies (as the depths of waters in the sea, and heaps of sand on the shore) run into confused heaps, as bodies uncapable to maintain an order in themselves.[12]

Political science for the Puritan was a required, engaging activity, emblematic and allegorical as well as historical, a study of high calling and importance.

The election sermon tradition began as an apologia for the indispensable cooperation of church and state, and although the eighteenth-century preachers gradually recognized the growing separation between the two, they continued to remind the politicians of their duties to God and to offer the guidance of the church in civil and political affairs. The cohesion of church and state was a concept bearing down on the election sermons with the authority of centuries, from the Old Testament to Canterbury's control under James and Charles. Orthodoxy in Massachusetts in the seventeenth century was not a new invention. The New England preachers were aware of the religious debates carried on in Europe between 1600 and 1660; Massachusetts was now free to put non-separating Congregationalism into practice—to make what had been theory in England, fact in America. The preachers were not going to miss any opportunity to announce the means of keeping the New England Way pure and functional. This, surely, is where minister and Magistrate saw eye to eye on the need for, and the subject matter of, the election sermon. The clergy would protect the authority of Governor and Magistrate; they in turn would see to it that civil law kept the churches clean, pure, and powerful. It was a masterful scheme until the Charter of 1691, and it was a great memory thereafter. The seventeenth-century preacher of an election sermon was in a unique, central position in the old Town House, surrounded by three audiences, all covenanted together, yet each seeing things in a slightly different light—the Magistrates (oligarchy), the Deputies (democracy), and the ministers (theocracy). It was his job to show them that their different lights might so blend as to produce one radiant white light of Puritanism. There is often a political edge to statements of order, as in this by William Hubbard in 1676:

> Let a body politic be never so well proportioned as to its constitution and form
> of government, and never so well furnished with wise and able men for its con-
> duct and guidance, yet if the several members be not well tuned together by a
> spirit of love and unity, there will never be any good harmony in their ad-
> ministrations. . . . In the beautiful system of the world, which yet is com-
> pounded of sundry elements and those of differing qualities one from the
> other, yet is there such a necessary and mutual connection between the parts
> that they are all so firmly knit one to another that it is altogether impossible to
> make any breach in their union; rather will those several bodies forget the
> properties of their own nature than there shall be any chasma or vacuum
> amongst them which would tend to a dissolution of the whole. Thus in the
> body politic, where it is animated with one entire spirit of love and unity and
> settled upon lasting and sure foundations of quietness and peace, all the
> several members must and will conspire together to deny or forbear the exer-
> cise of their own proper inclinations, to preserve the union of the whole, that
> there be no schism in the body, as the apostle speaks.[13]

Hubbard is telling the Deputies to remember their place. They must elect godly men as Assistants, and then leave them to govern. Factions and "backbitings" are disorderly.

The Representatives' power to elect the Councilmen (and the Governor until 1684) was viewed by the church with both pride and suspicion. If the right men were elected, such democratic power could be the strength of the Colony; but if the wrong men gained office, it could mean the Colony's undoing. That the Governor was appointed by the King and could veto the election of one or all of the elected Councilmen was, after 1684, another potential source of catastrophe. A Governor like Andros could destroy years of achievement in a few harsh strokes. (See the "Introduction" to Cotton Mather's *The Way to Prosperity*, 1689.) Thus it is easy to understand why the subject "The Character of a Good Ruler" (1694) became the most frequent topic in the election sermon tradition, accounting for over half of the printed sermons up to 1775. The electors must be reminded of the kind of man they should vote for and the Governor and candidates for Council must be reminded of the kind of man each should be. The people of Massachusetts have placed "great trust" in their Deputies, says Samuel Belcher in his election sermon of 1707, and they "do presume and expect that in the choice now before you, you will have a special regard" to elect only those who "have subjected themselves to the rule of Christ's kingdom."[14] "Let not private respects sway you in your elections, to be for those that are your friends or favorers," says James Allen in "A Word to the Freemen" in his sermon of 1679; rather, "see how men stand affected to religion and the common good of this people."[15] Peter Thacher in 1711 makes his point with a metaphor: "it is very proper for the sick to choose their own physician; and that is the work of this sick Province this day, to choose provincial healers."[16]

The ideal Councilman to be elected (and the ideal Governor whom, they hoped, the King had appointed) must be wise, godly, just. He must rule for the good of the people.

> Men in such a station should moreover approve themselves faithful to the interest of the people whose welfare as Councilors they are bound to endeavor. The prince and the people have not opposite interests; he that promotes the true interest of the one does so of the other also. A great emperor was wont to say, *Non mihi sed populo;* I am set in this high station not for myself but for the nation's sake.[17]

(This concept, lying dormant in the sermons all along, springs up as the guiding principle for resistance to George III in the sermons of 1770 and the following years of crises.) The good ruler must use his power with discretion. An example of this point occurs in Increase Mather's election sermon in 1693. Mather, acutely sensitive to criticism that he had failed as chief delegate to the Courts of James II and William to secure the Colony's old Charter privileges, leaves nothing to surmise about where he stands on the question of the Governor's veto. If there had been anyone else but the beloved "local son" Sir William Phips in the Governor's chair that day, Mather could have been accused of discourtesy approaching treason; as it was, it was all in the family.

> And as for yourself excellent Sir, whom God has made the captain over his people in this wilderness, it is a very great power which the divine providence has put into your hands, that you could have a negative on the elections of this day—a power which I confess neither you nor anyone else should have had if any interest that I was capable to make could have prevented it.[18]

A Councilman is a little god, says Ebenezer Pemberton in 1710; God would have him so, with appropriate titles, honors, power, and respect. But he must check any temptation to take advantage of power for luxury and personal gain; he is still a man, and like all men, he will die. Pemberton's discussion of the Magistrates' mutability is one of the high points in prose style in the Massachusetts election sermons.

> Their power can't overawe, nor their riches bribe death. Where are all those sons of fame, the mighty, rich, and honorable we read of in story! The kings and princes that filled their houses with gold and silver, and the counsellors of the earth! Are they not gone to sleep in those desolate places they built for themselves! Are not all the bright stars of the morning cover'd with the dark cloud of corruption! Where are those children of pride and oppression, who made the earth to tremble, shook kingdoms, made the world as a wilderness, and destroyed the cities thereof! How are they fallen, their pomp brought down to the grave, and becomes as weak as the meanest of their vassals! . . . Death causes all titles of honor to burst into air and nothing as empty bubbles. It disarms the great of all their power and they go naked into the other world. After all their pomp and parade on the stage of life, they drop into their graves, and nothing of all their glory descends after them. Death wrests the scepter out of the monarch's hand, plucks the crown from off his head, and turns his glory into noisesome putrefaction; and the very forethought of it will

stain the pride of all their glory. . . . This prospect will pall the unhallowed appetite of dominion and gain . . .[19]

The better election sermons up through 1730 are New World versions of *The Courtier, The Governour,* and *The Prince.*

The election sermons were not only political treatises on the nature of governor and governed, however; many of them, especially in the seventeenth century, contain qualities of myth and epic. For modern readers (as well as for writers like Hawthorne and Longfellow), these qualities are as interesting as their political ideals. The "desk" in the old Town House or the State House of 1713 served as a theater, as New England's "wooden O" where a priest dramatized—in soliloquy, but sometimes creating the voices of protagonist and antagonist, and in shifting tones and modes, history and prophecy, song and narrative—a great, epic story. Various sections of the audience might for political reasons listen to the sermon with cool detachment; but let the preacher begin to weave the magic spell of New England's "errand into the wilderness," and the blood began to tingle. . . .

IV

If a foreign student should ask where to begin in order to understand the meaning and development of "The American Dream," he could not be better advised than to study the environment of America's Age of Reason. The challenge of showing Europe that a democracy could be planned and executed by rational men surrounded by the confusion of war and disconnected from the British crown was successfully met. The Dream emerges in the writings, especially the letters, of Jefferson, Adams, Franklin, Madison, Paine, Hamilton, Freneau. Gilbert Chinard's excellent chapter "The American Dream" in the *Literary History of the United States* defines the phrase in terms of these men and this era. There is no mention of the Puritans.[20]

More recent studies take the Dream back to Puritan New England with illuminating results.[21] It is here that some of the essentials in the Dream first find expression when a group of displaced Europeans come to America to create their version of a great society and discover some unique features of being American.

The Puritan version of the Dream might be paraphrased as follows. God has offered his chosen people several opportunities to create the society he wishes for them. Adam and Eve failed to keep their covenant with God, and lost Paradise. The Israelites also fell away from their covenant with God, given to Moses on Mount Sinai; and after Moses, God sent many prophets, some of them great kings and leaders like Nehemiah and David, to warn, to help, to lead them from their apostasy. The second Adam, Christ, reaffirmed God's covenant with man, and the early little pockets of Christian churches after his death were as close to the ideal communities of God as history had, until 1630, shown. But it would seem impossible to preserve such purity for long; soon the church fell into decay, and entered upon a long sleep in the dark ages of Roman domination. Then the spirit of purification rose up out of its sleep in a baptism of fire; the Protestant revolution began a new chapter in the quest for God's covenanted society, and Cartwright and Ames in England carried the work of Luther and Calvin to theoretical perfection. England reformed, but failed to progress beyond a slightly improved church. At this point, when the energy and learning needed to create the long-awaited society were never more available, geography played its part. America was discovered—"a waste and howling wilderness," free of bishops, untainted (in the Puritans' view) except for Indians.

> Known unto God are all his works from the beginning of the world. And he that made this new world knoweth why he made it and what to do with it, though men do not. It is certain Antichrist boasted in his American eureka and conquest when he began to be routed in Europe by the reformation. And who can blame him to provide a new world against he lost his old one. But the Son of God followed him at the heels and took possession of America for himself. And this Province, so far as I know, is the very turf and twig he took possession by, as to the reformation and conversion of the natives and gathering of them into churches.[22]

> Where was there ever a place so like unto New Jerusalem as New England hath been? It was once Dr. Twiss his opinion that when New Jerusalem should come down from heaven America would be the seat of it. Truly that such a type and emblem of New Jerusalem should be erected in so dark a corner of the world is matter of deep meditation and admiration.[23]

The New England "city on a hill" was another opportunity to fulfill the challenge of the society which God desired and which man had been bungling since Adam.

This New England Dream was not a simple one, however; it was in part a myth of perfection, and in part a matter of practical politics on the first American frontier, and they soon split. The Dream had historical authority in Old and New Testaments and the imaginative attractions of myth. It looked homeward to the historical example of Israel and the early Christian churches in all their purity. Part of the energy of the Puritan Dream came from a renewal in a pure source, a purification which bypassed fourteen centuries of degenerate time in arriving at the meaningful center. "The first age was the golden age," says Cotton Mather in the "Introduction" to his epic history; "to return unto that, will make a man a protestant, and I may add, a Puritan."[24] Mircea Eliade has defined the impact of myth on a community as its attempt to recapture the integrity and energy of a past heroic act. All time which has flowed out from the great event—whether Prometheus' descent with fire or Moses' descent with the commandments of stone—is profane time, unmeaningful time.[25] The early American Puritans had a lively, daily sense of penetrating to the very center of a meaningful, compelling mythology. Their courts of law, their sermons, their primers and children's stories, their idiom—all re-enacted the days of Moses and the early Christians of the first century. The election sermon was a high point in the year when representatives of the people would gather to renew their spiritual energy by focusing on their errand.

But their Dream not only looked backward; it looked forward. If it was a return to the past, it was also a harbinger. If it worked, and the enclosed garden was created, kept clean and lovely, and its walls enlarged to include more people and more land, then it would be a "specimen" for the rest of the world.[26] The myths of utopias and Hesperides, the Golden Age and Atlantis, would now come true and New England would become a strong light that would reach over to Old England, the Low Countries, perhaps even the whole Latin world, illuminating their darkness and drawing some away.

> But behold, ye European churches, there are golden candlesticks (more than twice seven times seven!) in the midst of this outer darkness; unto the upright children of Abraham, here hath arisen light in darkness. And let us humbly speak it, it shall be profitable for you to consider the light which from the midst of this outer darkness is now to be darted over unto the other side of the Atlantic Ocean.[27]

The New England Dream was not only a fulfillment of an old prophecy; it was itself a new prophecy. The Puritans had a Whitmanesque sense of looking into the future, a view of a greater civilization for which they were laying the foundation and the guidelines. . . .

The Puritans wanted to fulfill the mission that the Israelites and early Christians began; they wanted to capture the elusive purity for which Moses delivered the guidelines; that was their "national idea." The ministers from 1660 to 1730 found that the people were slipping further and further away from these ideals; their "national idea" was out-traveling their experience. The preachers found themselves caught in the conflict between pressing on for a better, purer rendition of the Biblical blueprint, and holding fast to what they had because it might be as much as they were going to get. They called for a synod. By the time of the earliest election sermon reprinted here, perfection means a return unto the good old way of the first generation of New Englanders. Like Rip Van Winkle, New England had grown old much too fast; it changed too much in spite of the controls and in spite of the identity with Israel's pilgrimage. A communal wail arises, the chant of Ichabod: "the glory has departed." Increase Mather is the best example of many clergymen in the pulpits of 1660-1730; they appear early versions of Rip Van Winkle, trying to rub the strangeness from their eyes as if they had suddenly returned to a society which had left them behind and was full of new ways and strange gods.

> O generation, see the Word of the Lord! Is there any new way more eligible than that good old way (for the substance of it I mean) which the Lord's people have already tried, and have experimentally found to be the way of blessing from God? Shall we seek and enquire after any new found out way as the Lord speaks of new gods? . . . Upstart gods which our fathers knew not; should some of our fathers that are now asleep in Jesus and that have with so many

prayers and tears, hazards, and labors and watchings and studies night and day to lay a sound and sure and happy foundation of prosperity for this people, arise out of their graves and hear the discourses of some and observe the endeavors of others . . . crying "Rase it, rase it, even to the foundation!" (Psal. 137.7) by plucking up if they could that hedge that hath been here set to fence our all— would they not even rent their garments and weep over this generation?[28]

There are many ways in which this Puritan Dream of an iron grip on an old, pure formula was a dead end in America. Two later seminal Americans, Jefferson and Emerson, believed that the sons *should* rewrite the laws of the fathers, that change *was* the way of the world. Life was organic, like the growth of a plant, and must not be enclosed by walls, or thought of as immutably decreed in rock. There was no holding fast; there was only growth.

The errand sermons do illustrate, however, a continuous American motif. If Americans have never quite fulfilled their national dreams in fact in their literature they have made capital of the attempts. "Deracination" means uprooted. When the Puritans left England, they engaged in a longed-for uprooting—sad, but of epic greatness and hope. In America, they became deracinated in a far more serious way. Their Dream was still too compelling to throw over, and the actual achievement of a functional congregationalism and covenant was too solid to deny. But they never quite made the Dream come true. The wall around the enclosed garden showed gaps before it was fully built. Perhaps there never were any "good old days." The errand remained a quest, and became a national theme. If it could not flourish politically, the Dream found life in festival and art.

V

Any generalization about the style of the election sermon must begin with its rigid, logical, highly patterned form.[29] The sermon conformed to the general threefold division of Puritan sermons everywhere in the seventeenth century, a form which grew out of medieval traditions and was taught and perfected in centers of Puritan theological training such as Emmanuel and Christ's colleges, Cambridge, and Harvard.[30]

The sermon begins with a Biblical text followed by an "Explication" which "opens up" the text by a careful scrutiny of the words, including in some cases their derivations and their different meanings in context. The preacher may point out controversies among Biblical scholars over the proper English translation of the Hebrew or Greek, adding his own authority to the reading he is sure is correct. This meticulous examination of the text is often accompanied by a brief narrative of the historical events leading up to the time the words of the text were first spoken, whether by Samuel, Asa, Nehemiah, or Christ. Cotton Mather's *The Way to Prosperity* is a good example. Quite often this historical review plays a functional role in the sermon's success, for the preacher will emphasize incidents which his audience, trained to think in terms of typology and prophecy, will recognize as having an obvious parallel to their own life in America. The "Application" later in the sermon will come then as no surprise. The astute in the audience will early see what the preacher is driving at, and they will await the "Application" with something of the expectancy of the Greek audience watching a drama, the story of which they knew—they will want to see how the preacher does it, how well he will say what must be said. This pattern of expectancy in the audience would come only with training, but it was probably a real part of the aesthetics of the errand sermons; many in the audience, continuing members of the General Court, might hear several such sermons at election time.

With the philological and historical details explained, the preacher then announces the "Doctrine"—the second part of the sermon. Sometimes the word is set apart in large capitals as a separate heading in the printed texts; more often it is a small heading preceding a paragraph. In the seventeenth century the Doctrine is almost always italicized for emphasis. The heading was announced from the pulpit. Samuel Sewall's manuscript notes that he took during sermons show clearly the divisions "Doct." and "Prop. 2."[31] (In the 1728-31 years, these headings first begin to drop away as formal titles in the printed sermons. The word "Doctrine" may appear in the first sentence of a new paragraph, or be dispensed with entirely.)

In the section labeled "Doctrine," the preacher announces in his own words the lesson or law that he draws from the text. He works from the specific to the general, to the "maxims of wisdom"[32] that lie behind the specific words and context of the Biblical prophet. This general law is then broken down into several "Propositions" (or "Reasons"), each a slight expansion or variation of the central idea. It is here that the preacher makes his own contribution; here he is creative. He will show with ingenuity the various and often delicate shades of multiple meanings which open out from the text, once one sees the general law. He works carefully and logically through his propositions so that the audience can trace them easily. In print, the distinctions between propositions often look like hairsplitting in the worst traditions of scholasticism. (See the "Doctrine" of Cotton Mather's *The Way to Prosperity*.) The reader must keep in mind, however, that the sermon was intended for simple farmers as well as educated theologians. The preachers erred on the side of simplicity and repetition according to the old law of rhetoric that a listener must be led carefully and gently around each turn in a logical path, as if he were blind. Still, there are times when the reader of the election sermons gazes with amazement at the naïveté, wordiness, and circular repetition. The "Doctrine" part of a Puritan sermon had a built-in propensity to be plain to the point of foolishness, and some preachers succumbed.

[Prop.]3. To lead quiet and peaceable lives is to live quietly and peaceably together. When they are at peace among themselves and live quietly together, when families live peaceably and quietly, when there is peace and quietness in towns and churches and in all societies among a people, they may be said to lead quiet and peaceable lives.[33]

Sometimes a "Proposition" will be announced in a general heading, and subsequent paragraphs or groups of paragraphs united under a number will discuss the proposition. In these cases, the opening sentence of the first paragraph is often grammatically incomplete. The Puritans did not as a rule write incomplete sentences for rhetorical effect. Rather, such incomplete sentences are completions of the syntax of the proposition, or main point, made in a heading perhaps two or three paragraphs (or as much as a page or two) earlier. The modern reader must remember to keep a general proposition suspended in his mind while he attaches each unit developing it to its original syntax.

The third section of the sermon is the "Application" of the "Doctrine" and "Propositions" to present-day Massachusetts. It is usually expounded in several "Uses."[34] The Biblical past becomes an analogy to the present, and each is as close to, or equidistant from, the will of God. In the errand sermons, the "Use" is generally the relevancy of the text and its doctrine to the apostasy of New England. Sometimes the use can be blunt in its recommendations of curbs for specific abuses. Joseph Sewall in 1724 prevails on the Magistrates to create laws to curtail extensive traveling on Sundays and to shorten pub hours; three years later Joseph Baxter returns to the latter point by asking, "Is there nothing more to be done to keep town-dwellers from sotting away their time at taverns?"[35] Ebenezer Thayer in 1725 asks for magisterial support for higher salaries for ministers so that the profession will not fall into contempt. Requests for laws requiring congregations to honor their contracts with ministers so as not to take advantage of inflation and shifting standards of value, to the ministers' detriment, are often heard in the "Applications" of sermons in the 1720-50 years. Israel Loring, in an otherwise conservative election sermon advocating strict observance of Biblical and civil law, makes a unique request in 1737:

> There is one thing more which I would recommend to the serious considera-
> tion of this great and General Court; and that is whether there is not a great
> duty lying upon us respecting the transactions of the year 1692, when not only
> many persons were taken off by the hand of public justice for the supposed
> crime of witchcraft, but their estates also ruined and their families im-
> poverished. . . . the question is (if it be not beyond all question) whether a
> restitution is not due from the public to them, and we are not bound in justice
> to make it.[36]

Harvard College is also singled out continually as worthy of the Magistrates' special care; it is the "darling of the country," and a "nursery" which supplies the Colony with health-giving milk.

The sermon usually concludes with a direct word to each section of the audience. The Governor is praised, as are his sponsor the King, the House of Orange or Hanover (which through God's mercy has replaced the Stuarts), and the British Constitution (the best in the world). Some tributes to the Governor are dry and stereotyped; he is "damned with faint praise." Others are genuinely warm and well meant, such as John Barnard's in 1746 to William Shirley after the capture of Louisburg.[37]

After the tribute to the Governor, the House of Representatives is reminded of its duty to elect godly men to the Council. Finally, the ministers are acknowledged. (After 1747 they are merely mentioned, because a special sermon is to be preached the following day at their convention.)

That the preachers considered the election sermon a firm tradition is evident from frequent quotations and references to earlier election sermons and the "worthies" who preached them. Sometimes extensive quotations are incorporated, perhaps enlarged from the pulpit version for the pamphlet. Several append a few pages from earlier sermons to fill out a printer's form. Many phrases, such as "errand into the wilderness," "God's controversy with New England," "the noble vine," and "counsellors as at the beginning," recur frequently.

Because the format of the sermon is so rigid and the subject matter limited to several interrelated motifs, there is a sense in which any minister who graduated at the bottom of his class could put together a sermon mechanically and meet the occasion with some success. Some sermons read as if this is just what happened. As time went on, the challenge of saying the same old things vigorously and with meaning became more difficult. Several preachers in the eighteenth century freely admit the problem, such as John Prentice in 1735: "So many of my reverend fathers and brethren have gone before me in this service that there is but little room left to offer anything proper to the present occasion without repetition at least of the same thing. I have therefore omitted many things that I might have mentioned . . ."[38] By 1751, William Welsteed could wish with good reason that "the religious solemnities of this day never degenerate into an empty formality, nor sink away into vain flourish, cold and lifeless harangue upon politics."[39]

With a genre, an occasion, and a tradition contributing pressure for conformity and a highly conventional art form, it is surprising, not that there are as many poor sermons as there are, but that there are as many good ones. The sermons printed here, I submit, surmount the convention of time, place, and clichés with the ring of conviction, with passion as well as control. The familiar ideas find their perfect expression.

In the best errand sermons, the preacher transcends his role as a teacher of law, and becomes an actor. He has many roles to play. He may create different parts and speak them, as do Danforth in 1670 and Prince in 1730. He is a teller of tales, of great moments and epic quests in the history of his nation. He is to do for New England what Shakespeare did for his audience—bring the dead pages of history alive, with their shame and their glory, into significance and meaning. He will tell of heroes, Biblical as well as American, and he must recapture for his audience the idealism of the original errand to America—its innocence, its momentousness. The story must be told simply, but with passion, longing, and pathos. He must don the mask of the wise politician, of Samuel or Nehemiah or Asa. He must be like Portia in his understanding of the wise, sweet laws of God; yet he must also be like Bishop Carlisle in his wrath of exhortation and prophecy. It was not an easy task, and only a few did it well.

The biography of a Puritan sermon from conception to delivery appears in John Barnard's *Autobiography;* because it is so clearly spelled out by an able practitioner (his election sermon of 1734 appears in this collection), and because his practice must be representative of many of the ministers (he graduated from Harvard in 1707), it may be beneficial to close this brief review of the sermon's rhetoric by quoting it in full.

> Here suffer me to take occasion to show you the manner of my studying my sermons, which I generally pursued when I had time for it, and upon some special occasions I made use of even in my advanced years. Having in a proper manner fixed upon the subject I designed to preach upon, I sought a text of Scripture most naturally including it; then I read such practical discourses as treated upon the subject; I read also such polemical authors on both sides of the question as I had by me, sometimes having ten or a dozen folios and other books lying open around me, and compared them one with another, and endeavored to make their best thoughts my own. After having spent some time (perhaps two or three days) in thus reading and meditating upon my subject, I then applied myself to my Bible, the only standard of truth, and examined how far my authors agreed or disagreed with it. Having settled my mind as to the truth of the doctrine I had under consideration, I then set myself to the closest meditation upon the most plain and natural method I could think of for the handling the subject. Sometimes, not always, I penned the heads of the discourse. Then I took the first head and thought over what appeared to me most proper to confirm and illustrate it, laying it up in my mind; so I went through the several heads; and when I had thus gone over the whole in its several parts, then I went over all in my meditation, generally walking in my study or in my father's garden. When I thought myself ripe for it, I sat down to writing, and being a swift penman, I could finish an hour and a quarter's discourse, with rapid speaking, in about four hours' time. This manner of studying sermons cost me, 'tis true, a great deal of time, perhaps a week or fortnight for a sermon, and sometimes more; but I had this advantage by it, that there was a greater stock laid up in my memory for future use, and I found it easy to deliver my discourses *memoriter;* and by the full and clear view I had of my subject, I could correct the phraseology in my delivery. I kept indeed my notes open, and turned over the leaves as though I had read them, yet rarely casting my eye upon my notes, unless for the chapter and verse of a text which I quoted. When I was settled in the ministry, I found this method too operose, yet when called to special public services, if I had time I practised it, only penning head by head as I meditated on them. Observing also that the aged Mr. Samuel Cheever, with whom I settled, very much failed in his memory (for he was wholly a *memoriter* preacher), I thought I might be reduced to his circumstances if I lived to old age, and therefore betook myself to reading my notes; and I find the advantage of it, since it hath pleased God to spare me to a great old age.[40]

NOTES

[1]R. W. G. Vail, *A Check List of New England Election Sermons* (Worcester, 1936).

[2]Solomon Stoddard, *The Way for a People to Live Long in the Land That God Hath Given Them* . . . (Boston, 1703), 8.

[3]John Webb, *The Government of Christ Considered . . .* (Boston, 1738), 1.

[4]Ebenezer Thayer, *Jerusalem Instructed and Warned . . .* (Boston, 1725), 38.

[5]"From Edwards to Emerson," *Errand into the Wilderness* (Cambridge, 1956), 191-192 (reprinted in *Interpretations of American Literature,* ed. Charles Feidelson, Jr., and Paul Brodtkorp, Jr., New York, 1959, 114-136). See also the chapter "Hypocrisy," in Miller, *From Colony to Province,* 68-81.

[6]"Sion the Outcast Healed of Her Wounds," *Three Choice and Profitable Sermons,* 14. Cf. Larzer Ziff, *The Career of John Cotton,* 179-180.

[7]Samuel Danforth, *An Exhortation to All . . .* (Boston, 1714), 33.

[8]*The Ruler's Highest Dignity and the People's Truest Glory . . .* (Boston, 1739), 52.

[9]For discussions of colonial Puritan political theory see Perry Miller, "The Social Covenant," *The New England Mind: The Seventeenth Century* (New York, 1939), 398-431; Miller, "The Puritan State and Puritan Society," *Errand into the Wilderness,* 141-152; Edmund S. Morgan, "Introduction," *Puritan Political Ideas,* xiii-xlvii.

[10]Ebenezer Pemberton, *The Divine Original and Dignity of Government Asserted,* 13.

[11]*Ibid.,* 16.

[12]*The Happiness of a People . . .* (Boston, 1676), 8.

[13]*Ibid.,* 16. For a discussion of John Cotton's acceptance of theocracy, see Larzer Ziff, *The Career of John Cotton,* 97-98.

[14]*An Essay Tending to Promote the Kingdom of Our Lord Jesus Christ,* 18.

[15]*New England's Choicest Blessing . . .* (Boston, 1679), 7.

[16]*The Alsufficient Physician . . .* (Boston, 1711), 42-43.

[17]Increase Mather, *The Great Blessing of Primitive Counsellors,* 12.

[18]*Ibid.,* 19.

[19]*The Divine Original and Dignity of Government Asserted,* 59-60, 63, 65.

[20]Ed. Robert E. Spiller *et al.* (New York, 1948), 192-215. See also Theodore Hornberger, "The Enlightenment and the American Dream," in *The American Writer and the European Tradition,* ed. Margaret Denny and William H. Gilman (Minneapolis, 1950), 16-27.

[21]Frederic I. Carpenter, *American Literature and the Dream* (New York, 1955); Loren Baritz, *City on a Hill: A History of Ideas and Myths in America* (New York, 1964); Cyclone Covey, *The American Pilgrimage* (New York, 1961).

[22]Nicholas Noyes, *New England's Duty and Interest . . .* (Boston, 1698), 75; the pamphlet's "EYPHKA" has been changed here to "eureka."

[23]Increase Mather, *A Discourse Concerning the Danger of Apostasy . . .* issued with *A Call from Heaven* (Boston, 1685), 77-78.

[24]*Magnalia,* I, 25.

[25]*The Myth of the Eternal Return,* trans. Willard R. Trask (New York, 1954), 34-36.

[26]*Magnalia,* I, 25. See also Loren Baritz' discussion of Winthrop in *City on a Hill,* 3-44.

[27]*Magnalia,* I, 26.

[28]Thomas Shepard, *Eye-Salve,* 18; for comparable "Ichabod" passages in election sermons, see especially Benjamin Colman, *David's Dying Charge . . .* (Boston, 1723), 17ff; Ebenezer Thayer, *Jerusalem Instructed and Warned,* 19ff.

[29]For discussions of preaching and the sermon genre in New England, see Perry Miller, "Rhetoric" and "The Plain Style," *The Seventeenth Century,* 300-362; *The Puritans,* ed. Miller and Johnson, 64-74; Josephine K. Piercy, "The Sermon and Religious Discourse," *Studies in Literary Types in Seventeenth Century America (1607-1710)* (New Haven, 1939), 155-167; Babette M. Levy, *Preaching in the First Half Century of New England History* (Hartford, 1945); Kenneth B. Murdock, "The Puritan Literary Attitude," *Literature and Theology in Colonial New England* (Cambridge, 1949), 31-65; Howard M. Martin, "Puritan Preachers on Preaching: Notes on American Colonial Rhetoric," *Quarterly Journal of Speech,* L (Oct. 1964), 285-292.

[30]Louis B. Wright points out that about two-thirds of the sixty-five ministers who came to New England in the Great Migration were educated at Cambridge, and the majority of these were from "that great nursery of Puritanism, Emmanuel College." *The Colonial Civilization of North America 1607-1763* (London, 1949), 84-85. The most influential textbooks on preaching in seventeenth-century New England were William Perkins, *The Art of Prophecying . . . ,* trans. Thomas Tuke (London, 1607); Richard Bernard, *The Faithfull Shepheard . . .* (London, 1607; revised, London, 1621) William Ames, *The Marrow of Sacred Divinity . . .* (London, 1642).

[31]Some manuscript notebooks of Sewall's sermon notes are in the collection of the Massachusetts Historical Society. Such note-taking during sermons, often in shorthand, seems to have been a common activity. There are several anonymous manuscript books in the collections of Harvard and the Massachusetts Historical Society, in addition to sermon notes by Cotton Mather and other ministers.

[32]Nathaniel Appleton, *The Great Blessing of Good Rulers . . .* (Boston, 1742), 11.

[33]Joseph Baxter, *The Duty of a People . . .* (Boston, 1727), 7.

[34]For a discussion of the various "uses" in the application, see Levy, *Preaching in the First Half Century,* 95.

[35]Joseph Sewall, *Rulers Must Be Just . . .* (Boston, 1724), 55ff; Joseph Baxter, *The Duty of a People,* 32.

[36]*The Duty of an Apostatizing People . . .* (Boston, 1737), 51-52.

[37]John Barnard, *The Presence of the Great God in the Assembly of Political Rulers . . .* (Boston, 1746), 28.

[38]*Pure and Undefiled Religion . . .* (Boston, 1735), 27.

[39]*The Dignity and Duty of the Civil Magistrate . . .* (Boston, 1751), 28.

[40]*Collections of the Massachusetts Historical Society,* 3rd ser., V (Boston, 1836), 187-188.

6

Piety and Intellect in Puritanism

Robert M. Middlekauff

In the broad tradition of the Christian religion, there remains the perennial question of how belief is related to practice; and specifically, how the head interacts with the heart. Appreciation of Puritan intellectual life has made it important to recover insight into Puritan spirituality—and their interrelationship. In the following essay, Professor Robert Middlekauff, Department of History, University of California, Berkeley, discusses the elements of this issue.

What the Puritans knew as common sense about the mind has survived to be enshrined by historians as a theory of psychology. Puritans grew up thinking of the mind in terms of the faculties, such as "reason" and "will." Today we recognize that the Puritans had accepted the faculty psychology, a theory much older than they were. We have long since rejected this theory and have exhausted several others; yet we have not managed to divest ourselves of its vocabulary nor have we shaken off its underlying assumptions. Like the Puritans we still describe the mind's functioning with the familiar terms reasoning and willing. And, like them, we separate thought and feeling and ascribe a duality to the mind.

The assumption that the mind is a duality has proved especially important in the interpretation of Puritanism. If the Puritan mind was a duality the problem is one of establishing the relationship of the two parts—the

First published in the *William and Mary Quarterly*, 3rd Series, XXII (1965), pp. 457-470. Reprinted by permission of the author and the publisher.

religious emotion, or piety, and the ideas that historians agree informed the mind. Historians have approached this question with the familiar suppositions that emotion somehow produces ideas or, phrased in another way, that religious ideas are the articulations of piety. This proposition seems to defy more explicit statement and it does not exclude a second assumption, which may appear to be in conflict with it, that piety and intellect were historically in opposition to one another. Both assumptions may contribute to a disposition among historians of Puritanism to think of the psychic process in mechanistic terms—in this case as entailing "movement" from feeling to thought. Both hold that the mind was duality; and both imply that piety and intellect were separate.

With its descriptions of images shuttling back and forth among the faculties, the traditional Puritan psychology had obvious mechanistic overtones. If historians have found much of the old language antiquated, they have insensibly made use of the notion of a mechanical movement in which piety somehow yielded intellect. This view pervades Perry Miller's *New England Mind* where it is summed up in a splendid metaphor: "the emotional propulsion was fitted into the articulated philosophy as a shaft to a spearhead."[1] And Alan Simpson, declaring that Miller has told us too much about the Puritan mind and not enough about the Puritan's feelings, reveals a similar mode of thinking: "If the seventeenth century Puritan, with his formal training in scholasticism, usually tries to give a rational account of his faith, it is the stretched passion which makes him what he is. They are people who suffered and yearned and strived with an unbelievable intensity; and no superstructure of logic ought to be allowed to mask that turmoil of feeling."[2]

The use of terms such as "superstructure," which have mechanical connotations and the conception of the mind as a duality operating on a sequential basis, with emotion first in the sequence, gives the psychic process a deceptive neatness. These mechanical terms, after all, are abstractions which may establish relationships but they do not convey a state of mind. Rather they seem to suggest that emotions may be understood as any mechanical force can, perhaps even as uniformities. In this notion piety is an entity whose inception and expression parallel the action of any physical force.

Perhaps we cannot avoid thinking of the mind as a duality. The idea is embedded in our vocabulary, and we can in fact make meaningful distinctions between emotion and thought. But if we must acknowledge that thinking and feeling are different modes of the psychic process, perhaps we should give full importance to their connections, for these two modes do not exist apart from one another. Whatever else it is, the psychic process is not simply the sum of thinking and feeling; it is in some peculiar way their interaction. Men think within some emotional disposition and feel in a context that in part has been ordered by thought.

Perhaps, too, we should consider the possibility that creativity in the relationship of Puritan intellect and emotion may have arisen in the intellect. Puritanism, after all, offered an explicit philosophy covering all aspects of human existence. This philosophy defined man's place in the world with absolute clarity: it told him who he was and what he might become; and it told him what God expected of him.

But if man's fate was clear, the fate of individuals was not. In its doctrines of predestination and election, Puritanism offered a man the assurance that his future had been decided. But it gave him no infallible indication of the nature of the decision. All he could know with absolute certainty was that God in his justice had predestined some men for salvation and others for damnation.

These ideas reinforced a bent towards self-awareness in men eager to determine whether or not they were of the elect. Puritanism achieved the same result in yet another way—by explicitly demanding a self-consciousness that made a man aware of his emotions and sensitive to his attitudes towards his own behavior. It accomplished this by describing in elaborate detail the disposition of a godly mind. Sin, it taught, might be incurred as surely by attitudes as by actions. In the process of performing his religious duties a man might sin if his feelings were not properly engaged. Prayer, for example, was commanded of every Christian; but prayer without inward strain, even agony, is mere "Lip-labour," a formality that offends God.[3] Prayer for spiritual blessings without faith that those blessings will be granted implies a doubt of God's power and is equivalent to unbelief. Ordinary life, too, must be lived in a Christian habit of mind. A man getting his living in a lawful calling, though staying within the limits imposed by the state, might nevertheless violate divine imperatives by overvaluing the creatures, as Puritans termed excessive esteem for the things of this world. The "*manner* of performance," a Puritan divine once said, was the crucial thing in fulfilling the duties imposed by God.[4]

Puritanism thus bred a deep concern about a state of mind. The norms of good thought and feeling were clear, and every Puritan felt the need for effort to bring his consciousness into harmony with these norms. The most familiar figure among Puritans is the tormented soul, constantly examining his every thought and action, now convinced that hell awaits him, now lunging after the straw of hope that he is saved, and then once more falling into despair. He wants to believe, he tries, he fails, he succeeds, he fails—always on the cycle of alternating moods.

Consider, for example, Cotton Mather. By his own account he seems to have been completely at the mercy of his emotions: his *Diary* reverberates with his groaning, sighing, and panting after the Lord. From youth until death, his spirit fluctuated from despair to ecstasy. Between these emotions lay a vast number of others but for Cotton Mather few brought peace and repose.

If Mather's piety was more intense than most—in part because his familial heritage and his conception of his profession were unusual—its sources were similar to that of other Puritans. Mather lived in a world of ideas where God reigned, and man, diseased with sin, craved His dispensation. Only the Lord could save man and the Lord made His decisions about man's fate without consulting anyone. Man, helpless and sinful, did not deserve to be consulted. Evoking a world of uncertainty, these ideas engendered an anxiety in him that could be eased only by a conviction that he was somehow acceptable to God.

Cotton Mather never questioned the view of himself and of the world that these conceptions imposed. His description of himself would have satisfied any Puritan, for any Puritan would have recognized himself in it. All his life Cotton Mather accused himself of sin that rendered him indescribably filthy. He was a "vile" sinner, "feeble and worthless," suffering, he once told the Lord, from spiritual "diseases . . . so complicated, that I am not able so much as distinctly to mention them unto thee; much less can I remedy them."[5] He employed these terms in describing himself when he was an adolescent, apparently in the midst of an agonizing crisis of the soul. He survived this crisis and though years later he sometimes appeared complacent, he never lost his sense of sin. As an old man he confessed in a characteristic way his "Humiliation for my . . . Miscarriages" and called himself "as tempted a Man, as any in the World."[6]

The classic Puritan failures, idleness and waste, did not often contribute to his anxiety. He knew that he was rarely idle, that the little money he earned was not squandered; and he indulged in no false contrition on these scores. But he did recognize in himself pride and sensuality, the habits of mind that Christians had always considered evil.[7]

Mather's anxiety arose when he found himself unable always to bring his behavior and his state of mind into harmony with his ideas. A true Christian, he knew, was humble—not swelled with pride. A true Christian did not prize this world: he was to live in it and he was to give his best but at the same time the attention of his heart should be fastened upon God. Mather was pained by his failure to live up to this ideal. In his pride and in his sensuality, he disappointed both the Lord and himself. Falling short of the divine imperative rendered him ugly in the sight of God: truly Cotton Mather was a filthy creature.[8]

This conception of himself must certainly have helped induce the massive anxiety he endured for so long. From an early age Cotton Mather had learned of his sin; and by the time he reached maturity he did not have to be reminded of it, though he reminded himself often. After a few years of life he seems not to have required the specific accusation of sin to experience the unease; it probably was always there—a part of his consciousness or not far from it. The most trivial incident could set his fears in motion. When he had a toothache he asked: "Have I not sinned with my *Teeth*? How? By sinful, graceless excessive *Eating*. And by evil Speeches, for there are *Literae dentales* used in them?"[9]

The doctrine of predestination intensified Mather's anxiety. Mather knew that God, in a moment of power and justice, had resolved the eternal fates of all men. He knew too that all men were sinners deserving damnation; only those selected by the Lord would escape a punishment all merited. God had made His choice, nothing could be done to alter it, for predestination was a fact, not a theory.

He responded to this knowledge in several ways. Occasionally he achieved resignation, resolving "to resign all my Conserns unto Him, *without whom not* a little Bird falls unto the Ground." But more frequently he felt compelled to inventory his soul, to tabulate his worth. His *Diary* in one sense is an extended ledger of his merit and his failings. He longed to discover that the balance was on the side of his election.[10]

Just as conventional Puritan ideas about human nature and predestination evoked Mather's feeling about himself, so other related ideas helped him to cope with his anxiety. One set of ideas incited another: Cotton Mather was a sinful, helpless soul, but he could take comfort from the knowledge that God used the sinner for His own purposes. God chose him, Cotton Mather, for his vileness and used him for divine purposes. The choice demonstrated God's power: even a wretch like himself could be used in the Lord's work. In this way when Mather recognized the fact of his sin he was disconsolate and then when he remembered the power of the Lord to use even a vile sinner his anxiety was converted to joy. It was wonderful but the Lord worked in wonderful ways.[11]

Received ideas about God stimulated strong emotion. He longed for the Lord's blessing, begged for His aid, and strained to think, act, and feel in ways he imagined would earn His favor. "My highest Acquisition," Mather wrote in his *Diary*, "I will reckon to bee, a Likeness unto God. To *love* that which *God* loves, and *hate* that which God hates; to be *holy as God is holy* . . . . O That I may be conformable unto the *communicable* Attributes of God; and agreeable unto his *Incommunicable*."[12]

He would be like Christ. This idea proved to be psychically useful in a life filled with abuse from the external world. As the world grew increasingly hostile to Mather's values, he rejoiced in his suffering: "Yea, a Conformity to Him, in Sufferings, Injuries, Reproaches from a malignant World, makes me, even to rejoice in those Humiliations." He should not sorrow at attacks by evil men—had not evil men attacked Christ? He should glory in their abuse, for they were Satan's agents, and their enmity made him more like Christ.[13]

This mechanism did not always operate with perfection. Robert Calef's "Libel" nine years after the outbreak of witchcraft at Salem left Mather with an anger that smoldered. The best that Mather's attempt to "imitate and represent the Gentleness of my Savior" could achieve was a temporary "sweet calm" seven years after Calef's attacks.[14]

He was more successful in handling his emotions when he faced a twenty-year old widow who set her cap at him after the death of his first wife in December 1702. The young widow informed him in February 1703 that she had long valued his ministry and now wanted to share his life. The "highest Consideration" in her desire for marriage with Cotton Mather, she told him, "was her eternal Salvation, for if she were mine, she could not but hope the effect of it would be, that she should also be Christ's." Mather was delighted—and suspicious; he clearly found her sexually exciting—she was of a "Comely Aspect," he said—but her reputation was not unblemished.[15]

During the next two months he writhed in a confusion marked by desire and despair. He wanted the woman but he feared that her flattering offer was a snare laid by the Devil, who had long plotted to destroy Cotton Mather. He needed the comfort of his family and friends but they, evidently fearing that he was about to make a fool of himself, refused to listen to him talk of the widow. He would like to have had Boston's sympathy in his suffering but all he was likely to get—he sensed—was disapproval. Family, friends, the community, all proved interested but unwilling to come to his aid. The widow was hardly more helpful: when he warned her of the difficulty of life with a man who spent much of his time in fasting and praying, she replied that his way of living was precisely what had attracted her to him.[16]

Through his confusion Mather realized that neither his friends nor his family could help him. But within two weeks after the young widow approached him, the way out of his dilemma began to appear. In mulling over what to do Mather decided that he would have to be especially gentle. He admitted to himself that the girl's physical appeal "causes in me a mighty Tenderness" toward her; and of course good breeding demanded that she be treated with respect. "But Religion, above all, obliges me, instead of a rash rejecting her Conversation, to contrive rather, how I may imitate the Goodness of the Lord Jesus Christ, in His Dealing with such as are upon a Conversion unto Him." The problem was to find a Christ-like solution. Within three weeks he was to decide that rejection of the widow was a Christ-like action.[17]

During these three weeks his family and the community urged him toward action by impressing their disapproval upon him. They told him that bad company was often at the house of the widow's father, presumably visiting her. What was more frightening was a "mighty Noise" around the town that he was courting the widow. The rumor was false; all he aimed at— he told himself—was "conformity to my Lord Jesus Christ, and Serviceableness to Him, in my Treating of her."[18]

Cotton Mather could not bear to have his name besmirched, and he craved the approval of the community. But he could not reject the widow simply because Boston was outraged at his courtship. He would rebuff the widow but he would not be moved by "popular Slanders." Rather he discovered when he made his decision that he was moved "purely, by a religious Respect unto the Holy Name of the L[ord] Jesus Christ, and my Serviceableness to his precious Interests; which I had a Thousand Times rather dy, than damnify." His decision in fact was a victory, a victory over "Flesh and Blood," and suggested that he was regenerate. The girl was his "sacrifice" to Christ.[19]

The language Mather employed to describe this brief episode suggests how Christian values enabled him to act: the whole affair is cast into a conventional Christian form. He—the servant of the Lord—is tempted; he is denied resort to the ordinary comfort supplied by family and friends; his enemies in the community revile him. But strengthened by his conception of conforming to Christ, he disregards his enemies, overcomes the promptings of the flesh, and acts, sacrificing what is dear to him in the service of the Lord.

Phrasing his action in sacrificial terms eased the agony of rejecting in yet another way. His last entry in the *Diary* about the widow conveys a sense of the violence of his inner struggle. "I struck my Knife, into the Heart of my Sacrifice, by a Letter to her Mother." It also suggests that rejection in these terms, especially in the use of the word "knife" and the action described by the phrase "struck my Knife, into the Heart," released at least some small portion of his sexual urges.[20]

Christian ideas, for example the imperative to conform to Christ which had saved him from disaster in this extraordinary affair, also affected Cotton Mather in less spectacular ways. Problems of ordinary scale seemed less annoying when one considered Christ's responses to similar ones. Was his salary insufficient and was he reduced to wearing rags? Poverty presented the temptations of uncharitable anger and self-pity, but he resisted them. Christ's condition in the world had been distinguished by poverty and Christ was robbed of his garments. Why then should Cotton Mather complain of a poverty that left him and his children in want? "Anything that makes my Condition resemble His, tis acceptable to me!" Besides he had another, more desirable kind of garment, the robe of Christ's righteousness. The Lord had also used him to help clothe the poor. He gave from his own purse to the needs of the poor; he was honored by the Lord as "the happy Instrument of cloathing other people." This knowledge, he reported, left him "cheerful"; humiliation was banished, and he was strengthened to the point that he resolved to bear his trials with "the Frames of true, vital, joyful, Christianity."[21]

Not even Cotton Mather could keep the divine model constantly in mind; he, like most Puritans, sometimes experienced periods of "deadness," periods when neither ideas of sin nor of God could evoke emotional responses. This paralysis of thought and feeling never lasted long for it gradually built up anxiety until he was desperately searching for revived spirits. When in "an idle Frame of Soul," he found himself "filled with *Fears*, that the Spirit of God was going to take a sad *Farewell* of mee." In this state he would begin to pray. But his prayers were usually not answered immediately; the lethargy continued and he would find himself unable to believe in God. This feeling might persist for as long as a week, though he usually managed to dispel it in a few days. Horror and confusion filled these days; hope and joy returned only after Mather succeeded in completely humbling himself.[22] Following this state, which was reminiscent of the stage of humiliation in the conversion process, Mather began to feel hope once more. Hope arose when he found himself able to believe that the Lord would heed his plea if only he really believed. After all, God wanted to help him, and would; but he had to trust the Lord.

Although Cotton Mather did not ever comprehend the workings of his psyche, he did understand to some extent that his ideas might affect his emotions. The relationship of thought and feeling appeared most clearly in the case of a "particular faith." A particular faith was a promise given by God about future events. It was not given to everyone, rather "but *here* and *there*, but *now* and *then*, unto those whom a *Sovereign* GOD shall Please to Favour with it." All Christians of course may receive general reassurance when praying but a particular faith is granted only to a chosen few who approach the Lord with a specific request. The favored believer who goes to the Lord with his request receives, after strenuous prayer, assurance that he will get his wish. "The Impression is born in upon his mind, with as clear a light, and as full a Force, as if it were from Heaven *Angelically*, and even *Articulately* declared unto him."[23]

Convinced that the particular faith came from without, Mather insisted that "the Devout Believer cannot cause himself to Believe *What* and *When* he will"; but the fact is that he developed in the particular faith a technique to induce belief and feeling. At the same time he described the change wrought by a particular faith: the believer's feelings were altered. For example, he was sad and anxious before he pleaded for reassurance from God; afterwards, he lost his sadness and anxiety and his spirits revived. This was the theory; Cotton Mather's *Diary* reveals that he achieved the ideal in practice. He used such words as "afflatus" and "raptures" in describing his renewed feelings; at times his ecstasy became indescribable. More often his anxiety dropped away, and he found himself full of confidence and even joy. Not surprisingly he also felt physically rejuvenated.[24]

A typical experience with a particular faith occurred in April 1700 when he was to deliver the Thursday lecture, an important occasion when a minister strove to give his best. On this day he found himself "tired, and spent, and faint; especially with torturing Pains in my *Head*." Surely, he reasoned, on a day when he was to do work "to glorify my Lord Jesus Christ," the Lord would help him. And so he prayed for a particular faith—and received it: "I felt a wonderful Force from Heaven, strengthening, and assisting, and enlarging of mee."[25]

Psychologically, the conception of a particular faith was a way of expressing man's dependence upon God. Man required reassurance of the Lord's favor; to obtain it he must grasp the immensity of God's power in contrast to his own helplessness. Once he achieved this sense, usually after a prolonged period of humbling himself, the Lord might choose to speak. Man did not coerce the Lord, yet the Lord's response came only after man's extended plea. The answer confirmed God's power.[26]

Cotton Mather's inner life was peculiar and, in several ways, unique. His was a psychology of the extreme. If his peers felt a deep piety, he ached for union with Christ. When they were complacent, he was self-righteous. If they were filled with a mild dread, he was tormented by agonizing visions. If they enjoyed contemplating the divine, he experienced raptures. They gained reassurance by praying to the Lord, he received direct communication from an angel.

Samuel Sewall, a friend of Cotton Mather, lived a life in no way extravagant but one which revealed almost as clearly as Mather's, the role of Puritan ideas in creating piety. Like Mather, Sewall recognized that man was sinful and helpless and that only the Lord could save him. Like Mather, Sewall craved God's love; and he too wished to make his life conform to Christ's as closely as possible.[27]

Sewall did not comment on these convictions extensively or on any of the great ideas of Puritanism. Rather his ideas were masked by a life of placid success. There was his work, which followed an upward course after his marriage to the daughter of wealthy John Hull, and a long period as a Superior Court judge and a councillor, two positions he filled with dignity and skill. There was his service to family and friends and to his church which he performed with loving concern. And there was his interest in New England, an interest that propelled him into beliefs that some of his sophisticated contemporaries considered absurd: opposition to wigs, for example, and to the keeping of Christmas.[28]

The record of this life is set down in Sewall's *Diary*. It is a record largely unadorned by reflection, containing little more than his notes on his actions and the events of his world. Even dreadful accidents such as this one of August 10, 1686, stand unremarked: "Ridd to Braintrey in Company of Mr. Pain, and Mr. Joseph Parson, and home agen. 'Tis said a Groton Man is killed by 's cart, Bowells crushed out; and a Boy killed by a Horse at Rowley; foot hung in the Stirrup and so was torn to pieces; both about a week ago."[29] In Cotton Mather's feverish *Diary* such episodes were improved for all they were worth.

Sewall's emotional detachment was probably as great as the spare entries in the *Diary* indicate. His piety burned slowly and evenly throughout his life: it rarely flared as Cotton Mather's often did. Although Sewall knew that he should love God and reproached himself when he felt deadness to God's claims, neither his sense of sin nor his belief in divine power left him deeply anxious.[30]

Despite the absence of intensity in feeling, Puritan ideas patterned Sewall's responses in the approved way. In Sewall's uncomplicated mind ideas were applied simply and literally—in contrast to Cotton Mather's intricate, even tortured, use. They served to suppress doubt and inquiry and to provide reassurance that things were what they seemed to be, that God's universe was ordered and reliable. The lines that attitudes and emotions and behavior should follow were clear—God had traced them in the Scriptures, and Sewall never doubted for a moment that he, or one of Massachusetts's ministers, could follow them out to the Lord's satisfaction. Even the meaning of death, the worst that the world offered, was comprehensible, or at least man could know all he required about it in this life. Death should not become the occasion of wracking grief, or of philosophical speculation. Death was an affliction sent by God to make the living aware of their sin and to prepare them for their own ends. And death contained the promise of union with Christ. Sewall fronted death hundreds of times and though when relatives or close friends died he felt a grief we would recognize as a sense of loss, his emotions assumed other forms in response to his ideas. When a son died he told himself that God had chosen this way of humbling him; he had overvalued his son; his son had become an "Image" to him.[31] The death of his first wife prompted the reflection that "God is teaching me a new Lesson; to live a Widower's Life"; the death of his second left him "ashamed of my Sin."[32] In all these notions there was the assurance that death was a "righteous sentence upon one's self" and that it led ultimately to conformity to Christ.[33] This elaborate rationale controlled emotion, and made it supportable.

Emotional reactions to ordinary events were no less patterned by Puritan ideas. When he reacted, Sewall's response invariably reflected his conviction that all things occurred through the workings of Providence.

Happenings in the world around him drew his comment because he detected God's hand in them. Almost any incident could move him to connect the seemingly trivial to the divine: one day a child's ball clogged a rain spout on the roof causing a leak into a room; Sewall tried to clear the drain and failing put his servant to it. When the ball was poked out Sewall reflected, "Thus a small matter greatly incommodes us; and when God pleases 'tis easily removed." Spilling a can of water, he remarked "that our Lives would shortly be spilt."[34]

Long before Sewall's time making such connections became a Puritan convention. We are most familiar with it in the Puritan penchant for allegory. Cotton Mather, who made more out of the technique than anyone else in New England, saw in it a grand means of stimulating piety. "Daily spiritualizing," as he called it, could be done by anyone, in contrast to a particular faith which was reserved for a qualified few.[35]

The process served Sewall and Puritans like him in a manner they did not comprehend: it routinized their emotions. Savoring the divine was the end the technique proposed to make habitual, but the beginning point had to be the concrete and the immediate. This world must be pondered before the next was approached; and this world, as Sewall's record indicates, was endlessly intriguing. The shift to cosmic meaning was made but too often in perfunctory and spiceless terms. This world remained so fascinating that, instead of a renewed piety, Puritans found that they were still prone to complacency and even deadness in the face of the Lord's claims. The irony of such experience eluded Puritan ministers who had insisted that in a well-disposed mind the intellect must "frame, and shape, and mould" the emotions.[36] Ruminations on the things of the world were supposed to yield a new spirit, not a growing preoccupation with the creatures.

The failure did not arise from the convention but from the emotional framework in which it was exercised. Sewall and those Puritans who in their complacency resembled him were not fully self-conscious. They had not learned to examine every thought and every feeling for godliness. They had forgotten that sin inhered in attitude as well as in behavior. In their unthinking conformity to creed they were "secure," to use the seventeenth-century word that described an absence of tension.

Different as they were from Cotton Mather, men like Sewall were hardly less Puritan. Both types of Puritan felt what their ideas instructed them to feel. In both the intellect's application of a highly articulated moral code displaced certain kinds of emotion. At times raw, spontaneous feeling burst through—Mather's seething anger at Calef provides one such instance. But most of the time such spontaneity was absent: the model of what a Christian should be and how he should think and feel was too clear to escape. Even love of one's wife had to be carefully controlled: it should not become so absorbing as to divert one's attention from God. Knowing how they were supposed to respond as Christians, Puritans, at some level of their being, transmuted raw feeling into feeling sanctioned by their code.

The experience of Mather and Sewall suggests the great range in the quality of the emotional lives of Puritans. In these two men even the periods of "deadness" must have differed in tone. Yet both recognized deadness as a state of mind and both felt guilty while they endured it. And in each of them the Puritan conception of man served first to intensify the feeling and then to stimulate the guilt that enabled them to dispel it. Whatever the variation in quality of the feeling of each in these, and similar, periods, the process of emotional development was the same. This process involved a complex interaction of thought and feeling initiated by traditional Puritan ideas.

If this peculiar relationship of piety and intellect existed in Puritans as different as Mather and Sewall were, it probably should be regarded as one of the determinants of Puritan character. Certainly the Puritan was not born with a peculiar emotional bias, nor was his character defined somehow more basically by emotion than by intellect. If "stretched passion" made the Puritan what he was, ideas did much to evoke and control that passion. The traditional notion of the mind as a duality has obscured the connections of emotion and intellect and of the unity of the psychic process itself. This process was incredibly complex; and the interplay of ideas and feelings in Puritans can never be wholly reconstructed. This should not deter us from making the attempt, however. Once it is made, I suspect that it will reveal the pre-eminence of the intellect in Puritan mind and character.[37]

NOTES

[1]Perry Miller, *The New England Mind: The Seventeenth Century* (New York, 1939), 67.

[2]Alan Simpson, *Puritanism in Old and New England* (Chicago, 1955), 21.

[3]Increase Mather, *A Discourse Concerning Faith and Fervency in Prayer . . .* (Boston 1710), 82.

[4]Increase Mather, *Practical Truths Tending to Promote the Power of Godliness . . .* (Boston, 1682), 200. See also Urian Oakes, *New-England Pleaded With . . .* (Cambridge, Mass., 1673), 11-13; Urian Oakes, *A Seasonable Discourse Wherein Sincerity and Delight in the Service of God Is Earnestly Pressed Upon Professors of Religion . . .* (Cambridge, Mass., 1682), 4-5, 9, 17; William Stoughton, *New-Englands True Interests . . .* (Cambridge, Mass., 1670), 20-25.

[5]Cotton Mather, *Diary of Cotton Mather* (New York, [1957?]), I, 5, 9.

[6]*Ibid.*, II, 483.

[7]See, for example, *ibid.*, I, 15, 79-80, 224-225, 475.

[8]*Ibid.*, 24, 38, 62, et passim.

[9]*Ibid.*, 24.

[10]*Ibid.*, 60.

[11]*Ibid.*, 8-12, et passim.

[12]*Ibid.*, 61.

[13]*Ibid.*, 515.

[14]*Ibid.*, 172.

[15]*Ibid.*, 457.

[16]*Ibid.*, 458.

[17]*Ibid.*, 467.

[18]*Ibid.*, 470.

[19]*Ibid.*, 473-474.

[20]*Ibid.*, 474.

[21]*Ibid.*, II, 4-5.

[22]See *ibid.*, I, 7-12, an early example of "deadness."

[23]Cotton Mather, *Parentator* . . . (Boston, 1724), 189-190.

[24]*Ibid.*, 189; Mather, *Diary*, I, 343-355, 400, et passim.

[25]Mather, *Diary*, I, 344.

[26]I have learned much from Perry Miller's account of Mather's use of the idea of a particular faith in *The New England Mind: From Colony to Province* (Cambridge, Mass., 1953), 403-404. See also Cotton Mather, *Magnalia Christi Americana* . . . (London, 1702), Bk. IV, Pt. II, Chap. I.

[27]Samuel Sewall, *Diary of Samuel Sewall, 1674-1729* (Massachusetts Historical Society, *Collections*, 5th Ser., V-VII [Boston, 1878-82]), I, 46-47; II, 98, 212; III, 200.

[28]*Ibid.*, passim. For a modern account see Ola Elizabeth Winslow, *Samuel Sewall of Boston* (New York, 1964).

[29]Sewall, *Diary*, I, 146.

[30]For an example of "deadness," see *ibid.*, II, 189.

[31]*Ibid.*, 114.

[32]*Ibid.*, III, 144, 256.

[33]*Ibid.*, II, 212. See also *ibid.*, 172, 176.

[34]For the comment on the ball see *ibid.*, 388; for the comment on the spilled water, 404.

[35]Cotton Mather's *Diary* is filled with his attempts at daily spiritualizing. See also his *Winter Meditations. Directions How to Employ the Leisure [sic] of the Winter for the Glory of God* . . . (Boston, 1693); *Agricola, Or, the Religious Husbandman* . . . (Boston, 1727).

[36]Oakes, *New-England Pleaded With*, 11.

[37]For other examples of Puritans whose minds reveal the relationship of piety and intellect discussed in this article see John Hull, "The Diaries of John Hull," American Antiquarian Society, *Transactions and Collections*, III (Worcester, 1857), 109-316; M. G. Hall, ed., "The Autobiography of Increase Mather," in Amer. Arntiq. Soc., *Proceedings*, N.S., LXXI (Worcester, 1962), 271-360; Edmund S. Morgan ed., "The Diary of Michael Wigglesworth," in Colonial Society of Massachusetts *Publications*, XXXV (Boston, 1951), 311-444; *Winthrop Papers* (Boston, 1929——). John and Margaret Winthrop's letters in volumes I and II are especially revealing.

7

Underlying Themes in the Witchcraft of Seventeenth Century New England

John Demos

Interest in witchcraft at Salem is periodically revived. This essay and several other recent investigations, have directed insights derived from anthropological studies of witchcraft (especially in African societies) and contemporary psychological theories to the examination of New England's witchcraft phenomenon. As a result, the episodes open new perspectives on colonial life and the role religion has played within it. Professor Demos is a member of the Department of History, Brandeis University.

It is faintly embarrassing for a historian to summon his colleagues to still another consideration of early New England witchcraft. Here, surely, is a topic which previous generations of writers have sufficiently worked, indeed overworked. Samuel Eliot Morison once commented that the Salem witch-hunt was, after all, "but a small incident in the history of a great superstition"; and Perry Miller noted that with only minor qualifications "the intellectual history of New England can be written as though no such thing ever happened. It had no effect on the ecclesiatical or political situation, it does not figure in the institutional or ideological development."[1] Popular interest in the subject is, then, badly out of proportion to its actual historical significance, and perhaps the sane course for the future would be silence.

First published in the *American Historical Review*, LXXV (1970), pp. 1311-1326. Republished in Stanley N. Katz, ed., COLONIAL AMERICA (Boston, 1971), pp. 113-133. Reprinted (from the latter) by permission of the author, Professor of History, Brandeis University.

This assessment seems, on the face of it, eminently sound. Witchcraft was not an important matter from the standpoint of the larger historical process; it exerted only limited influence on the unfolding sequence of events in colonial New England. Moreover, the literature on the subject *does* seem to have reached a point of diminishing returns. Details of fact have been endlessly canvassed, and the main outlines of the story—particularly the story of Salem—are well and widely known.

There is, to be sure, continuing debate over one set of issues: the roles played by the various persons most directly involved. Indeed the historiography of Salem can be viewed, in large measure, as an unending effort to *judge* the participants—and above all, to affix blame. A number of verdicts have been fashionable at one time or another. Thus, the ministers were really the people at fault; or Cotton Mather in particular; or the whole culture of Puritanism; or the core-group of "afflicted girls" (if their "fits" are construed as conscious fraud).[2] The most recent and in some ways most sophisticated study of the Salem trials plunges right into the middle of the same controversy—and with yet another conclusion. Not the girls, not the clergy, not Puritanism, but the accused witches themselves are now the chief culprits. For "witchcraft actually did exist and was widely practiced in seventeenth century New England"; and women like Goody Glover, Bridget Bishop, and Mammy Redd were "in all probability" guilty as charged.[3]

Clearly these questions can still generate lively interest, but are they the most fruitful, the most important questions to raise about witchcraft? Will such a debate ever be finally settled? Are its partisan terms and moral tone appropriate to historical scholarship? And if, with Morison and Miller, we agree that witchcraft does not loom large as historians usually measure events, what significance remains for the old arguments about personal credit and blame? The outlook, on all counts, seems discouraging.

But this situation is not a hopeless one if only we are willing to look beyond the limits of our own discipline. There is, in particular, a substantial body of interesting and relevant work by anthropologists. Many recent studies of "primitive" societies contain chapters about witchcraft, and there are several entire monographs on the subject.[4] The approach they follow differs strikingly from anything in the historical literature. Broadly speaking, the anthropological work is far more analytic, striving always to *use* materials on witchcraft as a set of clues or "symptoms." The subject is important not in its own right, but as a means of exploring certain larger questions about the society and the individuals directly concerned. Thus witchcraft throws light on social structure, or the organization of families, or the inner dynamics of personality. The substance of such investigation is, of course, highly variable from one culture to another, but the framework, the informing purposes are roughly the same. To apply this framework and these purposes to historical materials is not inherently difficult. The data may be inadequate in a given case, but the analytic categories themselves are designed for any society, whether simple or complex, Western or non-Western, past or contemporary.

Consider, by way of illustration, the strategy proposed for the main body of this essay. The whole enterprise turns on a set of complex relationships between the alleged witches and their victims. The former group includes (for these purposes) all the persons accused of practicing witchcraft; and from henceforth let them be called, simply, "witches."[5] The category of victims, on the other hand, comprises everyone who claimed to have suffered from witchcraft. But note, too, an important distinction between different *kinds* of victims. As every schoolchild knows, some of them experienced "fits"—bizarre seizures that, in the language of modern psychiatry, closely approximate the clinical picture for hysteria. These people may be called "accusers," since their sufferings and their accusations seem to have carried the greatest weight in generating formal proceedings against witches. A second, much larger group of victims includes people who attributed to witchcraft some particular misfortune they had suffered: most typically, an injury or illness, the sudden death of domestic animals, the loss of personal property, or repeated failure in important day-to-day activities like farming, fishing, and hunting. This type of evidence was of secondary importance in actual trials of witches and was usually brought forward after the accusers had pressed their own more damaging charges. For people testifying to such experiences, therefore, the short-hand term "witnesses" seems reasonably appropriate.

Witches, accusers, and witnesses: here, then, are the three basic categories of participants in witchcraft proceedings. But just who were they? And how did their lives intersect with one another? And, most important, what attributes were generally characteristic of each group? These will be the organizing questions in the pages that follow. They will, however, demand answers of two distinct kinds, one that corresponds roughly to actual circumstances in the lives of the persons involved, and another which treats imaginary (or "irrational") materials. In short, the questions will point towards two most fundamental levels of human experience—external and internal, objective and subjective, social and psychological, define them as you will.

Consider, for example, the specific case of the witches. It is important to discover, if at all possible, their age, marital status, socio-economic position, visible personality traits, and so forth. And it is equally important to examine the chief characteristics *attributed* to witches by others (flying about at night, for instance, and transforming themselves into animals). In short, we can construct a picture of witches in fact and in fantasy; and we can make comparable efforts with accusers and witnesses as well. Analysis directed to the level of fact or "external reality" helps to locate certain points of tension or conflict in the social structure of a community. The fantasy-picture, on the other hand, reveals more directly the psychological dimension of life, the inner preoccupations, anxieties, and conflicts of individual members of that community.

An outline such as this looks deceptively simple—even, perhaps, easy to put into practice. In fact, it demands an unusual degree of caution, from writer and reader alike. The approach is explicitly cross-disciplinary, reaching out to anthropology for a strategy, and to psychology for theory. There is, of course, nothing new about the *idea* of a working relationship between history and the behavioral sciences. It is more than ten years since William Langer's famous summons to his colleagues, to consider this as their "next assignment."[6] But the record of actual output is still very meager. Hence all such efforts remain quite experimental—designed more to stimulate discussion than to prove a definitive case.

There is a final point about context and the larger purposes of this form of inquiry. Historians have traditionally worked with purposeful, conscious events, "restricting themselves," in Langer's words, "to recorded fact and to strictly rational motivation."[7] They have not necessarily wished to exclude non-rational, or irrational behavior; but it has mainly worked out that way in practice. Surely in our own post-Freudian era there is both need and opportunity to develop a more balanced picture. It is to these long-range ends that further study of witchcraft should be dedicated. For witchcraft is, if nothing else, an open window on the irrational.

The first witchcraft trial of which any record survives occurred at Windsor, Connecticut, in 1647,[8] and during the remainder of the century the total of cases ran to nearly 100. Thirty-eight people were executed as witches during this span of time; and a few more, though convicted, managed somehow to escape the death penalty. There was, of course, a variety of other outcomes as well: full dress trials resulting in acquittal, hung juries, convictions reversed on appeal, "complaints" filed but not followed up. Finally, no doubt, there were many unrecorded episodes touching on witchcraft, episodes of private suspicion or public gossip that never eventuated in legal action at all.[9]

This long series of witchcraft cases needs emphasis lest the Salem outbreak completely dominate our field of vision. Salem differed radically from previous episodes in sheer scope; it developed a degree of self-reinforcing momentum present in no other instance. But it was very similar in many qualitative aspects: the types of people concerned, the nature of the charges, the fits, and so forth. Indeed, from an analytic standpoint, *all* these cases can be regarded as roughly equivalent and interchangeable. They are pieces of a single, larger phenomenon: a "system" of witchcraft belief that was generally prevalent in early New England. The evidence for such a system, must, of course, be drawn from a variety of cases in order to produce representative conclusions. For most questions this is quite feasible: there is more evidence from a greater range of cases than can ever be presented in a single study.

Yet in one particular matter the advantages of concentrating on Salem are overwhelming. It affords a unique opportunity to portray the demography of witchcraft, to establish a kind of profile for each of the three basic categories of people involved in witchcraft, in terms of sex, age, and marital status. Thus the statistical tables that follow derive entirely from detailed work on the Salem materials.[10] The earlier cases do not yield the breadth of data necessary for this type of quantitative investigation. They do, however, provide many fragments of evidence that are generally consistent with the Salem picture.

There is at least minimal information about 165 people accused as witches during the entire period of the Salem outbreak.[11] (See Tables 1, 2, and 3.) These figures point to an important general conclusion: the witches were predominantly married or widowed women, between the ages of forty-one and sixty. The exceptions add up to a considerable number; but, significantly, most of them belonged to the *families* of middle-aged, female witches. Virtually all the young persons in the group can be identified as the children of previously suspected women, and most of the men as their husbands. In fact this pattern conformed to an assumption then widely prevalent that the transmission of witchcraft would naturally follow the lines of family or of close friendship. An official statement from the government of Connecticut included among the "grounds for Examination of a Witch" the following:

If ye party suspected be ye son or daughter the servt or familiar friend; neer Neighbor or old Companion of a Knowne or Convicted witch this alsoe a presumton for witchcraft is an art yt may be learned & Convayd from man to man & oft it falleth out yt a witch dying leaveth som of ye aforesd. heirs of her witchcraft.[12]

TABLE 1

Sex	Total
Male	42
Female	120
Total	162

TABLE 2

Marital Status	Male	Female	Total
Single	8	29	37
Married	15	61	76
Widowed	1	20	21
Total	24	110	134

TABLE 3

Age	Male	Female	Total
Under 20	6	18	24
21-30	3	7	10
31-40	3	8	11
41-50	6	18	24
51-60	5	23	28
61-70	4	8	12
Over 70	3	6	9
Total	30	88	118

In short, young witches and male witches belonged to a kind of derivative category. They were not the prime targets in these situations; they were, in a literal sense, rendered suspect by association. The deepest suspicions, the most intense anxieties, remained fixed on middle-aged women.

Thirty-four persons experienced fits of one sort or another during the Salem trials and qualify thereby as accusers. (See Tables 4, 5 and 6.)

TABLE 4

Sex	Total
Male	5
Female	29
Total	34

TABLE 5

Marital Status	Male	Female	Total
Single	5	23	28
Married	0	6	6
Widowed	0	0	0
Total	5	29	34

TABLE 6

Age	Male	Female	Total
Under 11	0	1	1
11-15	1	7	8
16-20	1	13	14
21-25	0	1	1
26-30	0	1	1
Over 30	0	4	4
Total	2	27	29

Here again the sample shows a powerful cluster. The vast majority of the accusers were single girls between eleven and twenty years old. The exceptions in this case (two boys, three males of undetermined age, four adult women) are rather difficult to explain, for there is little evidence about any of them. By and large, however, they played only a minor role in the trials. Perhaps the matter can be left this way: the core group of accusers was entirely composed of adolescent girls, but the inner conflicts so manifest in their fits found an echo in at least a few persons of other ages or of the opposite sex.

Eighty-four persons came forward as "witnesses" at one time or another during the Salem trials. (See Tables 7, 8, and 9.) Here the results seem relatively inconclusive. Three-fourths of the witnesses were men, but a close examination of the trial records suggests a simple reason for this: men were more likely in seventeenth-century New England, to take an active part in legal proceedings of any type. When a husband and wife were victimized together by some sort of witchcraft, the former would normally come forward to testify. As to the ages of the witnesses, there is a fairly broad distribution between twenty and sixty years. Probably, then, this category reflects the generalized belief in witchcraft among all elements of the community in a way that makes it qualitatively different from the groupings of witches and accusers.

TABLE 7

Sex	Total
Male	63
Female	21
Total	84

TABLE 8

Marital Status	Male	Female	Total
Single	11	3	14
Married	39	16	55
Widowed	3	1	4
Total	53	20	73

TABLE 9

Age	Male	Female	Total
Under 20	3	2	5
21-30	13	4	17
31-40	14	6	20
41-50	18	7	25
51-60	11	1	12
61-70	2	1	3
Over 70	2	0	2
Total	63	21	84

There is much more to ask about "external realities" in the lives of such people, particularly with regard to their social and economic position. Unfortunately, however, the evidence is somewhat limited here, and permits only a few impressionistic observations. It seems clear that many witches came from the lower levels of the social structure; but there were too many exceptions to regard this as a really significant pattern. The first three accused at Salem were Tituba, a Negro slave, Sarah Good, the wife of a poor laborer, and Sarah Osbourne, who possessed a very considerable estate.[13] Elizabeth Godman, tried at New Haven in 1653, seems to have been poor and perhaps a beggar[14]; but Nathaniel and Rebecca Greensmith, who were convicted and executed at Hartford eight years later, were quite well-to-do.[15] And "Mistress" Ann Hibbens, executed at Boston in 1656, was the widow of a wealthy merchant and former magistrate of the Bay Colony.[16]

What appears to have been common to nearly all these people, irrespective of their economic position, was some kind of personal eccentricity, some deviant or even criminal behavior that had long since marked them out as suspect. Some of them had previously been tried for theft or battery or slander.[17] Others were known for their interest in dubious activities like fortune-telling or certain kinds of folk-healing.[18] The "witch Glover" of Boston, on whom Cotton Mather reports at some length, was Irish and Catholic, and spoke Gaelic; and a Dutch family in Hartford came under suspicion at the time the Greensmiths were tried.[19]

More generally, many of the accused seem to have been unusually irascible and contentious in their personal relations. Years before her conviction for witchcraft Mrs. Hibbens had obtained a reputation for "natural crabbedness of . . . temper"; indeed she had been excommunicated by the Boston church in 1640, following a long and acrimonious ecclesiastical trial. William Hubbard, whose *General History of New England* was published in 1680, cited her case to make the general point that "persons of hard favor and turbulent passions are apt to be condemned by the common people as witches, upon very slight grounds." In the trial of Mercy Desborough, at Fairfield, Connecticut, in 1692, the court received numerous reports of her quarrelsome behavior. She had, for example, told one neighbor "yt shee would make him bare as a bird's tale," and to another she had repeatedly said "many hard words." Goodwife Clawson, tried at the same time, was confronted with testimony such as the following:

> Abigail Wescot saith that as shee was going along the street goody Clason came out to her and they had some words together and goody Clason took up stones and threw at her: and at another time as shee went along the street before sd Clasons dore goody Clason caled to mee and asked me what was in my Chamber last Sabbath day night; and I doe afirme that I was not there that night: and at another time as I was in her sone Steephens house being neere her one hous shee folowed me in and contended with me becase I did not com into her hous caling of me proud slut what — are you proud of your fine cloths and you love to be mistres but you neuer shal be and several other provoking speeches.[20]

The case of Mary and Hugh Parsons, tried at Springfield in 1651 affords a further look at some of these same questions. There is, for example, the record of a tax-rating taken at Springfield in 1646, which shows the land-holdings of most of the principals in the witchcraft prosecutions of five years later. When the list is arranged according to wealth, Parsons falls near the middle (twenty-fourth out of forty-two), and those who testified against him come from the top, middle, *and* bottom. This outcome tends to confirm the general point that economic position is not, for present purposes, a significant datum. What seems, on the basis of the actual testimonies at the trial, to have been much more important is the whole dimension of eccentric and anti-social behavior. Mary Parsons was very nearly insane. She succumbed repeatedly to periods of massive depression; and during the witchcraft investigations she began by testifying against her husband, and ended by convicting herself of the murder of their infant child. Hugh Parsons was a sawyer and brickmaker by trade, and there are indications that in performing these services he was sometimes suspected of charging extortionate rates.[21] But what may have weighed most heavily against him was his propensity for prolonged and bitter quarreling; many examples of his "threatening speeches" were reported in court.

One other aspect of this particular episode is worth noting: namely, the apparent influence of spatial proximity. When the names of Parsons and his "victims" are checked against a map of Springfield in this period, it becomes very clear that the latter were mostly his nearest neighbors. In fact, nearly all the people who took a direct part in the trial came from the southern half of the town. No other witchcraft episode yields such a detailed picture in this respect, but many separate pieces of evidence suggest that neighborhood antagonism was usually an aggravating factor.[22]

We can summarize the major characteristics of this—the "external"— side of New England witchcraft as follows. First, the witches themselves were chiefly women of middle age, and their accusers were girls of about one full generation younger. This may reflect the kind of situation which anthropologists would call a "structural conflict"—that is, some focus of tension created by the specific ways in which a community arranges the lives of its individual members. In a broad sense it is quite probable that adolescent girls in early New England were particularly subject to the control of older women, and this may well have given rise to a powerful underlying resentment. By contrast, the situation must have been less difficult for boys, since their work often took them out of the household and their behavior generally was less restricted.

There are, moreover, direct intimations of generational conflict in the witchcraft records themselves. Consider a little speech flung out by one of the afflicted girls during a fit and meticulously taken down by Cotton Mather. The words are addressed to the "spectre" of a witch, with whom the girl has been having a heated argument:

> What's that? Must the younger Women, do yee say, hearken to the Elder?—
> They must be another Sort of Elder Women than You then! they must not bee
> Elder Witches, I am sure. Pray, do you for once Hearken to mee.—What a
> dreadful Sight are You! An Old Woman, and Old Servant of the Divel![23]

Second, it seems notable that most witches were deviant persons—eccentric or conspicuously anti-social or both. This suggests very clearly the impact of witchcraft belief as a form of control in the social ordering of New England communities. Here indeed is one of the most widely found social functions of witchcraft; its importance has been documented for many societies all over the world.[24] The process operates in a fairly straightforward way on any individual who contemplates actions of which the community disapproves. He knows that if he goes ahead, he will make himself more vulnerable either to a direct attack by witchcraft or to the charge that he is himself a witch. Such knowledge is a powerful inducement to self-constraint.

What can be said of our third basic conclusion, that witchcraft charges particularly involved neighbors? Very briefly, it must be fitted with other aspects of the social setting in these early New England communities. That there was a great deal of contentiousness among these people is suggested by innumerable court cases from the period, dealing with disputes about land, lost cattle, trespass, debt, and so forth. Most men seem to have felt that the New World offered them a unique opportunity to increase their properties,[25] and this may have served to heighten competitive feelings and pressures. On the other hand, cooperation was still the norm in many areas of life—not only in local government, but for a variety of agricultural tasks as well. In such ambivalent circumstances it is hardly surprising that relations between close neighbors were often tense or downright abrasive.

"In all the Witchcraft which now Grievously Vexes us, I know not whether any thing be more Unaccountable, than the Trick which the Witches have, to render themselves and their Tools Invisible."[26] Thus wrote Cotton Mather in 1692; and three centuries later it is still the "invisible" part of witchcraft that holds a special fascination. Time has greatly altered the language for such phenomena—"shapes" and "spectres" have become "hallucinations"; "enchantments" are now a form of "suggestion"; the Devil himself seems a fantasy—and there is a corresponding change of meanings. Yet here was something truly remarkable, a kind of irreducible core of the entire range of witchcraft phenomena. And how much of it remains "unaccountable"? To ask the question is to face directly the other side of our subject: witchcraft viewed as psychic process, as a function of "internal reality."

These phrases are obvious signposts on the road from history to psychology, and they suggest the need for another brief comment on method. Ordinarily, the biggest obstacles to a joining of history and psychology are practical ones, involving severe limitations of historical data. Yet for witchcraft the situation is, on just these grounds, uniquely promising. Even a casual look at writings like Cotton Mather's *Memorable Providences* or Samuel Willard's *A briefe account,*[27] discloses material so rich in psychological detail as to be nearly the equivalent of clinical case reports. The court records on witchcraft are also remarkably full in this respect. The clergy, the judges, all the leaders whose positions carried special responsibility for combatting witchcraft, regarded publicity as a most important weapon. Witchcraft would yield to careful study and the written exchange of information. Both Mather and Willard received "afflicted girls" into their own homes and recorded "possession" behavior over long periods of time.

Of course, a wealth of evidence does not by itself win the case for a psychological approach to witchcraft. Further problems remain, problems of language, for example, and of validation.[28] There is, moreover, the very basic problem of selecting from among a variety of *different* theoretical models. Psychology is not a monolith, and every "psycho-historian" must declare a preference. In opting for psycho-analytic theory (as in the following pages), he performs, in part, an act of faith—faith that this theory provides deeper, fuller insights into human behavior than any other. In the long run the merit of such choices will probably be measured on pragmatic grounds. Does the interpretation "work"? Does it serve to explain materials which would otherwise lie inert? Is it consistent with different evidence in related subject-areas?

If, then, the proof lies in the doing, let us turn back to the New England witches and especially to their "Trick . . . to render themselves and their tools Invisible." What was the character of these spectral witches? What qualities were attributed to them by the culture at large?

First and definitely foremost in the minds of most New Englanders was the idea that witches gave free rein to a whole gamut of hostile and aggressive feelings. In fact most witchcraft episodes began after some sort of actual quarrel. The fits of Mercy Short (reported by Cotton Mather) followed an abusive encounter with the convicted witch Sarah Good. The witch Glover was thought to have attacked Martha Goodwin after an argument about some missing clothes.[29] Many such examples could be accumulated here, but the central message seems immediately obvious: never antagonize witches, for they will invariably strike back hard. Their compulsion to attack was, of course, most dramatically visible in the fits experienced by some of their victims. These fits were treated as tortures imposed directly and in every detail, by witches or by the Devil himself. It is also significant that witches often assumed the shape of animals in order to carry out their attacks. Animals, presumably, are not subject to constraints of either an internal or external kind; their aggressive impulses are immediately translated into action.

Another important facet of the lives of witches was their activity in company with each other. In part, this consisted of long and earnest conferences on plans to overthrow the kingdom of God and replace it with the reign of the Devil. Often, however, these meetings merged with "feasts"—the witches' main form of self-indulgence. Details are a bit thin here, but it is clear that the focus was on eating and drinking. The usual beverage was wine or beer (occasionally described as bearing a suspicious resemblance to blood); and the food was bread or meat. It is also worth noting what did *not* happen on these occasions. There were a few reports of dancing and "sport," but very little of the wild excitements associated with witch revels in continental Europe. Most striking of all is the absence of allusions to sex; there is no nakedness, no promiscuity, no obscene contact with the Devil. This seems to provide strong support for the general proposition that the psychological conflicts underlying the belief in witchcraft in early New England had much more to do with aggressive impulses than with libidinal ones.

The persons who acted as accusers also merit the closest possible attention, for the descriptions of what they suffered in their fits are perhaps the most revealing of all source materials for present purposes. They experienced, in the first place, severe pressures to go over to the Devil's side themselves. Witches approached them again and again, mixing threats and bribes in an effort to break down their Christian loyalties. Thus Elizabeth Knapp, betwitched at Groton, Massachusetts, in 1671, was alternately tortured and plied with offers of "money, silkes, fine cloaths, ease from labor"; in 1692 Ann Foster of Andover confessed to being won over by a general promise of "prosperity"; and in the same year Andrew Carrier accepted the lure of "a house and land in Andover." The same pattern appears most vividly in Cotton Mather's record of another of Mercy Short's confrontations with a spectral witch:

> "Fine promises!" she says, "You'l bestow an Husband upon mee, if I'l bee your Servant. An Husband! What? A Divel! I shall then bee finely fitted with an Husband: . . . Fine Clothes! What? Such as Your Friend Sarah Good had, who hardly had Rags to cover her! . . . Never Dy! What? Is my Life in Your Hands? No, if it had, You had killed mee long before this Time!—What's that?—So you can!—Do it then, if You can. Come, I dare you: Here, I challenge You to do it. Kill mee if you can."[30]

Some of these promises attributed to the Devil touch the most basic human concerns (such as death), and others reflect the special preoccupations of adolescent girls (such as future husbands). All of them imply a kind of covetousness generally consistent with the pattern of neighborhood conflict and tension mentioned earlier.

But the fits express other themes more powerfully still; and once again problems of aggression seem to occupy the central place. The seizures themselves have the essential character of attacks: in one sense, physical attacks by the witches on the persons of the accusers; and, in another sense, verbal attacks by the accusers on the reputations and indeed the very lives of the witches. This points directly toward one of the most important inner processes involved in the witchcraft, the process that psychologists call "projection" and define roughly as follows: "Projection is escape from repressed conflict by attributing . . . emotional drives to the external world."[31] In short, the dynamic core of belief in witchcraft in early New England was the difficulty experienced by many individuals in finding ways to handle their own aggressive impulses. Such impulses were not readily acceptable in terms of their culture and upbringing; but witchcraft accusations did provide one approved means of resolving the problem. Aggression was in this manner denied in the self and attributed directly to others. The accuser says, in effect, "I am not attacking you; you are attacking me!" In reality, however, the accuser *is* attacking the witch, and in an extremely dangerous fashion too. Thus witchcraft enables him to have it both ways: the impulse is denied and gratified at the same time.

And yet, too, the situation has another side, for the seizures of the afflicted children also permitted them to engage in a considerable amount of direct aggression. Of course, they were not held personally responsible; it was always the fault of the Devil at work inside them. Sometimes these impulses were aimed against the most important—and obvious—figures of authority. A child in a fit might act in a very disobedient way towards his parents, or revile the clergy who came to pray for his recovery.[32] The Reverend Willard of Groton, who ministered to Elizabeth Knapp during the time of her most severe fits, noted that the Devil "urged upon her constant temptations to murder her p'rents, her neighbors, our children . . . and even to make away herselfe & once she was going to drowne herselfe in ye well." The attacking impulses were quite random here, so much so that even suicide seemed a possibility. Cotton Mather reports a slight variant on this type of behavior in connection with the fits of Martha Goodwin. She would, he writes, "fetch very terrible Blowes with her Fist, and Kicks with her Foot at the man that prayed; but still . . . her Fist and Foot would alwaies recoil, when they came within a few hairs breadths of him just as if Rebounding against a Wall."[33] This little paradigm of aggression attempted, and then at the last moment inhibited, expresses perfectly the severe inner conflict that many of these people were acting out.

One last, extremely pervasive theme in the witchcraft data is more difficult to handle without having direct recourse to clinical models; and the summary word for it is "orality." It is helpful to recall at this point the importance of "feasts" in the standard imaginary picture of the witches, but the experience of the accusers speaks even more powerfully to the same point. The evidence is of several kinds. First, the character of the "tortures" inflicted by the witches was most often described in terms of biting, pinching, pricking; and, in a psychiatric sense, these modes of attack all have an oral foundation. The pattern showed up with great vividness, for example, in the trial of George Burroughs:

> It was Remarkable that whereas Biting was one of the ways which the Witches used for the vexing of the Sufferers, when they cry'd out of G.B. biting them, the print of the Teeth would be seen on the Flesh of the Complainers, and just such a sett of Teeth as G.B.'s would then appear upon them, which could be distinguished from those of some other mens.[34]

Second, the accusers repeatedly charged that they could see the witches suckling certain animal "familiars." The following testimony by one of the Salem girls, in reference to an unidentified witch, was quite typical: "She had two little things like young cats and she put them to her brest and suckled them they had no hair on them and had ears like a man." People assumed that witches were specially equipped for these purposes and searched their bodies for the evidence. In 1656 the constable of Salisbury, New Hampshire, deposed in the case of Eunice Cole,

> That being about to stripp [her] to bee whipt (by the judgment of the Court att Salisbury) lookeing upon hir brests under one of hir brests (I thinke hir left brest) I saw a blew thing like unto a teate hanging downeward about three quarters of an inche longe not very thick, and haveing a great suspition in my mind about it (she being suspected for a witche) desiered the Court to sende some women to looke of it.

The court accepted this proposal and appointed a committee of three women to administer to Goodwife Cole the standard form of examination. Their report made no mention of a "teate" under her breast, but noted instead "a place in her leg which was proveable wher she Had bin sucktt by Imps or the like." The women also stated "thatt they Heard the whining of puppies or such like under Her Coats as though they had a desire to sucke."[35]

Third, many of the accusers underwent serious eating disturbances during and after their fits. "Long fastings" were frequently imposed on them. Cotton Mather writes of one such episode in his account of the bewitching of Margaret Rule: "Tho she had a very eager Hunger upon her Stomach, yet if any refreshment were brought unto her, her teeth would be set, and she would be thrown into many Miseries." But also she would "sometimes have her Jaws forcibly pulled open, whereupon something invisible would be poured down her throat... She cried out of it as of Scalding Brimstone poured into her."[36] These descriptions and others like them would repay a much more detailed analysis than can be offered here, but the general point should be obvious. Among all the zones of the body, the mouth seems to have been charged with a special kind of importance for victims of witchcraft.

In closing, it may be appropriate to offer a few suggestions of a more theoretical nature. The reason for doing so is to indicate both the way in which an interpretation of New England witchcraft might be attempted and the kind of conclusions one can hope to draw from the witchcraft materials about the culture at large. But this is meant only as the most tentative beginning of a new approach to such questions.

Consider, first, an interesting set of findings included by two anthropologists as part of a broad survey of child-rearing practices in over fifty cultures around the world. They report that witchcraft belief is powerfully correlated with the training a society imposes on young children in regard to the control of aggressive impulses.[37] That is, wherever this training is severe and restrictive, there is a strong likelihood that the culture will make much of witchcraft. The correlation seems to suggest that aggression, if forcibly suppressed, will seek indirect outlets of the sort that witchcraft belief provides. Unfortunately, there is relatively little concrete evidence about child-rearing practices in early New England; but it seems at least consistent with what is known of Puritan culture generally to imagine that quite a harsh attitude would have been taken towards any substantial show of aggression in the young.[38]

The concept of "projection" has been sufficiently discussed already; but now it may be useful to speak also of the allied notion of "displacement." Only very few cases of witchcraft accusations occurred between members of the same family. But, as noted previously, the typical pattern involved adolescent girls accusing middle-aged women. It seems plausible, at least from a clinical standpoint, to think that this pattern masked deep problems stemming ultimately from the relationship of mother and daughter. Perhaps, then, the afflicted girls were both projecting their aggression and diverting or "displacing" it from its real target. Considered from this perspective, displacement represents another form of avoidance or denial; and so the charges of the accusers may be seen as a kind of double defense against the actual conflicts.

But how to locate the *source* of these conflicts is a more difficult and frankly speculative kind of issue. Indeed it leads farther and farther from the usual canons of historical explanation; the proof, such as it is, must come by way of parallels to certain findings of recent psychological research and, above all, to a great mass of clinical data. More specifically, it is to psychoanalytic theory that one may turn for insights of an especially useful sort.

Actually, the historical record does provide one more strong clue with the prominence it gives to oral themes and anxieties. This suggests that the disturbances which culminated in charges of witchcraft must be traced to the earliest phase of personality development. It would be very convenient to have some shred of information to insert here about breastfeeding practices among the early New Englanders. Possibly their methods of weaning were highly traumatic; but hard evidence does not exist, and there is simply no way to be sure.[39] What does seem plausible—if, once again, we accept the psychoanalytic model—is that many New England children were faced with some unspecified but extremely difficult psychic tasks in the first year or so of life. The outcome was that their aggressive drives were tied especially closely to the oral mode, and driven underground.[40] Then, years later, in accordance with changes normal for adolescence, instinctual energies of all types were greatly augmented; and this tended, as it so often does, to reactivate the earliest conflicts.[41] (The process is what Freud called, in a vivid phrase, "the return of the repressed.") But these conflicts were no easier to deal with in adolescence than they had been earlier; hence the need for the twin defenses of projection and displacement.[42]

One final problem must be recognized. The conflicts on which this discussion has focussed were, of course, most vividly expressed in the fits of the accusers. But the vast majority of people in early New England—subjected, one assumes to roughly similar influences as children—managed to get through to adulthood without experiencing fits. Does this pose any serious difficulties for the above interpretations? The question can be argued to a negative conclusion, in at least two different but complementary ways. First, the materials on witchcraft, and in particular on the fits of the accusers, span a considerable length of time in New England's early history. When taken all together, they strongly suggest that aggression and orality were more or less constant themes in the pathology of the period. Second, even in the far less bizarre testimonies of the witnesses—that category which has been taken to represent the community at large—the same sort of focus appears. Above all, it is significant that the specific complaints of the accusers were so completely credible to so many others around them. The accusers, then, can be viewed as those individuals who were somehow especially sensitive to the problems created by their environment; they were the ones who were pushed over the line, so to speak, into serious illness. But their behavior clearly struck an answering chord in a much larger group of people. In this sense, nearly everyone in seventeenth-century New England was at some level an accuser.

NOTES

[1]S. E. Morison, *The Intellectual Life of Colonial New England* (Ithaca, 1956), 264; Perry Miller, *The New England Mind: From Colony to Province* (Boston, 1961), 191.

[2]Examples of these varying interpretations may be found in Charles W. Upham, *Salem Witchcraft* (Boston, 1867); Winfield S. Nevins, *Witchcraft in Salem Village* (Salem, 1916); John Fiske, *New France and New England* (Boston and New York, 1902); W. F. Poole, "Witchcraft in Boston," in *The Memorial History of Boston,* ed. Justin Winsor (Boston, 1881); Marion L. Starkey, *The Devil in Massachusetts* (Boston, 1950); S.E. Morison, *The Intellectual Life of Colonial New England* (Ithaca, 1956), 259 ff.

[3]Chadwick Hansen, *Witchcraft at Salem* (New York, 1969). See especially x, 22ff., 64 ff., 226-27.

[4]Those I have found particularly helpful in developing my own approach toward New England witchcraft are the following: Clyde Kluckhohn, *Navajo Witchcraft* (Boston, 1967); E. E. Evans-Pritchard, *Witchcraft, Oracles, and Magic Among the Azande* (Oxford, 1937); M. G. Marwick, *Sorcery in its Social Setting*

(Manchester, 1965); *Witchcraft and Sorcery in East Africa,* ed. John Middleton and E. H. Winter (London, 1963); Beatrice B. Whiting, *Paiute Sorcery* (New York, 1950).

[5]This usage is purely a matter of convenience and is not meant to convey any judgment as to whether such people actually tried to perform acts of witchcraft. Chadwick Hansen claims to show, from trial records, which of the accused women were indeed "guilty"; but in my opinion his argument is not convincing. The testimony that "proves" guilt in one instance seems quite similar to other testimony brought against women whom Hansen regards as innocent. There may indeed have been "practicing witches" in colonial New England, but the surviving evidence does not decide the issue one way or another.

[6]William L. Langer, "The Next Assignment" [*American Historical Review,* LXIII (Jan. 1958), 283-304], in *Psychoanalysis and History,* ed. Bruce Mazlish (Englewood Cliffs, N.J., 1963).

[7]*Ibid.,* 90.

[8]See John M. Taylor, *The Witchcraft Delusion in Colonial Connecticut* (New York, 1908), 145 ff.

[9]Some of these episodes are mentioned, in passing, among the records of witchcraft cases that came before the court. See, for example, the references to Besse Sewall and the widow Marshfield, in the depositions of the Parsons case, published in Samuel G. Drake, *Annals of Witchcraft in New England* (Boston, 1869), 218-57. It is clear, too, that many convicted witches had been the objects of widespread suspicion and gossip for years before they were brought to trial.

[10]These findings are based largely on materials in the vital records of Salem and the surrounding towns.

[11]In some cases the information is not complete—hence the variation in the size of sample among the different tables. Still the total for each table is large enough to lend overall credence to the results.

[12]An early copy of this statement (undated) is in the Ann Mary Brown Memorial Collection, Brown University.

[13]The proceedings against these three defendants are included in the typescript volumes, *Salem Witchcraft, 1692,* compiled from the original records by the Works Progress Administration in 1938. These volumes, an absolutely invaluable source, are on file in the Essex County Courthouse, Salem.

[14]See *Records of the Colony of New Haven,* ed. C. J. Hoadly (Hartford, 1858), II, 29-36, 151-52, and *New Haven Town Records 1649-1662,* ed. Franklin B. Dexter (New Haven, 1917), I, 249-52, 256-57.

[15]Some original records from this trial are in the Willys Papers, Connecticut State Library, Hartford. For good short accounts see Increase Mather, *An Essay for the Recording of Illustrious Providences,* in *Narratives of the Witchcraft Cases,* ed. G. L. Burr (New York, 1914), 18-21, and a letter from John Whiting to Increase Mather, Dec. 10, 1682, entitled "An account of a Remarkable passage of Divine providence that happened in Hartford, in the yeare of our Lord 1662," in *Massachusetts Historical Society Collections,* 4th Ser., VIII (Boston, 1868), 466-69.

[16]See *Records of Massachusetts Bay,* ed. Nathaniel B. Shurtleff (Boston, 1854), IV, Pt. I, 269; William Hubbard, A *General History of New England* (Boston, 1848), 574; Thomas Hutchinson, *The History of the Colony and Province of Massachusetts Bay,* ed. Lawrence S. Mayo (Cambridge, Mass., 1936), I, 160-61.

[17]For example, Giles Corey, executed as one of the Salem witches, had been before the courts several times, charged with such offenses as theft and battery. Mary Parsons of Springfield was convicted of slander not long before her trial for witchcraft.

[18]For example, Katherine Harrison, prosecuted for witchcraft at Weathersfield, Connecticut, in 1668, was reported to have been given to fortune-telling; and a group of ministers called to advise the court in her case contended that such activity did "argue familiarity with the Devil." See John M. Taylor, *The Witchcraft Delusion in Colonial Connecticut* (New York, 1908), 56-58. Evidence of the same kind was offered against Samuel Wardwell of Andover, Massachusetts, in 1692. See the proceedings in his case in the typescript volumes by the Works Progress Administration, *Salem Witchcraft, 1692,* in the Essex County Courthouse, Salem. Margaret Jones, convicted and executed at Boston in 1648, was involved in "practicing physic." See John Winthrop's *Journal,* ed. J. K. Hosmer (New York, 1908), II, 344-45. Elizabeth Morse, prosecuted at Newbury, Massachusetts, in 1679, was alleged to have possessed certain occult powers to heal the sick. See the depositions published in Drake, *Annals of Witchcraft,* 258-96.

[19]Cotton Mather, *Memorable Providences, Relating to Witchcraft and Possessions,* in *Narratives,* ed. Burr, 103-06; Increase Mather, *An Essay, ibid.,* 18.

[20]Hutchinson, *History of the Colony and Province of Massachusetts Bay,* ed. Mayo, I, 160; Hubbard, *General History of New England,* 574.

[21]The tax list is published in Henry Burt, *The First Century of the History of Springfield* (Springfield, Mass., 1898), I, 190-91; a long set of depositions from the Parsons case is published in Drake, *Annals of Witchcraft,* 219-56; see especially 224-28, 242. Mary Parsons herself offered some testimony reflecting her husband's inordinate desire "for Luker and Gaine."

[22]See Burt, *First Century of the History of Springfield,* I, for just such a map; see Increase Mather, *An Essay,* in *Narratives,* ed. Burr, 18 ff., on the case of the Greensmiths. Also Richard Chamberlain, *Lithobolia, ibid.,* 61, on the case of Hannah Jones at Great Island, New Hampshire, in 1682.

[23]See Cotton Mather, *A Brand Pluck'd Out of the Burning,* in *Narratives,* ed. Burr, 270.

[24]See, for example, Whiting, *Paiute Sorcery;* Evans-Pritchard, *Witchcraft, Oracles, and Magic Among the Azande,* 117 ff.; and *Witchcraft and Sorcery in East Africa,* ed. Middleton and Winter.

[25]For material bearing on the growth of these acquisitive tendencies, see Philip J. Greven, Jr., "Old Patterns in the New World: The Distribution of Land in 17th Century Andover," *Essex Institute Historical Collections,* CI (April, 1965), 133-48; and John Demos, "Notes on Life in Plymouth Colony," *William and Mary Quarterly,* 3d Ser., XXII (Apr. 1965), 264-86. It is possible that the voluntary mechanism of colonization had selected unusually aggressive and competitive persons at the outset.

[26]Cotton Mather, *The Wonders of the Invisible World,* in *Narratives* ed. Burr, 246.

[27]Cotton Mather, *Memorable Providences,* in *Narratives,* ed. Burr, 93-143; Samuel Willard, *A briefe account of a strange & unusuall Providence of God befallen to Elizabeth Knap of Groton,* in Samuel A. Green, *Groton in the Witchcraft Times* (Groton, Mass., 1883), 7-21.

[28]The best group of essays dealing with such issues is in *Psychoanalysis and History,* ed. Mazlish. See also the interesting statement in Alexander L. George and Juliette L. George, *Woodrow Wilson and Colonel House* (New York, 1964), v-xiv.

[29]See Cotton Mather, *A Brand Pluck'd Out of the Burning,* in *Narratives,* ed. Burr, 259-60, and *Memorable Providences, ibid.,* 100.

[30]Willard, *A briefe account,* in *Groton in the Witchcraft Times,* ed. Green, 8; deposition by Ann Foster, case of Ann Foster, deposition by Andrew Carrier, case of Mary Lacy, Jr., in Works Progress Administration, *Salem Witchcraft, 1692;* Cotton Mather, *A Brand Pluck'd Out of the Burning,* in *Narratives,* ed. Burr, 269.

[31]This is the definition suggested by Clyde Kluckhohn in his own exemplary monograph, *Navajo Witchcraft,* 239, n. 37.

[32]See, for example, the descriptions of the Goodwin children during the time of their affliction, in Cotton Mather, *Memorable Providences,* in *Narratives,* ed. Burr, 109 ff., 119.

[33]Willard, *A briefe account,* in *Groton in the Witchcraft Times,* ed. Green, 9; Cotton Mather, *Memorable Providences,* in *Narratives,* ed. Burr, 108, 120.

[34]Cotton Mather, *Wonders of the Invisible World,* in *Narratives,* ed. Burr, 216-17.

[35]Deposition by Susannah Sheldon, case of Philip English, in Works Progress Administration, *Salem Witchcraft, 1692;* manuscript deposition by Richard Ormsbey, case of Eunice Cole, in *Massachusetts Archives,* Vol. 135, 3; manuscript record, case of Eunice Cole, *ibid.,* 13.

[36]Cotton Mather, *Memorable Providences,* in *Narratives,* ed. Burr, 131.

[37]John W. M. Whiting and Irvin L. Child, *Child Training and Personality* (New Haven, 1953), Chap. 12.

[38]John Robinson, the pastor of the original "Pilgrim" congregation, wrote as follows in an essay "Children and Their Education": "Surely there is in all children . . . a stubbornness, and stoutness of mind arising from natural pride, which must be broken and beaten down. . . . Children should not know, if it could be kept from them, that they have a will in their own: neither should these words be heard from them, save by way of consent, 'I will' or 'I will not.' " Robinson, *Works* (Boston, 1851), I, 246-47. This point of view would not appear to leave much room for the free expression of aggressive impulses, but of course it tells us nothing certain about actual practice in Puritan families.

[39]However, we can determine with some confidence the usual time of weaning. Since lactation normally creates an impediment to a new conception, and since the average interval between births in New England families was approximately two years, it seems likely that most infants were weaned between the ages of twelve and fifteen months. The nursing process would therefore overlap the arrival of baby teeth (and accompanying biting wishes); and this might well give rise to considerable tension between mother and child. I have found only one direct reference to weaning in all the documentary evidence from seventeenth-century New England, an entry in the Journal of John Hull: "1659, 11th of 2d. My daughter Hannah was taken from her mother's breast, and through the favor of God, weaned without any trouble; only about fifteen days after, she did not eat her meat well." American Antiquarian Society, *Transactions,* III (Boston, 1857) 49. Hannah Hull was born on February 14, 1658, making her thirteen months and four weeks on the day of the above entry. Was it perhaps unusual for Puritan infants to be "weaned without any trouble"? Also, does it not seem that in this case the process was quite abrupt—that is, accomplished entirely at one point in time? (Generally speaking, this is more traumatic for an infant than graudal weaning.) For a longer discussion of infancy in Puritan New England see John Demos, *A Little Commonwealth: Family-Life in Plymouth Colony* (New York, 1970), Chap. 8.

[40]I have found the work of Melanie Klein on the origins of psychic conflict in infancy to be particularly helpful. See *The Psycho-Analysis of Children* (London, 1932) and the papers collected in her *Contributions to Psycho-Analysis* (London, 1950). See also Joan Riviere, "On the Genesis of Psychical Conflict in Earliest Infancy," in Melanie Klein, *et al., Developments in Psycho-Analysis* (London, 1952), 37-66.

[41]See Peter Blos, *On Adolescence* (New York, 1962). This (basically psychoanalytic) study provides a wealth of case materials and some very shrewd interpretations, which seem to bear strongly on certain of the phenomena connected with early New England witchcraft.

[42]It is no coincidence that projection was so important among the defenses employed by the afflicted girls in their efforts to combat their own aggressive drives. For projection is the earliest of all defenses, and indeed it takes shape under the influence of the oral phase. On this point see Sigmund Freud, "Negation," *The Standard Edition of Sigmund Freud,* ed. J. Strachey (London, 1960), XIX, 237, and Paula Heimann, "Certain Functions of Introjection and Projection in Early Infancy," Klein *et al., Developments in Psycho-Analysis,* 122-68.

8

Jonathan Edwards as Great Man

Richard L. Bushman

Erik Erikson's Young Man Luther *(New York, 1958) has suggested the possibility that a leader in periods of severe social stress may be interpreted as embodying or living out the tensions of his age. If successful, these individuals achieve a new ordering of life: a pattern which resolves the tensions, and works for many people in the society as well as the pioneering self. Professor Richard Bushman, Department of History, Boston University, developed this study of Jonathan Edwards, as central figure in the "Great Awakening," from that point of view.*

I

Jonathan Edwards was born in 1703 in East Windsor, Connecticut, in the household of the Reverend Timothy Edwards.[1] East Windsor had separated from Windsor in 1694, and in the first year of its independence the parish settled Timothy Edwards as its minister. Fresh from Harvard, he soon married and moved into the house which his father, a prosperous Hartford merchant, built for him in the center of the village. Jonathan was his fifth child and first son, the only son, as it turned out, among eleven children.

The most evident import of Jonathan's genealogy is that he would be expected to attain to eminence. Differing circumstances on the ancestral lines of both mother and father pointed in the same direction: Jonathan

Reprinted by permission of the publisher from *Soundings, An Interdisciplinary Journal*, LII, 1, (Spring 1969), pp. 15-46 (abridged).

would have to be powerful and successful, especially intellectually, to fulfill his family's hopes. Jonathan's mother, Esther, was the daughter of Solomon Stoddard and Esther Warham Mather Stoddard, a very imposing pair of parents. Solomon Stoddard was the dominant ecclesiastical figure in the Connecticut Valley and a powerful man throughout New England. His voice could disturb the Mathers in their Boston stronghold and was regarded respectfully everywhere. Most noted for successfully challenging the "New England Way" of admitting only visible saints to communion, Stoddard believed that true saints could not be discovered and that upright and orthodox people should be accepted into the Church in the hope that communion would help convert them, a view that many churches in the Connecticut Valley adopted. Solomon was also renowned for the fervency of his preaching and for the recurrent revivals in his Northampton congregation, a tradition Jonathan was to inherit and culminate.

When Solomon accepted the pulpit at Northampton, he met and soon married his predecessor's widow. The daughter of a famed Connecticut minister, and a powerful person in her own right, Esther Stoddard was widely known for her vigorous mind, strength of will, and considerable learning, traits which, along with her name, she gave to Jonathan's mother.

Esther Edwards was remembered by her friends as "tall, dignified and commanding in her appearance," yet "affable and gentle in her manners." Solomon sent her to Boston for her education, and she became especially well acquainted with the Scriptures and with theological writers. After Timothy's death she would ask in the neighborhood ladies to listen to her comments on theology. Some of the listeners thought Esther Edwards surpassed her husband in "Native vigor of understanding."[2]

Knowing this much, it seems safe to say that Esther wanted Jonathan to embody the qualities notable in her father, her mother, herself, and the man she chose to marry. To please his mother fully Jonathan would have to be a man of unusual force and intellect. Values so thoroughly inbred and virtually unchallenged through at least two generations could exert an intense pressure, all the greater because Jonathan was the only son among eleven children. The hopes which only a man child could fulfill necessarily focused on a boy who arrived after four daughters, and the hopes grew more intense as six daughters followed.

A rivalry with the other Stoddard daughters may have heightened Esther's ambition for her son. A hint of this competition infuses all the family relationships. Perhaps the goal was to produce a worthy successor to Solomon; if so, Esther triumphed, for Jonathan was chosen to take the Northampton pulpit. But he paid dearly for his success. His cousins harried him whenever he was in trouble. During the dismissal proceedings at Northampton, one cousin, Joseph Hawley, was the leading spokesman for the opposition. Another, Solomon Williams, wrote the refutation of Edwards' plea for a church of visible saints, pointedly rebuking him for attacking his honored grandfather. Still another cousin, Isreal Williams, a powerful figure in civil and commercial affairs in Northampton, had a long record of opposing Edwards' ministry on various counts. As early as the college years, Elisha Mix, a roommate and a cousin on Esther's side, fell out with Jonathan and wanted to move. Jonathan's father complained to Elisha's mother of his bad conduct and reproved her for speaking ill of Jonathan before strangers.[3] This collective animus may measure the determination of the Stoddard daughters to have their sons achieve the stature of Solomon and the disappointment of Esther's sisters at seeing one who was not their own excel.

Timothy's predilections reinforced Esther's high expectations for Jonathan. Timothy was the first in his family to attend college in three generations. His great-grandfather, Richard Edwards, was an ordained minister, a university graduate, and the teacher in the Cooper's Company school in London. He died young, and his widow married a cooper. With him and William, her only son by Richard, she migrated to Connecticut. William would have gone to college had his own father lived, but in America he took up his stepfather's trade. Whatever educational values may have been transmitted across the generations were twice focused on only sons, for William's wife bore him a single son who was named Richard in memory of a father and perhaps of a way of life not wholly forgotten. Timothy remembered of this Richard that, beside the Bible, "Other Good books were in the Season thereof Much Read in his house," providing some evidence of values surviving.[4]

William could not afford college for his son, but in the cooper's shop Richard prospered. He also built up a mercantile business that eventually outgrew one warehouse and required another. Meanwhile he rose through town offices into colonial politics, holding positions as selectman, as deputy to the General Court, and in his later years as Queen's Attorney. When it came time to choose a career for his eldest son, Richard sent Timothy to Harvard to study for the ministry, and perhaps to recover the honor and refinement of the first Richard's station. Timothy's aspirations for Jonathan were at least tinged with the frustrated desires of two generations finally promised fulfillment in a brilliant scion.

After settling in East Windsor, Timothy became well known for his great skill in preparing boys for Harvard and Yale. He simply assumed that Jonathan would be a scholar too and assimilate his father's learning in Latin, Greek, and Hebrew. All of the Edwards children studied the classical languages under Timothy, and even the girls went on for more schooling. The desks lining the parlor were constant reminders of family expectations. Jonathan quite naturally began Latin at age six when his precocity was fast becoming evident. In the family of Esther and Timothy, the early discovery of Jonathan's great abilities only heightened the parents' hopes and intensified the pressure for achievement.

More remains than the meager information about Esther and Jonathan to tell us about the probable effects of Timothy's character on his son. Timothy was a compulsively exact and exacting man. He schooled his students so well because he tolerated no errors in their recitations, just as he allowed none to himself. He memorized every word of his sermons and delivered them letter-perfect. Measuring corn for barter or in lieu of money payment on his salary, he "made the negro sweep it up very clean" and then measured the sweepings.[5] He delighted in classifying thoughts, arranging them in numbered lists. His tribute to his father "ends with a list of seventeen mercies attending the manner of his death, separates his dying words into thirty-five items, works out six ways in which he glorified God at his death, and proceeds to supply numbered particulars under each."[6]

Timothy displayed all the classic compulsive traits, order, thrift, and obstinacy. When inflation depreciated the value of his salary, he prepared lengthy comparisons of purchasing power at the time he was settled and afterwards to prove he was being cheated. He was never one to yield in disputes with his congregation, either. In the 1730's a young man in town married a local girl without her parents' permission. Timothy wished to censor the boy, but the congregation refused to concur. Considering the case a matter of conscience, Timothy denied communion to the entire town for over three years while the controversy dragged on.

Jonathan's mind, though far more sweeping, poetic, and profound than his father's, bore the marks of its training under Timothy. Jonathan too refused to give an inch when challenged. In the dismissal controversy at Northampton he would not compromise with his parishioners, nor would he yield a point in the debate with Solomon Williams on admission to communion. In all intellectual disputes Edwards stubbornly beat down his opponents, demolishing even the slightest contradictions. He had to prove himself right in every detail. Even in non-combative writings, his arguments were exhaustive. What often appears as repetition was part of a massive effort to block every conceivable loophole. The careful definitions, the close reasoning, the piling up of proofs and illustrations were the natural ways of his thorough and fastidious mind. The truth had to be expressed immaculately and in perfect order, leaving no gaps for error to invade.

His father's parsimony shaped not only Jonathan's attitude toward money—he too argued with his parish over salary—but toward ideas. Ideas were poetry and power for Edwards; with them he negotiated his peace with the universe. But they were also things to be possessed. His delight in discovering Locke was greater "than the most greedy miser finds, when gathering up handsful of silver and gold, from some newly discovered treasure."[7] He pinned papers to his coat while riding as reminders of his thoughts so that none would be lost. All of his ideas, along with many he read, were written down and carefully preserved in notebooks that came to contain many thousands of pages. The productions of mind were hoarded and treasured as valued possessions in a vast miser's store of thoughts.

Timothy's exactions were moral as well as intellectual. He required perfect obedience as well as perfect accuracy. The detailed instructions contained in letters to his family were presumably no less thorough when he was at home. Jonathan's behavior for the most part appears to have satisfied his parents. In one letter, when Jonathan was eight, Timothy said, "I hope thou wilt take Special care of Jonathan that he dont Learn to be rude and naught etc., of which thee and I have Lately Discoursed."[8] But the tenor of the comment was that naughtiness was exceptional. Not until late adolescence did the strains which Timothy's high standards imposed come out. Jonathan gratefully acknowledged that his parents' "counsel and education" had been his "making," but confessed that "in the time of it, it seemed to do me so little good."[9] The entire diary testified of the "good" of that sort of upbringing. Timothy's education implanted a conscience as meticulous and demanding as his standards of scholarship. The comment "it seemed to do me so little good" speaks of long struggles in which part of the self was hopelessly resistant to the pressures of conscience. By the time of the diary, Jonathan had conquered all obvious forms of sin and was struggling with the fine points, like wanting to stop to eat when mealtime came and an occasional listlessness in his studies. But his conscience kept asking for perfection, and he obediently renewed the daily examinations of his soul. He thought once that he must live as if he were to be the only true Christian on the earth in his generation. Timothy's education placed that much of a burden on his boy. Throughout his life, Jonathan continued to abhor himself as a "miserable wretch," "base and vile," and unworthy of God.[10]

There is some evidence that a peculiar combination of fear and love enforced Timothy's exactions. He displayed an extraordinary anxiety for his children's physical safety. An excerpt from a letter to Esther illustrates the point.

> I hope God will help thee to be very careful that no harm happen to the little Children by Scalding wort, whey, water, or by Standing too nigh to Tim when he is cutting wood; and prithee take what care thou canst about Mary's neck, which was too much neglected when I was at home. . . . And Let Esther and Betty Take their powders as Soon as the Dog Days are Over, and if they dont help Esther, talk further with the Doctor about her for I wouldnt have her be neglected. . . . If any of the children should at any time Go over the River to meeting I would have them be exceeding carefull, how they Sit or Stand in the boat Least they should fall into the River.[11]

That passage may be read as the loving concern of an oversolicitous father, but, as Ola Winslow commented, "instead of quieting childish fears he raised them, as though parental guidance consisted in advance notice of potential disaster."[12] If the attitude was typical, Timothy's anxieties would have reinforced in the Edwards children the ordinary apprehensions of violent destruction. Perhaps on an unconscious level they sensed that under Timothy's apparent strength was a lively sense of the precariousness of existence. At the very least they imbibed a sense of their vulnerability. Small wonder that thunder terrified Jonathan and raised apprehensions of divine wrath.

Timothy's own vulnerability made resistance still more hazardous. Fears for his own destruction arose with anxieties about the children. The myth of his boyhood, based perhaps on fact, perhaps on his own febrile imagination, had him narrowly escaping calamities ranging from drownings and freezing to swallowing peach stones. His letters home from the military expedition which he accompanied as chaplain admonish Esther not to be "discouraged or over anxious concerning me," and follow with such quavering reassurances as, "I have still strong hopes of seeing thee and our dear children once again." His life, like the letters, was suffused with the conditional, "if I Live to come home." Or again: "Tell the children, that I would have them, if they desire to see their father again, to pray daily for me in secret."[13] The conventional sentiment may have had deeper significance in the Edwards household where the children were made to feel some of the responsibility for preserving his rather frail being, making resistance fraught with danger.

Timothy's fragility and perfectionism were slight defects, and the burdens he imposed on his children surprisingly light, considering the emotional hardships of his own childhood. Richard Edwards was one of the few men in seventeenth-century New England to seek and obtain a divorce. After three appeals and a special investigation, his complaints finally moved the magistracy. Timothy's mother, Elizabeth Tuttle, confessed pregnancy by another man three months after her marriage and was unfaithful periodically throughout the twenty-four years of her life with Richard. He never forgave her infidelity and besides bore other perversities "too grievous to forgitt and too mutch here to Relate."[14] Elizabeth's trouble was not mere weakness but a violent malice, bordering on or perhaps symptomatic of insanity. Her brother Benjamin killed their sister with an axe. Another sister killed her own son. Elizabeth threatened Richard with physical violence. Timothy grew up in the presence of distrust and hatred, dependent almost wholly on his father for steady affection and exposed to visible and explosive hostility in his mother. The insistence on rigid control and the precautions Timothy urged on the patient Esther out of fear for his own and his children's safety were modest demands from such a man.

The fear of destruction was always wrapped and muffled in love. Timothy Edwards was indeed an over solicitous parent, moved by genuine affection and concern. Another letter asks Esther to "remember my love to each of the children, to Esther, Elizabeth, Anne, Mary, Jonathan, Eunice and Abigail," in his usual thorough way naming each individually in order of birth, and then adding, "the Lord have mercy on the eternally save them all, with our dear little Jerusha," the most recent. The next sentence tells much about the warmth of his household: "The Lord bind up their souls with thine and mine in the bundle of life."[15]

Any contemplated disobedience faced this love as well as the implicit danger of destruction. Overt rebellion struck at the loving and loved parent. Jonathan's doctrine that sin was all the more heinous for offending a God who loved the sinner with infinite compassion expressed the anguish felt by rebels in the Edwards household. Unjustifiable resistance wholly deserved its punishment, even if it were complete destruction. All of the Edwards children remained loyal to their parents and their parents' values. The resentments arising from discipline were necessarily turned inward or diverted to other objects.

A chance event in the family history may have accentuated the apprehensions which Timothy aroused. When Jonathan was seven he passed through a rare naughty spell, resisting for a moment his father's strict control. Immediately afterwards Timothy left with the military expedition for Canada and soon wrote home his quavering hopes for a safe return and the admonitions to pray for his safety. Jonathan's wish to overthrow his father's government seemed to enjoy remarkable success. Suddenly his father was gone and Jonathan was the only male in the house, a situation perfectly designed to revive the furtive romance with the mother characteristic of boyhood a few years earlier. With his conscious mind, Jonathan knew well enough where his father was and that he intended to return, but the direct fulfillment of secret wishes heightened fantasies with immense appeal to the unconscious. When word came back that Timothy had fallen ill and nearly died, the rational faculty would have to struggle desperately to convince itself that those deep wishes had not come precariously close to fulfillment. The brief release of passionate hopes compelled the internal restraining forces to grow all the stronger. All this was stored away in the expanding armory of Jonathan's exceedingly aggressive conscience.

Recreating what we can, then, from the meager facts of Jonathan's childhood, a few themes begin to emerge:

1) Both father and mother had unusually high hopes for Jonathan's intellectual prowess and for the possibility of his becoming eminent.
2) Timothy exacted extraordinarily precise moral and intellectual behavior from his son.
3) Timothy's feelings for his children were an ambivalent mixture of high demands, intense love, and fear of destruction, both theirs and his own.

II

Three essays written by Jonathan, probably between his eleventh and thirteenth years, open a window on his character as it took shape amid the high expectations of the Edwards household. One was an unfinished set of observations on the rainbow, foreshadowing the later notes on natural science. The second was the famous essay on spiders, and the third a facetious rebuttal to the notion of a material soul. The hand of Timothy encouraging and guiding Jonathan's development is seen behind the spider essay, "Of Insects." Like many other New England ministers, Timothy cultivated English correspondents, offering them, in return for their interest, notes on natural phenomena in the New World. More ambitious for his son than himself, Timothy urged Jonathan to write up his observations and send them to England where conceivably they might impress "the Learned world."[16]

"Of Insects" demonstrates how precocious Jonathan was both intellectually and socially. In the letter accompanying the essay, he self-consciously presented himself in a stylized guise suitable for his tender age and also in accord with the conventional proprieties of authorship.

Forgive me, sir, that I Do not Conceal my name, and Communicate this to you by a mediator. If you think the Observations Childish, and besides the Rules of Decorum,—with Greatness and Goodness overlook it in a Child and

> Conceal Sir, Although these things appear very Certain to me, yet Sir, I submit it all to your better Judgment and Deeper insight. . . .[17]

Particularly the sentence, "Forgive me, sir, that I Do not Conceal my name, and Communicate this to you by a mediator," was an affectation entirely appropriate for his century, but one that had to be learned. Somehow from the books or the guests in the East Windsor parsonage Jonathan had picked up the mannerism and made it his own.

Obviously as Jonathan wrote this essay he did not think of himself as a young future pastor, as might be expected from his upbringing and later life. He accepted that role too; a contemporaneous letter to his sister triumphantly recounted the conversions during a revival time in East Windsor.[18] But in the essay on spiders he appeared as a natural philosopher, and the essay on the soul was weighted heavily with the gestures of an eighteenth-century man of letters.

> I am informed that you have advanced an Notion that the soul is materiall and attends the body till the resurection as I am a profest Lover of novelty you must immagin I am very much entertained by this discovery (which however [old] in some parts of the world is new to us) but suffer my Curiosity a Littel further I would know the manner of the kingdom before I swear alegance.[19]

The casual, satirical tone, so redolent of fashionable prose postures, stands in marked contrast to the earnest, straightforward style of Edwards' maturity and comes as something of a relief in an anthology of his writing. The two pages on "The Soul" suggest that he toyed with more sprightly life-styles and was for a moment light-hearted before settling down to the life and death issues.

The parenthetical comment, "which however [old] in some parts of the world is new to us," indicates that imitating English manners was more than an amusing posture. Jonathan was a provincial, painfully aware that there were brilliant centers of culture and learning where ideas had grown old before the provinces even heard them. He wanted access to those centers and recognition from them. The roles of man of letters or natural philosopher were acceptable in the capitals of the English community, and, with Timothy's help, Jonathan cultivated the parts. If Timothy's expertise was limited to ancient languages, he knew of larger fields for the mind and aspired to see his son enter them.

Jonathan's strategy is reminiscent of Benjamin Franklin's, to name but one of Edwards' contemporaries with a similar youthful outlook. Franklin too was industriously perfecting his style, using Addison and Steele as his masters, with the intent of winning the attention of great ones. Success in the *New England Courant* fostered high hopes which led first to Philadelphia and then to London, where he introduced himself to polite society with a philosophical essay and a natural curiosity, a piece of asbestos. Defeated for the most part in this first assault, Franklin returned to Philadelphia and built a solid provincial base before trying again and succeeding magnificently as a natural philosopher. His scientific experiments won the recognition of the learned world and helped to establish him as the most cosmopolitan of provincials. In social terms, scientific speculation and experimentation can be interpreted as providing entry to the intellectual life beyond the provinces. Far from being unique, Edwards and Franklin simply took more seriously activities in which many educated Americans dabbled. Science and letters were avenues which talented young men could follow into the great world.

In Edwards' case, the social opportunity must also be related to his personal situation. Ascent into the great world was the fulfillment of his parents' high expectations, or, more accurately, a natural sequel to the rewards his intelligence had won at home. As his parents' ambitions for him became his own ambitions for himself, success in meeting their expectations encouraged him to aspire to success in broader spheres.

The spheres he hoped to conquer grew ever larger after he entered Yale at age thirteen and learned about the marvels of Locke and Newton. Sometime during his college years he began the notes on mind and on natural science which reveal how seriously Edwards took the work of these two intellects. The natural science notes show Edwards exploring every physical phenomenon he observed and in his usual thorough and rational way explaining the facts of physics, biology, and astronomy. "The Mind" contained observations on psychology and metaphysics after the manner of Locke's *An Essay Concerning Human Understanding*. In it Jonathan laid the groundwork of his philosophical idealism.

Both sets of notes were meant to be more than a record of observations. Edwards planned two massive treatises for publication. At the head of the notes on "The Mind" is a formal title: "The Natural History of the Mental World, or of the Internal World: being a Particular Enquiry into the Nature of the Human Mind." The relationship of this work to the notes on natural science was to be explained in the introduction: "Concerning the two worlds—the External and the Internal: The External, the subject of Natural Philosophy; the Internal, our own Minds."[20] With his two volumes Edwards planned to encompass the whole of existence, the internal and external worlds. He aimed to enlarge upon and perhaps advance beyond Locke and Newton, grounding all in theological metaphysics. Edwards was well aware that his undertaking was presumptuous and cautioned himself "not to insert any disputable thing, or that will be likely to be disputed by learned men; for I may depend upon it, they will receive nothing, but what is undeniable, from me."[21] And yet confidence in his own powers and mastery of every intellectual task Connecticut had presented encouraged him to go ahead with his *Summa*. This young provincial aimed high.

The picture of Edwards thus far is relatively conflict-free. Past performance promised future fulfillment of his parents' hopes. His natural gifts and temperament suited perfectly the life they foresaw for him. Even the legacy of compulsive thoroughness and logic were put to the service of his identity as scholar and philosopher. In the family, at Yale, and hopefully in

the greater English community, society cofirmed his belief that the works of
his mind were worthy and important and would assure him a place of high
respect.

But the promise was not fulfilled exactly as forecast. The two treatises
were never published. Although Edwards steadily added to his scientific and
philosophical notes, they remained notes. He never publicly assumed the
role of natural philosopher, and he dropped the fashionable style of a man
of letters in favor of a more somber voice as preacher. His career as pastor
and divine absorbed his entire life. The early work was put aside except
when it served religion.

The main turning came during the conversion years, but the earliest
writings reflect the tensions conversion had to resolve. More was at stake, of
course, than boyish dreams of fame. The essay on spiders particularly points
to the pitfalls which the high-strung Edwards conscience created even for a
boy as obedient as Jonathan and which compelled him to change his life.
"Of Insects" is most useful to a biographer if it is read as an unconscious allegory of human existence. Such an interpretation is not far-fetched considering that later Edwards consciously made a spider the emblem of man's
plight. Aside from purely scientific curiosity, something held Edwards' attention on spiders hour after hour. During his observations he continually
drew parallels with people, and at the end he discussed the ways of God with
small creatures in the universal moral order.

The quality which first intrigued him was the "truly very Pretty and
Pleasing" ability of spiders to swim through the air from tree to tree and
float high in the sky toward the sun. By careful experimentation, he discovered that spiders emitted a fine web which the air bore upwards and
which, when it grew long enough, carried away the spider. He hypothesized
that it spun the web from "a certain liquor with which that Great bottle tail
of theirs is filled," and which dried and rarefied when exposed. He saw the
spiders on these webs "mount away into the air" and thought it afforded
them "a Great Deal of their sort of Pleasure." Their delight disclosed "the
exuberant Goodness of the Creator" who provided for the necessities and
also "the Pleasure and Recreation of all sort of Creatures."[22]

The pleasures of ascent, however, were short-lived, for as the spiders
mounted toward the sun in the fair summer weather, they were caught in the
prevailing westerly winds and carried to the sea with a great stream of other
insects to be "buried in the Ocean, and Leave Nothing behind them but
their Eggs." "The End of Nature in Giving Spiders this way Of flying Which
though we have found in the Corollary to be their Pleasure and Recreation,
yet we think a Greater end is at last their Destruction."[23] The "Greater end"
of the pleasing rise was eventual destruction.

The spider's nature made him worthy of this fate. At first appearance
"no one is more wonderful than the Spider especially with Respect to their
sagacity and admirable way of working." Its maneuvers were "truly very
Pretty." But the inner nature of the spider warranted a violent burial at sea,
for in essence it was "the Corrupting Nauseousness of our Air." Were
spiders in any number to die inland in winter, the spring sun would revive

"those nauseous vapours of which they are made up."[24] To prevent them from smelling up the country they were taught to rise and then destroyed.

Edwards here dwelt somewhat pathetically on two themes which sound again more stridently through the "Diary": a pleasurable ascent ends in destruction, and nauseousness lies beneath the pretty appearances. In the "Diary" Jonathan firmly renounced the pleasures of rising as he saw that pride led to destruction. His schemes to achieve eminence in the world had to be abandoned in favor of a life devoted wholly to religion. A loathing of his own vileness also came to obsess him. Later he spoke of sensuality as pollution. "How sensual you have been!" he told one audience. "Are there not some here that have debased themselves below the dignity of human nature by wallowing in sensual filthiness, as swine in the mire, or as filthy vermin feeding with delight on rotton carrion?"[25] "Of Insects" suggests that Jonathan's conscience was already disturbing his complacency in prideful achievement and that the underside of the compulsive perfectionism Timothy implanted was a fear of concealed filth.

Another portentous theme appeared in the early writings. Comparing spiders to humans, Edwards said, "the soul in the brain immediately Percieves when any of those little nervous strings that Proceed from it are in the Least Jarrd by External things." In the essay on the material soul, he asked facetiously if the soul is "a number of Long fine strings reaching from the head to the foot." The image of strings suggests how delicately responsive was his nervous system and how easily jarred. When the spiders were jarred in the course of the experiments, they spun a web and drifted off. The material soul was less mobile, and the main point of the essay concerned the discomforts it suffered "when the Coffin Gives way" and "the earth will fall in and Crush it." Or more excruciating, when other souls were buried in the same grave, they "Quarril for the highest place." "I would know whether I must Quit my dear head if a Superior Soul Comes in the way." When twenty or thirty souls occupied the spot, "the undergoing so much hard Ship and being deprived of the body at Last will make them ill temper'd."[26]

The satirical portrayal of a discontented, nervous soul, growing ill-tempered as it struggled for a place in the narrow confines of the grave, suggests some of the contrasting pleasures of Edwards' famous booth in the woods. The large family of girls, the guests, the students, and the watchful, demanding eyes of Timothy left little room in the house for peaceful worship. With his boyhood friends, Jonathan built a "booth in a swamp, in a very retired spot, for a place of prayer. And besides, I had particular secret places of my own in the woods, where I used to retire myself."[27] Personal relations all too easily jarred "the little nervous strings" proceeding from his brain, and Edwards struggled hard for mastery of his responses. His diary discloses that he suffered particularly from a "disposition to chide and fret." His own overweening conscience inclined him to snap at others' weaknesses and "to manifest my own dislike and scorn."[28] He eventually decided he could permit himself no evil speaking, not even that which he once thought to be righteous reproof. The dangers of slander or undue vehemence were all too apparent. Even public worship tried him, until by concerted effort he

learned to overcome his impatience.[29] Throughout his life he often walked in
the fields or rode in the woods, where alone under the sky he more easily
composed his soul and made peace with God.

In sum, these early writings confirm to some extent and elaborate the
previous speculations on the emotional import of Edwards' early life:

> 1) For a time anyway, Jonathan aspired to fulfill family expectations through
> his philosophic writings.
> 2) The pleasure and excitement of rising was counter-balanced by a fear of
> destruction because of unworthiness or inward filthiness.
> 3) The tendency to chide and fret made close personal relations uncomfor-
> table.

III

Edwards' conversion, which drew on all of these themes, occurred over
a period of years in his early manhood. Near the end of his college, a case of
pleurisy brought him "nigh to the grave" and shook him "over the pit of
hell." After that he grew steadily more uneasy about religion, going through
"great and violent inward struggles" until he finally broke off "all ways of
known outward sin." The "inward struggles and conflicts, and selfreflec-
tions" continued, and he made "seeking my salvation the main business of
my life" but still did not consider himself converted.[30] Meanwhile he was
studying theology in New Haven and preparing to take a temporary pulpit
in New York City.

Sometime in his eighteenth or nineteenth year began a series of experiences which he later believed to be gracious. Two slightly differing accounts survive. Edwards wrote the *Personal Narrative* nearly twenty years
later, after the first revivals in Northampton. What remains of the "Diary"
begins in December of 1722 when he was in New York City and when he
had reason to believe grace had already touched him. It records his struggles
with sin and his further experiences with grace.

In the "Diary" Edwards charted his cycles of spiritual decay and
recovery, the movement from spiritual dullness to the exhilarating moments
of rededication. On Saturday, January 12, 1723, in the morning, he enjoyed
one of the seasons of grace, and the comment he wrote directly afterwards
indicates the nature of the experience. The paramount issue was renunciation of self and complete surrender to God.

> I have this day, solemnly renewed my baptismal covenant and self-dedication,
> which I renewed, when I was taken into the communion of the church. I have
> been before God, and have given myself, all that I am, and have, to God; so
> that I am not, in any respect, my own. I can challenge no right in this under-
> standing, this will, these affections, which are in me. Neither have I any right
> to this body, or any of its members—no right to this tongue, these hands, these
> feet; no right to these senses, these eyes, these ears, this smell, or this taste. I
> have given myself clear away, and have not retained any thing, as my own. I
> gave them to God, in my baptism, and I have been this morning to him, and

told him, that I gave myself *wholly* to him. I have given every power to him; so that for the future, I'll challenge no right in myself, in no respect whatever.[31]

Edwards felt compelled to offer more than perfect obedience to God. He searched his soul to be sure nothing was left for himself; everything was given to God, his body and all its senses, all his powers, all enjoyments, the credit for all his efforts, the right to complain or rest, the right to seek anything for himself. He could not permit himself to be "in any way proud." At issue in conversion was the willingness to obliterate selfishness and give up all to God. During the controversy over admission to communion in Northampton, he summarized in a public profession what was expected of saints and put this surrender and the accompanying obedience at the heart. The profession read in the whole:

> I hope, I truly find in my heart a willingness to comply with all the commandments of God, which require me to give up myself wholly to Him, and to serve Him with my body and my spirit; and do accordingly now promise to walk in a way of obedience to all the commandments of God, as long as I live.[32]

The *Personal Narrative* shifted the stress somewhat to emphasize Edwards' reconciliation with the doctrine of "God's sovereignty, in choosing whom he would to eternal life, and rejecting whom he pleased, leaving them eternally to perish, and be everlasting tormented in Hell." Edwards did not consciously experience the intense fear of divine wrath which usually preceded conversion. He thought his "great and violent inward struggles" were not properly called terror, but as these comments reveal, the fear of punishment was there, probably buried too deep to be felt. The doctrine of election "used to appear like a horrible doctrine," and filled his mind with objections from his childhood up.[33]

For no discernible reason, Edwards suddenly became convinced of God's justice in election. Objections ceased and he rested easy in assurance of divine justice. In connection with this alteration, he tells of his first experience with "that sort of inward, sweet delight in God and divine things" that he later called grace. It came as he read the passage in Scripture saying, "Now unto the King eternal, immortal, and invisible, the only wise God, be honor and glory for ever and ever, Amen." As he read these words, there diffused through his soul "a sense of the glory of the Divine Being; a new sense, quite different from any thing I ever experienced before."[34] As far as Edwards could tell that was the moment of his conversion, and reconciliation with divine power was the critical issue. After that, the thunder that had once terrified aroused sweet contemplations of God's glory.

The two accounts of the experience with grace are easily reconciled, for they have in common a submission to God. The "Diary" stresses the surrender of self and renunciation of pride. The *Personal Narrative* emphasizes the discovery of beauty in God's sovereign right to punish. Both forms of submission can be seen as aspects of a single experience, especially if one remembers how some common vicissitudes of childhood could prepare the way for this very combination. While engaged in passionate rivalry with his father for the love of his mother, a boy imagines himself rising in pride and power to displace his father, thereby evoking paternal wrath. Peace negotiations require both the renunciation of pride and acceptance of the father's superior power, a double surrender morally symmetrical with the two issues in Edwards' conversion.[35]

Edwards' pride could easily have awakened these old memories and their attached apprehensions because his ambition was tied so closely to intellectual achievement, which was also his father's source of pride and a form of accomplishment his mother prized. In seeking to excel as a scholar he inevitably outdid his father and won the favor of his mother. The audacity of the act, though wholly symbolic and unconscious, released the fears which Timothy's compulsive demands and the implicit threats of destruction had formed in Jonathan's conscience. The "torments of hell" included the terror the Edwards children felt toward the imminent possibility of hurting and being hurt by their loving, profoundly fragile, and threatening father. In yielding all to God, Jonathan disclaimed the old rivalry, again symbolically and unconsciously, and placated his archaic fears. The danger of rising to destruction was averted.

Edwards wanted God to sanctify every level of his being, down to the deepest, and the glory of conversion was the comprehensive transformation it wrought. Its power lay in the affinity between theological notions and intimate personal tensions. In conversion Jonathan reconciled himself to God and universal being but the religious symbols also formed bonds with long forgotten memories and with buried conflicts too explosive for consciousness to touch. Conversion resolved tensions along the full range of experience. Until that moment God was the sovereign who judged and punished, shaking men over the pit until they obeyed. The relationship was one of king to subject. As the new "sense of the glory of the Divine Being" came over Edwards upon reading the first epistle to Timothy, he felt a happy yearning to enjoy God, to "be rapt up to him in heaven" and to be "swallowed up in him forever." He prayed "In a manner quite different" from before and "with a new sort of affection." The beauty and loveliness of Christ instead of the fierce power of God impressed his mind. All of Canticles occupied him and especially the verse, "I am the Rose of Sharon, and the Lily of the valleys." These symbols and the whole perception of the divine was softer, warmer, more sensuous.[36] The new relationship was one of lovers. At times the tone was frankly sexual. Some passages in the *Personal Narrative* overflow with a lover's passion.

> The inward ardor of my soul, seemed to be hindered and pent up, and could not freely flame out as it would. I used often to think, how in heaven this principle should freely and fully vent and express itself. Heaven appeared exceedingly delightful, as a world of love; and that all happiness consisted in living in pure, humble, heavenly, divine love.[37]

Or in a different mode: "My heart panted after this, to lie low before God, as in the dust; that I might be nothing, and that God might be ALL, that I might become as a little child."[38] One of the rewards of conversion was that feelings otherwise tightly suppressed flowed freely toward God.

The venting of emotion was possible because vileness was changed to sweetness. The nauseousness of the spider was banished. Whereas sensuality had been and under that name was still described as filth and defilement, the new "delights" were of a "pure, soul-animating and refreshing nature." The happiness of heaven where the inward ardor could "freely flame out" consisted "in pure, humble, heavenly, divine love." The "ravishingly lovely" beauty of holiness was "far purer than any thing here upon earth"; everything else was "mire and defilement" in comparison.[39] In grace emotions were sweet and calm and flowed freely without polluting. Sensuality was purely joyous.

One final issue came to resolution during conversion. Edwards overcame, partially at least, his uneasiness among people. His disposition to chide and fret had disturbed his personal relations, and he had found peace most easily in solitude. In conversion he still envisioned himself "alone in the mountains, or some solitary wilderness, far from all mankind, sweetly conversing with Christ, and wrapt and swallowed up in God." But loving and even ardent relations with other Christians were possible. Another of his poetic visions pictured the soul of a true Christian as "a little white flower" standing "peacefully and lovingly, in the midst of other flowers round about." In New York he drew very close to the two saintly people with whom he lived and delighted in long intimate discussions about heaven and holiness.[40]

Edwards' social discomforts did not disappear, for his "heart was knit in affection" only "to those, in whom were appearances of true piety." Indeed he "could bear the thoughts of no other companions, but such as were holy, and the disciples of the blessed Jesus." He disliked visiting among his parishioners where small talk of the world was a necessity. Instead he invited them to his study where he could keep the discussion on religion. The woman he married, Sarah Pierrepont, had been widely reputed for her piety, and even before he met her Edwards wrote a tribute to her "wonderful sweetness" and "singular purity."[41] He could enjoy the intimacies of marriage and friendship only with those whom grace had sanctified, but at least conversion afforded that measure of untroubled intercourse.

IV

The happy visitations of grace continued during his stay in New York and into the following summer spent at his father's house. By the fall of 1723 he had agreed to settle in Bolton, a new town not far from East Windsor, but before his installation, a tutorship opened at Yale, and Edwards persuaded Bolton to release him. From June of 1724, after a winter of private study, until September of 1726, he was the senior tutor and acting Rector, with responsibility to discipline the students as well as to instruct them. After one week on the job, "despondencies, fears, perplexities, multitudes of cares, and distractions of mind" weighed him down and convinced him "of the troublesomeness and vexation of the world." For the three years of his tutorship he was in a "low, sunk estate and condition, miserably senseless" about "spiritual things."[42] The only respite came in the fall of 1725 when he fell ill at North Haven on his way home and his mother came to nurse him.

For many reasons Edwards welcomed the offer which came in 1725 to assist aging Grandfather Stoddard in Northampton. The new position took him away from Yale, and it made him heir-apparent to Solomon Stoddard's immense power. Nothing could have thrilled his mother more. The summer following his ordination, Edwards married Sarah Pierrepont, whose piety he had admired from afar and whose life in the Northampton parsonage bore out the promise of her early godliness and aristocratic upbringing. She was deeply devoted to her husband—one of her deepest sorrows was to displease "Mr. Edwards"—and her saintliness fully matched his own.[43] A daughter, the first of eleven children, was born in 1728.

Solomon Stoddard died in 1729 and Edwards became chief pastor. He seems never to have regretted the subordination of his youthful ambitions to be a natural philosopher. A ministerial career was perfectly suited to the religious identity formed in conversion. In the pulpit the lonely quest for salvation entered onto a broad stage. His office permitted him to talk freely of God's wrath, of human defilement, and of the exquisite joys of grace. Speaking objectively as pastor, Edwards exposed his soul publicly as he could never do privately. The secret yearnings and dread so long stored in the recesses of his heart became the bread and wine of an open communion with the world. Even the disposition to chide and rebuke was dignified to a duty. When he admonished, he spoke for God, expressing the righteous wrath of a Holy Father, commanding rather than being commanded, pure instead of vile, terrifying rather than being terrified. And the whole was sanctified and purged of pride because done for God and not for self.

The congregation responded to his quiet, intense preaching. From time to time under Stoddard, revivals had brought unusually large numbers into the Church. Five years after Edwards became pastor, the town experienced a livelier concern with religion than any known before. Two sudden deaths contributed to "the solemnizing of the spirits" of the young, and a controversy over Arminianism set many to asking the true way of salvation. Before long "among old and young, and from highest to the Lowest; all seemed to be siezed with a deep concern about their Eternal salvation."[44] The concern spread from town to town until churches all up and down the Connecticut Valley were reporting revivals. The suicide of Edwards' Uncle Hawley in a fit of melancholy over his state slowed the work, but five years later in 1740, when Whitefield visited New England, Northampton and other towns were ripe. The concern spread more widely than ever, engaging thousands of souls this time, and Edwards was in great demand as a preacher and counselor.

Edwards identified these conversions as being of the same species as his own. People felt the same "utter helplessness, and Insufficiency for themselves, and their Exceeding wickedness and Guiltiness in the sight of God," each one considering himself worse than all others just as he had. They were eventually brought to "a Lively sense of the Excellency of Jesus Christ" and "to have their Hearts filled with Love to God and Christ, and a disposition to Lie in the dust before him." In the process of conversion people were also "brought off from their Inordinate Engagedness after the world," though obviously in different ways from Edwards' renunciation of achievement as a philosopher. The same love for others and concern for their souls, the same heightened sense of personal wickedness, the same variations in intensity of devotion all linked the common experience to Edwards' conversion.[45]

His personal influence, of course, does not begin to explain the prevalence of the revivals. All over New England people underwent rebirth in the period of a few years. They followed Edwards, or others like him, because they were ready, not because he personally overpowered them. Something common to all, some prevailing strain on their institutions, some pressure in the culture prepared people for the new life he urged upon them. They listened because the truth of his experience was also the truth of theirs.

I have treated the consciousness of this period at length elsewhere, but even in outline the parallels with Edwards can be seen.[46] In Edwards' psyche the most serious conflict leading to conversion was the tension between prideful ambition and the fear of suffering God's wrath for indulging in pride. Conditions in New England in the early eighteenth century put large segments of the population in a similar predicament. The paramount fact of the common life after 1700 was rapid expansion—in population, in the number of new settlements, in commercial opportunities and involvements, and in the economic horizons of the ordinary man. In Connecticut, for example, population grew nearly five times as fast in the thirty years after 1700 as in the thirty years before; the number of new towns settled doubled; the number of debt cases per capita—a measure of increasing prosperity and commercial growth—increased five times.

The most important and obvious effect on most lives was to broaden economic opportunities. The new towns offered a host of tantalizing possibilities for incipient merchants. The growing markets outside New England, in Newfoundland and Halifax, in the West Indies, and in Europe, along with the expanding needs of the prospering fishing fleet provided growing outlets for farmers, and the rapid growth of population made speculation in new land very enticing. These developments permitted young men to dream dreams utterly unfeasible earlier. New England had visited a few men with prosperity from the beginning, but very few ordinary men could hope for more than a decent living. William Edwards, for example, had carried on his trade without making great advances. Richard had fared better, building on his father's business, but in the seventeenth century he was exceptionally fortunate. Not everyone could elevate himself in the eighteenth century either, but new opportunities increased the incidence of success. Examples multiplied of small storekeepers who became wealthy merchants and of thrifty farmers who doubled their estates through speculation. By later standards the stakes were small, but the prospects dazzled the first generation of the new century.

Expansion stimulated the desire to rise in the world and yet implicitly threatened destruction, the very ambivalence prominent in Edwards' life. Commercial and agricultural expansion depended heavily on risk-laden speculations: natural disasters, debt foreclosures, and unforeseen calamities of various kinds could wipe out farmers and traders. The psychic hazards were as great as the economic ones. Puritan preachers urged men to follow their callings industriously and to rise through their enterprise. But they condemned men for setting their hearts on wealth and making it their god. The increasing luxury of the eighteenth century and its "Cursed Hunger of Riches" evoked the most bitter indictments. A man never knew exactly where he stood. At one moment he rested in the assurance of his virtuous diligence and of the prosperity heaven had bestowed. At the next a warning from the pulpit started fears that the lust for gold had hopelessly corrupted his soul. Men found themselves in a dilemma comparable to the plight of Robert Keayne, a Boston merchant of the seventeenth century. Keayne prospered in Boston and maintained a respectable reputation until he was accused of unfair dealing and reprimanded in the courts. The confrontation with his guilt put him in fear for his salvation. In hopes of recovering his peace of mind, Keayne wrote an interminable testament justifying his conduct.[47] In the seventeenth century distress like his hung over the few who prospered; in the eighteenth century economic expansion exposed the entire population to these unsettling apprehensions.

Conflicts with authority magnified the guilt and fears of the ambitious. Aspiring men fought with established authority at every level of government, in the town, in the church, and in the colonial government. With innumerable variations, involving large and small enterprises, the pattern repeated itself: ambitious men in pursuit of wealth broke through conventional restrictions and clashed with authorities bent on preserving order. The conflicts were psychically debilitating because the magistracy and ministry were thought to rule by virtue of divine investiture. Authority had a counterpart in individual consciences, and when men resisted they fought against themselves. Opposition, however well justified, partook of sinful rebellion.

Another theme in Edwards' life, his prickly relations with associates, appears in the social record also. New Englanders were notoriously litigious, quick to criticize, to sue, or to ask the church to censure. Economic expansion increased the occasions for misunderstandings and ill feeling. The competition for land and trade and for every conceivable economic advantage made enemies of former friends. Every debt case, for example, represented a dispute. A creditor always preferred to settle privately to avoid court costs. Only when prolonged appeals failed did he sue. The storekeeper or wealthy farmer grew exasperated at the delays in payment; the debtor for his part felt the terms unjust, the request for payment over-hasty, or the creditor unsympathetic. The fivefold increase in debt cases per capita in Connecticut between 1700 and 1730 represented at least as large an increase in personal quarrels arising for economic reasons.

The whole society suffered from a painful confusion of identity. People were taught to work at their earthly callings and to seek wealth; but one's business had to remain subservient to religion and to function within the bounds of seventeenth-century institutions. The opportunities constantly tempted people to overstep both boundaries, thereby evoking the wrath of the powerful men who ruled society. Even relations with neighbors deteriorated as expansion multiplied the occasions for hard feelings. At some indeterminate point social values and institutions stopped supporting the man who placed his confidence in worldly success and instead obstructed and condemned his actions. The pleasurable rise which prosperity afforded carried one at last to destruction.

A widespread uneasiness put people "upon Enquiring, with concern and Engagedness of mind, what was the way of salvation, and what were the Terms of our acceptance with God."[48] The revival preachers confronted their audience with the darkest possible view of their sins and hopeless future. They had fought against God, were filled with pride and vileness, and were worthy of unending torment in the pit of hell. This frank exposure of their dark inward side gave people the courage to being their sins and insecurity to the surface. The man in the pulpit assuring them that he understood their guilt and the presence of others publicly manifesting their anguish provided communal support for the agonizing confrontation.

The preachers required total humiliation and submission before promising peace. The only hope for reconciliation with God was to confess to utter helplessness and to depend wholly on his grace. For those who heard, moral rectitude and a measure of prosperity suddenly furnished neither peace in this world nor a promise of God's favor in the world to come. Men stood naked under the heavens, helplessly exposed to divine wrath. Edwards noticed people passing from despair to passivity as they recognized the impossibility of earning salvation and gave themselves up to be damned or saved at God's pleasure. Then almost surprisingly hope revived. The good news of the Gospel was heard as if for the first time. The gift of grace seemed sufficient to redeem, and the convert rejoiced in new confidence, founded now on God's loving mercy. They were brought to a "Lively sense of the Excellency of Jesus Christ" and "of the Truth of the Gospel." The sense of sin continued and increased, but now contrition was combined with love and joy.[49] Men felt that they were saved.

With a new identity founded in God's gracious love, converted men renounced their former sources of confidence. The world's wealth no longer appeared so enticing. Edwards noted that in Northampton "People are brought off from Inordinate Engagedness after the World, and have been Ready to Run into the other Extreme of Too much neglecting their wordly Business and to mind nothing but Religion." People seemed to "dread their former Extravagances" and wanted to strip themselves of worldly luxury.[50] After the frenetic itinerant James Davenport urged a New London audience to discard their wigs, fine clothing, and worldly books, the people piled their possessions in a public place and burned them.

Conversion also relieved tensions with neighbors and with authority. The infusion of God's love sweetened all personal relations. "Persons are soon brought to have done with their old Quarrels: Contention and Intermeddling with other mens matters seems to be dead amongst us," Edwards wrote. He cited a number of parishes where old contentions vanished and the congregation was "universally united in hearty affection to their minister." In 1735 his own people "Generally seem to be united in dear

Love, and affection one to another," and he "never saw the Christian spirit in Love to Enemies so Exemplified, in all my life." Indeed Northampton "never was so full of love, nor so full of distress as it has Lately been."[51] He composed a covenant to which his congregation subscribed in 1742, pledging themselves not to "overreach or defraud" their neighbors, or "wilfully or negligently" to default on their honest debts. They promised not to "feed a spirit of bitterness, ill will, or secret grudge," and in the management of public affairs not to let private interest and worldly gain lead them into "unchristian inveighings, reproachings, bitter reflectings, judging and ridiculing," but do everything with "christian humility, gentleness, quietness and love."[52]

The results of the revival deeply gratified Edwards. A barely suppressed elation runs throughout *A Faithful Narrative of the Surprising Work of God*, the essay in which he described the love of God and men which came over Northampton in 1735. The Spirit of God appeared to be creating an entire society of saintly men, submissive to God and exquisitely sensitive to religion, a society which confirmed and supported the identity Edwards had assumed in his own conversion. The resonance between Edwards and his people did not continue as perfect harmony. Eventually he demanded more saintliness than they could muster, and his congregation voted 200 to 23 to dismiss him. But for more than a decade, while his words shaped the innermost lives of the reborn, his heart and theirs were as one.

NOTES

[1] Three biographies of Edwards' life are useful for different purposes. Ola Elizabeth Winslow, *Jonathan Edwards, 1703-1758: A Biography* (New York, 1940), places Edwards in his social setting. Perry Miller, *Jonathan Edwards* (New York, 1949), is a brilliant interpretation of Edwards' thought with suggestive comments on the social structure in the Connecticut Valley. S. E. Dwight, *The Life of President Edwards* (New York, 1830), reprints much of the source material.

[2] Dwight, *Edwards*, pp. 16, 18.

[3] Jonathan Edwards to Timothy Edwards, Nov. 1, 1720; fragment of a letter from Timothy Edwards to Mrs. Mix. Both are in the Andover collection now on deposit at the Edwin J. Beinecke Library at Yale. I am grateful to Andover-Newton Theological Seminary for permission to refer to this letter and also to Miss Marjorie Wynne of the Beinecke Library for giving me access to it.

[4] Quoted in Winslow, *Edwards*, p. 16.

[5] Quoted in Winslow, *Edwards*, p. 21.

[6] Quoted in Winslow, *Edwards*, p. 22.

[7] Quoted in Miller, *Edwards*, p. 52.

[8] Winslow, *Edwards*, p. 41.

[9] From the "Diary," in Dwight, *Edwards*, p. 86.

[10] Ibid., pp. 81-83.

[11]Winslow, *Edwards*, pp. 41, 42.

[12]Ibid., p. 43.

[13]Dwight, *Edwards*, p. 14; Winslow, *Edwards*, p. 41.

[14]Quoted in Winslow, *Edwards*, p. 18.

[15]Dwight, *Edwards*, p. 14.

[16]Winslow, *Edwards*, p. 36.

[17]Ibid.

[18]Dwight, *Edwards*, p. 21.

[19]*Jonathan Edwards: Representative Selections, with Introduction, Bibliography, and Notes,* ed. Clarence H. Faust and Thomas H. Johnson, rev. ed. (New York, 1962), p. 11.

[20]The intended title page is reprinted in Dwight, *Edwards*, p. 664.

[21]From the "Notes on Natural Science," reprinted in Dwight, *Edwards*, p. 702.

[22]*Representative Selections,* pp. 3, 6, 7.

[23]Ibid., pp. 10, 8.

[24]Ibid., pp. 3, 10.

[25]*The Works of President Edwards, in Four Volumes* (New York, n.d.), IV, 234.

[26]*Representative Selections,* pp. 5, 11, 12.

[27]Ibid., p. 57.

[28]Dwight, *Edwards*, pp. 84-85.

[29]Ibid., pp. 85, 88, 89, 90, 94.

[30]*Representative Selections*, pp. 57, 58.

[31]Dwight, *Edwards*, pp. 78-79.

[32]*Works,* I, 202.

[33]*Representative Selections,* p. 58.

[34]Ibid., p. 59.

[35]A more elaborate explication of Edwards' conversion and the psychoanalytic elements involved may be found in Richard L. Bushman, "Jonathan Edwards and Puritan Consciousness," *Journal for the Scientific Study of Religion,* V (1966), 383-396.

[36]*Representative Selections*, pp. 59, 60.

[37]Ibid., p. 63

[38]Ibid., pp. 63-64.

[39]Ibid., pp. 62,63.

[40]Ibid., pp. 60, 63, 64, 65.

[41]Ibid., pp. 64, 65.

[42]Dwight, *Edwards*, pp. 103, 106.

[43]Ibid., pp. 171-172.

[44]*Representative Selections*, pp. 74, 75.

[45]Ibid., pp. 77, 78.

[46]Richard L. Bushman, *From Puritan to Yankee: Character and the Social Order in Connecticut, 1690-1765* (Cambridge, 1967).

[47]Bernard Bailyn, "The Apologia of Robert Keayne," *William and Mary Quarterly,* VII (1950), 568-587.

[48]*Representative Selections*, p. 74.
[49]Ibid., pp. 77, 78.
[50]Ibid., pp. 76, 77.
[51]Ibid., pp. 76-78.
[52]Dwight, *Edwards*, pp. 165-167.

9

The Great Awakening as Watershed

Alan Heimert

Alan Heimert argues that the Great Awakening (the intercolonial revival of religion in the 1740s) represents the first major transition in American religious and social history. In particular, the expectation that a millennial era would fulfil the yearnings of the faithful for a fraternal, democratic order became a powerful ingredient in emerging American nationalism. Professor Alan Heimert teaches American History and Literature at Harvard University.

I

The watershed in American history marked by the 1740's can be understood best in terms of the degree to which, after the Great Awakening, the American populace was filled with the notion of an impending millennium. From 1740 on, American thought and expression—or, more precisely, that of the evangelical American—was above all characterized by a note of expectation. Few Calvinist utterances of the period—and almost none of Edwards'—can be fully comprehended except as proceeding from the assumption that the "unspeakably happy and glorious" period of the "prosperity" of Christ's church and people was approaching and, more significantly, that it was attainable "through the ordinary processes of propagating the gospel."[1] Edwards' *Thoughts on the Revival* was, thus, far

Excerpted by permission of the author and publishers from *Religion and the American Mind: From the Great Awakening to the Revolution,* by Alan Heimert, Cambridge, Massachusetts: Harvard University Press, © 1966 by the President and Fellows of Harvard College.

more than the first and the best of many tracts in defense of emotional and "experimental" religion. It was inspired, Edwards reports, by the knowledge that the "people of God" were filled with "earnest desires, that the Work of God, now in the land," would be "carried on" until the Kingdom of the Messiah was established throughout the earth "as a kingdom of holiness, purity, love, peace, and happiness to mankind."[2] Edwards not only confirmed these expectations; he gave them substance by assigning tasks and duties to various elements of the people of Christ for establishing the Kingdom with the least delay and confusion. In sum, he announced confidently that the coming of the millennium might be hastened through the use of human instrumentalities.

The explosion of millenarianism in the Great Awakening was one of the symptoms of some Americans' dissatisfaction with the conditions of eighteenth-century life. Edwards described the world in which he lived as "for the most part a scene of trouble and sorrow,"[3] and, whatever the judgment of others, apocalyptic speculations persisted throughout the sixty years of American history after the Awakening.[4] Yet the revival of the 1740's also brought hope; the Great Awakening, like the revivals of 1800-1801, was preceded as well as accompanied by popular speculations and prophecies concerning "when Christ would appear and set up his true kingdom."[5] Such aspirations seem to have been fed in New England by underground Fifth Monarchy sentiments, largely unarticulated since the Revolutions of 1689 and their frustrating aftermath, and by chimney-corner traditions and recollections of New Haven colony, of Cotton, Vane, and Eliot. Perhaps they were sustained by a reading of such copies of Edward Johnson's *Wonder-Working Providence* as had survived the century; surely they were encouraged by Joseph Morgan's popular allegorical *History of the Kingdom of Basaruah* (1715), which held out the promise of the earthly Kingdom as a final solution to the intolerable hostilities of an emotionally parched New England and New Jersey.

In the first quarter of the century the Mathers had dilated on the "Universal Reign of Holiness and Righteousness" which the eighteenth century would surely see. They had predicted "horrid concussions, and wrecks in nature" as the attendants of the general judgment which, in their vision, was presumably to precede the millennium. But such chiliasm seems not to have persisted as a widely acceptable formula, at least not after the earthquake of 1727. When in 1734 a New England divine wrote of the final conflagration as occurring *"before the happy State* of the Church," he acknowledged that the contrary opinion generally prevailed: the earthly Kingdom was foreseen this side of judgment and cataclysm. The Great Awakening confirmed the American disposition against premillenarianism. James Davenport, to be sure, announced during the revival that "in a very short Time all these Things would be involv'd in devouring Flames."[6] But even he soon afterward understood what other Calvinists had seen, either by the New Light of the revival itself, or by the clearer light provided them by Edwards: that a shattering of the order of nature would not be required to introduce the era of earthly felicity.

In this regard the "Fort Hill Address" of eighteenth-century Calvinism was Edwards' *History of the Work of Redemption,* the thirty-nine sermons he delivered in 1739. Although the sermons were not published until the 1770's, they contained the axioms and postulates which, as expounded and expanded in such works as *An Humble Attempt to Promote Explicit Agreement and Visible Union of God's People* and *A Dissertation Concerning the End for which God Created the World,* sustained several American generations in a belief that the millennium was not a mere possibility but an imminent and attainable reality. The theory set forth in the *Work of Redemption* was postmillennial; that is, the thousand years of earthly felicity would come *before* the General Judgment. It has been suggested that the source of Edwards' millenarian theory was the chiliasm which arose out of late seventeenth-century interpretations of Newtonian physics. But the Edwardean metaphysic—a repudiation of the premillenarianism of the previous generation—seems rather to have been made intense belief and firm conviction by the revivals and the Great Awakening itself.

The revivals of the 1730's encouraged Edwards' inquiries into the "History of the Advancement of Christ's Kingdom," and his attention to its progress in the contemporary world.[7] Edwards presumably longed for the coming of the Kingdom well before 1735, but until then his sermons considered the Kingdom only as one into which men were to press as a matter of personal rather than corporate, and deferred rather than temporal, salvation. Such, at least, were the themes of his *Pressing into the Kingdom,* a sermon which preceded the Northampton revival of 1735. (And such were the themes of its Middle Colony counterpart, Tennent's discourse on *The Necessity of Religious Violence.)* But in 1739 Edwards, defining the "Work of Redemption" anew—as he put it, "more largely"—conceived of the Kingdom as an "evangelical state of things in the church, and in the world."[8] In *A History of the Work of Redemption* Edwards declared that from the "fall of man" onward the Kingdom had been advanced chiefly by such "remarkable communications of the spirit of God" as the people of Northampton had witnessed in 1735. In 1739 Edwards was not certain whether what had "already taken place," among the pietists of Germany and the followers of Frelinghuysen and the Tennents, as well as in the Connecticut Valley, constituted the "forerunners and beginning" of the triumphant Kingdom.[9] By 1741, however, he had more extensive data by which to test his hypothesis according to the rules of the inductive philosophy.

It was the Great Awakening itself that made non-cataclysmic millenarianism "the common and vital possession" of evangelical American Christians.[10] The prodigious accomplishments of George Whitefield on his first majestic tour of the colonies inspired both Calvinist ministry and populace with a new perspective on the tendency of history. The very first experience of the revival immediately rang a high and clear note of anticipation: "It looks as if some happy period were opening." Soon the question was not what "great things" were *"at the Birth"* but when, exactly, the "glorious day"—the millennium itself—would begin.[11] Samuel Finley an-

nounced that the showers of grace which had descended on the colonies
were "proof that the kingdom of Christ is come unto us this day." Edwards
himself was more cautious and could not in 1741 decide "whether the present work be the beginning of that great and frequently predicted coming of
Christ to set up his kingdom, or not." But a year later he publicly testified
(with what proved to be embarrassingly few qualifications) that the "*New
Jerusalem*" had "begun to come down from heaven" in 1740.[12] Eventually
Edwards confessed his conclusion to have been not only premature, but in-
opportune; still, he continued to affirm the revivals of 1740-41 to have been
"forerunners" of the millennium, which, he likewise insisted, must "needs
be approaching."[13]

The Awakening had clearly reversed the apparent course of history.
Calvinists ceased looking on the events of the past century as a tale of
mournful declension. Instead *The Christian History,* the magazine in which
accounts of the Awakening were assembled, in a series of articles on the
religion of the seventeenth century, noted the sins and afflictions of that age,
but only incidentally to what now seemed the more significant facts of the
past: "Some Former Instances of the Revival of Religion in New England."
In the course of the Awakening the themes of the jeremiad all but disappeared from Calvinist sermons. Thomas Foxcroft, who in 1730 had com-
memorated the first century of New England with a lamentation for
departed spiritual glories, greeted the year 1747 with a recapitulation of
Christian history in which the Reformation and the Puritan experiments
loomed as forerunners of the Spirit's triumphs in the Great Revival of the
1740's.[14] No longer did the tendency of history seem toward judgment, or
the thoughts of the pious bent on despair.

With the publication of Edwards' dissertations, *Will* and *God's End in
Creation,* the elements of American Protestantism for whom he spoke and
whom he profoundly influenced were committed, by his very postulates, to
an optimistic view of history. The crux of Edwardean theology was the inherent and necessary relation of the regenerating work of the Spirit to the
"erection, establishment, and universal extent of the Kingdom of the Messiah."[15] As Perry Miller has observed, Edwards' achievement in placing the
millennium "on this side of the apocalypse" was to provide Calvinism with
a formula in which the good society would and could be attained solely
through "natural causes." But the aspect of creation involved in the Work
of Redemption was, for Edwards, the "supernatural" realm—that portion
of the universe which was above and beyond nature, consisting in man's
"union and communion with God, or divine communications and
influences of God's spirit." The earthly Kingdom of the Calvinist Messiah
was not of the "natural, material" world: but "within men." It consisted not
"in things external," but in happiness and the "dominion of virtue" in the
minds and hearts of mankind.[16] The Work of Redemption was one with the
regeneration of humanity; it depended on no awful display of Divine power,
no shattering of the physical creation, but on the gradual restoration of the
influences of the Holy Spirit which had been withdrawn at the Fall.

II

Whether the millennial theory of post-Awakening Calvinism was intellectually respectable may be questioned, but what cannot be gainsaid is that the expectancy expressed in that theory controlled the mind of the period. Something of a key to the era is contained in one of Edwards' pronouncements of the 1740's:

> We are sure this day will come; and we have many reasons to think that it is approaching; from the fulfillment of almost every thing that the prophecies speak of as preceding it, and their having been fulfilled now a long time; and from the general earnest expectations of the church of God, and the best of her ministers and members, and the late extraordinary things that have appeared in the church of God, and appertaining to the state of religion.[17]

The heart and soul of Calvinism was not doctrine but an implicit faith that God intended to establish this earthly Kingdom—and to do so within the eighteenth century. The Awakening had brought history to a critical juncture, a discernible confluence which disposed the Calvinist mind to "look for the beginnings" of the millennium "from year to year."[18] And the faith of the 1740's sustained the Calvinists through dispensations of Providence which other Americans, less confident than they that Edwards had read God's plan aright, found both dark and bewildering.

In the sermons, the *Work of Redemption,* Edwards had portrayed mankind's progress as impelled by periodic impulses of the Spirit. But in the years of the Awakening, and those immediately following, he seemed to identify the beauty of history with what, in the *Notes,* he had defined as "proportion." The tempo of history in the early 1740's was seemingly such that God's purpose now promised to be fulfilled with ever-doubling acceleration, by geometric enlargement of the saintly host. But by 1747 history obviously no longer moved with its anticipated velocity, and such a vision proved untenable. It was then that Edwards adopted and announced a "cyclical" theory of history—one not of mere repetition, but of recurrence and periodically renewed and increased momentum. Outpourings of the Spirit were to be expected only in certain "times and seasons" roughly corresponding to each generation's coming of age. In such springtimes of the race, humanity's stagnant pools would once more become freshets, and the rivers of history would again be sent rushing on their way, each time etching more indelibly on the earth the courses through which they would at last hurtle to their destination.

Thus of all the "signs of the times," the most significant in the eyes of Calvinist watchmen was a "happy revival of religion." Well after Edwards himself acknowledged that the Awakening impulse was spent, his every statement continued to underscore the proposition that the "unspeakably happy" millennial era would be signaled by a "glorious day of religious revival" in which the experience of 1740-41 would be both infinitely exalted and indefinitely prolonged.[19] With the outbreak of the imperial wars, however, he began to seek other evidence of the fulfilling of God's grand design. Edwards was impressed by God's "dealings, both with Great Britain and the American plantations" in the conflict which culminated in the victory at fortress Louisburg—with its presumed consequences for the French fisheries and, thus, the revenues of the Papacy. But though he collected a body of notes on such contemporary events, and apparently planned to use them in the final version of his "History of the Work of Redemption," that history was ultimately written as *The End for which God Created the World.*[20] Battles and sieges were, after all, mere interludes in God's sublimest plot. Far from determining the course of history, their meaning—and the meaning of all temporal events—was subsumed in the grander tale of the spiritual transformation of mankind. . . .

The End for which God Created the World was Edwards' consummate effort to sustain such cosmic optimism in the dark years of the 1750's, a time of "lukewarmness" among God's people, of deaths and contention in the Church, and of natural catastrophies and imperial wars which threatened to impose on history a different, and contrary, meaning of their own. These years witnessed waverings of the Calvinist faith in certain circles, and even departures from it. In 1755 Jonathan Parsons, once Edwards' student, suffered a relapse into pre-Awakening thinking and jargon when he proposed that the Lisbon earthquake, which was felt throughout the colonies, was the beginning of "those terrible things in righteousness" that would culminate in general judgment.[21] A portion of the pious populace seemed also to be gripped by despair, for concurrently sectarians, indulging a renewed popular appetite for "millennial arithmetic," sought to fix the exact date of the Second Coming.[22] But the Calvinist mind quickly proved incapable of returning for long to premillenarianism. Indeed, by the close of the 1750's it seemed that historical pessimism was congenial only to the spokesmen of "enlightened" and rational religion.

The Calvinist questioned the Liberal cosmography, which seemed to reduce God to the role of an onlooker who, once He had set nature going, thereafter stood aside, no longer willing or able to influence the course of events. But it was not the purpose of Calvinist doctrine to vindicate the possibility of divine intervention in the order of nature, of arbitrary or violent repeal of its "laws." There were, to be sure, apparent exceptions, as when in the 1750's (and again in the 1770's), ministers attempted to console their flocks with the thought that God could and would reverse the earthly "scene" by turning "a single leaf in the volume of his decrees."[23] But such symptoms of flagging confidence represented a resignation from the abiding faith of post-Awakening Calvinism. The God of eighteenth-century evangelical Americans was not, like the one which Urian Oakes had invoked in a rapidly changing Restoration New England, disposed to providential caprice. The Calvinist, no less than the Liberal whose philosophy he despised, discerned a "pattern" in the order of nature as well as that of grace. When Edwards wrote of the "divine establishment" by which certain sequences were ordained or permitted, he was thinking, above all, of the great chain of events that constituted the Work of Redemption. That the universe was pervaded with the divine impulse was not for him a threat to an orderly succession of phenomena. Rather it provided assurance that no power was at work which operated contrary to, or even independently of, God's redeeming Will.

III

So emphatic was post-Awakening Calvinist insistence on the universality of Divine influence that its language often bordered on the transcendental. The instance of Edwards is too well known to require comment, but other Calvinists also portrayed nature as alive with Divine energy. Samuel Buell concluded one such depiction with the observation "that all nature is full of God, full of his perpetual, moving, guiding, and over-ruling influence."[24] Such doctrine differed widely, however, from the Emersonian. For the Calvinist entertained no thought of the charming happenstance that Emerson was to associate with what he called the "method of nature." That the divine influence descended "even to the very minutest particles, so as to give them all their variety of modes, properties and relations of every kind," did not serve the Calvinist as an argument for miracles—except, that is, for the ultimate miracle of grace. When the Calvinist contended that God's agency was discernible throughout the "whole universe," his emphasis was on God's "conducting" power, His efficacy in guiding the worlds both of nature and of man toward the fulfillment of His purpose.[25] The Calvinist God perhaps performed His wonders in various ways, but not deviously; and His ways, after all, were not more various than His single end in the creation of the world. . . .

That such was the import of Edwardeanism is perhaps most convincingly disclosed by the fact that his celebrated argument against the "freedom of the will" was set forth in a context of concern for the social salvation of mankind. "Unless God foreknows the future acts of men's wills," Edwards contended,

> all those great things which are foretold both in the Old Testament and the New, concerning the erection, establishment and universal extent of the *kingdom* of the *Messiah,* were predicted and promised while God was in ignorance whether any of these things would come to pass or no, and did but guess at them.[26]

The logic by which Edwards sustained such a predestinarianism is perhaps of less importance than the sense of urgency with which he strove to destroy the Arminian doctrines—doctrines which allowed individuals to be the initiators of action. To accept this possibility was to give the destiny of humanity over to those whose natures were so hopelessly corrupt that they sought to oppose the divine plan.

Though Edwards employed the doctrine of Divine "foreknowledge" to assure the coming of the millennium, he by no means committed Calvinism to the metaphor of the predetermined universal machine—or to the idea, implied thereby, that God was exclusively the first cause in history. His every pronouncement of the 1740's implies a belief that the future, as well as the past, is somehow a cause of the present.[27] But not until the *Freedom of the Will* did he develop a "scientific" vocabulary with which to account for the manner in which the transcendent became apparent. Employing the metaphor of the telescope, and conceiving of temporal relations in terms of distance, he concluded that it was necessary to "suppose future existences some way or another to have influence back, to produce effects beforehand."[28] Edwards' final statement of this proposition appeared, of course, in the *End in Creation,* wherein he declared that God was both "the first author" of humanity's "being and motion" and, at the same time, "the last end, the final term, to which is their ultimate tendency and aim."[29] His Deity was both the efficient and final cause of history—and, indeed, its formal and material cause as well.

Where Calvinists most commonly followed Edwards, however, was in his frequent depiction of the courses of history as a number of "large and long" rivers which "all unite at last, all come to the same issue, disgorging themselves in one into the same great ocean." In using this metaphor, Calvinists anticipated, in a sense, such social Darwinists as William Graham Sumner. "It is vain for men to attempt to turn back the stream," Edwards affirmed, "or put a stay to it."[30] But where Sumner mocked the absurdity of efforts to make the world over in defiance of the mainstream of history, Edwardeans conceived of Providence as a variety of "different streams"— all of them overturning and overturning as humanity was carried toward millennial felicity. "Not one of all the streams fail," Edwards affirmed.[31] The Calvinist Deity—both Alpha and Omega—stood not only at the beginning of history, supplying the waters and dispatching them on their downward course, but at the end of time, as an irresistible center of gravity.

The better part of Calvinist literature on the subject of causation was designed to undermine the smugness of Arminians in ascribing to "instruments" what was due only to the "efficient." It was employed in support of the ultimate truth that every being—whether a spider over a pit or a creature in the hand of God—had "nothing to support its Being, but its producing Cause."[32] But the Calvinist theory of causation was far more than a merely critical doctrine. That God was a motive force extending "to all actions of the creature—to natural, civil, supernatural. . . too all fortuitous and voluntary actions," was not, as Liberals incessantly complained, a hopeless and depressing proposition, but an optimistic and stimulating one.[33] It gave assurance that God did not only "sit at the helm and steer the ship," but, as it were, blew the gale.[34] In Newtonian terms, it implied that God gave direction as well as momentum to the lines of force which He had projected. In practical terms, it promised success to all who moved into the rushing streams of history.

The Republican persuasion of 1800—that mankind would witness the "coming of the Lord's Kingdom with power" only when all power and authority was "considered in the body of the people"—was in a sense the supreme fulfillment of the promise of the Great Awakening.[35] Out of the Awakening emerged a Calvinism which sought not merely to understand the course of history but rather to influence and control it, or at least to add momentum to it. Had the Calvinist mind, in the years after the Awakening, merely responded to events, neither the pace nor the direction of colonial history would have been so strikingly altered in the 1740's. What actually happened is that the Calvinists of America consciously undertook to advance the Work of Redemption.

In 1742 Edwards explained so all who ran might read that the days were "coming, when the saints shall reign on earth, and all dominion and authority shall be given into their hands." But the more remarkable of his propositions, and in all respects the most radical, was one set forth three years earlier in *The History of the Work of Redemption*. A view of the divine plan for redeeming the world, he declared, helped to make history comprehensible. But it was even more valuable as a means of inspiring men to action on behalf of the Kingdom. It was both testimony and summons to God's "friends and subjects"—who, Edwards proclaimed, were "capable of actively falling in with" the divine program and indeed of "promoting it."[36] Thereafter Edwards continued to descant on the "connection of one event with another, and the beautiful order of all things that come to pass," but it was never his sole purpose, in doing so, to explain the mysteries of Providence to the bewildered saints.[37] Nor for other Calvinists was the vision of God "conducting all things" to a predetermined end primarily "calculated to give consolation" to God's people. Its purpose was to assure them of the efficacy of their own endeavors on behalf of the Kingdom.

In its purer version, the Calvinist view of history was a stirring reminder that man's own efforts, God willing and assisting, were the only means of advancing the Kingdom. The Calvinist doctrine of the "means" was of course an inheritance from seventeenth-century Puritanism. But after the Awakening all "the ordinary means of grace," long focused on mere individual conversions, were incorporated into a strategy for advancing the earthly Kingdom. Chief among these was "the preaching of the Gospel," for the Calvinist, as a worker together with the Spirit, conceived progress the task primarily of those capable of communicating ideas.[38] Other devices—such as the establishment of seminaries of learning in order to train Christian ambassadors—were inspired by the belief that preaching was by far the most efficient means of exciting that revival, "far more pure, extensive, and glorious" than the Awakening, which would usher in the millennium.[39] It was generally in the context of hastening the "glorious day" that the eighteenth-century Calvinist best understood the efficacy of the means.

More importantly, perhaps, it was generally in such terms that he offered to his people an explanation of "how means become effectual, either in the natural or moral world." Eleazar Wheelock, for instance, thought of preachers as means for the "enlargement of the church of *God*" in terms both of greater population and of more extensive territory. He was confident, moreover, that either a handful of apostles among the Six Nations or a single evangelist sent to Virginia could somehow bring about the millennium, though the "means, by which this great event is to be brought about, seem to be in themselves but weak, and to bear but a small proportion to the greatness of the effects to be produced by them."[40] The doctrine of "constant providence" on which Wheelock's confidence was based seemed to make greater sense—as it did for a Calvinist chaplain of Revolutionary troops—in a context of "God's perfect scheme of universal government."[41] Its meaning, and the conviction which it carried to Calvinist audiences, was largely dependent on the relevance of the means to the felicity, not of individuals merely, but of the larger Kingdom.

Among the Calvinist means was one which in conception and practice was both consistent with the traditional Calvinist emphasis on the Spirit and yet revealing of the novel grandeur of Calvinist eschatology: the "Concert of Prayer." These quarterly meetings for prayer by the faithful throughout the world are commonly acknowledged to be among the more impressive institutions introduced to western Protestantism by the Awakening. Official credit for the idea is commonly given a group of Scotch Presbyterians associated with the dissenter revivals in and about Cambuslang, but a similar proposal had been broached three years earlier by Edwards in the *Thoughts on the Revival*. The venture was given publicity and meaningful metaphysic, moreover, in Edwards' *Humble Attempt to Promote Explicit Agreement and Visible Union of God's People in Extraordinary Prayer, for the Revival of Religion and the Advancement of Christ's Kingdom on Earth*. Here Edwards outlined a program whereby the people of God might be induced to manifest "a great spirit of prayer," which, as it tended gradually to "spread more and more, and increase to greater degree," would induce a great and general "revival of religion." This in turn would "be the means of awakening others," all of whom would then join again in prayer, until the process culminated in the "work of God's spirit" which would inaugurate "that glorious day of religious revival, and advancement of the church's peace and prosperity"—the millennium.[42]

This argument, though it was sustained by Edwards' faith in the final cause of history, contained within itself the premise that mankind could create within itself the very desires that were to accomplish and constitute the earthly Kingdom. It was, to be sure, the nearly perfect "spirituality" of this means that allowed Edwards to conclude that history would necessarily rise to a crescendo. For the Concert of Prayer represented a re-creation of the conditions of the revival and thus a stepping, as it were, into the clearly discernible mainstream of history. Yet Edwards' argument for the "fitness" of such a strategy can hardly disguise the truly radical notions embodied in his rationale for the Concert of Prayer. Edwards' crucial premise—that God is "at the command of the prayer of faith and in this respect, as it were, under the power of his people"—was, for all its modifications, a clear declaration that the achievement of millennial society was dependent on the collected will of God's people. Perhaps even more significantly, it depended more on the will of the multitude than on that of their pastors and leaders.

The program which Edwards outlined in the *Humble Attempt* served to chasten the "religion of the closet" which Cotton Mather had promoted in eighteenth-century New England, and even to overbear his own insistence on the value of private prayer and devotion. But despite the encouragement it gave to communal endeavor, the Concert of Prayer never fulfilled the whole of the hopes expressed in Edwards' title. It did, however, seem to induce some of the "happy *revivals* of *religion*" which Edwards expected it to accomplish.[43] The device produced its first apparent fruits in 1757, when the students of the College of New Jersey enjoyed the first revival in American history which "was not begun by the ordinary means of preaching."[44] For many years thereafter the better part of the Calvinist ministry continued to consider the Concert one of the most appropriate instruments for advancing the Kingdom. The fact that so many were in 1759 praying for the millennium gave Robert Smith the "Hope, that the Dawn of the foresaid glorious Day is not far off."[45] In 1763 and 1764 the prayers of the faithful seemed answered in an outpouring of the Spirit that spread through the colonies. The events of the next two decades altered everyone's millenarian calendar and strategy, but by 1795 Calvinists were again "calling the attention of the pious to an expectation of the introduction of this glorious day" by means of the Concert of Prayer.[46] The Congregationalists and many of the Baptists of New England were persuaded that the revival of 1799 was to be "traced, in its beginning, to these seasons for special prayer."[47] But even more significantly, the *Humble Attempt* inspired David Austin in the series of speculations and ventures by which he persuaded himself, and a large part of the dissenter population of New England and the Middle Colonies, to exert themselves on behalf of the election of Jefferson so the millennium might be inaugurated before the beginning of the nineteenth century.[48] . . .

IV

The Great Awakening had itself seemed for a moment nearly the final conflict in the eyes of the awakened. So evident were the bitter animosities released by the revival that an Anglican, writing to the Secretary of the Society for the Propagation of the Gospel in Foreign Parts, allowed that the "year of Enthusiasm," 1741, might be "as memorable as was 1692 for witchcraft for the converted cry out upon the unregenerated, as the afflicted did then upon the poor innocent wretches that unjustly suffered."[49] Quickly the battle lines were drawn, and both converts and the evangelical ministry were disposed to consider the chief enemies of the Kingdom those who were "raging" against the Awakening. The New Side Presbyterians needed no "further Witnesses" to the identity of Antichrist than the "furious Opposition to the Work of God in the Land." Both Finley and Edwards went far toward identifying opposition to the Awakening as the "unpardonable sin against the Holy Ghost," and, by doing so, impressed their critics as intending to draw up the populace of the colonies in battle array. In the pro-revivalists' view of history, the state of affairs in 1741 was, according to critics, placed on "a Level with the State of Things in the Days of Christ," and thus designed "to make those, who are (if you will) Enemies to the present Work, and violent Opposers of it, Sinners to the same Degree of Guilt, as were those, who opposed Jesus Christ himself." By design or otherwise, it appeared, the revivalists worked to make "the holy *Furioso*'s of the present Day hate, for God's Sake, all that are not in *their* wild Scheme."[50] At the height of the Awakening the strident censoriousness of the revival leaders sounded very much like a trumpet call to battle.

Jonathan Edwards clearly participated in such attitudes and encouraged the people of God to look on the revival as a holy war. Whereas in 1739 he had been more eclectic in his characterization of "Satan and all his instruments," two years later Edwards expressly defined the archenemies of the Work of Redemption as those who would "maliciously oppose and reproach" the revival. But by 1742 Edwards was working to suppress the antagonism that he as well as others had helped to arouse. In fact, even in 1741 Edwards wanted to restrain the impetuosity of the awakened—or at least to temper their vehemence of expression. Were the evil of those who opposed the revival "ten times so great as it is," he insisted, "it would not be best to say so much about it," nor call for "fire from heaven, when the Samaritans oppose us." His precise intentions in the 1740's are not always easy to discover; in one breath he would remind the people of God that "it becomes Christians to be like lambs," in the next, that they must be "wise as serpents."[51] Whether, then, his strictures against violence of word or deed, in the *Religious Affections*, were prudent counsel or deep conviction cannot be decided with absolute assurance. Obviously Edwards disclosed a temperamental aversion to violence, especially when he had reason to regret his own impetuous arrogance. But it is also clear that he was responding to the pride and pathos inherent in the partisans of the revival calling for heavenly judgment on those whom they judged the enemies of the Kingdom. Divine fire was simply not to be expected, and the complacent self-satisfaction of the awakened provided neither the kind of weapon necessary to turn their judgment to account, nor the discipline that would make Armageddon anything but a rout of mere unaided virtue.

In a broader perspective Edwards' denial of a need for conflict seems a strategy for dispelling the fears still lingering from the pre-Awakening era. The *Humble Attempt* was an effort to strengthen the hands of those on whom Edwards knew he must count to forward the Work of Redemption. He did so by encouraging the people, at a moment in history which might otherwise have seemed discouraging, to exercise their wills. The idea that a "slaying of the witnesses" was yet to come, he argued, would have to be dismissed because, quite simply, it was *practically* "of such hurtful tendency" to the cause of the Kingdom:

> If persons expect no other, than that the more the glorious times of Christ's kingdom are hastened, the sooner will come this dreadful time, wherein the

generality of God's people must suffer so extremely, and the church of Christ be almost extinguished, and blotted out from under heaven; how can it be otherwise, than a great damp to their hope, their courage and activity, in praying for, and reaching after the speedy introduction of those glorious promised times? As long as this opinion be retained, it will undoubtedly ever have this unhappy influence on the minds of those that wish well to Zion . . . So that this notion tends to discourage all earnest prayer in the church of God for that glorious coming of Christ's kingdom, till it be actually come; and that is to hinder its ever being at all.[52]

In the context of the 1740's, Edwards' declaration that a devastation of the godly was not to be expected served to instill with confident hope those on whose efforts the coming of the Kingdom depended. It would, Edwards believed, "be a great discouragement to the labours of nations, of pious magistrates and divines, to endeavour to advance Christ's kingdom, if they understood it was not to be advanced." More significantly, the hope of irreversible progress—or, more precisely, "the keeping alive such hopes"—had, as Edwards saw it, "a tendency to enliven all piety and religion in the general, amongst God's people."[53] Such a vision of unimpeded victory was for him the guarantor, because the inspiration, of the popular desires which alone could fulfill the promise of history.

It seems not to have been Edwards' purpose, at least in the years after the celebrated Enfield sermon, to frighten men into endeavors on behalf of the coming Kingdom by threatening to deprive them of its benefits. His observation in the *Thoughts,* that the magistrates and other "great men" of New England ought to assist in the Work of Redemption if they wished a share in its honors, probably carried an implicit threat. But by the late 1740's he clearly preferred to woo men into the Kingdom with the prospect of the millennium, the expectation of which should, he thought, be enough to "strongly excite" both pastors and people to be "such as God had promised to bless" in His day of earthly triumph. That Edwards was to acknowledge the failure of such methods is attested by the fact that, within two years of his dismissal from Northampton, he was reminding the Synod of New York that the world is a place of bitter conflict between "Christ's little children" and the followers of the Devil, "the chief enemy of God and Christ."[54] The emphasis on Satan and the indifference to the historical Antichrist were, of course, underscored in the next years by the polemical bitterness of Edwards' essays, *Will* and *Original Sin.* It was on the basis of the *Original Sin,* particularly, that Joseph Bellamy restored the prospect of a millennium inaugurated by an embattled host. As its captain he would lead the Church Militant to victories which seemingly overshadowed the achievements of Edwards as shepherd of the flock. But it should not be forgotten that it was Edwards, who having in the 1740's taught the pious of the colonies to behave like Christians, had given them the time and the will to acquire something of the stamina which Bellamy was able to call upon.

Throughout the second half of the eighteenth century the thought of Calvinism showed an impatience to return to the battle lines of 1742. Even in the *Humble Attempt,* Edwards quietly explained that though the spirit of prayer and the revival *might* finally spread "till the awakening reaches those that are in the *highest station*," the redeeming Spirit would necessarily first express itself in the lower reaches of society.[55] Such a suggestion as to where the greater number of saints were enrolled and enrollable reinforced, even as it sought to suppress, the sense of social cleavage aroused by the Awakening. Though in subsequent years ideas and events did mute momentarily the animosities of those who, in the Awakening, had taken such delight in conceiving their local enemies as "particular objects of divine displeasure,"[56] neither the literature nor the history of the decades after the revival can be wholly understood except as reflecting, in some manner, a fairly constant sense of social tension.

Even the missionary enterprise, which Chauncy no less than Edwards came to support, betrayed the antagonisms of the age. It was not merely that Liberals and Calvinists disagreed, and violently, over how missions were to be conducted, or by whom and for what ultimate purpose. Rather more significant is the fact that critics of the revival saw Indian missions as a means of turning the "fiery zeal" of the awakeners away from established institutions and to the "good use" of undermining the French hold on tribal allegiances.[57] While the Calvinist by no means consciously acquiesced in such blatantly diversionary attitudes, it is clear that his commitment to the missionary enterprise was a symptom of his inability to resolve satisfactorily the internal contradictions of colonial culture.

Such also was the case of the wars with France, which the awakened in the 1740's saw, and perhaps rightly so, as something of a red herring designed to blur the battle lines of the revival. Yet in 1754 Whitefield came to Boston to preach, not on the necessity of the New Birth, but on the "imminent Gallic menace."[58] He was awarded, on this occasion, a degree from the very Harvard which but ten years earlier had denounced him as a socially dangerous demagogue. This is not, however, to say that his cooperation, or that of any Calvinist leader, was consciously purchased by the colonial authorities. It required no such prompting for many Calvinists—among them some once suspicious even of Whitefield's blessing of the Louisburg fleet—to be caught up in the "crusade" against the French. Notable among them was James Davenport, the erstwhile contemner of iniquitous minions of Satan in high places in the colonies, who in 1755 expressed the belief that a British victory at Crown Point could "bring on the latter-day glory" by causing the Pope's reign to "come to its final period!"[59] And in the 1770's this history was recapitulated when George III was identified as the Antichrist of Revelation. Though ever conscious of being divided among themselves, Americans were seldom able to resist any opportunity to postpone a final reckoning.

Such a pattern of diversion and reunion is as much a part of the story of the pre-Revolutionary American mind as the schism in colonial society opened by the Awakening. Still, it must be emphasized that any consensus, however fascinating the process by which it was reached, was something of an interlude and a point of departure for a new division along the lines of 1740. Moreover, for forty years after the Awakening, Americans of all persuasions were supremely aware of a potential for discord within colonial society. Whatever the efforts of colonial preachers—Liberal and Calvinist—to move or mollify the people of the colonies, they ordered their thoughts and chose their words in the knowledge that the revival impulse had threatened the colonies, politically as well as intellectually, with revolution.

To Calvinists the Awakening was a revival of pure Christianity, and the crusade it launched was the perfection of God's age-old plan of redemption. Yet there may have been an unintended wisdom to Chauncy's thrust, made ironically enough as part of his effort to dispose of Calvinist millenarianism, that the "work of the SPIRIT is different now from what it was in the first days of Christianity."[60] The "spirit" at work in 1740 and after was indeed totally and essentially different from any before active on the face of the earth. To be sure, some of the avatars of the revival spirit sought to identify the Awakening with ancient causes and inherited slogans. For example, Alexander Craighead called on the Presbyterian awakened to renew the Solemn League and Covenant. But the Log College men refused to join him and, when Craighead complained that they "feared men" and lacked the courage needed to assail Episcopacy anew, answered that Craighead mistook the nature of the "cause." And indeed Craighead probably did, most particularly in thinking that the new spirit did not summon men "to leave their proper Stations in the World, such as, for Persons to run through the Country."[61] To the American revivalist, the cause was such that its goals could be achieved only through attitudes and institutions appropriate to the promise of the New World.

As waves of enthusiasm rolled against the parish hierarchies of colonial America, the true quality of the revival's millenarian aspirations was dramatically revealed. Not liberty, nor even equality, was, as it turned out, the essence of the Awakening, but fraternity. In the course of the eighteenth century many Calvinists were to be shocked as they saw the single end toward which all the streams of Providence and grace tended. But the spirit aroused in 1740 proved to be that of American nationalism.

NOTES

[1]C.C. Goen, "Jonathan Edwards: A New Departure in Eschatology," *Church History*, XXVIII (1959), 26.

[2]Edwards, *Thoughts on the Revival*, in *Works*, I, 377.

[3]Edwards, *A History of the Work of Redemption*, in *Works*, I, 613.

[4]Robert Ross, *A Plain Address to the Quakers, Moravians, Separatists, Separate-Baptists, Rogerenes, and Other Enthusiasts* (New Haven,[1762]), p. 45.

[5]Richard McNemar, *The Kentucky Revival; or, a Short History of the Late Extraordinary Outpouring of the Spirit of God in the Western States of America* ([2nd ed.], New York, 1846), p. 12.

[6]John White, *New England's Lamentations* (Boston, 1734), pp. 7-9; Ebenezer Pemberton, *Sermons on Several Subjects. Preach'd at the Presbyterian Church in the*

City of New York (Boston, 1738), pp. 79-83; Boston *Weekly News-Letter,* quoted, Chaucy, *Seasonable Thoughts,* p. 97.

[7]Edwards, "Personal Narrative," *Works,* I, clxxxix.

[8]Edwards, *Work of Redemption,* in *Works,* I, 584.

[9]*Ibid.,* pp. 539, 605.

[10]Niebuhr, *The Kingdom of God in America,* p. 143.

[11]Smith, *Character of Whitefield,* p. 20.

[12]Edwards, *Distinguishing Marks,* in *Works,* II, 272; *Thoughts on the Revival,* in *Works,* I, 380.

[13]Edwards, "The Church's Marriage to Her Sons and to Her God. Preached at the Instalment of the Rev. Samuel Buell . . . September 19, 1746," *Works,* II, 25.

[14]*The Christian History . . . for the year 1743* (Boston, 1744), pp. 106ff; Thomas Foxcroft, *A Seasonable Momento for New Year's Day* (Boston, 1747), pp. 54-57.

[15]Edwards, *Will,* p. 246.

[16]Miller, "The End of the World," *Errand,* p. 235; Edwards, *The Great Christian Doctrine of Original Sin Defended,* in *Works,* I, 218; Edwards, *Will,* p. 246.

[17]Edwards, "Church's Marriage," *Works,* II, 25.

[18]Jonathan Parsons, *Good News from a Far Country* (Portsmouth, N.H., 1756), p. 168.

[19]Edwards, *Humble Attempt,* in *Works,* II, 281, 287, 310.

[20]Edwards, *Works,* I, cxxviii; Ralph G. Turnbull, *Jonathan Edwards the Preacher* (Grand Rapids, Mich., 1958), p. 43.

[21]Parsons, *Good News,* p. 168.

[22]For example, *Questions & Answers to the prophetic numbers of Daniel and John Calculated . . . By an aged gentleman* (Boston, 1759).

[23]Samuel Buell, *Intricate and Mysterious Events of Providence, Design'd to Display Divine Glory* (New London, [1770]), pp. 11-12, 37; Parsons, *To Live is Christ,* pp. 23-24.

[24]Buell, *Intricate and Mysterious Events,* p. 12.

[25]N. Niles, *Perfection of God,* p. 23.

[26]Edwards, *Will,* p. 246.

[27]Edwards, *Humble Attempt,* in *Works,* II, 289.

[28]Edwards, *Will,* p. 266.

[29]Edwards, *A Dissertation Concerning the End for Which God Created the World,* in *Works,* I, 120.

[30]Edwards, *Images or Shadows,* p. 76.

[31]Edwards, *Work of Redemption,* in *Works,* I, 617.

[32]R. Smith, *Wheel in the Middle,* pp. 9-10; Buell, *Intricate and Mysterious Events,* pp. 12-13.

[33]Buell, *Intricate and Mysterious Events,* p. 12; Davies, "The Success of the Ministry," *Sermons,* II, 519-522.

[34]Parsons, *To Live is Christ,* pp. 22-25.

[35]McNemar, *Kentucky Revival,* pp. 59, 69.

[36]Edwards, *Thoughts on the Revival,* In *Works,* I, 387; *Work of Redemption,* in *Works,* I, 617-618.

[37]Edwards, "True Saints, when Absent from the Body," *Works*, II, 30.

[38]Edwards, *Work of Redemption*, in *Works*, I, 605.

[39]Edwards, "Church's Marriage," *Works*, II, 24.

[40]Eleazar Wheelock, *A Sermon Preached . . . June 30, 1763. At the Ordination of the Rev. Mr. Charles-Jeffry Smith . . . To which is Added, a Sermon Preached by Nathaniel Whitaker, D.D., after the Said Ordination* (London, 1767), p. 3.

[41]Israel Evans, *A Discourse, Delivered at Easton, on the 17th of October, 1779* (Philadelphia, 1779), p. 12; William Gordon, *The Separation of the Jewish Tribes . . . Applied to the Present Day, in a Sermon, Delivered on July 4th, 1777*, in Moore, *Patriot Preachers*, p. 160.

[42]Edwards, *Humble Attempt*, in *Works*, II, 310.

[43]*Ibid.*

[44]William Tennent II, quoted, "History of Revivals of Religion," *American Quarterly Register*, V (1833), 212.

[45]R. Smith, *Wheel in the Middle*, p. 26.

[46]David Austin, *The Voice of God to the People of These United States* (Elizabethtown, N.J., 1796), pp. 40-41.

[47]Thomas Baldwin, *A Sermon, Delivered . . . April 2, 1799; at a Quarterly Meeting of Several Churches for Special Prayer* (Boston, 1799), p. 23.

[48]Austin, *The Millennium . . . Shortly to Commence* (Elizabethtown, N.J., 1794), pp. v-vi; *The Millennial Door Thrown Open, or the Mysteries of the Latter Day Glory Unfolded in a Discourse, Delivered at East-Windsor, State of Connecticut, July Fourth, 1799* (East Windsor, Conn., 1799), *passim.*

[49]Charles Brockwell to Secretary of S.P.G., Feb. 18, 1741/2, in Perry, *Historical Collections, Massachusetts*, pp. 353-354.

[50]*The Wonderful Narrative: or, a Faithful Account of the French Prophets* (Boston, 1742), Appendix, p. 106; A—Z. (pseud.), *Mr. Parsons Corrected. Or, an Addition of Some Things to His Late Sermon* (Boston, 1743), p. 10; Chauncy, *Seasonable Thoughts*, p. 209; Philemon Robbins, *A Plain Narrative of the Proceedings of the Reverend Association and Consociation of New-Haven County* (Boston, 1747), pp. 19-22; Samuel Finley, *Clear Light Put Out in Obscure Darkness* (Philadelphia, 1743), p.72.

[51]Edwards, "Christ Exalted: or, Jesus Christ Gloriously Exalted Above All Evil in the Work of Redemption," *Works*, II, 216; *Distinguishing Marks*, in *Works*, II, 273, 276, 288; *Thoughts on the Revival*, in *Works*, I, 387.

[52]Edwards, *Humble Attempt*, in *Works*, II, 299; cf. *Works*, I, cxxiii.

[53]Edwards, "Miscellaneous Observations," *Works*, II, 474-475.

[54]Edwards, "Church's Marriage," *Works*, II, 474; "True Grace Distinguished from the Experience of Devils," *Works*, II, 42.

[55]Edwards, *Humble Attempt*, in *Works*, II, 281-282.

[56]Quoted, Joseph Tracy, *The Great Awakening* (6th ed., Boston, c1841), p. 322.

[57]Douglass, *Summary*, I, 249n.

[58]Carl Bridenbaugh, *Cities in Revolt. Urban Life in America, 1743-1776* (New York, 1955), p. 151.

[59]Quoted, Sprague, *Annals*, III, 91.

[60]Chauncy, *Enthusiasm Describ'd*, p. 16.

[61]Alexander Craighead, *A Discourse Concerning the Covenants* (Philadelphia, 1742), p. 18; Samuel Finley, *Satan Stripp'd of his Angelick Robe. Being the Substance of Several Sermons Preach'd at Philadelphia, January 1742-3* (Philadelphia, [1743]), p. vi.

10

From the Covenant to the Revival

Perry Miller

Perry Miller's interpretation of colonial Puritanism and the Great Awakening led to the question of what role this tradition played in the War for Independence and the develop-ment of the new nation. In this essay he delineates the metamorphosis from Edwards to Charles G. Finney, the prototypical nineteenth century American revivalist. Perry Mil-ler is late Professor of American Literature at Harvard.

I

On June 12, 1775, the Continental Congress dispatched from Philadelphia to the thirteen colonies (and to insure a hearing, ordered the document to be published in newspapers and in handbills) a "recommen-dation" that July 20 be universally observed as "a day of publick humilia-tion, fasting, and prayer." The Congress prefaced the request with a state-ment of reasons. Because the great "Governor" not only conducts by His Providence the course of nations "but frequently influences the minds of men to serve the wise and gracious purposes of his providential government," and also it being our duty to acknowledge his superintendency, "especially in times of impending danger and publick calamity"—therefore the Congress acts.

Selections from Perry Miller, "From the Covenant to the Revival," in *The Shaping of American Religion,* Vol. I, eds. James Ward Smith and A. Leland Jamison (copyright © 1961 by Princeton University Press), pp. 322-368 (abridged). Reprinted by permission of Princeton University Press.

What may elude the secular historian—what in fact has eluded him—is the mechanism by which the Congress proposed that the operation be conducted:

> ... that we may with united hearts and voices unfeignedly confess and deplore our many sins, and offer up our joint supplications to the all-wise, omnipotent, and merciful Disposer of all events; humbly beseeching him to forgive our iniquities, to remove our present calamities, to avert those desolating judgments with which we are threatened. . . .

The essential point is that the Congress asks for, first, a national confession of sin and iniquity, then a promise of repentance, that only *thereafter* may God be moved so to influence Britain as to allow America to behold "a gracious interposition of Heaven for the redress of her many grievances."[1] The subtle emphasis can be detected once it is compared with the formula used by the Virginia House of Burgesses in the previous month, on May 14:

> ... devoutly to implore the Divine interposition for averting the heavy calamity which threatens destruction to our civil rights, and the evils of civil war, to give us one heart and one mind firmly to oppose, by all just and proper means, every injury to *American* rights. . . .

Jefferson testifies that in Virginia this measure was efficacious. The people met with alarm in their countenances, "and the effect of the day through the whole colony was like a shock of electricity, arousing every man and placing him erect and solidly on his centre."[2] However gratifying the local results might be, it should be noted that this predominantly Anglican House of Burgesses, confronted with calamity, made no preliminary detour through any confession of their iniquities, but went directly to the throne of God, urging that He enlist on their side. The Virginia delegation in Philadelphia (which, let us remember, included Patrick Henry but *not* Jefferson) concurred in the unanimous adoption of the Congress's much more complicated—some were to say more devious—ritualistic project. Was this merely a diplomatic concession? Or could it be that, once the threatened calamity was confronted on a national scale, the assembled representatives of all the peoples instinctively realized that some deeper, some more atavistic, search of their own souls was indeed the indispensable prologue to exertion?

The question is eminently worth asking, if only because conscientious historians have seen no difference between the two patterns, and have assumed that the Congressional followed the Virginian.[3] And there are other historians, who may or may not be cynical, but who have in either case been corrupted by the twentieth century, who perceive in this and subsequent summonses to national repentance only a clever device in "propaganda."[4] It was bound, they point out, to cut across class and regional lines, to unite a predominantly Protestant people; wherefore the rationalist or deistical leaders could hold their tongues and silently acquiesce in the stratagem, calculating its pragmatic worth. In this view, the fact that virtually all the "dissenting" clergy, and a fair number of Anglicans, mounted their pulpits on July 20 and preached patriotic self-abnegation, is offered as a proof that they had joined with the upper middle-class in a scheme to bamboozle the lower orders and simple-minded rustics.

This interpretation attributes, in short, a diabolical cunning to the more sophisticated leaders of the Revolution, who, being themselves no believers in divine providence, fastened onto the form of invocation which would most work upon a majority who did believe passionately in it. This reading may, I suggest, be as much a commentary on the mentality of modern sociology as upon the Continental Congress, but there is a further observation that has been more cogently made by a few who have noted the striking differences in phraseology: the Congressional version is substantially the form that for a century and a half had been employed in New England. There, since the first years of Plymouth and the first decade of Massachusetts Bay and Connecticut, the official response in the face of affliction had been to set aside a day for public confession of transgression and a promise of communal repentance as the only method for beseeching the favor of Jehovah.[5] Hence some analysts surmise that the action of the Congress, if it was not quite a Machiavellian ruse for hoodwinking the pious, was at best a Yankee trick foisted on Virginia and New York. Leaving aside the question of whether, should this explanation be true, it might just as well have been a Virginian fraud, one which cost Patrick Henry and Peyton Randolph nothing, perpetrated to keep the New Englanders active, the simple fact is that unprejudiced examination of the records of 1775 and 1776 shows that New England enjoyed no monopoly on the procedure. The House of Burgesses might suppose it enough to petition Almighty God to redress their wrongs; the churches of the dissenters, and indeed most Anglican communities already knew, whether in Georgia, Pennsylvania, or Connecticut, that this was not the proper way to go about obtaining heavenly assistance. The Biblical conception of a people standing in direct daily relation to God, upon covenanted terms and therefore responsible for their moral conduct, was a common possession of the Protestant peoples.

However, there can be no doubt that New England had done much more than the other regions toward articulating colonial experience within the providential dialectic. Because, also, presses were more efficient there than elsewhere, and Boston imprints circulated down the coast, it is probable that the classic utterances of Massachusetts served as models for Presbyterians and Baptists as well as for "low-church" Anglicans. For many decades the Puritan colonies had been geographically set apart; the people had been thoroughly accustomed to conceiving of themselves as a chosen race, entered into specific covenant with God, by the terms of which they would be proportionately punished for their sins. Their afflictions were divine appointments, not the hazards of natural and impersonal forces.[6] Furthermore, the homogeneity of the Puritan communities enabled their parsons to speak in the name of the whole body—even when these were internally riven by strife over land banks, the Great Awakening, or baptism. Finally, this same isolation of the New England colonies encouraged a proliferation of the "federal theology" to a point where the individual's relation with God, his hope of salvation through a personal covenant, could be explicitly merged with the society's covenant. Hence in New England was most highly elaborated the theorem that the sins of individuals brought calamity upon the commonwealth.

In that sense, then, we may say that the Congressional recommendation of June 12, 1775, virtually took over the New England thesis that these colonial peoples stood in a contractual relation to the "great Governor" over and above that enjoyed by other groups; in effect, Congress added the other nine colonies (about whose status New Englanders had hitherto been dubious) to New England's covenant. Still, for most of the population in these nine, no novelty was being imposed. The federal theology, in general terms, was an integral part of the Westminster Confession and so had long figured in the rhetoric of Presbyterians of New Jersey and Pennsylvania. The covenant doctrine, including that of the society as well as of the individual, had been preached in the founding of Virginia,[7] and still informed the phraseology of ordinary Anglican sermonizing. The Baptists, even into Georgia, were aware of the concept of church covenant, for theirs were essentially "congregational" polities; they could easily rise from that philosophy to the analogous one of the state. Therefore the people had little difficulty reacting to the Congressional appeal. They knew precisely what to do: they were to gather in their assemblies on July 20, inform themselves that the afflictions brought upon them in the dispute with Great Britain were not hardships suffered in some irrational political strife but intelligible ordeals divinely brought about because of their own abominations. This being the situation, they were to resolve, not only separately but in unison, to mend their ways, restore primitive piety, suppress vice, curtail luxury. Then, and only thereafter, if they were sincere, if they proved that they meant their vow, God would reward them by raising up instruments for the deflection of, or if necessary, destruction of, Lord North.

Since the New Englanders were such old hands at this business—by exactly this method they had been overcoming, from the days of the Pequot War through King Philip's War, such difficulties as the tyranny of Andros, small-pox epidemics, and parching droughts—they went to work at once. For the clergy the task was already clear: beginning with the Stamp Act of 1765, the clerical orator who spoke at every election day, in May, surveyed the respects in which relations with England should be subsumed under the over-all covenant of the people with God. Charles Chauncy's *A Discourse on the good News from a far Country,* delivered upon a day of "thanksgiving" (the logical sequel to several previous days of humiliation) to the General Court in 1766, explained that repeal of the odious Stamp Act was a consequence not of any mercantile resistance but of New England's special position within the Covenant of Grace.[8] As the crisis in Boston grew more and more acute, successive election orators had an annual opportunity to develop in greater detail proof that any vindication of provincial privileges was inextricably dependent upon a moral renovation. Following the "Boston Massacre" of 1773, anniversaries of this atrocity furnished every preacher an occasion for spreading the idea among the people. The form of these discourses was still that of the traditional "jeremiad"—a threatening of further visitation upon the covenanted people until they returned to their bond by confession and reformation—but by the time the Congress issued its wholesale invitation, the New England clergy had so merged the call to repentance with a stiffening of the patriotic spine that no power on earth, least of all the government of George III, could separate the acknowledgment of depravity from the resolution to fight.

Everything the Congress hoped would be said in 1775 had already been declared by the Reverend Samuel Cooke of the Second Church in Boston at the election of 1770.[9] If that were not precedent enough, the General Court on October 22, 1774, confronting General Gage and the Boston Port Bill, showed how double-edged was the sword by proclaiming not a fast day but one of thanksgiving; it was illuminated by the sermon of William Gordon, from the Third Church in Roxbury, which was all the more memorable because Gordon had been English-born.[10] On May 31, 1775, six weeks after Lexington and Concord, Samuel Langdon, President of Harvard, put the theory of religious revolution so completely before the Court (then obliged to meet in Watertown) that the doctrine of political resistance yet to be formulated in the Declaration seems but an afterthought.[11] A few weeks before that assertion, on May 29, 1776, Samuel West of Dartmouth made clear to the General Court that what was included within the divine covenant as a subsidiary but essential portion had been not simply "British liberties" but the whole social teaching of John Locke.[12] After the evacuation of Boston, both Massachusetts and Connecticut were able to assemble as of old, and comfortably listen to a recital of their shortcomings, secure in the knowledge that as long as jeremiads denounced them, their courage could not fail. The fluctuations of the conflict called for many days of humiliation and a few for thanksgiving; in Massachusetts, the framing of the state constitution in 1780 evoked another spate of clerical lectures on the direct connection between piety and politics. Out of the years between the Stamp Act and the Treaty of Paris emerged a formidable, exhaustive (in general, a repetitious) enunciation of the unique necessity for America to win her way by reiterated acts of repentance. The jeremiad, which in origin had been an engine of Jehovah, thus became temporarily a service department of the Continental army. . . .

Though by now the Revolution has been voluminously, and one might suppose exhaustively, studied, we still do not realize how effective were generations of Protestant preaching in evoking patriotic enthusiasm. No interpretation of the religious utterances as being merely sanctimonious window-dressing will do justice to the facts or to the character of the populace. Circumstances and the nature of the dominant opinion in Europe made it necessary for the official statement to be released in primarily "political" terms—the social compact, inalienable rights, the right of revolution. But those terms, in and by themselves, would never have supplied the drive to victory, however mightily they weighed with the literate minority. What carried the ranks of militia and citizens was the universal persuasion that they, by administering to themselves a spiritual purge, acquired the energies God had always, in the manner of the Old Testament, been ready to impart to His repentant children. Their first responsibility was not to shoot redcoats but to cleanse themselves; only thereafter to take aim. Notwithstanding the chastisements we have already received, proclaimed the Congress on March 20, 1779—they no longer limited themselves to mere recommending—"too few have been sufficiently awakened to a sense of their guilt, or warmed with gratitude, or taught to amend their lives and turn from their sins, so He might turn from His wrath." They call for still another fast in April, 1780: "To make us sincerely penitent for our transgressions; to prepare us for deliverance, and to remove the evil with which he hath been pleased to visit us; to banish vice and irreligion from among us, and establish virtue and piety by his Divine grace." And when there did come a cause for rejoicing (almost the only one in four or five years that might justify their using other vestibule, the surrender of Burgoyne), patriots gave little thought to lengthening lines of supply or the physical obstacles of logistics; instead, they beheld Providence at work again, welcomed Louis XVI as their "Christian ally," and congratulated themselves upon that which had really produced victory—their success in remodeling themselves. Now more than ever, asserted the Congress on October 31, 1777, we should "implore the mercy and forgiveness of God, and beseech him that vice, profaneness, extortion and every evil may be done away, and that we may be a reformed and a happy people."[13]

II

Historians of English political thought have reduced to a commonplace of inevitable progression the shift of Puritan political philosophy from the radical extreme of 1649 to the genial universals of 1689. John Locke so codified the later versions as to make the "Glorious Revolution" seem a conservative reaction. As we know, Locke was studied with avidity in the colonies; hence the Congress used consummate strategy in presenting their case to a candid world through the language of Locke. . . .

Consequently, every preacher of patriotism was obliged to complicate his revolutionary jeremiad by careful demonstrations of exactly how the will of almighty God had itself always operated through the voluntary self-imposition of a compact, how it had provided for legitimate, conservative resistance to tyrants. Early in the eighteenth century, John Wise prophesied how this union of concepts would be achieved, but he seems to have had no direct effect on the patriot argument. Jonathan Mayhew was far ahead of his fellows; after his death in 1766 the others required hard work to catch up. In general it may be said that they started off serenely confident that of course the philosophy of the jeremiad, which required abject confession of unworthiness from an afflicted people, and that of the social compact, which called for immediate and vigorous action against an intruding magistrate, were one and the same. Then, discovering that the joining required more carpentry than they had anticipated, they labored for all they were worth at the task. Finally, by 1776, they triumphantly asserted that they had indeed succeeded, that the day of humiliation was demonstrably one with the summons to battle.

Political historians and secular students of theory are apt to extract from the context those paragraphs devoted solely to the social position, to discuss these as comprising the only contribution of the "black regiment" to Revolutionary argument.[14] To read these passages in isolation is to miss the point. They were effective with the masses not as sociological lectures but because, being embedded in the jeremiads, they made comprehensible the otherwise troubling double injunction of humiliation and exertion. In this complicated pattern (which could be offered as the ultimate both in right reason and in true piety), the mentality of American Protestantism became so reconciled to itself, so joyfully convinced that it had at last found its long-sought identity, that for the time being it forgot that it had ever had any other reason for existing.

A few examples out of thousands will suffice. Gordon's *Discourse* of December 15, 1774, runs for page after page in the standardized jeremiad vein: "Is not this people strangely degenerated, so as to possess but a faint resemblance of that godliness for which their forefathers were eminent?" Is it not horrible beyond all imagination that *this* people should degenerate, seeing how scrupulously God has befriended them according to the stipulations of their covenant with Him? Yet the ghastly fact is "that while there is much outward show of respect to the Deity, there is but little inward heart conformity to him." And so on and on, until abruptly, with hardly a perceptible shift, we are hearing a recital of the many palpable evidences that Divine Providence is already actively engaged in the work. Only by the direct "inspiration of the Most High" could the unanimity of the colonies have been brought about. From this point Gordon's cheerful jeremiad comes down to the utilitarian calculation that Americans are expert riflemen, wherefore "the waste of amunition will be greatly prevented"; after which he concludes by urging the people to "accept our punishment at his hands without murmuring or complaining"![15]

The elements woven together in this and other speeches can, of course, be separated one from another in the antiseptic calm of the historian's study, and the whole proved to be an unstable compound of incompatible propositions. What may be left out of account is the impact of the entire argument, the wonderful fusion of political doctrine with the traditional rite of self-abasement which, out of colonial experience, had become not what it might seem on the surface, a failure of will, but a dynamo for generating action. . . .

To examine the Revolutionary mind from the side of its religious emotion is to gain a perspective that cannot be acquired from the ordinary study of the papers of the Congresses, the letters of Washington, the writings of

Dickinson, Paine, Freneau, or John Adams. The "decent respect" that these Founders entertained for the opinion of mankind caused them to put their case before the civilized world in the restricted language of the rational century. A successful revolution, however, requires not only leadership but receptivity. Ideas in the minds of the foremost gentlemen may not be fully shared by their followers, but these followers will accept the ideas, even adopt them, if such abstractions can be presented in an acceptable context. To accommodate the principles of a purely secular social compact and a right to resist taxation—even to the point of declaring political independence to a provincial community where the reigning beliefs were still original sin and the need of grace—this was the immense task performed by the patriotic clergy.

Our mental image of the religious patriot is distorted because modern accounts do treat the political paragraphs as a series of theoretical expositions of Locke, separated from what precedes and follows. When these orations are read as wholes, they immediately reveal that the sociological sections are structural parts of a rhetorical pattern. Embedded in their contexts, these are not abstractions but inherent parts of a theology. It was for this reason that they had so energizing an effect upon their religious auditors. The American situation, as the preachers saw it, was not what Paine presented in *Common Sense*—a community of hard-working, rational creatures being put upon by an irrational tyrant—but was more like the recurrent predicament of the chosen people in the Bible. As Samuel Cooper declared on October 25, 1780, upon the inauguration of the Constitution of Massachusetts, America was a new Isreal, selected to be "a theatre for the display of some of the most astonishing dispensations of his Providence." The Jews originally were a free republic founded on a covenant over which God "in peculiar favor to that people, was pleased to preside." When they offended Him, He punished them by destroying their republic, subjecting them to a king. Thus while we today need no revelation to inform us that we are all born free and equal and that sovereignty resides in the people—"these are the plain dictates of that reason and common sense with which the common parent has informed the human bosom"— still Scripture also makes these truths explicit. Hence when we angered our God, a king was also inflicted upon us; happily, Americans have succeeded, where the Jews did not, in recovering something of pristine virtue, whereupon Heaven redressed America's earthly grievances. Only as we today appreciate the formal unity of the two cosmologies, the rational and the Biblical, do we take in the full import of Cooper's closing salute to the new Constitution: "How nicely it poises the powers of government, in order to render them as far as human foresight can, what God ever designed they should be, power only to do good."[16]

Once this light is allowed to play on the scene, we perceive the shallowness of that view which would treat the religious appeal as a calculated propaganda maneuver. The ministers did not have to "sell" the Revolution to a public sluggish to "buy." They were spelling out what both they and the people sincerely believed, nor were they distracted by worries about the probability that Jefferson held all their constructions to be nonsense. A pure rationalism such as his might have declared the independence of these folk, but it could never have inspired them to fight for it.

This assertion may seem too sweeping, but without our making it we can hardly comprehend the state in which American Protestantism found itself when the victory was won. A theology which for almost two centuries had assumed that men would persistently sin, and so would have to be recurrently summoned to communal repentance, had for the first time identified its basic conception with a specific political action. Then, for the first time in the life of the conception, the cause was totally gained. Did not a startling inference follow: these people must have reformed themselves completely, must now dwell on a pinnacle of virtuousness? But there was no place in the theology of the covenant for a people to congratulate themselves. There was a station only for degenerates in need of regeneration, who occasionally might thank God for this or that mercy He granted them, forgiving their imperfections. Where could Protestantism turn, what could it employ, in order still to hold the religious respect of this now victorious society?

III

An Anglican rationalist . . . would have no difficulty about the sequence of statements which said that by resisting England we would assure the future prosperity of the republic. The patriotic Jeremiahs also employed the argument, but they had to be more circumspect. Protestant political thinking had never doubted, of course, that God instituted government among men as a means toward their temporal felicity—or, at least toward their "safety." But it always based its philosophy upon the premise of original sin. Since the Fall, had men been left in a pure state of nature, all would have been Ishmaels; no man's life, family, or property would be secure. So, government was primarily a check on evil impulses; its function was negative rather than positive; it was to restrain violence, not to advance arts, sciences, technology. Yet, as Governor John Winthrop agreed during the first years of Massachusetts Bay, because *"salus populi suprema lex,"* there was a corollary (lurking out of sight) that government ought, once it restrained the lusts of these people, to do something more creative about making them comfortable.

In the negativistic emphasis of Protestant teachings, the reason for King George's violence and the consequent righteousness of resisting him were easy to make out. He and his ministers were violating the compact, so that he had become Ishmael. Law-abiding subjects were defending social barriers which, if once broken through, would cease to confine all social passions. By defying Britain they were preserving mankind from a descent into chaos. Resistance to a madman is not revolution; it is, in obedience to God, an exercise of the police power.

Yet what happens to particles of this logic when to it is joined the contention that by such resistance the righteous not only obey God but acquire wealth for themselves and their children? How can the soldier venture everything in the holy cause, after having confessed his depravity, if all the time he has a secret suspicion that by going through this performance he in fact is not so much repenting as gaining affluence for his society?

In most of the patriotic jeremiads the material inducement is entered—sometimes, we may say, smuggled in. It could not be left out. Yet once the machinery of national humiliation proved effective in producing the providential victory of the Americans, were they not bound to the prophecy that by their utilization of the form, they, and they alone, would bring about a reign of national bliss? But in that case how could a confession of unworthiness be sincere?

An uneasy awareness of the dilemma was present even in the early stages of agitation. Listen, for instance, to Samuel Williams, pastor of the Church in Bradford, delivering *A Discourse on the Love of Country,* December 15, 1774:

> As what should further confirm our attachment to our native country, it bids the fairest of any to promote *the perfection and happiness of mankind.* We have but few principles from which we can argue with certainty, what will be the state of mankind in future ages. But if we may judge the designs of providence, by the number and power of the causes that are already at work, we shall be led to think that the perfection and happiness of mankind is to be carried further in America, than it has ever yet been in any place.[17]

This passage is only one of hundreds in the same vein, and all wrestle with the same dubious contention: we have sinned, therefore we are afflicted by the tyranny of a corrupt Britain; we must repent and reform, in order to win the irresistible aid of Providence; once we have wholeheartedly performed this act, we shall be able to exert our freedom by expelling the violators of the compact; when we succeed we shall enter upon a prosperity and temporal happiness beyond anything the world has hitherto seen. But always implicit in this chain of reasoning was a vague suggestion that the people were being bribed into patriotism. And by universal admission, the occasion for a nation's deserting its Maker and surrendering to sensuality was always an excess of material comforts. So, was not the whole machinery an ironic device for bringing upon the children of the victors judgments still more awful than any that had previously been imposed?

The clergy had, in short, simplified the once massive complexity of the process of social regeneration by concentrating its terrorizing appeal upon a single hardship, the British government. Seventeenth-century theologians would have been more wary. They took pains to keep the list so long—draught, fires, earthquakes, insects, small-pox, shipwrecks—that while the people by their holy exertions might be let off this or that misery, they were sure to be tormented by some other. The Revolutionary divines, in their zeal for liberty, committed themselves unwittingly to the proposition that in this case expulsion of the British would automatically leave America a pure society. In their righteous anger, they painted gorier and gorier pictures of the depravity of England. Said President Langdon, "The general prevalence of vice has changed the whole face of things in the British government";[18] wherefore it had to follow that the sins of the colonial peoples, which brought down the Intolerable Acts, were in great part "infections" received from "the corruption of European courts." But then, once we innoculated ourselves against these contagions, would we not become a people washed white in the Blood of the Lamb?

These people, however, had for a long time been disciplined to the expectation of woe. The government of the Confederacy became mired in confusion, thus clouding once more any reading of God's design. While the States were devising a Constitution to correct this affliction, the blow was struck; but not in America—in Paris. At first, of course, the fall of the Bastille seemed to strengthen the alliance of social doctrine and religious hope. Shortly the fallacy became evident. Not that there was any serious threat in America of a reversion to the depraved state of nature which engulfed France in 1793; yet in this glorious republic the French Revolution brought home to the devout an immediate realization of the need for dissociating the Christian conception of life from any blind commitment to the philosophy of that Revolution. Indeed, they had no choice ultimately but to abandon the whole political contention of either of the two revolutions, and to seek at once some other program for Christian solidarity. They did not need to renounce the Declaration, nor even to denounce the Constitution, but only henceforth to take those principles for granted, yield government to the secular concept of the social compact, accept the First Amendment, and so to concentrate, in order to resist Deism and to save their souls, upon that other mechanism of cohesion developed out of their colonial experience, the Revival.

It took them until about the year 1800 to recast—or, as they believed, to recover—their history. Amid the great revivals which swept over Connecticut, Kentucky, and Tennessee in that year, which expanded into Georgia, Illinois, and for decades burned over northern New York, the Revolution was again and again presented as having been itself a majestic Revival. The leadership of Jefferson, Paine, and the rationalists was either ignored or explained away. The "Second Great Awakening" engendered the denominational forms of American Protestantism which still endure, but perhaps equally important was its work in confirming the American belief that the Revolution had not been at all revolutionary, but simply a protest of native piety against foreign impiety.

IV

Denominational historians tell us what the churches had to contend with following the Treaty of Paris. One fact seems indisputable: while Presbyterians and Congregationalists hesitated, Methodist itinerants rushed in. During the 1790's the major churches undertook a radical realignment of thinking, which for a century or more would determine their character.

The factors in this cultural crisis—complex though they were—can be, for narrative purposes, succinctly enumerated.

Despite the warnings of Provost Smith, the Protestant clergy preached so extravagant a Christian utopianism that with the end of the War they could only term what confronted them a demoralization beyond anything they had ever imagined. In 1795, for instance, the Methodist Church was calling for the resumption of fast days because of "our manifold sins and iniquities—our growing idolatry, which is covetousness and the prevailing love of the world . . . the profanation of the Sabbath . . . disobedience to parents, various debaucheries, drunkenness, and such like."[19] Relative to, say, the 1920's, the America of the 1790's may appear a reign of idyllic simplicity, but to organized religion it seemed morally abominable.

Coincident with this internal confusion came the French Revolution, that "volcano," as Robert Baird retrospectively called it in 1844, which "threatened to sweep the United States into its fiery stream."[20] It would not have set off such hysteria had not its excitements coincided with the frightening division of American society into parties, portending in the eyes of many an internal conflict. It is important, if we would make sense out of later developments, to insist that by no means all the religious—call them Calvinist, Evangelical, or simply Orthodox—went with Hamilton against Jefferson. On the contrary, multitudes were not alienated by Jefferson's Deism. The publicity given by Henry Adams to Timothy Dwight's insane fears over Jefferson's election—Dwight's certainty that all the virgins of Connecticut would be raped—has been so played up in our histories that we forget how the Evangelicals were worried not so much about the President as about the whole apocalyptical scene. The Presbyterian General Assembly in May, 1798, bewailed innovations in Europe, the parades of devastation and bloodshed, but saw these as ominous because along with them had come "a general dereliction of religious principle and practice among our fellow-citizens, . . . a visible and prevailing impiety and contempt for the laws and institutions of religion, and an abounding infidelity which in many instances tend to Atheism itself."[21] By this time the churches supposed themselves once more in the predicament Edwards had diagnosed in 1740: the nation, having prospered, had become slovenly. Each by itself, with connivance, concluded that it was high time for another outpouring of God's Spirit, and then to their surprise found themselves engaged in a common enterprise which owed nothing to political agitation or to governmental encouragement. "We rejoice," said the Stonington Baptist Association in 1798, "that many of our brethren of different denominations have united in concert of prayer, and meet at stated season, to offer up fervent [sic] supplications, that God would avert his judgments."[22]

There was a dimension to their anxiety, however, which had hardly been present in 1740—the terrifying West. Kentucky and Tennessee were opened up, the Ohio Valley was ready for the stampede. The churches—Congregational, Baptist, Presbyterian, Lutheran, even the insurgent

Methodist—were European institutions. In their several ways they had given religious sanction to the political break with Europe. Then, by 1800 or thereabouts, they had also to realize that they could no longer operate in terms of a provincial society huddled along the Atlantic coast, facing toward Europe; they had to find means for combating what everybody feared would be a plunge into barbarism, on the other side of the Appalachians, in a vast area stretching away from Europe. In the next decades the cry for saving the West swelled to a chorus of incitation infinitely more impassioned than had been the call for resistance to England. A view of the valleys of the two great rivers, said William Cogswell in 1833, is enough to make heaven weep, "enough to break any heart unless harder than adamant, and to rouse it into holy action, unless colder than the grave."[23]

To uncover the main spring of the "Second Great Awakening" one has to look in these directions, rather than to rest content with the conventional explanation that it was reaction against Deism and the Enlightenment. Actually, European Deism was an exotic plant in America, which never struck roots into the soil. "Rationalism" was never so widespread as liberal historians, or those fascinated by Jefferson, have imagined. The basic fact is that the Revolution had been preached to the masses as a religious revival, and had the astounding fortune to succeed. In a little more than a decade the Protestant conscience recognized anew that in the spiritual economy victory, especially the most complete victory, is bound to turn into failure. So the struggle had to be commenced once more. James McGready, Barton Warren Stone, and the two McGees were picking up at the end of the 1790's where the patriotic orators had relaxed. They were sustained by a sense of continuity.

There were, nevertheless, a few differences in their comprehension of the task. For these revivalists, it was no longer necessary to find space in their sermons for social theory. They might honor John Locke as much as George Washington, but could at best salute both in passing. Furthermore, they really had no way of holding the entire nation responsible for the observance of a covenant with Heaven. Clergymen of 1776 could plausibly present the tight little cluster of colonies as having been somehow all caught up within a special and particular bond, but after 1800, and even more after 1815, the country was too big, too sprawling, too amorphous. No Baptist, Presbyterian, or Methodist could pretend on national holidays to speak for the conscience of all churchmen. These two considerations so altered the bases of their campaign from what had served the First Awakening that they had to devise entirely new ones. They were required to risk an adventure unprecedented in history. Calling upon all the people to submit to a uniform moral law, they at the same time had to concede that American Christianity must and should accept a diversity of churches. We once, said the *Biblical Repository* in 1832, entertained Utopian ideas about great national religious institutions, but neither the state of the country nor the temper of the age will admit them: "Theological peculiarities and sectional feelings call for separate institutions."[24] If this configuration posed a threat of centrifugal force, then that had to be countered by the centripetal power of the Revival.

Therefore the technique of revivalism had to be remodeled to serve precisely this function. Thus accepting the liberal consequences of the Revolution in the form of republican governments, and so abandoning the dream of theocracy, and equally surrendering (except for rhetorical flourish) the idea of a people in a national covenant with their Maker, these insurgents proposed to salvage the Protestant solidarity by the main force of spiritual persuasion. They summoned sinners to the convulsions of conversion; what in fact they were doing, even though few quite understood, was asserting the unity of a culture in pressing danger of fragmentation. . . .

Thus it was evident that the salvation of the nation which the revivalists of 1800 and of the following decades burned to accomplish had to be won, if won it might be, by their own exertions, with no assistance from any civil authority. They undertook their task without trepidation. They were aware that they were attempting an "experiment" unprecedented in Christian history, against the success of which past experience testified. This consideration only encouraged them. In the colonies there had come about a multiplicity of churches, a knack of getting along together, and a formal separation of church and state, by a process so natural as to make them see nothing extraordinary in their situation. True, they did recollect that formerly there had been nasty struggles, but these they banished from mind and ceased to dream of an established or uniform orthodoxy. There was clearly no cause to fear that either the federal or state governments, though thoroughly secularized, would ever become enemies of Christianity. If the civil powers could not actively foment a revival, they could likewise not hinder it. So at first the spiritual leaders saw nothing incongruous in their continuing to speak as though the whole nation professed itself still in covenant, as a unit, with Providence. Indeed when President Washington proclaimed a day of thanksgiving for the inauguration of the Constitution in 1789, and another in 1795 over the suppression of the whiskey rebellion, the formula of national federation seemed still to prevail, and the churches promptly acted as of old. . . .

Between the Revolution and the Civil War an alteration was worked in the mind of American Protestantism which is in fact a more comprehensive revolution than either of the military irruptions. With the political order separated from the ecclesiastical, yet not set against it, the problem had become not how to enlist the community into a particular political crusade for any social doctrine, but how to preserve a spiritual unity throughout a multitude of sects amid the increasing violence of political dissension. On the one hand, the revival movement and the extension of the voluntary system could not prevent the Civil War, as conceivably the theology of the covenant might have; but what these forces could do was to formulate a religious nationalism which even the war could not destroy. Whatever blood was shed and scars remained, the battles were fought upon the assumption of a cultural similarity of the contestants, one with another, which could surmount the particular issues in dispute and thus become, after 1865, a powerful instrument of reunification.

VI

It is hardly too much to say that as the concept of the national covenant dissolved, depriving the jeremiad of its reason for being, the new form
of religious excitation, the revivalistic preaching, fed not on the terrors
which the population had passed but on the gory prospect of those to come.
Concealed within this curious device is a secret assurance that if religion can
be identified with nationality, or vice versa, then we can insure both
goodness and happiness. When Americans talked to each other, they made a
great show of the fear; when they turned to Europe, in order to explain this
peculiar and apparently insane American ecclesiastical order, they revealed
the confidence which inwardly sustained them. Robert Baird, for instance,
had spent years in France as an agent for the Presbyterian Church, before
his 1844 publication of *Religion in America*. Since it was addressed to an
English and European public, there was no need for him to shout impreca-
tions upon the disastrous consequences of prosperity, but simply and proud-
ly to explain the beauties of American revivals and the efficient workings of
the voluntary principle. By the time he was finished, foreign readers might
get at least a glimmer of how the miracle operated: in a free democracy, with
church and state entirely separated, amid what seemed a chaos of sects and
orgiastic convulsions, the society could be called a "Christian" community.
In fact, it was more thoroughly imbued with a Christian spirit than any in
Europe.[25] . . .

It is, of course, a matter of historical fact that the slavery question
proved so disruptive that not even this fervent religious nationalism could
keep the great evangelical bodies from separating into southern and
northern opponents. And from those prophetic divisions flowed eventually
secession and all its woes. In that sense, the instinct of the revivals had been
correct from their beginnings in 1800: that which should terrify religious
souls in America was not the past but the future. Men must seek the Lord
not because of what they have done or have suffered but so that they may be
prepared to endure what is approaching. But the federal theology, the
doctrine of the covenant and the call to humiliation as a method of gaining
relief from affliction, was a creation of what Schaff called venerable Europe,
and was supposedly extracted from the still more venerable Old Testament.
Its entire emphasis was retrospective: the covenant had been made with
Abraham, John Winthrop had committed the Puritan migration to a covenant back in 1630, the patriots of the Revolution called upon themselves to
repent so that God would restore them to a blessing from which their
transgressions had led them. The struggle was always to return, to get back
to what, theoretically, the people, the communities, had once been.
Therefore, among the many transformations wrought in the mentality of
America between the Revolution and the Civil War was precisely this turning of the gaze from what had been, and could therefore be defined, to the il-
limitable horizon of the inconceivable. No doubt, as Schaff remarked, this

achievement was not a result of the Americans' being more energetic or cleverer than other people (though they liked to boast that they were), but of circumstances—their isolation, their natural resources, their economic opportunity. Everything thus conspired to work an intellectual and moral transformation. In this drama the religious revolution plays a vital part, because in the pre-War society religion was all-pervasive. The piety that arose out of the process could not stave off the bloodshed. Perhaps we may even accuse it of prolonging the strife, of intensifying the ferocity. But it imparted a special character to this War which remains a part of its enduring fascination. Above all, by giving to American Protestantism an absolute dedication to the future, by leading it out of the covenant and into the current of nationalism, the religious experience of this period indelibly stamped an immense area of the American mind.[26]

NOTES

[1]B. F. Morris, *Christian Life and Character of the Civil Institutions of the United States*, Philadelphia, 1864, p. 525.

[2]*ibid.,* pp. 526-527.

[3]Cf., for instance, Arthur M. Schlesinger, *Prelude to Independence*, New York, 1958, pp. 31-32.

[4]Philip Davidson, *Propaganda and the American Revolution*, Chapel Hill, 1941, passim.

[5]Perry Miller, *The New England Mind: From Colony to Province*, Cambridge, Mass., 1953, pp. 19-26.

[6]Perry Miller, *The New England Mind; The Seventeenth Century*, New York, 1954, pp. 464-484.

[7]Perry Miller, *Errand into the Wilderness*, Cambridge, Mass., 1956, pp. 119-122.

[8]John Wingate Thornton, *The Pulpit of the American Revolution*, Boston, 1860, pp. 105ff.

[9]*ibid.,* pp. 147-186.

[10]*ibid.,* pp. 187-226.

[11]*ibid.,* pp. 227-258.

[12]*ibid.,* pp. 259-322.

[13]Morris, pp. 533-536.

[14]For example, Alice Baldwin, *The New England Clergy and the American Revolution*, Durham, N.C., 1928, a pioneer work of great value, but upon which later historians have unhappily depended. In this view, I should take Clinton Rossiter, *Seedtime of the Republic*, New York, 1953, as representing the strain of obtuse secularism.

[15]Thornton, pp. 208, 212, 225.

[16]Samuel Cooper, *A Sermon Preached . . . October 25, 1780*, Boston, 1780, pp. 2, 8, 11, 14, 15, 29.

[17]Samuel Williams, *A Discourse on the Love of Country*, Salem, 1775, p. 22.

[18]Thornton, p. 243.

[19]Nathan Bangs, *A History of the Methodist Episcopal Church*, New York, 1839, 11, 146.

[20]Robert Baird, *Religion in America*, New York, 1844, p. 102.

[21]Quoted in Charles R. Keller, *The Second Great Awakening in Connecticut*, New Haven, 1942, pp. 1-2.

[22]*ibid.*, p. 191.

[23]William Cogswell, *The Harbinger of the Millennium*, Boston, 1833, p. 102.

[24]*Biblical Repository*, IV, Andover, 1832, 79.

[25]Baird, pp. 105-129.

[26]See Philip Schaff, *America*, New York, 1855.

11

American Protestantism During the Revolutionary Epoch

Sidney E. Mead

In his essay, Sidney E. Mead is concerned with tracing the realignment of religious forces which occurred during the course of struggle for independence. The author repeatedly argues for the centrality of the Enlightenment to the interpretation of American religion in this and other essays. Professor Mead taught at the University of Iowa until retirement.

It is commonly said that the two live movements in European and American Christianity during the eighteenth century were rationalism and pietism. Both were rooted in the seventeenth century. And commonly their differences, which were real, are stressed to the point of making them appear to have been completely separate and even mutually exclusive developments. This obscures the fact that in origin they were but obverse sides of a single movement which gathered enough power and momentum during the eighteenth century to sweep in religious freedom and separation of church and state over the opposition of the great bulk of traditional orthodoxy in the churches.

Only *after* this achievement of one of the two great organizational revolutions of Christendom[1] did pietism discover its latent incompatibility with rationalism, divorce itself and remarry traditional orthodoxy.

First published in *Church History* XXII (1953), pp. 279-297. Reprinted by permission of *Church History* and the author.

American denominational Protestantism is the offspring of this second marriage living in the house of religious freedom built during the period of the first marriage. The child has always accepted and defended the house with ardor if not always with intelligence, but has generally exhibited great reluctance to admit that rationalists played a major part in building it.[2]

It is the purpose of this paper to examine some major developments during the Revolutionary Epoch which throw light upon this situation, and hence help us to understand some of the peculiar characteristics of the American religious scene.

I

The sixteenth and seventeenth centuries saw the hardening of a Protestant scholasticism which cramped the style of the learned, and a growing formalism in the churches which provided but dry food for the hungry souls of common people. Meanwhile Christendom was fragmented into absolutist rival faiths, and devastated by the religious wars between them.[3] As a consequence there developed a sheer weariness with divisions, a repugnance toward wars of extermination, and a widespread positive desire for peace and unity. And underneath it all was the growing suspicion that formal theological and liturgical differences were probably not of ultimate importance, and perhaps not even important enough to fight over. Small wonder that in this situation "a small number of divines and laymen . . . tried to introduce 'sweet reasonableness' into theological discussion," while others thought they had found a way more excellent than that provided by scholasticism "in the intuitive religion of the heart, and in the simplest and most primitive forms of faith, more or less independent of external ordinances and a 'form of words'."[4] These two movements may thus be seen as "mutually supplementary."[5]

Rationalist and pietist were alike in that both, each in his own way, managed to shrug off the theological questions that had divided their most Christian fathers, and each suggested and sometimes practiced his own way of unity. The rationalist, as befitted the learned, found that "the essentials of every religion" could be reduced to a set of intellectual propositions regarding God, immortality, and the life of virtue. And, as Benjamin Franklin put it, these being "found in all the religions we had in our country, I respected them all." This, plus "the opinion that the worst had some good effects, induc'd me to avoid all discourse that might tend to lessen the good opinion another might have of his own religion."[6] The pietist leader might be as learned in his generation as any rationalist, but his concern was for the hungry sheep in the Christian churches that might look up to but could not be nourished either on formal creeds and theologies or on intellectual propositions. All, however, could understand John Wesley's "heart strangely warmed" with "trust in Christ," and pietists found peace and a basis for unity in such personal religious experience. This they preached, spreading "scriptural religion throughout the land, among people of every denomination; leaving every one to hold his own opinions, and to follow his own mode of worship."⁷ So John Wesley could rhapsodize:

> Methodists do not impose in order to their admission, any opinions whatever. Let them hold particular or general redemption, absolute or conditional decrees; let them be churchmen or dissenters, Presbyterians or Independents, it is no obstacle. Let them choose one mode of baptism or another, it is no bar to their admission. The Presbyterian may be a Presbyterian still; the Independent and Anabaptist use his own worship still. So may the Quaker and none will contend with him about it. They think and let think. One condition and only one is required—a real desire to save the soul. Where this is it is enough; they desire no more; they lay stress upon nothing else; they only ask, "Is thy heart herein as my heart? If it be, give me thy hand."⁸

Thus rationalists appealed to the head, and concluded that all the multifarious differences over which Christian churchmen fought were matters of non-essential opinion, as pietists appealed to the heart and concluded that the differences over which Christians had battled and bled for a millennium were immaterial between those of like "heart." But while in opposition to traditionalists in the churches rationalists and pietists supplemented one another by sharing a common sentiment of reaction, they nevertheless represented basically different paths of life. And both, each in its own way, when separated from traditionalism were in danger of setting men adrift by breaking the continuity of Christian history and scattering the content of Christian faith.

II

The situation in America during the eighteenth century was such as to minimize the differences between rationalists and pietists, and even to accentuate their positive agreements. In the first place the American colonial rationalists, although numerous, were not fomenters of religious controversy, being "willing to leave the question of divine revelation alone,"⁹ in a genial respect for the unenlightened. While Deistic thinking permeated the air the intellectual world breathed,¹⁰ mature Deists were apparently mild, urbane and outwardly conforming. The prime example is Philadelphia's suave and impeccable Franklin, who "regularly paid my annual subscription for the support of the only Presbyterian minister or meeting we had,"¹¹ who urged his daughter to "go constantly to church, whoever preaches,"¹² and who punctiliously, as new meeting houses were erected in Philadelphia, contributed his "mite for such purpose, whatever might be the sect".¹³ And Jefferson, while pressing the Act for Religious Freedom in Virginia in 1777, exhibited the same spirit by writing and sponsoring subscription lists for the support of the clergy who were to be cut off from state support.¹⁴

In the second place, beginning during the third decade of the century, and under the impetus given by both native and imported leaders, great revivals swept the colonies from New England to the Carolinas. Everywhere they brought controversy as staunch defenders of the old order, the traditionalists, rose to defend their churches against the disintegrating inroads of rampant "enthusiasm." Whether among Congregationalists in New England, or Presbyterians in the middle colonies, or Anglicans in the South, the substance of the controversy was the same—a clash between the revivalists and the "right-wing"[15] supporters of the churchly patterns of clerical and ecclesiastical authoritarianism that had been transplanted from Europe.

The hold of these patterns had already been weakened by the inroads of transplanted "left-wing" sectarian groups which by this time were firmly entrenched in Rhode Island and the middle colonies and had gained a measure of tolerance in the other colonies. During the revivals the number of these groups was augmented by schisms from the "right-wing" churches (e.g. the Separate Congregationalists in New England), their membership was greatly increased, and they spread widely through all the colonies. This increase and expansion brought them into sharp conflict with the dominant or Established churches in every area.[16] These churches, although harassed and torn internally by the conflicts between revivalists and traditionalists, brought every possible ecclesiastical and civil weapon to bear against the sectarians and schismatics.[17] Under this widespread persecution anti-clerical and anti-ecclesiastical sentiments of the "left-wing" sectarians were welded together in a vigorous positive thrust for complete religious freedom.

Meanwhile the rationalist permeation of the intellectual and cultured classes meant that many men in positions of social and political leadership were Deists. These men, however much they might abhor "enthusiasm" were appreciative of the practical moral application of the revivalists' gospel, especially since it was based upon an appeal to the teachings and simple religion of Jesus. Rationalist and sectarian-pietist were agreed that religion was a matter between the individual and his God without institutional mediation, and hence that the church was a voluntary organization of like-minded and like-hearted individuals. They were united in opposition to the tradition of clerical and ecclesiastical authoritarianism manifested in the "right-wing" churches,[18] and they eschewed it with a denial of the binding power of the past. "As to tradition," wrote Jefferson in organizing his arguments against Episcopacy,

> if we are Protestants we reject all tradition, and rely on the scriptures alone, for that is the essence and common principle of all Protestant churches.[19]

This was sentiment dear to the heart of any sectarian-pietist.

Small wonder, then, that the sympathies of the Deistic political leaders, as they observed the controversies in and between the "religious sects" that were caused by the revivals, were with the sectarian-pietists from the beginning, and that they became their spokesmen and defenders in the legislatures—as, for example, James Madison and Thomas Jefferson in Virginia.[20]

Hence the struggles for religious freedom during the last quarter of the eighteenth century provided the kind of practical issue on which rationalists and sectarian-pietists could and did unite, in spite of underlying theological differences, in opposition to "right-wing" traditionalists. The positive thrust for the separation of church and state and the making of all religious groups equal before the civil law came from the sectarian-pietists both within and without the "ring-wing" churches, and from the rationalistic social and political leaders. It was indeed

> the leadership of such Lockian disciples as Jefferson and Madison, backed by an overwhelming left-wing Protestant public opinion, that was responsible for writing the clauses guaranteeing religious freedom into the new state constitutions and finally into the fundamental law of the land.[21]

This is an enlightening way of describing the complex alignment of forces during the eighteenth century that accomplished the declaration for national religious freedom, and the realignment of forces during the Revolutionary Epoch which had such tremendous effects upon the later development of Protestantism in America. For the very success of their alliance during the eighteenth century in effecting religious freedom removed the primary bond that had held rationalist and sectarian-pietist together, and the conditions which then brought theological questions to the fore forced their split and a realignment of sectarian-pietist with traditionalist against rationalist.[22]

III

Thus far we have stressed the likenesses and agreements of rationalists and sectarian-pietists which made it possible for them to work together so long as the pressing issue was practical and political, as it was down to the final acceptance of religious freedom. But in order to understand the realignment that took place during the Revolutionary Epoch their differences must be noted.

First was the sociological difference. Rationalism was of the classes, the aristocracy of birth, breeding, and wealth, with its tradition of paternalistic social responsibility, of learning and concern for fundamental intellectual problems. Such men, although feeling themselves superior to the "enthusiastic" religion of the common man, were nevertheless apt to frown upon the dissemination of their own religious views among the masses because of the possibly bad effect on morals. Benjamin Franklin spoke for them in typical fashion in a letter believed to have been addressed to Thomas Paine:[23]

> think how great a portion of mankind consists of weak and ignorant men and women, and of inexperienced, inconsiderate youth of both sexes, who have need of the motives of religion to restrain them from vice, to support their virtue, and retain them in the practice of it till it becomes habitual, which is the great point for its security.[24]

And Herbert M. Morais concluded that much of the later "vilification of Paine was due to the fact that he was guilty of carrying heresy to the people" and hence was a traitor to his class.[25]

It is obvious that any position which felt itself secure only within an aristocratic setting had a very questionable future in store for itself during a period when the outstanding trend was toward the equalitarianism that flowered in the age of President Jackson and the common man. Jefferson's democratic party lost its aristocratic leadership by the time of Jackson, and apparently had even lost Jefferson's concept of a responsible "natural aristocracy" grounded on "virtue and talents."[26] In brief, during this time the ethos that had sheltered Deism during the eighteenth century disintegrated, and Deistic thinking carried to the people in the popularized version of Thomas Paine's *Age of Reason* was soon found wanting.

Second, and more important, was the familiar theological difference, expressed as the necessity for a special and particular revelation in the Scriptures versus the complete sufficiency of human reason. During the eighteenth century in America conservative rational Christians—clergymen like "Gay, Briant and Bentley in Congregational surroundings and Johnson and Smith in Anglican circles" commonly "held that the authoritative basis of natural religion did not rest in reason alone but also depended upon the Christian revelation,"[27] and even those more radical in their views did not press the point publicly. Thus Benjamin Franklin, just a month before he died in 1790, when asked directly by Ezra Stiles the test question about his belief in the divinity of Jesus, replied charmingly in a way completely to avoid the issue,

> I have, with most of the Dissenters in England, some Doubts as to his Divinity; tho' it is a question I do not dogmatize upon, having never studied it, and think it needless to busy myself with it now, when I expect soon an Opportunity of knowing the truth with less trouble.

However, he added with disarming candor,

> I see no harm . . . in its being believed, if that Belief has the good consequence, as probably it has, of making his Doctrines more respected and better observed; especially as I do not perceive, that the Supreme takes it amiss, by distinguishing the Unbelievers in his Government of the world with any peculiar Marks of his Displeasure.[28]

Even an ardent champion of orthodoxy would have to have time on his hands in order to pick a quarrel with such a genial wit who contributed regularly to one church and gave his "mite" to all.

But looking back on the period we can see that once the practical political goal of religious freedom was achieved it would require only a situation that would accentuate the central theological difference between rationalists on the one hand and sectarian-pietists and traditionalists on the other to bring the groups into open conflict. Even so, it was only when rationalistic religious thinking assumed real or imagined social and political implications in America that controversy resulted. This happened when an interpretation of the French Revolution led to the conclusion that there was a direct cause-and-effect relationship between "infidel" thinking and the later phases of the revolution; and when during the rise of the Jeffersonian party the religious views of Jefferson and other leaders of the party could be labeled "French" with enough popular plausibility to make the label stick.

The rise of the Jeffersonian party in America coincided with the events of the French revolution. America was still oriented to Europe and the struggles in the Old World were reflected in the New. Hence from the beginning of the definition of differences within the first Cabinet of the new government, symbolized by the names of Hamilton and Jefferson, the former reflected sympathies with England, the latter with France—at least, and this was sufficient, so it was widely supposed.[29]

Jefferson and his cohorts were not, of course, theologians or religious leaders. They were political reformers with typical eighteenth century theories about the nature of man and hence about the social and political institutions most suited to him as a rational being. Basic was the notion that man's present deplorable situation was largely due to the enslavement of his natural reason in the interests of selfish and privileged individuals and groups in the society. Jefferson merely echoed the opinion of his group when he said:

> My opinion is that there would never have been an infidel, if there had never been a priest. The artificial structure they have built on the purest of all moral systems, for the purpose of deriving from it pence and power, revolt those who think for themselves, and who read in that system only what is really there.[30]

Hence they concluded that reform depended upon the freeing of man's natural reason from such enslavement—largely by opening all the channels of communication through freedom of speech, freedom of the press, freedom to assemble and petition, so that every opinion could have a hearing, errors ceasing "to be dangerous when it is permitted freely to contradict them."[31] This is the theory that lies back of the great reforming zeal and thrust developed during the eighteenth century.

This reforming thrust found directly across its path in France, to which all eyes were directed, the twin institutions of monarchy and church. And of the two the church came to be regarded as the more culpable because it seemed to the reformers that it was the church that really operated the machinery for the enslavement of the minds of the people. The principles of Jesus, said Jefferson, "were departed from by those who professed to be his special servants, and perverted into an engine for enslaving mankind, and aggrandizing their oppressors in church and state." These men, he continued, warped "the purest system of morals ever before preached to man . . . into a mere contrivance to filch wealth and power to themselves."[32]

Thomas Paine, a more excellent or less cautious pamphleteer, put it more briefly and bluntly:

> All national institutions of churches, whether Jewish, Christian or Turkish, appear to me no other than human inventions, set up to terrify and enslave mankind, and monopolize power and profit.[33]

Hence the church came under attack as the first institution that must be broken in the interests of freedom and reform. And there were two obvious ways of undermining the control of the church over the minds of the people.

The first was to attack the existing churches as institutions reared not upon the "pure religion of Jesus" but upon the historical corruptions of that pure religion. The prime example of this sort of attack is Joseph Priestley's two volume *History of the Corruption of Christianity,* first published in 1782. Priestley conceived the work as "researches into the origin and progress" of the corruptions of Christianity, in such manner as will tend to give all the friends of pure Christianity the fullest satisfaction that they reflect no discredit on the revelation itself.[34] In the interests of the true Christian faith, he thought, it was necessary "to exhibit a view of the dreadful corruptions which have debased its spirit, and almost annihilated all the happy effects which it was eminently calculated to produce."[35]

This attack on the existing churches, even though launched by a rationalistic Unitarian, was in essence the same kind of attack that was dear to the hearts of anti-clerical and anti-ecclesiastical sectarian-pietists, and hence it found a wide appeal in America. And even in more extreme form it did not push the crucial issue regarding revelation versus reason to the front.

Among the political leaders this was, as intimated in the quotations above, the view of Thomas Jefferson, who is said to have read Priestley's work through once a year from the time of its publication, and to have recommended it as required reading for students in the University of Virginia as the work most likely to wean them from sectarian narrowness. His own attempt while president, and later, to distill from the four gospels "The Philosophy of Jesus of Nazareth . . . for the use of the Indians, unembarrassed with matters of fact or faith beyond the level of their comprehension" was his positive contribution in the form of a definition of the "pure religion of Jesus." "We must," he said, "reduce our volume to the simple Evangelists: select, even from them, the very words of Jesus." This, he added, he had performed for his own use

> by cutting verse by verse out of the printed book, and arranging the matter which is evidently his and which is as easily distinguished as diamonds in a dunghill.

These diamonds mined out of the dunghill constituted

> the most sublime and benevolent code of morals which has ever been offered to man . . . forty-six pages of pure and unsophisticated doctrines such as were

professed and acted upon by the unlettered Apostles, the Apostolic Fathers, and the Christians of the first century.[36]

Sectarian pietists could have little quarrel with this.

But this attack on the church, depending as it did upon the ability to keep in mind the distinction between the pure religion of Jesus and the religion of the existing churches, was too subtle for use during the excitements of social and political upheaval. Hence the more radical attack—always latent in deistic thinking[37]—namely, the direct attack on the orthodox Christian view of revelation itself, on the basis that the church held its great power over the minds of the people because it claimed to be the sole guardian and interpreter of God's saving revelation to man. The notable popularized version of this kind of attack is Thomas Paine's *Age of Reason.* Said Paine,

> Every national church or religion has established itself by pretending some special mission from God communicated to certain individuals. The Jews have their Moses; the Christians their Jesus Christ, their apostles and saints; and the Turks their Mahomet, as if the way to God was not open to every man alike.[38]

The motivating thought in the mind of the author here is clear—if the people's belief in the idea of revelation as held by the orthodox could be completely undermined, the whole structure of the church would collapse,[39] and the way be cleared for the true religion founded upon the true revelation of God in "CREATION." For, since

> all corruptions . . . have been produced by admitting of what is called *revealed religion*, the most effective means to prevent all such evils and impositions is not to admit of any other revelation than that which is manifested in the book or creation, and to contemplate the creation as the only true and real word of God that ever did or ever will exist; and that everything else, called the word of God, is fable and imposition.[40]

Here, then, the real theological issue was raised and the direct claims of "natural" as over against "revealed" religion were laid bare. But as the exponents of natural religion had become so explicit in their claims only when goaded into doing so through the pressures to promote their reforms, the theological issue was inextricably bound up with the social and political issues and all but lost to sight.[41]

What could be clearly enough sensed by religious leaders of all groups, even by the most heart-happy pietists, was that this attack undermined not only the traditionally authoritarian churches, Catholic and Protestant, but Christianity itself as they conceived it. And this prospect could be made alarming not only to leaders in the several churches, including sectarian pietists, but also to many intellectuals who, while nominally, at least, Deists themselves, deplored the undermining of the people's simple faith.

At this juncture of events, as befitted the new republic, the battle became one for the allegiance of the masses of the people. Works like Ethan

Allen's *Reason the Only Oracle of Man* (1784), and Paine's *Age of Reason* (1794) carried the issues to the people through popularization. And defenders of orthodox Christianity—men like Timothy Dwight and (later) Lyman Beecher in Connecticut—followed suit, as, being experienced revivalists, they were eminently prepared to do. Such heated discussion conducted in the vernacular did not admit of subtle distinctions. Hence the tendency on both sides greatly to oversimplify the issues. It is necessary to keep this in mind in order to understand the ensuing conflict. It cannot be understood simply as an intellectual controversy, but is better regarded as all-out ideological warfare.

The striking revolutionary developments of the period provide the context. The European political situation loaned itself to the interpretation that an Infidel International was deliberately fostering the overthrow of all religion and all government—that it had been successful in France and was pushing out from there. Jedediah Morse of the First Church in Charlestown, Massachusetts, became an outstanding spokesman for this view in his Fast Day sermon preached in Boston on May 9, 1789. He took his cue from a work published by Professor John Robinson of the University of Edinburgh in 1798, the title of which is sufficiently explanatory of the contests:

> Proofs of a Conspiracy against all Religion and Governments of Europe carried on in Secret Meetings of Free Masons, Illuminati, and Reading Societies.[42]

Morse claimed that branches of the Order were already established in America, suggested that Paine's *Age of Reason* was one of their products, and held that the Democratic Societies were spending the principles of illuminism through the land.

This simplified interpretation of the situation in America, although vehemently and soundly disputed by some, was of a nature to become widely accepted. It was picked up and broadly echoed through sermons and speeches until, as Vernon Stauffer concluded, "there was probably not a solitary Federalist leader in the United States who did not believe that French ministers and agents were in secret league with influential representatives of the Democratic party."[43]

Meanwhile the Federalists who, understandably enough, identified their continued well being and control of the government with the continued well being of the new nation, had in effect declared "war upon the ideas of the French Revolution" in the Sedition Act of 1798.[44] Such men easily recognized in the party led by Thomas Jefferson the American instrument of the Infidel International. Jefferson was known to have consorted with French Infidels during his five years in France, and although seemingly always cautious of his public pronouncements on religion, enough was known of his Deistic views to give popular plausibility to the notion that he was a thoroughgoing Infidel with diabolical designs on American institutions.[45] This view of Jefferson and his party seemed to be confirmed by the concurrent organization of radical Deistic Societies in several American cities, the publication and circulation of several outspoken Deistic papers, and the attempt on the part of Deistic speakers—notably for example the renegade Baptist preacher, Elihu Palmer—to work up a definitely anti-Christian, or, rather, anti-church crusade among the people.[46]

It was in New England that the controversy became hottest, and the most effective anti-infidel party line was developed by colorful and able leaders. There the Congregational churches were established, and their clergy Federalist almost to a man and inclined to identify true religion with the Standing Order. Hence they soon constituted the chief bloc of opposition to the rising Jeffersonian party. Naturally that party in its thrust for power attacked this "political Congregationalism" which stood in its way, and seemed to bear out the reformer's notion that the church was the primary support of conservative and reactionary government. Hence disestablishment became one of its main objectives. This development served further to confuse the theological and political issues, for disestablishment early gained the support of the "sects" who suffered some restrictions and more humiliations under the Establishment, and threw them into the party of the "infidels" politically, while theologically they belonged with the clergy of the Establishment. Disestablishment also gained significant support from the unchurched who were apt to resent having to pay taxes for the support of the Congregational churches.

This is why Lyman Beecher, outstanding defender of the Congregational order at the time, could say that "democracy as it rose, included nearly all the minor sects, besides the Sabbath breakers, rum-selling, tippling folk, infidels, and ruff-scuff generally."[47] To Beecher at the time it apparently seemed clear enough that if this Sabbath-breaking, rum-selling, tippling ruff-scuff could be reformed into temperate Congregationalist observers of the Sabbath they would automatically cease to be democrats and a threat to the Standing Order. Thus "infidelity" would be overthrown and true religion, good morals and sound government continue to prevail.[48]

So long as the issue was the practical one of religious freedom the sectarian-pietists thus aligned themselves with the rationalists against the traditionalists. And true to form, when disestablishment finally came in Connecticut the realignment of sectarian-pietist with traditionalist against rationalist immediately took place. Then even Beecher saw that political defense of the Standing Order caused a false alignment of religious forces. For he noted that by the repeal of the law compelling everyone to pay toward the support of some church, "the occasion of animosity between us and the minor sects was removed and the infidels could no more make capital with them against us." Then indeed, those of the minor sects "began themselves to feel the dangers of infidelity, and to react against it, and this laid the basis of cooperation and union of spirit."[49]

Here is a microcosm of what happened in America generally once the political issue of religious freedom was acceptably settled. Then the sectarian-pietist lamb snuggled up against the lion of traditionalism for protection against the infidel wolves. But there the metaphor breaks down, for the "lion" and the "lamb" produced offspring—the American Protestant denominations.

It is important to note that the theological issue which formed the basis of this union of traditionalist and sectarian-pietist in America, and constituted their real difference with the Deists, was all but lost sight of in the excitement of the controversy. Rather the effective argument against "infidelity" was moral and political, not theological—the argument namely, that "infidel" thinking directly and necessarily led to personal immorality and chaos in society. This has been labeled the "argument from tendency"—a viewing with alarm that was very effective in gaining popular support, but which meant that the issue between natural and revealed religion was never really discussed on a theological level at all.

IV

Out of this kind of attack on infidelity, plus organized efforts to carry the appeal to as many people as possible, the new revivalism was born. The vivid presentation of the two alternatives, Christianity and Infidelity, with the simplified version of the moral, social, and political tendencies of each, and the fervid insistence that the individual could and must choose between them, was its substance. And men like Timothy Dwight had a way of making what he called "Infidelity" as vivid and repulsive for his generation as Jonathan Edwards at Enfield had made hell fire for a previous generation.

The substance of the new revivalism, although clothed in less learning on the frontier than in New England, was the same the country over, and the story of how Infidelity was drowned in the great tidal wave of revivalism that swept the country early in the nineteenth century has been made familiar enough.[50]

This welter of controversy and revivalism eventuated in a realignment of forces and movements that was to condition the development of Protestantism in America for more than a century, and to stamp it with characteristics that almost baffle analysis. But all are related to the fact that pietism came to dominate overwhelmingly in all the denominations.

Once religious freedom had been won, these denominations were confronted by the great problem posed by a rapidly growing and westward moving population about ninety percent of which was unchurched. Revivalism, developed during the Colonial period, proved the most effective technique, and was adopted by all the denominations. It was revivalism, stressing "evangelism more than creed"[51] that "terminated the Puritan and inaugurated the Pietist or Methodistic age of American church history."[52]

And pietism, or "Methodism," for reasons suggested above, was peculiarly amorphous and intellectually uncritical.[53] The pietist was not inclined to make logical consistency a test of either doctrine or fellowship, and in every period was not likely to permit basic theoretical differences to stand in the way of cooperation with those who seemed to be of like heart in working for "good" social and political ends. And he was likely to equate, as the Methodists put it, "spreading scriptural holiness over these lands" with reforming the nation, assuming that "if the man's soul was saved fundamental social change would inevitably follow."[54] Hence pietists have been apt to endorse any current reform movement that seemed likely to accomplish "good" ends, and as apt to defend any social order that gave free range to evangelism.

Pietists acted in this fashion during the eighteenth century when working with rationalists for religious freedom. In the revolutionary period they vehemently rejected the rationalists' religious position, but retained much of their social and political views. Hence while sectarian-pietists aligned themselves with traditional orthodoxy theologically, they by and large clung to the rationalists' social and political program,[55] for which there was little theoretical foundation in the orthodoxy they now professed.

It is this underlying schizophrenia of nineteenth century pietistic American Protestantism that makes its activities so difficult to understand.[56] Recognition of it, for example, throws light upon F. O. Matthiessen's observation that the many reform movements of the eighteen forties "marked the last struggle of the liberal spirit of the eighteenth century in conflict with the rising forces of exploitation."[57] This seems implausible at first glance because so many of the reformers were evangelical Protestant Christians. But it is less implausible when the conflict is seen as one taking place in the jelly-like intellectual structure of pietistic reformers themselves.

So far as the bulk of American Protestantism was concerned the "struggle" eventuated in a victory for "the rising forces of exploitation." These forces provided the apologetic ideology for their "acquisitive society" delineated by Ralph Gabriel in his discussion of "The Gospel of Wealth of the Gilded Age."[58] And pietistic religious leaders accepted and sanctioned this ideology as easily as their predecessors had aligned themselves with rationalists in the eighteenth century and with the traditionally orthodox early in the nineteenth.

Meanwhile, insofar as the defenders of traditional orthodoxy concerned themselves with such matters, they were solidly conservative. All of which offers substantiation for the view that "at least from the time of the battle with the Enlightenment, religious social doctrine [in America] offered a powerful and uncompromising support to the status quo."[59] So it was then when critics of the social and economic order began to emerge in the denominations they soon discovered, like Walter Rauschenbush, that if they were to embark upon *Christianizing the Social Order* they must first create or reconstruct *A Theology for the Social Gospel*. But at the time adequate materials for such a theology were not obviously present.

If on the one hand, the roots of the religious and social activities of the American Protestant denominations were thus made ambiguous during the revolutionary period, on the other hand their intellectual life was rendered fuzzy and inconsistent. For although there was at the time a theological issue important enough to divide honest and able men, the nature of the controversy was such that it was not discussed or settled on its own merits. Timothy Dwight's eminent men who were finally persuaded and began to insist that Christianity "was absolutely necessary to good Government, liberty and safety" were not necessarily convinced because they were persuaded that revealed religion was true and natural religion was false. There is considerable evidence to indicate that they may have been convinced only that it was more expedient. An English traveler in America in 1822-1823 observed that

> Instances of openly avowed deism are rare. Persons who hold deistical opinions generally either keep them to themselves, or veil them under the garb of flimsy hypocrisy . . . In many parts a man's reputation would be seriously injured if he were to avow himself one.[60]

This testimony could be multiplied many times, and it suggests that "Infidels" were not so much convinced as driven underground.[61] Protestantism thus laid on the table a large item of unfinished intellectual business.

Further, the effectiveness of the argument from tendency depended upon slurring over many important distinctions and tilting the whole scale of values so that everything that could be dubbed "infidelity" was put on an incline and viewed with alarm as irresistibly sliding toward atheism, immorality, and chaos. This meant that intellectual issues were transformed into moral issues, and intellectual challenges were not met as such. Pietists were inclined to make the moral character of the speaker the test of the truth of what was said, and the absence of petty individualistic vices the test of moral character. Thus American Protestantism largely fell into the murky habit of seldom meeting or solving basic intellectual problems (as distinct from technical problems), substituting for this irksome task the criticism of the moral character of those who raised them. It is notable that almost every subsequent religious and social critic in America has been called immoral or atheistic at one time or in one way or another, and many cogent criticisms thus easily met.

But the great item of unfinished intellectual business confronting the Protestant denominations was and is the problem of religious freedom. And here the situation is almost desperate as increasingly it becomes clear that the problem cannot be solved simply by maligning the character of those who question the American practice.

Is it not passing strange that American Protestantism has never developed any sound theoretical justification of or theological orientation for its most distinctive practice? Today we should probably have to agree with the writer of 1876 who said that

> we seem to have made no advance whatever in harmonizing (on a theoretical level) the relations of religious sects among themselves, or in defining their common relation to the Civil power.[62]

The reasons for this lacuna have been suggested in this paper. There is no getting around the fact that the fundamental documents of American religious freedom are James Madison's *Memorial and Remonstrance on the Religious Rights of Man* of 1784, and Thomas Jefferson's *An Act for Establishing Religious Freedom,* which was written in 1779 and enacted in Virginia in 1786.[63] Both of these documents are oriented in a theological rationalism. Hence when Protestantism vigorously rejected eighteenth century rationalism during the revolutionary period, it cut itself off from the theoretical justification for the religious freedom it ardently espoused in practice. And it has never been made clear that the practice can be given theoretical justification on the premises of traditional orthodoxy which the bulk of the denominations have professed to accept. Hence at present the strange inclination of Protestant guardians of separation of church and state against real or imagined Roman Catholic "threats" to accept as their own the purely "secular" defenses being promulgated, and in a way that implies the equation of Protestantism with secularism. There seems to be too little realization that identification with secular defenses of this "good" cause could be as disastrous for Protestantism as for Roman Catholicism.[64]

Again we are confronted with an underlying schizophrenia. It puzzled Ralph Gabriel who noted correctly enough that although

> during the Middle Period, the secular faith in democracy and the religious faith of evangelicalism were not only closely interrelated but were mutually interdependent . . . [and] complemented one another,[65]

yet they were never really merged and given over-all meaning in an inclusive intellectual structure. It is suggested here that this did not take place because, although their theoretical foundations were unreconciled and perhaps unreconcilable, yet the nature of the predominant pietistic Protestantism was such that "mere" theoretical considerations did not trouble its leaders even though they constituted the foundations of their religious and civil house.

In conclusion, the alignment of traditionalism and sectarian-pietism against rationalism during the revolutionary period gained a tremendous victory for Christianity in the popular arena, and placed the marks of its peculiar strengths and weaknesses on all subsequent American Protestantism. Its strengths produced "The Great Century [1814-1914]" celebrated by Professor K. S. Latourette in his massive *History of the Expansion of Christianity*. Its weakness effectively scuttled most of the intellectual structure of Protestantism. When the tremendous growth and innumerable good works of American Protestantism are celebrated, it must also be noted that "no theologian or theology of first rank issued from the nineteenth century Christianity of the United States."[66]

The lush century of expansion and growth in the midst of apparently unlimited resources produced an American Protestant dinosaur, huge and impressive, but now, its pietistic heart's blood changing rapidly into routine moralism, it is in danger of perishing from a lack of intellectual power.

NOTES

[1]"On the administrative side, the two most profound revolutions which have occurred in the entire history of the church have been these: first, the change of the church, in the fourth century, from a voluntary society . . . to a society conceived as necessarily coextensive with the civil community and endowed with the power to en-

force the adherence of all members of the civil community; second, the reversal of this change . . . in America." W. E. Garrison, *Annals of the American Academy of Political and Social Science,* CCLVI (1948), 17.

²Robert Baird, *Religion in America* (New York: Harper & Brothers, 1845), 110-111.

³See Roland H. Bainton, "The Struggle for Religious Liberty," *Church History,* X (June 1941), 97.

⁴M. Kaufman, "Latitudinarianism and Pietism," *Cambridge Modern History* (New York, 1908), V, 742.

⁵*Ibid.,* 763.

⁶Frank L. Mott & Chester E. Jorgenson, *Benjamin Franklin. American Writers Series* (New York, 1936), 70.

⁷John Wesley, *Sermons on Several Occasions* (New York, 1851), I, 392.

⁸Quoted in William W. Sweet, *The American Churches, An Interpretation* (Nashville, 1948), 46-47.

⁹Herbert M. Morais, *Deism in Eighteenth Century America* (New York, 1934), 13.

¹⁰Note for example how easily the youthful Franklin, brought up "piously in the Dissenting way . . . soon became a thorough Deist simply by reading orthodox refutations of Deism." Mott and Jorgenson, *Benjamin Franklin,* p. 55.

¹¹*Ibid.,* 12.

¹²Letter to Sarah Franklin, Nov. 8, 1764, in Nathan G. Goodman (ed.), *A Benjamin Franklin Reader* (New York, 1945), 237.

¹³Mott and Jorgenson, *Benjamin Franklin,* 70.

¹⁴Gilbert Chinard, *Thomas Jefferson, Apostle of Americanism* (Boston, 1944), 103-104.

¹⁵The phrases "right wing" and "left wing" of the Reformation have come into quite general use since the publication of the article by Roland H. Bainton, "The Left Wing of the Reformation," in the *Journal of Religion,* XXI (April 1941), 124-134.

¹⁶Note for example the "New Lights", Separate Congregationalists, and Baptists in New England, the "New Side" Presbyterians in the Middle Colonies, and the Presbyterians and Baptists in the Anglican South.

¹⁷See for example Connecticut's "Act for Regulating Abuses and Correcting Disorders in Ecclesiastical Affairs" of 1742, and the struggle for recognition of dissenters' rights under the English Toleration Act in Virginia.

¹⁸Compare with W. W. Sweet's "comparison . . . between the basic ideas of the popular religious bodies and those held by the intellectual liberals" in "Natural Religion and Religious Liberty in America," *Journal of Religion,* XXV (Jan. 1945), 54-55.

¹⁹Saul K. Padover (ed.), *The Complete Jefferson* (New York, 1943), 940.

²⁰It is said that Madison and Jefferson were intrigued by the practice of democracy in the Baptist churches and no doubt their interest in religious freedom was stimulated by their observation of the persecution of the Baptists in Virginia.

²¹William W. Sweet, *Annals of the American Academy of Political and Social Science,* CCLVI (Mar. 1948), 45. The argument is more fully developed in the article noted above, note 18.

²²Compare the position of John M. Mecklin in *The Story of American Dissent* (New York, 1934), 36.

[23]Morais, *Deism in Eighteenth Century America,* 20.

[24]Thomas C. Hall, *The Religious Background of American Culture* (Boston, 1930), 172.

[25]Morais, *Deism in Eighteenth Century America,* 121.

[26]See Jefferson's letter to John Adams, October 28, 1813, in Stuart G. Brown (ed.), *We Hold These Truths* (New York, 1941), 114.

[27]Morais, *Deism in Eighteenth Century America,* 15.

[28]Mott and Jorgenson, *Benjamin Franklin,* 508-509.

[29]See John C. Miller, *Crisis in Freedom; the Alien and Sedition Acts* (Boston 1951), *passim.*

[30]Letter to Mrs. M. Harrison Smith, August 6, 1816, quoted in W. W. Sweet, *Journal of Religion,* XXV (Jan. 1945), 52-53.

[31]Jefferson's "An Act for Establishing Religious Freedom," in Padover, *The Complete Jefferson,* p. 947. Jefferson argued consistently that where "reason and experiment have been indulged . . . error has fled before them. It is error alone which needs the support of government. Truth can stand by itself." (*Ibid.,* 675). In his Second Inaugural he pointed out the salutary effects of such freedom (*Ibid.,* 413).

[32]Quoted in Adrienne Koch, *The Philosophy of Thomas Jefferson* (New York, 1943), 26.

[33]Quoted from *The Age of Reason,* in Arthur W. Peach (ed.), *Selections from the Works of Thomas Paine* (New York, 1928), 232.

[34]Joseph Priestley, *An History of the Corruptions of Christianity* (2d ed., Birmingham, 1793), I, v.

[35]*Ibid.,* xv.

[36]See Henry Wilder Foote, *Thomas Jefferson; champion of religious freedom, advocate of Christian morals* (Boston, 1947), 51-52.

[37]"Always latent" because to the deistic way of thinking the orthodox view of revelation was particularistic—that is, given to a particular group at a particular time and place and hence not readily available for all mankind. See Arthur O. Lovejoy, *The Great Chain of Being* (Cambridge, 1936), 288-289, 292, for a discussion of this aspect of rationalism. Compare Paine, *Age of Reason,* in Peach, *Selections,* 250-51.

[38]In Peach, *Selections,* 232. *The Age of Reason* was written in France and as much to stem the trend toward atheism as to undermine the church.

[39]Compare Morais, *Deism in Eighteenth Century America,* 129: "the deism of Paine, Volney and Palmer, presented in a popular form was designed to reach the masses in order to destroy their faith in traditional Christianity with its priesthood, dogmas and supernatural revelation. Its ultimate end was to replace the Christian religion by the religion of nature with its three-fold creed—God, Virtue and Immortality, a creed believed in even by devout Christians."

[40]In Peach, *Selections,* 250, 263 note.

[41]The theological issues raised by Paine's *Age of Reason* apparently received only a very few replies on a "rational and scholarly plane." Most of the "replies" were primarily personal attacks on Paine. See Morais, *Deism in Eighteenth Century America,* 163-67.

[42]See Vernon Stauffer, *New England and the Bavarian Illuminati* (New York, 1918), 229 ff; Jones, *America and French Culture,* 398-99.

[43]Stauffer, *N. E. and the Bavarian Illuminati*, 126-27; 272 ff.

[44]Miller, *Crisis in Freedom*, 74.

[45]Jones, *America and French Culture*, 402-403.

[46]This ground has been made familiar by the studies of Vernon Stauffer, Charles Hazen, Herbert M. Morais, G. Adolf Koch and Howard Mumford Jones which are referred to elsewhere in this paper.

[47]Beecher, *Autobiography*, I, 342.

[48]See Sidney E. Mead, *Nathaniel William Taylor 1786-1858: a Connecticut Liberal* (Chicago, 1942), chapters iv and vi.

[49]Beecher, *Autobiography*, I, 543.

[50]See Jones, *America and French Culture*, chap. xi; Koch, *Republican Religion*, chap. viii; Morais, *Deism in Eighteenth Century America*, chap. vi.

[51]Garrison, *The Annals*, 19-20. For the development of revivalism during the period following the Revolution, see W. W. Sweet, *Religion in the Development of American Culture 1765-1840* (New York, 1952), chapters iv and v.

[52]Robert E. Thompson, *A History of the Presbyterian Churches in the United States* (New York, 1895), 34; Leonard W. Bacon, *A History of American Christianity* (New York, 1900), 176. Both of these books are in the *American Church History Series*.

[53]"The great Methodist movement . . . can appeal to no great intellectual construction explanatory of its modes of understanding. It may have chosen the better way. Its instinct may be sound. However, that may be, it was a notable event in the history of ideas when the clergy of the western races began to waver in their appeal to constructive reason." A. N. Whitehead, *Adventures of Ideas* (New York, 1933), 27-28.

[54]Wade C. Barclay, *History of Methodist Missions*, volume II, *To Reform the Nation* (New York, 1950), 8.

[55]Compare, Morais, *Deism in Eighteenth Century America*, 22: "In New England God-fearing Baptists and Methodists were usually Jeffersonians but at the same time were backbone of the evangelical movement which more than anything else was responsible for the decline of deism." And see Koch, *Republican Religion*, 281-82.

[56]Compare J. H. Randall and J. H. Randall, Jr., *Religion and the Modern World* (New York, 1929), 26-27: "Western society confronted the disruptive forces of science and the machine with a religious life strangely divided. On the side of moral and social ideals and attitudes . . . Christianity had already come to terms with the forces of the modern age. . . . On the side of beliefs, however, Christianity in the early 19th century had not come to terms with the intellectual currents of Western society. It found itself, in fact, involved in a profound intellectual reaction against just such an attempt at modernism."

[57]*American Renaissance*.

[58]*The Course of American Democratic Thought* (New York, 1940), Part III.

[59]Henry F. May, *Protestant Churches and Industrial America* (New York, 1949), 263.

[60]Quoted in Jones, *America and French Culture*, 410.

[61]That this was really the case is borne out by Albert Post's study of *Popular Freethought in America, 1825-1850* (New York, 1943). See my review in *Journal of Religion*, XXIV (Oct. 1944), 293-94.

[62]J. L. Diman, "Religion in America, 1776-1876," *North American Review*, CXXII (Jan., 1876), 42. This view is confirmed by Wilhelm Pauck, "Theology in the Life of Contemporary American Protestantism," *The Shane Quarterly*, XIII (April, 1952), 37-50.

[63]See my "Church and State in the United States" a review-article dealing with A. P. Stokes three volumes of that title, in *Religion in Life*, XX (Winter, 1950-51), 41.

[64]I have developed this idea in my review of R. Freeman Butts, *The American Tradition in Religion and Education* (Boston, 1950) in the *Journal of Religion*, XXXII (April, 1952), 141-142.

[65]*Course of American Democratic Thought*, p. 38.

[66]K. S. Latourette, *History of the Expansion of Christianity*, IV, 415.

12

The Republic and the Millennium

James F. Maclear

From the outset, a chief strand in American self-understanding concerned the place of the New World society in universal history. The millennium was the traditional Christian symbol for the culminating period in the process of salvation, and to many the new American republic seemed, in one or another way, to represent that era. Professor James F. Maclear, Department of History, University of Minnesota, Duluth, offers this analysis of these beliefs.

In May 1777 the historian Jeremy Belknap, described by a modern historiographer as "rationalist" and "close in spirit to the modern historian," excitedly turned to Scripture to uncover the true meaning of the American Revolution. Using the best writers on prophecy, he found assurance in Daniel and Revelation that no "rotten toe of Nebuchadnezzar's image" or "proud horn of the seven-headed beast" should ever "exercise dominion over this country."

Neither in method nor in patriotic conclusion was Belknap unique. Other spokesmen of the Revolutionary age also hastened to locate the new American nation in a grand apocalyptic interpretation of universal history, the only conceptual framework acceptable to a people still rooted in the providential assumptions of the English Reformation. In most evangelical

First published in Elwyn A. Smith, ed., *The Religion Of The Republic* (Philadelphia, Fortress Press, 1971), pp. 183-216 (abridged). Reprinted by permission of Fortress Press and the author.

minds this conviction rapidly became part of a complex of religious-political assumptions which long influenced American Protestantism and which helped shape the common national myths of the American people. The nation was an elect people, a new Israel, providentially prepared for a redemptive historical role, bound in covenant with God faithfully to perform his will, and summoned to lead all the nations to a millennial fulfillment. Viewed thus, the American vocation inspired a conjoined patriotic and theocratic emotion. "This country," stressed Samuel Worcester, "which, with such an emphasis of grateful significance we may call *our own,* is still *not our own.* God owns it all. And it is ours only in the covenant of his gracious Providence, that it may be beautified with holiness."[1]

These motifs have long been recognized as central nineteenth century concepts of American self-consciousness and mission. But historians have recently given much greater emphasis to the power of millennial ideas in the Awakening, their role in the Revolution, and their continuing importance in the evolution of American nationhood. Hence it may be appropriate in discussing the religion of the Republic to survey the relation between the mythology of a national redemptive and millennial mission and the shaping of American religion.[2]

The destiny of the American Republic to lead the world to millennial glory was claimed immediately on the birth of the new nation. For men who, under the sway of the Great Awakening, had expected God to bring forth some new stage of universal history in the Western world, the Revolution could be no mere political convulsion. Within a few months of the clash at Lexington, an interpretative literature, chiefly sermons and histories, began to develop, arguing that the Revolution was "big with such consequences of glory or terror" for the whole Christian world that the apocalyptic prophecies might, "not unaptly, be applied to our case, and receive their fulfillment in such providences as are passing over us."[3] With independence, the establishment of the Republic, and victory, the conviction became irresistible that a final and American stage preparatory to the millennium had now commenced. To all these interpreters, the Revolution was the greatest revealing moment since the Reformation, illuminating the past and pointing to a future in which the nations would increasingly adopt "our wisdom, liberty, and happiness," knowledge and religion would be diffused throughout the earth, and mankind would be prepared "for the universal REIGN of the SON OF GOD in the glories of the latter day."[4]

These claims were most commonly presented from pulpits in New England, where they served to revitalize the province's ancient and deep sense of vocation, but they were heard in every section, particularly where the Reformed tradition was strong. Always the same elements were present: the new grasp of divine providences; the conjunction of freedom and religion, twin ideals which America was to preserve, perfect, and propagate through the world; and the assurance of national greatness beyond worldly glory and secular patriotism. Thus, at a time when national consciousness was still half formed, some patriotic divines were advancing a focused historical perspective on the past and a vital and coherent interpretation of national purpose for the future. But despite the rooting of these hopes in the piety of the Awakening, a fundamental change had here passed over the millennial conception itself. An earlier evangelical hope that God's people in America might be granted the spiritual power to prepare the world for Christ's kingdom now passed, in some of these statements, into a conviction of the high destiny of the United States. The millennium was to be related not only to contemporary American history but to the particular political and national structure which American patriots were now erecting.

Despite its importance, the tradition born here has only recently begun to receive serious historical analysis. It is now more than thirty years since Richard Niebuhr published *The Kingdom of God in America* with its brilliant elucidation of one central conception in the development of American religion. But while Niebuhr's work has not been superseded, neither did it attempt detailed treatment of the history and scope of the millennial argument nor deeply examine its political implications. Since then, most of the students of American identity have touched on religious backgrounds, but their interest has been given principally to national destiny and vocation in terms of republican and democratic ideals, and they have seldom been drawn to eschatological literature.[5] Increasingly, however, religious historians studying diverse problems have found it necessary to come to terms with American Protestantism's fascination with the millennium—in colonial thought, in the Awakening and Revolution, and in the evangelism and reforms of the nineteenth century. Finally, E. L. Tuveson, building on his earlier study *Millennium and Utopia,* has most recently sought to evaluate the ideology of the *Redeemer Nation* and place it in the total context of the millennial tradition.[6] From these developing critical accounts, as well as from the vast primary literature, it is now possible to summarize the several factors which contributed importantly to the formation and popularization of this version of the American purpose.

First, throughout the American states, though most definitely in New England, a particular Protestant view of history had long been widespread. This view rested partly on the usual Protestant interpretation of papist apostasy and Reformation renewal of the church and partly on English and Scottish convictions that the British kingdoms harbored a people chosen by God for unusual service in advancing his providential plan.[7] American settlers made their peculiar appropriation of this tradition by impregnating the idea of providential guidance with their own sense of historic mission. Evident even in southern colonial rhetoric, this claim was raised to high art in the New England historical style. Histories of New England were never fundamentally parochial because they were ruled by the conviction that the church in the New World was joined in a historic continuum with the Old Testament patriarchs and the apostles and was leading the people of God in their modern pilgrimage. These assumptions, broadened, amalgamated, invigorated, and politicized by the Revolution, stood behind the popular image of the American Israel, with all its implications of special election, vocation, and guidance. Hence Christian patriots saw nothing incongruous in linking Moses and Winthrop with Washington, who "with his worthy companions and valiant band, were instrumental in the hand of JESUS, the King of Kings, to deliver this American Israel from their troubles."[8]

Second, this self-consciousness was given new dimension by the growing importance and changing meaning of the millennial scheme of history in the eighteenth century. Expectation of a glorious consummation to history, a thousand-year reign of Christ and the saints, was, in orthodox Reformed tradition, primarily a seventeenth century addition to the apocalyptic story.[9] Though capable of causing upheaval, this millennial doctrine had more often served as consolation, promising that though God's people might have to wander until the far-off end of history, Christs's second advent would ultimately banish oppression and suffering and inaugurate the blessed millennium antecedent to the final judgment. But by the end of the eighteenth century, millennial thought was not only more central in theology but had altered in structure, most significantly in the tendency to expect Christ's coming after rather than before the millennial age. Thus the genuine eschatological states did not commence until after the church's enjoyment of the millennial blessing, which was expected within history and which was to be realized by the ordinary means of propagating the gospel in the power of the Spirit. By the same shift the future marked by tribulation, expected by tradition, was transformed into a future of hope, overcoming psychological obstacles to prayers for the swift completion of history. "Postmillennial" exegesis, usually traced to the Anglican scholar Daniel Whitby, was widely disseminated in America through the influence of the great Edwards and his disciples, but even without their recommendations it would have become widespread through such popular English works as those of Moses Lowman, Thomas Scott, Adam Clarke, and David Bogue.[10] Such millennial interpretation had the effect of teaching many Americans to expect some coming perfection of history, achieved by progressive stages, to which comtemporary events, first the Awakening and later the Revolution, must be the prelude.

Third, the evangelical impulse, both in colonial and later revivals, worked a change of emphasis whereby the millennium ceased to be primarily a stage in formal eschatology and instead became the object of intense speculation, anticipation, and longing. Many besides Samuel Hopkins lived "in a region of imagination, feeding on visions of a holiness and happiness which are to make earth all but heaven."[11] This shift from doctrine to popular piety was fundamental in preparing the millennial hope to serve as a dynamic ideology. Further, this very ardor and the visible evidence of the Spirit's work in America suggested both an American location for the millennial dawn and its imminent appearance. That Edwards and others perceived the hoped-for signs in New England conversions is well known. And this perspective gave to all succeeding American events a continuing cosmic importance. Thomas Prince saw the French and Indian War as "opening a way to enlighten the utmost regions of America" preparatory to the millennial reign.[12] Revolutionary preachers in their turn found the prophecies unfolding in the triumph of independence and liberty; their successors discovered them in the growth and perfection of the American Republic. . . .

Finally, the Revolution turned much millennial speculation in the direction of justifying the nation's existence. This development, though immediately appearing, as we have seen, was also powerfully reinforced by a more gradual perception of the full significance of independence. The new nationality, attained in the cultural context of the Enlightenment, presented a double challenge to conservative Protestants and at length evoked a determined and sustained reaction. By the turn of the century a new republican nationalism was becoming defined, and religious leaders were concerned lest this spirit be separated from older religious ideologies, which were often burdened with a narrowly provincial outlook.

To take the most obvious example, what did the Puritan errand into the wilderness mean to the United States? In time, New England as a discrete society and civilization would pass away, just as particular New England values would be submerged in ideals common to the entire American community.[13] Second, the danger appeared to be far more acute when account was taken of the rationalist environment in which the United States had indeed been established. The founding fathers had been little concerned with divine providences and had entrusted no religious role to the Republic. Instead, their utterances had implied a self-created union, invoked by social compact, venerating the rights of man, and following the "simple principles of nature." Yet this Republic claimed a universal appeal in offering a gospel of liberty for all mankind. Religious leaders of the Jeffersonian era were well aware that the natural rights philosophy, originally aristocratic, was now advancing into a popular liberal version of the American purpose. Even without the vulgarizations of the school of Thomas Paine, this version was bound to develop because expositors such as Franklin and Jefferson and revered texts such as the Declaration of Independence stood at the center of the national myth. To sharpen anxiety, the dread example of the infidel nationalism of revolutionary France hovered always in the background. "The crisis, then, has come," said Lyman Beecher in 1812. "By the people of this generation—by ourselves, probably—the amazing question is to be decided, whether the inheritance of our fathers shall be preserved, or thrown away."

In this atmosphere of continuing crisis the older themes of providential creation, covenanted relationship with God, and theocratic mission terminating in millennial glory were elaborately restated and made relevant to the new nation's destiny. The work was aided by the reaction against European rationalism, the powerful evangelical renewal, and the great though gradual realignment of interests whereby sectarian religion abandoned an earlier alliance with rationalists and gravitated toward stronger ties with the conservative churches.[14] The success achieved was only partial, for millennial vocation remained only one explanation of the national role. But it was also enduring. Reverence for the Christian Republic commanding the advance of history toward prophesied millennial blessings won a lasting place beside other American dreams of destiny which were less informed by religious ideals. The millennial version was assured prominence, not only because it reconciled the Republic with revered historic and religious values, but because it was spread by clergymen, authors, and educators possessing a disproportionate influence on cultural life.

Thus, from the very beginning of the nation's existence, providential and millennial themes in American religion offered some check to whatever dangers lay in republican ideology and successfully accommodated the United States in the grand design of religious history. Yet it was ironic that, this having been done, American churches were henceforth bound to regard the nation as having extraordinary religious significance. The American achievement was peculiarly God's handiwork, and American history was evolving into the millennium of Christ. Accordingly, from its inception, the religion of the republic was unusually open to the American experience.

What was the effect of this relation on the course of American religion? Probably the most successful years of postmillennialism in the concept of national mission were those between 1815 and the Civil War. During this era the idea of the redemptive nation may be observed conferring some unity and identity on the pluralistic American religious tradition and reinforcing its activism and optimism. At the same time it is apparent that the millennial hope was itself adjusted and acculturated by common ideas and values. Hence the history of millennial doctrine reflected the broader story of Protestantism's endeavor to penetrate American culture and its reverse penetration by that culture.

The concept of an American Christianity emerged in these years, and to a large degree it rested on the belief in national religious mission. At the Revolution the religious complexion of the colonies was already diversified; it became even more so with the decline of the conservative churches, sectarian expansion, and renewed immigration. The apparent confusion of traditions, polities, and doctrines never failed to perplex foreign observers. But common participation in the American enterprise and common conviction of its millennial denouement gave American churchmen an opportunity for greater unity than that implied in the mutual recognitions of denominational theory. Like the tribes of Israel, the American churches shared a special relation with God and a special destiny on earth which conferred on them a singularity eclipsing their disparate origins, histories, and confessions. It was this common mission which dominated countless Independence Day sermons, inspired the great interdenominational societies, and informed the principal American church histories from Benjamin Trumbull to Leonard Woolsey Bacon.[15]

It seems clear also that commitment to the vision of America as a redemptive instrument strengthened the public activism of evangelical Protestantism. As the bearer of history's promise, the Republic and its political life could never be consigned to a secular sphere free from religious direction. Rather, they were to be progressively perfected and spiritualized, and the religious resources for this task were to be mobilized by expectations of imminent victory. This vision intensified the theocratic determination to keep the United States a Christian republic even though legal ties between church and state were soon broken. The state, though no longer explicitly Christian by confession, would remain so by vocation. In practical terms, this outlook helped preserve religious influence in the ecclesiastically neutral state. The prospect of a millennial perfection to be won through human exertions reinforced, stabilized, and sustained the evangelical impulse, especially during those periods when revival fervor was temporarily on the wane. . . . The prospect before Americans was that of *finishing* the millennial order, fired by the certainty of impending and glorious reward.

Yet as the Civil War approached some observers also noted that the millennium itself had begun to lose religious definition as it had become more entangled in American life. Loss of focus was perhaps inevitable for another reason. Evangelicalism inclined toward emphasis on the conversion of souls as the sufficient basis for the kingdom's coming, and accordingly it less clearly envisioned social structures appropriate for millennial society. While generating reforms, it also tended to accept and then to sanctify basic American institutions and social values. In any case by 1850 Mark Hopkins, weighing the evidence of the coming millennium, significantly joined "the benevolent and reformatory movements" of the time with "the attempt to realize . . . the liberty and rights of the individual man" and "the subjugation of the powers of nature to the use of man."[16] In doing so he confirmed the widespread coalescence of the millennial conception with both the prevailing republican enthusiasm and the cult of progress.

The "republicanism" of American Protestantism, inevitable as the corollary of the idea of the American Israel, rested partly on the ancient assurance that those who covenanted with God covenanted also with one another, and revivalism sought to universalize such covenant membership in the Republic. But after 1815 Protestant republicanism became more rationalized in arguments which attempted to harmonize human and divine sovereignty, natural liberty and Christian dedication. The usual theme was mutal dependence. Just as the hope of a successful experiment in popular government rested on moral restraints that the Bible alone could supply, so also the pure Christianity of the future could thrive only in a republican society where religious freedom and personal decision prevailed. Preachers regularly demonstrated the biblical origins of republican government—Beecher traced the American polity to Moses—and decried the fatal alliance in Europe between authoritarian regimes and degenerate Christianity. These arguments reflected a settled belief that free government was a mark of true religion, while liberty and piety were alike the concerns of the American church.[17] . . .

Even more broadly, the millennial convergence of American and Christian history committed churchmen to pursue religious meanings in the total national experience. The close inspection of American culture which this logic required was incidentally furthered also by the particular cultural situation of the United States in the first half of the nineteenth century. The time was one of impressive technological advance, literary venture, and humanitarian reform, while Western "barbarism" increasingly forced the church to promote civilizing institutions for a new society. Even at the beginning of the century millennial preachers had spoken hopefully of the providential advantages to the gospel of the new developments in science, transportation, and communication, and by 1818 Joseph Emerson's popular account of the millennium prophesied how "every cottage will be irradiated with science, as well as with religion" and "every peasant will be able not only to read the bible but to read the stars."[18]

. . . These various strands were gathered together in the most reasoned and systematic exposition of America's millennial destiny by President Francis Wayland of Brown. In 1830 Wayland, possibly the most influential figure in college education in his time, preached before the American Sunday School Union in Philadelphia. His sermon, "Encouragements to Religious Efforts," has never received the attention given to his 1825 address, *The Duties of an American Citizen,* yet both are essential to his discussion of the American purpose. In his earlier work Wayland had described the American political and religious system—the rule of law and a free Christianity—and contrasted these with European autocracy and Catholic oppression. But revolutions abroad were pressing irresistibly for change, and in the coming reorganization of the world the nations would look to the United States—"the first that taught them to be free; the first that suffered in the contest."[19] The later Philadelphia sermon related the same messianic purpose to a broader analysis of the meaning of the nineteenth century. The physical condition of man, he declared, was undergoing sweeping changes with steam technology, wider distribution of wealth, and increasing leisure for the ordinary man. Similarly, educational reforms were showing how men's minds could be more easily strengthened for rational and moral decision. Together both changes pointed to the coming victory of free government and pure religion in a historic transformation far more important than the Reformation. To the United States fell the glory of leading this wondrous upheaval. There the number of "truly religious persons" was greatest. There "perfect civil and religious freedom" reigned. There sound institutions, religious revivals, and moral societies were molding a new public mind. All the evidence yielded but one conclusion: "Never have there been presented so many or so great encouragements for a universal effort to bring the world into cordial subjection to Jesus Christ." Wayland's peroration disclosed the millennial enthusiasm which sprang from this assessment of the American scene. "Why stand we here all the day idle?" he asked, when with sincere effort

> a revival of piety may be witnessed in every neighbourhood throughout the land; the principles of the Gospel may be made to regulate the detail of individual and national intercourse; and high praises of God may be heard from every habitation; and perhaps before the youth of this generation be gathered to their fathers, there may burst forth upon these highly-favored States the light of Millennial Glory. What is to prevent it? . . . I do believe that the option is put into our hands. It is for us . . . to say, whether the present religious movement shall be onward, until it terminate in the universal triumph of the

Messiah, or whether all shall go back again. . . . The church has for two thousand years been praying "Thy kingdom come." Jesus Christ is saying unto us, "It shall come if you desire it."[20]

With these words—with all of their activist and optimistic undertones—the Americanization of the millennial tradition was far advanced. To many Americans the rapid development of the United States—moral, political, cultural—was now bringing to pass the era foretold in prophecy. In this expectancy, this presumption that America was both the locus and the instrument of the great consummation, lay some of the seeds of the democracy-and-progress faith of later American Christianity.

Beginning about 1840 the millennial ideology relating American Protestantism to the Republic was disturbed by a rapidly mounting crisis. The threat was twofold. First, the structure, survival, and identity of the Republic were brought into question as rising sectional animosities threatened an approaching disruption. And, second, the millennial heritage was itself rendered increasingly insecure through theological changes.

The first trend found expression in the note of uncertainty introduced into sermons and orations on America's role and purpose. Even the repeated assurances that God's former providences proved his future intentions toward the Republic masked an insecurity inspired by the political threat to the Union. The disunity had other effects. It fostered the growth of disparate versions of the once-common faith so that while millennial strivings fired Northern abolitionists, Southern churchmen came to see the national mission as the preservation of slavery and to see covenant-loyalty as an exact regard for the limitations of the general government.[21] And while revivals and crusades continued, politics grew more insistent, antislavery eclipsed other reforms, and churches divided.[22]

More significant was the second trend, the intellectual changes which caused some erosion of the traditional postmillennial doctrine itself. This shift is still largely uninvestigated and must be dealt with speculatively. But it is clear that by the end of the Civil War millennial anticipations in religious literature had often separated from former doctrinal and biblical supports. For this, natural science seems to have been only indirectly responsible. Geology, it is true, had already begun to undermine the reliability of the biblical cosmology, but its controversy tended to fix on Creation and the Genesis account (while its speculations on a final destruction of the earth could be regarded as congenial to traditional eschatology).[23] Another possible influence, the debate over the flamboyant Adventism of the 1840s, has never been properly assessed, but its influence was probably disturbing. That it gave new prominence to premillennial interpretation was perhaps of minor consequence, though some men not otherwise attracted to Millerism were apparently persuaded. Of greater moment may have been the unfavorable publicity which the Adventist movement drew upon the expectation of a millennium. Miller's religious opponents were not skeptics. They equaled him in enthusiasm for the millennium and agreed that the last age had indeed come. Accordingly, they too may have been placed at some disadvantage by prevalent journalistic ridicule.[24] In any case, in the 1840s orthodox references to the millennium tended to become more cautious and defensive, disclaiming sensual delights, precise prediction of times, and "fanaticism." Even the term *millennium* was sometimes replaced by a euphemism.

The most serious undermining of postmillennial eschatology may have been the work of the new biblical critics. American criticism was still in its infancy, but scholars had already provided Daniel and Revelation with historical exposition which related their prophecies to the context of their age. The Adventist sensation compelled critics to write popular explanations asserting, as in the title of Calvin Stowe's tract, "the utter groundlessness of all the millennial arithmetic." Moses Stuart's *Hints on the Interpretation of Prophecy* is the most important example of this literature, since the author's scholarship and orthodoxy were widely respected. . . Further, to know the time of the millennium would destroy endeavor; if its coming were far distant, men would regard labor as vain, and, conversely, if it were divinely ordained for the present age, men would complacently await the miracle. Only through a benevolent ignorance of the time would Christian effort be fruitful. Last, Stuart warned against enthusiastic representations of the millennium induced by biblical imagery. Sin, pain, civil government, ecclesiastical institutions—all would continue, though divine compassion would be shed abroad to an extraordinary degree as well.[25] The effect of [his] interpretation. . . was further to historicize the millennium, remove it from meaningful relation to biblical apocalyptic, and center attention on the march of progress rather than on the glorious termination.

Finally, the decline of traditional postmillennialism was probably related to the appearance of a nascent theological liberalism in the very quarter of the American ministry which had been most articulate in promoting a theocratic patriotism. Though patriotic and optimistic, this liberalism also sought to escape the confinement of biblical or credal literalism. . . .

As a consequence of these factors, the millennial function of the United States seemed to be losing adequate religious basis just at the time when doubts about its secure nationhood and confusion about its role began to perplex. Yet so fundamental were the millennial assumptions of religious people in America that no real breakdown of consensus was evident. The basic concepts continued to receive ritual expression in the 1850s on every appropriate occasion. Then by the 1860s this millennial nationalism was immeasurably deepened by two profound experiences which bestowed new and poignant meaning on God's commission to his American people. In 1858 began the powerful evangelical renewal which enveloped American cities and produced anew a passionate longing for perfection, reform, and the millennial dawn. And second, the American Civil War re-created an intense emotional commitment to the Union and to its responsibility for the renovation of the world. In the vast sermon literature of the war all the earlier themes were once again heard, charged with new sincerity and conviction. God's judgment on his people was truly righteous, cleansing and purging were necessary for his future service, but the baptism by blood was also a reanointing for the task of fulfilling his will in history. When men heard Lincoln invoke "this last, best hope of earth" and armies sang "Mine eyes have seen the glory of the coming of the Lord," the two experiences merged into a single faith.[26]

Thus it is not possible to dismiss this consecration of the Republic with the passing of the older, antebellum America. Just after the war Henry Ward Beecher—patriot, liberal, progressive—gave expression to the persistent millennialism (coupled with indifference to doctrine) of Protestants of the new age: "We must believe . . . that somehow 'in the ages to come' when there is a new heaven and a new earth, righteousness will dwell in them. By what road we are coming to it, by what process the work shall be done, we cannot say. . . . If it be not the literal millennial glory which men have counted upon, it will be in some form the substance of which that is a sign and symbol."[27] A long epilogue was beginning in which attenuated but modernized millennial patterns would continue to invest the Republic with religious meaning.

Discrete millennial themes in the national culture are more difficult to trace in the modern period. On the one hand, American nationalism finally was rendered pervasive and secure by the Civil War. Just as the older Federalism disappeared in a new and unprecedented assertion of central power, the former dedication to the Union gave way to a novel but irresistible sense of organic unity. This nationalism no longer had the same need for the older mythic unity supported by religious sanctions. Henceforth patterns of religious patriotism might still prove comfortable embellishments to nationalism, but they would not again serve as a resource of critical importance. Moreover, the sweeping transformations in America's society and world position in the later nineteenth century independently assured the prominence of "progressive" motifs in any national self-appraisal. Mastery of machine technology, the rise of northern wealth, population increase, the great-power role in global politics—all these made inevitable the expectation of an advancing triumph even without the aid of the religious tradition. On the other hand, while faith in a coming era of the Lord remained fervent in large areas of the Protestant community, such faith generally ceased to rely on the language, doctrine, or exegesis of Scripture prophecy. While some persons professed confusion or indifference concerning the means of the kingdom's advent, others tended to reclothe the millennial faith in organic imagery, relying on such appropriate biblical allusions as the parable of the mustard seed. This change had decided apologetic advantages. Friction with science and biblical criticism was avoided, and religious faith was brought closer to the idiom of the prevailing Darwinism. But in the process Protestant liberalism tended to draw even closer to culture, lose independent religious insight, and become preoccupied with progress of every kind—biological, technological, and cultural, as well as spiritual and moral. Hence its persistent millennial motif could not readily be distinguished from progressive assumptions arising from Darwin or Spencer.

Because of these conditions, the primary characteristic of a millennial ingredient in the American sense of mission in the modern era was its diffuseness. And this very diffuseness facilitated its adaptability and ready integration with other modern trends in American Christianity. While the various modifications comprehended much of the history of liberal theology, it is possible here only to select for brief emphasis three features of this modernization of the tradition.

First, though the religious impetus after the Civil War stemmed from the evangelical revival, the dominant theological course in the middle-class churches was set by the "New Theology" which developed under the leadership of such nationally known preachers as Henry Ward Beecher and Phillips Brooks. Sensitive to the religious problems raised by recent scholarship, this school was eager to state a Protestant view of history in terms that were modern, "philosophical," and congenial to the age. This they attempted to do by stressing such ideas as divine immanence, the fruition of the divine purpose in the natural order, and the redemptive character of the cultural process. When they appropriated the millennial inheritance, they found its affirmation of "progress" appealing, but often inclined to place it in a natural context rather than preserve or reconstruct its scriptural basis. In doing so they achieved the ultimate historicization of the millennium. The millennial blessing was no longer beckoning at the end of the human story but was located in the inexorably progressive tendencies of history itself. Furthermore, in relying on a universal redemptive process, this restatement tended to become vague about the role of Christianity and the church. All humanity, rather than the people of God, was pressing toward a perfection that was more than spiritual. In this work the nation, representing the entire community, could be a more appropriate redemptive organ than the church.[28]

Consequently, Protestant liberals were ready to embrace and expand the idea of American leadership in the total cultural ascent of mankind, an idea which had been heard even before the war. Impressed by the triumphs of nineteenth century progress, they also sensed that the United States was now destined to become the master and leader of modern civilization. Hence they expressed enthusiasm for all aspects of the new America—its machines and wealth, its democracy, its popular culture, and its religion. . . .

Second, late nineteenth century Protestants, no less than their antebellum predecessors, were preoccupied with the quest for a Christian America. The modernization of this pursuit which led, practically, to such experiments as the institutional church or the YMCA also led, theoretically, to urgent redefinitions of the Republic's redemptive work in the contemporary world. These versions owed much to the profoundly evangelical backgrounds of many Protestant liberals and to the new focus in religious thought on the kingdom of God as a comprehensive biblical concept adequate to ground undiminished "postmillennial" expectations. They attained prominence because they attempted to make traditional beliefs relevant to the new American conundrum—the paradoxical fulfillment of national strength and vitality for remaking the world at the very time when a new industrial and pluralistic society jeopardized the old Protestant America. Past testimony about the nation's universal role had included both the foreign missions emphasis on world crusade and a more isolationist but equally evangelical stress on America as a providential refuge and example of true Christianity.

So it was again. Classic modern expressions of these versions were supplied by Josiah Strong and Washington Gladden.

Strong wrote partly in response to the expansionist mood of the late nineteenth century, when the country had begun to take seriously its global role and opinion had became more cosmopolitan, aware of the conflict of cultures and the "competition of races." But his rise to prominence was also closely related to conservative America's confrontation with the alien cultures of the "new immigration," neither Anglo-Saxon nor Protestant in composition. Once again inherited values were likely to be lost, and once again Protestant America was ready to respond to an enthusiastic portrayal of the religious mission of the Republic.

Strong's *Our Country* (1885) has been analyzed many times. What has not always been recognized is its skill in blending traditional and modern thought. In the main the message was the ritual one: evangelize both the (urban) frontier at home and foreign lands with the twin gospel that would perfect the world—free government and pure Christianity. God's providential care, the chosen race, the world mission, the critical hour, the appeal for action—all were part of the established antebellum pattern. What was new was the modern intellectual context in which these were placed by his fresh assessment of America's contemporary situation, more "scientific" social survey, and notorious adoption of fashionable Darwinian language concerning the competitive struggle of races. Strong's hope for the future rested on Protestant Saxondom, of which the United States was the effective instrument. Soon this race, led by a divinely prepared Republic, "with all the majesty of numbers and the might of wealth behind it—the representative, . . . of the largest liberty, the purest Christianity, the highest civilization—having developed peculiarly aggressive traits calculated to impress its institutions upon mankind will spread itself over the earth." Some peoples and cultures would suffer extinction, but the ultimate effect would be admirable as well as inevitable. Indeed, "our plea is not America for America's sake; but America for the world's sake." And though Strong addressed his appeal to Christians of the United States, he saw the American nation as the chief means to this end. "For, if this generation is faithful to its trust, America is to become God's right arm in his battle with the world's ignorance and oppression and sin."[29]

In obscuring the distinction between church and world, glorifying American humanity, and trusting in the ascending impulse of history, Strong revealed his debt to newer theological fashions. When in a much later volume he presented a bill of particulars against premillennialism, he made his own modernized millennialism even clearer. That unworthy creed, he complained, was "hostile to the scientific spirit" and to biblical criticism, unsympathetic to "modern culture and the new civilization," "skeptical of all progress," and "hopeless as to the success of God's moral government of the world." Instead, Strong taught, "the coming of Christ is progressive, and is hastened by all true progress in the world."[30]

Gladden, like Strong, was a pioneer in the social gospel, but his emphasis fell more on the revival of another millennial theme, that of the exemplary nation. Though basically optimistic, many Protestant liberals were troubled by the evidence of social injustice and distress accompanying the adolescent industrial capitalism of the United States. Hence they returned to the plea for national righteousness, seeking now the perfection of the American community through moderation of competition and adherence to justice, service, and brotherhood. In achieving this harmony, the nation would enlighten all mankind. They, like their forebears, still expected the United States to conduct all peoples to the kingdom. . . .[31]

Last, modern versions of the nation's millennial destiny were no longer exclusively, nor—in time—even predominantly, the property of Protestant heirs of the tradition. By its very diffuseness modern "millennialism" had been readily absorbed by Americans of every creed or none in the increasingly pluralistic post-Civil War society. It mattered little that thousands were Catholic or Jewish, unchurched "Protestants" or premillennial fundamentalists. All could share the inchoate conviction that the Republic constituted a divinely favored nation, fundamentally honest in a guilty world, doing God's will and fulfilling a worthy mission in directing all peoples to democracy, progress, and civilization. While a long succession of clerical and rabbinical patriots voiced these ideas, the real beneficiary was the "fourth faith," the growing phenomenon of generalized religion clustering about American democracy. Though certainly not new, this democratic faith had become more visible in the twentieth century as a genuinely catholic confession for Americans troubled by religious pluralism, the decline of the churches, and finally the subsidence of the older Protestant nationalism.[32]

Here statesmen and journalists, guardians of the public faith, were the appropriate evangelists. Always present in patriotic editorial and public ritual, this faith became most explicit when threatened. During World War II, in the only sermon ever composed by federal bureaucracy, clergy of all faith were instructed to show how "free men in the excellent fellowship of faith, we can go forward not only to create a nation dedicated to liberty but to build a world of brotherhood fit to be called the Kingdon of God."[33] The subsequent cold war contest with "godless communism" offered further opportunitites for recital of America's mission to advance God's will for democracy, civil and religious freedom, and international harmony. "You know what makes America great?" asked Richard Nixon in 1960.

> What makes her great is not our military strength, nor our economic richness, but the fact that we believe in the right things—our faith—our faith in God, our faith in the rights of man; that those rights to freedom, to independence, don't come from men, but come from God, and, therefore, can never be taken away by any man; our belief that America came into the world 180 years ago not just to have freedom for ourselves, but carry it to the whole world. . . . Strengthen the faith of America. See that our young people grow up with faith in God, recognizing that this is a great country, recognizing that the ideals that we have belong not just to us, but to the world, recognizing that America has a mission, and that mission is to keep the peace. That mission is to stand for freedom for ourselves and for others as well. That mission is to lead the world

to a world in which all men can live together in friendship, in which all men can have the right to worship God, in which all men can have freedom.

And Nixon, fresh from travels across the country, claimed universality for "this belief, this idealism of the American people, . . . a shining idealism that I see . . . on the faces of millions throughout America."[34]

"American religion is distinctive . . . precisely for the fact that the aspirations it nurtured have found profane embodiments."[35] This thesis may find fresh support in the career of the millennial idea. Today, faith in America's world-redemptive mission is largely a secularized confidence, without sense of grace or judgment alike, while religious opinion, distrustful of the earlier easy nationalism and utopianism, has all but abandoned the theme. Yet for over a century the idea of the elect Republic played a significant role in imparting a distinctive quality to American religion.

Its success in winning this consensus was in large measure related to its breadth and utility. To the novelty and rootlessness of American history it brought a compensating historical grandeur. On diverse peoples and churches it conferred a unifying trust. By it the dynamic of theocratic reform and the conservative instinct were held together. Men labored zealously for the coming kingdom, yet the coming kingdom also affirmed the worth of existing institutions as acceptable bases for the growth to perfection. Most importantly, it seemed to balance and join divergent aspects of national experience—convictions of divine and human sovereignty, theocracy and liberty, providence and nature, reverence for the Pilgrim fathers and for the founding fathers.

In substance, that career underscores an essential continuity in American religion throughout the nineteenth century. Recent reinterpretation of church history has stressed the integrity of the period between the Second Awakening and the Great Depression, despite the "great divide" of the Civil War.[36] Here was the search for a Christian America, and the vision of the nation as "protomillennium" gave verve and confidence to the quest. At length, however, the great change came. Religious recession in the 1920s signaled a coming transformation, prevailing liberal assumptions fell victim to the disastrous succession of twentieth century calamities and a new theological realism, and America passed into the post-Protestant decades.[37]

By the 1960s the relation of American Christianity to a partially deconsecrated Republic was not yet clear, nor had credible new forms of national or religious self-identification been established. Although religious testimony varied, it seemed that the churches generally expressed a new critical and theological awareness fatal to visions of worldly millennia or national innocence and were more genuinely sensitive to the limits of history and the failures of men and institutions. Correspondingly, there appeared to be some growing recognition that the passing of the older myth offered fresh opportunities for recovering a sense of the integrity of the Christian community and redefining the church's relation to the general culture. From that vantage point Americans could look back with some detachment, wonder, and perhaps nostalgia on the deep sense of special vocation and promise long confessed in their churches:

> BEHOLD the expected time draw near,
> The shades disperse, the dawn appear;
> Behold the wilderness assume
> The beauteous tints of Eden's bloom.[38]

NOTES

[1]Michael Kraus, *The Writing of American History* (Norman: University of Oklahoma Press, 1953), pp. 73-74. Jeremy Belknap, *A Sermon Delivered on the Ninth of May, 1798* (Boston, 1798), pp. 17-19. However, Belknap did not identify Christ's kingdom with the American state. Samuel M. Worcester, *Our Country and Our Work* (Salem, 1843), pp. 7-8.

[2]This essay surveys only one strand of the incredibly rich postmillennial tradition in America. I have made no effort to view the place of millennial thinking in the various utopian and communitarian experiments or in such enduring churches as the Mormons, the Campbellites, or the Jehovah's Witnesses. This sketch principally treats articulate spokesmen of middle-class Protestant denominations—often ministers, professors, or college presidents of Presbyterian, Congregational, Episcopal, Methodist, or Baptist backgrounds. Because of the Puritan heritage of mission and the New England predominance in much of the life and thought of these denominations, representatives from this area have figured more prominently. Lastly, it should not be supposed that all enthusiasts for the millennium reserved distinction therein for the United States. Yet the views described in this essay were so common as to be almost canonical.

[3]See, e.g., Samuel Sherwood, *The Church's Flight into the Wilderness* (New York, 1776), p. 18. This sermon was preached on January 17, 1776.

[4]Benjamin Trumbull, *A Sermon Delivered at North-Haven December 11, 1783* (New Haven, 1784), p. 22.

[5]H. Richard Niebuhr, *The Kingdom of God in America* (Chicago: Willett, Clark, & Co., 1937).

[6]Ernest Lee Tuveson's *Millennium and Utopia: A Study in the Background of the Idea of Progress* (Berkeley: University of California Press, 1949) and *Redeemer Nation: The Idea of America's Millennial Role* (Chicago: University of Chicago Press, 1968) provide the best guide to the evolution of the millennial tradition. However, these works are brief interpretations, and a comprehensive examination of millennial literature and argument still awaits an author.

[7]See William Haller, ed., *The Book of Martyrs and the Elect Nation* (New York: Fernhill House, 1963).

[8]Seth Stetson, *The Substance of a Discourse Preached in the Second Parish, Plymouth, December 22, 1806* (Boston, 1807), p. 7.

[9]Its entry into the English orthodox Reformed tradition may be the Savoy Declaration's promise that "in the later days . . . the Churches of Christ being inlarged, and edified through a free and plentiful communication of light and grace, shall enjoy in this world a more quiet, peaceable, and glorious condition than they

have enjoyed." See chapter 26, "Of the Church," in Williston Walker, *The Creeds and Platforms of Congregationalism* (New York, 1893), p. 396. The Westminster Confession does not so hint at a millennium.

[10]This statement of the alteration of millennial doctrine in the eighteenth century is much simplified. For fuller accounts of changing interpretation with reference to biblical commentary, see Miller, "The End of the World," in *Errand into the Wilderness*, Tuveson, *Redeemer Nation*, pp. 26-73; Froom, *The Prophetic Faith*, 2:640-796, 3:9-259; C. C. Goen, "Jonathan Edwards: A New Departure in Eschatology," *Church History*, vol. 28, no. 1 (1959), pp. 25-40.

[11]The characterization was that of William Ellery Channing, in his *Works*, 10th ed. (Boston: American Unitarian Assn., 1849), p. 427. For Hopkins' "Treatise on the Millennium," see *The Works of Samuel Hopkins*, D.D., 3 vols. (Boston, 1852), 2:223-364. The work was dedicated "TO THE PEOPLE WHO SHALL LIVE IN THE DAYS OF THE MILLENNIUM."

[12]Thomas Prince, *Six Sermons* (Edinburgh, 1785), p. 28.

[13]The attempt to broaden the New England tradition to embrace the United States is apparent in Stetson, *The Substance of a Discourse:* "It is probable that no nation under heaven resembles God's chosen Israel, more than the United States of America; especially New England" (p. 4).

[14]Beecher, *Works*, 2:99-102.

[15]Benjamin Trumbull's *General History of the United States of America* (Boston, 1810) bore the subtitle, *Sketches of the Divine Agency, in Their Settlement, Growth, and Protection, and Especially in the Late Revolution;* Leonard Woolsey Bacon, *A History of American Christianity* (New York, 1895), p.2.

[16]See Emerson Davis, *The Half-Century* (Boston, 1851), p. xvi.

[17]Beecher, *Works*, 1: 176, 331; 2: 92-95.

[18]Joseph Emerson, *Lectures on the Millennium* (Boston, 1818), p. 18.

[19]Francis Wayland, *The Duties of an American Citizen* (Boston, 1825), esp. pp. 19-25.

[20]Francis Wayland, "Encouragements to Religious Efforts," in *American National Preacher*, vol. 5, no. 3 (1830), esp. pp. 39-46.

[21]See, e.g., *The Collected Writings of James Henry Thornwell, D. D., LL.D.* (Richmond, 1873), 4: 510-48; and B. M. Palmer, *Slavery a Divine Trust* (New York, 1861), pp. 6-7.

[22]Note the dirge of Laurens P. Hickock, *A Nation Saved from Its Prosperity Only by the Gospel* (New York, 1853).

[23]See discussion in Arthur Alphonse Ekirch, *The Idea of Progress in America, 1815-1860,* Studies in History, Economics, and Public Law (New York: Columbia University Press, 1944), pp. 120-25; Conrad Wright, "The Religion of Geology," *New England Quarterly*, 14 (1941): 335-58.

[24]See discussion in Froom, *The Prophetic Faith*, 4:738-60; Francis David Nichol, *The Midnight Cry: A Defense of William Miller and the Millerites* (Washington: Review & Herald Pub. Assn., 1944), pp. 427-53.

[25]Calvin Stowe, *Letter to R. D. Mussey, M.D., on the Utter Groundlessness of All the Millennial Arithmetic* (Cincinnati, 1843); Moses Stuart, *Hints on the Interpretation of Prophecy* (Andover, 1842), pp. 140-42.

[26]See William A. Clebsch, *Christian Interpretations of the Civil War* (Philadelphia: Fortress Press, 1969); William John Wolf, *The Almost Chosen People:*

A Study of the Religion of Abraham Lincoln (Garden City: Doubleday & Co., 1959); and Smith, *Revivalism and Social Reform*, pp. 63 ff.

[27]Henry Ward Beecher, "The Ages to Come" (preached April 30, 1871), in *The Sermons of Henry Ward Beecher, in Plymouth Church, Brooklyn*, Sixth Series (New York, 1872), pp. 160-61.

[28]Winthrop Still Hudson provides useful summaries of "New Theology" in *The Great Tradition of the American Churches* (New York: Harper & Bros., 1953), pp. 157-94, and in *Religion in America* (New York: Charles Scribner's Sons, 1965), pp. 263-76.

[29]Josiah Strong, *Our Country* (New York, 1885), pp. 213-18, 253-54; Henry Farnham May, *Protestant Churches and Industrial America* (New York: Harper & Bros., 1949), pp. 113-16.

[30]Josiah Strong, *The New World-Religion* (New York, 1915), pp. 284-85, 299.

[31]The postmillennial fervor of the social gospel is apparent in James Dombrowski, *Early Days of Christian Socialism in America* (New York: Columbia University Press, 1936), pp. 22ff.; and Charles Howard Hopkins, *The Rise of the Social Gospel in American Protestantism, 1865-1915*, Studies in Religious Education, 14 (New Haven: Yale University Press, 1940).

[32]See Martin E. Marty, *The New Shape of American Religion* (New York: Harper & Row, 1959), pp. 67 ff. for analysis. A sophisticated plea for democratic religion is in J. Paul Williams, *What Americans Believe and How They Worship* (New York: Harper & Bros., 1952), pp. 363-75.

[33]The sermon outline, entitled "Religion and Democracy," was issued by the U.S. Office of Civilian Defense, November 3, 1941. It sought to demonstrate that (1) religion is the source of democracy; (2) democracy gives religion its best opportunities; and (3) democracy and religion can together build the good society. The text is printed in Anson Phelps Stokes, *Church and State in the United States*, 3 vols. (New York: Harper & Bros., 1950), 3:893 ff.

[34]Richard M. Nixon, in a speech at Wheaton College Field, Illinois, on October 29, 1960, published in *The Final Report of the Committee on Commerce, United States Senate . . . . Part II: The Speeches, Remarks, Press Conferences, and Study Papers of Vice President Richard M. Nixon, August 1 through November 7, 1960* (Washington: Government Printing Office, 1961), p. 878.

[35]William A. Clebsch, *From Sacred to Profane America: The Role of Religion in American History* (New York: Harper & Row, 1968), p. 14.

[36]See Robert T. Handy, *The Protestant Quest for a Christian America, 1830-1930* (Philadelphia: Fortress Press, 1967); and Winthrop Still Hudson, *American Protestantism* (Chicago: University of Chicago Press, 1961).

[37]Paul A. Carter, *The Idea of Progress in Most Recent American Protestant Thought, 1930-1960* (Philadelphia: Fortress Press, 1969).

[38]*Psalms and Hymns Adapted to Social, Private, and Public Worship in the Presbyterian Church in the United States of America* (Philadelphia, 1843), hymn 561.

13

The Second Great Awakening as an Organizing Process, 1780-1830

Donald G. Mathews

The religious ferment of the early national period was so pronounced that the period became identified as the second *Great Awakening. Professor Donald Mathews, Department of History at the University of North Carolina, Chapel Hill, proposes that this event must be interpreted as an important aspect of the formation of the new nation.*

The "Second Great Awakening" is one of those happily vague generalizations which American historians use every now and again to describe a movement whose complexity eludes precision. The term usually includes monumental changes such as the "break-up of Calvinism," an event which, like the thawing of northern rivers in the spring, heralded a new burst of creativity, energy and warmth. The Awakening is also understood as a conservative assertion of a new mode of religious authority by ministers who, fearful of losing their traditional role in New England society, tried to tame the rising democracy. It provided new channels not only for social control, but also for social service which some scholars have said was but a manifestation of the former. It burned in white-hot emotionalism in Kentucky, spreading along the frontier like a prairie fire, sweeping even beyond the backfires set by cautious seaboard ecclesiastics who had hoped to control it. It was an expansion of religious feeling unknown in American history.

First published in the *American Quarterly*, XXI (1969), pp. 23-43. Reprinted by permission of the *American Quarterly*, published by The University of Pennsylvania. Copyright, 1969, Trustees of the University of Pennsylvania.

To be able to say so much about the Awakening might be taken as evidence that it is not such a vague term after all. Yet there are too many unsettling things about the literature relating to it to conclude that present interpretations are sufficiently comprehensive. The difficulties are a mixture of too much emphasis upon the truly intricate and challenging intellectual problems of the New England theology, and a certain awesome impressionability in regard to the non-rational phenomena of revivalism in the burned-over districts of New York and Vermont, and the camp meeting grounds of the South and West. In fact, it is emotionalism and devout piety, heart over reason, commitment as opposed to disinterestedness which characterizes the revival for many scholars. And it is its impact upon Congregationalist-Presbyterian dogmas of "inability" which invites the scrutiny of intellectual historians who quite rightly are concerned with the metamorphosis of ideas. Considering both these problems, historians of American religion have, by and large, been interested in one or two aspects of the Second Great Awakening—either its western phase or its New England manifestations. To be sure, some, perhaps most, have identified both as in some way being a part of the other because they both included revivals and because leaders of both were interested in each others' activities as evidence of the power of God. Impressed by the changes which the revivals forced upon theological discussion, most historians consider the Second Great Awakening a transformation from Predestinarianism to Arminianism. And at this point they often discuss the tracts defending revivalism written in the 1830's by such moderate Presbyterians as William B. Sprague. The "heroes" of this transformation are Timothy Dwight who saved Yale from infidelity, Nathaniel William Taylor who made the intellectual shift from inability to commitment possible, and Lyman Beecher, political prophet of the new American church. In spite of a few observations reserved for acknowledging the emotionalism of Baptists and the circuit riding of Methodists, students of the Second Great Awakening have usually explained it from the viewpoint of one theological tradition. Most historians apparently assume, Timothy L. Smith to the contrary notwithstanding, that the Holy Spirit came to the New World by way of Geneva, Cambridge and Boston only.[1]

Another major problem with conventional views of the Second Great Awakening is that they focus rather persistently upon revivalism as an emotional or intellectual problem. The spectacular character of revivals as exceptional outbursts in a presumably otherwise undramatic process of ecclesiastical development has encouraged historians to explain the Second Great Awakening as characterized primarily by revivals. They cite outbursts in Vermont, and never fail to examine the Cane Ridge Revival of 1803 when literally thousands of people met in a model of evangelistic activity that affected the vision of the western churches for years afterward. It is assumed that revivals in the West were the same as revivals in New England. It is assumed that churchmen, impressed as they were by such phenomena, believed that the great revival was the proper goal of ministerial activity and therefore epitomized the Awakening. Now, to be sure, churchmen such as

Francis Asbury wanted great revivals; they were depressed when there seemed to be a lack of religious intensity, when revivals did not occur, and people were "dead" to religion. But many of them also realized what scholars have overlooked; namely, that revivals are a *re*-vitalizing of religion, a repeat performance, that they do not introduce religion into a region, that it is simply impossible to have a revival unless there is some institutional and ideational framework that has provided a meaningful context for the revival in the first place. That is, one cannot have a revival without churches. Furthermore, church life simply cannot be sustained psychologically in a constant state of excitation; the institutional framework is necessary to maintain the everyday life of a Christian community. Thus the sporadic revival, although an interesting phenomenon, might possibly be a ritualistic dramatization of religious life necessary to sustain the hopes of the clergy and to relieve the anxieties of the laity and still not be the basic, essential peculiarity of the Second Great Awakening. One might possibly better ask how the churches got established in the first place.

A major reason for believing that revivalism was not the quintessence of the Second Great Awakening is that the phenomenon had appeared before in the First Great Awakening. That outburst had worked something of a crisis in colonial society by bringing many people, through the confirmation of their own experience, into what seemed to be a more significant relationship with the church. The leadership of the movement had been diverse and somewhat incongruous—the brilliant theologian, Jonathan Edwards; the errant priest and Methodist, George Whitefield; and that unbelievable reincarnation of Amos, James Davenport of Long Island. These men, and others, quickened the revival with the help of improved communications, public curiosity, a sense of social rebellion and those psychological tensions which in the right context increased the susceptibility of crowds. Picturing human destiny in such a way as to induce guilt and fear and then offering means of release from resulting anxieties, revivalists brought many people to an emotional and religious experience. The news of one outburst of religious emotion raised expectations of another and made more people susceptible to the same excitement elsewhere. Wherever the eloquent Whitefield went he seemed to bring Pentecost again, and soon there were various facsimiles of the revivalist, making the Awakening very general indeed.

New churches were organized outside the establishment because the revived Christians thought that the visible church should be a holy community based not on geography but repentance and faith in Christ. Congregationalists separated in New England, the dissidents providing a later increase among the Baptists. Presbyterians divided in the middle colonies, and both they and the Baptists helped maintain revivalism by sending missionaries to Virginia. Those missionaries provided a link between the First and Second Awakenings. Samuel Davies almost singlehandedly kept evangelical Presbyterian theology and faith active in Virginia, but he and his few brethren were never so effective as the Separate Baptists. These enthusiasts made many people, whom the establishment could not reach, into participating members of society at large in an age when church membership provided social as well as religious standing. By their annoying ubiquity and visibility they also accustomed the people of Virginia and North Carolina to the language and values of evangelical Christianity. This revivalist process was intensified in the middle 1770's by the Methodists who, had they been solely Virginian would have continued to be part of a provincial revival. They were, however, on the way to becoming more national than any of the other sects in the sense that they soon spread, unevenly at first, over the entire United States. And while they had many characteristics in common with the revivalists of the First Great Awakening, they possessed one important difference. From the end of hostilities with Great Britain they were intent upon organizing the revival in a new way as we shall see.

Since revivalism, because of its persistence since the middle of the 18th century, could not be a distinguishing innovation of the Second Great Awakening, the social historian must look elsewhere. That revivalism in the Second Great Awakening developed differently from the First, is of course true, but the development was not so significantly different as to require a distinction between the two eras of social history. What was different was the social function of each Awakening. Whereas the First demanded a rethinking of church authority without subsequent general expansion of the churches, the Second Awakening was most noticeable in the undeniable quantitative fact that the Methodist and Baptist sects were not restructuring church life so much as extending it—they were recruiting new Christians by the tens of thousands. By the time of Alexis de Tocqueville's celebrated tour of the United States, evangelical religion was widespread—the statement is a truism of American historiography. What is clearly lacking in the literature that deals with the period of the Second Great Awakening, however, is a successful explanation of the origins and process of mass evangelization prior to 1825. Seymour Martin Lipset, in his study of the first new nation, exemplifies the problem. He maintains that Americans have always been religious and to prove it tries to demonstrate that nearly everyone in Tocquevillian America was either a church member or "constituent." (The rest were presumably backsliders who owned taverns, kept their stores open on Sunday, or secretly read Tom Paine while everyone else was at church.) What is surprising and not a little distressing about Lipset's study of a changing and growing new nation is that he never explained how it got to be so religious.[2] Perhaps it never actually was; but Lipset's problem is that of most students of Jacksonian religion. No one is really sure just how the Second Great Awakening began or why it continued over so long a period of time.

A search for the social origins and context of the Second Great Awakening need not imply a diminution of interest in theological change or ecclesiastical adjustment. But it does imply that there may be social components in the Second Great Awakening which have nothing to do with theological issues. It is, in fact, the thesis of this paper that one of the major determinants of the Second Great Awakening was irrelevant to theological issues and can be studied apart from them, that the Awakening in its social aspects was an organizing process that helped to give meaning and direction to people suffering in various degrees from the social strains of a nation on the move into new political, economic and geographical areas.

A short article cannot provide a definitive statement about the Awakening, but it may suggest where we now are in scholarship and where we could profitably go. Fortunately, historians labor not only under the burdens outlined above but also with keen insights bequeathed them by some of their more incisive predecessors. We are aware, for example, that the Second Great Awakening was characterized by *unity*, as well as *organization*, and demonstrated the dynamics of a *movement*. The first of these marks of the Awakening, unity, was discussed by Perry Miller, who, in two separate studies, described the emergence and character of the evangelical foundations of American thought. The process began with the Revolution which was preached from the pulpits of patriotic clergymen with what, theologically speaking, was disastrous success. Interpreting the world from the assumption of covenant theology, the preachers explained the Revolution and King George as afflictions placed upon Americans for their sins. These afflictions could be removed by acts of contrition and monumental exertion coupled with faith in the mercy of Almighty God who promised judgment upon the wicked and victory for the virtuous. When the Americans won, it was not terribly difficult for them to guess who the virtuous were. The preachers in their Whiggish enthusiasm had "committed themselves unwittingly to the proposition that . . . expulsion of the British would automatically leave America a pure society." Pure society or no, Americans still suffered afflictions thought to be sent by the French Revolution but actually resulting from internal social change with its accompanying anxieties and frustrations. Frightened, the pious turned to save themselves with the Revival, rewriting the history of the Revolution to make it a "protest of native piety against foreign impiety." In preaching this new revival, American "Protestantism" hoped to reaffirm the faith and meet the threat of barbarism that it perceived in the opening of the West. The significant result of this shift was the abandonment of the idea of national covenant and the adoption of "Protestant solidarity by the main force of spiritual persuasion." Only in this way could the cultural unity of America be achieved. And in the process, the Revival jerked men away from the covenant's preoccupation with what had been to a glorious vision of what might be.[3] Miller's synthesis was imaginative but it lacked precision. He thought of American Protestantism as having the presumed unity of New England theology, but it is extremely doubtful that even New England acted so purposefully as did his "Protestantism" in moving from the covenant to the revival. As an intellectual model, Miller's essay is brilliant and stimulating; as historical explanation, it leaves out the social patterns and untidy non-intellectual events of the Second Great Awakening.

In his posthumously published intellectual history of developing America, Miller discussed the revival as one of the major events of the 19th century. Observing that New England's Second Awakening was a "local phenomenon," he was nevertheless tangled in the basic problems of New England theology. At the heart of the Revival, he said, was the resolution to escape "the trammels of 'inability.' "[4] Certainly that was true of Presbyterian and Congregationalist revivalists like Finney, but not of hundreds of their predecessors who, although religious, were far from being theological. Miller's Great Revival of the pre-Civil War generation, broad in conception as it is, is still an analysis of the intellectual metamorphosis of but one strain of American religious history which was never so predominant in the South, West and Chesapeake area as it was in New England. The process was important for the history of American thought, but of less consequence for the development of American society than the revivals triggered and led by men whose reverence for American Calvinism was little greater than their meager knowledge of it. There is no denying, however, that Miller's main point is as well taken as it was made. American religious history, broken into denominationalism, has often neglected the essential unity of ecclesiastical-social development.[5]

In addition to unity, the Second Great Awakening is known to have exhibited the marks of a vast process of *organization* which William Warren Sweet described. Although tending to believe that in America Christianity had been "frontierized," Sweet also emphasized the reverse effect—how the churches tamed the frontier. However much abused he may be for his fascination with the West, Sweet understood the remarkable growth of the evangelical churches as something more than a purely religious phenomenon. The churches were also socializing institutions, helping to create a new society out of the frontier, but Sweet left later scholars to fuse these two aspects into a thoroughly integrated interpretation.[6] Although Sweet's involvement with the Awakening on Turner's frontier did not blind him to the necessity of trying to connect it with the revivals in the East, he actually did little more than mention that the two were going on at the same time. Nor did he ever really come to grips with why people might have been drawn to the churches although he knew that it had something to do with the displacement of the westward movement.

T. Scott Miyakawa has tried to explain the latter problem in his suggestive book, *Protestants and Pioneers: Individualism and Conformity on the American Frontier,* a study which will facilitate a re-evaluation of the Second Great Awakening. By strengthening many of Sweet's contributions and correcting some of his faults, Miyakawa has, through sociological analysis, brought illuminating insight to the study of American religious history. Emphasizing the evangelical socialization of the Old Northwest, he has shown how the churches provided elementary "disciplined formal organizations" which created a society accustomed to working through voluntary associations for common goals. The churches were the most effective organizations of acculturation in the West, using their power through a kind of group therapy and social control to make normative the evangelical ideal of egalitarianism and the democratic prejudice of anti-intellectualism. One may argue with some of Miyakawa's assumptions and conclusions, or even crankily complain about his avoidance of "original sources," but he has nevertheless demonstrated how, in a mobile society, the churches could become for a great many people the focus of "individual integration" and "social unity."[7] Since the evangelical sects were growing so rapidly throughout the United States between 1780-1830, they may well have provided similar functions in other areas.

The third mark of the Awakening, which could well include the other two, is its characteristic as a *movement*. This category is suggested by the writings of one of the most imaginative of the scholars who have wrestled with the meaning of American Christianity, H. Richard Niebuhr. Professor Niebuhr emphasized that Protestantism itself is essentially a movement, and especially in the United States.[8] It has, according to Niebuhr, moved one strand of Christianity from the "mode of life primarily interested in structure to one primarily directed toward action"[9]—a point made also by Sidney Mead in his essay on denominationalism as the shape of American religion.[10] Protestantism as movement has been essentially innovating, coming into conflict with the existing order only when the latter sought to keep Protestantism from realizing its essentially dynamic character. Niebuhr also emphasized that Protestantism was order—that in each movement there is an inner direction toward stability.[11] Here we have a major clue to the Awakening. We know that it was a movement that converted hundreds of thousands of people and that it had some kind of profound social implications. But too often scholars have examined religion without taking its dynamism and stability seriously as *social* phenomena—a mistake which should be corrected.

The Awakening's aspects of *organization* and *unity* can well be subsumed under the category of *movement* because its dynamism was made relevant to its recruits through local organization, and also because the unity that transcended localism is in the final analysis what gives a movement its continuity. Professor Niebuhr's observations and the well-known but little explained great mobilization of people undertaken by the evangelical churches after the Revolution suggest that scholars might possibly achieve a new perspective of the Second Great Awakening by considering it, as is done in the following section, as a general social movement that organized thousands of people into small groups. To assist historians in the analysis of movements is an ever growing literature in the social sciences on the nature of social movements and collective behavior. One grave danger in trying to "apply" sociological analysis to historical events is that historians often work on the basis of evidence that would be deemed inadequate by social scientists, and historians are often ill acquainted with the sophisticated rigor which a great fund of data allows (or enforces upon) their brethren in related disciplines. Thus what follows does not pretend to be a prescriptive formula for analyzing the Second Great Awakening, but a tentative, perhaps suggestive venture into it from a new perspective: it is simply a hypothesis.

Certainly the Awakening had many of the attributes of a general movement. To be sure, it had less form than the later, more clearly defined reform, "nativist" and abolition movements, and its primary goals were certainly not consciously to effect a major change in the social structure. Furthermore, it was institutionalized in different "denominations" and in the end tended to be almost identical with the population in general. But these are not damaging admissions since the Awakening also had most of the requirements for a general social movement. In the first place it grew from a few converts to an expanding organization of Americans in small groups all over the country. Secondly, its expansion was in large part the work of a dedicated corps of charismatic leaders who proposed to change the moral character of America. Moreover, as the movement grew, a new corps of administrators "routinized" the charisma, created new institutional forms and standardized what once had been spontaneous. Before that happened, however, an ideology of personal "salvation" and moral responsibility had produced a sense of purpose and participation that divided the sheep from the goats—the ingroup from the out, the saved from the damned—and provided common standards for evaluating and enforcing behavior. There were other characteristics as well, unique to the time and situation of the movement; but whatever its peculiarities, it was more than a series of religious "crazes" and camp meetings. Mobilizing Americans in unprecedented numbers, it had the power to shape part of our history.

The origins of the Second Great Awakening have usually been grounded in a New England suffering the intellectual contortions of theological transmutation and the social adjustments demanded by the Age of the Democratic Revolution, especially its French phase. But the Awakening demonstrated the evangelicals' ability to recruit people throughout the United States, even in places where the New England theology had never been predominant, nor Thomas Jefferson anything less than a folk hero. The conventional view has to its credit, however, that it understood that a relationship existed between social uneasiness and the Awakening. What it has not appreciated is that the people who joined as well as the people who led the movement might have found the Awakening meaningful. Too much attention has, as usual, been paid to the articulated fears of a few New England clerics.

Students of collective behavior and social movements agree that the latter often develop under conditions of social strain. This may be rapid economic change, the reshaping of social relationships, uncertainty about the direction and lasting quality of political institutions, and geographical mobility—anything that disorients people. But the strain is often ambiguous, the threat vague and the future uncertain—the anxieties are not focused upon an obvious enemy or an unequivocal situation. If the threat to people were clearly perceived as in war or depression, energies could be channeled into the immediate problem-solving of fighting or redirecting economic activity provided proper institutions were available. Without such social institutions to give meaning and direction to the afflicted, however, anxiety could create a situation that would spawn a social movement. Even victory in war is no guarantee that social stress will be avoided, as the United States found after the major wars of the 20th century as well as after the War for Independence from Great Britain.

Historians of the Revolutionary era are presently paying more attention to the extraordinary social strain and dislocation which afflicted the United States toward the end of the 18th century. They have described how the events which drew Americans into war came to be interpreted through extant Whiggish ideas that lent a revolutionary aspect to the War for Independence as it progressed. Bernard Bailyn has called the process "the contagion of liberty," a happy phrase which suggests the nature of the impact of Revolutionary ideas.[12] But in the rhetoric which represented the metamorphosis of rebels into revolutionaries, Gordon Wood has discovered the relatively great extent of fears, anxieties and changes in orientation—general social strain—which plagued Americans in that time of great change.[13] It should be emphasized that during the Revolution, the fears for the future, the uneasiness at changing economies, and the vague anxieties about the course of American society could be resolved in the demanding necessity of fighting the war. Then there would be no need for significant movements or organizations to give direction and meaning to life so long as the uncertain future could be met with the purposeful activity of fighting the enemy. But when peace came, there were more problems than ever.

American society after the Revolution was undergoing more strain than ever before. Winning the war had placed new demands upon American politicians. They were not now vying with the Crown, but with history—they were not reacting to royal decisions, but making significant decisions of their own as to what kind of constitutional structure the new nation would have. Furthermore, with the development of a federal government and the innovation of political parties came an awareness of more differences among Americans than had been previously anticipated; differences became political and social issues, and issues entailed further conflict. In this process of trying to create new governments, attempting to develop a national economy and finding voluntary organizations for achieving what government seemed unable to achieve, there was a joyous sense of optimism, to be sure, but simultaneously there was grave social strain. The violence of the political rhetoric, its suspicion, intolerance and hatefulness, is particularly remarkable, not at all the kind of public discourse one would suggest represented placidity. With the violent words came also violent actions; Shays' Rebellion, Jacob Fries' "Rebellion," the Whisky Rebellion. And the Federalist government, too, beset by fear, anxiety and resentment against its political enemies resorted to the violence of repressive measures in the Alien and Sedition Acts—again, not the sort of action expected of a government ruling over an untroubled people. This repression was accepted by many as justified because the revolutionary ideology of human equality was undermining the "deferential society" of pre-Revolutionary America while Deism threatened the presumed orthodoxy of the New England churches. The norms of the old life were changing; its stimuli were gone, its manners inapplicable, its conventions often incapable of being reinforced. For many people there were no educational or religious institutions which automatically acted upon them in the same old-shoe familiar way. The Revolution had created great anticipation for the future; but the kind of future people wanted was not easily realized. The result was a vague uneasiness that created a general susceptibility to social movements.

As Americans faced new strains imposed by independence and intellectual turmoil, they were also busily engaged in attempting to impose order upon their society. Although Revolutionary optimism may have helped to encourage the organization of voluntary societies, the need to have order and definite goals in the midst of strain undoubtedly assisted the epidemic of organization that followed the war. Americans organized not only to promote "useful knowledge" and the arts, but also medicine, commerce, charity and security through professional, business and "mutual benefit" societies. Usually bringing together the "better sort" of people, these predominantly urban groups did not exist in any great numbers prior to the Revolution. It was only after the war that these societies together with the new state and federal governments literally reorganized American society.[14] But these societies, no matter how prolific, were superseded in number of new members by an even more persuasive and pervasive organizing force under which the societies themselves could be subsumed, i.e., the Second Great Awakening.

The process may be summarized by reference to the simple formula offered by Hadley Cantril in his pioneering study of *The Psychology of Social Movements.* He explains that people are most susceptible to suggestion in two instances: first of all, when they have no adequate world view or general standards by which to explain life in general and special events or situations in particular. The extreme opposite situation leads to a similar susceptibility. That is, people are highly suggestible when their general standards of interpretation ("mental context") are so rigid that situations are automatically judged by these standards without reflection or perspective.[15] Thus, people oppressed by the ambiguous social strains of the 1780s and 1790s would be susceptible to evangelical preaching if they had had no religious orientation but desperately needed one—or if they had one so rigid that social pressure merely strengthened it. Actually, Cantril's model is only an approximating formula which should not be used as a Procrustean device to provide a "pat" answer to a very difficult problem. The model is not a prescription, but an invitation to look beyond religious phenomena; it is a suggestion as to how out of a period of religious doubt and irrelevance, one strand of Christianity could help to reshape society within the span of a single generation.

The Revival in this general social strain promised a "positive outcome in an uncertain situation" for it proposed to make men better by putting them into direct contact with God. It also provided values or goals for which to work and codes which regulated behavior giving ideological as well as social order to life. The ambiguity of the post-Revolutionary situation further helped the revivalists because it precluded a precise solution for problems, thus permitting a religious solution for social as well as religious uneasiness. The fact that the Revival proposed to change individuals, not institutions, was equally conducive to its growth because movements with such goals do not invite counter-pressures against them from people or institutions jealous of their power and influence. Such movements are also less dependent on a correct evaluation of and response to political or economic aspects of community life and can therefore adapt to the changing environment better than movements offering specific solutions for social problems. It is true that New England with its heritage of "theocracy" was less susceptible to the Revival than other areas because of the social and political standing of the Congregational churches, but with the increasing strength of the Awakening as a reviver of religion came semi-respectability and final acceptance. Not until the movement had commended itself to the "standing order" by the "transformation" of literally countless individuals did it begin to affect institutions and by then the opposition was almost powerless.

Another reason for the success of the Revival was that it could, under the impact of Revolutionary patterns of thinking, be understood as the Revolution at work in religion. Conversely, the Revolution could be understood as a partial vindication of the evangelical ideal of a society of individuals who were equal by virtue of participating in a common experience. It was not that ideas of equality were consciously knit together from two strands in the minds of converts, for the Second Great Awakening was not in the first instance an intellectual movement. Rather, in the work of readjusting the relationship of Church to State in the South, and in explaining the Revolution as an event which gave them control over their own destiny, many Americans could find it relatively easy to participate in the only organization which sought them out, made them responsible for ordering a new holy community, and built the entire structure upon their own personal experience. Both Revolution and Revival put it to the people—would they be free or no? If they answered affirmatively, they were expected to order themselves accordingly into a new society, whether a *novus ordo seculorum* or a church. The Revolution then provided a political and social world view which was conducive to building a new religious community based on common participation in a holy life. The Revolution had dethroned George III; the Revival as organized "enthusiasm" had "removed from God much of the aristocratic and esoteric aura of his remoteness and function as pure Being."[16]

The measure of the success of the Awakening was not in the length of various periods of enthusiasm, however, even though many ministers of the time thought so. The measure was in the number of new churches organized which could persist when enthusiasm had died down, the number of converts who remained in the churches once their emotions had been channeled from public ecstasy into private devotion. The Awakening was a recruiting impulse. It brought people into the church in unprecedented numbers, and the first and most spectacular increases were among the Methodists. It was the organization of Methodism rather than the hopes, fears or decisions of a mystical "Protestantism" that marked the beginning of the Second Great Awakening, for with this development churches everywhere began to learn that they must be an organizing impulse reaching throughout the society rather than a stabilizing institution located in one place. Formalized as a church during the last days of 1784, the Methodists had already been multiplying at a rapid rate for three years. Their new organization was supremely suited to the new era in religion since it was not based on theological exposition of the nature of the church as were the Anglican and Calvinist communions, but upon pragmatic necessity. That is, it was necessity if one thought that the ministry's purpose was to organize new societies of Christians—if the church was primarily a missionary organization. Methodists thought so, and the success of their pragmatism affected Baptists, who were known to suspend theological objections to supralocal organizations long enough to employ the more effective aspects of the Methodist itineracy.

The Methodist leadership was topped by an episcopacy that was primarily administrative, but was in part charismatic. It oversaw a ministry noted primarily for its ability to arouse a following and to create new societies. The ministry had a "seniority system" of various stages of apprenticeship that trained a constantly increasing corps of men. This elite merged almost imperceptibly with a hierarchy of lay leadership to guarantee strong guidance even when the itinerants were absent on their circuits. The emphatic peculiarity of the Methodist Episcopal Church was that its preachers were not settled. They were sent out to call churches into existence, not to wait for a church to call them. Professional organizers, they literally went from house to house looking for anyone who would listen. And if the roving evangelist found two or three people willing to hear prayer and preaching, he appointed a subordinate responsible for leading the new group in worship and discipline. Thus leadership begat leadership in an unending series. And it should be emphasized that what made the Methodists so successful during the early days of the Awakening was not the intellectual content of their preaching, which was meager, but their ability to do what voluntary societies, state governments and even political parties would soon do—organize people.

In this they were extremely successful. From 1781 to 1791 they increased from 10,500 "friends" (members) to 76,150. No other organization in America increased so rapidly over so large an area in so short a time—a statement that would apply to Methodism for the next fifty years. Between 1781 and 1786 this new movement erupted, making overall gains of 90 per cent, pushing membership up in New Jersey by 150 per cent, in Maryland by 70 per cent or better and in the Carolinas by 225 per cent. Only the latter area was on the frontier. Statistics for the second half of the decade were even more impressive. Between 1786 and 1791 the denomination grew roughly 270 per cent with New Jersey and the Carolinas up 150 per cent or more, Virginia up 220 per cent and the invasion of New England and New York bringing absolute gains incalculable in terms of percentages. The most dramatic growth, however, occurred from 1790 to 1791 when religious excitement in the Old Dominion swept about twenty thousand converts into the fold. Once the Methodist vanguard began the process, Baptist itinerant preachers began once more to enliven Baptist churches and to create new ones. The Methodists' growth was contagious; it acted as an example, prod and guide to the Baptists who used their associations "to receive petitions and to appoint preachers to travel into new places where the Gospel was likely to flourish."[17] The Baptists multiplied after 1785 following the same kind of pattern used by Methodists—only less formally—and in a single ten-year period the combined strength of the two popular denominations jumped from 45,000 to 121,000. From Maine to Georgia the people of the new nation were being recruited into the various local organizations of a vast social movement. This was not the old church being rejuvenated, but a new church providing a pattern of thinking and social organization familiar enough to enlist people and new enough to enforce allegiance.

The movement's growth was all the more spectacular when one considers the religious situation after the Revolution. By all accounts it was disheartening: churches had been destroyed, congregations dispersed and ministers sent scurrying. The fact that there were only 1,499 ministers and about 1,965 churches for over three million Americans was indicative of the religious demoralization which seemed to have settled over the former colonies after the exodus of the British. Even more appalling to revivalists were the church members who had not come to a crisis in their "spiritual" lives—apathetic souls who had not been "born again" or had the "witness of the Holy Spirit" that their sins were forgiven and that they could "go on to perfection." But by 1791 there was reason to believe that the moribund state of religion in the new world had been enlivened.

Once the Methodists had demonstrated the value of an extensive effort to organize new churches, the process which promised a hopeful future was about the same for both evangelical churches and their various branches. What had once made the Methodists unique—their rapid organization of small societies—soon became the chief characteristic of the Second Great Awakening. Indeed, perhaps too much has been made of the self-conscious differences between Baptist and Methodist churches—the latter being in connection with others and the former being autonomous. In the period of organization the two churches were, as movement organizations, essentially the same. Although the Methodist organization was more formalized, the Baptists were quite capable of superimposing an associational system upon themselves in order to provide for more rapid expansion. They sometimes sent out traveling evangelists; and one well-known Baptist missionary urged his coreligionists to adopt formally the Methodist system which they had informally adapted to Baptist needs in the West.[18] If a successful Baptist denomination was in part Methodist, the successful Methodist society was in part Baptist, for the Methodists were always members of small, local, and for all intents and purposes autonomous groups. For example, nothing in the entire hierarchy of preachers' meetings could make the Amelia circuit fight slavery if its members were not so inclined.

This purposive or evangelical conception of the church and ministry was what Sidney Mead describes as the denominational mode and what sociologists have called the essence of a social movement organization. Movement organizations differ from complex or formal organizations in that they are a purposive and collective attempt to change society. The new church had no social program, but it was nevertheless intent upon change.

The old church had been an organic part of traditional society with a small membership and no orientation toward a goal. Rather it was occupied with maintaining spiritual and moral order. With the advent of the evangelical itinerants, however, there was beginning to develop a new conception of the church as a society of people dedicated to changing their own lives and, by recruitment, those of their neighbors. With this new idea and its indefatigable propagandists began a social movement.

In 1792 the Methodists faltered, but the Awakening did not. Arguments among the Wesleyans as to the nature of the ecclesiastical elite and the delegation of power led to schism as the Methodist movement entered a stage of more complex organization with its attendant strains. But the Awakening was not reliant upon one organization—the social uneasiness that made Methodism attractive was conducive to Baptist conversions as well. And the members whom the main Methodist body lost were still very much a part of the general awakening of religion. Indeed, the Revival, once begun, seemed to generate its own momentum as Baptists and Presbyterians, aroused by the religious excitement of newly created Methodist groups, began holding meetings throughout the South. Geographical as well as denominational divisions crumbled under the onslaught. Methodists penetrated New York and New England between 1791 and 1796 gaining about three thousand converts. This growth was hardly spectacular. But in Vermont and Connecticut where Methodists and Baptists participated actively in the Second Great Awakening their successful recruitment did not go unnoticed. When in the next four years Methodists managed to double their numbers in Congregationalist strongholds, they demonstrated to the establishment once again the effectiveness of revivalism in reasserting the waning power of its churches.

The results of the organizational process of the Awakening had important implications for the course of American society. Professor Miyakawa has done much to explain the impact not only for the frontier and Northwest, but by an extension of his arguments, for the Awakening throughout the nation. If the pattern of organizing new societies provided for group unity, socialization, and greater "participatory democracy" in the rural West, it may also be concluded that it did the same wherever new churches were built. By multiplying church units throughout the nation, the Revival was facilitating democracy in much the same way as did the new organizational possibilities of Turner's frontier as interpreted by Elkins and McKitrick.[19] At the same time the Revival was, by its universality, also helping to create a more integrated American society as opposed to a confederation of provincial societies. It was, in other words, a nationalizing influence. Robert Cooley Angell in *The Integration of American Society* has pointed out how a "common world of experience" makes society possible, and a common world of experience was what the Revival was helping to create. This process was not an exclusive one, to be sure, for it was complementary to the other nationally creative forces of political involvement and economic interaction. The constant visitation of evangelical preachers and their preaching the same values, norms and vision of society throughout the

United States helped to create a distinct moral community. Thus the Revival helped make religion one of the major determinants of public discourse everywhere in the country. And it is not surprising that the period 1794-1825 was the great period of founding religious magazines and papers. Through the almost indecent persistence of its professional organizers and an increasing control of the means of public communication, the Awakening was one of the unifying factors of American national life.[20]

Along with this nationalization and democratization went provision for "structural" social mobility. Seymour Martin Lipset and Hans L. Zetterberg have explained how industrialization facilitates mobility by the multiplication of specialized, higher status jobs. The expansion and creation of institutions provides more positions of responsibility into which people from hitherto lower status occupations may move.[21] The same process was occurring in the Second Great Awakening. Church membership which had in some areas of the country signified a higher status was now being opened to more people. The ministry which had formerly been reserved for an educated elite was now opened to new recruits by the simple process of creating new churches. Of course, there would be different strata of clergymen, but in an age of advancing democracy it would be a rather delicate question to decide who commanded what prestige from whom. If traditional society had its elites and status levels, so did the democracy. And if there were more Methodists and Baptists than Congregationalists and Presbyterians, perhaps being a self-taught evangelical commanded a higher status value than being a puny, mealy mouthed, sermon-reading, settled clergyman. The "people" would know.

The pulsation of organization and movement—order and mission—persisted for about fifty years. After the early 1790s the Awakening became more general, affecting each section of the new nation with its values and language until all America seemed to have become a "revivalistic" society: a community quickened by appeals to mission, ordered by reproaches of sin and saved by personal exertion in doing good and doing well. This accomplishment was made possible by the persistent combination of social strain, ecclesiastical turmoil and purposeful leadership. Because of the ubiquity of the latter and the flexibility of their appeal, the Awakening provided something for everyone. There was orderly benevolence for those in the older churches, a stimulating emotional catharsis for others. There was the *promise* of perfection for some, and the *example* of it for the more sanguine.

In New England the establishment was taught the powers of persuasion before it was taught the necessity of it. The Awakening through Methodist and Baptist organizations helped to give social and religious direction to those disaffected from the establishment. The latter, having already fulfilled a vital function in ordering society, turned to making its religious life more relevant to a people afflicted by a general social malaise. This search for relevance is often interpreted as a conservative counteroffensive against a rising democracy, and some Federalist clerics may well have understood it as such—social movements are contrivable for such purposes even if not so conceived initially. The Awakening may have been on the other hand a process whereby the conservative clergy became resigned to the democracy. In either event, the interpretation of the Awakening as a conservative (or liberal) movement is really beside the point. For it was a mobilization of people by religiously oriented movement organizations that had democratic implications. If churchmen fought change on principle they had to yield to it when they accepted the Awakening. And if they yielded to keep the church abreast of change, they were simply doing what institutional elites had done before them. In fact, they were also doing what ecclesiastical leaders had done in American Quakerism when faced with social and political change in the 18th century.

Even for New England, the Awakening was much more than retrenchment. For the Congregational churches it was not so much a device for recruiting new members as a way of making the old ones more aware of religious obligations as social obligations. Where Baptists and Methodists united social and religious functions in organizing thousands of new religious societies, Congregationalists and Presbyterians united the two in organizing hundreds of missionary and benevolence societies. In 1801 the two latter denominations even united in the West to provide an itinerant ministry for that section, in effect imposing a Methodist superstructure upon a Congregational-Presbyterian polity. Later, when the benevolence empire came into its own, it also perpetuated the Methodist ideal of an itinerant elite of professional organizers.[22] It was this benevolence empire that led the Awakening in search of social responsibility—although some scholars apparently dislike the manner in which it was done. And it was not until the more popular denominations created their own benevolence systems like that of the Congregationalist-Presbyterian combine, and the latter adopted and transformed the techniques of fifty years of previous evangelism that the Awakening became unified. It was also unified by the social strain of rapid economic growth and increased geographic mobility, for these made people susceptible to the pattern of movement and order that in turn enabled them to deal with ambiguity and discontent. Out of the continuing social strain, however, came also pressures for more specific goal-oriented movements than the generalities of the Second Great Awakening. As ambiguities became unequivocal threats fixed in definite conspiracies (such as that of the "slavocracy") and as the values of the Awakening became social programs that threatened rather than reinforced orderly society (such as "modern abolitionism") the movement achieved unity just in time for the abolitionists to tear it apart.

Having said all this, it must be admitted that the hypothesis of the Second Great Awakening as an organizing process and social movement requires more explanation than can be accomplished in a single article. We need to explain the interaction between different subgroups of the movement, and other social movements and institutions. We would like to describe precisely the social significance of who was being organized by the new movement, for it seems to have been a rising middle class in general and women in particular. Indeed, it may have been the greatest organization and mobilization of women in American history. We would also like to analyze the ideology that ritualized not awe but experience and reinforced the value structure of men who were developing an industrial future as well as those who clung to a paternalistic, slaveholding past. And it should be fruitful to explain more precisely than has been done previously the relation of revivalistic ideology to reform movements, distinguishing between what revivalism caused, what it provided channels for and what it merely made possible through its universality. And there are other more sophisticated questions yet to be formulated and tested.

Nevertheless, what we can know about the Second Great Awakening is very significant for understanding the development of the new nation. 1) In the first place, it should be clear that the Revival began as an organizing movement, not as a Calvinist reaction, and that it was successful precisely because it adopted Methodist trappings of organization and conception of the church as missionary movement. Once this fact is taken seriously, one can see 2) that the Revival began in the early 1780s and continued to grow over more than a generation, involving not merely one section, but the entire nation. 3) Because the Revival enveloped the entire country, it was a nationalizing force that created a "common world of experience." It was not a strong national organization that helped to make the churches important in the development of an American community, but the relatively strong local churches that shared common values and norms with their counterparts throughout the United States. The experience of participating in a small, local organization was more meaningful for Americans than any identification with a supralocal agency. The latter body, by sending out professional organizers and literature merely made sure that the local churches would be more or less alike. American nationalism in part, therefore, rested not on the power of a national institution so much as the relevance, power and similarity of thousands of local organizations that helped to create "a common world of experience."

The advantages of viewing the Second Great Awakening as an organizing process are numerous despite the admitted tenuousness of any new thesis ventured for the sake of academic discussion. To explain the Revival in this manner enables students to see the social impact of what is too often presumed to be a purely religious movement, sometimes guided by men who deeply resented the future. To see the Awakening as a social movement is also to see how and why the churches became an integral part of American society and to suggest that disestablishment was not so significant for determining the future of American social and ecclesiastical history as for writing finis to part of the past. That is, the creation of a new movement was previous to and more significant than the destruction of the old order. By the same token, the Awakening is seen not as the result of a threat to religious institutions so much as the appeal of a religious movement for men troubled by social cleavage. The Second Great Awakening as a general phenomenon not limited by institutional or denominational lines was a vast mobilization of people. It was so vast in fact, that if a similar mobilization were to take place in any of the developing nations of the 1960s, there is no doubt that it would be duly recorded and analyzed as evidence of grave social unrest and reorganization. It was precisely that in early America, and it profoundly affected our history for years afterward.

NOTES

[1]Timothy L. Smith, *Revivalism and Social Reform in Mid-Nineteenth Century America* (New York, 1957), pp. 32-33

[2]Seymour Martin Lipset, *The First New Nation: The United States in Historical and Comparative Perspective* (New York, 1963), pp. 140-69.

[3]Perry Miller, "From the Covenant to the Revival," in *The Shaping of American Religion*, eds. James Ward Smith and A. Leland Jamison (Princeton, 1961), pp. 332-68 esp. pp. 346, 350, 367-68.

[4]*The Life of the Mind in America from the Revolution to the Civil War* (New York, 1965), p. 34.

[5]*Ibid.,* pp. 61, 69 ff. One significant exception to the tendency to differentiate needlessly is of course Sidney Mead's intelligent syntheses concerning American religious institutions, which have been collected in *The Lively Experiment: The Shaping of Christianity in America* (New York, 1963).

[6]For an example of Sweet's argument, see his *Religion in the Development of American Culture 1765-1840* (New York, 1952), pp. 153 ff; 160 and *Revivalism in America: Its Origin, Growth, and Decline* (New York, 1944), pp. 112 ff, 119, 138 ff. These are but two books on a long bibliography of pioneering works.

[7]*Protestants and Pioneers: Individualism and Conformity on the American Frontier* (Chicago, 1964), *passim* and pp. 213 ff.

[8]*The Kingdom of God in America* (New York, 1937), chap. 3. Also Niebuhr, "The Protestant Movement and Democracy in the United States," in *Shaping of American Religion*, eds. Smith and Jamison, pp. 20-71.

[9]"The Protestant Movement and Democracy," p. 31.

[10]*Lively Experiment*, pp. 103-33.

[11]"The Protestant Movement and Democracy," pp. 36 ff.

[12]"The Transforming Radicalism of the American Revolution," in *Pamphlets of the American Revolution, 1750-1776*, ed. Bernard Bailyn (Cambridge, 1965), I, 139-202.

[13]"Rhetoric and Reality in the American Revolution," *William and Mary Quarterly,* 3rd Ser., XXIII (Jan. 1966), 3-32.

[14]Frank Warren Crow, "The Age of Promise: Societies for Social and Economic Improvement in the United States 1783-1815" (unpublished doctoral thesis, University of Wisconsin, 1952), *passim*. See also Eugene P. Link, *Democratic-Republican Societies 1790-1800* (New York, 1942), pp. 74 ff.

[15]*The Psychology of Social Movements* (New York, 1941), pp. 64-77.

[16]Joe Lee Davis, "Mystical versus Enthusiastic Sensibility," *Journal of the History of Ideas,* IV (June 1943), 304.

[17]Robert B. Semple, *A History of the Rise and Progress of the Baptists in Virginia,* rev. ed. by G. W. Beale (Richmond, 1894), pp. 64 ff., 91. One of the most surprising things one discovers in this early Baptist history is how Baptists reacted to

Methodist successes by adapting some of their rivals' practices to their own purposes without doing any denominational or theological damage.

[18]John Mason Peck, *Forty Years of Pioneer Life: Memoir of John Mason Peck, D.D.,* ed. Rufus Babcock (Philadelphia, 1864), p. 124. Also Albert Henry Newman, *A History of the Baptist Churches in the United States* (New York, 1915), pp. 323-32. Semple, *History of the Baptists,* pp. 64 ff., 91, 114.

[19]Stanley Elkins and Eric McKitrick, "A Meaning for Turner's Frontier," *Political Science Quarterly,* LXIX (Sept. 1954), 321-53. Miyakawa, *Protestants and Pioneers,* pp. 199 ff., 213 ff.

[20]Angell, *The Integration of American Society* (New York, 1941), pp. 8 ff., 17.

[21]Seymour Martin Lipset and Reinhard Bendix, *Social Mobility in Industrial Society* (Berkeley, 1959), chap. 2, esp. pp. 57 ff.

[22]See John Lytle Myers, "The Agency System of the Antislavery Movement 1832-1837, and Its Antecedents in other Benevolent and Reform Societies" (unpublished doctoral thesis, University of Michigan, 1961), pp. 1-91.

14

Religious Benevolence as Social Control: A Critique of an Interpretation

Lois W. Banner

As a counter to interpretations of religious benevolence as manipulative and expressive of latent interests, this essay emphasizes the basic commitment to Christian republicanism which suffused the ranks of the religious humanitarians. Professor Banner, Douglass College, Rutgers University, argues that the manifest ideals and theories of this generation must not be lightly dismissed or interpreted away.

Among social historians of the last two decades it has become standard to classify the post-Revolutionary generation of religious humanitarians as conservative and self-serving. Fearful of rising currents of secularism and egalitarianism in the new nation, these churchmen, so many students would have it, mounted a campaign of religious evangelism and created a system of local and national religious and benevolent societies in order to preserve their own declining status and to regain their earlier colonial position as the moral arbiters of American society. Such a conclusion about the nature of religious humanitarianism was first advanced in 1954 by John R. Bodo and Charles C. Cole. Charles I. Foster and Clifford S. Griffin offered in 1960 important variations on the main theme: Each approached the subject from a different perspective. While Bodo and Cole organized their studies around individual representatives from the clergy and focused on sermons as their sources, Foster and Griffin centered on both ministerial and lay members of

First published in the *Journal of American History*, LX (June 1973), pp. 23-41 (notes abridged). Reprinted by permission of the Organization of American Historians.

the interdenominational societies and focused on the societies' reports. Yet all agreed that when these religious humanitarians founded Bible and tract societies, or promoted temperance and Sabbath observance, or tried to aid the urban poor, what they wanted in reality was to gain power over society for their own conservative, if not reactionary, ends. It was the desire for "social control," not social improvement, which lay behind their seemingly benevolent schemes.[1]

Moreover, it has recently been customary to stress the differences rather than the similarities in ideology and motivation between these religious humanitarians and the later antislavery reformers, thereby isolating the former from the historical plaudits now accorded the latter. In the past two decades few figures who would be classified as reformers have escaped the sweeping and often profound criticism of the American reform tradition launched by a generation of historians of the right and left. The abolitionists, however, have been more fortunate. Attacks against them for racism, for fanaticism, for ideological rigidity and methodological naiveté have been powerfully resisted and in large measure turned back.[2] And, as if further to maintain the abolitionists' claim to moral integrity, some historians have found it important to deny their connection with the earlier Protestant humanitarians of the century. For example, building on arguments first advanced by Bodo, Cole, Foster, and Griffin, John L. Thomas has argued that Protestant benevolence before the 1820s was in no sense humanitarian. This earlier generation, according to Thomas, was interested solely in furthering Christianity and morality, not humane improvements. Not until the flowering of liberal theology in Unitarianism and Transcendentalism and of Christian perfectionism under Charles Grandison Finney, Thomas argues, did Protestants become truly humanitarian and reform-minded. From Thomas' perspective, the connection between the abolitionists and their religious predecessors in reform was only indirect. The earlier generation was the last dying gasp of an old order rather than the herald of a new. Their influence was negligible, and their motives were suspect.[3]

Yet however satisfying to the liberal conscience such criticism may be, it ignores some significant factors about the genesis and goals of religious humanitarianism. The not-surprising devotion of these men to Protestant morality, their attachment to the capitalist economy, and their fear of democracy comprised only one strand in a complex of attitudes toward politics and society. To abstract this one strand as their "real" motivation is to fall into the error which plagued the Progressive historians: the belief that reality is always mean, hidden, and sordid and that men normally act not out of generosity but from fear and from considerations of status and gain. Equally important, the historians who advance such a thesis have for the most part failed to take into account a large literature on the subject written by sympathetic students, beginning with Robert Baird in 1844 and continuing more recently to Perry Miller and Sidney Mead. These authors argue that, rather than trying to control the steady growth of egalitarianism in America, the men of the older order were trying to adjust to it.[4] Above all, their studies suggest that there are some major weaknesses within the "social control"argument.

These weaknesses warrant analysis. Foster, Griffin, Bodo, and Cole suggest that the religious humanitarians comprised a group of Calvinist clergymen whose roots lay in New England; who drew their inspiration directly from Congregationalist Samuel Hopkins' notion of "disinterested benevolence"; whose status in the community was in decline; who were bent on establishing some sort of theocratic control over society and politics; and whose most characteristic representative was Lyman Beecher. All these assertions are highly debatable.

First, the idea of benevolence was a general inheritance from a number of eighteenth-century sources and was not of narrow New England origin. The Scottish philosopher Francis Hutcheson, the Quakers, and Anglican reformers like George Whitefield and John Wesley all presented versions of it.[5] Moreover, the self-assertive New Englanders aroused as much hostility as imitation among their Protestant coreligionists. In part out of personal and denominational rivalry and in part because Hopkins substituted universal salvation for Calvinist determinism, even the Presbyterians in the middle region came to reject Hopkinsianism.[6] That historians have singled out Hopkins as the originator of religious benevolence has much to do with Congregational allegiance to their own men and ideas, to the strength and vitality of the organizations they established, to the popularity of their American Board of Commissioners for Foreign Missions (ABCFM)—the first organization of its kind in America—and to the romantic story of its founding in 1810, through the efforts of six college students who, inspired by Hopkins' theories, subsequently became the first American Foreign missionaries under the auspices of ABCFM.[7] Moreover, there were important institutional precedents for post-Revolutionary humanitarianism in the Anglican's Society for the Propagation of the Gospel and in Quaker and Moravian charitable societies, not to mention the organizations for fraternity and for social improvement which Benjamin Franklin and others had established throughout the colonies. Institutional needs and goals, as well as ideologies, can powerfully affect motivation and action.[8]

Second, it is also questionable whether the clergy of the early republic considered their authority to be on the decline. Here, too, scholars have appropriated certain well-known Congregational complaints to explain the attitudes and situation of the entire ministerial profession.[9] Those Congregational ministers who nurtured the romantic version of an idyllic, theocratic past may have felt such status anxieties, but none of the other denominations looked back to such a golden era from which to draw inspiration and example. Their way had always been beset by that inattention to spiritual matters which the new and unorganized continent engendered: the revivalism of the so-called "Second Great Awakening" was on one level a well-tested response to a familiar situation of religious indifference. Moreover, most ministers, even among Presbyterians and Congregationalists, came from farming families of moderate means.[10] To these families the ministry represented a significant social advance.

Moreover, no other profession offered such extensive scholarship funds and part-time work opportunities to its practitioners in training. In some places and among some groups ministers may have been scorned, but in a shifting social order so were doctors and lawyers. To no less a degree than the latter, clergymen had access to local prominence and community deference.[11]

Third, it was the Presbyterians and not the Congregationalists who dominated the boards of the two major post-Revolutionary interdenominational societies—the American Bible Society and the American Sunday School Union. Presbyterianism, despite what seems an almost common assumption, was not a replica of Congregationalism. Most important, Presbyterianism, except for some areas in New Jersey, was a dissenting church. Unlike Congregationalism, it did not have a tradition of establishment in America. Religious diversity had always characterized the situation in the middle states. Presbyterians had always lived in cooperation and competition with a variety of other churches, and in Virigina, where there was an Anglican establishment, the Presbyterians had vigorously fought for disestablishment.[12] As if to underscore this diversity, the American Bible Society and the American Sunday School Union always tried to preserve an interdenominational character: Methodists, Baptists, Quakers, and Episcopalians were always included on their boards of directors, and representatives of all these churches—at least until the 1830s, when denominationalism began to predominate—participated in the decision-making and activities of these two societies.[13] In contrast, the two major Congregational societies, the American Education Society and the American Board of Commissioners for Foreign Missions, could lay little claim to interdenominationalism.[14] Centered at midcontinent and with a more diverse membership, the "Presbyterian" societies were more truly interdenominational in character.

To institute denominational control over the state was not the goal of midstate and southern Presbyterians, Baptists, and Methodists. Nor were they intent on gaining some sort of direct control over political affairs. Scholars base too many interpretations upon Beecher's famous 1818 statement that before disestablishment in Connecticut the clergy controlled politics and after disestablishment they seized on the voluntary societies as an indirect means of political control. What is in fact significant about Beecher's claim is its uniqueness.[15] No other clergyman left such witness. Rather, one of the more important themes of clerical thought under the early republic was a distaste for politics, a belief that political life in America was corrupt, that acrimonious political divisions were undermining national unity, and that the clergy had no business in the political arena.[16] Historians like Griffin, who argue that the clergy were politicians with a Machiavellian cunning that would do credit to the most sophisticated party leader, overlook these themes.

Among the dissenting sects and on the frontier, it is true, ministers did run for elective office, and no clergyman would freely relinquish his traditional right of commenting on politics from his pulpit or fail to utilize the petition, that time-honored tool of registering popular attitudes, in favor of religious campaigns like temperance and Sabbath observance. Few, however, were willing to go further. Scholars have vastly overrated the importance of Ezra Stiles Ely's published appeal in 1828 that denominations and groups of Christians issue statements backing political candidates, for it found little open support among the ecclesiastical community.[17] It was not until the 1840s that a reform group was able to overcome the anti-political bias of American Protestantism and to launch a genuine political movement in the Liberty party.

Finally, the "social control" school has erred in identifying the membership of religious benevolence in the antebellum years so closely with the Congregationalists and Presbyterians. To do good works was a universal Christian sentiment, to fear secularism was a common reflex among Protestants after the Revolution.[18] Historians of benevolence who slight this fact do so because they have not paid sufficient attention to the large body of writing on the development of the denominations in America—works which suggest that the structure and dimension of benevolence during the years of the early republic were greatly influenced not only by the political, social, and ideological factors which most social historians have stressed, but also by the institutional needs and growth patterns of the American Protestant denominations themselves. It is axiomatic to social scientists that an important determinant of individual action lies within the norms and standards of the groups with which the individual identifies himself.[19]

In explaining motivation, the institutional dimension cannot be overlooked. Congregationalists, for example, took up benevolence several decades before the Methodists largely because they had earlier reached a more complex stage of institutional development. By the 1800s their churches were formed; their ministers were settled; but their associations and consociations too often lacked vigor or were prevented from taking decisive action because of the Congregational devotion to the autonomy of local churches. New leaders were tired of old habits, were desirous of advancing themselves, and, given the massive defections to the Baptist faith and to liberalism which the Great Awakening of the eighteenth century had produced, were eager to find some new way of assuring the loyalty and sustaining the enthusiasm of a newly "awakened" constituency. Voluntary societies for missions, for distributing Bibles and tracts, and even for broader humanitarian ends suited all these purposes.[20] As for the Quakers and Anglicans in the eighteenth century, organizational innovation plus new and broadened religious objectives became the way to translate piety into action, to bypass indecision and conflict in regular organizations, and to gain new respect and influence in the community at large.[21]

Methodism, however, which had not appeared on the American continent until 1767, in the early 1800s still preserved its unified sectarian zeal. Within its tightly centralized and hierarchical structure, conflicts of opinion had not yet appeared; there was still no discontent with Methodist programs for enlisting and retaining church members through the preaching of itinerant pastors who served a number of churches and who were transferred to a different section of the country each year. In short, the denomination had not yet experienced a sense of failure.[22] Because Methodist ministers kept aloof from secular affairs, did not preach political sermons, and did not hold settled pastorates, they did not make the kind of local connections which might have increased their interest in extra-ecclesiastical matters. Nor was Methodism strong in those urban areas where human suffering was concentrated. Methodist preachers missed the cosmopolitan influences, the wide-ranging contacts, the air of change and experimentation that the city brought to the clergy of other denominations. Like Baptists, Congregationalists, and Presbyterians, they held revivals, but instead of forming missionary and benevolent societies as a result of revivals, they formed churches.[23] When it suited their purposes they utilized the interdenominational societies, but they did not become deeply involved with them.

Moreover, the organization of individual Methodist churches was directed toward individual piety, not social improvement. Individuals met in groups called "classes" and "bands," not to discuss missions or to give Sunday instruction to the young, but to seek for the state of holiness, unique at this point to the Methodist church, called "Christian perfection." The duty of the early Methodist was to perfect himself and to help others attain sanctification, not to engage in benevolence as a means of social improvement. Society would be perfected only when all its individual members were.

By the 1820s, however, as its early sectarian zeal waned, Methodist development began to parallel that of Congregationalism. Its ministers demanded settled pastorates; conflict appeared in the hierarchy; and a group of younger New York City ministers successfully agitated for the formation of denominational missionary and religious benevolent societies. Subsequently, Methodists began to exhibit a strong interest in temperance and African colonization. Indeed, that equal temperance and antislavery causes spread so rapidly in the late 1820s and 1830s when they had previously met with indifference had much to do with Methodist espousal of them, since by then Methodism was the largest denomination in the country.[24] In the final analysis, one can make a strong case that Congregationalists and Methodists took up benevolence because it suited the particular institutional needs of denominations trying to make the best possible adjustment to the conditions of religious life in America.[25]

Historians of religious benevolence have not only slighted the denominational dimension of their subject but also have not made clear exactly what projects were included as part of the broad movement of religious humanitarianism nor to what extent and where secular and religious humanitarianism intersected in personnel and programs. For the most part, those who advance the "social control" thesis give the impression that men of religion were interested in little beyond their missionary, Bible, and tract societies, except for those few reforms—like temperance, poor relief, and African colonization—through which they could extend their plans to manipulate society for conservative ends. Except for the Quakers and Unitarians, who have always had their staunch champions, the prevailing literature often suggests that, indeed, secular and religious reform associations had little in common except the accident of proximity in time. Yet it is clear that the various churches' enthusiasm for voluntarily joining behind social programs, their desire to institutionalize the revival and gain increased social relevancy, and certain ideological concerns like millennialism and nationalism may have been more crucial to the genesis of many more humanitarian movements than historians have heretofore realized.

Clerical involvement in education is a useful example. Assuredly, one cannot deny that the inculcation of morality often seemed to take precedence over goals more strictly educational in the schools that the religious humanitarians established and that eventually, in a number of locales, they chose to oppose the public schools over the issue of Bible instruction. Yet to stress these features is too often to overlook the real variety and number of educational innovations they supported. In most cities of the nation, benevolent leaders established free school systems for the children of the poor, who previously had received little or no education.[26] They chided legislatures for not providing sufficient funds for public systems of education.[27] They pressured local governments into establishing special juvenile reformatories where youthful convicts could learn the rudiments of education, a trade, and the tenets of Christian morality. They established libraries for young mechanics and apprentices and in a number of areas were the major force behind the founding of lyceums, for which they were in constant demand as speakers.[28] They founded Sunday schools as centers for religion and education.[29] And throughout the nation, pastors of all churches conducted elementary schools, often as a way of supplementing inadequate salaries, but also because of clerical concern that Americans be educated at a time when the public authorities had not yet assumed full responsibility for public education.[30] Not the least of their activities on behalf of education was the founding of the majority of American colleges and universities in existence at that time.

Moreover, religious benevolence for many was a transitional activity on the way to humanitarian reform. Local Bible, tract, and particularly missionary projects did not always remain stagnant endeavors. Missionaries to the Cherokee and Choctaw Indians found, for example, that the tribes were often more interested in learning the white man's methods of cultivating crops and organizing his civilization than in listening to Christian preaching or acquiring Bibles.[31] There was also a dynamic interaction between those men and women who distributed Bibles and tracts in the cities and the subjects of their charity. Often these benevolent partisans met with hostility, but until the 1820s, in New York City at least, it was they, and not public officials, who toured the poverty wards and came into contact with the disadvantaged. It was from their reports that the directors of the many private welfare organization in existence in a city like New York—men who in addition often headed the religious benevolent societies—planned their schemes to establish schools, churches, savings banks, juvenile reformatories, and asylums.[32] Throughout the nation the columns of religious periodicals were consistently filled with news of humanitarian organizations of every variety because their readers were interested in and involved with these organizations.

Furthermore, one suspects that restless Americans, enthused by their ministers' nationalist and millennial rhetoric to expect rapid social improvement in their country free from the vices of Europe, would not long remain satisfied with the obvious inability of Bible and tract distribution to accomplish the revolutionary social effects their promoters claimed for these charities. When it became clear, especially after the excitement over the extensive and highly publicized campaigns to provide every family in the United States with a Bible in the early 1830s died down, that simply putting the Bible into the hands of all Americans was not sufficient to convert them to Christianity and to eliminate poverty and other social ills, many supporters of religious benevolence obviously were attracted toward reforms, like temperance and antislavery, whose potential to effect social change was without question greater. And in the case of the many women who, because of their piety and leisure time, were often the benevolent societies' most faithful workers, employment outside the home in contact with the disadvantaged often made them more cognizant of their own disabilities. They formed the ranks from which the emerging women's rights movement would later draw its members.[33]

Similarly, it is becoming increasingly apparent that a prime consideration in the motivation of many early American reformers was their religious background and training.[34] Thomas Hopkins Gallaudet, for example, founder of the first asylum and school for the training of the deaf in the United States, was an ordained Congregational minister and a graduate of the Andover Seminary, which was renowned as a center for missionary training. Recruited by a number of prominent laymen from his home town of Hartford, Connecticut, Gallaudet spent a year in Europe learning the most advanced techniques in the field and returned to the United States in 1817 to apply what he had learned abroad. Gallaudet would have disavowed the scholarly custom of classifying his efforts as "secular" humanitarianism. He had chosen a career in humanitarianism rather than the ministry because he wanted to be a part of "the great system of good" which looked forward to "the millennium." And that his endeavors were conducted along "Christian principles" was, he judged, crucial to their very nature.[35] Just as so many of his classmates from Andover chose to become missionaries, so Gallaudet defined his work as a mission to a particular group of the disadvantaged at home.

And who more than the missionary personified to American society the self-abnegation and concern for others which reform itself demanded? To a generation raised on romantic tales of the lives of eighteenth-century Indian missionaries like David Brainerd—who died an early death from smallpox and left behind a pietistic and popular diary—and eagerly followed the exploits of youthful missionaries to foreign lands, most of whom died tragically after a few years of service, the missionary life was the acme of heroic self-sacrifice for society's greater good. It was characteristic, for example, that when future antislavery lecturer Marius Robinson was converted to Christian service in Finney's revivals in 1827, he could at first think of no more idealistic pursuit to follow than foreign missionary service.[36] And it was only through the extraordinarily persuasive powers of Theodore

Dwight Weld that he and other students at Lane Seminary, to which many of Finney's converts had transferred, were persuaded to substiture anti-slavery for missionary activity as their life work.[37] The shift in careers, however, was in reality much less sharp than it has often appeared. Many antislavery reformers had previously worked as missionary agents for tract, temperance, and Bible societies, and their antislavery careers of constant traveling, preaching, and converting resembled nothing so much as that of the missionary.[38] They were the itinerants of a new sectarian faith, the radical sons of liberal fathers who had learned about humanitarianism and its methods from the older generation but who, without the institutional at-tachments of their fathers, could more easily take up new reform and career pursuits.[39]

Finally, in addition to overemphasizing the Puritan origins of religious humanitarianism and underemphasizing its full extent and its denominational setting, some historians have been less than fair in discuss-ing the ideological content of the humanitarians' appeal. Behind all clerical revivals and benevolent endeavor lay several major concerns which historians anxious to expose the failings of their subjects have overlooked. The foremost of these—a theme which religious historians stress and which historians like Bodo, Foster, and Griffin ignore—was millennialism.[40] The second, which parallels an underlying and recently discovered theme of political discourse during the young republic, can be called "Christian republicanism."[41] Both millennialism and republicanism were central to the humanitarians' conception of their role in America, and one cannot com-pletely understand their motivation and their actions without taking these concepts into account.

The belief that Christ was to come to earth, eradicate all social ills, and reign for a thousand years before the final judgment had been a standard Christian belief since the time of Saint Paul and had played a role in Edwar-dian and Wesleyan doctrines. But the eighteenth-century revolutions, the birth of the American Republic, and the beginnings of a worldwide Protes-tant missionary movement seemed to give it special urgency in the early nineteenth century. By about 1800 the Protestant community had largely abandoned Edwards' postmillennialism (the belief that human society had already entered the millennial age); but whether Protestants saw its initia-tion as imminent or in the future, the millennial belief colored all their mis-sionary and benevolent activities.

The doctrine itself had a double-edged effect on them. First, as Alan Heimert has argued with regard to the eighteenth century, the society they imagined was clearly utopian and often radical in its implications. Timothy Dwight, in a typical description of the future age, predicted that there would be neither poverty nor illness, neither wars nor civil strife. There would be no need for politicians, for "all distinctions of party and sect, of name and nation, of civilization and savageness, of climate and colour, will finally vanish."[42] But as different from the present as the future was to be, by the early nineteenth century clerics generally did not expect that radical human actions would precede the millennium's appearance. Rather, they interpreted their Bible and missionary societies to be God's special way of converting the world to Christianity and inaugurating the millennial age. "We have all been praying for the coming of the Millennium," explained James Blythe, speaking in 1814 before the Presbyterian Synod of Kentucky in Lexington, "and by most Christians it has been thought to be very nigh at hand; but who until a few years ago, apprehended that an high way for our God was to be prepared among the heathen, simply by *multiplying the Bible,* or that this great event was to be ushered in by awakening a *missionary spirit,* and the erection of *theological schools?*"[43]

Those critics who might scoff at such a naive program for effecting social change were irrelevant to them, for they were certain that behind their endeavors lay what might be called a "powerful magic." When Lewis and Arthur Tappan, the New York philanthropists, were criticized by their brother Benjamin, an Ohio politician and religious skeptic, for supporting senseless causes like Bible and tract distribution in addition to their more worthwhile ventures into education and antislavery, they retorted that in God's sight all humanitarian endeavors were of equal importance. What was needed for the divine favor, they explained, was simply that the "benevolent principle" be in operation.[44] Millennialism was a powerful spur to benevolence; but it was just as much a stimulus to unrealistic thought on the matter. For since the coming of the millennial age was inevitable as long as men worked and prayed for its appearance, religious humanitarians could justify any legitimate action, however foolhardy, that seemed to further the Christian hope for a perfect society.

In addition to millennialism, clerical ideas about the nature of the American polity underlay most benevolent actions. It was not simply that most Protestant clerics were, as many historians point out, devoted nationalists, but they were also ardent republicans as well. Like the Federalists and Jeffersonians who governed the new nation, their reading of history and their own experience during the troubled post-Revolutionary years had demonstrated to them that a republic could survive the constant threat of demagoguery and dictatorship only if its citizens were alert and self-reliant. Virtue was the key, in the republican point of view, to the maintenance of a successful state. Yet on all sides they saw impending disaster. Politics had quickly degenerated into division, and politicians had become sycophants, not statesmen. Political differences had degenerated into that political factionalism which had heralded the downfall of all previous republics, and the parties themselves had become little more than vehicles for personal ambition. Politicians had no concern for the "intelligence and virtue of coming generations," and electoral contests had "cast a shade over our national character, wasted our strength, endangered our union, assaulted the basis of our constitution, and placed in jeopardy our existence as a nation."[45]

Such lack of concern for the true national interest, however, only reflected, according to Protestant analysts, the prevailing attitudes of the citizenry. Too many Americans, clerics judged, had little concern for their own souls, for their fellow men, or for their country. Too many men lusted after power, fame, or wealth. "We must be rich," wrote one spokesman with scorn, "and that in a few years."[46] No longer could humanitarians view the individual accumulation of wealth as an unmixed blessing, for behind the actions of the rising entrepreneurs, professionals, and politicians too often lay a ruthless self-aggrandizement to which virtues like humility and philanthropy seemed irrelevant. The national ideal seemed no longer the self-reliant and honorable merchant and mechanic which these Protestant clerics envisioned—a man whose life was simple and whose charity was manifold; a man who had the strength of character to scorn prevailing social customs and styles; and a man behind whose entrepreneurial ambition lay the desire to help others. Instead, men of position and wealth were attacking the religious humanitarians as theocrats, refusing to support their charities, paying little attention to their strictures against materialism and high-living, and devoting their energies to the more self-satisfying and less morally demanding requirements of the worlds of business and politics, while men of lesser rank who aspired after success followed their example. The Tappans as philanthropists, who confessed that their sole reason for making money was to enable them to do good, were the exception, not the rule.[47]

From their perspective, three remedies to the evils they diagnosed suggested themselves. First was the establishment of effective systems of education, where young and old could learn republican virtues such as civic responsibility, personal simplicity, and charity. Like Thomas Jefferson and many nineteenth-century liberal reformers, Protestant humanitarians looked on education as a panacea for many social ills: it was, for example, the "universal antidote" to end poverty. For if Americans—and particularly the young, still impressionable and idealistic—were effectively taught right conduct in schools, in prisons, in reformatories, and through public lectures and lyceums, there was a chance they could transcend their natural selfishness and licentiousness and work together to achieve that millennial utopia which Protestant thought envisioned. If ignorance, according to Protestant humanitarian De Witt Clinton, was "the cause as well as the effect of bad governments," then education was the way to achieve a successful republican state. Educator Philip Lindsley agreed: "The want of it [education] has occasioned most of the misery and crime which have been inflicted on our world under the specious names and imposing authority of religion and liberty."[48]

Religion, too, was the key to a successful republican state. No matter the inaccuracy of their analysis, Protestant humanitarians believed that Christianity and especially the liberating spirit of the Reformation had been responsible for all the liberal achievements of their era, including the founding of the American colonies and the formation of the United States itself. In freeing men from Catholicism, the Protestant Reformation had liberated them from their attachment to the feudal state and had stimulated them to develop representative governments and liberal societies. Contained everywhere in the religious journals of the early republic are highly selective and self-interested studies comparing the progressive institutions of Protestant countries with the decadent and despotic institutions of pagan states.

As one speaker before the Baltimore Women's Sunday School Society, drawing on an undeniably partisan interpretation of human history and human character, exulted, "The obvious tendency of our holy religion is to make men republicans."[49]

For not only did the Protestant faith teach men humility and humanitarianism but also it taught them, according to its apologists, to be self-motivated and self-reliant. Unlike the professional man or the politician, anxious to please demanding clients and constituencies and intent on gratifying desires dictated by social customs and fads, the Christian was truly independent; he was subject only to God's law. Among Christians, the primary effect of the Reformation had been "the emancipation of the mind from subjection to every restraint but that which common sense and truth imposes...." "Few men in any profession or party ever think for themselves," wrote Lindsley; it was the Christian alone who followed his reason and his conscience. Benevolent partisans could not often comprehend the quite legitimate attacks on their humanitarian activities, like temperance or Sabbath observance, for being authoritarian: it was not, according to one Unitarian source, the temperance reformers who were establishing a new orthodoxy, but rather the "self-styled gentlemen" who set the fashion for drink. Religious humanitarians saw themselves as the last survivors of that slowly dying American who acted according to universal and time-honored standards and who did not adopt current fad and fashion as his guide. Religion made men republicans; it also made them individualists.[50]

In addition to religion and education, the third major ingredient of "Christian republicanism" was the voluntary association. It was a form of organization long employed to give permanency to citizen initiative and group endeavor. Many reformers came to view the voluntary society as the perfect means whereby benevolence could be institutionalized without granting additional and potentially dangerous powers to the central government.[51] It was, moreover, a way of involving citizens with their government and thus insuring that democracy would actually function within the republican framework, of bringing together in harmony people of the various competing classes and sections, and of providing stable organizations and a sense of community within a society in continual flux. In sum, the benevolent leaders planned their societies as workshops in republicanism, which could "bind together as with a cord of love the citizens of this great country" and which could "divert the attention of enlightened minds from the visions of political speculation, and the angry disputes of party, to the substantial good of lessening the miseries and multiplying the comforts of human life."[52]

Benevolent spokesmen envisioned that employer and worker, wealthy and poor, would participate in these voluntary associations and that through this "true American Union" the wealthy would learn frugality and charity and the poor would learn self-reliance and industriousness. William Ellery Channing, often incorrectly cited as a critic of voluntarism because he, unlike others involved in benevolence, saw the potential danger to the republic from large-scale organizations which could be perverted to political ends, in reality supported their aims. He looked "with interest and hope on the spirit of association" for he regarded the central government with suspicion. "Our social principles and relations are the great springs of improvement, and of vigorous and efficient exertion," he wrote. When united with others, he observed, the individual's resolve became firm, and men became conscious of unknown powers.[53] Voluntary associations, then, could be an important contribution to the success of republicanism.

In their analyses of voluntary organization, men like Channing offered an important contribution to the republican ideology of their age. Many literate Americans after the Revolution regarded the republican form of government with apprehension. Only too often such fears limited the ability of republican theorists to view American institutions from other than a negative perspective: they were concerned with how to check power, not how to create it. The most representative minds of the American enlightenment, Jefferson and James Madison, judged that society could best protect itself against the destructive energy of factions, the corrupting influence of power, and the evil inherent in all men by federalizing territorial states and by dividing the powers and functions of government among many branches. The benevolent leaders, however, ventured in a more positive direction. Excluded from politics, they looked toward society to find their solution to the supposed defects inherent in the republican order. The mechanistic division of power they left up to political theorists; what concerned them was how best to channel social power for useful democratic ends.

Such was the theory of voluntarism which underlay their benevolent organizations. In practice, of course, it did not often work out as they had planned. Individuals could easily enough be persuaded to join their societies; the problem was to maintain interest for any period of time. Rather than acting as coordinators for active local chapters, however, directors of the national religious societies spent their time as publicity agents, as fund raisers, and as employers of paid agents sent out to invigorate local auxiliaries and to try to form new ones. Nor was the hope that the wealthy and the poor might learn from one another any more than a romantic and naive vision. Men of position quickly assumed prominence in the societies, and, although they did not hesitate to proclaim their own values to the poor, one wonders to what extent they put into practice in their own lives their rhetorical commitment to virtues like humility, asceticism, and self-abnegation.

Like many groups dedicated to a common purpose, the religious humanitarians were often blind to those evils in their own organizations which they saw clearly in the associations of others. They had little conscious desire to control society or to resurrect an older social order in which clerical wisdom was supreme. They wanted rather, like their Federalist and Jeffersonian contemporaries, to insure the success of the American republic and ultimately to attain a stable democratic order. But because their organizations were subject to all the frailties of human institutions, it was inevitable that their results would fall far short of the goals they had set for themselves and that, from the perspective of history, their moralism would seem to outweigh their benevolence. Yet when they excoriated materialism and called for humanitarian endeavor, they provided a signal service for their generation. Few men in that age were willing to challenge the universal devotion to wealth; few men were able to see that contemporary materialism had in it a ruthlessness which disregarded spiritual and humane qualities. The religious humanitarians of the early nineteenth century called into question the goals of America and forced their generation to examine their values. Not the least of the results of this examination was to direct the thoughts of many Americans toward reform.

NOTES

[1] John R. Bodo, *The Protestant Clergy and Public Issues, 1812-1848* (Princeton, 1954); Charles C. Cole, Jr., *The Social Ideas of the Northern Evangelists, 1820-1860* (New York, 1954); Charles I. Foster, *An Errand of Mercy: The Evangelical United Front, 1790-1837* (Chapel Hill, 1960); Clifford S. Griffin, *Their Brothers' Keepers: Moral Stewardship in the United States, 1800-1865* (New Brunswick, 1960).

[2] For criticism of the abolitionists, see David Donald, "Toward a Reconsideration of Abolitionists," *Lincoln Reconsidered: Essays on the Civil War Era* (New York, 1956), 19-36; Stanley M. Elkins, *Slavery: A Problem in American Institutional and Intellectual Life* (Chicago, 1959), 140-206; and Avery Craven, *The Coming of the Civil War* (rev. ed., Chicago, 1957), 134-50. For defenders of the abolitionists, see Martin Duberman, "The Northern Response to Slavery," Martin Duberman, ed., *The Antislavery Vanguard: New Essays on the Abolitionists* (Princeton, 1965), 395-413; Merton Dillon, "The Abolitionists as a Dissenting Minority," Alfred E. Young, ed., *Dissent: Explorations in the History of American Radicalism* (DeKalb, 1968), 83-108; Aileen Kraditor, *Means and Ends in American Abolitionism* (New York, 1967).

[3] John L. Thomas, "Romantic Reform in America, 1815-1865," *American Quarterly*, XVII (Winter 1965), 656-81.

[4] Robert Baird, *Religion in America; Or, an Account of the Origin, Process, Relation to the State, and Present Condition of the Evangelical Churches in the United States. With Notices of the Unevangelical Denominations* (New York, 1844); Sidney E. Mead, *The Lively Experiment: The Shaping of Christianity in America* (New York, 1963); Perry Miller, *The Life of the Mind in America: From the Revolution to the Civil War* (New York, 1965).

[5] Miller, *Life of the Mind in America*, 78; Edward A. Park, *Memoir of the Life and Character of Samuel Hopkins* (Boston, 1854), 120.

[6] For the negative reaction to Hopkinsianism, see Edmund S. Morgan, "The American Revolution Considered as an Intellectual Movement," Arthur M. Schlesinger, Jr., and Morton White, eds., *Paths of American Thought* (Boston, 1963), 11-33.

[7] Clifton Jackson Phillips, *Protestant America and the Pagan World: The First Half Century of the American Board of Commissioners for Foreign Missions, 1810-1860* (Cambridge, Mass., 1968), 1-31.

[8]For voluntary organizations, see Arthur M. Schlesinger, "Biography of a Nation of Joiners," *American Historical Review*, L (Oct. 1944), 1-25; Carl Bridenbaugh, *Cities in the Wilderness: The First Century of Urban Life in America, 1625-1742* (New York, 1938); Carl and Jessica Bridenbaugh, *Rebels and Gentlemen: Philadelphia in the Age of Franklin* (New York, 1942).

[9]Historians of the "social control" persuasion have relied too heavily on Lyman Beecher's famous lament of the passing of "cocked hats, and gold-headed canes." Barbara M. Cross, ed., *The Autobiography of Lyman Beecher* (2 vols., Cambridge, Mass., 1961), I, 253.

[10]*Christian Spectator*, V (Jan. 1823), 16-17. For biographies of early nineteenth-century ministers of all denominations, see William B. Sprague, *Annals of the American Pulpit; Or Commemorative Notices of Distinguished American Clergymen of Various Denominations, from the Early Settlement of the Country to the Close of the Year Eighteen Hundred and Fifty-Five* (9 vols., New York, 1857-1869.)

[11]Baird, *Religion in America,* 306; Sidney E. Mead, "The Rise of the Evangelical Conception of the Ministry in America (1607-1850)," H. Richard Niebuhr and Daniel D. Williams, eds., *The Ministry in Historical Perspectives* (New York, 1956), 234.

[12]For the history of Presbyterianism, see E. H. Gillett, *History of the Presbyterian Church in the United States of America* (2 vols., Philadelphia, 1864); Leonard J. Trinterud, *The Forming of an American Tradition: A Reexamination of Colonial Presbyterianism* (Philadelphia, 1949); William Warren Sweet, *Religion on the American Frontier: The Presbyterians; A Collection of Source Materials* (New York, 1936); Walter Brownlow Posey, *The Presbyterian Church in the Old Southwest, 1778-1838* (Richmond, 1952); Ernest Trice Thompson, *Presbyterians in the South* (2 vols., Richmond, 1963); Elwyn A. Smith, "The Forming of a Modern American Denomination," *Church History,* XXXI (March 1962), 74-99; Fred J. Hood, "Presbyterianism and the New American Nation, 1783-1826: A Case Study of Religion and National Life" (doctoral dissertation, Princeton University, 1968).

[13]See American Bible Society, *Annual Reports* (New York, 1817-1840); American Sunday School Union, *Annual Reports* (Philadelphia, 1825-1840).

[14]Although one apologist for the Congregationalists contended that the directors of American Board of Commissioners for Foreign Missions (ABCFM) had tried without success to enlist representatives of other denominations. *Address to the Public on the Proposed Union between the American Board of Commissioners for Foreign Missions and the United Foreign Missionary Society* (Boston [1826]), 6.

[15]Cross, ed., *Autobiography of Lyman Beecher,* I, 253. Elwyn A. Smith significantly modifies the common notion that even Beecher was intent on some sort of "social control." Elwyn A. Smith, "The Voluntary Establishment of Religion," Elwyn A. Smith, ed., *The Religion of the Republic* (Philadelphia, 1971), 154-82.

[16]See Lois W. Banner, "The Protestant Crusade: Religious Missions, Benevolence, and Reform in the United States, 1780-1840" (doctoral dissertation, Columbia University, 1970).

[17]Moreover, the sermon does not prove that the benevolent community was anti-Jackson and, thus, "anti-democratic." Ely endorsed neither candidate in the sermon, and he added an appendix to the 1828 printed version of the 1827 sermon, in which he admitted a preference for John Quincy Adams, but he thought that Andrew Jackson was a "friend and supporter of Christianity" and deserved the presidency in the future. Ezra Stiles Ely, *The Duty of Christian Freemen to Elect Christian Rulers: A Discourse Delivered on the Fourth of July 1827.* (Philadelphia, 1828).

[18]Bangs, *History of the Methodist Episcopal Church* I, 26-27; Charles Roy Keller, *The Second Great Awakening in Connecticut* (New Haven, 1942), 191; Isaac Backus, *A History of New England with Particular Reference to the Denomination of Christians Called Baptists* (2 vols., Newton, Mass., 1871), II, 385.

[19]Robert Bierstadt, *The Social Order: An Introduction to Sociology* (New York, 1957). For a historian who takes cognizance of the denominational dimension, see Foster, *Errand of Mercy.*

[20]Data on the Congregationalists is vast and scattered. For developments in Massachusetts, see Evarts B. Greene, "A Puritan Counter-Reformation," *Proceedings of the American Antiquarian Society,* 42 (April, 1932), 17, 46; Samuel Worcester, *The Life and Labors of Rev. Samuel Worcester D.D., Former Pastor of the Tabernacle Church, Salem, Mass.* (Boston, 1852); William Sprague, *The Life of Jedidiah Morse D.D.* (New York, 1874); and James King Morse, *Jedidiah Morse: A Champion of New England Orthodoxy* (New York, 1939). On Connecticut, see Keller, *Second Great Awakening in Connecticut;* M. Louise Green, *The Development of Religious Liberty in Connecticut* (Boston, 1905); Richard J. Purcell, *Connecticut in Transition, 1775-1818* (Washington, 1918). The two histories of Congregationalism as a denomination, Williston Walker, *A History of the Congregational Churches in the United States* (New York, 1894), and Gaius Glenn Atkins and Frederick L. Fagley, *History of American Congregationalism* (Boston, 1942), are unsatisfactory.

[21]For a study of the institutional development from sectarianism to denominationalism and benevolence, see Sydney V. James, *A People Among Peoples: Quaker Benevolence in Eighteenth-Century America* (Cambridge, Mass., 1963).

[22]For this discussion of Methodism, see Bangs, *History of the Methodist Episcopal Church;* Wade Crawford Barclay, *Early American Methodism, 1769-1844* (2 vols., New York, 1949); Elizabeth K. Nottingham, *Methodism and the Frontier: Indiana Proving Ground* (New York, 1941); William Warren Sweet, *Religion on the American Frontier, 1783-1840: The Methodists* (Chicago, 1946); Walter Brownlow Posey, *The Development of Methodism in the Old Southwest, 1783-1824* (Nashville, 1933); W. M. Gewehr, "Some Factors in the Expansion of Frontier Methodism, 1800-1811," *Journal of Religion,* VIII (Jan. 1928), 98-120; Elmer T. Clark, J. Manning Potts, Jacob S. Payton, eds., *The Journal and Letters of Francis Asbury* (3 vols., London, 1958); Nathan Bangs, *An Authentic History of the Missions under the Care of the Missionary Society of the Methodist Episcopal Church* (New York, 1832).

[23]Donald G. Mathews, "The Second Great Awakening as an Organizing Process, 1780-1830: An Hypothesis," *American Quarterly,* XXI (Spring 1969), 23-43, (reading number 13).

[24]Barclay, *Early American Methodism,* II, 37.

[25]The institutional imperatives behind Presbyterian benevolence were much the same as for the Congregationalists. For a discussion of the general relationship between denominationalism and benevolence, see Banner, "The Protestant Crusade."

[26]Rush Welter, *Popular Education and Democratic Thought in America* (New York, 1962), 34. See also Timothy L. Smith, "Protestant Schooling and American Nationality, 1800-1850," *Journal of American History,* LIII (March 1967), 679-95.

[27]John Romeyn to John Van Shaack, Feb. 2, 1800, Gratz Collection (Pennsylvania Historical Society).

[28]William B. Sprague, *A Discourse, Delivered on Sabbath Evening, March 17, 1833, in St. Peter's Church, in Aid of the Albany Apprentices' Library* (Albany, 1833). On the lyceum, see Carl Bode, *The American Lyceum: Town Meeting of the Mind* (New York, 1956), 31.

[29]*Twelfth Annual Report* (Philadelphia, 1836), 29. See also *Religious Intelligencer,* I (May 17, 1817), 805.

[30]Walter Brownlow Posey, *Frontier Mission: A History of Religion West of the Southern Appalachians to 1861* (Lexington, Ky., 1966), 409.

[31]Thompson, *Presbyterians in the South,* I, 189-203; Jedidiah Morse, "Journal of a Mission to the Isle of Shoals, performed at the request and expense of the Society for Propagating the Gospel among the Indians and Others," Aug. 5-15, 1800, Jedidiah Morse Papers (New York Public Library).

[32]According to Baird, in distributing Bibles and tracts, members of voluntary associations often discovered cases of poverty and disease and reported them to associations or individuals qualified to attend to them. Baird, *Religion in America,* 177. See Mohl, *Poverty in New York,* 121-58.

[33]Keith Melder, "Ladies Bountiful: Organized Women's Benevolence in Early 19th-Century America," *New York History,* XLVIII (July 1967), 231-54; R. Pierce Beaver, *All Loves Excelling: American Protestant Women in World Missions* (Grand Rapids, 1968).

[34]Thomas, "Romantic Reform in America," 159.

[35]Henry Barnard, *Tribute to Gallaudet. A Discourse in Commemoration of the Life, Character and Services, of the Rev. Thomas H. Gallaudet L.L.D., Delivered before the Citizens of Hartford, January 7, 1852* (Hartford, 1852); Thomas H. Gallaudet, *A Sermon Delivered at the Opening of the Connecticut Asylum for the Education and Instruction of Deaf and Dumb Persons, April 20, 1817* (Hartford, 1852), 169.

[36]Russel B. Nye, "Marius Robinson, A Forgotten Abolitionist Leader," *Ohio State Archaeological and Historical Quarterly,* LV (April-June 1946), 139.

[37]See Gilbert Hobbs Barnes, *The Antislavery Impulse, 1830-1844* (New York, 1933), 64-73.

[38]John Lytle Meyers, "The Agency System of the Anti-slavery Movement, 1823-37, and its Antecedents in Other Benevolent and Reform Societies" (doctoral dissertation, University of Michigan, 1961).

[39]Lois W. Banner, "Religion and Reform in the Early Republic: The Role of Youth," *American Quarterly,* XXIII (Dec. 1971), 677-95.

[40]For millennialism, see Elsbree, *Rise of the Missionary Spirit;* Ira V. Brown, "Watchers for the Second Coming: The Millenarian Tradition in America," *Mississippi Valley Historical Review,* XXXIX (Dec. 1952), 441-58; David E. Smith, "Millenarian Scholarship in America," *American Quarterly,* XVII (Fall 1965), 535-49; Ernest Lee Tuveson, *Redeemer Nation: The Idea of America's Millennial Role* (Chicago, 1968); and J. F. Maclear, "The Republic and the Millennium," Elwyn A. Smith, ed., *The Religion of the Republic* (Philadelphia, 1971), 183-216, reprinted as reading 12.

[41]For republican thought after the Revolution, see John R. Howe, Jr., "Republican Thought and the Political Violence of the 1790's," *American Quarterly,* XIX (Summer 1967), 147-65; Gordon S. Wood, *The Creation of the American Republic, 1776-1787* (Chapel Hill, 1969); James M. Banner, Jr., *To the Hartford Convention: The Federalists and the Origins of Party Politics in Massachusetts, 1789-1815* (New York, 1970).

[42]Alan Heimert, *Religion and the American Mind: From the Great Awakening to the Revolution* (Cambridge, Mass., 1966); Timothy Dwight, *A Sermon Delivered in Boston, Sept. 16, 1813, before the American Board of Commissioners for Foreign Missions at Their Fourth Annual Meeting* (Boston, 1813), 7.

[43]James Blythe, *A Portrait of the Times; Being a Sermon, Delivered at the Opening of the Synod of Kentucky . . . Sept. 7, 1814* (Lexington, Ky., 1814).

44Lewis Tappan to Benjamin Tappan, Sept. 26, 1829, Jan. 8, 1833, Benjamin Tappan Papers (Manuscripts Division, Library of Congress).

45*Panoplist*, II (May 1807), 570; *Weekly Recorder*, III (July 30, 1817), 413.

46*An Address, from the Convention of Massachusetts Congregational Ministers*, 1799, *Panoplist*, II (Aug. 1806), 117. See also *Evangelical and Literary Magazine*, I (July 1818), 323; *Connecticut Evangelical Magazine*, VI (Nov. 5, 1805), 171; *Methodist Magazine*, XII (Oct. 1830), 402; *New York Evangelist*, VII (July 30, 1836), 121.

47For evidence of the societies' difficulties in retaining members and in raising money, see Mathew Carey, *Essays on the Public Charities of Philadelphia: Intended to Vindicate Benevolent Societies from the Charge of Encouraging Idleness, and to Place in Strong Relief, before an Enlightened Public the Sufferings and Oppression under which the Greater Part of the Females Labour, Who Depend on Their Industry for a Support for Themselves and Children* (Philadelphia, 1830), 13-14; Barck, ed., *Letters from John Pintard*, II, 155-56; J. Orin Oliphant, *Through the South and the West With Jeremiah Evarts in 1826* (Lewisburg, Pa., 1956), 84-87; Bela Bates Edwards, *Memoir of the Rev. Elias Cornelius* (Boston, 1833), 297. On the motivation of the Tappans, see Lewis Tappan to Benjamin Tappan, Sept. 26, 1829, Jan. 8, 1833, Benjamin Tappan Papers.

48*Quarterly Christian Spectator*, II (June 1830), 221; Charles Fenton Mercer, *A Discourse on Popular Education; Delivered in the Church at Princeton, . . . the evening before the annual commencement of the College of New Jersey, Sept. 28, 1826* (Princeton, 1826), 36; De Witt Clinton's address to Free School Society, Dec. 11, 1809, William W. Campbell, ed., *The Life and Writings of De Witt Clinton* (New York, 1849), 312; Philip Lindsley, "The Cause of Education in Tennessee: An Address Delivered to the Young Gentlemen Admitted to the Degree of Bachelor of Arts, at the First Commencement of the University of Nashville, Oct. 4, 1826," LeRoy J. Halsey, ed., *The Works of Philip Lindsley, D.D.* (3 vols., Philadelphia, 1866), I, 126.

49"Extracts from an Address, Delivered before the Managers and Teachers of Female Union Society of Baltimore, for the Promotion of Sabbath-Schools, Nov. 3, 1828," *American Sunday-School Magazine*, VI (Jan. 1829), 3.

50Philip Lindsley, "Baccalaureate Address Pronounced on the Evening of the Anniversary Commencement of the University of Nashville, October 3, 1827," Halsey, ed., *Works*, I, 186-201; Albert Barnes, *The Power of Holiness in the Christian Ministry. A Discourse Delivered before the Directors, Professors, and Students of the Theological Seminary of the Presbyterian Church at Princeton, September 29, 1834* (Philadelphia, 1834), 8; *Christian Examiner*, XIV (July 1833), 273-78.

51Mead alone notes that there was an ideological thrust behind the formation of voluntary societies. See Sidney Mead, *Lively Experiment*, 92.

52*Virginia Evangelical and Literary Magazine*, II (Feb. 1819), 91-92; *Christian Monitor*, II (Oct. 26, 1816), 49-51.

53For a representative statement of the "true American Union" idea, see Heman Humphrey, *The Way to Bless and Save our Country: A Sermon, Preached in Philadelphia at the Request of the American Sunday-School Union, May 23, 1831* (Philadelphia, 1831), 15. William Ellery Channing subscribed to the idea of a "fraternal union" of classes. See William Ellery Channing, *Memoir of William Ellery Channing: With Extracts from his Correspondence and Manuscripts* (3 vols., Boston, 1848), III, 38. For Channing's discussion and criticism of voluntary organization, see *Christian Examiner*, VII (Sept. 1829), 105-40.

15

The Emergence of Immediatism in British and American Antislavery Thought

David Brion Davis

In analyzing the impact of evangelical Protestantism, historians have frequently focused on the relationship between revivalism and the abolitionist movement. In the following essay, David Brion Davis, Professor of History at Yale University, analyzes the reasons for the escalation of abolitionist goals from gradual to immediate emancipation, and the corresponding change in tactics. Further, comparing Great Britain to the United States, Professor Davis suggests how evangelicalism and romanticism combined to influence the debate over slavery.

In the history of reform few slogans have brought forth such confusion and controversy as "immediate emancipation."[1] To the general public in the 1830's the phrase meant simply the abolition of Negro slavery without delay or preparation. But the word "immediate" may denote something other than a closeness in time; to many abolitionists it signified a rejection of intermediate agencies or conditions, a directness or forthrightness in action or decision. In this sense immediatism suggested a repudiation of the various media, such as colonization or apprenticeship, that had been advocated as remedies for the evils of slavery. To some reformers the phrase seemed mainly to imply a direct, intuitive consciousness of the sinfulness of slavery, and a sincere personal commitment to work for its abolition.[2] In this subjective sense the word "immediate" was charged with religious overtones and

First published in the *Mississippi Valley Historical Review*, XLIX (September 1962), pp. 209-30 (notes abridged). Reprinted with permission of the Organization of American Historians.

referred more to the moral disposition of the reformer than to a particular plan for emancipation. Thus some reformers confused immediate abolition with an immediate personal decision to abstain from consuming slave-grown produce; and a man might be considered an immediatist if he were genuinely convinced that slavery should be abolished absolutely and without compromise, though not necessarily without honest preparation.[3] Such a range of meanings led unavoidably to misunderstanding, and the antislavery cause may have suffered from so ambiguous a slogan. The ambiguity, however, was something more than semantic confusion or the unfortunate result of a misleading watchword. The doctrine of immediacy, in the form it took in the 1830's, was at once a logical culmination of the antislavery movement and a token of a major shift in intellectual history.

A belief in the slave's right to immediate freedom was at least implicit in much of the antislavery writing of the eighteenth century. If Negro slavery were unjust, unnatural, illegal, corrupting, and detrimental to the national interest, as innumerable eighteenth-century writers claimed, there could be no excuse for its perpetuation.[4] Several of the *philosophes* held that since masters relied on physical force to impose their illegal demands, slave revolts would be just;[5] Louis de Jaucourt went so far as to argue that slaves, never having lost their inherent liberty, should be immediately declared free.[6] Anthony Benezet advanced a similar argument, asking what course a man should follow if he discovered that an inherited estate was really the property of another: "Would you not give it up immediately to the lawful owner? The voice of all mankind would mark him for a villain, who would refuse to comply with this demand of justice. And is not keeping a slave after you are convinced of the unlawfulness of it—a crime of the same nature?"[7]

In England, Granville Sharp denounced slavery as a flagrant violation of the common law, the law of reason, and the law of God. After exhorting Lord North to do something about the plight of the slaves, he warned: "I say immediate redress, bacause, *to be in power,* and to neglect . . . even a day in endeavoring to put a stop to such monstrous injustice and abandoned wickedness, must necessarily endanger a man's *eternal* welfare, be he ever so great in *temporal* dignity or office."[8] Sharp, who argued that "No Legislature on Earth . . . can alter the Nature of Things, or make that to be lawful, which is contrary to the Law of God,"[9] secured a judicial decision outlawing slavery in England. Americans like James Otis, Nathaniel Appleton, and Isaac Skillman took a similarly uncompromising stand before the Revolution;[10] by the 1780's the doctrine of natural rights had made the illegality of slavery an established fact in Vermont and Massachusetts.[11]

But the natural rights philosophy was not the only source of immediatism. Officially, the Society of Friends showed extreme caution in encouraging emancipation, but from the time of George Keith a latent impulse of moral perfectionism rose to the surface in the radical testimony of individual Quakers, who judged slavery in the uncompromising light of the Golden Rule. For such reformers slavery was not a social or economic institution, but rather an embodiment of worldly sin that corrupted the souls of both master and slave; emancipation was not an objective matter of social or political expediency, but a subjective act of purification and a casting off of sin.[12]

Immediatism, in the sense of an immediate consciousness of the guilt of slaveholding and an ardent desire to escape moral contamination, is similarly evident in the writings of men who differed widely in their views of religion and political economy. John Wesley's combined attack on the opposite poles of Calvinism and natural religion could also be directed against slavery, which some defended by arguments similar to those that justified seeming injustice or worldly evils as part of God's master plan or nature's economy. In 1784 Wesley's antislavery beliefs were developed into a kind of immediatism in the rules of American Methodists: "We . . . think it our most bounden duty to take immediately some effectual method to extirpate this abomination from among us."[13] A related source of immediatism can be traced in the development of the romantic sensibility and the cult of the "man of feeling," which merged with Rousseau and the French Enlightenment in the writings of such men as Thomas Day and William Fox.[14]

In the light of this evidence we may well ask why immediatism appeared so new and dangerously radical in the 1830's. The later abolitionists charged that slavery was a sin against God and a crime against nature; they demanded an immediate beginning of direct action that would eventuate in general emancipation. Yet all of this had been said at least a half-century before, and we might conclude that immediatism was merely a recurring element in antislavery history.

But if immediatism was at least latent in early antislavery thought, the dominant frame of mind of the eighteenth century was overwhelmingly disposed to gradualism. Gradualism, in the sense of a reliance on indirect and slow-working means to achieve a desired social objective, was the logical consequence of fundamental attitudes toward progress, natural law, property, and individual rights.

We cannot understand the force of gradualism in antislavery thought unless we abandon the conventional distinction between Enlightenment liberalism and evangelical reaction. It is significant that British opponents of abolition made little use of religion, appealing instead to the need for calm rationality and an expedient regard for the national interest. Quoting Hume, Lord Kames, and even Montesquieu to support their moral relativism, they showed that principles of the Enlightenment could be easily turned to the defense of slavery.[15] A belief in progress and natural rights might lead, of course, to antislavery convictions; but if history seemed to be on the side of liberty, slavery had attained a certain prescriptive sanction as a nearly universal expression of human nature.[16] Men who had acquired an increasing respect for property and for the intricate workings of natural and social laws could not view as an unmitigated evil an institution that had developed through the centuries.

Though evangelicals attacked natural religion and an acceptance of the world as a divinely contrived mechanism in which evils like slavery served a legitimate function, they nevertheless absorbed many of the assumptions of conservative rationalists and tended to express a middle-class fear of sudden social change.[17] Despite the sharp differences between evangelicals and rationalists, they shared confidence, for the most part, in the slow unfolding of a divine or natural plan of historical progress. The mild and almost imperceptible diffusion of reason, benevolence, or Christianity had made slavery—a vestige of barbarism—anachronistic. But while eighteenth-century abolitionists might delight in furthering God's or nature's plan for earthly salvation, they tended to assume a detached, contemplative view of history, and showed considerable fear of sudden changes or precipitous action that might break the delicate balance of natural and historical forces.[18]

There was therefore a wide gap betwen the abstract proposition that slavery was wrong, or even criminal, and the cautious formulation of anti-slavery policy. It was an uncomfortable fact that slavery and the slave trade were tied closely to the rights of private property, the political freedom of colonies and states, and the economic rewards of international competition. Yet from the 1790's to the 1820's British and American reformers were confident that they understood the basic principles of society and could thus work toward the desired goal indirectly and without infringing on legitimate rights or interests. Frequently they seemed to think of slavery as a kind of unfortunate weed or fungus that had spread through the Lord's garden in a moment of divine inattention. As expert horticulturalists they imagined they could gradually kill the blight without injuring the plants. The British reformers focused their attention on the slave trade, assuming that if the supply of African Negroes were shut off planters would be forced to take better care of their existing slaves and would ultimately discover that free labor was more profitable. In America, reform energies were increasingly directed toward removing the free Negroes, who were thought to be the principal barrier to voluntary manumission. Both schemes were attempts at rather complex social engineering, and in both instances the desired reform was to come from the slaveowners themselves. Antislavery theorists assumed that they could predict the cumulative effects and consequences of their limited programs, and since they never doubted the goodness or effectiveness of natural laws, they sought only to set in motion a chain of forces that would lead irresistibly to freedom.[19]

This gradualist mentality dominated antislavery thought from the late eighteenth century to the 1820's. Though French thinkers had been among the first to denounce slavery as a crime, the emancipation scheme which they pioneered was one of slow transformation of the slave into a free laborer.[20] Even the *Amis des Noirs* feared immediate emancipation; and the French decree abolishing slavery in 1794, which was the result of political and military crisis in the West Indies, seemed to verify the ominous warnings of gradualists in all countries.[21] The years of bloodshed and anarchy in Haiti became an international symbol for the dangers of reckless and unplanned emancipation.

British abolitionists were particularly cautious in defining their objectives and moving indirectly, one step at a time. When outlawing the slave trade did not have the desired effect on colonial slavery, they then sought to bring the institution within the regulatory powers of the central government by limiting the extension of slavery in newly acquired islands and by using the crown colonies as models for gradual melioration;[22] and when these efforts failed they urged a general registration of slaves, which would not only interpose imperial authority in the colonies but provide a mechanism for protecting the Negroes' rights.[23] By 1822 these methods had proved inadequate and the British reformers began agitating for direct parliamentary intervention. Even then, however, and for the following eight years, British antislavery leaders limited their aims to melioration and emancipation by slow degrees.[24]

Between British and American antislavery men there was a bond of understanding and a common interest in suppressing the international slave trade and finding a home in Haiti or western Africa for free Negroes.[25] But in America the antislavery movement was given a distinctive color by the discouraging obstacles that stood in the way of even gradual emancipation. While states like New York and Pennsylvania provided tangible examples of gradual manumission, they also showed the harsh and ugly consequences of racial prejudice.[26] Americans, far more than the British, were concerned with the problem of the emancipated slave. Even some of the most radical and outspoken abolitionists were convinced that colonization was the inescapable prerequisite to reform. Others stressed the importance of education and moral training as the first steps toward eventual freedom.[27]

In America the gradualist frame of mind was also related to the weakness and limitations of political institutions. British abolitionists could work to enlist the unlimited power of a central Parliament against colonies that were suffering acute economic decline. But slavery in America was not only expanding but was protected by a sectional balance of power embodied in nearly every national institution. A brooding fear of disunion and anarchy damped down the aspirations of most American abolitionists and turned energies to such local questions as the education and legal protection of individual Negroes. Antislavery societies might call for the government to outlaw slavery in the District of Columbia or even to abolish the interstate slave trade, but in the end they had to rely on public opinion and individual conscience in the slave states. While British abolitionists moved with the circumspection of conservative pragmatists, their American counterparts acted with the caution of men surrounded by high explosives. For many, the only prudent solution was to remove the explosives to a distant country.

But if British and American abolitionists were gradualist in their policies and expectations, they did not necessarily regard slavery as simply one of many social evils that should be mitigated and eventually destroyed. The policy of gradualism was related to certain eighteenth-century assumptions about historical progress, the nature of man, and the principles of social change; but we have also noted a subjective, moral aspect to antislavery thought that was often revealed as an immediate consciousness of guilt and a fear of divine punishment. During the British slave trade controversy of the 1790's the entire system of slavery and slave trade became identified with sin, and reform with true virtue.[28] Though antislavery leaders adopted the gradualist policy of choosing the slave trade as their primary target, they bitterly fought every attempt to meliorate or gradually destroy the African trade. It was the determined opponents of the slave trade who first gave popular currency to the slogan, "immediate abolition," which became in the early 1790's a badge of moral sincerity.[29] When uncompromising hostility to the slave trade became a sign of personal virtue and practical Christianity, the rhetoric of statesmen acquired the strident, indignant tone that we associate with later American abolitionists. Charles James Fox made scathing attacks on those who pled for moderation; he even said that if the plantations could not be cultivated without being supplied with African slaves, it would be far better for England to rid herself of the islands. "How shall we hope," asked William Pitt, "to obtain, if it is possible, forgiveness from Heaven for those enormous evils we have committed, if we refuse to make use of those means which the mercy of Providence hath still reserved to us for wiping away the guilt and shame with which we are now covered?"[30]

This sense of moral urgency and fear of divine retribution persisted in British antislavery thought and was held in check only by a faith in the certain and predictable consequences of indirect action.[31] Whenever the faith was shaken by unforeseen obstacles or a sense of crisis, there were voices that condemned gradualism as a compromise with sin. Granville Sharp, who interpreted hurricanes in the West Indies as supernatural agencies "to blast the *enemies* of *law* and *righteousness*," called in 1806 for direct emancipation by act of Parliament, and warned that continued toleration of slavery in the colonies "must finally draw down the Divine vengeance upon our state and nation!"[32] When William Allen, Zachary Macaulay, and James Cropper became disillusioned over the failure to secure an effective registration scheme and international suppression of the slave trade, they pressed for direct though gradual emancipation by the British government.[33] The British Anti-Slavery Society remained officially gradualist until 1831, but individual abolitionists, particularly in the provinces, became increasingly impatient over the diffidence of the government and the intransigence of colonial legislatures.[34] From 1823 to 1832 the British Caribbean planters violently attacked the government's efforts to meliorate slavery. They not only devised schemes to nullify effective reform but threatened to secede from the empire and seek protection from the United States.[35] Though the evils of West Indian slavery were probably mitigated in the 1820's, the planters' resistance convinced many abolitionists that gradual improvement was impossible.

The most eloquent early plea for immediate emancipation was made in 1824 by a Quaker named Elizabeth Heyrick, who looked to the women of Great Britain as a source of invincible moral power, and who preached a massive consumers' crusade against West Indian produce. The central theme in Mrs. Heyrick's pamphlet, *Immediate, Not Gradual Abolition,* was the supremacy of individual conscience over social and political institutions. Since antislavery was a "*holy war*" against "the very powers of darkness," there was no ground for compromise or for a polite consideration of slaveholders. Like the later American immediatists, she excoriated gradualism as a satanic plot to induce gradual indifference. It was a delusion to think that slavery could be gradually improved, for "as well might you say to a poor wretch, gasping and languishing in a pest house, 'here will I keep you, till I have given you a capacity for the enjoyment of pure air.' "[36] For Mrs. Heyrick the issue was simple and clearcut: sin and vice should be immediately exterminated by individual action in accordance with conscience and the will of God.

In 1824 such views were too strong for British antislavery leaders, who still looked to direct government action modeled on the precedent of the Canning Resolutions, which had proposed measures for ameliorating the condition of West Indian slaves as a step toward ultimate emancipation.[37] Abolitionists in Parliament continued to shape their strategy in the light of political realities, but by 1830 several prominent reformers had adopted the uncompromising stand of Elizabeth Heyrick. The shift from gradualism to immediatism is most dramatically seen in James Stephen, who possessed a mind of great clarity and precision and who, having practiced law in the West Indies, had acquired direct experience with slavery as an institution. For a time Stephen adhered to the principle of gradualism, transferring his hopes from the slave registration scheme to a "digested plan" of abolition by stages, beginning with domestic servants. By 1830, however, he was convinced that debate over alternative plans merely inhibited action and obscured what was essentially a question of principle and simple moral duty. It would be a tragic mistake, he felt, for the abolitionists to propose any measure short of "a general, entire, immediate restitution of the freedom wrongfully withheld." Lashing out at the moral lethargy of the government, he denounced the principle of compensation to slaveowners and rejected all specific gradualist measures such as the liberation of Negro women or the emancipation of infants born after a certain date. Stephen's immediatism was based ultimately on a fear of divine vengeance and an overwhelming sense of national guilt. "We sin remorselessly," he said, "because our fathers sinned, and because multitudes of our own generation sin, in the same way without [public] discredit."[38]

On October 19, 1830, the Reverend Andrew Thomson, of St. George's Church in Edinburgh, delivered a fire-and-brimstone speech that provided an ideology for George Thompson and the later Agency Committee.[39] Beginning with the premise that slavery is a crime and sin, Thomson dismissed all consideration of economic and political questions. When the issue was reduced to what individual men should do as moral and accountable beings, there was no possibility of compromise or even controversy. The British public should "compel" Parliament to order total and immediate emancipation. With Calvinistic intensity he exhorted the public to cut down and burn the "pestiferous tree," root and branch: "You must annihilate it,—annihilate it now,—and annihilate it forever." Since Thomson considered every hour that men were kept in bondage a repetition of the original sin of man stealing, he did not shrink from violence: "If there must be violence, . . . let it come and rage its little hour, since it is to be succeeded by lasting freedom, and prosperity, and happiness."[40]

Taking its cue from men like Stephen, Thomson, and Joseph Sturge, the Anti-Slavery Society reorganized itself for more effective action and focused its energies on raising petitions and arousing public feeling against slavery.[41] While Thomas Fowell Buxton sought to make the fullest use of public opinion to support his campaign in Parliament, he found himself under mounting pressure from abolitionists who refused to defer to his judgment. People's principles, he told his daughter, were the greatest nuisance in life.[42] When the government finally revealed its plan for gradual and compensated emancipation, the Anti-Slavery Society committed itself to vigorous and aggressive opposition.[43] But once the law had been passed, the antislavery leaders concluded that they had done as well as possible and that their defeat had actually been a spectacular victory. They had achieved their primary object, which was to induce the people to support a tangible act that could be interpreted as purging the nation of collective guilt and proving the moral power of individual conscience.

In America the developing pattern was somewhat similar. Despite the conservatism of most antislavery societies, a number of radical abolitionists branded slaveholding as a heinous sin, which, if not immediately abandoned, would bring down the wrath of the Lord. A few early reformers like Theodore Dwight, David Rice, Charles Osborn, and John Rankin, were well in advance of British antislavery writers in their sense of moral urgency and their mistrust of gradualist programs. As early as 1808, David Barrow, although he denied favoring immediate abolition, anticipated the later doctrine of the American Anti-Slavery Society by refusing to recognize the lawfulness of slavery or the justice of compensation. Holding that slavery was the crying sin of America, he urged a prompt beginning of manumission in order to avert the retribution of God.[44] Three years earlier Thomas Branagan, who opposed "instantaneous emancipation" if the freed Negroes were to remain within the United States, contended that his plan for colonization in the West would bring a speedy end to slavery and avert the divine judgment of an apocalyptic racial war.[45] In 1817 John Kenrick showed that colonization could be combined with a kind of immediatism, for though he proposed settlement of free Negroes in the West, he went so far as to suggest that the powers of the central government should be enlarged, if necessary, in order to abolish slavery. "If slavery is 'a violation of the divine laws,' " Kenrick asked, "is it not absurd to talk about a gradual emancipation? We might as well talk of gradually leaving off piracy—murder—adultery, or drunkenness."[46]

The religious character of this radical abolitionism can best be seen in the writings of George Bourne, an English immigrant who was to have a deep influence on William Lloyd Garrison. In 1815 Bourne condemned professed Christians who upheld the crime of slavery. "The system is so entirely corrupt," he wrote, "that it admits of no cure, but by a total and immediate, abolition. For a gradual emancipation is a virtual recognition of the right, and establishes the rectitude of the practice." But while Bourne associated slavery with the very essence of human sin, his main concern was not the plight of Negroes but the corruption of the Christian church:

> Had this compound of all corruption no connection with the church of Christ; however deleterious are the effects of it in political society, however necessary is its immediate and total abolition, and however pregnant with danger to the *Union,* is the prolongation of the system; to Legislators and Civilians, the redress of the evil would have been committed. But *Slavery* is the *golden Calf,* which has been elevated among the Tribes, and before it, the Priests and the Elders and the *nominal* sons of Israel, *eat, drink, rise up to play, worship and sacrifice.*[47]

Thus for Bourne "immediatism" meant an immediate recognition of the sin of slavery and an immediate decision on the part of Christians to purge their churches of all contamination. He was far more interested in the purification of religion than in slavery as an institution.

In 1825 the Boston *Recorder and Telegraph* published a long correspondence that further clarifies the origins of immediatism. After arguing that slavery was unlawful and suggesting that slaves might have a right to revolt, "Vigornius" [Samuel M. Worcester] asserted that *"the slave-holding system must be abolished;* and in order to the accomplishment of this end, immediate, determined measures must be adopted for the ultimate emancipation of every slave within our territories."[48] This was the position of the later Kentucky and New York abolitionists, but Vigornius combined it with strong faith in the American Colonization Society. He was bitterly attacked by "A Carolinian," who accused him of believing in "an entire and immediate abolition of slavery." "Philo," the next contributor, said he opposed immediate emancipation on grounds of expediency, but recognized the right of slaves to immediate freedom; he advocated, therefore, "immediate and powerful remedies," since "We are convinced, and if our Southern brethren are not convinced, we wish to convince them, and think with a little discussion we could convince them, that to postpone these prospective measures a day, is a great crime . . . and moreover, we wish to state directly, that this postponement is that, in which we consider the guilt of slavery, so far as the present proprietors are concerned, to consist."[49]

A Southerner, who called himself "Hieronymus," defended Vigornius and tried to avoid the ambiguities that were later to cloud discussions of immediate abolition. Vigornius, he wrote,

> pleads, it is true, for *speedy* emancipation, and immediate preparatory steps. But immediate and speedy are not synonimous [*sic*] expressions. One is an absolute, the other a relative or comparative term. An event may in one view of it be regarded as very speedy, which in another might be pronounced very gradual. If slavery should be entirely abolished from the United States in 30, 40, or even 50 years, many . . . will readily admit, that it would be a speedy abolition; while every one must perceive, that it would be far, very far, from an immediate abolition. In a certain sense abolition may be immediate; in another, speedy; and in both, practicable and safe. There are not a few blacks now at the South, qualified for immediate emancipation, if Legislatures would permit, and owners would confer it.[50]

Hieronymus, who had read and been impressed by Elizabeth Heyrick's pamphlet, agreed with Vigornius that colonization was the only practicable solution to the nation's most critical problem.

These ardent colonizationists believed that slavery was a sin that would increase in magnitude and danger unless effective measures were adopted without delay. Yet by 1821 Benjamin Lundy and other abolitionists had come to the opinion that the American Colonization Society was founded on racial prejudice and offered no real promise of undermining slavery. Lundy thought that slavery could not be eradicated until his fellow Americans in both North and South were willing to accept the free Negro as an equal citizen.[51] But in the meantime the institution was expanding into the Southwest and even threatening to spread to such states as Illinois. In the face of such an imposing problem, Lundy called for the swift and decisive use of political power by a convention of representatives from the various states, who might devise and implement a comprehensive plan for emancipation.[52]

The American antislavery organizations absorbed some of this sense of urgency and mistrust of palliatives. The Pennsylvania Society for the Abolition of Slavery was cautious in its approach to the national problem, but in 1819 it approved a declaration that "the practice of holding and selling human beings as property . . . ought to be *immediately* abandoned."[53] In 1825 the Acting Committee of the American Convention for Promoting the Abolition of Slavery advocated the "speedy and entire" emancipation of slaves, a phrase later used by the British Society.[54] The Convention showed little confidence in any of the specific proposals for gradual abolition but at the same time rejected direct emancipation by act of Congress as an impossibility. Alert always to the need for conciliating the South and remaining within the prescribed bounds of the Constitution, the Convention considered every conceivable plan in a rationalistic and eclectic spirit.[55] In the South, however, there was an increasing tendency to see the most conservative antislavery proposals as immediatism in disguise.[56] By 1829 the gradualist approach of the American Convention had reached a dead end.[57]

It is a striking coincidence that both the British and American antislavery movements had come to a crucial turning point by 1830.[58] In both countries the decline of faith in gradualism had been marked in the mid-1820's by enthusiasm for a boycott of slave produce, a movement which promised to give a cutting edge to the moral testimony of individuals.[59] In both countries the truculence and stubborn opposition of slaveholders to even gradualist reforms brought a sense of despair and indignation to the antislavery public. To some degree immediatism was the creation of the British and American slaveholders themselves. By accusing the most moderate critics of radical designs and by blocking the path to many attempted reforms they helped to discredit the gradualist mentality that had balanced and compromised a subjective conviction that slavery was sin.[60] The sense of crisis between 1829 and 1831 was also accentuated by an increasing militancy of Negroes, both slave and free.[61] In 1829 David Walker hinted ominously of slave revenge; groups of free Negroes openly repudiated the colonization movement; and in 1831 bloody revolts erupted in Virginia and Jamaica. In that year a new generation of American reformers adopted the principle of immediatism, which had recently acquired the sanction of eminent British philanthropists.[62] But while American abolitionists modeled their new societies and techniques on British examples, the principle of immediatism had had a long and parallel development in both countries.

In one sense immediatism was simply a shift in strategy brought on by the failure of less direct plans for abolition. Earlier plans and programs had evoked little popular excitement compared with parliamentary reform or Catholic emancipation in England, or with tariff or land policies in the United States. As a simple, emotional slogan, immediate abolition would at least arouse interest and perhaps appeal to the moral sense of the public. As a device for propaganda it had the virtue of avoiding economic and social complexities and focusing attention on a clear issue of right and wrong.[63] If the public could once be brought to the conviction that slavery was wrong and that something must be done about it at once, then governments would be forced to take care of the details.

But immediatism was something more than a shift in strategy. It represented a shift in total outlook from a detached, rationalistic perspective on human history and progress to a personal commitment to make no compromise with sin. It marked a liberation for the reformer from the ideology of gradualism, from a toleration of evil within the social order, and from a deference to institutions that blocked the way to personal salvation. Acceptance of immediatism was the sign of an immediate transformation within the reformer himself; as such, it was seen as an expression of inner freedom, of moral sincerity and earnestness, and of victory over selfish and calculating expediency.[64] If slaveholders received the doctrine with contempt and scathing abuse, the abolitionist was at least assured of his own freedom from guilt. He saw the emergence of immediatism as an upswelling of personal moral force which, with the aid of God, would triumph over all that was mean and selfish and worldly.[65]

There are obvious links between immediate emancipation and a religious sense of immediate justification and presence of the divine spirit that can be traced through the early spiritual religions to the Quakers, Methodists, and evangelical revivals.[66] The new abolitionism contained a similar pattern of intense personal anxiety, rapturous freedom, eagerness for sacrifice, and mistrust of legalism, institutions, and slow-working agencies for salvation. It was no accident that from the late seventeenth century the boldest assertions of antislavery sentiment had been made by men who were dissatisfied with the materialism and sluggish formality of institutionalized religion, and who searched for a fresh and assuring meaning of Christian doctrine in a changing world.[67] To the extent that slavery became a concrete symbol of sin, and support of the antislavery cause a sign of Christian virtue, participation in the reform became a supplement or even alternative to traditional religion.[68] As a kind of surrogate religion, antislavery had long shown tendencies that were pietistic, millennial, and anti-institutional. By the 1830's it had clearly marked affinities with the increasingly popular doctrines of free grace, immediate conversion, and personal holiness. According to Amos A. Phelps, for example, immediatism was synonymous with immediate repentance: "All that follows is the carrying out of the new principle of action, and is to emancipation just what sanctification is to conversion."[69]

Immediate emancipation was also related to a changing view of history and human nature. Whereas the gradualist saw man as at least partially conditioned by historical and social forces, the immediatist saw him as essentially indeterminate and unconditioned. The gradualist, having faith in the certainty of economic and social laws, and fearing the dangers of a sudden collapse of social controls, was content to wait until a legal and rational system of external discipline replaced the arbitrary power of the slaveowner. The immediatist, on the other hand, put his faith in the innate moral capacities of the individual. He felt that unless stifling and coercive influences were swept away, there could be no development of the inner controls of conscience, emulation, and self-respect, on which a free and Christian society depended.[70] His outlook was essentially romantic, for instead of cautiously manipulating the external forces of nature, he sought to create a new epoch of history by liberating the inner moral forces of human nature.[71]

It falls beyond the scope of the present essay to show how immediatism itself became institutionalized as a rigid test of faith, and how it served as a medium for attacking all rival institutions that limited individual freedom or defined standards of thought and conduct. It is enough to suggest that immediatism, while latent in early antislavery thought, was part of a larger reaction against a type of mind that tended to think of history in terms of linear time and logical categories, and that emphasized the importance of self-interest, expediency, moderation, and planning in accordance with economic and social laws. Immediatism shared with the romantic frame of mind a hostility to all dualisms of thought and feeling, an allegiance to both emotional sympathy and abstract principle, an assumption that mind can rise above self-interest, and a belief that ideas, when held with sufficient intensity, can be transformed into irresistible moral action.[72] If immediate emancipation brought misunderstanding and violent hostility in regions that were charged with racial prejudice and fear of sectional conflict, it was nevertheless an appropriate doctrine for a romantic and evangelical age.

NOTES

[1] For the dispute over which American abolitionist had been the first to preach the doctrine, see George W. Julian, "The Genesis of Modern Abolitionism," *International Review* (New York), XII (June, 1882), 538, 542; A. T. Rankin, *Truth Vindicated and Slander Repelled* (Ironton, Ohio, 1883), 2-15; and the Parker B. Osborn Papers (Ohio Historical Society, Columbus).

[2] See Gilbert H. Barnes, *The Antislavery Impulse, 1830-1844* (New York, 1933), 48-49, 66-67, 102-104, 248; Gilbert H. Barnes and Dwight L. Dumond (eds.), *Letters*

of Theodore Dwight Weld, Angelina Grimké Weld, and Sarah Grimké, 1822-1844 (2 vols., New York, 1934), I, vii-x. While Barnes shows that Americans were mainly preoccupied with the sin of slavery, he tends to overemphasize the British origins of immediatism and ignores the historical development of the doctrine in both countries. This criticism applies also to Stanley M. Elkins, *Slavery: A Problem in American Institutional and Intellectual Life* (Chicago, 1959).

[3]In both England and America immediatists denied that they opposed careful preparation for full freedom. See, for example, the influential speech of Joseph Sturge at the Society of Friends' London Meeting of 1830, printed in Henry Richard, *Memoirs of Joseph Sturge* (London, 1864), 87-88.

[4]Frank J. Klingberg, "The Evolution of the Humanitarian Spirit in Eighteenth Century England," *Pennsylvania Magazine of History and Biography* (Philadelphia), LXVI (July, 1942), 261-65; Klingberg, *The Anti-Slavery Movement in England* (New Haven, 1926), 25-69; Wylie Sypher, "Hutcheson and the 'Classical' Theory of Slavery," *Journal of Negro History* (Washington), XXIV (July, 1939), 263-80; Edward D. Seeber, *Anti-Slavery Opinion in France during the Second Half of the Eighteenth Century (Johns Hopkins Studies in Romance Literatures and Languages,* Extra Volume X, Baltimore, 1937), *passim;* Thomas Clarkson, *The History of the Rise, Progress and Accomplishment of the Abolition of the African Slave-Trade by the British Parliament* (2 vols., London, 1808), I, 83-126, 185-89, 461-67.

[5]Seeber, *Anti-Slavery Opinion,* 71-72; F. T. H. Fletcher, "Montesquieu's Influence on Anti-Slavery Opinion in England," *Journal of Negro History,* XVIII (October, 1933), 414-26; Shelby T. McCloy, *The Humanitarian Movement in Eighteenth-Century France* (Lexington, Ky., 1957), 86-92.

[6]Louis de Jaucourt, "Traite des Negres," *Encyclopedie, ou Dictionnaire Raisonné des Sciences, des Arts et des Métiers, par une Societé de Gens de Lettres* (Neufchastel, 1765), XVI, 532-33.

[7][Anthony Benezet], *An Address to the Inhabitants of the British Settlements in America, upon Slave-Keeping* (Philadelphia, 1773), 20-21.

[8]Granville Sharp to Lord North, February 18, 1772, printed in Prince Hoare, *Memoirs of Granville Sharp, Esq., Composed from His Own Manuscripts* (London, 1820), 79.

[9]Granville Sharp, *An Appendix to the Representation* (London, 1772), 25.

[10]Mary S. Locke, *Anti-Slavery in America from the Introduction of African Slaves to the Prohibition of the Slave Trade* (Boston, 1901), 19-20; Lorenzo J. Greene, "Slave-Holding New England and Its Awakening," *Journal of Negro History,* XIII (October, 1928), 523-25; Herbert Aptheker, "Militant Abolitionists," *ibid.,* XXVI (October, 1941), 440.

[11]In Vermont, slavery was effectually prohibited by the state constitution; in Massachusetts the courts supported the claims to liberty of individual Negroes.

[12]Samuel W. Pennypacker, "The Settlement of Germantown, and the Causes Which Led to It," *Pennsylvania Magazine of History and Biography,* IV (1880), 28-30; George Keith, "An Exhortation & Caution to Friends Concerning Buying or Keeping of Negroes," *ibid.,* XIII (1889), 265-70; Society of Friends, Philadelphia Yearly Meeting, *A Brief Statement of the Rise and Progress of the Testimony of the Religious Society of Friends, against Slavery and the Slave Trade* (Philadelphia, 1843), 21-24, 44-56.

[13]Lucius C. Matlack, *The History of American Slavery and Methodism from 1780 to 1849* (New York, 1849), 15-20.

[14]Ronald S. Crane, "Suggestions Toward a Genealogy of the 'Man of Feeling,' " *English Literary History* (Baltimore), I (December, 1934), 205-206, 216, 225, 229-30; Wylie Sypher, *Guinea's Captive Kings: British Anti-Slavery Literature of the XVIIIth Century* (Chapel Hill, 1942), 10, 77-85, 193-98; Thomas Day and John Bicknell, *The Dying Negro* (London, 1773); William Fox, *An Address to the People of Great Britain, on the Consumption of West India Produce* (London, 1791).

[15][Edward Long], *Candid Reflections upon the Judgment Lately Awarded by the Court of King's Bench* (London, 1772); [Gordon Turnbull], *An Apology for Negro Slavery; or the West-India Planters Vindicated from the Charge of Inhumanity* (2nd ed., London, 1786); [Robert Norris], *A Short Account of the African Slave Trade* (Liverpool, 1787).

[16]This was a problem recognized by Montesquieu and Burke, among others. See Fletcher, "Montesquieu's Influence," *Journal of Negro History*, XVIII, 422; Seeber, *Anti-Slavery Opinion*, 14-16, 28-33.

[17]For the influence of naturalism and the idea of progress on English theology in the eighteenth century, see Ronald S. Crane, "Anglican Apologetics and the Idea of Progress, 1699-1745," *Modern Philology* (Chicago), XXXI (February, 1934), 281-306, 349-79; Leslie Stephen, *History of English Thought in the Eighteenth Century* (2 vols., New York, 1949), I, 70-91; James Stephen, *Essays in Ecclesiastical Biography* (4th ed., London, 1860), 440-45.

[18]For the connection between gradualism and the idea of progress, see John Millar, *The Origin of the Distinction of Ranks* (3rd ed., London, 1781), 304, 320-47; William Paley, *The Principles of Moral and Political Philosophy* (London, 1785), 197-98; James Ramsay, A MS Volume, Entirely in Ramsay's Hand, Phillipps MSS, 17,780 (Rhodes House, Oxford). For the conservative approach of the Church of England to slavery, see Edgar L. Pennington, *Thomas Bray's Associates and Their Work among the Negroes* (Worcester, Mass., 1939), 10-12; J. Harry Bennett, Jr., "The Society for the Propagation of the Gospel's Plantations and the Emancipation Crisis," in Samuel C. McCulloch (ed.), *British Humanitarianism* (Philadelphia, 1950), 16-29. For cautious gradualism in America, see "The Appeal of the American Convention of Abolition Societies," *Journal of Negro History*, VI (April, 1921), 200-201; "American Convention of Abolition Societies Documents," *ibid.*, VI (July, 1921), 323-24, 363-64.

[19]E.g. [William Belsham], *Remarks on the African Slave Trade* (London, 1790), 14-15. It is true, of course, that American reformers also devoted considerable attention to the slave trade.

[20]For the economic considerations behind French gradualism, see Gaston Martin, "La doctrine coloniale de la France en 1789," *Cahiers de la Révolution francaise* (Paris), III (1935), 25, 38-39; Martin, *Histoire de l'esclavage dans les colonies francaises* (Paris, 1948), 130-42, 164-65, 189-90, 251-59.

[21]Martin, *Histoire de l'esclavage*, 190, 209-26; McCloy, *Humanitarian Movement*, 114-25. Abolition became associated with the worst excesses of the French Revolution.

[22]Wilberforce, *Correspondence*, I, 328-29.

[23]This had been proposed in 1788 by the Reverend F. Randolph, *A Letter to the Right Honourable William Pitt . . . on the Proposed Abolition of the African Slave Trade* (London, 1788), 44-46.

[24]The gradualism, however, was combined with a sense that slavery was the ultimate of all evils. See Society for the Mitigation and Gradual Abolition of Slavery

Throughout the British Dominions, *Prospectus* (London, 1823), v-vii; James Cropper, *A Letter Addressed to the Liverpool Society for Promoting the Abolition of Slavery* (Liverpool, 1823), 31-32.

[25]E.g., *Twelfth Report of the Directors of the African Institution . . . April, 1818* (London, 1818), 35-37, 130-40.

[26]E.g., Edward R. Turner, *The Negro in Pennsylvania* (Washington, 1911), 143-68; Charles H. Wesley, "The Negroes of New York and the Emancipation Movement," *Journal of Negro History,* XXIV (January,1939), 65-103; Wesley, "The Concept of Negro Inferiority in American Thought," *ibid.,* XXV (October, 1940), 540-60.

[27]*Emancipator* (reprint), vii, ix-x; "Appeal of American Convention," *Journal of Negro History,* VI, 215-18; Drake, *Quakers and Slavery,* 114-15; Turner, *Negro in Pennsylvania,* 210-12; [William Griffith], *Address of the President of the New Jersey Society for Promoting the Abolition of Slavery* (Trenton, 1804), 8-9.

[28]E.g., Clarkson, *History,* I, 1-29, 158-66; II, 119-20, 347, 581-86.

[29]William Wilberforce, *A Letter on the Abolition of the Slave Trade* (London, 1807), 301-302; Wilberforce, *Life,* I, 345-46, 351; *Debate on the Motion for Abolition of Slave Trade . . . 1792* (Wilberforce speech), 47-48.

[30]*Debate on the Motion . . . 1792,* pp. 116-17, 132-34, 164-65.

[31]Granville Sharp, *The Case of Saul, Shewing that His Disorder was a Real Spiritual Possession* (London, 1807), preface to 1807 ed., iii-iv.

[32]Sharp, *Serious Reflections,* 38; Sharp, *"Systems of Colonial Law,"* 13.

[33]For the formation of the British Anti-Slavery Society, see David B. Davis, "James Cropper and the British Anti-Slavery Movement," *Journal of Negro History,* XLV (October, 1960), 241-58.

[34]In the 1830's American abolitionists claimed that the British Anti-Slavery Society had adopted the principle of immediatism in 1826, and later historians have repeated the same error. It was only in 1831 and 1832 that immediatism gained widespread support, and even then the more conservative leaders looked to the government for an effective but gradual working plan.

[35]Ragatz, *Fall of the Planter Class,* 287, 332, 412-48; Claude Levy, "Barbados: The Last Years of Slavery, 1823-1833," *Journal of Negro History,* XLIV (October, 1959), 316-22.

[36]Elizabeth Heyrick, *Immediate, Not Gradual Abolition; or, An Inquiry into the Shortest, Safest, and Most Effectual Means of Getting Rid of West Indian Slavery* (London, 1824), 8, 14-18.

[37]But on June 8, 1824, the General Committee of the Anti-Slavery Society instructed its secretary to procure a dozen copies of the Heyrick pamphlet for distribution to interested members; and some of the Society's members were reported at the same time to favor immediate abolition. Minutes, I, 111-12.

[38]James Stephen, *The Slavery of the British West India Colonies Delineated* (2 vols., London, 1824-1830), II, 387, 390-401; Minutes, III, 132-33.

[39]Raymond English, "George Thompson and the Climax of Philanthropic Radicalism, 1830-1842" (unpublished dissertation, Cambridge University), 33. I am indebted to Mr. English for lending me a copy of his manuscript.

[40]Andrew Thomson, *Immediate Emancipation: Substance of a Speech Delivered at the Meeting of the Edinburgh Society for the Abolition of Slavery* (Manchester, 1832), 4, 11, 24.

[41]While many members of the parent society favored immediate emancipation, it was the Agency Committee that popularized the doctrine. See e.g., *The Tourist: A Literary and Anti-Slavery Journal* (London), I (1832-1833), 16, 94, 108, 124, 173, 231, 266, 308.

[42]Frank Carpenter Stuart, "A Critical Edition of the Correspondence of Sir Thomas Fowell Buxton, Bart., with an Account of his Career to 1823" (2 vols., M.A. thesis, Institute for Historical Research, London, 1957), II, 24-29, 45-46, 244.

[43]Society for the Abolition of Slavery Throughout the British Dominions [Circular Letter to Provisional Organizations], April 4, 1833, pp. 1-2; [Anon.], *Some Remarks on Mr. Stanley's Proposed Bill for the Abolition of Colonial Slavery* (n.p., 1833), 1-7; Minutes, IV, 54-55, 61; Richard, *Joseph Sturge*, 106-107.

[44]David Barrow, *Involuntary, Unmerited, Perpetual, Absolute, Hereditary Slavery, Examined; on the Principles of Nature, Reason, Justice, Policy and Scripture* (Lexington, Ky., 1808), 13-14, 42.

[45]Thomas Branagan, *Serious Remonstrances*, 35, 64; Branagan, *Buying Stolen Goods Synonymous with Stealing* (2nd ed. [printed with *The Penitential Tyrant]*, Philadelphia, 1807), 233-39.

[46]John Kenrick, *Horrors of Slavery* (Cambridge, Mass., 1817), 38-39, 58-59.

[47]George Bourne, *The Book and Slavery Irreconcilable: With Animadversions upon Dr. Smith's Philosophy* (Philadelphia, 1816), 7-8, 16-19, appendix. Bourne's appeal for unconditional emancipation attracted the attention of William Allen, the English philanthropist who was later instrumental in founding the British Anti-Slavery Society.

[48][Samuel M. Worcester], *Essays on Slavery: Re-Published from the Boston Recorder & Telegraph, for 1825, by Vigornius, and Others* (Amherst, 1826), 24-25.

[49]*Ibid.*, 32-33.

[50]*Ibid.*, 46-47.

[51]*Genius of Universal Emancipation* (Greeneville, Tenn.), I (September, 1821), 33; (October, 1821), 49-52.

[52]*Ibid.*, I (September, 1821), 35; (February, 1822), 118-20; (March, 1822), 135. Lundy favored colonization at public expense of Negroes wishing to leave the country but he also called on the North to receive emancipated slaves without restriction, and exhorted the South to repeal laws discriminating against free Negroes.

[53]Turner, *Negro in Pennsylvania*, 216. In 1819 the Pennsylvania Society sent a message to the American Convention, calling for the "total and most early abolition of slavery, consistent with the interest of the objects of your care." American Convention, *Minutes of the Sixteenth Session of the American Convention* (Philadelphia, 1819), 6-8.

[54]American Convention, *Minutes of the Nineteenth Session of the American Convention* (Philadelphia, 1825), 30.

[55]"Appeal of American Convention," *Journal of Negro History*, VI, 235-40; "American Convention Documents," *ibid., passim.*

[56]Glover Moore, *The Missouri Controversy, 1819-1821* (Lexington, Ky., 1953), 303-304; [Worcester], *Essays on Slavery*, 29; William S. Jenkins, *Pro-Slavery Thought in the Old South* (Chapel Hill, 1935), 67-80.

[57]This is perhaps most clearly seen in the memorial drawn up by a committee of the American Convention on December 11, 1829. See "American Convention

Documents," *Journal of Negro History,* VI, 351-57. Also, Drake, *Quakers and Slavery,* 134-39; Alice Dana Adams, *The Neglected Period of Anti-Slavery in America* (Boston, 1908), 116-17, 154-57, 175-76.

[58]This parallel development of British and American antislavery movements was recognized by Benjamin Lundy. See *Genius of Universal Emancipation,* New Series (Baltimore), III (November, 1832).

[59]E.g., *The Philanthropist: A Weekly Journal* (Mount Pleasant, Ohio), II (August 21, 1819), 297-99; II (September 4, 1819), 324-25.

[60]William B. Hesseltine, "Some New Aspects of the Pro-Slavery Argument," *Journal of Negro History,* XXI (January, 1936), 8-13; *Philanthropist, A Weekly Journal,* VII (April 20, 1822), 353-55.

[61]Aptheker, "Militant Abolitionists," *Journal of Negro History,* XXVI, 444-48; Wesley, "Negroes of New York," *ibid.,* XXIV, 68-81; Bella Gross, " 'Freedom's Journal' and the 'Rights of All,' " *ibid.,* XXVII (July, 1932), 241-62; Herbert Aptheker, *The Negro in the Abolitionist Movement* (New York, 1941), 33-36, 40-42. The crisis was also intensified by the tariff and nullification controversy in America and by the mounting pressure for political reform in Britain.

[62]Barnes, *Antislavery Impulse,* 32-33, 42-44; Roman J. Zorn, "The New England Anti-Slavery Society: Pioneer Abolition Organization," *Journal of Negro History,* XLII (July, 1957), 159-73; David M. Ludlum, *Social Ferment in Vermont, 1791-1850* (New York, 1939), 142-44.

[63]See, for example, the letter in *The Liberator* (Boston), I (January 22, 1831), 13, suggesting that a special juvenile department would help correct prejudice in adults: "For there is, perhaps, no better way of removing error, than by leading the mind back to the first simple view of a subject, which you would present to a child."

[64]Barnes and Dumond (eds.), *Weld-Grimké Letters,* I, 97-103, 116, 132-35, 140-46; *Liberator,* I (January 8, 1831), 7; *Philanthropist, A Weekly Journal* (Mount Pleasant, Ohio), II (September 4, 1819), 324-25; *The Philanthropist* [an earlier journal published by Charles Osborn] (Mount Pleasant, Ohio), I (December 5, 1817), 114; Bourne, *The Book and Slavery,* 20-21, 58, 74-75, 139-40, Appendix; Heyrick, *Immediate, Not Gradual Abolition,* 34-36.

[65]"Letters of William Lloyd Garrison to John B. Vashon," *Journal of Negro History,* XII (January, 1927), 36-38; Thompson, *Three Lectures on British Colonial Slavery,* 4-5, 7; *Tourist,* I, 84, 124; William Allen to Charles Babbage, December 1, 1832, Add. MSS, 37,187, fols. 255-56.

[66]Rufus M. Jones, *Spiritual Reformers in the 16th and 17th Centuries* (Boston, 1959 [1st ed. 1914]), xviii-xlvii, 44-45, 234, 288-98; William C. Braithwaite, *The Beginnings of Quakerism* (London, 1955 [1st ed. 1912]), 49-50; Rufus M. Jones, *The Later Periods of Quakerism* (2 vols., London, 1921), I, 23-37, 78, 81-83; Wade C. Barclay, *Early American Methodism* (2 vols., New York, 1949-1950), I, xxii-xxiii; William G. McLoughlin, *Modern Revivalism* (New York, 1959), 103-105. It should also be noted that the issue of gradual versus immediate emancipation followed a long religious controversy over gradual versus immediate, instantaneous conversion.

[67]For an expression of the religious motives of antislavery, see Wilberforce, *Life,* V, 156-59. There is a clear relationship between antislavery and religious anxiety in the lives of many abolitionists. Obviously, most religious anxiety found other outlets than antislavery; but the writings of abolitionists in both Britain and America show that the cause satisfied religious yearnings that could not be fulfilled by the traditional institutions of the church.

[68]This point is made convincingly by Barnes, *Antislavery Impulse,* 104-107.

[69]Amos A. Phelps, *Lectures on Slavery and Its Remedy* (Boston, 1834), 179. For the relation between antislavery and revivalism, see Barnes and Dumond (eds.), *Weld-Grimké Letters,* I, 40-52, 94-97; McLoughlin, *Modern Revivalism,* 23-31, 53-54, 86, 107-12; Charles C. Cole, *The Social Ideas of the Northern Evangelists, 1826-1860* (New York, 1954), 101-25, 196, 231-38.

[70]For the rise of new values concerning work, authority, and the development of inner disciplinary controls, see Reinhard Bendix, *Work and Authority in Industry: Ideologies of Management in the Course of Industrialization* (New York, 1956), 34, 60-62, 72-73; Adam Smith, *An Inquiry into the Nature and Causes of the Wealth of Nations* (Modern Library ed., New York, 1937), 364-66.

[71]For the relation between this romantic anthropology and the liberal theology of men like Nathaniel W. Taylor and Albert Barnes, see McLoughlin, *Modern Revivalism,* 45-69. Stanley Elkins correctly discerns the anti-formal and anti-institutional character of immediatism (*Slavery,* 189-92), but he relates it to the fluid social structure in the United States; the same characteristics had been present in British and French antislavery literature from the eighteenth century, and their accentuation by the 1830's would seem to have been part of a major ideological development.

[72]Walter J. Bate, *From Classic to Romantic* (Cambridge, Mass., 1946), 176-77; Walter E. Houghton, *The Victorian Frame of Mind* (New Haven, 1957); Meyer H. Abrams, *The Mirror and the Lamp* (New York, 1953).

16

The Formation
of the Catholic Minority
in the United States,
1820-1860

Thomas T. McAvoy, C.S.C.

American Catholicism during the nineteenth and early twentieth centuries has been described as a "ghetto culture," in that, personal and group identities were fostered that were independent of and separate from the mainstream of American society. In his analysis, Thomas T. McAvoy, C.S.C., traces the development of this separatist mentality into the early nineteenth century. Until his death in 1969, Father McAvoy taught at the University of Notre Dame.

No minority group in the United States is probably as formless and yet at the same time as rigid as the American membership of the Roman Catholic Church. The rigidity of the Catholic organization arises from the fact that there has never been a real heresy during the three centuries and more of Catholic life within the boundaries of the present United States. Even the so-called heresy of Americanism[1] existed more in the minds of European theologians than in the Catholics of the new world. There have been divergencies among American Catholics on such questions as the application of Gregory XVI's condemnation of the slave trade,[2] the timeliness of the declaration of papal infallibility[3] or the extent of the papal condemnation of secret societies,[4] but there has been no difference on the essential doctrines involved in these disputes. In startling contrast to this unity in dogma and morals has been the extreme divergence among American

First published in the *Review of Politics*, X (1948), pp. 13-34 (abridged). Reprinted with the permission of the *Review of Politics*.

Catholics in political beliefs and in economic and social status. What there is of a distinctive Catholic culture is the result of the interaction between the doctrinal unity and this political, social and economic divergence. It took its dominant form during the stormy years immediately before the Civil War.

In matters of theology the historian has little difficulty determining the American Catholic position. The doctrinal uniformity can be ascribed to several sources such as the fact that the Church in the United States took form after the great theological controversies of western Europe, that the American people have been so completely absorbed with the practical problems of settling an unconquered country that they are not accustomed to theological speculations, and that the Catholic immigrants have been mostly downtrodden and persecuted peoples who have clung un-questionably to their religious faith as the chief hope in trial. One should also remember that the existing separation of church and state has eliminated the chief sponsor of heretical and dogmatic divisions—political interference. Some disciplinary problems among the American Catholics arose as soon as these immigrants began to enjoy the freedom of the United States, but these scandals resulting from undisciplined clergymen and lay trusteeism had been reduced to a minimum before the greater growth of Catholicism began. By 1829, the date of the first Provincial Council of Baltimore, dogmatic and disciplinary uniformity had been established in nearly all details. Later councils merely confirmed and developed these foundations. Catholics of all political parties, despite wide differences of economic and social status and of national origins, have quickly rallied to the defense of the common faith just as they have rallied to the defense of American social and political institutions. In all these diverse kinds of Catholic citizens there has developed a common element, founded upon their religious faith and the common loyalty to the American state yet embracing all these differences, which can be called an American Catholic culture. That this culture has not been as perfect as it might be is a matter of common observation. In most critical judgments, Catholic educational in-stitutions[5] have been made to carry most of the blame for this low cultural level, but in so judging the critics have shown little understanding of the fac-tors of peasant origins and frontier handicaps which have been almost in-superable obstacles to the success of Catholic education.

Roughly, all American cultural ideals are compounded of two ele-ments, the European traditions brought by the immigrant and the effects of the American frontier—in a broad sense of the term—on these immigrants. American Catholic culture has been no exception to the process, but the Catholic minority history differs from the history of the majority Protestant group because the Catholic immigrants have been overwhelmingly non-English. American Catholic culture has undergone a series of rises and declines under the effect of successive waves of non-English migrations and has not completely solved the problems of its later immigrants even today. Yet, the essential characteristics of American Catholic culture were deter-mined by the generation of Catholics in America during the great immigra-tion from 1830 to the Civil War. Unwittingly the nativistic and anti-Catholic reaction of forties and fifties furnished the hammer and the anvil by which this distinctive Catholic cultural unity was created; and this cultural unity has slowly absorbed all the later immigrations since the Civil War.

In most of the historical accounts of the Catholic body in the United States the cultural composition of the group has been generally misunderstood. No one, for example, has explained why the cultural and social position of English-speaking Catholics before 1835 was higher than it has ever been since that time. Some writers do not recognize the existence of the group before the eighteen-thirties. Because the Catholic body achieved national importance only when the number of Catholics had been suddenly swollen by Irish and German immigration in the second quarter of the nineteenth century, most historians of American social and cultural life have tended to classify Catholicism as a foreign importation,[6] almost out of harmony with the dominant Anglo-American culture. This is understandable, for no one can deny that the dominant American culture is actually English and Protestant, although greatly modified by the frontier and by American experience. The supposition that American culture is essentially Protestant, however, overlooks the fact that since 1636, at least, there has always been an English Catholic minority, truly Catholic and truly American according to the times, within the present United States. That minority has always accepted all the essentials of English culture while remaining loyal to their Catholic faith. The members of this Anglo-American Catholic group were never very numerous. They were scarcely thirty thousand in three million in 1790,[7] but they were accepted as fully American, even though their faith was not approved. This Catholic minority of Maryland and Pennsylvania had absorbed many non-English Catholics even before the Revolution without changing its character, because these earlier Irish, German, and French immigrants had adopted generally the cultural standards of the English Catholics and were quite indistinguishable from them after a generation in the United States.

The number of Irish, French, and German immigrants in this Anglo-American Catholic minority prior to 1820 actually was scarcely greater in relation to the English Catholics than the non-English immigrants were in relation to the total English population of the country during this early period. The relation of the Anglo-American Catholic group towards the non-Catholic majority, on the other hand, can be described roughly as the relation of the Catholic minority in England towards the English majority, minus the legal disabilities of English Catholics. Catholics in England[8] since the Gunpowder Plot in 1605 had ceased to hope for a corporate reunion of England with the Church of Rome. They bore as best they could the social and economic persecution which cut more deeply than the political disbarment, and saw their numbers frequently lessened—before the Oxford revival—by the usual wearing away at the edges of Catholics whose faith had weakened under the strain. Nevertheless, English Catholics remained loyal to their country as well as to their Catholic friends and sought to attain the position of a select cultured minority. American Catholics before 1820, however, had higher hopes than English Catholics because they had attained equality before the law and because they had been reenforced especially by a group of cultured French priests who had fled into exile from the persecution of the French Revolution.

A second and perhaps more important reason for the usual misinterpretation of the cultural relation between the Catholic minority and the majority group in the United States has been the insistence of certain Catholic historians, particularly John Gilmary Shea[9] and Monsignor Peter Guilday,[10] on identifying the Irish Catholic with the Catholic minority chiefly because the more numerous Irish spoke English and had adopted the United States as their country once they had landed. Such a theory, which was apparently accepted by many Irish Catholic leaders a hundred years ago, will hold in the political sphere but culturally overlooks completely the difference between English and Irish cultural ideals in the nineteenth century. It also ignores the existence of the definite Anglo-American Catholic minority in that early period. This viewpoint too hastily considered all opposition to the Irish immigrant to be based on religious belief alone. Actually the continued existence and growth of the Anglo-American Catholic group in the larger Catholic group is the chief connecting link between the history of the Catholic immigrant and that of the native Protestant and is the basic element in our distinctive American Catholic culture.

In American ecclesiastical history of the first two decades of the nineteenth century the existence of a number of French clerical exiles and their opposition to the immigrant Irish clergyman has been a source of confusion in evaluating the Catholic group of the period. These French clergy have been accused of plotting a Gallic domination of the American Church, where they were actually defenders of the Anglo-American group against an Irish invasion. That these Irish immigrants of the day, especially among the clergy, regarded themselves as more American than the French who spoke only broken and accented English was understandable. But it must be borne in mind that in the broader American scene the French Huguenots, such as the Jays, the Faneuils, the Legarés, and the Pettigrues, and the Swiss Albert Gallatin were accepted as part of the majority group without too much objection. And the Catholic French clergymen were readily received by the Anglo-American Catholics and even by American non-Catholics because of their learning and culture. Abbé Jean Cheverus and Abbé Francis Matignon[11] were revered by the New England Yankees who despised the Irish immigrant, and Abbé Jean Dubois in Virginia and Abbé Gabriel Richard in Michigan were accepted as honorable citizens. The sympathy of these French priests was naturally with the native Americans with whom they generally associated, expecially those of some social position. The Irish[12] on the contrary were generally antagonistic toward the English, had even lost most of the traditions of ancient Irish culture and had little social position. The French clergymen, particularly Archbishop Ambrose Maréchal of Baltimore, looked upon the Irish as just as much foreigners as themselves and wanted the control of the clergy in the hands of American clergymen. Further, his antagonism toward some of the Irish clergy was based upon several cases of clerical disobedience and misconduct. Actually, most of our knowledge of the Catholic minority at this time arises from the troubles between the French Archbishop and his Irish suffragans, but these troubles are symbolic of the cultural conflict within the Catholic group of that time.

Partly, perhaps, because the Irish were the most active Catholics in the English speaking world and partly because of some ecclesiastical intrigue in Rome, the Sacred Congregation of the Propaganda had been prevailed upon to appoint several Irish bishops to the American episcopate, thus giving the new Irish immigrants spokesmen for their opinions in the government of American Catholics. Father John Connolly, O.P., of Ireland was named bishop of New York in 1815, and Fathers Henry Conwell, Patrick Kelly and John England, also from Ireland, were named to the sees of Philadelphia, Richmond and Charleston, respectively. None of these men had even been in the United States before their appointment and all had been elected without any recommendation from the American bishops. Archbishop Amborse Maréchal of Baltimore was alarmed at this action. He had proposed American-born Benedict Fenwick for Charleston and wanted either men experienced in America or, perhaps, Englishmen[13] appointed to the other sees. He began at once to petition the Sacred Congregation against further appointments without the consultation of the American bishops. To Maréchal the increasing Irish immigration and the growth in the number of Irish priests and bishops constituted the first threat of a real foreign domination of the American church, and he felt called upon by his position to prevent such a situation. To the Irish, however, the activities of Maréchal and the other French clergymen looked rather like an attempt at Gallic domination. The care of the Anglo-American Catholics as such and the promotion of their interests seem to have rested mostly with the French clergymen since the natives had not produced enough native priests to care for their own needs.

Bishop John England, the foremost of the new Irish clergymen, was undoubtedly an outstanding ecclesiastic possessing exceptional gifts as an orator and as a journalist. Despite the fact that he was situated in a diocese containing few Catholics and away from the other Catholic centers, he began at once to influence the whole Catholic minority. He visited other Catholic congregations along the coast and founded the first really Catholic newspaper in the United States, the U.S. Catholic Miscellany, in 1822 for the exposition of the Catholic faith. He so delighted Catholics and non-Catholics by his oratory as to receive countless invitations to speak to American audiences throughout the country—once speaking before the Congress of the United States. Although England had been an outstanding Irish nationalist as a clergyman and editor in Ireland, he became an honest, zealous American as soon as he arrived in this country. If he seemed extremely pro-Irish in his activities it was because he felt that the Irish were the chief Catholics in the English-speaking world, European or American, and were being attacked chiefly because of their faith. He and his fellow Irish immigrants accepted American citizenship and considered themselves entitled to all American social privileges as well. Actually, he and his confreres from Ireland were not as much a part of the American Catholic group as the French-speaking Maréchal and the French Sulpicians of St. Mary's Seminary. In the columns of the *Miscellany*[14] even England admitted that the Irish immigrants were not all the social equals of the older English inhabitants of the country. He had, however, no great respect for the culture of the French archbishop and his Sulpician associates who, he maintained, would never be accepted by Americans because of their foreign language and accent.[15] . . .

Meanwhile, as a result of the heavy Irish and German immigration between 1830 and 1850 the Catholic group in the United States had become overwhelmingly immigrant, chiefly Irish in the eastern cities and German in the colonies in the Middle West. The violence of the nativistic reaction continued. In vain did the American Bishops Timon, McGill and Whelan seek a native American for Archbishop of Baltimore when Samuel Eccleston died in 1851.[16] Their only candidates were Chanche and Timon and they did not compare in ability to the Irish-born prelates. Rome, at the request of most of the American bishops, named Francis Patrick Kenrick of Philadelphia to the Baltimore see. Thus, when the first Plenary Council of Baltimore was convened in 1852, the American hierarchy consisted of six foreign-born archbishops and seventeen foreign-born bishops. There were no American-born archbishops and only nine of the bishops had been born in the United States. The chief archepiscopal sees—New York, Baltimore, Cincinnati, and St. Louis—were occupied by prelates of Irish birth. In point of fact this Irish domination represented the numerical composition of the Catholic body at this time. Of the Catholic population, those in New England and the Middle Atlantic states were almost solidly Irish and were in control of nearly all the Catholic press. The English Catholics who had increased only by conversions and by natural growth were chiefly in the upper South although many groups of them had gone to various farming regions in the Ohio valley. The German Catholic immigrants were increasing rapidly in the north central states but because of language difficulties exerted little influence on the general Catholic body.

This change in the hierarchy to Irish domination did not imply any political maneuvers by the Irish or other foreign-born ecclesiastics. The bishops were rightly chosen from the more capable of the clergy in the field and were the nominees of the other bishops both native and foreign-born. There was already some discussion of the need of separate organizations for the German faithful, who did not speak English, but Archbishop Cajetan Bedini,[17] the papal legate who visited the country in 1853, disapproved of such a separation. There was, however, an increase in the German bishops. Altogether, then, the change in the hierarchy actually represented in a proper way the change in the cultural and national origins of the Catholic population. The cultural unity of the Catholic minority before 1830 was gradually reestablished on the foundations of the common faith and sacraments, but while the English and native-born Catholics provided the cultural leadership, the numerical predominance of the immigrant group had changed the quality and character of the whole group.

There are few manifestations of strictly cultural character by which one can estimate the cultural accomplishments of the Catholic group of that day. Outside of a few converts there were few writers or thinkers of note.[18] The Catholic lawyers such as Roger Taney and William Read of Maryland and the Spaldings and Elders of Kentucky were examples of the continued growth of the Anglo-American Catholic group throughout the period. It is also significant that for Catholic opinions on the great national problems of the day even the immigrants took their leadership from these border states. Brownson and other Yankee converts could complain of this, but they actually preferred that leadership in most affairs to dictation from the immigrant. The oratory and the Catholic press of the eastern cities were on a much lower cultural plane and were devoted rather to political than to cultural pursuits. Numerically the Catholic population was chiefly in the ports of entry and the mill towns of the North. These northern Catholics, however, were mostly poor immigrants struggling for a livelihood in the less desirable section of the towns and buffeted by the storms of nativism. Naturally their pastors were gravely concerned with their welfare and defended them not in literary journals but in the press and from pulpit and platforms. Around New York Catholic leadership in public affairs had passed into the hands of Bishop Hughes, whose diocese became the center of most of the public controversy. Closely associated with him in this work was Bishop Kenrick in Philadelphia and Bishop Fenwick and later Bishop Fitzpatrick in Boston; but no other prelate commanded the attention of the Irish immigrant and of the American public as easily as Bishop Hughes. In him the Irish immigrant group found its cleverest and most potent expression. He sought to protect the immigrants from the nativists and to direct their efforts for their own good. He exerted this protection chiefly in the field of politics and oratory where the impoverished immigrant could best be marshalled. He saved his flock from physical persecution in the riots of 1844 but he kept them in the cities where progress and cultural development for the lower classes came hardest.[19] In general the Catholic bishops were conspicuously absent in the movement against slavery, the temperance movement or in the other social reforms of the day. They could not concern themselves with these things as long as their flocks lacked religious care and economic security.

Considering the poverty of most of the Catholic immigrants it is easy to see that the chief burden of the Catholic clergy during the three decades before the Civil War was not to build up universities or other institutions of higher culture. They were absorbed in the immediate task of giving the sacraments and essential Catholic instruction to these impoverished immigrants and of protecting them so far as possible from the fury of the nativistic movement.[20] That this nativism was to a great extent a religious persecution is amply proven in the controversial literature of the day. But at the same time it was a cultural reaction to the influx of immigrants. So long as the dominant cultural group was so hostile to the Church, it is understandable that the defenders of the Irish immigrants were the Catholic clergy and that Bishop (Archbishop after 1850) Hughes and his fellow bishops should object to the efforts of Orestes Brownson and other native American Catholics to produce harmony between the immigrant Catholics and the nativists. Indeed, for the Irish immigrant who had fled from English oppression the combination of religious and political persecution was not new. He was not surprised to find the English descendant in America attempting to carry on the same persecution but he did appeal to his rights as guaranteed by American law. In his appeal to the law the immigrant was sustained but socially and culturally there remained a division between the immigrant and the nativist which only generations of living together could overcome.

The native-born Catholics, including the older Irish, looked forward to the day when the immigrant would cease to be looked upon as a foreigner. Brownson,[21] a militant Yankee, wanted to eliminate this distinction at once. Archbishop Hughes objected to Brownson's reasonings because he feared that the loss in faith in a hasty adoption of American ways would outweigh any social gain. Later on the Americanized Irish would use the Brownson argument against the Germans, Poles, and French Canadians. In the case of the Irish immigrant, the absence of a language difficulty did not prevent Archbishop Hughes from realizing that there was a cultural difference between the immigrants and the native Americans.[22] But like the defenders of later national groups he failed to see the advantages of a quicker Americanization. The cultural conflict in the forties and fifties, as had been anticipated by Maréchal, was the first great manifestation of a foreign nationalism in the American church. Culturally the policy of Hughes set back the progress of the Irish immigrant at least a generation, as such policies have set back other Catholic groups wherever they have manifested themselves. In some instances, it is true, the opposition to the immigrant of the earlier period included local political feeling because the immigrant had become the tools of politicians,[23] and there was, also, some economic feeling manifested by the incipient labor unions against foreign labor competition. These latter, however, were minor items in a struggle that was mainly religious and cultural.

Since the cultural opposition to the Irish immigrant during the second quarter of the nineteenth century was chiefly on religious grounds, it was to the religious advantage of the Catholic group that the clerical leaders who defended the immigrant were men from Catholic countries where no compromise in religious matters was the order of the day. In the Catholic unity moulded by the nativistic opposition, American Catholicism acquired a new aggressive characteristic. Even though the more dominant immigrant groups were of a lower strain culturally, their staunch defense of their religion created in this country the most militant Catholic organization in the English speaking world. Before this change the Anglo-American Catholics, like their English brethren, did not show themselves active apologists of the Catholic position, and in striving to advance the faith by Catholic preeminence in cultural matters they had continued the defeatist attitude of the English minority group of colonial days. The Irish and German Catholic leaders, who were unaccustomed to make any compromises in their relations with non-Catholics, insisted instead on their full rights in all public matters. The position of Bishop Francis Patrick Kenrick in Philadelphia and of Bishop John Hughes in New York on the public schools and on the use of the Catholic Bible in those schools may be open to question on the grounds of strategy,[24] but the uncompromising defence of their flocks by these bishops was in the best Catholic tradition. Since that time American Catholicism has never retreated to the position of a defeatist minority. Nevertheless, since the opposition to the immigrants was based on more than religious disagreements there were bound to be some differences within the ranks of the Catholic reaction to the nativistic movement.

Bishops Hughes and Kenrick were not native Americans and represented the immigrant point of view in the public discussions, and the circumstances of the times would not allow any public manifestations of a different point of view by the native-born bishops. Yet there has always been some nativism among the American Catholics. Their patriotism could have no other results, although Hughes and other episcopal defenders of the immigrants failed to understand that even a Catholic could resent the immigrant invasion. Brownson, as he showed in his *Review*,[25] felt strongly this Yankee resentment towards the immigrant and, in Louisiana, Abbé Adrien Rouquette[26] expressed in French poetry an Americanism that opposed the Irish immigrants and led him to associate with the American Party. And there were other manifestations of this internal cultural conflict in the Catholic group.

Perhaps the locality in which to observe most clearly the amalgamation of these cultural strains into an American Catholic culture was the Middle Western frontier.[27] There the immigrant groups living away from the cities yielded more quickly to the general cultural trends. At least the Catholics in these western settlements—if we except the German mass colonies which were comparable to the Irish groups in the cities—were quickly Americanized. It was noted by the early missionaries in the Middle West that there was less bigotry on the frontier so long as the common problem of conquering the wilderness and the prairies gave little occasion for internecine cultural differences. Generally, the bigotry that appeared on the frontier was an importation from the older settlements, deliberately propagated by missionary societies.[28]

The Americanization of the immigrant Catholic away from the concentrations on the seaboard is shown best in the Kentucky Catholic group which was augmented by Catholics of other nationalities as it spread across the Ohio and Mississippi to found new centers of settlement. These frontiersmen were joined by Irish canal and railroad workers and by German farmers. These English Catholic families—many dating back their arrival to 1681 in Maryland—built up first the communities of Bardstown, Loretto, Holy Cross and the like with Catholic colleges and a seminary, three communities of religious women and a Dominican monastery. Many of these families, such as the Spaldings, Wathens, Coomes, Haydens, Clements and Mattinglys, remained in Kentucky, some at Bardstown and others in more prosperous communities. The same families are also found in Daviess County, Indiana, and in early Catholic communities at Paris, Illinois, and

Lancaster, Ohio, and in Tennessee and Missouri. They have given to the Church many bishops and priests and prominent lawyers and physicians. Sometimes when they moved into less Catholic communities they achieved positions of local importance, although the propaganda of the anti-Catholic movements of the forties and fifties usually prevented this. In most communities where Catholics lived, the church or mission chapel with a pastor of almost any national origin was the center of a growing Catholic culture. Usually the Anglo-American element furnished the social leadership of the group and frequently a professional vocation; to this the Irish added spirit and religious fervor and the Germans a devotion to the parish organization and to the parochial school. Seldom were the Catholics the wealthy persons of the community and only the few English or Yankee Catholics were welcomed socially by their non-Catholic neighbors, who wondered at their devotion to Catholic dogma and the Sunday Mass. Only in the completely German communities and in the compact Irish settlements of the eastern cities was the English element lacking, with a resultant cultural isolation that delayed the Americanization of the group.

In the nativist Catholic group there has always been an important small, but vigorous, number of converts and their children. In estimating how many converts there were to the Church among the native Americans during the first two quarters of the century there are no statistics, but some estimates are quite high.[29] These converts were frequently of a higher social position and were less inclined to apologize for their religious differences with the majority. They became far more active than the native Catholics in the propagation and defense of their religion. Notable, besides Eccleston, in the hierarchy, Bishop Josue M. Young of Erie and Bishop James F. Wood of Philadelphia, were converts and there were other notable clerical and lay converts active in the religious discussions of the day. Perhaps none of these outshone in their zeal Isaac Thomas Hecker and Orestes A. Brownson, both of whom became notable for the efforts to show that Catholicism and Americanism were not only compatible but complementary.

In Brownson, particularly, the nativistic attacks on the Irish produced two distinct reactions. Examining the religious attacks on the immigrant, Brownson charged that such attacks were un-American. But to the cultural attack upon the Irish immigrant Brownson was in a certain sense sympathetic, not, as he vehemently insisted, because he was anti-Irish but because he felt that the Irish could best prosper if they joined themselves to the American cultural majority in culture and public practice. Brownson saw only prosperity and advancement for the Irish if they would combine their religious zeal and the advantages of American civilization. But to the Irish American press and to Archbishop John Hughes, for whom Catholicism in the English speaking world and Irish origins had become almost synonymous, writings of this nature from the pen of Brownson amounted to a betrayal of the faith. The Catholic press attacked Brownson and Archbishop Kenrick allowed his letter of approval of the *Brownson's Review* to be withdrawn. Archbishop Hughes publicly rebuked Brownson at a commencement at Fordham in 1856,[30] to the glee of Thomas D'Arcy

McGee's *American Celt*. Disclaiming publicly any intention to injure Brownson, Hughes nevertheless wrote privately to Brownson, ordering him to cease his efforts to make Americanism and Catholicism compatible. Brownson fought vainly against the tide and eventually, after making other tactical errors, had to suspend his *Review* in 1864. Likewise, the concentration of the minds of the American people on the issue of slavery and the approaching Civil War caused a slackening of the interest in the nativistic movement until some years after the war.

Irish immigration never again reached the peak it had attained in the fifties. The Irish who had moved away from the ports of entry and the industrial concentrations tended to assimilate themselves to the more native groups in which they lived, although the compact communities in the eastern cities were more resistant to American culture. The Germans, who generally had sufficient means to buy farmlands, tended to settle in rural communities in the Middle West.[31] As their numbers increased some also settled in Cincinnati, Milwaukee, Chicago, and St. Louis. Only later, as their cultural isolation began to break down, did they feel the effects of this cultural amalgamation and offer resistance to the Americanizing process, particularly in the so-called Cahensly movement.

During the Civil War the Catholics followed the communities in which they lived to fight for the North or the South. The War lifted for a while the nativistic pressure against the immigrant. Outside of the German communities the leadership was divided between the Irish and their descendants and the old Maryland-Kentucky group, with the latter supplying most of the cultural leaven. Public changes symbolized this fact. During the Civil War Archbishop Hughes was succeeded by the American-born John McCloskey, the first American cardinal, and Archbishop Francis Kenrick was succeeded by the Kentucky-born Martin John Spalding. At the close of the conflict the two groups of native-born and second generation Irish immigrants, together with the other groups not living in compact immigrant groups, had united to form a distinctive American Catholic cultural group. With renewed Irish immigration after the War, American Catholics remained dominantly Irish in numbers and in public policy but the Catholic culture of the whole group became increasingly American. Later conflicts were to arise; first, between the dominantly Irish hierarchy and the foreign language groups, and then between these Americanized groups on the one side and the Irish of the cities and the foreign language groups of the northwest on the other. But throughout these later decades the Americanized Catholic culture remained basically the same as that of 1860 with later immigrants balanced in number by new generations of American-born.

There were other characteristics developed in the formation of this American Catholic culture. The common element, of course, has been the fidelity of the whole Catholic group to hierarchial rule and to sacramental practices. The sternness of the American Protestant majority in rejecting Catholics for public office and the continuous propaganda against the Church, however, have added to this religious solidarity. The labors of

French, German and Irish religious organizations to give Catholic education to the impoverished immigrant have magnificently supplemented the efforts of the native-American Catholic to remove any social stigma from the Catholic group. Only the serious financial burden of maintaining Catholic churches, separate schools and hospitals out of the lesser material resources has prevented greater progress in raising the level of this American Catholic culture.

To isolate the contributions of the native-born or the immigrant in the formation of this American Catholic culture is difficult because the common faith of both groups led necessarily to a great uniformity in life and practice. The immigrant did lower the cultural level of the group. The earlier Catholic group was also outside the majority religious groups of the country, but where some of these native-born Catholics had before 1830 achieved some social and political position in dominantly non-Catholic communities, the later immigrants and Catholics generally have achieved such positions only within their own immigrant locality. Nor did this condition change quickly. The accident of birth in the United States was not sufficient alone to raise the new generation socially above its parents. As a matter of fact the children of immigrants who remained in the immigrant milieu did not always attain the cultural level of their parents. Frequently, also, social distinctions brought from the old country disappeared in the general low level of a mass of immigrants.

Where the immigrant had the means to seek his fortune in the richer opportunities of the West, he usually developed the characteristics of the American pioneer, just as the early English Catholic frontiersmen had done in Kentucky, Indiana, and Ohio. Likewise, where the immigrant settled in communities possessing Catholic educational institutions, such as the colleges at Bardstown, Georgetown, and Emmitsburg, he usually competed more successfully with the Americans of earlier immigration. But where the immigrant's poverty kept him among crowds of other impoverished immigrants and deprived him of all improvements except that achieved by mere numbers, as in politics, the immigrant failed to improve or to become Americanized in the fullest sense.

Subsequent attempts by the descendants of these Irish immigrants to Americanize later immigrants met with resistance. Already, in 1860 in the Catholic minority there was a growing number of immigrants who spoke another language instead of English. They were at first chiefly from Germany but later included some immigrants of south and central Europe. Their amalgamation with the English speaking Catholic group was consequently slower and at times they rebelled against the efforts of the dominantly Irish Catholics to assimilate them. They, perhaps better than the Irish themselves, saw the difference between American culture and the culture of the Irish immigrant. They, too, objected to Americanization and offered to the English and Irish Catholics of American birth and culture the same resistance offered by the Irish in 1850.

There were some definite advantages and disadvantages in this composite American Catholic culture that was created before 1860. If the Anglo-

American group, led by Maréchal, Whitefield and Eccleston and later by Spalding, Bayley and Elder and signalized by activities of such converts as Hecker and Brownson, had retained the dominance over the Catholic minority, perhaps Catholic colleges and an American Catholic literature in English might have flourished more readily. Instead, the energies of this smaller American group that might have developed into higher cultural forms were absorbed in educating and absorbing a larger group which was without means and, in great numbers, had been deprived of education for generations. Likewise, Catholics in politics might even have advanced more quickly in public office if they could have escaped the stigma of foreign culture which the confusion of religion and politics of the nativistic period ascribed to all Catholics. On the credit side, the aggressive American Catholicism which manifests itself in public demonstrations, the frequentation of the sacraments, and the insistence on Catholic parochial schools can be attributed to the tradition of the non-English immigrants, Irish, German, Polish, and the like, who came from Catholic regions of Europe and who saw more quickly the dangers to religious faith in the nonreligious public schools and the advantages of a Catholic milieu.

Both natives and immigrants benefited from the freedom of frontier America but the native who was able to remain away from the industrialized urban conditions acquired more quickly a distinctly American spirit. The fact that Catholics who congregated in compact Irish or German settlements in the mill towns, in the larger cities, or even in the immigrant colonization projects of the west made slower progress in accepting American cultural ideals can be explained chiefly by the absence in their communities of members of the Anglo-American Catholic group which had formed the leaven of the Maryland and Kentucky communities. Brownson's analysis of this fact was received angrily in the 1850's. But even then, there were some who sensed the formation of a distinctly American Catholic culture. The writer "M" in the January 1857 *Metropolitan*,[32] the chief Catholic magazine of the time, commenting critically on Brownson's essays on nativism, sized up the situation quite well despite his sympathy for the immigrant group. "The native Catholics of Maryland and Kentucky furnish their full quota of priests and religious, and before there is an increase in the number of native priests there must be an increase in the number of native Catholics. As a general thing Irish priests *ceteris paribus,* are the best for the Irish people and it will be found most likely that the relative number of native priests and native Catholics will under God's providence, augment in proper ratio."

Like so many of the Irish Catholics of the period, "M" did not fully understand that Brownson and Bishops Timon and McGill and Whelan had no doubt of the faith or of the patriotism of the immigrant Catholic. But these native Americans did recognize that there was a distinction between American culture and that of the immigrant. They were convinced that the immigrant could profit by the social and cultural spirit of Americans. The attitude of the Irish immigrant of the fifties was best personified by Archbishop John Hughes. Archbishop Hughes did not seem to understand fully that there had always been American Catholics or that there was no conflict between being an Anglo-American and being a Catholic.[33] Faced with American nativists who were hostile to their religion, the Catholic immigrants can be excused for not realizing that to prefer the ideals of the Anglo-American Catholics was perhaps a greater loyalty to Catholicism and certainly a better service to American Catholic culture. Repelled by the nativists, the immigrants who dominated numerically the Catholic group held back from the common culture and suffered some of the cultural evils which Brownson had predicted as a result of this partial isolation. For the eighty years since 1860 American Catholic culture has risen just as quickly as the immigrant group has been able to Americanize its cultural tradition. Similarly the non-Catholic religious people have shown a better understanding of Catholic culture just in proportion as they have been able to see that the foreign elements of the Catholic culture are the accidents of history and not part of their universal faith. Those who reject that faith have other reasons for rejecting American Catholic culture. But the gradual Americanization of the masses of non-English Catholic immigrants, with the old Anglo-American Catholic group as a nucleus, is an understandable process and one as American as all the other combinations of immigration and the frontier which constitute our American civilization.

NOTES

[1]Cf. my article in the *Review of Politics,* (July, 1943), V: 275-301 and in *The Catholic Historical Review* (July, 1945), XXXI:133-153.

[2]Madeleine Hooke Rice, *American Catholic Opinion in the Slavery Controversy* (New York, 1944), pp. 62-72.

[3]Raymond J. Clancy, C.S.C., "American Catholic Prelates in the Vatican Council" in *U.S. Cath. Hist. Records & Studies,* XXVIII:8-135.

[4]F. J. Zwierlein, *The Life and Letters of Bishop McQuaid.* 3 vols. (Rochester, N.Y., 1926) II:378-474, and Fergus Macdonald, C.P., *The Catholic Church and the Secret Societies in the United States* (New York, 1946), especially Chapter VI.

[5]James M. Campbell, "The Catholic Contribution to the American College" in *Vital Problems in Catholic Education in the United States,* ed. by Roy J. Deferrari (Washington, 1939) pp. 84-107.

[6]Cf. Merle Curti, *The Growth of American Democratic Thought* (New York, 1943), pp. 316-7, 492-3.

[7]Sister M. Augustina Ray, B.V.M. *American Opinion of Roman Catholicism in the Eighteenth Century* (New York, 1936) traces the decline of political opposition to Catholicism under the influence of the Revolution and the granting of political toleration; cf. especially pp. 292-3.

[8]David Mathew, *The Jacobean Age* (New York, 1938), pp. 11-16; also, Philip Hughes, *The Catholic Question* (New York, 1929), pp. 122-141.

[9]Shea in *The History of the Catholic Church within the United States* (4 vols. New York, 1886-92) is less given to this devotion to the Irish immigrants than Mon-

signor Guilday because of his adherence to a more strictly hierarchical history and because of his broader perspective.

[10]Cf. Guilday's *The Church in Virginia (1815-1822)* (New York, 1924) and *The Life and Times of John England, First Bishop of Charleston 1786-1842* (2 vols. New York, 1927).

[11]R. H. Lord, J. E. Sexton, and E. T. Harrington, *History of the Archdiocese of Boston,* (3 vols. New York, 1946), I:619-631.

[12]The best account of the Irish immigrants of this period is that of W. F. Adams, *Ireland and Irish Emigration to the New World from 1815 to the Famine* (New Haven, 1932), especially Chapter VII "The Fruits of Emigration." Noteworthy on the cultural conflict is M. W. Hansen's essay "Immigration and Puritanism" in *The Immigrant in American History* (Cambridge, 1940), pp. 97-128, reprinted in this collection as reading 21.

[13]Guilday, *Life and Times of John England,* I:251-2.

[14]*U.S. Catholic Miscellany* (Aug. 3, 1825) V:80.

[15]*Idem* (Sept. 14, 1825) V. 17:5-6.

[16]Letter of Bishop Richard V. Whelan of Wheeling to Bishop John McGill of Richmond, May 15, 1851, Richmond Diocesan Archives.

[17]John G. Shea, *History of the Catholic Church within the U.S.* III:364-5.

[18]This is clearly brought out in a prize essay on "Catholic Literature in the United States" in *The Metropolitan* (Baltimore) of 1854; II:69-75; 133-139; 198-204.

[19]Cf. *The Metropolitan* (Baltimore), IV:251-3. The letter of "Oliver" on the Buffalo Convention of 1856 for the promotion of Irish colonization in the west shows that some at least disagreed with Hughes.

[20]The Bishop's Pastoral Letter of 1852 stressed the great material handicap involved in caring for these poorer immigrants in estimating the future prospects of the Church in the country. *National Pastorals of the American Hierarchy (1792-1919),* pp. 187-191.

[21]Brownson's more notable essays on this topic are in the *Brownson Quarterly Review* of January (XI:I-29) July (XI:328-353) and October (XI:447-486), 1854 and January, 1857 (XIV:114-141).

[22]In his "Lecture on the Present Condition and Prospects of the Catholic Church in the United States" *(Complete Works* [New York, 1864], II, pp. 102-121) Hughes distinguishes the original Maryland group, the immigrants and the converts in the growth of the Church in this country.

[23]Oscar Handlin, *Boston's Immigrants 1790-1865* (Cambridge, 1941), stresses this political backwardness but shows a serious lack of appreciation for the religious faith of the immigrants.

[24]Ray Billington, *The Protestant Crusade (1800-1860)* (New York, 1938), especially Chapter XII "The Catholic Church Blunders." Billington considers this aggressiveness a blunder.

[25]There are several rough drafts of Brownson letters supporting his position on this point in the Brownson Mss., U. of Notre Dame Archives.

[26]D. R. Lebreton, *Chala-Ima, The Life of Adrien-Emmanuel Rouquette* (Baton Rouge, 1947), pp. 187-198.

[27]A capable study of this Kentucky group after 1815 and its filial settlements in the neighboring states has not been made.

[28]Cf. Thomas T. McAvoy, *The Catholic Church in Indiana 1789-1834*, pp. 126-8, 141-2, 158-9, 200-1; also George M. Stephenson, "Nativism in the Forties and Fifties, with special Reference to the Mississippi Valley" in *Miss. Valley Hist. Review,* IX:185-202.

[29]Cf. "Bishop Bruté's Report to Rome in 1836" ed. by T. T. McAvoy in *Catholic Historical Review* (July 1943) XXIX:177-233. Bruté estimated the number of converts very highly. His successor, Bishop Celestine de la Hailandière was of the same opinion. The chief defect of G. M. Shaugnessy's *Has the Immigrant Kept the Faith?* (New York, 1925) is his failure to estimate properly these converts.

[30]Henry F. Brownson, *Orestes A. Brownson's Latter Life from 1856 to 1876* (Detroit, 1900), pp. 66-75.

[31]Sister Mary Carol Schroeder, O.S.F., *The Catholic Church in the Diocese of Vincennes, 1847-1877.* (Washington, 1946), pp. 70-114, studies this immigration in Indiana; also Emmet H. Rothan, O.F.M. treats the German Catholic immigration in *The German Catholic Immigration in the United States (1830-1860)* (Washington, 1946), especially chapter VIII "German Catholics and Rural Communities."

[32]*The Metropolitan* (Baltimore) January, 1857 (pp. 720-723). This editorial is a comment on the article of Archbishop Hughes on the Catholic press in the December, 1856 issue (pp. 629-661) and on Brownson's criticism of the Archbishop's statement in the January, 1857 issue of *Brownson's Quarterly Review* (XIV:114-141).

[33]In his "Lecture on the Present Condition and Prospects of the Catholic Church in the United States" he does recognize the existence of the early Maryland Catholics, but when he speaks of Catholics in the American Revolution he mentions only Irish names.

17

Religion and Resistance Among Antebellum Negroes, 1800-1860

Vincent Harding

Was the Christian religion an "opiate" which served to make slaves docile and obedient? Or was it a source of resistance, and even rebellion, in the slave community? Vincent Harding raises these questions which resonate beyond the study of slavery to the civil rights movement of the mid-twentieth century. Professor Harding teaches Afro-American Studies at Spellman College.

In these days of ecumenism among the academic disciplines, it would likely be both fair and appropriate to describe the state of our historical understanding of Negro religion in America as a variety of cultural lag. This is clearly the case when we try to assess the role of black religion in the antebellum period of American history, and especially when an attempt is made to understand its relationship to acts of protest and resistance.

Stated in simplest terms, the situation may be described in this way: Thanks to the crucial work of Aptheker, the Bauers, Stampp and others we have moved beyond a naive and often distorted view of happy or indifferent Negro slaves whose docility was a sight to behold.[1] Indeed the movement towards the new theme of slave rebellion and resistance has often been so strong that the inevitable reconsiderations and revisions have already set in.[2] But it would appear unlikely that even such fascinating and worthy caveats as those raised by Elkins, Wade and Genovese will drive us back to the old

First published in August Meier and Elliott Rudwick (eds.), *The Making of Black America* (New York, 1969), pp. 179-97. Reprinted with permission of the author.

dominions—if for no other reason than the uneasiness our increasingly black-oriented age feels with such interpretations. So the new slaves seem to be a permanent fixture. On the other hand, we have not yet been released from the traditional views of black religion which supported the older generalizations concerning submissive and humble slaves. Here precisely is the lag.

Much of current historical opinion about the role of religion among antebellum southern Negroes still follows the classic lines set out in Benjamin Mays' *The Negro's God,* which claimed that the Negroes' idea of God "kept them submissive, humble and obedient."[3] Repeatedly Mays referred to this religion as "otherworldly" and "compensatory," inclining its votaries "to do little or nothing to improve their status here . . ."[4] Even so shrewd and perceptive a scholar as E. Franklin Frazier later adumbrated the theme in his important work on *The Negro Church.*[5] There the antebellum Negroes—especially in the South—were identified with a religion that "turned their minds from the sufferings and privations of this world to a world after death where the weary would find rest and the victims of injustice would be compensated."[6]

The views of Mays and Frazier are representative of most discussions of the black religion that developed before the Civil War. In many ways these men helped to set the theme. Their views, of course, represented an American adaptation of the classic statement by Karl Marx:

> Religion is the sign of the oppressed creature, the heart of the heartless world . . . the spirit of a spiritless situation. It is the *opium* of the people.[7]

In this essay what we question is not the applicability of such an understanding of religion to a majority of antebellum Negroes. Indeed, the traditional view often has much support in the records. For instance, it was not accidental that a slaveholder said in the 1830's, "The deeper the piety of the slave, the more valuable he is in every respect."[8] This was a widespread opinion. Nor was that eloquent refugee from slavery, William Wells Brown, wrong when in 1850 he claimed that religious instruction for his fellow-bondsmen consisted "in teaching the slave that he must never strike a white man; that God made him a slave; and that when whipped he must find no fault . . ."[9]

That was likely an accurate description of most instruction, and many slaves seemed to live by it. (Generally, of course, they had no other choice than to give at least an impression that they did.) However the present dispute does not center there. Rather this paper seeks to raise the issue of the ambiguity, the doubleness, of black religious experience, indeed of all religious experience. It seeks not to deny the opiate quality of much slave religion but to offer the suggestion that there were significant, identifiable black responses to religion which often stormed beyond submissiveness to defiance.

Perhaps Frederick Douglass best sets the scene for an understanding of this ambiguous and two-edged Negro reaction to religious teaching. In one of his autobiographical writings, this most famous of fugitive slaves, recorded words which scarcely covered his underlying scorn. He said,

> I have met, at the south, many good, religious colored people who were under the delusion that God required them to submit to slavery and to wear their chains with meekness and humility.

Then he added, "I could entertain no such nonsense as this . . ."[10] For Douglass, as for countless others, the requirements of God pointed in other directions, and black religion led them away from slavery. Often it led to protest, resistance and death. . . .

II

It has seemed wise for the present to confine this statement to the period 1800–1860, and to focus on Negroes in the South. Therefore, it may be significant to note that it was in 1800 that South Carolina's legislature indicated a keen awareness of the possible connections between black rebellion and black religion, an awareness that was apparently the property of many southern white persons. In that year the legislature passed one of the first of those countless nineteenth century laws restricting black religious services. This one forbade Negroes

> even in company with white persons to meet together and assemble for the purpose of . . . religious worship, either before the rising of the sun or after the going down of the same.[11]

Magistrates were given the power to break up all such gatherings. Behind the legislation was obviously a fear that these religious meetings might lead to trouble, especially if they were held at hours when they could not easily be monitored.

If the fear needed substantiation it was soon available. In Virginia's Henrico county Tom Prosser's slave, Gabriel, and Gabriel's brother, Martin, were then gathering slaves and free Negroes at strange hours and making strange uses of "religious services." Gabriel was plotting insurrection, and building a force that had evidently mounted into the thousands by 1800. At their religious services it was said that both Martin and Gabriel— what fitting names!—regularly set forth

> an impassioned exposition of Scripture . . . The Israelites were glowing portrayed as a type of successful resistance to tyranny; and it was argued, that now, and then, God would stretch forth his arm to save, and would strengthen a hundred to overthrow a thousand.[12]

The black men of Henrico county were the new Israelites. Gabriel was their Moses. Would they follow?

It is not known how deeply this appeal from the Old Testament moved the persons who gathered in those secret meetings, nor which of them joined the attempted rebellion in response to it. But the analogy to the Israelites was a traditional one in the black community, and it continued to have great force among the slaves. Therefore it would not be too much to expect that some of the men who set themselves on the path of rebellion in those Virginia meetings were responding to a profoundly religious call, as well as to the news from Santo Domingo, or to the stirring cries of "Death or Liberty." Haiti was a good example, and the political motto was a moving cry, but it surely helped to believe as well that the God of Israel would "stretch forth his arm" to intervene on behalf of the blacks.[13]

When the insurrection was foiled by the sudden downpour of torrential rains, the white residents of Virginia would, of course, have been justified in thinking that divine intervention was indeed present—on their side.[14] But they were likely caused to be suspicious about other religious matters as the trials of the rebels revealed that Methodists and Quakers—as well as Frenchmen—were to be spared the vengeful swords of Gabriel's band.[15] What could that mean?

Religion and its relationship to black rebellion continued to be a matter for concern and for questions in Virginia, even before the coming of Nat Turner. For instance, one Richard Byrd of that state wrote to his Governor in May, 1810, to express his conviction that "slave preachers used their religious meetings as veils for revolutionary schemes," and he cited a "General Peter" from Isle of Wight as an example of the danger.[16]

Six years later this kind of fear was given solid ground in the Old Dominion again, but it was a white preacher who now seemed to be using black religion for seditious purposes. George Boxley, proprietor of a county store, was a regular participant in the religious meetings held by the Negroes of Spottsylvania and Louisa counties. Soon he began telling them "that a little white bird had brought him a holy message to deliver his fellowmen from bondage. . . ."[17] Again the promise of divinely aided deliverance found active response, and Phillips says that Boxley "enlisted many blacks in his project" for messianic insurrection. Unfortunately for the black believers, as was so often the case, the plot was betrayed. Some Negro followers were hanged, others were sold out of the state, but Boxley escaped from jail.[18] Perhaps the message of deliverance had been meant only for him. After all, it was a white bird.

The pattern of religious connections to rebellious movements continued consistently into South Carolina in the same year—1816. There, in Camden, a plot had evidently been maturing, and when the almost inevitable betrayal and arrests finally came, a local newspaper offered its own version of the relationship between religion and resistance:

> It is a melancholy fact [the editor said] that those who were most active in the conspiracy occupied a respectable stand in one of the churches, several were professors [i.e., avowed Christians], and one a class leader.[19]

Camden was not the only place in South Carolina where black Christians and class leaders were making life difficult for the keepers of the established order. Charleston was having its difficulties with the darker variety of Methodists, trouble that would eventually lead into deep distress.[20]

The Negroes in the port city's Methodist congregations had long outnumbered their white brethren by ten to one. They had known a sense of significant independence through their own quarterly conference and as a result of the control they exercised over finances and the discipline of their members. In 1815 alleged "abuses" had led to the loss of these privileges as well as much of the independence that went with them. But black church leaders like Denmark Vesey, Peter Poyas and Jack Pritchard (Gullah Jack) had no intentions of accepting such debilitating penalties without offering direct and open response.

They led agitation among the Negro members, rounded up a thousand new members and sent two of their leaders up to Philadelphia to be ordained by the African Methodist Episcopal bishops there. Then in 1818 a dispute over their burial ground provided the occasion for more than 4000 of the 6000 black Methodists to withdraw their membership *en masse* from the white Charleston congregations. With ordained ministers of their own they now moved ahead to build a meeting house and establish an independent congregation called the African Church of Charleston.

It is in this context that we may speak more precisely of rebellion. Here the crucial issue is not the nature of what happened in 1822, not the matter of whether widely organized insurrection was being planned.[21] At this juncture it is of critical importance simply to see that organized rebellion on another level had already been built deeply into the structure of black church life in Charleston. The agitation from 1815 to 1818 and the concerted withdrawal from the white congregations in the latter year took significant courage for the slaves. The raising of an independent house of worship implied not only the gathering of financial resources, but it is clearly an act of defiance for the world to see. The municipal officials knew this and responded accordingly with harassments, arrests, banishments, and finally with the closing of the church in 1821.[22] It is, then, essential to note that the sense of black solidarity was imbedded in the organization of the Negro church. Attempts to dilute this or break it down met inevitably with resistance, resistance centered in that church's life.

Did the defiance include a wider plan for insurrection? It is not the purpose of this essay to enter into the argument that has been interestingly raised by Mr. Wade. However, my own examination of available evidence leads me to suspect that the plot was "more than loose talk by aggrieved and embittered men."[23] These men had already given evidence of impressive skill in organizing black discontent for action. They had followers in their defiance, and their leadership was evidently trusted. There was no reason for them to be content with "loose talk" by 1822.

Whatever the extent of the new action being planned, it seems clear that some continuing organizing was going on, that it was centered in the membership of the African Church and that the charismatic Denmark

Vesey was at the heart of the affair.[24] Now, for our purposes it is necessary only to continue to deal with the role of religion as it participated in a movement that went beyond the defense of church-oriented prerogatives to new and likely bolder concerns. If, as seems probable, an insurrection was being planned, Vesey surely knew how to continue to use themes that had led the blacks to organize for independent church status.

His focus was regularly on religion. One witness testified that this leader's "general conversation . . . was about religion, which he would apply to slavery." Indeed, "all his religious remarks were mingled with slavery," according to the testimony.[25] Was this surprising? For the most part these were church members who were being addressed, and they were also slaves. What other focus was more natural? These were also persons whose extant religious records indicate that they were profoundly attracted to the analogy between their condition and the condition of the Hebrews in Egypt. As a class leader, Vesey surely knew all this very well. So one of the alleged conspirators was probably quite accurate when he said that Denmark Vesey "read to us from the Bible, how the *children of Israel were delivered out of Egypt from bondage* . . ."[26] Nor did the persuasive exhorter stop there. It is said that he made it clear to the bondsmen that it was imperative to their faith that slaves "attempt their emancipation, 'however shocking and bloody might be the consequences.' " And on the strength of his magnificent authority as a class leader—and as a man—he declared that such efforts would be "pleasing to the Almighty," and that their success was thereby guaranteed.[27]

If, as we are suggesting, religion did play a critical role in the motivating of his followers, then Vesey chose wisely (or was fortunate, if he did not make the choice himself) when he gained an accomplice like Jack Pritchard, better known as Gullah Jack. This black man of Angolan background provided an excellent counterpoint to Vesey's Old Testament theme. For he was not only a member of the African Church but a conjurer, a medicine man in the African tradition. Therefore Vesey had the best of both religious worlds, and we are told that Gullah Jack exerted tremendous influence over the other members of his ancestral group.[28]

This, of course, does not mean that Vesey did not seek to rally his forces through the use of other issues as well. The tradition of Santo Domingo, the debate over Missouri, the general mistreatment of the Negroes by the city authorities and by some of their masters—these were all part of the strategy.[29] But it would be derelict to fail to note how crucial was the religious issue, especially in the light of the post-1814 church experiences. Was this not the significance of the note found in Peter Poyas' trunk after he was arrested: "Fear not, the Lord God that delivered Daniel is able to deliver us."[30]

Then in the summer of 1822, when deliverance appeared to have been aborted and the gallows were heavy with black bodies, it was fitting that the city should demolish the First African Church.[31] This was not only a rehearsal of more modern southern church treatment, but it was a testimony to the significant role the people of that congregation had played in carrying the contagion of rebellion. Nor was it surprising that an Episcopalian minister boasted that such things could never happen among black Episcopalians because their Negroes "were not allowed to exhort or expound scriptures in words of their own . . . and to utter . . . whatever nonsense might happen into their minds."[32]

Regardless of how we see such matters now, it was evidently clear to most Charlestonians of the time that "religious enthusiasm" had been one of the motivating forces in Vesey's action. So all preachers of the gospel to slaves—white and black—were suspect.[33] And a Charleston editor condemned the white Christian missionaries who

> with the Sacred Volume of God in one hand scattered with the other the firebrands of discord and destruction; and *secretly* dispensed among our Negro Population, the seeds of discontent and sedition.[34]

Though he saw much, the editor did not see that the firebrands and the seeds were often in the same hand as "the Sacred Volume," but he surely must have known that the hands were often black.

At least this was the case with Nat Turner, who carried his own Volume, fire and seeds. Whatever doubts we may entertain about the authenticity of Vesey's rebellion, Turner leaves us with no choice. Even more important for our present concerns is the central theme of Turner's *Confession*—the theme of a black, avenging Messiah, urged into action by nothing less than the repeated calling of God.[35] Here was religion and resistance that would not be separated.

Based primarily on the *Confession,* the story develops. As a child he became convinced that he was "intended for some great purpose." Evidently he nurtured the search for his destiny through arduous prayer and fasting and the development of an austere personal life. Turner claimed to be directed many times by "the Spirit" as it spoke to him in his lonely vigils or as he worked in the fields. A major theme of that direction was "Seek ye the kingdom of Heaven and all things shall be added unto you." When asked later about this "Spirit," the 31year-old prisoner made it clear that he stood self-consciously in the prophetic tradition, for he said that he had been visited by "The Spirit that spoke to the Prophets in former days."

Eventually the young mystic became fully confirmed in his sense of ordination to some "great purpose in the hands of the Almighty," and he went through his own Wilderness experience—thirty days in the forests of Virginia as a runaway slave. Then the Spirit drove him back for his great encounter with the future. In 1825 Turner saw his first major vision suggestively describing his ultimate calling. White and black spirits were battling in the air. Thunder rang out, the sun was darkened, and he watched in awe as blood flowed through the land. The same Spirit promised him the wisdom and strength needed for the task.

After a fascinating variety of other visions, the critical revelation came in May, 1828. According to Nat,

> I heard a loud noise in the heavens and the Spirit instantly appeared to me and said the Serpent was loosened, and Christ had laid down the Yoke he had

borne for the sins of men, and that I should take it on and fight against the Serpent, for the time was fast approaching when the first should be last and the last should be first.

The Spirit also revealed to him that there would be adequate signs in nature to let him know when he should begin the messianic work for which he was ordained, when to "arise and prepare myself to slay my enemies with their own weapons." In an eclipse of the sun—that most ancient of signs—Nat Turner found his signal to begin. He ate a last supper with some of his followers and went forth to carry out his own version of the work of Christ, using the weapons of the Old Testament, drenching the ground with blood, for "neither age nor sex was to be spared." And when he was asked if he thought himself mistaken as he faced execution at the end, Turner's response came fittingly enough: "Was not Christ crucified?" To the charge of dastardly crime, his plea, of course, was "Not Guilty."

Obviously Nat Turner was one of those religious charismatics who arise in a variety of settings, from the walls of Münster to the fields of Southampton County.[36] He was not a "preacher" in any formal sense of the word, and evidently belonged to no structured church group. But he was an "exhorter," and he clearly convinced his fellow slaves by the power of his message and the strange sense of his presence that he was the anointed one of God for their deliverance—a deliverance for which slaves never ceased to yearn.

No other explanation will open the intricacies of Nat Turner. Thus, when they were wounded and waiting to die, it was said of his companions that some of them "in the aggonies [sic] of Death declared that they was going happy fore that God had a hand in what they had been doing. . . ."[37] They still believed that "Prophet Nat" was sent from God.

When all the dyings were over, after the fierce retaliations had taken place, the conviction and the legend lived on. Black people believed and remembered, and some acted. The religion of Nat Turner, the religion of black rebellion became part of their tradition.[38] Whites, on the other hand, believed variations of the black themes and acted in their own ways. Their response was well summed up by a writer in the Richmond *Enquirer* who said then:

> The case of Nat Turner warns us. No black man ought to be permitted to turn a preacher through the country. The law must be enforced—or the tragedy of Southampton appeals to us in vain.[39]

In the minds of blacks and whites alike religion and rebellion had been welded into one terrifying—or exalting—reality through the black body of Nat Turner.

So the laws set off by fear swept through the states, forbidding Negroes to preach, in many places interdicting all meetings, attempting as it were to exorcise so troubling a religious spirit.[40] The Mississippi law of 1831 provided a good example when it ruled that "It is 'unlawful for any slave, free Negro, or mulatto to preach the gospel' under pain of receiving thirty-nine lashes upon the naked back of the . . . preacher."[41]

... It may be that the ambiguous nature of American religion, as it related to antebellum blacks, was best seen by a visitor to this land, one who had become a heroic figure among abolitionists by 1841. This was Joseph Cinquez, the African who had led a rebellion aboard the vessel *Amistad*, as it carried a load of slaves along the coast of Cuba in 1839.[42] In the course of the revolt the captain and the cook had been killed by the rebels, the ship was steered to American shores and Cinquez had been brought to New England with his fellow slaves. There they were exposed to American Christianity with all of its contradictory potentials.

Then, in 1841, just before leaving for his native continent Cinquez was given the rare opportunity to apply this nation's religion to his rebellion—after the fact. One of his fellow rebels said to a group of Christians, "We owe everything to God; he keeps us alive and makes us free." Filled with enthusiasm, another went on to claim that he would now pray for the Captain and cook rather than kill them if the rebellion were to be done over again. We are told that "Cinquez, hearing this, smiled and shook his head. When asked if we would not pray for them, he said: 'Yes I would pray for 'em, an' kill 'em too.' "[43]

III

While the religion of some slaves could lead them to pray and kill, and though the Jesus of Southampton beckoned black men through streams of the masters' blood, there were other bondsmen who were evidently no less religiously motivated but who were led to seek different alternatives in their struggle. The Bauers have reminded us of the many levels of resistance to slavery that existed in the South, and they have indicated that some slaves who shed blood as an act of protest were known to draw their own or to take the lives of their children.[44] Death and self-mutilation were preferred to slavery, and one of the accounts of such death may offer some hint concerning the religious motivation involved here.

In Kentucky it was reported that "a father and mother, shut up in a slave baracoon and doomed to the southern market . . . did by mutual agreement send the souls of their children to Heaven rather than have them descend to the hell of slavery, and then both parents committed suicide."[45] No one may be sure that the theology of the contemporary writer was shared by the parents he described, but is it impossible to conceive that a religion which stressed the reality of heaven after death might strengthen slaves to leave their bondage for the freedom they had heard was ahead? If the "other world" was really so good, why allow children to suffer the agonies that parents had known?

In spite of the possible force of such reasoning, especially in extreme situations, it is certain that the action of the Kentucky parents was not typical. Perhaps a more common religious response to slavery was simply the act of refusing to believe the Christian teachings that justified the system of exploitation. A most striking instance of this alternative was found in Georgia shortly before 1830. In Liberty County a group of slaves were listening to a white minister hold forth on a staple topic—the escaped slave, Onesimus, and his return to his master. According to the report from Georgia, half of the Negro group walked out when the point of the sermon became clear, and "the other half stayed mostly for the purpose of telling [the preacher] that they were sure there was no such passage in the Bible."[46]

Because action could often be more costly than thoughts it is likely that many more slaves were involved in the kind of resistance to such religion that was identified by a former slave who said that Negroes simply refused to believe "a pro-slavery doctrine."[47] But Henry Bibb went on to point to what might have been an even more significant kind of defiance when he said that "This kind of preaching has driven thousands into infidelity."[48] Bibb's observations were supported by a southern Presbyterian minister who noted that many white ministers had assumed that Negroes "are an unsophisticated race" only to discover among them "deism, universalism, skepticism, and all the strong objections against the truth of God . . . which he may perhaps have considered peculiar only to the cultivated minds . . . of critics and philosophers."[49]

May we not suggest that the turn to "deism, universalism" and other unapproved forms of southern faith on the part of the slaves was in itself a profoundly religious act of protest against a system that seemed to be supported by all the correct lines of doctrine? Thus one may possibly speak of both protest and accommodation, if the accommodation were carried out under the new religiously protestant ground rules, rules that needed perforce to remain largely interior, but nonetheless real for that.

We are, however, concerning ourselves here with the more exterior, reportable, forms of resistance, and it is clear that one of the most obvious of these was the act of running away from slavery. It was not an act lightly taken up nor easily accomplished, and a sampling of fugitive slave narratives readily reveals the level of inner conviction and strength that was most often necessary for a slave to strike out for freedom. The difficulty of the path and the disobedience of the act provided good testing grounds for the nature of religious faith.

Frederick Douglass recalled his own struggle with the issue of escape as an older man continued to speak to him of the great things that he thought Douglass was meant to do in the world. Young Frederick responded: "I am a slave, and a slave for life, how can I do anything?" To this "Uncle Lawson" replied:

> The Lord can make you free, my dear; all things are possible with him . . . If you want liberty, ask the Lord for it in faith, and he will give it to you.[50]

From that point on Douglass began asking—in his own unorthodox way—and planning, until he felt he had freedom grasped securely in his hands. This was why the religion of chains and submission seemed like "nonsense" to him.

Samuel Ringgold Ward, another fugitive who became a brilliant abolitionist lecturer, lived the struggle through his mother. When he was a child this matriarch had to decide whether she would remain in Maryland and likely be sold further south or whether she would encourage her husband to lead them all to freedom. The will of God was discussed at that point, and the strong, single-minded black woman decided that they should leave. As Ward later described it,

> Submission to the will of God was one thing, she was prepared for that, but submission to the machinations of Satan was quite another thing; neither her womanhood nor her theology could be reconciled to the latter.[51]

In one of the most famous of the antebellum slave narratives William Wells Brown spoke of the same issue—the relationship of his mother's God to freedom. He told of how he confided in her his own plans for escape from slavery in St. Louis just as she was being sold into the deep South. Without any hesitation she urged him to go, and her last word may have expressed her theology of slave rebellion: "God be with you."[52]

There is only one woman whose journey from Southern slavery to freedom is readily available, and that story—half legend by now—is a religious pilgrimage in itself.[53] Harriet Tubman grew up on the stories of the Hebrew children, heard the whispered descriptions of Nat Turner, and sang the songs of impossible hope. Like Turner she saw visions and dreamed dreams of struggle and conflict and searching for freedom. Like him she prayed and talked with God and became fully convinced that her God willed freedom. Indeed, one of her more radical biographers said that by the time she escaped from her native Maryland in 1849 "she was ready to kill for freedom, if that was necessary, and defend the act as her religious right."[54]

The year after Harriet's arrival in the North her fellow black runaways were cast in a new light as a result of the Compromise of 1850 and its Fugitive Slave law. Therefore, while Douglass and Harriet Tubman gained most lasting fame as fugitives, it was a slave who arrived north in 1854—Anthony Burns—whose case became the *cause célèbre* of his time.[55] As a result of the notoriety resulting from the Boston abolitionist furor, Burns received a letter of rebuke and excommunication from the white Baptist church he had joined as a slave in Virginia. In his response we have one of the best statements of the religious apologia for resistance through flight. Burns wrote,

> You charge me that, in escaping, I disobeyed God's law. No, indeed! That law which God wrote upon the table of my heart, inspiring the love of freedom, and impelling me to seek it at every hazard, I obeyed, and by the good hand of my God upon me, I walked out of the house of bondage.

Then, in response to the inevitable citation of Paul and Onesimus which had been in the church's letter, Burns said he would be glad to return if he had any reason to believe that he too would be received in the brotherly spirit that Paul had requested for Onesimus. But Burns said that he did not believe in such a possibility, and was staying North. Finally he stated his basic defense and comfort in the terms of his faith: "You have thrust me out of your church fellowship. So be it. You cannot exclude me from heaven . . ."[56]

Such was the religion of the runaways. They were obviously a self-selective group, but an important and impressive one too. None of them was willing to wait for Frazier's "world after death" to find their rest or to gain compensation for their condition, and they had thousands of brothers in their impatience. (Even heaven-oriented Anthony Burns wanted to try out Boston before confirming his reservation in heavenly places.)

Indeed, persons like Brown, Ward, Douglass and Harriet Tubman (to say nothing of their Northern-born counterparts) seemed unwilling to accept rest anywhere. Their religion was a restless one while slavery existed in the South and segregation shamed the North. The extreme form of this eternally protesting religion was expressed, of course, by Harriet Tubman shortly after her arrival in Philadelphia. There, upon being asked to settle in the city, she was quoted as having said,

> There are three million of my people on the plantations of the south. I must go down, like Moses into Egypt, to lead them out.[57]

Such a spirit breeds legends and makes history difficult to write, but Harriet Tubman did return and she delivered some small, but important fragment of the waiting people. She returned often enough to end up with rewards amounting to $40,000 being offered for her. Just as her own escape from slavery was the Lord's doing in her mind, so too did a sense of divine obsession now drive Harriet Tubman to continue this strange and courageous work of deliverance.[58] She too knew how to exhort, sing spirituals and carry a gun.

If the sparse evidence available is any guide, Harriet Tubman's efforts were child's play compared to a plan that was already at work in the South when she was escaping. It was a plan that revived memories of Gabriel and Vesey and Prophet Nat, expanding them beyond imagination. According to the Reverend Moses Dickson, the founder of a post-Civil War Negro benevolent society, in 1846 he had been instrumental in forming a group of twelve young men who called themselves the twelve Knights of Tabor.[59] They vowed in that year to spend the next decade organizing an army of liberation throughout the South, and were preparing to strike for the freedom of the slaves sometime after 1856. The Old Testament name was self-consciously chosen, Dickson said, for it "gave the members courage."[60]

According to his story, they were encouraged because they knew that

> God was with Israel, and gave the victory to the bondsmen, though they were opposed by twenty times their number. Our cause was just, and we believed in the justice of the God of Israel and the rights of man. Under the name of Tabor we resolved to make full preparation to strike the blow for liberty.[61]

With this sense of divine calling the members supposedly organized within ten years more than forty thousand recruits who were "well drilled, with ample arms and ammnunition." They were located in all the slave states except Texas and Missouri. The larger group was dubbed Knights of Liberty.[62]

In 1857 they were prepared, by Dickson's account, to gather more followers and converge on Atlanta with 150,000 troops. They were to spare women and children, but "march, fight, and conquer was the command, or leave their bodies on the battle field." Their flag was to have a cross made up of twelve stars. Then when all was prepared, just before an unidentified "Chief" was about to give the command to march, Dickson says, "it was plainly demonstrated to [the leader] that a higher power was preparing to take part in the contest between the North and South . . ." So the group was told to hold off, and it disbanded when the Civil War came.[63]

If this account is true, America was on the verge of experiencing the work of a Holy Liberation Front. So far it has not proved possible to go beyond one or two documentary sources related to this movement. However, it is important to note that if such a movement was indeed on foot, it was self-consciously arrayed in the train of Nat Turner. Event or legend, it testified to the fact that there was a strong tradition of religious rebellion among antebellum blacks.

While the Knights of Liberty failed to march, John Brown did not fail. His religious self-image is well known. Less known is the fact that many Negroes took John Brown's insurrectionary action and fitted it into their understanding of religion without any apparent difficulty.

For instance, Frances Ellen Watkins, a gifted writer who published constantly in the cause of Negro freedom, wrote these words to Brown as he awaited execution:

> The Cross becomes a glorious ensign when Calvary's . . . sufferer yields up his life upon it. And, if Universal Freedom is ever to be the dominant power of the land, your bodies may be only her first stepping stones to dominion.[64]

A writer representing "The Colored Women of Brooklyn" became even more explicit in setting the messianic theme as she wrote, "We . . . recognize in you a Saviour commissioned to redeem us, the American people, from the great National Sin of Slavery . . ."[65]

Harriet Tubman had meant to march with Brown, but became ill and was evidently on her way to meet him when the old man was captured. Out of the religious world in which she moved it was clear that she spoke honest words when she said after his death: "It was not John Brown that died at Charleston . . . It was Christ—it was the savior of our people."[66] The black cross had passed from Nat Turner to John Brown. Therefore it was fitting that a traditional Negro tune should be used to carry the words of "John Brown's Body."

IV

Though "John Brown's Body" is not a spiritual, its presence bears a reminder that it is impossible to conclude any discussion of black religion without at least a reference to those songs. They represent the most profound verbal expression of Afro-American religious experience. As W. E. B. DuBois has said, they are "the siftings of centuries . . ."[67]

In spite of their significance it will not be fitting to attempt any lengthy exposition of them here—neither time nor skill allows that. However, it should be noted that these songs have been subjected to much of the same difficulties that we encountered at the outset of this discussion of black religion. Frazier is found again speaking of them as "essentially religious in sentiment and . . . otherworldly in outlook," thereby suggesting that he had missed the point of much of the greatest religious sentiments of man.[68] (Perhaps he was not blessed to hear Paul Tillich's definition of religion.)

Mays also describes most of the spirituals as expressing "compensatory" and heaven-oriented attitudes, but he faces the texts and is willing to admit that some of them clearly bespeak real protest in the present world. Especially does he cite "Go Down Moses" and "Oh Freedom" in this vein.[69] But the author of one of the most carefully wrought attempts to set the spirituals in a historical context goes much further, and develops a theme concerning the spirituals quite similar to the one being suggested here for all of Negro religion.

Miles Mark Fisher sees black religion so closely allied to protest that he suggests that some of the spirituals were likely the creation of Nat Turner, Denmark Vesey, and Harriet Tubman.[70] Especially provocative is Fisher's suggestion that "Steal Away" emerged directly out of Nat Turner's vision of 1825, when the call of God came to him through convulsions in the elements, as he grew increasingly convinced that his great future task would lead him away from all that he had known before.[71] By this Fisher does not mean to deny that many persons have sung that haunting song with longings for a heavenly place, but he affirms that it may well have originated in a marvelously earthbound experience, an experience of affirmation and rebellion.

This recognition that the spirituals surely bore many possible meanings for many persons is strongly supported by Frederick Douglass, who sang so many of them while they were yet fresh in the air. As he later recalled his youth, Douglass pointed to two examples of the potential for profound ambiguity which rested at the center of the songs. There was one with the words

> O Canaan, Sweet Canaan
> I am bound for the land of Canaan.

In Douglass' experience, as he put it, "The North was our Canaan." There was no doubt about that. He says, too, that a song with the words "I don't expect to stay much longer here" (probably a variant of "Steal Away") was another favorite and had "a double meaning." He explained the duality in this way: "On the lips of some it meant the expectation of a speedy summons to a world of spirits, but on the lips of our company [of young men in Maryland] it simply meant a speedy pilgrimage to a free state, and deliverance from all the evils and dangers of slavery."[72]

It would then appear that even in the midst of so community-oriented an experience as the singing of spirituals, many men may have sung out of many varied visions. For some—perhaps for most—the visions took them beyond this earth entirely, and made the experiences of their surroundings fade in importance. For other black persons the music and the faith it expressed—and engendered—filled them with a sense of God's awesome calling for their present moment, and supplied new determination to struggle, build, and resist here.

This dual function of religion should not be surprising. Speaking of another oppressed people in another time, Reinhold Niebuhr has reminded us that "The radical sectarians [of the Reformation period] appropriated Messianism to make of it an instrument of social revolt, while the more conservative religious forces used otherworldly hopes to beguile men from injustices in history."[73]

Unless we grasp that common historical truth and apply it to the black experience in America we shall not only be unprepared to meet those Negroes who break out of the pages of Aptheker and Stampp, but we shall certainly fail to understand so recent and lately controversial a phenomenon as Martin Luther King. He stands in a long tradition of black exhorters whose lives and whose religion can neither be spiritualized, captured, or denied. They can, however, be understood, and that is our task.[74]

NOTES

[1]See especially Herbert Aptheker, *American Negro Slave Revolts,* Paperback edition (New York: International Publishers, 1963); Raymond A. Bauer and Alice H. Bauer, "Day to Day Resistance to Slavery," *Journal of Negro History,* xxvii, 4 (October, 1942), 388-419; Kenneth M. Stampp, *The Peculiar Institution,* Paperback edition (New York: Vintage Books, 1956), particularly Chap. III.

[2]Some of the most persuasive concerns are raised in Stanley M. Elkins, *Slavery,* Paperback edition (New York: Grosset and Dunlap, 1963); Richard C. Wade, *Slavery in the Cities* (New York: Oxford University, 1964); also Wade's "The Vesey Plot: A Reconsideration," *Journal of Negro History,* xxx, 2 (May, 1964), 143-161; Eugene D. Genovese, "The Legacy of Slavery and the Roots of Black Nationalism," *Studies on the Left,* vi, 6 (November-December, 1966), 3-26.

[3]Benjamin E. Mays, *The Negro's God as Reflected in His Literature* (Boston: Chapman and Grimes, 1938), 26.

[4]*Ibid.,* 24.

[5]*The Negro Church in America* (New York: Schocken Books, 1964).

[6]*Ibid.,* 45.

[7]Karl Marx and Friedrich Engels, *On Religion* (New York: Schocken Books, 1964), 42; quoted from the "Introduction to Marx's Contribution to the Critique of Hegel's Philosophy of Right."

[8]Quoted in Haven P. Perkins, "Religion for Slaves: Difficulties and Methods," *Church History,* x, 3 (September, 1941), 228-245.

[9]*Narrative of the Life of William Wells Brown* (London: Charles Gilpin, 1850), 82-83.

[10]*Life and Times,* Paperback edition (New York: Crowell-Collier, 1962), 85.

[11]Quoted in W. E. B. DuBois (ed.), *The Negro Church* (Atlanta: The Atlanta University Press, 1903), 22.

[12]Harvey Wish, "American Slave Insurrections Before 1861," *Journal of Negro History,* xxii, 3 (July, 1937), 311; Thomas Wentworth Higginson, *Travellers and Outlaws* (Boston: Lee and Shepard, 1889), 1899; Aptheker, *Slave Revolts,* 220-224.

[13]*Ibid.,* 220.

[14]See citations in note 12.

[15]Aptheker, *Slave Revolts,* 224.

[16]*Ibid.,* 246.

[17]Ulrich B. Phillips, *American Negro Slavery,* Paperback edition (Baton Rouge: Louisiana State University, 1966), 476.

[18]*Ibid.*

[19]Aptheker, *Slave Revolts,* 258.

[20]The story of the pre-1822 struggles of the black Methodists of Charleston is developed most fully in Phillips, *American Negro Slavery,* 420-421.

[21]Richard Wade, in his works cited in note 2 above, expresses strong doubts about the extent and significance of the insurrectionary plans.

[22]Phillips, *loc. cit.*

[23]Wade, "The Vesey Plot," 160.

[24]See Aptheker, *Slave Revolts,* 268-276; Higginson, 215-275; John W. Lofton, Jr., "Denmark Vesey's Call to Arms," *Journal of Negro History,* xxxiii, 4 (October, 1948), 395-417; Sterling Stuckey, "Remembering Denmark Vesey," *Negro Digest,* xv, 4 (February 1966), 28-41—a direct response to Wade's questions; Marion L. Starkey, *Striving to Make It My Home* (New York: W. W. Norton and Company, 1964), 152-210; Corporation of Charleston, *An Account of the Late Intended Insurrection* (Charleston: n.p. 1822).

[25]Higginson, 228.

[26]Corporation of Charleston, 34 [italics in original].

[27]Higginson, 404.

[28]On Gullah Jack see especially Starkey and Corporation of Charleston, as cited in note 24.

[29]Corporation of Charleston, 39.

[30]Wish, 410.

[31]Phillips, 421.

[32]Quoted in Perkins, "Religion for Slaves," 232.

[33]Donald G. Mathews, *Slavery and Methodism* (Princeton: Princeton University Press, 1965), 41.

[34]*Ibid.,* 42.

[35]Turner's *Confession, Trial and Execution* was originally published in 1881 by T. R. Gray in Petersburg, Virginia. However it is most accessible in Herbert Aptheker, *Nat Turner's Slave Rebellion* (New York: Humanities Press, 1966). I have used the same text as it appeared in "The Confession, Trial and Execution of Nat Turner," *Negro Digest,* xiv, 9 (July, 1965), 28-48. The source will not be cited again until it seems appropriate in the development of Turner's story.

[36]For the story of the Münsterites see George H. Williams, *The Radical Reformation* (London: Weidenfeld and Nicolson, 1962), 362-386.

[37]Aptheker, *Nat Turner's Slave Rebellion,* 38.

[38]From the lives of Frederick Douglass and Harriet Tubman to "The Ballad of Nat Turner" in a recently published book of poems by Robert Hayden, *Selected Poems* (New York: October House, 1966), the tradition has been carefully and faithfully maintained.

[39]Quoted in George Washington Williams, *History of the Negro Race in America,* 2 vols. (New York: G. P. Putnam's Sons, 1883), II, 90.

[40]DuBois (ed.), *The Negro Church,* 25.

[41]*Ibid.*

[42]A brief account of the *Amistad* story is most conveniently found in Louis Filler, *The Crusade Against Slavery 1830-1860* (New York: Harper and Row, 1963), 167-168.

[43]Quoted in Williams, *History,* II, 96.

[44]See reference to the Bauers' work in note 1 above, especially pp. 415-418.

[45]*Ibid.,* 417.

[46]Perkins, 236.

[47]Henry Bibb, *Narrative of the Life and Adventures of* (New York: the author, 1850), 24.

[48]*Ibid.*

[49]Quoted in Perkins, 237.

[50]Douglass, 91.

[51]Samuel Ringgold Ward, *Autobiography of a Fugitive Negro* (London: John Snow, 1855), 19. The family ran away in 1820.

[52]Brown, *Narrative,* 79.

[53]Three of Harriet Tubman's most widely read biographers tend to encourage the legendary aspects: Henrietta Buckmaster, *Let My People Go* (Boston, Beacon Press, 1959); Earl Conrad, *Harriet Tubman* (Washington, D.C.: Associated Publishers, 1943); and Dorothy Sterling, *Freedom Train: The Story of Harriet Tubman* (New York: Doubleday and Company, 1954). In a recent study of the Underground Railroad, Larry Gara attempts to suggest Harriet's real life size. See his *The Liberty Line* (Lexington, University of Kentucky Press, 1961).

[54]Conrad, 35.

[55]See Buckmaster for an account of Burns' situation, especially 230-236.

[56]Herbert Aptheker (ed.), *A Documentary History of the Negro People in the United States,* 2 vols. (New York: Citadel Press, 1965), I, 372.

[57]Sterling, 81.

[58]See references in note 53 above.

[59]For an account of this fascinating story, see Aptheker, *Documentary History,* I, 378-380 and Moses Dickson, *Manual of the International Order of Twelve* (St. Louis: A. R. Fleming, 1891), 7-17.

[60]*Ibid.,* 15.

[61]*Ibid.,* 16.

[62]Aptheker, *Documentary History,* I, 380.

[63]*Ibid.*

[64]*Ibid.,* 441.

[65]*Ibid.*

[66]Sterling, 129-133.

[67]DuBois, *The Souls of Black Folk* (Greenwich, Conn.: Fawcett Publications, 1961), 183. DuBois' justly famous work contains a number of important essays on black religion. See especially chapters X, XII and XIV.

[68]Frazier, 12.

[69]Mays, 28-29.

[70]Miles Mark Fisher, *Negro Slave Songs in the United States,* Paperback edition (New York: Citadel Press, 1963), 66-67, 181-185.

[71]*Ibid.,* 67.

[72]Douglass, 159-160.

[73]Introduction to Marx and Engels, *On Religion,* viii.

[74]After I completed this paper my attention was called to a sociological study which attempts to relate Negro religion to protest in the modern era: Gary T. Marx, *Protest and Prejudice* (New York: Harper and Row, 1967).

18

The Negro Church: A Nation Within a Nation

E. Franklin Frazier

After the War between the States, the "invisible institution" of the black church under slavery became visible. Like the Roman Catholic Church in the United States, it developed separately from the white Protestant churches and along different lines. E. Franklin Frazier, a sociologist who has studied numerous aspects of Afro-American life and culture, describes how the black church responded to the hostility of white society and the problems of the black community following Emancipation. The late Professor Frazier taught at Howard University.

The Civil War and Emancipation destroyed whatever stability and order that had developed among Negroes under the slave régime. An educated mulatto minister of the African Methodist Episcopal Church who went from the North to the South following Emancipation wrote:

> The whole section (in the neighbourhood of Charleston, South Carolina) with its hundreds of thousands of men, women and children just broken forth from slavery, was, so far as these were concerned, dying under an almost physical and moral interdict. There was no one to baptize their children, to perform marriage, or to bury the dead. A ministry had to be created at once—created out of the material at hand.[1]

Reprinted by permission of Schocken Books Inc. from *The Negro Church in America/The Black Church Since Frazier* by E. Franklin Frazier/C. Eric Lincoln. Copyright © 1963 by The University of Liverpool, © 1974 by Schocken Books Inc.

The "material at hand" was, of course, those Negroes among the slaves who had been "called to preach." In answer to the criticism that neither men nor money were available for creating a ministry, the minister just quoted wrote that "God could call the men; and that the A.M.E. Church had the authority to commission them when thus called." This represented the fusion of the "invisible institution" of the Negro church which had taken root among the slaves and the institutional church which had grown up among the Negroes who were free before the Civil War.

The most obvious result of the merging of the "invisible institution" of the church which had grown up among the slaves with the institutional church of the Negroes who were free before the Civil War was the rapid growth in the size of the Negro church organization. But there was a much more important result of this merger which is of primary concern to our study. The merger resulted in the structuring or organization of Negro life to an extent that had not existed. This becomes clear when we recall that organized social life among the transplanted Negroes had been destroyed by slavery. The traditional African clan and family had been destroyed and in the environment of the New World the development of a structured family life was always nullified by the exigencies of the plantation system. Any efforts towards organization in their religious life was prevented because of the fear of the whites of slave insurrections. Even any spontaneous efforts towards mutual aid on an organized basis was prevented for the same reasons. There was, to be sure, some social differentiation among the slaves based upon the different roles which they played in the plantation economy. But this did not result in the structuring of the social life among the slaves themselves. Among the slaves themselves one may note the germs of stratification based upon their different roles in the plantation, but no system of stratification ever came into existence that became the basis of an organized social existence.

This was all changed when the Negro became free and it is our purpose here to show how an organized religious life became the chief means by which a structured or organized social life came into existence among the Negro masses. The process by which the "invisible institution" of the slaves merged with the institutional churches built by the free Negroes had to overcome many difficulties. These difficulties arose chiefly from the fact that there were among the free Negroes many mulattoes and that they, as well as the unmixed Negroes, represented a higher degree of assimilation of white or European culture. This was often reflected in the difference in the character of the religious services of those with a background of freedom and those who were just released from slavery. In fact, in the social stratification of the Negro population after Emancipation, a free and mulatto ancestry became the basis of important social distinctions.[2] It should be pointed out, however, that these cultural and social distinctions were reflected in the denominational affiliation of Negroes. The Negro masses were concentrated in the Methodist and Baptist churches which provided for a more emotional and ecstatic form of worship than the Protestant Episcopal, Presbyterian, and Congregational churches. But even in the Methodist and Baptist denominations there were separate church organizations based upon distinctions of colour and what were considered standards of civilized behaviour. In the Methodist and Baptist churches in which the vast majority of Negroes were communicants, it was impractical to organize separate churches which would be congenial to the way of life of the small Negro elite. Nevertheless, some of the educated leaders were not in sympathy with the more primitive religious behaviour of the masses. The attitude of educated leaders of even Methodist and Baptist churches was expressed by a Bishop in the African Methodist Episcopal Church even before Emancipation. He opposed the singing of the Spirituals which he described as "corn field ditties" and songs of "fist and heel worshippers" and said that the ministry of the A.M.E. Church must drive out such "heathenish mode of worship" or "drive out all intelligence and refinement."[3]

Despite the difficulties, the integration of the "invisible institution" which had emerged among the slaves into the Negro church organization established by the free Negroes was achieved. This provided an organization and structuring of Negro life which has persisted until the present time. We shall begin by considering the relation of the organization of the religious life of the Negro to building up of social control.

In dealing with the Negro church as an agency of control we shall focus attention upon the relation of the church to the Negro family and sex life during the years following Emancipation. In order to understand the important role of the Negro church, it is necessary to have a clear conception of the situation which confronted organized religion. Under slavery the Negro family was essentially an amorphous group gathered around the mother or some female on the plantation. The father was a visitor to the household without any legal or recognized status in family relations. He might disappear as the result of the sale of slaves or because of a whimsical change of his own feelings or affection. Among certain favored elements on the plantation, house slaves and skilled artisans, the family might achieve greater stability and the father and husband might develop a more permanent interest in his family. Whatever might be the circumstances of the Negro family under the slave régime, family and sex relations were constantly under the supervision of the whites.

The removal of the authority of masters as the result of the Civil War and Emancipation caused promiscuous sex relations to become widespread and permitted the constant changing of spouses. The daughter of a planter family who has idealized the slave régime nevertheless tells a story which illustrates the disorder. "Mammy Maria," she wrote, "came out in the new country as 'Miss Dabney,' and attracted, as she informed her 'white children,' as much admiration as any of the young girls, and had offers of marriage too. But she meant to enjoy her liberty, she said, and should not think of marrying any of them."[4] Some of the confusion in marital relations was due, of course, to the separation of husbands and wives during slavery and the social disorganization that resulted from Emancipation.

The problem of monogamous and stable family life was one of the most vexing problems that confronted northern white missionaries who undertook to improve the morals of the newly liberated blacks. These missionaries undertook to persuade the freedmen to legalize and formalize their marriages. There was resistance on the part of many of the slaves since legal marriage was not in their mores. Sometimes missionaries even attempted to use force in order that the freedmen legalize their sexual unions. There were, of course, many cases in which the marriage ceremony was a confirmation of a union that was based upon conjugal sentiment established over a long period of association. Marriage and an institutional family life could not be imposed by white missionaries. Marriage and the family could acquire an institutional character only as the result of the operation of economic and social forces within the Negro communities.

A large proportion of the Negro families among the freedmen continued after Emancipation to be dependent upon the Negro mother as they had been during slavery. But the new economic conditions which resulted from Emancipation tended to place the Negro man in a postion of authority in family relations. The freedmen refused to work in gangs as they had done during slavery and a man would take his wife and children and rent and operate a farm on his own account.[5] The man or husband in the family was required to sign the rent or work agreements. Sometimes the wives were also required to sign but the husband or father was always held responsible for the behaviour of his family. The more stable elements among the freedmen who had been in a position to assimilate the sentiments and ideas of their former masters soon undertook to buy land. This gave the husband and father an interest in his wife and children that no preaching on the part of white missionaries or Negro preachers could give. But it would be a serious mistake to overlook the manner in which the new economic position of the man was consolidated by the moral support of the Negro church.

There was, of course, moral support for a patriarchal family to be found in the Bible and this fact contributed undoubtedly a holy sanction to the new authority of the Negro man in the family. However, there were more important ways in which the Negro church gave support to Negro family life with the father in a position of authority. As we have pointed out, after Emancipation the Negro had to create a new communal life or become integrated into the communities created by the Negroes who were free before the Civil War. Generally, this resulted in the expansion and complete transformation of these communities. The leaders in creating a new community life were men who with their families worked land or began to buy land or worked as skilled artisans. It is important to observe that these pioneers in the creation of a communal life generally built a church as well as homes. Many of these pioneer leaders were preachers who gathered their communicants about them and became the leaders of the Negro communities. This fact tends to reveal the close relationship between the newly structured life of the Negro and his church organizations.

The churches became, and have remained until the past twenty years or so, the most important agency of social control among Negroes. The churches undertook as organizations to censure unconventional and immoral sex behavior and to punish by expulsion sex offenders and those who violated the monogamous mores. But it was impossible to change immediately the loose and unregulated sex and family behaviour among a people lacking the institutional basis of European sexual mores. Very often the churches had to tolerate or accommodate themselves to sexual irregularities.[6] A bishop in the African Methodist Episcopal Church in recounting the task of "cleaning up" irregular sex behavior among the members of the church where he served said that his church became "the Ecclesiastical Court House, as well as the Church."[7] Let us not forget, however, the control exercised by the Negro was exercised by dominating personalities. Frequently, they were the preachers who had become leaders of Negroes because of their talents and ability to govern men. Very often they were self-made men.[8] In the Baptist churches in which the majority of the Negroes have always been concentrated there was even greater opportunity for self-assertion and the assumption of leadership on the part of strong men. This naturally resulted in a pattern of autocratic leadership which has spilled over into most aspects of organized social life among Negroes, especially in as much as many forms of organized social life have grown out of the church and have come under the dominant leadership of Negro preachers.

As DuBois pointed out more than fifty years ago, "a study of economic co-operation among Negroes must begin with the Church group."[9] It was in order to establish their own churches that Negroes began to pool their meagre economic resources and buy buildings and the land on which they stood. As an indication of the small beginnings of these churches, we may note that the value of the property of the African Methodist Episcopal Church in 1787 was only $2,500. During the next century the value of the property of this organization increased to nine million dollars.[10] The Negroes in the other Methodist denominations, and especially in the numerous Baptist Churches, were contributing on a similar scale a part of their small earnings for the construction of churches. At the same time, out of the churches grew mutual aid societies. The earliest society of this type was the Free African Society which was organized in Philadelphia in 1787.[11] [This] Society was organized by Absalom Jones and Richard Allen, the two Negroes who led the secession from the Methodist Church. At the time the Society was organized, Negroes were migrating to Philadelphia in large numbers and the need for some sort of mutual aid was becoming urgent. The Society became a "curious sort of ethical and beneficial brotherhood" under the direction of Jones and Allen who exercised a "parental discipline" over its members. The avowed purpose of this organization was to "support one another in sickness, and for the benefit of their widows and fatherless children."

In the cities throughout the United States numerous beneficial societies were organized to provide assistance in time of sickness or death.[12] Many of these beneficial societies, like the Free African Society, were connected with churches. These societies continued to be established throughout the nineteenth century. For example, in Atlanta in 1898 there were nine beneficial societies which had been founded from soon after the Civil War up to

1897.[13] Six of these beneficial societies were connected with churches. The names of these beneficial societies are not without significance. At the Wheat Street Baptist Church, for example, there were two beneficial societies—the Rising Star and the Sisters of Love, while at the Bethel (Methodist) Church was the Daughters of Bethel. These associations for mutual aid which were generally known as beneficial societies were often the germ out of which grew the secular insurance companies.

The role of religion and the Negro church in more elementary forms of economic co-operation among Negroes may be seen more clearly in the rural mutual aid societies that sprang up among freedmen after Emancipation. They were formed among the poor, landless Negroes who were thrown upon their own resources. These societies were organized to meet the crises of life—sickness and death; consequently, they were known as "sickness and burial" societies. The important fact for our study is that these benevolent societies grew out of the Negro church and were inspired by the spirit of Christian charity. They were supported by the pennies which the Negroes could scrape together in order to aid each other in time of sickness but more especially to insure themselves a decent Christian burial. The influence of the simple religious conceptions of the Negro folk and the Bible is revealed in the names of these mutual aid societies which continue to exist in the rural South. They bear such names as "Love and Charity," "Builders of the Walls of Jerusalem," "Sons and Daughters of Esther," "Brothers and Sisters of Charity," and "Brothers and Sisters of Love."[14]

These "sickness and burial" societies should be distinguished from the fraternal organizations which played an important role in early economic co-operation among Negroes. Fraternal organizations like the Negro Masonic Lodge and the Odd Fellows came into existence among the free Negroes in the North as the result of the influence of the white fraternal organizations.[15] On the other hand, Negroes began before the outbreak of the Civil War to organize fraternal organizations which reflected their own interests and outlook on life. One such secret society, the Knights of Liberty, was organized by a preacher, Moses Dickson, who was born in Cincinnati in 1824.[16] This organization was active in the underground railroad and claimed to have nearly 50,000 members in 1856. Dickson joined the Union Army and after the Civil War he disbanded the Knights of Liberty. In 1871 he organized the first Temple and Tabernacle of the Knights and Daughters of Tabor in Independence, Missouri. The object of this secret society was "to help to spread the Christian religion and education" and its members were advised to "acquire real estate, avoid intemperance, and cultivate true manhood." At the end of the nineteenth century this society claimed to have nearly 200,000 members in eighteen jurisdictions scattered from Maine to California and from the Great Lakes to the Gulf of Mexico.

The organization and development of the Grand United Order of True Reformers provides a better example of the manner in which an organization under the leadership of a preacher fired with religious zeal played an important role in economic co-operation and the accumulation of capital. The founder of the organization was a Reverend Washington Browne who was born a slave in Georgia in 1849.[17] During the Civil War he ran away from a new master and made his way to the North where he received a meagre education. After Emancipation he returned to Alabama where he joined a movement of the Good Templars against the whisky rings. But after observing the various benevolent and burial societies among Negroes, he decided that Negroes should have a separate organization adapted to their special needs. In 1876 he succeeded in bringing together in a single organization, known as the Grand Fountain of True Reformers, twenty-seven Fountains with 2,000 members. Although he was not successful in creating a mutual benefit society, through his paper, *The Reformer,* he attracted the attention of the Organization of True Reformers in Virginia. He was invited to Richmond and became the Grand Worthy Master of the Virginia organization.

The True Reformers organized a variety of enterprises, including a weekly newspaper, a real estate firm, a bank, a hotel, a building and loan association, and a grocery and general merchandising store. The True Reformers took the lead in incorporating an insurance feature in its program for the benefit of its members, an example of which was followed by the other fraternal organizations among Negroes. The insurance ventures failed because they did not have sound actuarial basis and were not under government supervision.[18] Nevertheless, the Negro gained a certain experience and training which prepared him for his more successful business ventures.

The educational development of Negroes does not reflect to the same extent as their churches and mutual aid associations the racial experience and peculiar outlook on life of Negroes. Education, that is Western or European education, was something totally foreign to the Negro's way of life. This was because, as Woodson has written, "The first real educators to take up the work of enlightening American Negroes were clergymen interested in the propagation of the gospel among the heathen in the new world."[19] In fact, the purpose of education was primarily to transmit to the Negro the religious ideas and practices of an alien culture. In the North the strictly religious content of education was supplemented by other elements, whereas in the South limitations were even placed upon enabling the Negro to read the Bible. By 1850 there were large numbers of Negroes attending schools in northern cities. Then, too, individual Negroes managed to acquire a higher education and most of these were men who were preparing to become ministers.

This does not mean that Negroes took no initiative in setting up schools and acquiring an education. The free Negroes in the cities contributed to the support of schools for Negro children. Generally, the support which the free Negroes provided was greater in southern cities like Baltimore, Washington, and Charleston, South Carolina, than in New York and Philadelphia. As early as 1790, the Brown Fellowship Society in Charleston maintained schools for the free Negro children. An important fact about the schools which the free Negroes maintained was that many of them were Sunday schools. On the eve of the Civil War, "There were then in

Baltimore Sunday schools about 600 Negroes. They had formed themselves into a Bible Association, which had been received into the convention of the Baltimore Bible Society. In 1825, the Negroes there had a day and night school giving courses in Latin and French. Four years later there appeared an 'African Free School,' with an attendance of from 150 to 175 every Sunday."[20] Although the Sunday schools represented before the Civil War one of the most important agencies in the education of Negroes, nevertheless the churches through their ministers urged parents to send their children to whatever schools were available.

After Emancipation the initiative on the part of Negroes in providing education for themselves was given a much freer scope. This was because of the great educational crusade which was carried on by northern white missionaries among the freedmen. As the Union armies penetrated the South, the representatives of northern missionary societies and churches sent funds and teachers in the wake of the advancing armies. The majority of the men and women or "school marms," as they were called, were inspired by a high idealism and faith in the intellectual capacity of Negroes. They laid the foundation for or established most of the Negro colleges in the South. Working with the Freedmen's Bureau which was created by an Act of Congress in 1865 to aid the freedmen in assuming the responsibilities of citizens, they also laid the foundation for a public school system for the newly emancipated Negro. It was Negroes trained in these schools supported by northern churches and philanthropy who became the educated leaders among Negroes.

The schools—elementary, secondary, and those which provided the beginnings of college education—were permeated with a religious and moral outlook. The graduates of these schools went forth as missionaries to raise the moral and religious level of the members of their race. Many of the men were preachers or became preachers. A preacher who was a graduate of a Baptist college founded by white missionaries and who had helped to make the bricks for the buildings of the college, said that when he was graduated, the white president addressed him as follows: "I want you to go into the worst spot in this State and build a school and a church."[21] This minister followed the instructions of his white mentor and established the school that provided the primary school and later the only secondary school for Negroes in the country and four Baptist churches. This is typical of the manner in which the Negro preacher who was often the best educated man in the community took the initiative in establishing schools.

An educated and distinguished bishop in the African Methodist Episcopal Church who was the father of the most distinguished American Negro painter, wrote in his history of the Church in 1867: "For it is one of the brightest pages in the history of our Church, that while the Army of the Union were forcing their victorious passage through the southern land and striking down treason, the missionaries of our Church in the persons of Brown, Lynch, Cain, Handy, Stanford, Steward, and others, were following in their wake and establishing the Church and the school house. . . ."[22] The work of the Negro preacher in establishing schools was especially important since the southern States provided only a pittance of public funds for the education of Negro children. When the Julius Rosenwald Fund contributed to the building of more than 5,000 schools for Negroes in the South in order to stimulate the public authorities to appropriate money for Negro schools, Negro churches played an important role in making possible the schools aided by the Rosenwald Fund. Negroes contributed 17 percent of the total cost of the schools which amounted to over $28,000,000. They raised much of their share in this amount through church suppers and programmes under the auspices of their churches.[23]

The impetus among Negroes to build institutions of higher education was due primarily to their need for an educated ministry. But the desire on the part of the masses for an educated ministry was far from universal. The masses of Negroes were still impressed by the ignorant and illiterate minister who often boasted that he had not been corrupted by wicked secular learning. Soon after the "invisible institution" of the slaves was integrated into the institutional church, it was feared that a schism would occur in the African Methodist Episcopal Church as the result of the conflict between the ignorant and intelligent elements in the church.[24] Nevertheless, the African Methodist Episcopal Church succeeded in establishing a number of so-called colleges and universities.[25] The African Methodist Episcopal Zion Church and the Colored Methodist Episcopal Church also established schools. The Baptists had to depend upon local efforts. In South Carolina the Negro Baptists who became dissatisfied with the white control of the college for Negroes finally established their own school.

The schools and colleges maintained by the Negro church denominations have never attained a high level as educational institutions. They have generally nurtured a narrow religious outlook and have restricted the intellectual development of Negroes even more than the schools established for Negroes by the white missionaries. This has been due only partly to lack of financial resources. It hardly needs to be emphasized that there was no intellectual tradition among Negroes to sustain colleges and universities. The attendance of Negro students at private colleges has reflected the social stratification of the Negro community. The children of the upper class in the Negro community have generally attended the schools established by the Congregational Church and the better type of schools supported by the white Methodists and Baptists for Negroes. Nevertheless, the Negro church has affected the entire intellectual development and outlook of Negroes. This has been due both to the influence of the Negro church which has permeated every phase of social life and to the influence of the Negro preacher whose authoritarian personality and anti-intellectualism has cast a shadow over the intellectual outlook of Negroes.

It was inevitable that preachers who had played such an important role in the organized social life of Negroes should become political leaders during the Reconstruction period when the Negro enjoyed civil rights.[26] The career of Bishop Henry M. Turner of the African Methodist Episcopal Church will enable us to see how these leaders in the religious life of Negroes became, after Emancipation, leaders in politics. He was born in South

Carolina of free ancestry in 1834.[27] On his mother's side he was the grandson of an African prince. He was able to acquire some education through private instruction. When fourteen years of age he joined the Methodist Church and later became a chaplain in the United States Army. After the Civil War he transferred to the African Methodist Episcopal Church in which he advanced from a position of an itinerant preacher to that of an elder. During this time he became active in politics. He organized Negroes in the Republican Party in Georgia and was elected to the Georgia legislature. Turner was expelled from the Georgia legislature when "white supremacy" was restored in Georgia and as the result of persecution he was forced to resign as postmaster of Macon, Georgia, a position to which he had been appointed by President Grant. Turner abandoned politics and devoted his life to the Church.

During the Reconstruction period a number of outstanding leaders in the Baptist and in the other Methodist denominations became outstanding as leaders of Negroes in politics. Bishop James W. Hood of the African Methodist Episcopal Zion Church was elected president of a convention of Negroes in North Carolina which was perhaps the first political convention called by Negroes after they gained their freedom. He served as a local magistrate and later as a Deputy Collector of Internal Revenue for the United States.[28] Hood was also appointed Assistant Superintendent of Public Instruction of the State of North Carolina. These ministers who became the political leaders of Negroes were all Republicans and shared on the whole the conservative political philosophy of that party.

It should be noted that of the twenty Negroes elected to the House of Representatives of the United States from the South during the Reconstruction period only two were preachers, but one of the two Negroes who were elected to the Senate was a preacher.[29] Senator Hiram R. Revels, one of the two Negroes elected from Mississippi, was born a free Negro in North Carolina in 1822. He moved to the North and was ordained in the African Methodist Episcopal Church. When the Civil War broke out he assisted in organizing two Negro regiments in Maryland. He worked with the Freedmen's Bureau and, like other preachers, engaged in the establishment of churches and schools before entering politics in Mississippi. Revel's career in politics, like that of other Negro preachers, was of short duration because of the re-establishment of white supremacy in the South. After elimination from politics in the South, the Negro preachers generally devoted themselves to their church though in some cases they became heads of Negro schools.

As the result of the elimination of Negroes from the political life of the American community, the Negro church became the arena of their political activities. The church was the main area of social life in which Negroes could aspire to become the leaders of men. It was the area of social life where ambitious individuals could achieve distinction and the symbols of status. The church was the arena in which the struggle for power and the thirst for power could be satisfied. This was especially important to Negro men who had never been able to assert themselves and assume the dominant male role, even in family relations, as defined by American culture. In the Baptist churches, with their local autonomy, individual Negro preachers ruled their followers in an arbitrary manner, while the leaders in the hierarchy of the various Methodist denominations were czars, rewarding and punishing their subordinates on the basis of personal loyalties. Moreover, the monetary rewards which went with power were not small when one considers the contributions of millions of Negroes and the various business activities of the churches.

The Negro church was not only an arena of political life for the leaders of Negroes, it had a political meaning for the masses. Although they were denied the right to vote in the American community, within their Churches, especially the Methodist Churches, they could vote and engage in electing their officers. The election of bishops and other officers and representatives to conventions has been a serious activity for the masses of Negroes. But, in addition, the church had a political significance for Negroes in a broader meaning of the term. The development of the Negro church after Emancipation was tied up, as we have seen, largely with the Negro family. A study of Negro churches in a Black Belt county in Georgia in 1903 revealed, for example, that a large proportion of the churches were "family churches."[30] Outside of the family, the church represented the only other organized social existence. The rural Negro communities in the South were named after their churches. In fact, the Negro population in the rural South has been organized in "church communities" which represented their widest social orientation and the largest social groups in which they found an identification. Moreover, since the Negro was an outsider in the American community, it was the church that enlisted his deepest loyalties. Therefore, it was more than an amusing incident to note some years ago in a rural community in Alabama, that a Negro when asked to identify the people in the adjoining community replied: "The nationality in there is Methodist." We must remember that these people have no historic traditions and language and sentiments to identify them as the various nationalities of Europe. For the Negro masses, in their social and moral isolation in American society, the Negro church community has been a nation within a nation.

In providing a structured social life in which the Negro could give expression to his deepest feeling and at the same time achieve status and find a meaningful existence, the Negro church provided a refuge in a hostile white world. For the slaves who worked and suffered in an alien world, religion offered a means of catharsis for their pent-up emotions and frustrations. Moreover, it turned their minds from the sufferings and privations of this world to a world after death where the weary would find rest and the victims of injustices would be compensated. The Negroes who were free before the Civil War found status in the church which shielded them from the contempt and discriminations of the white world. Then for a few brief years after Emancipation the hopes and expectations of the black freedmen were raised and they thought that they would have acceptance and freedom in the white man's world. But their hopes and expectations were rudely shattered when white supremacy was re-established in the South. They were excluded from participation in the white man's world except on the basis of inferiority. They were disfranchised and the public schools provided for them were a mere travesty on education. The courts set up one standard of justice for the white and another standard for the black man. They were stigmatized as an inferior race lacking even the human attributes which all men are supposed to possess. They were subjected to mob violence involving lynchings and burnings alive which were justified even by the white Christian churches.

Where could the Negro find a refuge from this hostile white world? They remembered from their Bible that the friends of Job had counselled him to curse God and die. They remembered too that Samson when blinded had torn down the Temple and destroyed himself along with his tormentors. Had not one of their leading ministers in his disillusionment and despair cried out against the flag of the nation he had served in the Civil War, "I don't want to die under the dirty rag." But the Negro masses did not curse God and die.[31] They could not pull down the Temple upon the white man and themselves. They retained their faith in God and found a refuge in their churches.

The Negro church with its own forms of religious worship was a world which the white man did not invade but only regarded with an attitude of condescending amusement. The Negro church could enjoy this freedom so long as it offered no threat to the white man's dominance in both economic and social relations. And, on the whole, the Negro's church was not a threat to white domination and aided the Negro to become accommodated to an inferior status. The religion of the Negro continued to be other-worldly in its outlook, dismissing the privations and sufferings and injustices of this world as temporary and transient.[32] The Negro church remained a refuge despite the fact that the Negro often accepted the disparagement of Negroes by whites and the domination of whites. But all of this was a part of God's plan and was regarded just as the physical environment was regarded. What mattered was the way he was treated in the church which gave him an opportunity for self-expression and status. Since the Negro was not completely insulated from the white world and had to conform to some extent to the ways of white men, he was affected by their evaluation of him. Nevertheless, he could always find an escape from such, often painful, experiences within the shelter of his church.

NOTES

[1]Theophilus G. Steward, *Fifty Years in the Gospel Ministry* (Philadelphia, 1915), p. 33.

[2]See E. Franklin Frazier, *The Negro Family in the United States* (Chicago, 1939), Chapter XIX, "Old Families and New Classes."

[3]Quoted in Fisher, *Negro Slave Songs in the United States,* pp. 189-90.

[4]Susan Smedes, *A Southern Planter* (Baltimore, 1887), p. 179.

[5]See Frazier, *The Negro Family in the United States,* Chapter IX, "The Downfall of the Matriarchate."

[6]In one case of accommodation which was unique only because of the rationalization which the Negroes used to reconcile their habitual unregulated sex behaviour with Christian morality regarding premarital sex relations, the Negroes evolved the doctrine of "clean sheets." According to this "doctrine" it was not wrong for two *Christians* to have sex relations outside of marriage since both were "clean sheets," and could not soil each other as would be the case if one or both were unconverted or sinners.

[7]L. J. Coppin, *Unwritten History* (Philadelphia, 1920), p. 127.

[8]See Benj. T. Tanner, *An Apology for African Methodism* (Baltimore, 1867), p. 123.

[9]W. E. Burghardt DuBois, *Economic Cooperation Among American Negroes* (Atlanta, 1907), p. 54.

[10]*Ibid.,* p. 57.

[11]W. E. B. DuBois, *The Philadelphia Negro* (Philadelphia, 1899), pp. 19-20.

[12]In 1790 the Brown Fellowship Society was organized among the "free brown men" of Charleston, South Carolina, to relieve widows and orphans in "the hour of their distresses, sickness, and death. . . ." The membership of the Society was restricted to fifty person who paid an admission fee of fifty dollars. See E. Horace Fitchett, "The Traditions of the Free Negroes in Charleston, South Carolina," *Journal of Negro History,* Vol. 25, pp. 139-52.

[13]DuBois, *Economic Cooperation Among American Negroes,* p. 94.

[14]See Arthur Raper, *Preface to Peasantry* (Chapel Hill, 1926), p. 374.

[15]See Harold Van Buren Voorhis, P. M., *Negro Masonry in the United States* (New York, 1940), pp. 3-22; and Charles H. Brooks, *A History and Manual of the Grand United Order of Odd Fellows in America* (Philadelphia, 1893), pp. 19-20.

[16]*Why You Should Become a Knight and Daughter of Tabor,* p. 13. Pamphlet in the Moorland Foundation, Howard University, Washington, D.C.

[17]W. P. Burrell and D. E. Johnson, *Twenty-five Years History of the Grand Fountain of the United Order of True Reformers* (Richmond, Va., 1909), p. 12.

[18]W. J. Trent, Jr., *Development of Negro Life Insurance Enterprises,* Master's Thesis (University of Pennsylvania, 1932), p. 32.

[19]Carter G. Woodson, *The Education of the Negro Prior to 1861* (New York, 1915), p. 18.

[20]*Ibid.,* pp. 140-1.

[21]Secured during an interview.

[22]Tanner, *An Apology for African Methodism,* p. 251.

[23]Frazier, *The Negro in the United States,* p. 429.

[24]See Woodson, *The History of the Negro Church,* p. 172.

[25]See Perry, *op. cit., passim.*

[26]See Woodson, *The History of the Negro Church,* Chapter XI, "The Call of Politics."

[27]Henry M. Turner, *Life and Times of Henry M. Turner* (Atlanta, 1917), p. 23.

[28]Woodson, *The History of the Negro Church,* pp. 236-8.

[29]Samuel D. Smith, *The Negro Congress, 1870-1901* (Chapel Hill, 1940), p. 8.

[30]DuBois, *The Negro Church,* p. 57.

[31]The suicide rate among Negroes, it may be noted here, has always been much lower than among whites.

[32]See Charles S. Johnson, *Shadow of the Plantation* (Chicago, 1934), Chapter V, for description of Negro church services and sermons of Negro preachers in rural Black Belt County in Alabama. See also J. Mason Brewer, *The Word on the Brazos* (Austin, Tex., 1953), for Negroes' reaction to their preachers.

19

A Critical Period in American Religion, 1875-1900

Arthur M. Schlesinger, Sr.

The extraordinary development of American society in the last quarter of the nineteenth century confronted religious groups with a series of challenges internal to the traditional bodies and from the culture as well. Arthur M. Schlesinger, Sr., outlines the nature of these challenges and a variety of religious responses and suggests how this critical period transformed American religious life. Professor Schlesinger, who died in 1965, taught in the History Department at Harvard University for several decades.

From early colonial times the life of American Christianity has consisted in its capacity for adaptability and change. Its history has been marked by recurrent conflicts between orthodoxy and heterodoxy, between fundamentalism and modernism, with every hard-won peace a truce and the battle line ever advancing to new fronts. However disturbing to defenders of the old-time religion, this ceaseless bending of creeds and practices to the changing needs of society has been the price of survival. Perhaps at no time in its American development has the path of Christianity been so sorely beset with pitfalls and perils as in the last quarter of the nineteenth century. The validity of the Bible itself seemed at stake in the light of new pronouncements of science and scholarship. Darwinism, the emerging science of biblical criticism, the increasing knowledge and study of other great religions—such threats to orthodoxy could not be ignored, yet how were

First published in the *Massachusetts Historical Society Proceedings,* LXIV (1930-32), pp. 523-46 (abridged). Reprinted with the permission of Arthur M. Schlesinger, Jr.

they to be met? But this was not all. In an age of rapid, not to say fearful, urban and industrial development, the church was fast losing its appeal for the wage-earning masses, though such folk asked emotional, not intellectual, satisfaction of their spiritual guides. Was Protestantism to be sequestered in the small towns and rural districts, or could it adjust itself to the requirements of megalopolis? These two great challenges to organized religion, the one to its system of thought, the other to its social program, form the main themes of the discussion that follows.

The religious controversy over biological evolution reached its most critical stage in the late 1870's, for by that time American scientists stood a solid phalanx in its support, and many of the thoughtful public had been won over by the persuasive writings of Spencer, Huxley, and Fiske. It no longer sufficed for theological disputants to castigate Darwinism with such epithets as "materialistic" and "atheistic." If evolution was the "bestial hypothesis" of man's origin, it was only too easy to retort in kind that the biblical account was the "mud-man theory" of creation. Reason must be appealed to as well as inherited belief.[1] An analysis of the turbid flood of argument which poured from the press during the eighties reveals a steady advance—or retreat—from a position of pure emotional obscurantism to one of concession and accommodation. Some found the way out by asserting that religion and science belonged to mutually exclusive spheres; that the Bible was a rule of conduct and a guide to faith, not a scientific cyclopedia. Others held that the account in Genesis, when allegorically construed, really anticipated and supported Darwin's thesis. Still others contended that genuine religion remained unaffected by what was, at most, a conflict between science and theology.

Gradually, an increasing number of ministers, influenced by the example of Henry Ward Beecher in his Brooklyn pulpit and by Lyman Abbott's sermons and writings in the *Christian Union* (later the *Outlook*) and elsewhere, came to embrace evolution as a new and grander revelation of the mysterious way God moves his wonders to perform.[2] Mark Twain's facetious proposal, early in the eighties, of a monument to Adam before that great progenitor of mankind should be wholly supplanted by Darwin's simian was decidedly premature. But unmistakable evidence of a sweeping change of sentiment among thoughtful religionists appeared when, after another decade of discussion, the great New York Chautauqua gave over its platform in 1893 to a series of lectures by the well-known Scotch evolutionist Henry Drummond. "It is a sign of the times which no observer can neglect," commented the *Nation*.[3]

Like the doctrine of natural selection, textual criticism of the Bible also called into question the infallibility of the Scriptures. Imported from German university centers, the higher criticism, as it was known, subjected Holy Writ to rigorous historical analysis. According to the new findings, the sixty-six books, far from being all of one piece and inspired throughout, comprised a storehouse of history, folklore, discourses, poetry, and prophecy brought together over a period of a thousand years.[4] Popular acceptance of the new point of view was somewhat facilitated by the appearance of a revised version of the King James Bible in 1881 and 1885, a laborious enterprise carried through by a group of English and American scholars. So great was the public interest that two hundred thousand copies of the New Testament were sold in New York alone within less than a week, and the *Chicago Times* and the *Chicago Tribune* printed the text entire.

While ministers and churchgoers accustomed themselves to changed readings and often changed meanings of treasured passages, liberal theologians wrote books and articles to disseminate the teachings of the higher critics. President Orello Cone, of Buchtel College, for example, published in 1891 his *Gospel Criticism and Historical Christianity,* the ablest work in its field from an American pen. All was not smooth sailing, of course. Dwight L. Moody, the famous evangelist, venting contempt on those who found inconsistencies and contradictions in the Scriptures, shouted to vast audiences with all the force of his two hundred and eighty pounds: "The Bible was not made to understand."[5] Professor W. H. Green, of Princeton Seminary, stoutly defended the orthodox position in a notable debate with President Harper, of Chicago, and many a household and congregation continued to find solace in an unquestioning acceptance of the King James version. Yet the reception accorded Washington Gladden's *Who Wrote the Bible?,* published in 1891, indicates the broad appeal of the more advanced attitude. A summary and popularization of the newer studies, it not only enjoyed the largest sale of any of his widely read books, but became a manual for Bible classes and Young Men's Christian Associations.[6] Sober reflection was convincing even many of the earlier objectors that, if critical analysis stripped the Bible of its vesture of infallibility, it revealed it as a work of literary, spiritual, and ethical power, a veritable book among books.[7]

The crumbling of orthodoxy was furthered by certain byproducts of American missionary enterprise in the Orient. Thousands of Christian workers, brought into contact with the great faiths of Asia, learned that Christianity and religion were not coextensive, that all good was not monopolized by their own system of belief. At the same time the work of secular scholars in the realms of mythology, folklore, psychology and anthropology suggested points of departure for an understanding of religious phenomena. James Freeman Clarke's sympathetic portrayal of *Ten Great Religions* made such an impression upon the public that in the fifteen years after 1871 it passed through twenty-one editions. Comparative religion became not only a preoccupation of scholars but a new measuring rod for Christianity. As dramatic evidence of the widened horizon, a World's Parliament of Religions, the first of its kind in history, was convened during the Columbian Exposition of 1893. More than one hundred and fifty thousand people attended its sessions. While all was not harmony, the animating spirit of the great assemblage was expressed in the words of Malachi, which served as its motto: "Have we not all one Father? hath not one God created us?"[8] In the light of fuller knowledge the old misunderstanding and intolerance once accorded non-Christian faiths was beginning to wane.

If these new intellectual currents little touched the average mind, they deeply affected the thinking of more intelligent readers. In 1881, the American Institute of Christian Philosophy was formed in New York state for the purpose of producing and distributing literature upon the relations of science and the Bible. Magazines, both religious and secular, gave generous space to appraisals of the new learning. Even more significant was the discussion of theological issues in certain notable works of fiction. The best sellers of the year 1888 were Margaret Deland's *John Ward, Preacher,* described by a contemporary as "a profound outcry against the intolerance of the creeds," and Mrs. Humphry Ward's *Robert Elsmere,* an English novel of similar import which sold more copies in America than in the author's own country.[9] Here and there theological schools introduced courses dealing with the relations of science and religion and with the study of comparative religion.

Traditionalism, however, maintained a stubborn front where it could. In 1878, the geologist Alexander Winchell was dismissed from the Methodist-controlled Vanderbilt University, with the exultant pronouncement of the Tennessee Methodist Conference—anticipating the state of mind behind the Dayton "monkey trial" of 1925—that "our university alone has had the courage to lay its young but vigorous hand upon the mane of untamed Speculation and say, "We will have no more of this.' "[10] Not to be outdone in good works, the Southern Baptist Seminary at Louisville followed Vanderbilt's example within a year by forcing Professor C. H. Toy's resignation because of his attempts to interpret the Old Testament from the viewpoint of modern science. Five years later Dr. James Woodrow was driven from his post in the Presbyterian Theological Seminary at Columbia, South Carolina, for avowing the truth of evolution; and in 1891, W. J. Alexander was dropped from the chair of philosophy at the state university because of unorthodox views regarding the divinity of Christ.[11]

Such bigotry, however, was not confined to the South or to three denominations. In 1882, Dr. E. P. Gould was obliged to resign from Newton Theological Institution (Baptist) in Massachusetts as a result of doctrinal differences with the president. The next year the Reverend R. Heber Newton of All Souls' Protestant Episcopal Church, New York City, was charged with heresy at the instance of Bishop H. C. Potter and other divines, the case later being allowed to drop. In 1886, a fire that for several years had been smoldering at Andover Theological Seminary (Congregational) in Massachusetts burst into flame when the Board of Visitors tried five professors for theological liberalism and declared one of them guilty.

Even more rancorous than the "Andover controversy" was the storm that rose in 1891 within Presbyterian ranks over the transfer of Professor Charles A. Briggs, a distinguished exponent of the higher criticism and long an ornament of Union Theological Seminary, to the new chair of biblical theology. More than seventy presbyteries protested the appointment. Although the New York presbytery recommended that in the interests of "the peace . . . of the Church" no action be taken, the General Assembly in 1893 suspended Briggs from the ministry for heresy. The peace of the church was indeed involved. In Albany a clergyman resigned because of the decision, while Professor H. P. Smith was suspended from Lane Theological Seminary in Cincinnati for supporting Briggs's views.

The harm to the cause of religion inflicted by such incidents was greater than that to the cause of science and learning. Yet the wayward religious tendencies of the times help explain the fears of the pious that, once old moorings were cut, the people would drift into uncharted seas. Untold thousands listened receptively to the eloquent and pungent discourses of Robert G. Ingersoll, the "notorious infidel"; many a village Jacques won his reputation for bold speculation by filching the doughty Colonel's iconoclastic shafts. Himself a minister's son, in lifelong revolt against his father's extreme Calvinism, Ingersoll was an agnostic, not an atheist: "I do not deny. I do not know—but I do not believe."[12] A relentless foe of dogmatism and illiberalism, he inveighed against Old Testament terrors and New Testament miracles, finding good in all the great religious systems and extolling science as "the only true religion, . . . the only Savior of the world." Starting from much the same position, Dr. Felix Adler, like Ingersoll a clergyman's son, though of the Jewish faith, rejected Ingersoll's negative attitude and sought to erect ethical purpose as the vital principle of living without reference to any kind of theological doctrine.[13] With this as his aim he founded in 1876 the Society for Ethical Culture which presently attracted small bands of intellectuals, usually of Jewish extraction, in the great cities of the East and of the Middle West.

Whatever Ethical Culture lacked in mysticism was supplied in full measure by another sect which sought disciples during these years. Originated by Helena P. Blavatsky, an obese Russian woman of somewhat unsavory antecedents, Theosophy was a curious blend of spiritualism and certain occult doctrines derived from the Brahmanic and Vedic literatures of India.[14] The Theosophical Society, formed in New York in 1875, was to be the spearhead of the new movement, but, converts remaining few, Madame Blavatsky three years later transferred her colorful activities to India and Europe. Meantime the cult managed to maintain a tenuous existence in America and was temporarily stirred to a flurry of activity in the 1890's by the arrival of numerous swamis at the time of the World's Fair.

If these new religions lacked warmth of appeal, their plight was shared to some extent by the older, Protestant sects whose ministers, immersed in intellectual controversy, often failed to satisfy deeper spiritual needs. Even more harmful was the failure of the church to adjust itself to the unprecedented conditions created by rapid urban and industrial growth.[15] American Protestantism, the product of a rural middle-class society, faced a range of problems for which it had neither experience nor aptitude. In the cities the building of church edifices lagged behind the advance of population while the shifting of residential districts left once prosperous houses of worship stranded and abandoned on the bleak shores of factory and slum neighborhoods. In the twenty years preceding 1888 seventeen Protestant churches moved out of the district below Fourteenth Street, New York, though two hundred thousand more people crowded into it.[16] In the decade after 1878 twenty-two thousand residents in the thirteenth ward of Boston were without a single Protestant church, and it was said that in the heart of Chicago sixty thousand people had no church, either Protestant or Catholic. It was generally true of large cities that those parts which needed most religious attention got least.

When better accommodations existed, the working class commonly regarded the church—with its fine upholstery, stained-glass windows and expensive choirs—as an institution where ill-clad worshipers were unwelcome and where the Nazarene himself would have been snubbed.[17] As someone has observed, in religion nothing fails like success. The pulpit, increasingly beholden to contributions from the rich, ordinarily ignored or condoned the terrible injustices from which the wage-earning multitude were suffering. In one instance, reported by Professor Ely, when the bakers' union petitioned five hundred clergymen of New York and Brooklyn to preach sermons against compulsory Sunday labor, all but half a dozen ignored the appeal.[18] Even popular sects like the Baptists abandoned their contempt for wealth. In 1890, the Indiana state Baptist convention "thankfully recognized the rich blessing of the Great Head of the Church in the recent gift of Brother John D. Rockefeller to the Baptist Seminary in Chicago."[19] To laborites, religion seemed a sort of capitalistic soothing-syrup. Samuel Gompers bluntly charged that the intellect and talent of the ministry had been suborned by the plutocratic oppressors of the poor.[20] . . .

"Go into an ordinary church on Sunday morning," declared a Protestant clergyman in 1887, "and you see lawyers, physicians, merchants, and business men with their families . . . but the workingman and his household are not there."[21] Of the older faiths the Roman Catholic and the Jewish alone knew how to attract and hold the laborer and the immigrant newcomer. Evangelistic endeavors might temporarily bridge the chasm in the case of Protestants; but even such ardent harvesters of souls as Dwight L. Moody and Ira D. Sankey found their chief work among laggard members of existing congregations and did little to reach the unchurched masses. The Catholic Church, on the other hand, reared its edifices where humanity was densest, and thronged its pews three or four times each Sunday with worshipers whose hands and clothing plainly betrayed their humble station.

Another token of alienation from the church appeared in the growing secularization of the Sabbath. This, too, was largely a city phenomenon, for in rural communities, and notably in the South, the people continued to regard the day as one set aside for religious observance and rest. In urban centers, on the other hand, the pressure of life turned the toiling masses to thoughts of pleasure on their one free day, while, to satisfy their desire thousands of their fellows needs must operate trains and street cars and provide the means of recreation. The altered attitude owed much to the practices of immigrant groups unfamiliar with the strait-laced American Lord's Day—the Germans with their Continental Sabbath, the Irish and other aliens with their Catholic Sunday, and the Jews who observed Saturday as their holy day. "Where is the city in which the Sabbath day is not losing ground?" asked one sad voice. "To the mass of the workingmen Sunday . . . is a day for labor meetings, for excursions, for saloons, beer-gardens, baseball games and carousals."[22]

The change in Sabbath habits had little relation to Sabbath legislation. Such laws existed in almost every state and were usually very strict, forbidding all labor except works of necessity and charity and, in many cases, banning also travel and nearly every kind of amusement. As late as 1885 Vermont and South Carolina required church attendance on Sunday, and in Pennsylvania the stay-at-home was liable to the penalty of sitting in the stocks. But if rural majorities in the legislatures insisted on retaining the laws, they seemed strangely indifferent to lax law enforcement in the cities. Indeed, certain strongly urban states like New York (1883) and Massachusetts (1887) markedly relaxed their statutes; and in California in 1883, after a thorough public discussion of the issue, the legislature repealed all the Sabbath blue laws. The running of passenger trains was a particular affront to sabbatarians who, however, saw each year an increasing number on the tracks.

The portentous spread of Sabbath desecration brought a revival of militant efforts to restore its sanctity. In 1884, the W. C. T. U. established a department of Sabbath observance, and four years later the American Sabbath Union, formed by several evangelical churches, began organizing local branches to arouse opinion. In addition, the International Sabbath Association and the Sunday League of America were in the field. But even such bodies reflected a changed attitude on the subject. Their main plea was less a religious than a humanitarian one: Sabbath breaking was condemned not so much as an offense against God as against man.[23] In other words, a rational regard for a secular day of rest was supplanting the old idea of a day exclusively for religious consecration. For this reason their efforts often won support from powerful labor groups like the Knights of Labor, the Brotherhood of Locomotive Engineers, and the American Federation of Labor.

It was a union of these forces which bombarded Congress from 1887 to 1889 with memorials, said to represent fourteen million people, for a cessation of dispensable Sunday labor in interstate commerce, in the postal and military services, and also in the territories and the District of Columbia. The desired measure was introduced by Senator H. W. Blair on May 21, 1888, hearings were held, but the bill mysteriously never came to a vote.[24] On the matter of Sabbath recreation, however, laborites parted company with the professional sabbatarians. The question of opening the World's Fair on Sunday proved the occasion for a pitched battle. The management vacilated and, when finally it opened the gates but with incomplete exhibits, the attendance was so poor that after a few weeks they were shut again.[25]

Whether or not a more vibrant religious message would have kept more people within bounds on the Lord's Day, the older Protestant churches, as we have seen, were not prepared to give it. To help the common man rekindle the altar fires of his faith two new religions, however, made their appearance. One was a British importation, the other an authentic American creation. The Salvation Army had been organized in London by

William Booth in an effort to adapt the Methodist revivalistic technique to the needs of the city wilderness. Extended to America in 1879, it grew by leaps and bounds in the next two decades.[26] Its uniformed bands, parading the down-town districts with bass drum and trombone, gathered knots of the curious at the street corners and preached to "rumdom, slumdom and bumdom" the exciting gospel of repentance and reform. After 1889, the Army added social service to its evangelism. By means of its employment bureaus, "slum brigades" to work with tenement-house families, cheap lodgings for vagrants, and rescue homes for fallen women, it carried on an essential work of Christian service.[27]

The rise of Christian Science is inseparably bound up with the life and personality of its founder, Mrs. Mary Baker Glover Patterson Eddy. Of New England Puritan descent and a prey from childhood to ill health and recurrent hysteria, she had dabbled in mesmerism, spiritualism, and hydropathy until she found relief from a distressing spinal malady at the hands of P. P. Quimby, a mental healer of Portland, Maine. Upon his death in 1866 she presently set up as a practitioner in her own right. At first an avowed Quimbyite, using one of his manuscripts as the fount of her teachings, she gradually evolved a system which she came to regard as wholly her own and which she put into print in 1875 under the title *Science and Health*.[28] "Disease is caused by mind alone," and matter is an illusion—this was the essence of the newly proclaimed Christian Science. "You can prevent or cure scrofula, hereditary disease, etc., in just the ratio you expel from mind a belief in the transmission of disease" by working in harmony with the Eternal Mind as revealed through Jesus Christ.[29]

The founder gathered about her a small band of adherents in Lynn, Massachusetts, consisting mostly of factory workers and other artisans, "their hands stained with the leather and tools of the day's occupation."[30] She also provided for the training of healers by setting up the Massachusetts Metaphysical College in 1881, with herself as the faculty. Converts coming too slowly to suit her, she next changed her base of operations to Boston eight miles away. Though the period of struggle was not yet over, the removal to a large population center proved the turning point. Attacked by foes both within and without the church and harried by delusions of persecution, this frail, spectacled, ill-educated woman, already past sixty, proceeded to build up a solid support in Boston and to spread her doctrines afar. As a philosophy Christian Science would probably have had little appeal, but as a system of therapeutics it assured nerve-racked urban dwellers of the immediate cure of their bodies as well as the ultimate cure of their souls.

By 1890, there were over two hundred Christian Science groups with nearly nine thousand members, a majority of them in the larger cities of the Middle West. The number of local bodies doubled in the next decade while the membership perhaps quadrupled.[31] Meanwhile, as Mrs. Eddy became increasingly well-to-do and many of her practitioners acquired economic security, the cult sloughed off its working-class origins, directing its chief appeal to members of other denominations at higher income levels. This transition to a religion of the comfortable may be said to have been completed in 1895 when the First Church of Christ, Scientist, built at a cost of two hundred thousand dollars, opened in Boston as the "Mother Church" of the faith.

Unlike the Salvation Army, the Christian Scientists did not develop social work as one of their interests, since poverty, like disease, was regarded as an illusion of mortal mind. Meantime, however, leaders in some of the older Protestant sects were awakening to a sense of responsibility for the world about them. Those most active in the effort to liberalize religious thought were usually also at the forefront of the effort to socialize religious practice. Notable among them were Lyman Abbot, Beecher's successor at the Plymouth Church in 1888; his neighbor on Manhattan, R. Heber Newton; and Francis G. Peabody, who from 1881 to 1886 was Parkman Professor of Theology, and from the latter year occupied the chair of Christian Morals at the Harvard Divinity School. Particularly influential were Josiah Strong, general secretary of the Evangelical Alliance from 1886, author of an eloquent book on social Christianity, *Our Country* (1885), which sold a half-million copies in twenty years, and Washington Gladden, Congregational minister in Columbus, Ohio, whose voice and example made him perhaps the great outstanding leader.[32] The more liberal theological schools responded by introducing courses in economics and sociology, and even in some cases, as at Andover Seminary and the Chicago Theological Seminary, encouraging their students to get practical experience in social work. In the last years of the century it was possible to say that the "theological seminary of today . . . is a totally different institution from that of a generation ago."[33]

At the same time efforts began to be made by Protestant bodies to minister to the religious and practical needs of immigrants when they landed in the great Atlantic ports. In 1883, the interdenominational American Home Missionary Society organized German, Scandinavian, and Slavic departments for this purpose. Of single sects the Lutherans in particular vied with the Catholics and the Jews in watching over the alien newcomer.[34] More significant was the steady tendency of Protestant churches in downtown districts to develop "institutional" features, that is, conduct organized philanthropic and educational work among the poor and unchurched.

Thus, St. George's Episcopal Church in New York, the People's Temple (Congregational) in Denver, and Russell H. Conwell's Baptist Temple in Philadelphia began in the eighties to provide reading rooms, gymnasiums, social clubs, day nurseries, sewing classes, and manual-training courses which, along with religious instruction, were available throughout the week to all comers. By 1894, the number of institutional churches was sufficiently large to justify the organization of an Open and Institutional Church League on an intercity and interdenominational basis. The success of the new methods was attested by phenomenal increases in religious membership. St. George's Episcopal Church, which had but seventy-five communicants in 1882 when it started institutional work, numbered over four thousand in 1897; Berkeley Temple (Congregational) in Boston grew in seven years from three hundred to eleven hundred; and the Ninth Street Baptist Church of Cincinnati added nearly nine hundred members in four years. It was reported in 1900 that over a period of six years Congregational churches employing institutional methods had increased six times as fast as those which did not do so.[35]

To give the new social tendencies a wider backing various organizations were formed, one of the most influential being that among the Episcopal clergy known as the Church Organization for the Advancement of the Interests of Labor (1887). Two years later some of the more radical religionists of Boston, inspired by the Reverend W. D. P. Bliss of Grace Church (Episcopal), founded the Society of Christian Socialists in order "to awaken members of the Christian churches to the fact that the teachings of Jesus Christ lead directly to some specific form or forms of Socialism."[36] Though the movement did not prosper widely, the Congregationalists and Baptists in the early nineties formed national agencies to direct attention to social and economic problems, and two interdenominational societies, the Christian Social Union (1891) and the American Institute of Christian Sociology (1894), gave further impetus to the cause. In the latter year, too, the Evangelical Alliance of the United States, largely as a result of Josiah Strong's efforts, turned definitely to a social prgram.

These attempts to socialize Christian thought and practice, of course, represented the efforts of energetic minorities. "We were few and we shouted in the wilderness," a pioneer of the social gospel later wrote of this time.[37] Yet that a rich harvest awaited beyond the turn of the century was plainly indicated by the extraordinary interest excited among the lay public by the appearance of *In His Steps,* a book written by the Reverend C. M. Sheldon, of Topeka, in 1896. It told the story of a congregation which resolved to live for a year, regardless of consequences, in accordance with the teachings of Jesus. Its wider message was inescapable: "If the church members were all doing as Jesus would do, could it remain true that armies of men would walk the streets for jobs, and hundreds of them curse the church, and thousands of them find in the saloon their best friend?"[38] Within a year sixteen different publishers were issuing the book to meet a demand that showed no sign of appeasement.

Since early colonial times clergymen had often lifted their voices at critical public junctures, but never before had religious ethics been so sharply challenged by the practices of the business order, or the ministry so apparently helpless before the economic masters of society. Yet, despite Gompers' sweeping denunciation of churchmen, individuals stood forth who, not content with "making faces at the devil from behind the pulpit"[39] or with treating symptoms rather than the disease itself, strove to cope with the deeper forces responsible for the conditions. Few went so far as Bliss when he became a Master Workman of the Knights of Labor and candidate for lieutenant governor on the Massachusetts Labor ticket; nor were many willing to risk the obloquy which befell the Methodist pastor, W. H. Cawardine of Pullman, Illinois, when he flayed the Pullman corporation for precipitating the strike of 1894.[40]

Washington Gladden, on the other hand, showed how actively a minister might concern himself with industrial relations without forfeiting the confidence of even a well-to-do congregation. During the Hocking Valley coal strike of 1884 he preached the "right and necessity of labor organizations" to a congregation which included high officers of the corporation involved. Two years later, while a fierce street-car strike raged in Cleveland, he journeyed thither from Columbus and spoke to a great meeting of employers and employees on "Is It Peace or War?", again declaring the right of wage-earners to organize. A little later he headed a committee of Ohio Congregationalists to investigate employment conditions in the state in an effort to promote better understanding between capital and labor. He saw the solution of the difficulties in an "industrial partnership" in which the toilers would receive "a fixed share of the profits of production."[41]

The attitude of the Roman Catholic clergy toward the labor problem was greatly influenced by the course of Cardinal Gibbons of Baltimore. Thoroughly American in outlook and deeply sympathetic with the workingmen who composed the great bulk of his church, he made an eloquent plea to Rome in 1886 which saved the Knights of Labor from papal condemnation and ultimately secured the reversal of an edict against the organization in Canada.[42] He also resisted the recommendation of Archbishop Corrigan of New York that Henry George's *Progress and Poverty* be put upon the Index, again winning his point in Rome. Of other Catholic ecclesiastics Archbishop Ireland of St. Paul was notable for the pacificatory part he took in two great railway strikes in 1894 in the Northwest. Catholic liberalism received high sanction in 1891 from the encyclical *Rerum Novarum* in which the pope, while denouncing socialism, defended the dignity of labor and declared that the problem could be solved only through the application of religious ethics.

Despite the many difficulties, theological and practical, which beset the path of religion, the last two decades of the century witnessed a substantial gain in church membership. Protestant communicants increased from ten million to nearly eighteen; the Roman Catholic population from well over six million to more than ten; the number of Jews from less than a quarter million to approximately a million. It was a striking testimonial to the vitality of organized religion that the growth was proportionately greater than the general advance of population, though, as was to be expected, less than the rate of increase of the urban wage-earning class. Of the Protestant communicants the Methodist bodies represented a third of the total throughout the period, followed in order by the Baptists, Presbyterians, Lutherans, and Congregationalists. At all times, however, the Catholics outnumbered any Protestant group, being nearly twice as strong as the Methodists.

The geographic distribution of the sects remained substantially as before. The East continued to be the seat of Catholicism, Congregationalism, and Episcopalianism, with a strong infusion of Presbyterianism, while the Methodists and Baptists, numerous everywhere, dominated the religious life of the South. In the Middle West all faiths flourished—Chicago was the most Catholic of American cities—and in that section, too, the Lutherans had their principal stronghold. The most conspicuous religious feature of the Great West was the Mormon community in Utah. As might be expected, the great Scandinavian influx shot up the numbers of Lutherans, while it was the anti-Semitic persecutions in Russia, Austria-Hungary, and Roumania that made the Jewish church for the first time an important American religion.

Roman Catholicism, however, garnered the richest harvest from among the immigrant newcomers, notably those from Ireland, Germany, Austria-Hungary, Italy, Poland, and French Canada. The heightened importance of the American church was signally recognized by the creation of a pontifical university in Washington, the appointment of an American cardinal, and, in 1893, the sending of an apostolic delegate to Washington. On the other hand, many Americans, particularly in the Middle West, viewed with mounting alarm the rapid accretion of Catholic power. They took amiss the agitation to secure public funds for parochial schools and regarded even the labor encyclical of 1891 as a sinister move by the Vatican to gain American working-class support.

As in the 1830's and 1840's, the fear and misunderstanding took the form of organized bigotry, embodied this time principally in the American Protective Association, a secret oath-bound order founded in 1887 by H. F. Bowers, a sixty-year-old lawyer of Clinton, Iowa. Cradled in the heart of agricultural America, the anti-Catholic animus was vaguely mingled with the long-standing rural antagonism toward the great cities where, of course, the citadels of Romanism were to be found. The A. P. A. gained adherents slowly at first, having only seventy thousand members in 1893. Then, spurred by fear of immigrant competition for jobs during the hard times and a sudden flaming resentment on the part of urban dwellers against Irish machine politicians, the movement had a mushroom growth in the cities, probably commanding a million members in 1896.[43]

All the familiar phenomena of the earlier Know-Nothing movement were reproduced. The members of the order swore not to vote for or employ Catholics. "Escaped nuns" and "converted priests" told their harrowing tales to any who would listen. Forged documents were circulated to expose the designs of Rome against free America, one of them, an alleged papal encyclical, ordering the faithful to "exterminate all heretics" at the time of the feast of Ignatius Loyola (July 31) in 1893.[44] In a similar spirit stories were whispered of the gathering of arms in the basements of Catholic churches; and in at least one instance, that of the Toledo council of the A. P. A., a quantity of Winchester rifles was purchased as a measure of self-defense—a fact revealed by the dealer's suit for nonpayment.[45] At Dallas, Keokuk, and elsewhere, mob outrages occurred, the riot in East Boston on July 4, 1895, causing the death of one man and the injury of forty others.[46]

As the movement turned to political action, its stronghold was shown to be a zone extending through northern Ohio, eastern Michigan, and northern and central Illinois into the southern half of Iowa, northern Missouri, and eastern Kansas and Nebraska, an area originally peopled largely by religionists of New England Puritan background.[47] The anti-Catholic groups held the balance of power in many local elections, controlled the Ohio Legislature, and helped pile up a triumphant majority for William McKinley in 1893 when he ran for governor. By 1896, however, free silver and Bryanism made the Catholic menace seem the veriest specter. Both major parties snubbed the A. P. A., and the movement withered as suddenly as it had grown. By bringing to the defense of Catholicism and fair play such respected figures as Gladden, Roosevelt, and Senator Hoar, the church issued from the conflict in a stronger position before the public than when the attack began. Within a few years it could be written: "Old feuds between Protestant and Catholic have ceased to be as imporant as their united battles against moral decay."[48] Organized religion had made great strides in the two decades, not the least of which was an enhanced appreciation of the common spiritual ideals for which all faiths stood.

NOTES

[1] Among the efforts to rationalize the antievolutionist position should be noted *Creation or Evolution?* (New York, 1887) by the well-known publicist and legal scholar George Ticknor Curtis, who found Darwin's reasoning "ingenious but delusive" (p. x).

[2] Beecher introduced evolution into his sermons as early as 1880. Lyman Abbott, *Henry Ward Beecher* (Boston, 1903), 317-324.

[3] A. B. Paine, *Mark Twain* (New York, 1912), II. 707-709; editorial in the *Nation,* LVII. 21 (July 13, 1893).

[4] George Harris, *A Century's Change in Religion* (Boston, 1914), chap. iv; C. A. Briggs, *Whither?* (New York, 1889), 277-285; A. D. White, *A History of the Warfare of Science with Theology* (New York, 1896), II. chap. XX.

[5] E. J. Goodspeed, *A Full History of the Wonderful Career of Moody and Sankey in Great Britain and America* (Ashland, Ohio, 1877), 315.

[6] Washington Gladden, *Recollections* (Boston, 1909), 320-321.

[7] Lyman Abbott, *Reminiscences* (Boston, 1915), 460-462; C. W. Shields, "Does the Bible Contain Scientific Errors?," *Century* (1892), XLV. 126-134; C. A. Briggs, "Works of the Imagination in the Old Testament," *North American Review* (1897), CLXIV. 356-373.

[8] F. H. Stead, "The Story of the World's Parliament of Religions," *American Review of Reviews* (1894), IX. 299-310.

[9] Anon., "The Books of 1888," *Publishers' Weekly,* XXXV. 205, 208 (Feb. 9, 1889); anon., "The Influence of the Religious Novel," *Nation,* XLVII. 329-330 (Oct. 25, 1888); anon., "Theology in Fiction," *Atlantic Monthly* (1888), LXII. 699. Sarah B. Elliott's novel *The Felmeres,* published in 1879, was of the same *genre,* as was also the widely discussed *The Damnation of Theron Ware* (1896), by Harold Frederic.

[10] White, *Warfare of Science with Theology,* I. 313-316.

[11]G. F. Moore, "An Appreciation of Professor Toy," *American Journal of Semitic Languages and Literatures,* XXXVI. 3-5; White, *Warfare of Science with Theology,* I. 316-318; F. B. Simkins, *The Tillman Movement in South Carolina* (Duke University, *Publications,* Durham, 1926), 142, 144.

[12]For a summary of his views, see R. G. Ingersoll, "Why Am I an Agnostic?," *North American Review* (1889), CXLIX. 741-749; (1890), CL. 330-338.

[13]His work *Creed and Deed* (New York, 1877) sets forth his view that the essence of religion is "fervent devotion to the highest moral ends."

[14]For her exposition of the tenets of Theosophy, see *Isis Unveiled* (New York, 1877) and *The Secret Doctrine* (London, 1888).

[15]Awareness of this failure is expressed in books like Washington Gladden, *Applied Christianity* (Boston, 1886), 146-179; S. L. Loomis, *Modern Cities and Their Religious Problems* (New York, 1887), esp. chap. iii; Strong, *New Era,* chap. X; and W. T. Stead, *If Christ Came to Chicago!* (Chicago, 1894), 389-405.

[16]Data in regard to the distribution of churches in urban centers are summarized in Loomis, *Modern Cities,* 7-9, 88-89, and Strong, *New Era,* 197-201.

[17]The total amount paid for music by three hundred and fifty churches in New York City in 1876 was estimated at $590,000. *Arthur's Illustrated Home Magazine* (Philadelphia, 1876), XLIV. 290.

[18]R. T. Ely, *Social Aspects of Christianity* (rev. edn., New York, 1889), 44-45. In at least one case on record, that of a Lutheran congregation in Oshkosh, Wisconsin, in February, 1894, trade unionists were excluded from the church on the ground that membership in a labor organization violated the law of God. Stead, *If Christ Came to Chicago!,* 394-395n.

[19]R. H. Johnson, "American Baptists in the Age of Big Business," *Journal of Religion,* XI. esp. 72.

[20]H. F. Perry, "The Workingman's Alienation from the Church," *American Journal of Sociology* (1898-1899), IV. esp. 622.

[21]Loomis, *Modern Cities,* 82.

[22]*Ibid.,* 104.

[23]See, for example, W. R. Crafts, "Valid Grounds for Sabbath Observance," *Our Day* (1888), II. 262-275.

[24]"Notes of a Hearing . . . on the Petitions . . . ," *Miscellaneous Senate Documents,* no. 108, 50 Cong., I sess.; "Sunday Rest Bill," *Miscel. Senate Docs.,* no. 43, 50 Cong., 2 sess.; *Our Day* (1889), III. 51-53, 192, 310.

[25]W. R. Crafts, "Sunday Closing of the Columbian World's Fair," *Our Day* (1891), VIII. 259-267; "Jesus, the Church, and the World's Fair," *Arena* (1892), VI. 250-260; Elizabeth C. Stanton, "Sunday at the World's Fair," *North American Review* (1892), CLIV. 254-256; J. W. Chadwick, "Why the Fair Must Be Open on Sunday," *Forum* (1892), XIV. 541-550; *Nation,* LVII. 39 (July 20, 1893).

[26]F. W. Farrar, "The Salvation Army," *Harper's Magazine* (1891), LXXXII. 897-906; C. A. Briggs, "The Salvation Army," *North American Review* (1894), CLIX. 697-710.

[27]A schism within the ranks led in 1896 to the establishment of the Volunteers of America which had less military autocracy in its form of organization but was otherwise devoted to a similar mission.

[28]Unadulterated Quimbyism became the basis of the New Thought movement which began to emerge toward the end of the century.

[29]Moreover, "Healing the sick through mind instead of matter, enables us to heal the absent as well as the present." Edn. of 1875, 334, 348, 398. Conversely, vindictive persons, through malicious animal magnetism ("M.A.M."), can produce disease or misfortune in others—a doctrine which first appeared in the edition of 1878.

[30]Sibyl Wilbur (O'Brien), *The Life of Mary Baker Eddy* (New York, 1907), 198; see also 155-160, 199-201, 223-224, 227.

[31]*U.S. Eleventh Census* (1890), XVI. 297-298; *Christian Science Journal,* (1900), XVIII. 202.

[32]Besides discussing modern social problems from the pulpit, all these men aired their views in magazines and books. Professor R. T. Ely, though not a cleric, also wielded great influence, especially through his volume *Social Aspects of Christianity.*

[33]The Chicago Seminary, one of the most progressive, offered courses on the labor movement, ethics of the family, penology, charity organization, child saving, city evangelization, and municipal reform. John Tunis, "Social Science in the Theological Seminaries," *Lend a Hand* (1896), XVI. 3-10; anon., "Sociology and the Church," *Nation,* LIII. 114 (Aug. 13, 1891).

[34]Helen M. Sweeney, "Handling the Immigrant," *Catholic World* (1896), LXIII. 497-508. Early in the eighties Jewish charitable agencies began to look after the needs of their Russian co-religionists; and when the strain upon their resources proved too great, Baron de Hirsch, in 1890, established a fund of $2,400,000 for this and allied uses. E. J. James and others, *The Immigrant Jew in America* (New York, 1906), 64-66, 79, 84-85.

[35]Strong, *Religious Movements,* 31-33.

[36]*The Dawn* (Boston, 1889), I. no. I, 3. R. Heber Newton became president of the New York branch. The strength of the movement is difficult to determine. Though in January, 1890, its organ *The Dawn* asserted that at least twenty-one California clergymen had declared for Christian Socialism, five years later *The Dawn,* lacking adequate financial support, turned Episcopalian.

[37]Walter Rauschenbusch, *Christianizing the Social Order* (New York, 1912), 9.

[38]Edition of 1899 (Street & Smith, New York), 261. In 1925, it was estimated that over eight million copies had been sold in the United States and twelve million more in the British Empire. The author received little financial return because of a defective copyright. C. M. Sheldon, *His Life Story* (New York, 1925), chap. IV.

[39]Stead, *If Christ Came to Chicago!,* 269.

[40]More typical of the pulpit's attitude toward the strike is Z. S. Holbrook, "The American Republic and the Debs Insurrection," *Bibliotheca Sacra* (1895), LII. 135-152, 209-231.

[41]Gladden *Recollections,* 291-293, 300-305; same author, *Applied Christianity,* 1-37, 102-145.

[42]A. S. Will, *Life of Cardinal Gibbons* (New York, 1922), I. chaps. XVIII-XX.

[43]In Chicago, in 1894, the mayor, chief of police, fire chief, city attorney, a number of judges, forty-five aldermen, nine out of ten policemen, four fifths of the fire department, and two thirds of the school teachers were said to be Catholics. Stead, *If Christ Came to Chicago!,* 265. It was alleged that the municipal offices of New York, St. Louis, New Orleans, San Francisco, and other important cities were also largely under Catholic control. W. H. J. Traynor, "The Aims and Methods of the A. P. A." *North American Review* (1894), CLIX. 69. Traynor, the national president, claimed a membership of two and a half million for the A. P. A.

[44]Gladden, "The Anti-Catholic Crusade," *Century* (1894), XLVII. 789-795; T. J. Jenkins, "The A. P. A. Conspirators," *Catholic World* (1893), LVII. 685-693.

[45]Anon., "The Purchase of Guns by the A. P. A.," *Public Opinion* (1893-1894), XVI. 621.

[46]*Iowa State Register* (Des Moines), March 16, 1894; "Echoes of the Boston Riot," *Public Opinion* (1895), XIX. 201-202.

[47]The movement also possessed strength in Massachusetts and Rhode Island and in parts of the Great West.

[48]H. D. Sedgwick, Jr., "The United States and Rome," *Atlantic Monthly* (1899), LXXXIV. 445-458.

20

Protestantism and the American Labor Movement: The Christian Spirit in the Gilded Age

Herbert G. Gutman

Generally, it has been argued that in the late nineteenth century Protestant churches became increasingly aligned with values of the middle and upper-middle classes in America. In a study of the labor movement of that period, Herbert G. Gutman notes how several themes in American Protestantism were used by the workers to formulate a different understanding of Christian social responsibility. Professor Gutman is a member of the History Faculty at the City University of New York.

Labor historians and others have puzzled over precisely how and why American workers, especially those critical of the new industrial order, reacted to the profound changes in the nation's social and economic structure and in their own particular status between 1850 and 1900, but in seeking explanations they have studied almost exclusively working-class behavior and trade-union organization and have neatly catalogued the interminable wranglings between "business" unionists, "utopian" dreamers, and "socialist" radicals. Although their works have uncovered much of value, the "mind" of the worker—the modes of thought and perception through which he confronted the industrialization process and which helped shape his behavior—has received scant and inadequate attention. American workers, immigrant and native-born alike, brought more than their "labor" to the factory and did not view their changing circumstances in simple

First published in the *American Historical Review*, LXXII (1966-67), pp. 74-101. Reprinted with the permission of the author.

"economic" terms. So narrow an emphasis ignores the complexity of their lives and experiences and, in general, distorts human behavior. "Events, facts, data, happenings," J. L. Talmon reminds us, "assume their significance from the way in which they are experienced."[1] These pages examine one of several important but overlooked influences on the disaffected worker's thought: the way certain strands of pre-Gilded Age Protestantism affected him in a time of rapid industrialization and radical social change.

Before 1850 relatively few Americans had direct contact with an industrial *society,* but after that date rapid industrialization altered the social structure, and the process left few untouched. Depending upon circumstance, these social changes meant more or less opportunity for workers, but nearly all felt greater dependence and profoundly different patterns of work discipline. In addition, urbanization and immigration changed the structure and composition of the working class and affected its style of life. In ways that have not yet been adequately explored, class and status relationships took on new meaning, too.[2] And a new ideology that sanctioned industrial laissez faire emerged because, as Ralph Gabriel has perceptively written, "the mores of a simpler agricultural and commercial era did not fit the conditions of an age characterized by the swift accumulation of industrial power."[3] The era found much "truth" in the frequent judgments of the Chicago *Times* that "the inexorable law of God" meant that "the man who lays up not for the morrow perishes on the morrow," that "political economy" was "in reality the autocrat of the age" and occupied "the position once held by the Caesars and the Popes," and that cheapened production counted for so much that men did not inquire "when looking at a piece of lace whether the woman who wove it is a saint or a courtesan."[4]

Legal and political theory, academic economics, amoral "social science," and institutional Protestantism emphasized that in industrial America interference with the entrepreneur's freedom violated "divine" or "scientific" laws, and historians have given much attention to the many ways Gilded Age social thought bolstered the virtues of "Acquisitive Man."[5] Two seemingly contradictory ideas especially sanctioned industrial laissez faire. Related to the decline of traditional religious sanctions and the growing importance of secular institutions and values, the first insisted that no connection existed between economic behavior and moral conduct. Gilded Age business practices, Edward C. Kirkland has argued, cannot be understood without realizing that for most entrepreneurs "economic activity stood apart from the sphere of moral and personal considerations."[6] Much contemporary evidence supports this view.[7] The second concept, identified with traditional Calvinist doctrine, reinforced the business ethic by equating poverty and failure with sin.[8] Evidence gathered primarily from national denominational weekly and monthly periodicals, together with a Gilded Age premillennial evangelism (typified by the popular Dwight Moody) that insisted that "until Christ returned none of the basic problems of the world could be solved," convinces its historians that the Protestant denominations and their leaders mostly "lost their sense of estrangement from society" and "began . . . to bless and defend it in a jargon strangely compounded out of the language of traditional Christian theology, common-sense philosophy, and *laissez-faire* economics."[9] Henry May, Aaron Abell, and Howard Hopkins have shown that a small but quite influential group of Protestant clergymen and lay thinkers broke free from institutional Protestantism's social conservatism and traveled a difficult route in pioneering the social gospel,[10] but in the main Gilded Age Protestantism is viewed as a conformist, "culturebound" Christianity that warmly embraced the rising industrialist, drained the aspiring rich of conscience, and confused or pacified the poor. The writings of an articulate minority suggest to historians that the wealthy busied themselves memorizing Herbert Spencer's aphorisms and purchasing expensive church pews, that the middle classes chased wealth and cheered Horatio Alger, and that the wage earners, busy laboring, found little time to ponder existential questions and felt separated from institutional Protestantism. Workers wandered from the fold, and the churches lost touch with the laboring classes.

Accurate in describing certain themes characteristic of Gilded Age social and religious thought, this view nevertheless tells little about the relationship between Protestantism and the working class because the many functions of religion, particularly its effects on the lower classes, cannot be learned by analyzing what leading clergymen said and what social philosophy religious journals professed. Unless one first studies the varieties of working-class community life, the social and economic structure that gave them shape, their voluntary associations (including churches, benevolent and fraternal societies, and trade-unions), their connections to the larger community, and their particular and shared values, one is likely to be confused about the relationship between the worker, institutional religion, and religious beliefs and sentiments.[11] It is suggested, for example, that a close tie between laissez faire and Gilded Age Protestantism developed partly because the post-Civil War "burst of technological and industrial expansion . . . created unbridled cheerfulness, confidence, and complacency among the American people" and because "the observational order coincided in a high degree with the conceptual order and . . . such coincidence defines social stability."[12] Such was probably the case for successful entrepreneurs and many lesser folk who benefited from rapid industrialization and the era's massive material gains, but the same cannot be inferred for those whose traditional skills became obsolete, who felt economic dependence for the first time, who knew recurrent seasonal and cyclical unemployment, and who suffered severe family and social disorganization in moving from farm and town to city and in adapting to industrial and urban priorities and work discipline patterns different from traditional norms. Day-to-day experiences for many such persons ("the observational order") did not entirely coincide with the religious and secular ideas and values ("the conceptual order") they carried with them from the immediate past. Some withdrew from the tensions stirred by such conflict, and others changed their beliefs. Many found in Gilded Age Protestantism reason to cheer material progress or comfort in premillennial evangelism. But some, especially trade-unionists and labor reformers and radicals, discovered that preindustrial ideology heightened rather than obliterated the moral dilemmas of a new social order and that the Protestantism of an earlier America offered a religious sanction for *their* discontent with industrial laissez faire and "Acquisitive Man." A preindustrial social order had nurtured particular religious beliefs that did not disappear with the coming of industrialism and did not easily or quickly conform to the Protestantism of a Henry Ward Beecher or a Dwight Moody and the secular optimism of an Andrew Carnegie or a Horatio Alger. The material conditions of life changed radically for these workers after 1850, but not the world of their mind and spirit. They saw the nation transformed, but were not themselves abruptly alienated from the past. Older traditions and modes of thought (religious and secular in origin) did not succumb easily to the imperatives of a disorganized industrial society, but, depending upon particular circumstances, often clung tenaciously and even deepened tensions generally characteristic of an early industrializing society.

The recent perspective emphasized by British historians of early industrial England helps clarify the particular relationship between Protestantism and Gilded Age labor reform. "In order to understand how people respond to industrial change," Asa Briggs has written, "it is necessary to examine fully what kind of people they were at the beginning of the process, to take account of continuities and traditions as well as new ways of thinking and feeling."[13] Edward P. Thompson has gathered and organized a mass of data in *The Making of the English Working Class* to argue persuasively that the English working class was not "the spontaneous generation of the factory-system" and that the early social history of industrial England was more than "an external force—the 'industrial revolution'—working upon some nondescript undifferentiated raw material of humanity."[14] Applied to the United States, this general point is quite simple although its particular American characteristics demand a level of conceptualization and a method of research not yet typical of "labor history." Protestantism in its many and even contradictory forms but particularly the Christian perfectionism of pre-Civil War evangelical and reform movements lingered on among many discontented *post-bellum* workers.[15] It was no different in the United States than in Great Britain where labor and religious historians have documented the close relationship between Protestant Nonconformity, especially Methodism, and labor reform.[16] None of this should surprise students of social movements. "The bulk of industrial workers in all countries," Eric Hobsbawm notes, "began . . . as first-generation immigrants from preindustrial society . . . and like all first-generation immigrants, they looked backwards as much as forwards." The new industrial world "had no pattern of life suited to the new age," and so men and women often "drew on the only spiritual resources at their disposal, preindustrial custom and religion."[17]

An additional point stressed in Thompson's recent work offers insight into the Gilded Age labor reformer. "Behind every form of popular direct action," Thompson notes, "some legitimising notion of right is to be found."[18] Thus Boston labor leader and editor Frank K. Foster insisted in

1888: "The dry names and dates furnish but a small part of the history of the labor movement. To understand its real meaning one must comprehend the spirit animating it."[19] Leaders and followers of social movements that challenge an established order or question the direction of a rapidly changing society (such as the United States after the Civil War) are usually "animated" by a "spirit" that sanctions and legitimizes the particular alternative they espouse. It is not enough for them merely to criticize and to offer alternatives. This is the case whether they advocate trade-unions in a society hostile to collective activity or urge even more thorough and fundamental social reorganization. They must *feel* that what they propose is justified by values that transcend the particular social order they criticize. For this reason, they often crudely reinterpret the historical past. They either project "new" values or, as is more frequently the case, reinterpret vague and broadly shared national values to sanction their behavior. Then, they can argue that their critique of the dominant order and its ideology is "consistent with very basic values."[20] Such was the case with the generation of trade-unionists, labor reformers, and labor radicals who felt the transition from a preindustrial to an industrial society and who bore the social, economic, and psychological brunt of the American industrializing process after 1860.

Two broadly shared preindustrial national traditions especially offered the discontented nineteenth-century American worker a transcendent and sanctioning "notion of right." The first—the republican political tradition—is beyond the scope of these pages. The second was traditional American Protestantism. Frank Foster could explain in 1887: "John on Patmos, Jack Cade at the head of the populace, . . . Krapotine indicting Russian imperialism, the rising wrath of American Democracy—these are all of kinship." Commenting on the American labor movement, Foster went on:

> The "cross of the new crusade" is the cross of an old crusade, old as the passions of the human heart. An idea may take different forms of expression and its ethical purport may be the same, and in whatever direction men may strive for this ambiguous thing we call social reform, if they mean anything at all, they but echo—be they Jew or Gentile, Greek or Christian, Deist or Atheist, Knight of Labor or Socialist—that carol of welcome which was sung to greet the coming of the Carpenter's Son in the centuries long gone by, "peace on earth, good will to men."

"Looking afar off, over the broad ocean of time and space," the Boston editor concluded, "we have faith, like St. Simon at death's door, [we] may exclaim, 'The future is ours.' "[21] Similarly, the *Union Pacific Employees Magazine* comforted fearful trade-unionists by reminding them that after the Crucifixion "the rabble rejoiced." "Time," this journal insisted in explaining the difficulties encountered by trade-union advocates, "corrects errors. . . . The minority continue to urge their views until they become the majority or the fallacy of them be proven. Advance is made only thus. Time must be had to prepare the way for every step."[22] In another connection, the

American Railway Union's *Railway Times* called "sublime idiocy . . . the idea that workingmen of the present, or of any other century, were the first to call attention to the rapacity of the rich." Instead, "The arraignment of the rich by God Himself and His Son, the Redeemer, set the pace for all coming generations of men who would be free from the crushing domination of wealth." Labor's complaints had "the unequivocal indorsement of the Holy Writ."[23] Here, then, was a religious faith that justified labor organization and agitation, encouraged workers to challenge industrial power, and compelled criticism of "natural" economic laws, the crude optimism of social Darwinsim, and even the conformist Christianity of most respectable clergymen.

Protestantism affected the American working class in many ways, and a brief article cannot encompass its varied manifestations. But it is possible to indicate some of them.

A subordinate but distinct theme drew from pessimistic premillennialism the apocalyptic tradition that prophesied doom and imminent catastrophe before "redemption." In a period of rapid, unpredictable social and economic change, change itself meant decay and destruction to some. For them, the Christian prophetic tradition did not buoy up the spirit and command reform, but stimulated withdrawal. A Massachusetts ship joiner predicted destructive world-wide war as the result of "the sin of the people, 'covetousness.' "[24] A regular *Coast Seaman's Journal* columnist more than once made the same point.[25] Readers of the Denver *Labor Enquirer* learned from several sermons by Mrs. P. C. Munger of "The World's Final Crisis." She urged violence to speed the end of an evil social order and praised dynamite as a "blessing" from God:

> Socially, the ruling world is a dead leper. In the name of God and man bury it deep in the earth it has corrupted. . . . Dynamite in its line is the last scientific fruit of the Holy Ghost. . . . It is in every way worthy of the giver—God. . . . I thank, I praise, I bless God for dynamite. It is the blast of Gabriel's trumpet. . . . It does the deeds of God. . . . Its fruits are peace, love, joy, goodness, gentleness, meekness, and truth displayed in decent life and government. Is not this boon of heaven worth a blow; worth a blast on the trumpet of doom? . . . Dynamite is a weapon to win; a weapon to conquer, a weapon to kill. It is your only one. God Himself allows you no other; use it or tamely submit and sign your death warrant.[26]

Such violent and apparent psychotic anguish, however, was not typical of even the most extreme premillenarian visionaries. More characteristic was the complaint of an Indiana coal miner's wife who believed that "according to history" a "visitation" took place every two thousand years and quietly complained, "I have heard my mother talk about her girlhood days and how good and religious people were." The world had changed for the worse. "It is no wonder," she feared, "that God sends His voice in thunder through the air as wicked as this world stands to-day. . . . We are living in a land where shadows are continually falling in our pathway."[27] The extraordinary psychological strains of early industrialism thus found expression in the rejection of the secular order and the acceptance of a Protestantism of doom, despair, and destruction.[28]

More widespread than these premillennial prophecies was a postmillennial Christian justification of trade-unionism and even more radical social reform. Conservative trade-unionists and radical anarchists and socialists (except for the zealous followers of Daniel De Leon) often appealed to Christianity for its sanction. A pre-Civil War utopian and afterward a Knight of Labor and builder of cooperatives, John Orvis claimed "the labor question" was "here in the Providence of Almighty God" and meant "the deliverance, exaltation, and ennobling of labor and the laboring classes to the first rank."[29] Conservative craft unionist and president of the Amalgamated Association of Iron, Steel, and Tin Workers, John Jarrett told a gathering of clergymen that "the climax of the mission of the Savior, beyond a question, . . . is that He came here so that the gospel would be preached to the poor."[30] After being sentenced to death in the aftermath of the Haymarket affair, German immigrant anarchist August Spies linked his beliefs to Thomas Münzer. "He," Spies said of Münzer, "interpreted the Gospel, saying that it did not merely promise blessings in heaven, but that it also commanded equality and brotherhood among men on earth." Spies insisted that "the spirit of the Reformation was the 'eternal spirit of the chainless mind,' and nothing could stay its progress."[31] This sentiment—radical criticism and labor discontent sanctioned by an appeal to Christian tradition—did not diminish by the end of the nineteenth century and remained as common in the 1890's as in the 1860's. No apparent connection existed between a particular brand of labor reform and Christianity; all shared in it.

Prophetic Protestantism offered labor leaders and their followers a transhistoric framework to challenge the new industrialism and a common set of moral imperatives to measure their rage against and to order their dissatisfactions. The intensity of religious commitment varied among individuals: it depended upon particular life experiences, and its sources drew from the many strands that made up the web of Protestant tradition. But the influence of the Christian perfectionism and postmillennialism identified with Charles G. Finney and other pre-Civil War and preindustrial evangelical revivalists seems predominant.[32] Even this tradition, which emphasized God's redemptive love and benevolence and insisted that "progress, in all its forms, was divinely directed toward the perfection of the world," took many forms.[33] A few examples suffice. In the 1860's, William Sylvis, that decade's most prominent trade-unionist, pitted the God of Christian perfectionism against Malthusian doctrine and asked: "Is it not reasonable, is it not Christian, to suppose that the all-wise Being who placed us here, and whose attributes are benevolence and love, could find other means of controlling population than by war, famine, pestilence, and crime in all its forms?"[34] More than thirty years later, George E. Ward hailed the coming of the American Railway Union by arguing that "God is infinite and eternal justice" so that "he who strives to promote and establish justice upon earth is a co-worker with God." It followed that union men were "the rapidly-evolving God-men—the *genus homo* vivified by the eternal truths and energizing principles of the gospel of Christ."[35] Another perfectionist strain, more "emotional," told of man's "sin," but was nevertheless distinctly postmillennial. Celebrating Thanksgiving, a midwestern worker assured the Chicago *Knights of Labor:*

> God has given the earth to the children of men; that a few have stolen it all and disinherited the masses, is not fault of God's, but the wickedness of man. . . . We could not know the wickedness of man, could we not see the goodness of God. . . . It is perfectly safe to pray for His kingdom to come, and in that prayer you anathematize the present system as bitterly as words could do it. . . .[36]

"Pumpkin Smasher," a Newcomb, Tennessee, coal miner, typified extreme labor evangelism:

> Labor has made this country into a bed of roses so that a few may lie therein, and bask in the beautiful God-given sunshine, while the laborer or the creator of all this splendor is roaming in rags all tattered and torn. . . . Cheer up, my brothers, the longest night comes to an end. It may end by an honest use of the ballot box, but as that can never be until the great and glorious millennium with all its attendant beauties set in, brothers we need not look for deliverance through the medium of the ballot box. But it will come just the same. It may come like it did to the Israelitish serfs from down yonder in Egypt, or it may come like it did in France in those long days of rebellion. Or, my brothers, it may come as it did to the colored slaves of the South by sword and fire. Let us be ready to eat the Paschal lamb at any moment the trumpet sounds.[37]

Even the more "conservative" *American Federationist* found room for labor evangelism. A contributor to the American Federation of Labor's official journal asked for nothing less than "A living Christ moving, living, breathing and dominant in the hearts of a people, not a dead Christianity, dreaming of a dead Christ, but live Christians as live Christs, scattering the table of the money changers in the temples, . . . going down in the poverty-stricken alleys of the robbed industrial slaves, and raising up its victims." This Christianity he called *"the real article!"*[38]

Not surprisingly, the labor evangels found the most essential characteristics of the rapidly developing new industrial social order un-Christian and violative of God's will. As early as the 1860's "Uncle Sam" told readers of *Fincher's Trades Review* that "the present system of labor . . . is a system begotten by the *evil one, hell-born"* and that it "warred against the heaven-born creation, the system instituted by *God* for the good of man."[39] And the Boston *Daily Evening Voice* justified a living wage and condemned the maldistribution of wealth by appealing to God: "It is because He has made of one blood all men—because all are brethren—that the differences instituted by men—the chief of which is the money difference— are so morally disastrous as they are. . . . The elevation of a false god dethrones the real one."[40]

Self-protection and trade-unionism especially enjoyed the blessings of God. A Louisville cigar maker argued: "The toilers are coming out of darkness into light and . . . have dared to organize, to come in closer touch with our Lord's will and the teachings of Jesus Christ." He prophesied: "The time is not far distant when the wage earners shall stand on the rock of independence and sing, 'Nearer, My God, to Thee.' We need not fire and sword, but [to] organize, unionize. . . ."[41] During the bitter bituminous coal strike of 1897 the *United Mine Workers' Journal* editorialized: "Blessed are the union men. They are the salt of the earth which keeps uncontaminated the pure principles of brotherhood in the breast of their fellow toilers, and which, if allowed to die, would make us doubt the fatherhood of God."[42] Biblical "history" served well J. A. Crawford, Illinois district president of the United Mine Workers, as he preached the divinity of unions:

> The first labor organization mentioned in history, either profane or divine, was the one founded just outside of the historic Garden of Eden, by God Himself; the charter members being Adam and Eve. . . . Noah's campaign among the Antediluvians favorably reminds us of the organizing campaigns of the United Mine Workers. . . . The third attempt at organizing labor was made by the authority of Jehovah, instituted and carried to a successful termination by "The Walking Delegates," Moses and Aaron, for the purpose of redeeming Israel from Egyptian task-masters. . . . The next labor movement of importance recorded in sacred history, begins with the beginning of the ministry of the "Nazarene," opposed to all forms of oppression of the poor and antagonistic to the operation of "Wall street" in the house of His Father, the sanctuary of worship. . . . Choose you this day whom you shall serve. If plutocracy be God, serve it; if God be God, serve Him.[43]

A *Railway Times* writer summed it up by insisting that "so-called 'labor agitators,' who are such, *not* for the love of money, but for the love of humanity, are true followers of Christ and are striving to establish upon earth the kingdom of God, for which disciples are taught to pray."[44] Labor organizers had only to push ahead. "Brother Knights," a fellow unionist advised, "allow me to say that Moses, while fleeing from bondage and endeavoring to deliver his people from the hands of the Egyptian destroyer, received the imperative command from God, to 'go forward.' The same injunction still comes to us, 'go forward.' "[45]

The historic and divine person of Jesus Christ loomed large in the rhetoric and imagery of labor leaders. He served as a model to emulate, a symbol to inspire. An Illinois coal miner later elected to the state assembly admiringly described trade-unionist Richard Trevellick: "While not a preacher of Jesus and Him crucified, yet he was one of His most exemplary followers. . . . My wife thought Dick Trevellick the second Jesus Christ."[46] Much was made of the argument that "the Saviour Himself" had associated "with common fishermen and carpenters."[47] A West Coast seaman reminded his brothers that "Peter and James and John, . . . three sailors, were the chosen of our Saviour."[48] *Railway Times* called Jesus "an agitator such as the world has never seen before nor since, . . . despised and finally murdered to appease the wrath of the ruling class of His time."[49] William Mahon, the international president of the motorman's union, lectured the Businessman's Bible Class of the Detroit First Congregational Church that Christ was "crucified for disturbing the national order of things . . . [by] the conservative goody good people, whose plans Jesus spoilt." The businessmen learned that the speaker belonged to "the organizations. . . fighting for the very principles laid down by Jesus Christ."[50] The *Coast Seaman's Journal* explained Christ's death:

> Christ taught that all men had souls and were therefore equal in the finality of things. For that He was put to death. But it was not for preaching the doctrine of a common equality before God that the Saviour suffered. The Powers have never objected to changing the conditions and relations of the future: it is the conditions and relations of today they object to altering. Christ was crucified because the doctrine of common equality hereafter, which He preached, led inevitably to the doctrine of common equality now. This is the essence of Christ's teaching.[51]

Christ in an industrializing America would suffer as a labor leader or even a "tramp" suffered. "Had Christ lived in Connecticut, he would have been imprisoned for asking for a cup of water," believed the Washington *Craftsman*.[52]

If Gilded Age businessmen make sense only when it is realized that for them "economic activity stood apart from moral considerations," the opposite is true for most Gilded Age labor leaders. Protestantism helped many of them restore what Oscar Handlin calls "the sense of human solidarity infused with religious values."[53] Prominent Gilded Age trade-unionists, labor reformers, and even radicals—with the notable exception of Samuel Gompers and De Leon—shared a common faith in a just God, effused perfectionist doctrine, and warned of divine retribution against continuing injustice.[54] They often condemned the insensitivity of institutional Protestantism to the suffering brought about by rapid industrialization, but their speeches and writings also made frequent allusion to essential religious "truths" that gave meaning to their lives and that sanctioned organized opposition to the new industrialism.[55] Trade-unionists and reformers from Catholic backgrounds such as Joseph P. McDonnell, who had studied for the priesthood, and Terence V. Powderly frequently quoted the Sermon on the Mount.[56] Important trade-unionists and labor radicals reared as Protestants did the same. Sylvis found no contradiction between his sympathies for the First International and his belief that the worker's "task" was "to found the universal family—to build up the City of God" through trade-unions which Sylvis called an "association of souls" formed by "the sons of God." America's distinctiveness rested for Sylvis on "God's ordained equality of man . . . recognized in the laws and institutions of *our* country."[57] Early trained for the Baptist ministry, Knights of Labor founder Uriah Stephens called excessive hours of work "an artificial and man-made condition, not God's arrangement and order" and insisted the Knights build upon "the immutable basis of the Fatherhood of God and the logical principle of the Brotherhood of Man." Labor organizations had come "as messiahs have ever come, when the world was ready for them." The Knights brought workers together in local assemblies:

> The tabernacle—the dwelling-place of God—is among men. No longer shall men pine for justice, or perish for lack of judgment. "And He will dwell with them, and they shall be His people." "God and Humanity." How inseparably connected! God, the Universal Father; Man, the Universal Brother![58]

Trevellick found in God reason to ennoble human labor and asked: "Is He less because His mechanical hand formed the mountains? . . . No fellow toilers; He is not less because He worked; neither are you."[59] Eugene V. Debs bristled with Christian indignation at human suffering and cannot be understood outside that framework. From his prison cell after the Pullman debacle, Debs publicly celebrated Labor Day by declaring that it "would stand first in Labor's Millennium, that prophesied era when Christ shall begin in reign on the earth to continue a thousand years."[60] He compared his jailing with Daniel's treatment by the Persians.[61] Released from Woodstock jail, Debs told an admiring Chicago throng in an oration punctuated with religious images and analogies:

> Liberty is not a word of modern coinage. Liberty and slavery are primal words, like good and evil, right and wrong; they are opposites and coexistent. There has been no liberty in the world since the gift, like sunshine and rain, came down from heaven, for the maintenance of which man has not been required to fight. . . . Is it worth [while?] to reiterate that all men are created free and that slavery and bondage are in contravention of the Creator's decree and have their origin in man's depravity?

Courts, like the Supreme Court, had been "antagonizing the decrees of heaven since the day when Lucifer was cast into the bottomless pit." "God Himself had taught His lightning, thunderbolts, winds, waves, and earthquakes to strike," and men, too, would strike, "with bullets or ballots," until they walked "the earth free men." "Angels" had "transplanted" "sympathy," one of the "perennial flowers of the Celestial City" and the mainspring of human compassion for Debs, "in Eden for the happiness of Adam and Eve," and then "the winds had scattered the seed throughout the earth." Without sympathy, Debs concluded, there could be "no humanity, no elevating, refining, ennobling influences."[62]

The most eloquent Gilded Age labor reformer, George E. McNeill, was an abolitionist turned staunch American Federation of Labor trade-unionist and Christian socialist. He was also an essential link between preindustrial American reform and the Gilded Age labor movement. McNeill rarely spoke or wrote without imparting a deep Christian fervor.[63] In 1876 he complained in the socialist *Labor Standard:* "It is the old, old story. . . . Have the Pharaoh's descendants nothing to learn from Pharaoh's fate?"[64] At a meeting eleven years later to condemn the hanging of Albert Parsons, McNeill announced: "I believe in the passive force of non-resistance as 'Him of old.' . . . I come here tonight as a Christian."[65] In 1890 he once again tied labor reform to Christian ethics:

> The Pilgrim leaven still works, true to the fundamental principles of the great Leader of men. . . . The influence of the teachings of the Carpenter's Son still tends to counteract the influence of Mammon. In this movement of the laborers toward equity, we will find a new revelation of the Old Gospel, when the Golden Rule of Christ shall measure the relations of men in all their duties toward their fellows. . . . Though the Mammon-worshippers may cry, "Crucify Him! Crucify Him!", the promise of the prophet and the poet shall be fulfilled . . . by the free acceptance of the Gospel that all men are of one blood. Then the new Pentecost will come, when every man shall have according to his needs.[66]

Three years later, McNeill found "the religious life" of the labor movement nothing less than "a protest against the mammonizing interpretation of religious truth." He wanted "the kingdom of Heaven (of equity and righteousness) to come on earth," but, more importantly, argued that "religious truth," adapted to the realities of industrial society, had meaning for his America. "A new interpretation of the old truth, 'That the chief end of man is to glorify God and to enjoy him forever,' reads that the glorification of God is the reinstatement of man in the likeness of God; that to enjoy God forever all things must be directed toward the securing for all the largest measure of happiness."[67] McNeill never changed. In 1902, sixty-five years old, he reaffirmed his continued faith in the supremacy of "moral power," but nevertheless warned: "Submission is good, but the order of God may light the torch of Revolution."[68]

Evangelical Protestantism that emphasized the possibility of perfect holiness in this world found expression among trade-unionists of less importance than McNeill and other national leaders. Negro activists in the early United Mine Workers of America (1890-1900) reveal such an influence.[69] A preacher and coal miner, William Riley won election in 1892 as secretary-treasurer of the Tennessee district and importuned fellow Negroes to join the union:

> Continue to battle on for the right, seek wisdom and be wise, act honest men and by so doing both white and colored men will love to respect you, and God Himself will bless you. . . . Yes, my people, wake up and ask yourselves these questions: How long am I to live in ignorance? How long am I to be a pullback to my race? How long am I to be a stumbling block for the cause of labor, justice, and humanity? Say as the prodigal did: I will arise and join the labor unions and rally for its [sic] rights, defend its [sic] cause and be known among my own craftsmen as a man among men.[70]

The tensions between an active, just God and the day-to-day realities of a Negro coal miner's life strained William E. Clark, a Rendville, Ohio, miner. He reported:

> My mind has wandered from world to world. My first wonder, was, I wonder if the other worlds were inhabited? Did they have the same kind of law and government that we have? And my next wonder was, was this world of ours the hell we read about in the good book? If it is not, how can a man stand the punishment twice, and then live through eternity? They burn men alive, skin them, lynch them, shoot them, and torture them. . . ."[71]

The most important early UMW Negro leader, Richard L. Davis, elected to the National Executive Board in 1896 and 1897, penned many letters that suggested the influence of evangelical imperatives. He found in the union a secular church that promised redemption from an evil social order. He gave to his work the zeal and devotion expected of a dedicated missionary. Miners who threatened to quit the UMW heard from him the words of Paul in the New Testament: "Except those abide in the ship, ye cannot be saved." Preachers designated the "ship as a church," but Davis called the UMW "the ship" and insisted: "I now exhort you that except ye abide in the ship ye cannot be saved."[72] A common religious rhetoric helped Davis war against factionalism. He denied the charge of fellow Negroes who called the UMW "a white man's organization" and told them: "You yourselves are men and . . . have the same interest at stake as your white brother, because . . . I believe in the principle of the fatherhood of God and the brotherhood of all mankind no matter what the color of his [sic] skin may be." Davis' evangelical fervor was not otherworldly. "I know," he addressed these same Negroes, "that in former days you used to sing 'Give me Jesus, give me Jesus, you may have all the world, just give me Jesus.' But the day has now come that we want a little money along with our Jesus, so we want to change that old song and ask for a little of the world as well."[73] Urging compact labor organization, Davis argued that "we are taught by teachings of the Holy Writ that in unity there is strength."[74] The acquittal of a Pennsylvania sheriff involved in the shooting of several Polish anthracite miners in 1898 caused Davis to lament: "It is as we expected. . . . The miner has no rights that the coal barons are bound to respect. Surely, oh Heaven, this condition of things will not last forever."[75]

Just as Christianity motivated so many labor leaders who organized the reaction against the radical transition from preindustrial to industrial America, so, too, did it serve to condemn particular aspects of that new society and its ideology. A few examples illustrate. The *United Mine Workers' Journal* felt that legal convict leasing of coal miners proved "the laws of Tennessee . . . in conflict with Christianity, civilization and government."[76] Exploitative child factory labor caused the Chicago *Knights of Labor* to explode: "When Jesus said, 'Suffer little children to come unto me,' He did not have a shirt or cloak factory, nor a planing mill, that He wanted to put them into at 40 cents per day. He wanted to bless them and show them the light."[77] The San Francisco Manufacturer's and Employer's

Association defense of "free contract" led Andrew Furuseth, secretary of the Sailors' Union of the Pacific, to exclaim indignantly: "If the present system be right, then Christianity is a lie; if the present system be right, then Robert Ingersoll is not a censer-boy in the Temple of Mammon, but the prophet of a new dispensation."[78] Critics of Labor Day learned that "Labor Day is one of the signs of the millennium."[79]

Those who saw in Christianity justification for industrial laissez faire especially felt the sting of labor critics. The *Locomotive Firemen's Magazine* declared the "theory" that "God assigns anyone a station in life . . . preposterous, repulsive, and degrading to God and man."[80] Men who argued that "labor, like flour or cotton cloth, should always be bought in the cheapest market" did so because "an All-wise God, for some inscrutable purpose, has created them" so that workers could see "to what viciousness the antagonism to labor has arrived" and then "beat back to its native hell the theory that . . . laborers . . . are merchandise to be bought and sold as any other commodity—as cattle, mules, swine. . . ."[81] Clergymen who upheld the competitive system learned: "The church which allows the competitive system of each for himself, without a never-silent protest, is not a living Christian church; for 'each for himself' is a gospel of lies. That never was God's decree."[82] And the argument that poverty enjoyed God's blessings met the retort: "Do you think it is anything short of insulting to God to pretend to believe He makes of ninety-nine paving material for the one to walk into Heaven over?"[83] Paul's directive to Titus to "obey magistrates" was rejected. If followed "by the patriots of '76," explained the *Locomotive Firemen's Magazine,* "a new nation would not have been born."[84]

Christian example and religious exaltation proved especially important in times of severe discontent and defeat and in challenging dominant Gilded Age "myths." Two examples suffice. After the Pullman strike and boycott and Debs's imprisonment, a Portland, Oregon, railroad worker drew inferences and analogies only from sacred history:

> Were Moses now living, and the Almighty should send him to a General Manager's office to protest against corporation robberies, he would be forthwith arrested and thrown into jail, and if Moses should appeal to the Supreme Court, the infamous proceedings would be sustained and declared constitutional; and therefore, the way I look at it, the corporation slaves of the United States are in a worse condition than were the slaves of Pharaoh. But in the case of Pharaoh, God put a curse upon him. The corporation Pharaohs are not to have their way always. There may be a Red Sea just ahead—but beyond it is the promised land.
>
> Egypt had only one Pharaoh at a time on the throne. Here we have probably a hundred of the abnormal monsters, all engaged in enslaving working people. . . . The Egyptian Pharoah did not send Moses to prison. . . . He could have done it. He had absolute power. He was a despot with a big D. . . . Here a labor leader is condemned and thrown into prison by a decree of one small contemptible Pharaoh at the suggestion of a General Manager Pharaoh . . . and there is no appeal except to the Buzzards Bay Pharaoh [Grover Cleveland's Summer White House was in Buzzard's Bay.], which would be like appealing from a pig stealing coyote to a grizzly bear.[85]

The second example concerns Andrew Carnegie and his belief in the "Gospel of Wealth," the notion of "stewardship." At the time of its enunciation, the *Locomotive Firemen's Magazine* scorned the "Gospel of Wealth" as "flapdoodle" and "slush." Of Carnegie, it said: "While asserting that the ' "Gospel of Wealth" but echoes Christ's words,' [he] endeavors to wriggle out of the tight place in which Christ's words place him." It required "patience" to read about "the 'right modes of using immense fortunes' known to be the product of cool, Christless robbery."[86] The Homestead conflict in 1892 caused the same journal to call Carnegie and Henry Clay Frick "brazen pirates [who] prate . . . of the 'spirit of Christ' [and] who plunder labor that they may build churches, endow universities and found libraries."[87] In 1894 the conservative *National Labor Tribune* joined in mocking Carnegie's professions:

> Oh, Almighty Andrew Philanthropist Library Carnegie, who are in America when not in Europe spending the money of your slaves and serfs, thou are a good father to the people of Pittsburgh, Homestead and Beaver Falls. . . . Oh, most adorable Carnegie, we love thee, because thou are the almighty iron and steel king of the world; thou who so much resembles the pharisee. . . . We thank thee and thy combines for the hungry men, women and children of the land. We thank thee and thy combines for the low price of iron and steel and the low price in iron and steel works. . . . Oh, master, we thank thee for all the free gifts you have given the public at the expense of your slaves. . . . Oh, master, we need no protection, we need no liberty so long as we are under thy care. So we command ourselves to thy mercy and forevermore sing thy praise. Amen![88]

Such language could not be misunderstood.

Although the evidence emphasized in these pages indicates the existence of a working-class social Christianity and suggests that Protestantism had a particular meaning for discontented Gilded Age labor leaders, social radicals, and even ordinary workers, it is hazardous to infer too much from it alone about the working class. Too little is yet known about nineteenth-century American Protestant workers. Evidence on church affiliation, for example, is contradictory. While many contemporaries like D. O. Kellogg, general secretary of the Charity Organization of Philadelphia, frequently worried over the "widespread skepticism and alienation from Christianity prevalent among the workingmen" and complained that institutional Protestantism often was "out of the poor man's reach," inadequate but significant statistics for church affiliation among the general population, not just workers, show an increase from 16 per cent in 1850 to 36 per cent in 1900.[89] Until more is known about particular groups of workers and their relations to institutional and noninstitutional religious sentiment and belief, however, it remains impossible to reconcile such seemingly contradictory evidence. Scattered but still inconclusive evidence hints at an apparent close connection between youthful religious conversion and subsequent labor militancy among certain workers.[90] The considerable but as yet largely neglected variations in the experience and outlook of factory workers and skilled craftsmen and of self-educated artisans and casual day laborers as well as the different social environments of small, semirural factory and mining villages, industrial cities, and large urban centers suggest other important analytic problems in exploring the relationship between Protestantism and the "working class."[91] And there are additional complexities. It is risky to assume too close a relationship between religious sentiment and rhetoric and everyday behavior, and it is equally perilous to view church attendance and affiliation as proof of religious belief or not attending church as presumptive evidence of the opposite. An example of the confusion that might result was the response of an unidentified worker when asked in 1898: "Why are so many intelligent workingmen non-church goers?" "Jesus Christ," he replied, "is with us outside the church, and we shall prevail with God."[92]

Despite these many difficulties, a perspective over more than one or two generations suggests tentative connections between the religious mode of expression of many Gilded Age trade-unionists and labor radicals and the behavior of larger numbers of disaffected Gilded Age Protestant workers. Except for those unions that drew support primarily from workers living in small towns and semirural or other isolated areas, the language of labor leaders and social radicals and the tone of their press after 1900 displayed a marked decline in religious emphasis when compared to the labor speeches, editorials, and letters penned between 1860 and 1900. In part this difference suggests the growing secularization of the national culture, but it also makes possible a particular view of Gilded Age workers, seeing them as a transitional generation that bridged two distinct social structures and was the first to encounter fully the profound strains accompanying the shift to an urban and industrial social order. Not separated emotionally or historically from a different past, they lived through an era of extreme social change and social disorder, but carried with them meaningful and deeply felt traditions and values rooted in the immediate and even more distant past. This process was not unique to the United States, but occurred at different times in other rapidly changing societies and greatly explains the behavior of the "first generation" to have contact with a radically different economic and social structure.[93] Although it is an exaggeration to argue that the violent and often disorganized protest characteristic of so much Gilded Age labor agitation resulted only from the tension between the outlook the worker brought to the Gilded Age and that era's rapidly changing economic and social structure, it is not too much to suggest that the thought and the behavior of Gilded Age workers were peculiar to that generation.

Vital in both pre-Civil War reform movements and evangelical crusades, perfectionist Christianity carried over into the Gilded Age and offered the uprooted but discontented Protestant worker ties with the certainties of his past and reasons for his disaffection with the present by denying for him the premises of Gilded Age America and the not yet "conventional wisdom" of that day. In 1874 the secretary of the Miners' Protective and Progressive Association of Western Pennsylvania, George Archbold,

called the trade-union a "God-given right" and warned fellow unionists of
employer opposition: "The Philistines are upon you, and the fair Delilah
would rob you of your locks and shear you of your power."[94] Twenty-three
years later and not in entirely dissimilar language, West Coast labor
organizer and sailor Andrew Furuseth celebrated the twelfth anniversary of
the Sailors' Union of the Pacific:

> Congress may rob us of our rights as men, and may make us bondsmen. The
> Judiciary may say "Well done" and uphold them. Yet we have our manhood
> from nature's God, and being true to our best interests we shall yet as free men
> turn our faces to the sun. . . . We must organize ourselves and align ourselves
> with the forces which in our country are making for that brotherhood for
> which Jesus died. So we must as individuals forget home, self and life if need
> be, to reconquer our liberty, to preserve the sacredness of our bodies, which by
> Paul were called "the temples of the living God."[95]

Such an emphasis was common to men who disagreed on other matters such
as trade-union strategy and the long-range purposes of labor organization
and reform. That it is found among "business" unionists, Knights of Labor,
and socialist and anarchist radicals and is as prevalent in the 1890's as in the
1860's suggests that it characterized no particular segment of organized
labor, but was common to a generation of disaffected workers. Even the
German Marxist immigrant Adolph Douai revealed its influence. Although
he worried that "enthusiasm without reason engenders fanaticism and thus
baffles the noblest purposes," Douai nevertheless pleaded in 1887: "Our age
needs religious enthusiasm for the sake of common brotherhood, because
infidelity is rampant and hypocrisy prevails in all churches—an infidelity of
a peculiar kind, being a disbelief in the destiny of men to be brothers and
sisters, in their common quality [sic] and rights." Douai depicted the Gilded
Age labor movement as "*the* religion of common brotherhood."[96]

Preindustrial Christian perfectionism offered Gilded Age labor
reformers absolute values in a time of rapid social change and allowed the
labor reformer or radical to identify with "timeless truths" that legitimized
his attack on the absolutes of Gilded Age social thought—the determinism
of Spencerian dogma, the sanctity of property rights and freedom of contract, and the rigidity of political laissez faire.[97] "Conditions" had changed,
but the "issues" remained as of old, wrote the *Printer's Labor Tribune,* immediate forerunner to the important Pittsburgh *National Labor Tribune,* in
arguing that "the war between capital and labor" was being "fought all the
time, and [was] . . . identical with civilization itself." Privilege and monopoly were not new. "When Adam commenced business as a farmer, he enjoyed
a monopoly, and the same might be said of Noah, but this could not continue," wrote the *Tribune* in 1873. Industrialism merely altered the terms of
a historic conflict. "The age of steam, electricity and progress generally
shows up a new phase of this old war. We have to fight against the old
enemy of the masses, only under a new shape."[98] Coal miner and union

organizer W. H. Haskins could declare: "Brothers, the principles of organized labor are as old as the old gray rocks and sand of Mt. Sinai."[99] And Knights of Labor leader Charles Litchman could promise:

> If you ask me to say how this system is to be changed, when the emancipation of the toiling millions on earth is to come, I can only say, "I know not *when* it will come, but I know it will come," because in the sight of God and God's angels the wrongs of the toiling millions on earth are a curse and a crime, and that as God is mercy and God is love, in His own good time the toiler will be free.[100]

Although the labor press frequently complained that institutional Protestantism had "come down to the level of merchandise, and our modern Levites worship the golden calf and offer their wares, like fakirs, to the highest bidder,"[101] the *United Mine Workers' Journal* printed on its first page a sermon by Baptist minister J. Thalmus Morgan for good reason. Morgan warned from his Ohio mining village pulpit:

> God's laws of right and wrong are ever the same and cannot be changed until God and man's moral nature shall be changed. Opinions may change, but truth never. Truth is truth to the end of all reckoning. What was right in the time of Moses, Mordecai and Ehud will be right forever. . . . God shall judge the poor of the people; He shall save the children of the needy, and shall break into pieces the oppressor. Yes, He will do the poor justice, for He will delight in doing them good. . . . And [He] shall break into pieces oppression. He is strong to smite the foes of His people. Oppressors have been great breakers, but their time of retribution shall come, and they shall be broken themselves.[102]

The transcendent values that organized labor found in such postmillennial Christian exhortation helped steel it in a transitional era of deep crisis. "The mandate, 'Thou shalt glorify me in thy works,' is Labor's first article of faith," concluded the *Coast Seaman's Journal.*[103]

Although trade-unionists and labor radicals were not the only critics of Gilded Age industrial America, the social Christianity they espoused was different from the more widely known and well-studied social gospel put forth by middle- and upper-class religious critics of that society. Both groups reacted against the early disintegrating consequences of rapid industrialization and drew from the same broad religious tradition. But parallel developments are not necessarily synonymous even though they occur at the same time and share a common mode of expression. The available evidence suggests few formal connections between the two "movements" and for several reasons. Before the 1890's, the two groups, so different in their social composition and in the way industrial and social change affected them, rarely addressed each other and usually spoke to different audiences. Despite many diversities (its "radical" and "conservative" fringes), the essential attributes of the early social gospel movement are characterized by

Henry May in a way that makes it possible to distinguish it from its working-class counterpart:

> The Social Gospel of the American nineteenth century . . . did not grow out of actual suffering but rather out of moral and intellectual dissatisfaction with the suffering of others. It originated not with the "disinherited" but rather with the educated and pious middle class. It grew through argument, not through agitation; it pleaded for conversion, not revolt or withdrawal.[104]

Critical of business behavior and the individualist ethic of their time and anxious to infuse all social classes with a meaningful Christian ethic, few early advocates of the social gospel identified closely with organized labor and its particular forms of collective organization and protest. Few shared Henry George's belief that "the revolt everywhere" against the "hard conditions of modern society is really the religious spirit."[105] They sought first to mediate between the competing classes and frequently failed to understand the "immediacy" of labor discontent. Only a small number, May finds, arranged "a successful working relation between their ultimate confidence in the new social spirit and the drab realities of day-to-day struggle."[106] Even the young Richard T. Ely and Washington Gladden, both so typical of the mainstream social gospel movement and both profoundly at odds with the materialism of their times, found it difficult at the start to associate themselves with working-class organizations and their methods and objectives.[107] Of the early social gospel movement, C. Howard Hopkins concludes that its "inclusive panacea" was "Christianity itself." Quoting Gladden, he adds, " 'the power of Christian love' was declared to be strong enough 'to smooth and sweeten all relations of capitalists and labor.' " Society would change mainly "through the converted individual whose changed character would produce a social transformation."[108] Such thought and argument stimulated numerous middle- and upper-class reformers in late nineteenth-century America, but what May calls its "facile optimism" and its "fatal tendency to underestimate difficulties and to neglect mechanism" cut it off from working-class critics of industrial society.[109]

Protestantism in Gilded Age America permeated the social structure and the value system of the nation more deeply and in different ways than heretofore emphasized by that era's historians. The careers and writings of Henry Ward Beecher, Dwight Moody, Mary Baker Eddy, Washington Gladden, and the trade-unionists and labor radicals described in these pages illustrate the complexity of the relationship between religious belief and organization and the component parts of a particular social structure. Although what has been written here must not be interpreted as a single explanation for the little-studied subject of nineteenth-century working-class thought and behavior, it should be clear that the social gospel early found expression among those who professed to speak for the discontented lower classes and that the behavior of these critics of industrial capitalism cannot be understood without first exploring the religious (and secular) dimensions of their thought. For some workers and their leaders, including some of the most prominent Gilded Age trade-unionists and radicals, a particular strand of Protestantism offered what Hobsbawm calls "a passion and morality in which the most ignorant can compete on equal terms" and what Liston Pope describes as a religion "intimately related to the everyday struggles and vicissitudes of an insecure life" and "useful for interpretation and succor."[110] In 1893 one American pondered existential questions:

> While man is nothing more than a human, he has feeling. . . . While I am not a preacher nor one among the best of men, I am one who believes in Christ and His teachings and endeavor each day to live the life of a Christian. . . . My way is not everybody's way, and it would be wrong to even suppose it should be. . . . Now, what is my motive? . . . My reasoning is after this manner: Can man within himself accomplish as much while self exists as when he considers, Am I the only being that lives? and finds in answer, no. But I am one among millions, a pitiful drop in the bucket he thinks at once. . . . Am I right? Man wants everything but that which is best for him and his brother.[111]

These were not the words of Henry Ward Beecher, Russell Conwell, Mary Baker Eddy, Dwight Moody, William Lawrence, Lyman Atwater, John D. Rockefeller, Andrew Carnegie, or even Washington Gladden; they were penned by an unidentified but troubled Belleville, Ohio, coal miner.

NOTES

[1]J. L. Talmon, "The Age of Revolution," *Encounter*, XXI (Sept. 1963), 14.

[2]Evidence on differing contemporary estimates of the status of industrialists and workers in large cities and small industrial towns is found in H. G. Gutman, "The Worker's Search for Power: Labor in the Gilded Age," in *The Gilded Age: A Reappraisal*, ed. H. Wayne Morgan (New York, 1963), 38-68.

[3]Ralph Gabriel, *The Course of American Democratic Thought* (New York, 1956), 154.

[4]Chicago *Times*, Aug. 24, 1874, Aug. 26, 1876.

[5]An able summary of the defense of laissez faire in the Gilded Age is found in Sidney Fine, *Laissez Faire and the General-Welfare State: A Study of Conflict in American Thought, 1865-1901* (Ann Arbor, Mich., 1956), 3-166. On the process of legitimizing newly achieved power, see Max Weber, *Essays in Sociology*, tr. and ed. H. W. Gerth and C. W. Mills (New York, 1946), 271.

[6]Edward C. Kirkland, "Divide and Rule," *Mississippi Valley Historical Review*, XLIII (June 1956), 3-17.

[7]See Fine, *Laissez Faire*, 54, 56, 103; Kirkland, "Divide and Rule"; and Thomas Cochran, *Railroad Leaders, 1845-1890: The Business Mind in Action* (Cambridge, Mass., 1953), 436-37.

[8]This view is identified most frequently with Henry Ward Beecher and Russell Conwell. See Henry F. May, *Protestant Churches and Industrial America* (New York, 1949), and William G. McLoughlin, Jr., *Modern Revivalism: Charles Grandison Finney to Billy Graham* (New York, 1959), 267-68.

[9]Sidney E. Mead, "American Protestantism since the Civil War," *Journal of Religion,* XXXVI (Jan. 1956), 1-15. See also Winthrop Hudson, *American Protestantism* (Chicago, 1961), 136-40. Hudson also relates these developments to the new theology, "the doctrine of Incarnation, interpreted as divine immanence, which sanctified the 'natural' man and invested the culture itself with intrinsic redemptive tendencies." The new theology therefore surrendered "any independent basis of judgment." Excellent analysis of the post-Civil War evangelism typified by Dwight Moody is found in McLoughlin, *Modern Revivalism,* 166-281, and Bernard A. Weisberger, *They Gathered at the River: The Story of the Great Revivalists and Their Impact upon Religion in America* (Boston, 1958), 160-219.

[10]May, *Protestant Churches, passim,* but esp. 91-111, 163-203; A. I. Abell, *The Urban Impact on American Protestantism, 1865-1900* (Cambridge, Mass., 1943), *passim;* and C. H. Hopkins, *The Rise of the Social Gospel in American Protestantism, 1865-1915* (New Haven, Conn., 1940), *passim.*

[11]See the penetrating and original study of the role of voluntary associations and community institutions among Irish immigrant workers and their children in Newburyport, Massachusetts, between 1850 and 1880 in Stephan Thernstrom, *Poverty and Progress: Social Mobility in a Nineteenth Century City* (Cambridge, Mass., 1964), 166-91.

[12]Hudson, *American Protestantism;* Mead, "American Protestantism."

[13]Asa Briggs, review of Edward P. Thompson, *The Making of the English Working Class, Labor History,* VI (Winter 1965), 84.

[14]Edward P. Thompson, *The Making of the English Working Class* (London, 1963), 194 *et passim.*

[15]See esp. Timothy L. Smith, *Revivalism and Social Reform in Mid-Nineteenth Century America* (New York, 1957), *passim*; and C. E. Olmstead, *History of Religion in the United States* (Englewood Cliffs, N.J., 1960), 352; W. G. McLoughlin, "Pietism and the American Character," *American Quarterly,* XVII (Summer 1965), 163-86.

[16]Thompson, *Making of the English Working Class,* 350-400; Eric Hobsbawm, *Labouring Men: Studies in the History of Labour* (London, 1964), 23-33; Robert F. Wearmouth, *Methodism and the Working-Class Movements of England, 1800-1850* (London, 1937), *passim.*

[17]E. J. Hobsbawm, *Social Bandits and Primitive Rebels: Studies in Archaic Forms of Social Movement in the 19th and 20th Centuries* (Glencoe, Ill., 1959), 108, 130.

[18]Thompson, *Making of the English Working Class,* 68.

[19]*Labor Leader* (Boston), Sept. 15, 1888.

[20]Alvin and Helen Gouldner, *Modern Sociology* (New York, 1963), 634-36.

[21]*Labor Leader,* Aug. 27, 1888.

[22]*Union Pacific Employees Magazine,* n.d., reprinted in the *Journal of the Knights of Labor* (Philadelphia), July 16, 1891. The Crucifixion was but one example this journal cited. It also pointed to the mobbing of William Lloyd Garrison, the hanging of John Brown, and the jailing of Voltaire.

[23]*Railway Times* (Chicago), June 15, 1896.

[24]*Labor Standard* (Boston), Feb. 22, 1879.

[25]*Coast Seaman's Journal* (San Francisco), Nov. 28, 1888, Jan. 30, 1889.

[26]*Labor Enquirer* (Denver), Apr.-May 1883.

[27]*United Mine Workers' Journal* (Columbus, Ohio), Mar. 8, 1900.

[28]Hobsbawm, *Labouring Men,* 376.

[29]*American Workman* (Boston), June-July 1869.

[30]*Labor: Its Rights and Wrongs* (Washington, D.C., 1886), 252-61.

[31]*The Accused, the Accusers. The Famous Speeches of the Eight Chicago Anarchists in Court . . . On October 7th, 8th and 9th, 1886* (Chicago, 1886), 5-6.

[32]McLoughlin, *Modern Revivalism* 65-165; Smith, *Revivalism, passim;* Olmstead, *History of Religion,* 347-62.

[33]McLoughlin, *Modern Revivalism,* 167.

[34]James Sylvis, *Life, Speeches, Labors and Essays of William H. Sylvis* (Philadelphia, 1872), 152-65.

[35]*Railway Times,* Jan. 15, 1894.

[36]*Knights of Labor* (Chicago), Nov. 20, 1886.

[37]*United Mine Workers' Journal,* Mar. 29, 1894.

[38]Louis Nash, "Is This A Christian Civilization?" *American Federationist,* I (Jan. 1895), 252.

[39]*Fincher's Trades Review* (Philadelphia), Feb. 2, 1864.

[40]Boston *Daily Evening Voice,* Sept. 2, 1865.

[41]*Cigar-Makers' Official Journal,* XIX (Jan. 1894), 3.

[42]*United Mine Workers' Journal,* Sept. 30, 1897.

[43]*Ibid.,* June 15, 1893.

[44]*Railway Times,* Jan. 15, 1894.

[45]*Journal of United Labor* (Philadelphia), Sept. 1882.

[46]O.T. Hicks, *Life of Richard Trevellick* (Joliet, Ill., 1898), 198-200.

[47]*Craftsman* (Washington, D.C.), May 30, 1885.

[48]*Coast Seaman's Journal,* Feb. 25, 1891.

[49]*Railway Times,* Feb. 1, 1897.

[50]*The Motorman and Conductor,* V (Jan. 1899), 1-3.

[51]*Coast Seaman's Journal,* Feb. 22, 1897.

[52]*Craftsman,* Dec. 19, 1885; see also W.J.M., "Christmas Greeting," *Coast Seaman's Journal,* Dec.21,1887. The identification of Christ with "tramps" occurred earlier, too, especially during the antitramp hysteria of the middle and late 1870's. Defending "tramps," the *Weekly Worker* reminded readers: "About the only consolation left the truly unfortunate tramp is the thought that Christ was a tramping vagabond. . . ." (*Weekly Worker* [Syracuse, N.Y.], Aug. 15, 1875.) The *National Labor Tribune* and other labor journals echoed this point in the 1870's. "Christianity," the *Tribune* insisted, "was ushered into existence by tramps. . . . Great movements come from the bottom layer of society, who [sic] possess the truest instincts and noblest instincts. Our tramps are but the beginning of a worn-out system." (*National Labor Tribune,* Dec. 23, 1876.)

[53]Oscar Handlin, *The Americans* (Boston, 1963), 308.

[54]See Hopkins, *Rise of the Social Gospel,* 85, and Bernard Mandel, *Samuel Gompers: A Biography* (Yellow Springs, Ohio, 1963), 9-12.

[55]May, *Protestant Churches,* 216-23.

[56]See, e.g., Powderly's speeches in the *Journal of United Labor,* July 17, 1890, Dec. 28, 1892, and McDonnell's editorials in the Paterson *Labor Standard,* Dec. 24, 1881, May 15, 1886, and in *Baker's Journal,* Dec. 1, 1888.

[57]Sylvis, *Life . . . of William H. Sylvis*, 96-117, 443-46.

[58]Terence V. Powderly, *Thirty Years of Labor* (Columbus, Ohio, 1886), 160-72, 176-77.

[59]*National Labor Tribune*, Mar. 18, 1882.

[60]*Writings and Speeches of Eugene V. Debs*, ed. Arthur M. Schlesinger, Jr. (New York, 1948), 4-6.

[61]*Labor Leader*, Oct. 12, 1895.

[62]*Union* (Indianapolis), Jan. 17, 1896.

[63]Arthur Mann, *Yankee Reformers in the Urban Age* (Cambridge, Mass., 1954), 178-84, contains perceptive comments on the career and importance of McNeill, but most labor historians have minimized his importance.

[64]*Labor Standard*, Nov.-Dec. 1876.

[65]*Labor Enquirer*, Nov. 27, 1887.

[66]*Labor Leader*, Feb.-Mar. 1890.

[67]George E. McNeill, *The Philosophy of the Labor Movement* (Chicago, 1893), unpaged pamphlet.

[68]*American Federationist*, IX (Sept. 1902), 479-80.

[69]Further details on the role of Negroes in the early United Mine Workers of America are found in Herbert G. Gutman, "The Negro and the United Mine Workers. The Career and Letters of Richard L. Davis and Something of Their Meaning: 1890-1900," in *The Negro and the American Labor Movement*, ed. Julius Jacobson (New York).

[70]Riley to the editor, *United Mine Workers' Journal*, Sept. 8, 1892.

[71]Clark to the editor, *ibid.*, Aug. 9, 1894.

[72]Davis to the editor, *ibid.*, Aug. 15, 1895.

[73]Davis to the editor, *ibid.*, Apr. 18, 1892.

[74]Davis to the editor, *ibid.*, Feb. 11, 1897.

[75]Davis to the editor, *ibid.*, Mar. 3, 10, 1898.

[76]*Ibid.*, Dec. 8, 1892.

[77]*Knights of Labor*, Sept. 25, 1886.

[78]*Coast Seaman's Journal*, June 29, 1892.

[79]*Railway Times*, June 1, 1895.

[80]*Locomotive Firemen's Magazine*, XI (Apr. 1887), 207-208.

[81]*Ibid.*, X (Sept. 1886), 519-20.

[82]*Journal of United Labor*, Sept. 13, 1888.

[83]*Ibid.*, Sept. 20, 1888.

[84]*Locomotive Firemen's Magazine*, XVIII (Sept. 1894), 877-79.

[85]*Railway Times*, Aug. 15, 1895.

[86]*Locomotive Firemen's Magazine*, XIV (Feb. 1890), 104-106.

[87]*Ibid.*, XVI (Aug. 1892), reprinted in *Writings and Speeches of Eugene V. Debs*, ed. Schlesinger, 378-82.

[88]*National Labor Tribune*, n.d., reprinted in *Coming Age*, Feb. 10, 1894. Such satiric use of traditional religious forms recurred in these years. See, for example, "A Miner's Prayer . . . ," *United Mine Workers' Journal*, May 16, 1895: "Oh! Almighty and allwise and powerful coal barons who art living in great and glorious palaces,

when thou art not in secret meeting working for our interest and welfare, we hail thy blessed name as the great philanthropist of our commercial world to-day. We bow before thee in humble submission. . . . We are Americans of the modern type, not like Jefferson, Hancock and Washington. . . . We are your fools, liars, suckers; spit in our faces and rub it in. We have no business to want an education for our children or ourselves. We ain't got any sense. We don't want any; it don't take any sense to load coal for thee. . . . Did Dred Scott ever serve his master better? . . . Amen".

[89]D. O. Kellogg, "Some Causes of Pauperism and Their Cure," *Penn Monthly*, XI (Apr. 1878), 275-76, 281-82; Olmstead, *History of Religion*, 447.

[90]Hobsbawm, *Social Bandits and Primitive Rebels*, 140; Gabriel, *Course of American Democratic Thought*, 208-11.

[91]Asa Briggs, *The Making of Modern England, 1784-1867* (New York, 1965), 287.

[92]H. Francis Perry, "The Workingman's Alienation from the Church," *American Journal of Sociology*, IV (Mar. 1899), 626.

[93]Hobsbawm, *Social Bandits and Primitive Rebels*, 1-12, 126-49; Thompson, *Making of the English Working Class*, 356 ff.; and Marc Bloch, *The Historian's Craft* (New York, 1964), 185-87.

[94]*National Labor Tribune*, Jan. 31, 1874.

[95]*Coast Seaman's Journal*, Mar. 17, 1897.

[96]*Workmen's Advocate* (New Haven, Conn.), May 14, 1887.

[97]Vittorio Lanterari, *The Religion of the Oppressed: A Study of Modern Messianic Cults* (New York, 1965), x.

[98]*Printer's Labor Tribune* (Pittsburgh), Nov. 27, 1873.

[99]*United Mine Workers' Journal*, Jan. 17, 1895.

[100]*Journal of United Labor* (Philadelphia), Aug. 27, 1888.

[101]*Coast Seaman's Journal*, Oct. 18, 1893.

[102]*United Mine Workers' Journal*, June 28, 1894.

[103]*Coast Seaman's Journal*, Aug. 29, 1894.

[104]May, *Protestant Churches*, 235.

[105]*Labor: Its Rights and Wrongs*, 261-68.

[106]May, *Protestant Churches*, 231-35.

[107]R. T. Ely, *The Labor Movement in America* (New York, 1886), v-xiii; John L. Shover, "Washington Gladden and the Labor Question," *Ohio Historical Quarterly*, LXVIII (Oct. 1959), 335-52.

[108]Hopkins, *Rise of the Social Gospel*, 70, 89, 325.

[109]May, *Protestant Churches*, 233.

[110]Hobsbawm, *Social Bandits and Primitive Rebels*, 132; Liston Pope, *Millhands and Preachers* (New Haven, Conn., 1942), 86.

[111]*United Mine Workers' Journal*, June 29, 1893.

21

Immigration and Puritanism

Marcus L. Hansen

Students of American history have often puzzled over the question of why immigrants who condoned such practices as beer drinking in their native countries espoused temperance or prohibition upon their arrival in the United States. In the following essay, the late Marcus L. Hansen analyzes how the impulse toward "puritanism" is closely associated with the process and experience of immigration and suggests another perspective on why puritanism is held to be so influential in American history. Professor Hansen is known for his extensive work in the history of immigration to America and was, at his death, in the Department of History at the University of Illinois.

A strange and undefined authority pervades American social and intellectual life, and occasionally its influence extends into the realm of politics. This sovereign force bears the name Puritanism. It has no definition and every person gives it his own meaning. Whenever a patriot honors great men and mighty deeds he says that they were inspired by Puritanism; whenever a critic of society or art bemoans the dullness and uniformity of the national scene he traces them back to the blighting effects of Puritanism. Any sort of restraint established by the government or decreed by the customs of the community is Puritanism. Any intolerance in the world of ideas is Puritanism. A human prejudice, a stern injustice, an annoying regulation are all derived from the same source. And then, when occasionally a robust

First published in *Norwegian-American Studies and Records,* IX (1936), pp. 1-28 (abridged). Reprinted with permission of the Norwegian-American Historical Association.

pioneer society breaks all the bounds of propriety and runs into license, the evildoers are personally excused on the plea that this was merely a reaction to Puritanism. . . .

The term Puritanism has . . . been applied to administrative policies which have sometimes been expressed in state and federal legislation and sometimes have been the product of judicial decisions or the decrees of officials. What this means is well known: the censorship of literature by a customs inspector; the censorship of the theater by a policeman temporarily taken off his regular beat; the interpretation of what is art and what is indecency by a judge who knows nothing about the canons of culture. In the same category fall the state laws and city ordinances that have laid down precise rules as to how the Sabbath day is to be kept holy; and, finally, the legal code adopted to preserve temperance, ending in a prohibition amendment to the Constitution. This is what the average citizen refers to as Puritanism: a program that seeks to regulate morals by preventive legislation. Such an attempt has not been unknown in other countries, but in the United States it has been more persistent and more drastic; and out of its presence have come many of the predominant features of American social life.

So obvious has this national distinction been that the popular mind possesses a standard explanation of its origin and development. It runs about as follows: the most successful colonizers of the North American continent were English Purtians who left the decadent society of the homeland to plant a Bible commonwealth beyond the sea. Permeated through and through by Calvin's theology, they found in the Old Testament the spirit of their government and the text of many of their laws. To preserve this ideal state they did not hesitate to hang Quakers and drive dissenters into the wilderness; and their sons and daughters were reared in an ecclesiastical atmosphere as harsh as New England's climate. Time softened somewhat the administration of these ideals, but the spirit remained. From its home in the northeastern states Puritanism was introduced to the West and Southwest by migrating settlers, and the wealth that the merchants accumulated was devoted to the establishment of colleges. From these institutions came one generation of ministers after the other who gradually captured control of most of the Protestant churches and stamped their teachings upon the pattern of village and country life. The Civil War (which in many ways was an attempt of the South to escape this domination) was a great victory for the ministers and, elated by success, their ambitions led them on until at last morality was written into the fundamental law of the land in the Eighteenth Amendment. . . .

Who were the Puritans of New England? Much learning has failed to yield satisfactory answers to questions regarding their education, material possessions, and practical motives in seeking new homes. Perhaps they were fanatics; on the other hand, they may have been ordinary individuals who, not being deeply concerned with religion, left discipline to the leaders. But whatever they were in spiritual matters, in temporal affairs they were colonists, settlers who were obliged to devote most of their time, thought, and energy to chopping down forests, building homes, and planting and reaping harvests. They were immigrants, and most of their policies must have been typical immigrant reactions. Whether the European crossed the Atlantic in 1630, 1730, or 1830, the all-absorbing problem that faced him was that of getting settled, with the result that his social life, in all of its aspects, was colored by the needs of his pioneer status. In a group of settlers these individual needs, multiplied many times over, inevitably became an essential part of community policy.

If an investigator will make a thorough study of the experiences of the millions of nineteenth-century immigrants, saturate himself in their problems, and then turn back to the original records of seventeenth-century Massachusetts and study the pages without the assistance of any traditional interpretations, he will be amazed to note how familiar the passages sound. Every one of the later immigrant settlements was troubled by its Roger Williams and its Anne Hutchinson, who had to be cast out for the sake of religious peace. Each group had its statesmen who sacrificed to build a college lest the people be left to an illiterate ministry. Each had its fanatics in social philosophy and religious practice, and Puritanism was the spirit that permeated all. So striking is the parallel that one hesitates to doubt that the Germans, Swedes, Finns, and all the rest of them would have been just as intolerant in their laws if they had possessed the same legal rights of self-government as the Fathers of New England. The vocabulary of Calvin may have provided the phrases in which the ideals were expressed but those ideals were only an outgrowth of the necessities of daily life.

The *Journal* of John Winthrop, many times governor of Massachusetts Bay, provides an enlightening passage which may be taken as a starting point. Winthrop is remembered as one of the milder and more humane of the Fathers and the regime of which he was a part never had his complete approbation. But crime and disorder appeared in a startling degree among the settlers. The authorities were obliged to take action; dispute arose as to how severe the action should be. The ministers went into conference, and the passage continues, "The next morning they delivered their several reasons, which all sorted to this conclusion, that strict discipline both in criminal offences and in martial affairs, was more needful in plantations than in a settled state, as tending to the honor and safety of the gospel."[1] To repeat the significant words: "strict discipline . . . more needful in plantations than in a settled state." This is the clue to immigrant Puritanism.

Why a stricter discipline? In the Old World a person was more likely to lead a respectable life because he was surrounded by the restraints of family and tradition. But in the New World these restraints were gone; no one knew him; life was harder and former pleasures were not available. Moral standards had been an outward prop, not an inner support, and now the prop was gone. Law had to do for the individual what he could not do for himself; and law did it, not primarily for the individual's good but for the protection of society. Every frontier lived through its period of lawlessness before government caught up; and when the miners of California formed vigilance committees and hanged horse thieves and claim-jumpers they were merely being puritanical in their own way. The famous Blue Laws are also understandable. No person to smoke more than two pipes a week—because the few acres already cleared must be planted to wheat, not tobacco, or starvation might be the result; no cooking on Sunday, because during the long hours when the family was in church the embers might flare up and put the whole settlement ablaze; no loitering or fishing in the woods on the part of the young men, because the Indians might fall upon them, seize their rifles, and have the settlers at their mercy. Thus we can page through the code and reason out a practical, every-day explanation of the regulations that now seem so strange.

Occasionally a reader chances upon one of the intimate diaries in which a Puritan recorded the duties and pastimes of his fleeting hours. Before many paragraphs are covered there comes the inevitable exclamation: "But these saints weren't so puritanical after all." There were picnics and dinner parties and courtships and ordinations—especially ordinations. The bill for refreshments (port, sherry, and also the harder varieties) always amounted to a total that certainly would have cared for all the poor of the parish for many years. When a church was dedicated, when the ministers gathered in annual conference, when the judges met in conclave, there were not many restrictions or inhibitions evident.[2] All this illustrates what may be called the practical aspect of Puritanism. Regulations were adopted not so much for the moral good of those who did the regulating but because there were many in society who could not be trusted to restrain themselves. The first temperance society in America was founded in 1789 by the farmers of Litchfield County, Connecticut, who took the pledge; but note what they pledged: they agreed not only to abstain themselves but also to refuse their hired hands any liquor as part of the rations. That was the essence of practical Puritanism—restriction of *others*.[3]

New England Puritanism had its ups and downs. As the influx of colonists ceased and life became more settled the early regime was relaxed, only to be revived in a more bitter and unnatural form whenever some danger loomed. Shortly before 1700 war with France and the threat of invasion led to a Puritan outburst that sought to free the land of all the evil spirits that had lodged in the mortal frames of old women.[4] In the 1740's there was again war with France, and every frontier community lived in terror of Indian massacre. Again the ministers could preach the need of reformation, and the Great Awakening sought to restore the piety of earlier days. But when the emergency had passed and the evangelizing zeal had cooled, sinners could continue along the broad way in peace.

After the expulsion of the French from North America and the achievement of independence New England reached social maturity. Puritanism was still a tradition that provided the ideal for many of the forms of life but officials and public opinion condoned scenes and standards that give to the age an aspect of unrestrained license. There was religious indifference. The Sabbath was desecrated. Business morals were low and Yankee traders bore an unsavory name in most of the ports of the seven seas. Drunkenness was a prevailing vice.[5] John Harriott, whose *Struggles through Life* presents a varied picture of a seaman's career in the latter days of the eighteenth century, found in Boston "more private debauchery than I ever knew in any other part of the world."[6] Contemporary moralists blamed the condition onto the laxness attending the war of the Revolution, and others ascribed the degeneration to the vogue of French philosophy and infidelity. Is it not more realistic to suppose that the conditions that had nourished Puritanism had disappeared and the Puritan Age had run its course?

A more pleasing aspect of the change was the liberalism that appeared in all intellectual circles. A theater was opened in Boston and (what would probably have shocked the ancestors more) a Catholic chapel was erected. Tolerance of opinions and practices was the mark of a gentleman. The pioneer Catholic clergy of New England were elected to learned and select societies, and Protestants flocked to the services to hear the creed of the church expounded.[7] Puritan doctrine was softened into Unitarianism and Unitarianism was further softened into Universalism. Many gave up all religion and became humanitarians of the literary variety. For over a generation this spirit reigned and finally in the 1830's and 1840's it blossomed out into the so-called "golden age" of New England—a period of literature and philosophy when continental scholars received a welcome in the universities that had hitherto been narrow in personnel and teaching, and their theories were eagerly absorbed by the clergymen who no longer found satisfaction in the spiritual food of their fathers.

Perhaps it was too good to last. New England was doomed to be something other than an agricultural commonwealth. Nature had provided power, and two centuries of industry and parsimony had accumulated capital. In the years that followed the War of 1812 commercial ports and rural villages were industrialized. Local capitalists constructed cotton and woolen mills, and every country girl spent a few months or a year or two tending the spindles until she had earned a dowry. But there was other labor to be done—heavy, dirty work that no New Englander would perform for the pittance offered: canals to be dug, foundations to be laid, dams to be constructed. And so the Irishman came.

In no other part of the United States at the time would the Irishman have felt himself more of a stranger and received less of a welcome. Two hundred years before, twenty thousand Englishmen had founded the Puritan colonies. Since that first influx the current of immigration had practically passed them by. A few hundred families from Ulster had come shortly after 1700 but their descendants could not be counted upon to extend a cordial greeting to the Catholic Celt. Nevertheless, no hardship could daunt them and no ridicule discouraged their persistence. The son sent for his father and the father for his wife and children. They crowded together in the garrets of the cities and built "shanty towns" wherever a vacant lot and discarded boxes and timbers could be discovered.

No matter how sympathetic one might feel towards these new colonists he could not overlook the practical problems created by their presence. Passage from Ireland was not expensive. Often fifteen shillings secured a berth in a timber vessel bound for New Brunswick. A few shillings more brought the immigrant in a coasting schooner to Boston. Thence transportation was on foot and usually food was provided by the charity of kind housewives. When at last the newcomer reached the vague destination, too often the expected work was not available or the job was done. There was no use in proceeding further. Penniless and hungry and often sick, the new resident's first acquaintance in the community was the officer whose duty it was to relieve the poor. Even when employment was obtained, the Irishman remitted such a large percentage from the small wage that he received to his native land that poverty and squalor seemed to be his perpetual state. In the eyes of his American neighbors he was the representative of a thriftless and improvident race whose coming had destroyed the standards of living and the aspect of comfort that had previously prevailed.[8]

Honest poverty the Yankee might have condoned but this unfortunate state, he believed, was the result not of divine affliction but the working of the devil drink. The immigrant gulped American whisky and found it excellent in taste and effective in results. Not the least of the virtues was its price. In a letter in which he described the advantages of the New World, one of them wrote, "Give my very kind love to Father, and tell him if he was here he could soon kill himself by drinking if he thought proper . . . .I can go into a store, and have as much brandy as I like to drink for three half-pence, and all other spirits in proportion."[9] This advantage the immigrants did not hesitate to make the most of. The fatigue of heavy labor demanded a stimulant; fever and ague wanted an antidote; homesickness had to be dispelled. For all these ailments whisky provided a universal remedy. It was, however, a remedy that was taken socially and produced the reckless conviviality that exiles always inspire in one another when they meet over the cup in a foreign clime. Payday was Saturday night, which Puritan custom considered part of the Sabbath; but on that evening shouts of happiness and sounds of strife came from the hovels and arose from the streets of shanty town.[10] As has been indicated, this was a time of intemperance in New England, but the Yankee drunkard was of the Rip Van Winkle type, the easy-going, humorous village character, the friend of children and dogs. He became more and more stupefied and finally reached a fitting end. Immigrant drunkenness was violent and as dangerous to innocent bystanders as to the circle of drinkers. For this description it is not necessary to depend upon the biased criticism of the natives. Catholic priests who followed parishioners to the labor camps fought against intemperance as the supreme immigrant vice and their warnings and sermons are source materials as vivid as the complaints of any outraged Congregational clergyman.[11]

At first the only official measures prompted by this situation were directed against the burden of poverty. Every incoming foreign passenger was forced to pay a head tax, and from the fund thus accumulated the towns were reimbursed for any expense incurred.[12] The social difficulties were neglected on the theory that American institutions would cure anything. In the meantime the immigrants established their own institutions, and by 1850 New England was the home of two peoples, each of whom possessed its own manner of living, its own standards of conduct, and its own intense hostility towards the other. With the large invasion of hungry Irishmen in 1847 and thereafter, the natives arose in revolt. Economic jealousy, religious bigotry, and simple, unprejudiced worries united in secret societies collectively designated in history the "Know-Nothing Movement."[13]

The title was an unfortunate choice. Every American schoolboy can explain that it received its name because the participants replied, "I don't know," when quizzed regarding their objectives. The objectives, however, did not long remain secret. Politically, the movement sought to restrict immigration and hinder naturalization. Unofficially, it aimed to curb the growth of the Catholic church. But socially it became a part of the revival of Puritanism that occurred at this time, and it was one of the strongest factors leading to that revival.

Earlier in this discussion attention was drawn to the distinctive feature of American Puritanism: The regulation of the morals and actions of those whom the regulators considered dangerous to society because they were unable to take care of themselves. Here was a situation that would encourage the reapplication of this principle, and the statute books of every New England state record the revival.[14] In 1851, Maine adopted a law prohibiting the manufacture and sale of intoxicating liquor; that is, state prohibition. During the next five years practically every northern state battled over similar proposals and many of them borrowed the "Maine Law" as a weapon against intemperance. This, it is true, was not an official plank of the Know-Nothing program and the agitation had arisen apart from that movement. But it appealed to the moderate and most practical element who followed the advice of a writer in the sedate magazine, the *New Englander*. Persecution of aliens, he urged, will do no good; ostracism cannot change their habits. "Beget about them a pure moral atmosphere," he wrote, "so they and their children will grow up strong in the virtues that constitute a good citizen."[15]

Both the temperance agitation and the Know-Nothing Movement met an inevitable reaction. But the spirit of Puritanism that both had fostered was again breathed into the life of the churches. When many of the states repealed the prohibitory laws, the clergymen and their faithful cohorts were not discouraged. A return to state-enforced prohibition remained a constant hope. An impetus was given by the hard times that followed the panic of 1857. Moralists pointed to the hardships and suffering that immigrant families, in particular, endured, and blamed the difficulties upon the improvidence of a drinking father. The despair of the period also strengthened religious zeal, and the outburst of enthusiasm known as the "revival of 1858" stamped the reborn Puritanism upon a rising generation of ministers and people. For the time being, the full effects could not be seen because the anti-slavery crusade obscured everything but the status of the Negro. But ten years later, when that issue had been fought out in the Civil War, the churches returned to the earlier conflict and inaugurated a new era of reform with the nation, instead of the state, as the object of their endeavors.

In this new offensive the churches that had been Puritanized by the New England influence were aided by allies who came from a quarter in which little assistance would normally have been expected. Thus far, New England has dominated our thoughts. There were, however, immigrants other than the Irish. Germans and Scandinavians colonized the rising West, and wherever they settled, personal and community problems appeared to vex immigrants and natives alike.

The foreigner who set out to establish a home in a pioneer agricultural region obviously found himself in an environment different from that which surrounded the New England Celt. Out on the prairie or deep in the forest American institutions were often entirely lacking or, if present, they were too weak to be effective in enforcing any local standards. Many of the settlers were as respectable in conduct as any eastern deacon, but the tide of migration had carried in a class of native Americans who rejoiced in the freedom of the West and disported themselves riotously in the crossroads taverns.[16] It was with this social class that the immigrant from abroad was naturally thrown. Here was American liberty with a vengeance, and he proceeded to cast off all the restraints that European society had bred into him. As elsewhere, homesickness and dreary labor were incentives to conviviality and the comradeship offered by the native rowdies was eagerly accepted. The physical and social mortality among people unaccustomed to such ways of living was high, and in a large number of cases immigration, instead of being a step upward, was a plunge downward. As successive groups of any nationality arrived, the young men among them at once accepted the company and adopted the standards of their predecessors. The history of every immigrant settlement reveals that at some time it passed through this stage of drunkenness and revelry.[17]

When the first clergyman of the faith that these foreigners had professed at home appeared upon the scene, his work was cut out for him. To baptize and confirm was not so important as to conduct a clean-up campaign. Irrespective of his past inclinations this clergyman was forced to adopt a program of reform and to forbid pastimes and pleasures that the ecclesiastical rules of his early training had condoned. Thus the immigrant church was started out upon a career of Puritanism which, at first, had absolutely no connection with the saints at Boston, the fountain head from which all such American tendencies are supposed to flow.

In dealing with the immigrant church a distinction must be made between the Roman Catholic church, a world-wide organization with more than a thousand years of experience in pioneering, and the Protestant denominations that were suddenly called upon to enter into undertakings for which no machinery existed. This latter group may be considered first.

A continental state church looked with no favor upon emigration. As an organ of the government it often sought to discourage expatriation. Among the arguments presented to the head of a family who was anxiously considering the step was the danger involved in bringing up sons and daughters in a country which was described as a spiritual waste.[18] Every letter that came from across the Atlantic with its account of the drunkenness and misery in the immigrant settlements illustrated this point. These same letters prompted others to urge that clergymen, supported by church funds, be sent out to gather together the scattered faithful and organize congregations that would restore the moral atmosphere of the homeland. These requests were refused. Action of this kind, it was stated, would be interpreted as governmental encouragement of emigration. The more hardhearted among officials argued that those who deliberately separated themselves from their native country and its benevolent institutions should suffer the consequences of their folly.[19]

What state churches refused to do was, therefore, undertaken by benevolent and serious individuals. Sometimes it was the enterprise of a private person, sometimes of an association formed for the purpose. Methods that had been evolved for subsidizing missionaries in India and China were now applied for the benefit of benighted emigrants. Among the clergymen, candidates offered themselves for this field as others had volunteered for service in heathen lands; and, as in the latter case, they tended to be men of more zeal, with stricter standards of conduct, than their fellow ministers who remained at home in the comfortable security of an ecclesiastical position as strong as the state. As a result, the immigrant church started out under the leadership of men with a strong bent towards Puritanism.[20]

This inclination was firmly fixed as a permanent trait when the missionary entered upon his duties. Responsibility rested heavily upon the shoulders of the Lutheran or Reformed pastor who found himself the moral leader in a settlement of fellow countrymen intoxicated with the ideas and the liquor of the Republic. His coming was welcomed by the sober members of the colony. They organized themselves into an ecclesiastical body, sacrificed to build a church, and set out to restore the good name of German, Swede, or whatever it might be.

In this endeavor Puritanism received another impetus. To be successful, even among its own constituency, an immigrant institution had to have the good will of the native Americans. But the respectable, middle-class American looked with suspicion upon an organization which was, he thought, a branch of a monarchical government. In his opinion a state church was no church because the individual was born into it. But every American church was a union of believers who, deliberately, under no compulsion, chose to belong to it, to contribute to its support, and to pattern their daily life upon the code of morality that it decreed. These American churches undertook to proselyte among the immigrants and they argued that the adopted citizen, along with his new-found glory as a political individual, should also acquire religious individuality and separate himself from the group that had no meaning except as an association of people who happened to be of the same blood.[21]

Accordingly, in self defense, the immigrant church was forced to adopt standards that conformed to the ideals of the prevailing denominationalism.

An illustration or two are in order. It was a hot July Sunday in Madison, Wisconsin, in 1857. Fifty or sixty Scandinavians attended religious services and then rowed across the lake and enjoyed a picnic afternoon and evening—eating, probably drinking, singing and, probably, engaging in some country dances. The event was observed by many, but the picnickers were not prepared for the barrage of criticism that appeared in the local paper, warning them to behave like respectable Americans if they wanted to enjoy the privileges of the country. A worse blow followed when their own clergyman sided with the natives and forbade the faithful to repeat the enjoyment. Thereupon a debate ensued in the columns of the Norwegian paper. The revelers asked: such Sunday pastimes are a common custom in Norway; the clergymen do not condemn; in fact, they partake therein; why does the church forbid in America what is encouraged in Norway? Is not a sin in one place a sin in another? The reply of authority was: we do not argue this on the basis of intrinsic right or wrong; the fact is clear that such practices bring our church into disrepute and whatever weakens the position of the church is wrong.[22]

The second incident is drawn from the autobiography of one of the immigrant missionaries. He came to the New World at considerable personal sacrifice in order that he might organize the scattered congregations into some uniformity in theology and administration. It was not long before he became aware that his success was being hindered by the rumor that he was a drunkard and a Sabbath-breaker. Investigation revealed the origin of these charges. The first was based upon his habit of stopping while on long horseback journeys to refresh himself with a glass of wine at a country tavern; the second was the result of his calling together a congregational meeting on a Sunday afternoon to consider the worldly question of how much salary the church could raise for the support of a settled minister. Being a practical person he at once "reformed" and determined, at the first opportunity, to reveal the strictness of his code. The opportunity came. In the ranks of one congregation was a member who had fallen into evil ways. Admonition did no good and so he was excluded from the fellowship of the church. This was a procedure which in Europe was reserved for only the most despicable of conduct and which rendered the victim almost a social outcast. This stigma the accused one refused to bear and argued that the congregation had no authority to exclude. To maintain his point he boldly appeared at the next business session. The minister who presided announced that when all strangers had withdrawn they would proceed. No one left. Thereupon, the minister, addressing him by name, told him (in proper ecclesiastical language) to get out and stay out. He didn't budge. At once the clergyman descended from his place, seized the sinner by the collar, and hurled him through the door out into the world. This was not the last of the incident. The minister was summoned before the nearest justice of the peace, charged with assault and battery, found guilty and fined. In recording the outcome he made no complaint regarding American justice. On the contrary, there is a note of triumph in the account, for never again did anyone in the community say there was no discipline in the Lutheran church. The conduct of its members was as irreproachable as any Methodist, Baptist, or Presbyterian could demand.[23]

This is what may be described as spontaneous immigrant Puritanism. It was reinforced by a closer association with the American churches. The problem of money was preeminent. Comparatively little support was received from Europe and when the undenominational American Home Missionary Society offered a struggling pastor a subsidy of a hundred dollars a year there was no reason for him to refuse. But this society insisted that only earnest souls were to be tolerated in the membership of the congregation that received help, and although no definition of "earnestness" was provided prudent pastors knew that conduct was considered a necessary quality and exercised discipline accordingly.[24] From this beginning the relations with the institutions of the country were expanded. Young men who were educated for the ministry were often sent to a theological seminary in New England, and when the immigrant churches founded colleges to train pastors for their congregations those institutions could not escape the forms or the spirit that prevailed at Harvard, Yale, and Princeton.

The process of Puritanization can be followed by anyone who studies the records of a congregation or the minutes of a synod. Discipline became more and more strict. One after the other, social pleasures that were brought from the Old World fell under the ban. Temperance and Sunday observance were early enforced. Then card playing and dancing were prohibited. Simplicity in dress and manner of living were praised as virtues. The children of the immigrants were the object of much concern. When they began to forget the language of their parents and absorb the culture of their American contemporaries an effort was made to prevent all mingling in surrounding society by decreeing the sinfulness of any pastime that tempted such association. By the last quarter of the nineteenth century the Protestant immigrant churches had adopted so much of the New England atmosphere that clergymen who came from the European seminaries of the various denominations were strangers in theology and ecclesiastical practice.[25]

That part of the Irish immigration that settled in the West and the large number of Germans who were of the Catholic faith were subjected to a regime mild in comparison with that of their Protestant neighbors. When the settlers arrived upon the scene the Catholic church was already present. Over a century before, missions had been established among the Indians and the flexible framework of the church was ready to expand as soon as the need for another kind of service was apparent. When the immigrants arrived priests were not far behind. Sometimes they were in the van of the movement, provided with funds with which to build a church that would act as a magnet encouraging the newcomers to locate within sight of the steeple. The rapid multiplication of dioceses in the region beyond the mountains testifies to the efficiency of the system.

Accordingly, the church was more concerned with prevention than with cure and less drastic measures were necessary. The person who went astray could not so universally blame his fall upon the absence of spiritual advisers. Once lost, he was lost for good. Those who from the beginning identified themselves with the church at once felt at home, and all the restraining influences of their native village were in operation. No new prohibitions were added to the commandments they had known from youth. Moreover, the Catholic church was less sensitive to the opinion of the Americans. It realized that it was viewed with suspicion. A certain amount of persecution was taken for granted. The oldest institution in western civilization was not going to revise its program because a few Yankees looked upon it with disfavor.

In the growth of that body of restrictive laws and customs called Puritanism, the Catholic church is usually accounted a retarding force. Never did it enter whole-heartedly into the campaign to make people moral by police regulations. This desirable end could be achieved by other methods.[26] In the course of time, however, the American hierarchy realized that they were dealing with a situation that had no precedent. Not only did many members of their congregations succumb to the prevailing immigrant vice but some of the most prosperous of the parishioners were key men in the liquor trade. Who could produce better beer than the brewer from Munich? And he was a Catholic. Who was a more genial and efficient bartender than the Irishman? And he was a staunch supporter of his religion. The American Protestant press associated the two facts, and the church, for the sake of its public honor, had no alternative but to take action.[27]

Organized and encouraged by bishops and priests, a temperance agitation which left unaffected no one in the constituency was set under way. The archbishop of St. Paul, in whose province so many Catholic immigrants were settled, assumed the leadership of the movement and under his direction public opinion was changed. Men connected with the liquor trade were retired from their positions as lay leaders and all efforts which sought to secure reform by imposing high licenses and restricting hours received church support. The archbishop was frank in his declaration that if improvement were not secured by these measures he would not hesitate to support the policy of prohibition.[28] This attitude, it is true, was not generally accepted. The majority had faith in the ultimate success of less drastic means; but the Catholic church, like the other immigrant churches, helped to form that ecclesiastical sentiment which was the largest single element in bringing about the final triumph of national prohibition.

It is not necessary to recount the steps by which this end was achieved. To complete the picture, however, it is necessary to consider a third section of the country—the South—from which many of the strongest impulses came. Can that source, also, be related to immigration?

If the theory propounded at the beginning of the discussion, that colonial Puritanism was more practical than theological, is sound, then it should have appeared outside New England. It did. In what phase are we interested? Sunday observance? The resident of Virginia who failed to attend the established service on the Sabbath incurred a penalty of fifty pounds of tobacco. The law of New Netherland decreed that not only were ordinary labor, hunting, and fishing prohibited on that day but also "going on pleasure parties in a boat, car, or wagon before, between, or during divine service"—a regulation that covered most contingencies. Or shall we consider orthodoxy? A man might be sentenced to death for blasphemy in Maryland as well as in New Haven.[29] Or is our interest in intolerance? Massachusetts was not the only place where Quakers could expect opposition. In the Virginia records appear items such as, "Quakers whipped," "Quaker fined for entertaining a Quaker," "June 10, 1658, general persecution of Quakers directed."[30]

But south and west of the Hudson the system did not assume any theological aspect and it did not become an honored tradition. New York remained a colony of two parts: the sleepy valley of the Hudson River where Dutch farmers smoked peacefully and, if they ever contemplated any excesses, never got around to action; and the city of New York that was constantly thronged with rowdy sailors—but no one, not even Puritans, ever attempted to reform sailors on shore leave. New Jersey and Pennsylvania possessed a large Quaker element, of which each person governed himself; and the largest contingent of early immigrants was made up of German sectarians bound together in communistic societies that were ruled by an authority more severe than any Boston theocracy would presume to decree. The other large immigration was of Presbyterians from Ulster who brought with them a severe code and a strict discipline.

Below the Mason and Dixon Line, however, the evolution is more enlightening. Reference has already been made to some of the legislation in Virginia and Maryland. The statute books of both colonies abound with enactments which, had they appeared in Massachusetts or Connecticut, would have been considered evidences of Puritan bigotry. But the South did not remain Puritan in its society. Laws were allowed to fall into disuse. Virginia, in particular, became the scene of a civilization which in comfort and tolerance is always taken as the direct antithesis of everything Puritan. The horse-racing parson, the plantation master who loved his mint juleps, the gay gatherings of young and old in the provincial capital at Williamsburg are evidences of a society beyond the pioneer state. They are evidences of something else as well. The small farm had been superseded by the large plantation. Economic life revolved around tobacco, and slaves had taken the place of white servants.

In a history of Puritanism in America, slavery deserves a chapter because, from the definition that has been adopted, slavery was Puritanism raised to the nth degree. When the labor class (or it may be designated the lower class) consisted of slaves, no code of moral behavior was necessary. The upper ranks of society curbed the lower, not by state laws but by personal decrees. Every master established the standards of morality to which his Negroes must submit and he determined the punishment to be meted out in case of infraction. In any matter his will was stronger than the ties of marriage or family and his decisions were superior to the precepts of religion. Only occasionally did the law interfere between owner and slave and then the presumption was that the former was in the right.

It is not surprising that the South with a social system of this nature did not feel the wave of Puritanism that arose in the 1850's. The Maine Law agitation affected it only slightly. But twenty-five years later the situation was reversed. Then the southern states were the leaders in the movement for prohibition and it was evident that a change of far-reaching influence had taken place. That change, of course, was the abolition of slavery; with its disappearance chaos entered into the relations of black and white, rich and poor, pious and wicked. Restraint of some sort was necessary and, now, in the South as before in the North, the state undertook duties in the realm of moral supervision.[31] . . .

The movement for temperance gathered force with each decade that followed the Civil War. The annual influx of foreigners increased rapidly and finally it passed the million mark. A million new inhabitants each year lived through all the temptations and all the disillusionments that had been the lot of their predecessors. The Puritans struggled with a situation that constantly became more difficult. Most of the states experimented with various remedies, but after their failure came a return to the discarded practice of prohibition by state law. In this movement the South, which had done more experimenting than any other section of the country, was the leader. In less than a year four of these states became "dry." In the succeeding period other commonwealths in the North and West followed the same policy.[32] State prohibition, however, encountered difficulties in enforcement because of the ease of interstate transportation.

Accordingly, the Puritans took their agitation to Congress. Here the representatives of the three elements met: congressmen from the North who had inherited the strict principles of New England forefathers; congressmen from the West who did not dare oppose the desires of the immigrant churches that had such great control over their constituents; congressmen from the South who desired to make national a policy which both religion and practice championed. By 1913, they had secured a law controlling the interstate shipment of liquor but this was an enactment that could be repealed by any change in congressional sentiment. They argued: while the mood is on let us put it where it cannot be tampered with. So the agitation was continued and, finally, when the war gave an added impetus to governmental control of life and property the Eighteenth Amendment was adopted.

The Eighteenth Amendment will long be remembered as a social experiment, an experiment of which many of the American people are not proud. But to consider the Puritanism that inspired it the twentieth-century child of seventeenth-century bigotry is the most superficial of views. It was a Puritanism that arose out of nineteenth-century conditions, and in the formation of those conditions the millions of immigrants had as vital a part as any other factor of thought or practice.

NOTES

[1]John Winthrop, *History of New England from 1630 to 1649,* 1:212 (Boston, 1853).

[2]The drinking habits of the New England clergy are illustrated by Frank O. Erb, *The Development of the Young People's Movement,* 3-5 (Chicago, 1917).

[3]This pledge is printed in Daniel Dorchester, *The Liquor Problem in All Ages,* 166 (New York, 1884).

[4]G. L. Kittredge, *Witchcraft in Old and New England,* 371, 372 (Cambridge, 1928); Richard M. Bayles, *History of Windham County, Connecticut,* 42 (New York, 1889).

[5]*History of Middlesex County, Connecticut,* 272 (New York, 1884). One of the early nineteenth-century German writers on America warned emigrants that the evil effects of the Revolution were still noticeable. Ernst L. Brauns, *Praktische Belehrungen und Rathschläge für Reisende und Auswanderer nach Amerika,* 226 (Braunschweig, 1829).

[6]John Harriott, *Struggles through Life,* 36 (London, 1808).

[7]The tolerance of the educated New Englanders is commented upon in *The Jesuit* (Boston), March 19 and July 23, 1831; and in *The United States Catholic Intelligencer* (Boston), September 21, 1832.

[8]M. L. Hansen, "The Second Colonization of New England," in *The New England Quarterly,* 2:539-560 (Baltimore, 1929).

[9]G. Poulett Scrope, ed., *Extracts of Letters from Poor Persons Who Emigrated Last Year to Canada and the United States,* 23 (London, 1831). Warnings regarding the disasters that followed cheap liquor are numerous in all immigrant literature. See, for example, S. H. Collins, *The Emigrant's Guide and Description of the United States of America,* 168 (Hull, Massachusetts, n.d.).

[10]Such disturbances, during the course of one year, are reported in the *Boston Courier,* January 19, April 8, 11, June 20, August 3, September 5, 12, 1848. Innumerable riots taking place at the railroad camps are also recorded.

[11]*The Catholic Herald* (Philadelphia), November 5, 1840; *The United States Catholic Intelligencer,* February 17, 1832; *Boston Pilot,* September 1, 1838, July 24, 1841.

[12]The shortcomings of this system as it operated in Massachusetts are explained in the "Report on Foreign Paupers" in *Massachusetts House Documents,* 1835, no. 60 (Boston, 1835).

[13]This antagonism is reflected in the reports of the city missionaries whose attitude had hitherto been distinctly tolerant. Executive Committee of the Benevolent Fraternity of Churches, *Seventeenth Annual Report,* 21-24, and *Eighteenth Annual Report,* 24 (Boston, 1851, 1852).

[14]George H. Haynes, "A Know Nothing Legislature," in American Historical Association, *Annual Report for the Year 1896,* 1:177-187 (Washington, 1897); "The Doings of the Last Connecticut Legislature on Temperance and Liberty" in *The New Englander,* 12:449-456 (New Haven, 1854).

[15]"Immigration; Its Evils and Their Remedies" in *The New Englander,* 13:262-276 (New Haven, 1855).

[16]The gloomy religious and moral prospects of the new settlements predominate in the communications sent to the missionary societies. See, for example, *The Home Missionary and American Pastor's Journal,* 1:10, 29, 48, 88, 167, 168 (New York, 1828-29).

[17]Fredrika Bremer, *The Homes of the New World,* 1:635 (New York, 1853). A missionary who visited the Norwegian settlement in Dane County, Wisconsin, in 1850, reported, "Such gross immorality I never witnessed before—it was offensive to come within the sphere poisoned by their breath." *The Home Missionary,* 23:120 (New York, 1850).

[18]Gunnar J. Malmin, ed., "Bishop Jacob Neumann's Word of Admonition to the Peasants," in Norwegian-American Historical Association, *Studies and Records,* 1:95-109 (Minneapolis, 1926).

[19]The attitude of the Prussian government is indicated in a memoir by the minister for internal affairs, dated February 17, 1845, in the Prussian archives at Berlin-Dahlem, under the classification AA III R 1, Auswanderung aus Europa, 11, vol. 1, no. 1458.

[20]This tendency is illustrated in the career of the Reverend T. N. Hasselquist, one of the founders of the Swedish Augustana Synod. His pietistic leanings were evident at the beginning of his ministry in Sweden. O. F. Ander, *T. N. Hasselquist: the Career and Influence of a Swedish-American Clergyman, Journalist and Educator,* 7 (Rock Island, Illinois, 1931).

[21]H. R. Niebuhr, *The Social Sources of Denominationalism,* 200-235 (New York, 1929). Chapter 8 is entitled "The Churches of the Immigrants."

[22]*Emigranten* (Madison, Wisconsin), January 20, 1858.

[23]J. W. C. Dietrichson, *Reise blandt de norske emigranter i de forenede nord-amerikanske fristater,* 38, 70 (Stavanger, 1846).

[24]See the letter of Reverend T. N. Hasselquist to the Home Missionary Society dated Galesburg, Illinois, February 3, 1854. Gunnar Westin, ed., *Emigranterne och kyrkan,* 70-73 (Stockholm, 1932).

[25]Indications of the strictness of the code may be found in G. M. Stephenson, *The Religious Aspects of Swedish Immigration,* 174, 199, 267 (Minneapolis, 1932). Knut Hamsun was surprised to note that the ministers, instead of discussing theology, preached "Boston morals." Knut Hamsun, *Fra det moderne Amerikas aandsliv,* 210 (Copenhagen, 1889).

[26]"Prohibitory Legislation: Its Cause and Effect" in *The Catholic World,* 27:182-204 (New York, 1879).

[27]John Ireland, "The Catholic Church and the Saloon," in *North American Review,* 159:498-505 (New York, 1894).

[28]John Ireland, *The Church and Modern Society,* 287 (New York, 1897).

[29]Edward Channing, *History of the United States,* 1:530, 535, 536 (New York, 1917).

[30]Conway Robinson, "Notes from the Council and General Court Records," in *The Virginia Magazine of History and Biography,* 8:166 (October, 1900).

[31]Leonard S. Blakey, *The Sale of Liquor in the South* (New York, 1912). How the presence of Negroes and "poor whites" fostered the growth of prohibition sentiment is explained in an article by John E. White, "Prohibition: The New Task and Opportunity of the South," in *The South Atlantic Quarterly,* 7:130-142 (Durham, North Carolina, 1908).

[32]E. H. Cherrington, *The Anti-Saloon League Year Book,* 1909, p. 179-180 (Chicago).

22

Lay Initiative in the Religious Life of American Immigrants, 1880-1950

Timothy L. Smith

Historians of American religion have frequently focused on American religious groups and their leaders, often failing to give attention to the role of lay people. In this essay, Timothy L. Smith examines the many churches established by eastern European immigrants of the late nineteenth century and explores how Old World traditions were adapted to the American situation by the immigrants themselves. Professor Smith is a member of the Department of History at The Johns Hopkins University.

Growing scholarly appreciation of the ways in which the beliefs and practices of Protestants of English backgrounds have reinforced certain democratic tendencies in American society[1] has recently begun to inform reexaminations of the religious history of Catholic, Protestant, and Jewish immigrants whose first large contingents arrived in this country during the middle decades of the nineteenth century.[2] It has as yet awakened little curiosity, however, as to whether commitments to freedom of belief and association, to equality of opportunity, and to the right of individuals to participate in decisions which affect their lives also stemmed from the faith and worship of the groups once called "new immigrants," whose large-scale migration from Central and Southern Europe began about 1880. These in-

Timothy L. Smith's "Lay Initiative in the Religious Life of American Immigrants, 1880-1950" in *Anonymous Americans: Explorations in Nineteenth-Century Social History,* edited by Tamara K. Hareven, © 1971, pp. 214-249. Reprinted by permission of Prentice-Hall, Inc., Englewood Cliffs, New Jersey.

clude Slavs, Magyars, and Romanians of Roman Catholic, Byzantine Catholic, Eastern Orthodox, or Protestant persuasions; Jews from Romania and from the Russian and Austro-Hungarian empires; Lutherans from what are now Finland, Slovakia, or Transylvania; Italian and Portuguese Roman Catholics; Greeks and Albanians of Byzantine Catholic or Eastern Orthodox faith; and Christian or Moslem Syrians, Turks, Lebanese, and Armenians.

Historical and sociological interpretations of the role of religion among these latter groups continue to perpetuate the prejudices with which the established Protestant, Catholic, and Jewish leadership greeted the arrival of their first representatives.[3] The older Americans assumed, as does Professor Robert Cross in his introduction to *The Church and the City,* that the faith of the newcomers stemmed from blind adherence to village or ethnic traditions which were irrelevant in a commercial or industrial society. They believed that Old World Bishops and the rabbis and pastors who accompanied the displaced villagers to America used superstition and fear to persuade them to continue their support of institutions and beliefs whose chief function was to perpetuate clerical power. And they considered the alliances, synods, or dioceses which eventually united the congregations of each group in the New World to be sectarian anachronisms which met neither the emotional, intellectual, nor social needs of their membership. To convince the newcomers that they should reject these old traditions seemed to many of their confessional kinsmen among the older American population, whether they were Catholics, Protestants or Jews, an act of religious charity.[4]

A survey of the contemporary evidence available to one who reads only English, French, and German, coupled with several brief forays in company with translators in regional and town archives and village church records in Eastern Slovakia, Transylvania, and Slovenia, has pressed upon me a diametrically opposite framework of interpretation. Village religion in Central and Southern Europe on the eve of the mass migrations to America was by no means a bastion of social or ecclesiastical privilege. On the contrary, laymen often played key roles in both local and regional religious affairs and expected priests, bishops, and rabbis to support lay social and political interests. Moreover, the earliest religious organizations that immigrants from these areas formed in America greatly enlarged the scope and significance of lay responsibility and initiative, making their congregations appear in retrospect as "democratic" as those of the Methodist, Presbyterian, or Hebrew Reformed faith. Finally, the national ethnoreligious organizations which eventually emerged to bind together each group's congregations were at least as responsive to popular will as were the governments of their Protestant denominational counterparts. "New" immigrant and Protestant sects differed chiefly in the degree to which transatlantic confessional or ethnic ties broadened the horizon of the former.

Associated with this interpretation is a general hypothesis about urbanization which this essay does not attempt to demonstrate so much as, by illustration, to suggest. The social and cultural changes which occurred among immigrant groups in America seem to have been more a consequence of their urbanization than the result of conflicts with the "host" culture. The myopic concept of "Americanization" distorts an understanding of what really happened. The most bitter conflicts arose among rival groups of the same nationality. The social role of religion among them resembles to a marked degree its role in the lives of native Americans, both white and black, who were moving to some of the same cities at the same time. And it also resembles what I have been able to learn about the role of religious beliefs and institutions among their fellow European villagers who chose to settle in cities of the Old World instead of the New. Moreover, the changes of religious attitude and of institutional structure which urbanization involved began some time before the migrants left their fathers' hearthsides. For that as well as other reasons, the extensive adjustments they made in their new homes seemed to participants to have grown naturally out of their past experiences, rather than to have been imposed upon them by the host society.

VILLAGE RELIGION ON
THE EVE OF MIGRATION

The belief that monolithic state churches dominated both religion and culture in the Old World has distorted understanding by American scholars of the situation in Central and Southeastern Europe, particularly in agricultural villages, from where most emigrants to the United States departed. Even when a region knew only one faith and nationality, as in Roman Catholic Sicily or Slovenia, Orthodox Greece or Lutheran Finland, parishes rooted in peasant societies often reflected the needs and aspirations of the villagers as much as the traditions or prerogatives dear to their ecclesiastical overlords.[5] Such a situation was even more likely when ethnic and religious diversity prevailed, as was the case in the areas from which the overwhelming majority of the immigrants from the Austro-Hungarian Empire came to North America. These included what is now Southeastern Poland and the adjoining portions of the Ukraine, which before World War II comprised the Austrian provinces of Galicia and The Bukovina; The Subcarpathian Ukraine and Eastern Slovakia, which in the same period were the northeastern counties of the Old Kingdom of Hungary; Transylvania, Vojvodina, the Banat, and the Croatian borderland with Bosnia, now in Romania and Yugoslavia, but then also part of the Old Kingdom; and the Dalmatian coast, which was then under Austrian administration. Previous migrations into these regions which had given them their multiethnic character produced intense political and economic rivalries which found expression in the life of religious congregations. The Magyarization policies which the Kingdom of Hungary put in operation after 1867 compounded these rivalries. Thereafter, lay people of many faiths identified their religious with their ethnic commitments, and the varied economic and political strategies which these inspired. Priests, bishops, or rabbis who would not support those commitments risked alienating many of their followers.[6]

In the Austrian province of Galicia, for example, Rusin Catholics of the Byzantine Rite, ancestors to the great majority of Americans now called Ukrainians, shared with Jews of several traditions and with lesser numbers of Poles, Russians, and German Lutherans the cultural borderland between Roman Catholic Poland and Orthodox Russia. During the latter half of the nineteenth century, while Poland was partitioned among Russia, Germany, and Austria, an ethnic awakening took place among the Rusins in this province. Priests and lay leaders, a growing number of whom called themselves Ukrainians, promoted educational and cultural activities and popularized the new phonetic spelling of their language, in order both to counter the political power of Poles in Galicia and to help Rusins beyond the border eastward resist the efforts of the Orthodox Church of Russia to swallow up the Byzantine Rite.[7] They also established mutual benefit and savings and loan societies so as to lessen their dependence upon Jewish merchants and moneylenders for capital with which to buy land. These societies soon were active in financing short trips to industrial Silesia or longer ones to the United States through which peasants' sons hoped to earn such capital.[8] Galician Jewish congregations had for generations maintained similar associations for mutual aid in cultural and economic matters.[9] Polish Roman Catholics who had remained or planted themselves in areas largely Rusin followed similar strategies, learning rapidly (as did the Poles settled among Germans in Pomerania or Silesia) to sustain by voluntary action parochial schools, cultural associations, and mutual benefit societies. Priests and rabbis were always mainstays of these congregational efforts at mutual aid.[10]

Farther east, in The Bukovina, a more nearly balanced population of Orthodox Romanians, Greek Catholic and Orthodox Rusins, Lutheran Germans, and Jews enjoyed a remarkably even-handed support from their Austrian rulers, as did the relatively much smaller groups of Poles and Magyars. Congregational action in behalf of lay interests was a principal characteristic of Bukovinian life, as it continued to be in Western Canada, where so many migrants from that region settled. . . . [11]

The great majority of America's "Hungarian Jews" are descended from the Magyarized Jews whose ancestors had, during the previous centuries, crowded into these same northern counties of the Old Kingdom. The forebears of some of these had come from Germany with the merchants whom Maria Theresa settled in her eastern lands. Far more of them, however, were offspring of migrants from Galicia who spoke either Yiddish or Ashkenazi Hebrew. Their ancestors had moved southward across the mountains by the hundreds in the seventeenth and eighteenth centuries, and by thousands in the nineteenth. In Mukačevo, one of the largest and wealthiest towns of the region, Jewish culture, ranging in variety from the Chassidic to the fully assimilationist Neolog sect, was by the midnineteenth century so predominant that the city was called the "Jewish Rome."[12]

Although most Jews of the sub-Carpathian region were strictly Orthodox, they developed the practice of cultural pluralism into an ethnic art. By 1900, for example, at the ancient Lutheran academy John Amos

Comenius had founded in Prešov, the 19 Jewish boys from that town and the 18 others from the surrounding region outnumbered by almost two to one the Slovak Protestants enrolled in the first-year class.[13] In other towns, such as Humenné, Jewish congregations founded for boys and girls both academic and business schools which gentile students often attended. They organized welfare and work relief societies for their own people, and joined interfaith ladies' clubs and cultural associations.[14] Long accustomed to using the German language as a means of advancement in the educational and professional as well as the economic affairs of the Hapsburg realm, rabbis and leading Jewish laymen even in isolated villages accepted Magyar speech and identity after 1867, in return for the favor of government officials, for tavern and brewery licenses, or for educational or professional advantage. As happened later in America, religious loyalty, relatively uncomplicated by linguistic and national aspirations, served to maintain the identity and to promote through educational and economic cooperation the group interests of Hungarian Jews. . . .[15]

Hungarian law recognized the right of each village congregation to maintain an elementary school, though public officials steadily increased their efforts to enforce and expand the scope of the statutes requiring instruction in Magyar language and history. All the religious hierarchies were, moreover, firmly pro-Magyar. The assimilationist pressures emanating from the great Reformed center at Debrecen, from the Lutheran National Synod in Budapest, and from the Roman Catholic Archbishops of Estergom made loyalty to a minority ethnic tradition a congregational rather than a confessional matter, just as happened later in America. Among the minority congregations of all faiths, except possibly the Greek Catholic, lay associations operating both on a local and a regional basis helped to maintain church buildings and support schools, engendered pride in language and culture, and attempted to maintain and extend members' land holdings in the villages or their economic opportunities in cities.[16] German and Slovak Lutherans enjoyed a somewhat stronger tradition of lay prerogative than other Christian groups. The electing of teachers, the maintenance of regional teachers associations, the appointment for each district of a lay "director" to advise the clerical "senior," and participation by members of a congregation in the formulation of the evaluations bishops made on their occasional visitations were all ritualized expressions of Lutheran doctrine of the priesthood of believers.[17]

The processes of urbanization, though slower in this region than elsewhere in Europe, made each large town a mosaic of ethno-religious groupings. In ancient Bardejov, nestled beneath the Carpathians, Slovak Roman Catholics worshiped in the fourteenth century cathedral recovered from the Protestants during the Catholic Reformation, while Germans and Magyars met together in another church nearby. A large Lutheran population, one part German and Magyar and one part Slovak, maintained two congregations; two or three synagogues served various sects of Jews; Rusins worshiped in a relatively new Byzantine Rite Catholic church; and at least one congregation of Slovak Catholics worshiped in their own church rather than in the cathedral.[18] Prešov's population and church organizations displayed an almost identical variety, its distance from Rusin villages being compensated for by the fact that a Byzantine Rite bishop was seated there, and a seminary for the training of priests stood across the street from his cathedral.[19] Košice, farther south, boasted fine buildings for the same Slovak, German, Rusin, and Jewish contingents, as well as others for the Slovak Reformed, Hungarian Reformed, and Hungarian Roman Catholic groups. Most of these congregations maintained a school. All, save possibly the Greek Catholic Rusins, sponsored cultural and mutual benefit societies of some sort.[20] Both in the complexity and intensity of their religious pluralism, then, Prešov and Košice were in 1910 like South Pittsburgh and East Cleveland: cultural artifacts of the Kingdom of Hungary's ethnic diversity.

So also were the villages and towns of the Banat and the Batchka, from whence many Romanians and some Croats, Serbs, Slovaks, and Catholic Germans emigrated to America. A variegated pattern of ethnic and religious settlement developed there from the eighteenth century onward, as agriculturalists of many nationalities crowded into the rich region to reclaim lands from the Danube swamps. As in Eastern Slovakia, villages of two to five thousand souls often had Protestant, Roman Catholic, Orthodox, and Byzantine Rite Catholic congregations, and occasionally a tiny synagogue of Jews as well. Each congregation was the center of educational and cultural activities aimed to help its laymen seize and hold as large a share as possible of economic and political power. The religious edifices in larger towns, such as Zrenjenen, display to this day a variety similar to what one finds in American industrial cities like Scranton or Passaic. Yet the congregations date back in many cases 200 years or more.[21] In Croatia-Slavonia, and especially along the old military border South of Zagreb from where so many American Serbs and Croats emigrated, the majority population was Catholic and Croatian, and the only substantial minority were the Orthodox Serbs. The language of the two ethnic groups was the same, but their identities and, therefore, their rivalries, whether for land, political power, or cultural achievement, were defined by their religious differences. . . .[22]

Two institutional arrangements, one confessional and the other congregational, helped preserve religious order in the multinational Austro-Hungarian Empire. Each gave laymen of the several faiths important preparation for their future in America. In the early seventeenth century, Lutheran and Reformed Protestants had secured from their Catholic rulers statutes of autonomy which provided for representative government of their religious institutions. Each parish elected a council of elders, to which the pastor and the teacher belonged. These units in turn chose representatives to the first level of a hierarchy of confessional assemblies, at the head of which stood the Reformed "General Conventus" and the Lutheran "National Synod." The monarch's confirmation of the decisions of the annual meetings of these two latter organizations was necessary, but he could not alter them. Somewhat later, the Serbian and the Romanian archbishops were able to secure comparable statutes of autonomy which provided for lay representation in governing bodies at each level of Orthodox church administration. In these cases, however, the crown enjoyed the right to prorogue, dissolve, or veto the calling of a national congress. Jews eventually established similar unifying institutions, but their national organization was not officially recognized in the Kingdom of Hungary until 1896, their chief Rabbi meanwhile sitting in the House of Magnates not by right but as a nominee of the crown.[23]

The second arrangement was the system of parish organization illustrated in the Obysovce case [in which different groups maintained separate parishes and schools]. It prevailed among Protestant, Roman Catholic, Byzantine Rite, Eastern Orthodox, and Jewish groups, in all the multiethnic village societies. Since the members were scattered and always poor, rarely could those of the same faith in a single village support a pastor or rabbi. Instead, a parish or congregation usually comprised a parent organization with its filial congregations in villages from a mile to ten or more miles distant and scattered groups in other villages which were too small to justify a chapel or synagogue of their own. One pastor or rabbi served the entire congregation. The people usually maintained only one parochial school, located in the village where their numbers were largest, electing their schoolmaster and paying many expenses by voluntary subscription. A leading layman in each village watched over the property of this segment of the congregation. He forwarded news of need or tragedy to the pastor, priest, or rabbi, led in the observance of sacred days and, in general, symbolized the unity of the faithful who lived in out-of-the-way places. On the most important holy days, members of a congregation often assembled from their several villages at the central house of worship, renewing by rituals both sacred and secular the ties which bound them to one another and to their spiritual leaders.[24]

FOUNDING CONGREGATIONS
IN THE NEW WORLD

Little wonder that when laymen of these various backgrounds reached America, they did not wait for the arrival of a pastor or a rabbi to organize a religious congregation, but undertook the task themselves. Social and psychological need as well as the shortage of clergymen—severe in all cases but that of the Slovenes—prompted them to build upon and extend those aspects of their traditions which emphasized lay leadership. Those from multiethnic regions, accustomed to a large degree of initiative, seem to have set the pace. Laymen of all groups, however, retained long after the shortage of pastors ended many of the enlarged prerogatives they had assumed in their earliest years in the New World.

The shortage of clergymen stemmed in part from the voluntary and economic nature of the decision to emigrate and in part from the dispersion and constant movement of laborers among small mining and industrial towns in America. The first local groups to organize in such places as Scranton or Toledo were at the outset too poor to support a minister. The canonical tangle afflicting Eastern Orthodox and Byzantine Catholic administrations in America deterred Romanian, Rusin, and Serbian priests from answering such calls as were made, just as suspicions of Irish and German bishops caused Roman Catholic priests from Sicily, Dalmatia, and Poland to hesitate. Young Lutheran clergymen in Finland and Slovakia and graduates of the Hungarian Reformed seminary in Debrecen realized that, in American pastorates, they would be much more dependent upon the voluntary support of lay people. They often sought ironclad guarantees of salary and housing which the tiny New World congregations were unable to give.[25]

Thus Rusins from south of the Carpathians who began settling in Minneapolis in the early 1880's worshiped first in the Polish Roman Catholic parish, but soon began meeting separately, reciting from memory the rituals of the Byzantine Rite. A parish committee made plans for a church building and requested their Bishop in Prešov to send them a pastor. Father Alex Toth arrived in due time, only to find that Roman Catholic Archbishop John Ireland was unwilling to permit a married priest to administer the sacraments in his diocese. Shortly thereafter, two laymen returned from a trip to San Francisco, where they had chanced upon the Russian Orthodox cathedral and received from the archbishop who resided there an offer to accept their congregation under his care and to provide a regular subsidy for the support of a pastor. Father Toth and the entire Minneapolis congregation thereupon decided to forsake the ancient union which had tied their European parishes to Rome and became the first permanent Russian Orthodox organization east of the Rocky Mountains.[26] Father Toth soon left Minneapolis to seek the conversion to Orthodoxy of Byzantine Catholic Rusins who had settled in the anthracite towns around Scranton, Pennsylvania. The Minneapolis congregation continued to flourish, despite the strange ways of their Great Russian pastors. Its parish committee constructed a fine building, modeling it upon pictures of a provincial church in Russia, which was quite unlike anything in their own homeland. They operated a parochial school after public school hours weekdays and on Saturdays, and in 1907 the first Orthodox theological seminary in the United States began classes in the parish hall.[27]

Meanwhile, single men and a few families of Slovak or Hungarian Protestant persuasion, some Lutherans and others Reformed, followed one another from villages in the northern counties of Hungary to such industrial or mining communities as Raritan and Passaic, New Jersey, Mount Carmel and Braddock, Pennsylvania, and Streator, Illinois, as well as to the cities of Cleveland, Minneapolis, Pittsburgh, and Chicago. Long accustomed to relying upon religious associations to sustain social and cultural goals, they moved at once to organize congregations and mutual benefit insurance societies, even though many of their members planned to return home after a few years. A diverse company established at Pittsbugh in 1890 a congregation which bore the ecumenical name, "First Hungarian and Slovak Evangelical and Reformed Church of St. Paul." Heirs of the two national and two confessional traditions worshiped together successfully for almost a year in the Grand Avenue Lutheran Church, Pittsburgh, in services led by a Hungarian layman, Gustav Hamborszky. Each group maintained a separate "religious society" for mutual aid, however, and language and perhaps other differences soon forced the congregation itself to divide. The Lutheran Slovaks built a house of worship on Braddock Street and the Reformed Hungarians erected another on Bates Street.[28]. . .

Among Orthodox Romanians from Transylvania, the first bonds of friendship and association in the New World likewise stemmed from their common origins. The pioneer group in each American town or city usually came from two or three clusters of homeland villages. Newcomers in succeeding years often went directly to the homes of men they had known or were related to in their own or neighboring villages in Transylvania, the Banat, or the Bukovina. Those in Chicago early formed the habit of singing chants and responses together on Sunday, gathering for this purpose at the saloon which was their social center on weekdays. They soon realized that among them they were able to reconstruct from memory most of the Orthodox service. So without waiting for liturgical books to arrive from Romania they began in a room at the back of the tavern the rituals of worship which they shared, without benefit of clergy until sometime after 1908, when the Orthodox Bishop of Sibiu sent them a priest. Meanwhile, they had organized, as had other Orthodox Romanians in Cleveland and Indiana Harbor, Michigan, a mutual benefit insurance society which paved the way in both sentiment and practice for the formation of a religious congregation. The Cleveland society sponsored the formal organization of St. Mary's parish there in 1904, two years before the first priest arrived. The homeland custom of a single priest ministering to a central church and its daughter congregations in nearby places was easily transferred to the New World. Here, however, each one of the clustered congregations was independently organized and its parish society incorporated, so as to enable it to purchase property, erect a building, and establish a parish school.[29]. . .

During the same decades, Hungarian, Czech, Italian, Slovenian, Finnish, Polish, and Greek laymen who had recently arrived from lands which knew only one faith and nationality established mutual benefit societies and congregations in a similar pattern.[30]. . .

Brief reflection upon these patterns of congregation-founding will suggest the tenuousness of the argument that Jews from Central and Eastern Europe were more sophisticated in the use of formal organization or, by reason of the persecution they had suffered, more alert to the advantages of communal solidarity than other immigrants. The hundreds of storefront synagogues which Romanian, Galician, and Hungarian Jews founded in America, and the mutual aid societies which sustained both their congregations and their schools, seem in retrospect to reflect a lay initiative which was both in motive and form closely comparable to that which prevailed among Magyars, Italians, and Slavs. The initiative stemmed from a similar reaction to the prejudice which the older German Jewish community showed toward the newcomers from Central Europe.[31]

When Magyarized Jews from Hungary arrived in Cleveland during the Civil War, they established a "Hungarian Aid Society," and in October 1866 formed the Orthodox "Hungarian Congregation Bene Jeshurun," disdaining the Bohemian and the German synagogues already in existence. Chief among the founders of the new congregation was Herman Sampliner, presumably a native of Zemplin County in Northeastern Hungary. The group first met in his home, renting a large hall for high holidays, then moved to a succession of storefronts and halls. When, at the dedication of a new temple purchased in 1887 from another Jewish congregation, sermons by visiting Reformed rabbis, including Dr. A. Friedman of Cleveland and Isaac M. Wise from Cincinnati, urged the "Hungarians" to lay aside outmoded traditions, the pastor spoke out firmly in opposition, and the congregation continued in its Orthodox way. The story was repeated hundreds of times in cities large and small.[32]

Moreover, the notion that the establishment of immigrant congregations depended upon the action of ecclesiastical leaders either in America or the home countries contradicts not only the evidence of their founding but that of their financing as well. Laymen employed attorneys to help them incorporate congregational organizations under state laws, and in most cases raised every dollar used to purchase lots and build churches, synagogues, and rectories. Peter Roberts reported in 1903 that of the 143 Catholic parishes which worshiped in their own buildings in the anthracite towns, almost half were either Polish, Rusin, Slovak, Lithuanian, or Italian. Their members had paid for their buildings amost entirely by voluntary contributions, while securing and supporting pastors of their own nationality.[33] A few years later, Roberts noted that Poles, Lithuanians, Croats, and Serbs living in Pittsburgh's south side had accumulated, after only 20 years of residence there, church property valued at three-quarters of a million dollars, most of it paid for. The priests kept in close touch with newcomers, taking a census each year, and assisted laymen in promoting mutual benefit societies and building and loan associations. Though women were yet few in their communities, Slavic men often went to confession at six in the morning so as to be ready for mass on the following day. "I have seen in Pittsburgh a congregation of 1,000 men, all in the prime of life," Robert wrote, "so intent upon the religious exercises that the least movement of the priest at the altar found immediate response in every member of the audience."[34]

THE EMERGENCE OF
NATIONAL RELIGIOUS ORGANIZATIONS

These manifold lay initiatives in local religious association led very early to the establishment under predominantly lay auspices of denominational and quasi-denominational organizations which sustained and united the scattered units of each group. The idea of congregational independence never took root among the "new immigrants." Instead, almost from the moment of the formation of their congregations, lay leaders of mutual benefit societies pressed upon the flocks and their newly arrived pastors the necessity of forming national alliances which, whether uniting congregations or lodges, aimed to bring together all immigrants of the same ethnic and confessional commitments in one American organization. Contributing to this outcome was the great mobility of pastors and of laymen during the early years of settlement. The rapid development of newspapers, almanacs, and other means of communication, including intercity travel among widely separated settlements, also played a part, as did the tradition that a religious congregation must depend upon an authority higher and broader than its own to legitimize and sustain its existence.

The governments of these national organizations depended far more upon lay participation and leadership than the synods and dioceses of the Old World. They were more responsive to popular impulses, in my judgment, than were the governments of mainstream Protestant communions, and their responsibilities were the same: to promote the founding of new congregations and to sustain struggling ones; to keep each local unit abreast of matters of interest to all; to publish newspapers and yearbooks, as well as special magazines for women and children; to provide materials for the education of the young in both religious and secular aspects of their parents' way of life; and to recruit and assign pastors to the congregations which needed them. They often carried out these functions in a manner opposed to the traditions of ecclesiastical government which had prevailed among the parent communions in the Old World.

Immigrant Protestant sects such as the Slovak Evangelical Lutheran Church revealed explicitly the extensions of lay prerogative which were implicit in the organizations which emerged to serve Catholic and Orthodox minorities. The eight or more Slovak Lutheran mutual benefit societies which had helped establish congregations in various cities and towns between 1890 and 1893 coalesced in the latter year in a lay organization called "The Slovak Evangelical Church and Sick Benefit Union of the Augsburg Confession." One of the local units, the Holy Trinity Society organized at Cleveland in 1892, included in one body a congregation and an insurance brotherhood, as did another organized at Raritan, New Jersey, two years later. Members of local brotherhoods which adhered to the Union soon withdrew from the nonsectarian National Slovak Society. By that action they opted for a specifically Lutheran basis of their Slovak identity in the New World, just as Stefan Furdek's followers had chosen a Catholic definition of their identity two years earlier. The few Slovak Lutheran pastors in the country in the 1890's were active members of the Union, but lay leaders long held the initiative in both church and fraternal affairs. The pastoral "seniorate" formed in 1893 reported its business to the annual meeting of the Union. The seniorate died of neglect, partly from differences among the pastors as to whether their congregations should be associated with the Evangelical Lutheran Synod of Missouri. The lay officers of the Union thereupon invited all pastors to attend the convention of 1899 at its expense, and persuaded them to form a "pastoral conference." Under its constitution, the Union's officers were to approve plans for the division of the field in which each pastor was to work, as well as to oversee the adjudication of misunderstandings among pastors and of complaints against those charged with behavior unbecoming a minister.[35]

With continuous prodding from the laymen in charge of the Union, the "Slovak Evangelical Church of the Augsburg Confession" finally came into being in September 1902 at a joint meeting of pastors and lay delegates in Connellsville, Pennsylvania. The synod thereafter decided upon a wide range of questions brought to its attention from congregations, many of them dealing with clarification of the rights and duties of pastors and people. The lay office of "church inspector" was widely introduced, according to the custom then prevailing in Slovakia. The Union meanwhile increased its annual contributions to the support of Slovak Lutheran students of theology, shared the expenses and often the editorship of the synod's publications, and continued for some years to discuss church affairs at its annual meetings as though they were its primary business. Eventually, however, a separation of responsibilities emerged, the professed reasons being the synod's opposition to dancing and other forms of "worldliness" in lodge activities, the insistence of the pastors upon doctrinal and confessional purity, and their sharp opposition to a fraternal ritual containing "non-Christian" funeral prayers. But the pattern of lay prerogative in both church and society was fully established in these early years.[36]

Perhaps the largest of the Protestant movements emanating from Central Europe is the Hungarian Reformed. Its earliest congregations in America united first in what was called a "classis" of the Reformed Church in the United States. Many of the congregations organized later affiliated with the Presbyterian Church, U.S.A. Most also maintained close ties with the Reformed Conventus in Budapest, however, receiving visitations from Magyar church officials, securing their pastors from the theological seminary in Debrecen, and following in their American publications detailed accounts of religious developments in Hungary. In 1904 the lay president of the Conventus visited the American settlements and provoked a crisis among them, resulting in the creation of three separate denominational or quasi-denominational structures. One group associated closely with the Reformed Church in the United States, another with the Presbyterian Church, U.S.A., and a third adhered officially to the Old World communion. In all three, lay leaders and clergymen who were responsive to lay initiatives seem to have exercised a controlling influence. After World War II, the Reformed Church in the United States received into its ranks most of the congregations which had been up to then subject to the Conventus in Budapest, and an independent Free Magyar Reformed Church came into existence to provide a home for the rest.[37] . . .

The lay-directed national fraternal societies which provided Roman Catholic ethnic minorities a measure of religious autonomy indicate with equal clarity the relationship between migration and voluntarism. Such organizations as the Polish Roman Catholic Union, the Croatian Catholic Union, the First Catholic Slovak Union, the Grand Carniolian (Slovenian) Catholic Union, and the first Greek Catholic Union competed directly with non-sectarian, secular, or socialist societies which appealed for membership on a purely ethnic or political basis. These Catholic societies, like the Protestants, Eastern Orthodox, and Jewish ones which I treat in this essay, defined their purposes in specifically religious terms, restricted their membership to practicing communicants, and spent a substantial portion of their money and energies in promoting their faith. Their activities included founding and supporting congregations, recruiting pastors from the Old World and arranging their appointments in the New, publishing Sunday School and other religious periodicals, sponsoring parochial schools, and defending the ethnic version of their faith from attacks within as well as from outside their nationality. The national officers of some of them performed for many years all but the specifically spiritual functions of a bishop, securing when possible canonical approval and support for their actions, and when that was not possible, managing by some means to give the congregations the help they needed. The little-known history of these societies dramatizes the diversity of real power which has long flourished beneath the externally monolithic structure of authority in American Catholicism.

Even when clergymen were the principal founders of such organizations, as was true for Catholic Slovaks and Slovenes, laymen were soon in effective control. The Slovenian congregation in Joliet referred to above was host in 1893 to a meeting of delegates from lay brotherhoods which priests had helped form in the multiethnic mining town parishes of northern Michigan and Minnesota and in Chicago and Cleveland. The Joliet pastor, F. S. Šušteršič, accepted the first presidency of the national body. The leader of a group of immigrant seminarians at St. Paul Theological Seminary, Mat Šavs, was elected secretary. However, laymen soon replaced clergymen in all the national offices, as well as in the editorship of the weekly newspaper which Father Joseph Buh edited at Tower, Minnesota, from 1891 until 1899. Only the office of "Spiritual Advisor" remained an important priestly function. The clergyman who held it sat on the "Supreme Board" and hence shared in all decision-making, but he rarely exercised anything like a controlling influence.[38]

The proliferation of an elaborate array of officials with high sounding titles gave to the national boards of such brotherhoods a ritualistic appearance which belied the pragmatic functions the officers served. All were subject to annual reelection by representatively constituted national conventions. The "supreme presidents" and "supreme secretaries" were salaried professionals, charged with promoting not only cultural and religious goals but also the enrollment of members in the mutual benefit insurance program. The treasurers soon became responsible for the administration of very large sums of money held in reserve against future insurance claims. Every society published a newspaper circulated automatically to each member. The editors, also elected annually at the national conventions, filled their columns with news of the home country and of lodges in America, as well as with accounts of the deeds of immigrant pastors and laymen and of the work of lay or religious organizations in establishing parish schools. A Slav or Magyar reader of such a newspaper saw Catholicism or Orthodoxy from the perspective of his own ethnic interests, and America as a land where he should combine traditional ways of acting and thinking with newly-acquired ones. To a Slovenian Catholic immigrant, the most important churchman was neither his local bishop nor an archbishop or cardinal of the American church, but the monsignor of his own nationality who was spiritual advisor to his fraternal order, usually the pastor of either St. Vitus parish, Cleveland, or St. Joseph's in Joliet.[39]. . .

American Roman Catholics of Polish, Lithuanian, Croatian, and Hungarian backgrounds fashioned similar national societies, drawing in many cases upon the example set earlier by Czech and German Catholics. The histories of two unusual "denominations," the Polish National Catholic Church and the First Greek Catholic Union, seem in the light of the foregoing examples unique only in the extent to which they made explicit the meaning of their religious experimentation.

Within two years of the founding of the independent St. Stanislas Polish Catholic Church in Scranton, Father Hodur answered appeals from lay groups at nearby Dickson City, Duryea, Wilkes-Barre, and Nanticoke, Pennsylvania, to help them form parish committees and establish sister congregations. He also received into his fellowship a congregation organized at Baltimore, Maryland, in 1898, and two others located at Fall River and Lowell, Massachusetts. In December 1900, Hodur announced that he would celebrate the Christmas Mass at Scranton in the Polish language. Latin thereafter disappeared from Polish National Catholic worship. The first meeting of a formal synod took place in 1904. Sixteen priests and 130 lay delegates from the parishes and ethnic societies supporting the National Church movement gathered at Scranton that year, chose Hodur their bishop, and voted to establish a theological seminary to train young men for the priesthood, all amidst scenes, as a *Scranton Times* reporter put it, in which "people embraced one another, kissed one another, shouted, the church bells pealed," and "the throngs gathered on the street around the Convention Hall" were "carried away with . . . sincere feelings of joy."[40] Soon after Hodur organized the Polish National Union, a fraternal insurance society. It brought lay communicants together in local lodge meetings and in regional and national conventions, and nurtured through its newspaper and other publications, through its evening school in Scranton and through its advocacy of social justice for workers the community of religious conviction which the new denomination required.[41]

Equally illuminating is the story of the "Greek Catholic Union of Rusin Brotherhoods," as it was first called, organized at Wilkes-Barre, Pennsylvania, in February 1892. The founding convention, attended by six priests and lay representatives from 14 local mutual benefit societies scattered from Bridgeport, Connecticut, to Streator, Illinois, declared that the aim of the Greek Catholic Union was to spread love and friendship among the Rusin people in America, to provide insurance against death and accidents, to educate the people in "national and religious requirements," and "to aid churches and schools." The founders began issuing a weekly newspaper and adopted a constitution which provided equal lay and clerical

membership on a supervisory commission. The early years of the organiza-
tion were wracked by controversy, rooted in the fact that Rusins from
Galicia resisted identification with those from sub-Carpathian Hungary.
The Galicians founded a competing national organization open to persons
who were not practicing Greek Catholics, which eventually became the
Ukrainian National Union.[42] Meanwhile, local groups of Rusins from both
sides of the Carpathians followed Father Alexander Toth into the Russian
Orthodox fold. They soon formed two competing national unions of Rus-
sian Orthodox brotherhoods, both of which maintained units in some
Orthodox congregations.[43]

In the years which followed, the Greek Catholic Union became in all
but formalities a separate denomination. Although the membership
remained overwhelmingly Rusin, it welcomed to its rolls lodges associated
with congregations of Slovak or Hungarian Greek Catholics. Until 1906 the
officers of the Union performed all of the functions of a bishop: recruitment
of pastors from the Old World and their assignment in the New; adjudication of controversies between lay parish organizations and their pastors; encouragement of parochial schools, and provision of literature for them;
sponsorship of affiliate religious societies for women, children, and youth;
and the publication of a weekly newspaper which gave to the Carpatho-
Rusins their understanding of America, of their own Greek Catholic
culture, of affairs in their homeland, and of the Roman Catholic Church of
which they were in form but never in feeling a part. Having misunderstood
the depth of the ethnic division which separated the Ukrainians from the
Carpatho-Rusins, the Roman Curia in 1906 appointed a bishop to serve all
Greek Catholics in the United States. The bishop, Stephen Ortinsky, a
native of Galicia, strove for ten frustrating years to unite the two groups,
but the net result was to increase the insistence of laymen upon the
prerogatives which they perceived as their only sure means of protecting
their congregations and lodges from aggression by the other side.[44]. . .

RELIGIOUS ORGANIZATIONS AND
URBAN SOCIETY: A HYPOTHESIS

Thus did the local and national religious organizations established by
immigrant groups in America after 1880 come to resemble in structure and
function as well as in their intergroup relationship those organizations
which had for many decades served the native Protestant population. In
retrospect, evidence that the newcomers borrowed ideas of lay prerogative
or democratic procedure from the host society is less persuasive than that
which suggests that new social and psychological conditions prompted them
to cultivate and extend traditions of lay participation and initiative which
were rooted in their past experience in Central or Southern Europe. Immigrant pastors and laymen sometimes fought sharp battles with entrenched
leaders of their own faith and, because newcomers were generally economic
underdogs, the lines of conflict often paralleled those which delineated
social privilege. Nevertheless, what the innovators fought for was not a new

religious order tailored to the demands of the disinherited, but freedom to participate on their own terms in the system of denominational pluralism which already prevailed here.

Viewed thus from its religious underside, the social history of immigrant workingmen in America displays a striking unanimity of preference for what scholars persist in labeling the middle class way. That this preference should have prevailed in that area of their lives which was perhaps least subject to legal or other coercions suggests how broad are the foundations of the social consensus of which the nation's religious institutions are but one facet.

The events I have described also raise the question whether the religious aspects of this consensus stem more from general urban than from specifically American conditioning. The role of ethnic congregations and of ethno-religious denominations has become increasingly important in the cities of the homeland from which the newer immigrant groups hailed. Moreover, tendencies toward voluntarism, lay initiative, and denominational pluralism in religion seem to have grown steadily in all urban societies during the last century, not only on both sides of the North Atlantic but on opposite shores of the South Atlantic, the Pacific, and the Indian Oceans as well—wherever urban expansion has rested upon the decision of large numbers of men to move to cities in search of a new start for themselves and their children. To be sure, the early renunciation in America of the state-church tradition, the comparative freedom allowed minority groups to conduct parochial schools, the specific support which state laws gave congregations engaged in battles with bishops or other central authorities, and the extensive second-stage mobility of immigrants during the years after they had settled in the United States all reinforced the principle of religious voluntarism which the first arrivals of each group had found compelling. The contrasts, however, between the pattern of religious organization which prevails today in, for example, Pittsburgh and those prevailing in Budapest, Beirut, Buenos Aires, Durban, Singapore or El Monte, California, do not seem large enough to substantiate the claim that ethno-religious pluralism, denominationalism, voluntarism, or lay prerogative give to the history of religion in America a special mystique. Events in ancient Hellenistic and in modern Oriental and Israeli cities suggest, moreover, that neither modernity nor a predominantly Christian setting is essential to the emergence of such a pattern.

The mobility and diverse origins of their populations require urban societies to be publicly and officially secular. Religion does not lose its force in such an environment merely because its support and structuring rest upon voluntary choice. Communities of faith may by that circumstance acquire enlarged vitality, developing new modes of winning adherents, sustaining new patterns of association which cut across traditional class lines, and showing in both idea and structure more responsiveness to the needs and wishes of their members than either established or dissenting sects in old commonwealths display. True, many elements of traditional structure persist. Romantics on the inside and social critics on the outside often identify these with conservative interpretations of religious doctrine which seem to sanctify the privileges of urban elites. But to conceive religious organizations in cities either as united fronts for the privileged or as arenas of conflict between the elite and the disinherited is to obscure their main purpose.

The centuries-long experience of urban migration required adherents of America's older faiths to make profound changes in the structures, beliefs, and ethical rules which they had inherited. The process began in colonial Boston, New York, and Philadelphia long before the migrants whom this essay describes arrived in search of the freedom and affluence which America promised. What these new citizens demanded in their religious life, once they had determined to stay here, was the right to do what their predecessors of the three major faiths had done—to fashion religious communities suited to their own needs. They conceived those needs in new as well as in traditional terms, with earthly as well as heavenly ends in view. None should be surprised that once the right was granted or gained, the congregational and denominational organizations they founded resembled those which earlier settlers, enjoying similar freedom and like aspirations, had established for themselves.

NOTES

[1] Sidney Mead's title essay for Jerald C. Brauer et al., Reinterpretation in American Church History (Chicago, 1968), 185-192, is a thoughtful restatement of one aspect of this view.

[2] Philip Gleason, The Conservative Reformers: German-American Catholics and the Social Order (Notre Dame, Indiana, 1968), 76-82, 91-102; Robert D. Cross, The Emergence of Liberal Catholicism in America (Cambridge, Mass., 1958); Aaron I. Abell, American Catholicism and Social Action: A Search for Social Justice, 1865-1950 (Garden City, N.Y., 1960).

[3] See, for example, Rudolph J. Vecoli, "Prelates and Peasants: Italian Immigrants and the Catholic Church," Journal of Social History, II (Spring 1969), 228-235, 248-251; Fred L. Strodtbeck, "Family Interaction, Values and Achievement," in David C. McClelland et al., Talent and Society: New Perspectives in the Identification of Talent (Princeton, N.J., 1958), 149-158.

[4] Robert D. Cross (ed.), The Church and the City, 1865-1910 (New York, 1967), xx-xxi, 115; Henry J. Browne, "The 'Italian Problem' in the Catholic Church of the United States, 1880-1900," United States Catholic Historical Records and Studies, XXXV (New York, 1946), 46-72; and Testimony of Mr. Simon Wolf, past vice-president of B'nai B'rith, in U.S. Industrial Commission, Reports . . . Volume 15 . . . (Washington, 1901), 245-249.

[5] Theodore Saloutos, Greeks in the United States (Cambridge, Mass., 1965), 18-19, 97; Donald Treadgold, "The Peasant and Religion," in Wayne S. Vucenich (ed.), The Peasant in Nineteenth Century Russia (Stanford, 1968); Uuras Saarnivaara, The History of the Laestadian or Apostolic-Lutheran Movement in America (Ironwood, Mich., 1947), 13-15, summary of a more detailed work in Finnish published the same year.

⁶Summaries of religious aspects of the history of minority problems in Hungary up to 1918 in Carlile A. Macartney, *Hungary and Her Successors: The Treaty of Trianon and Its Consequences, 1918-1937* (London, 1937), 83-94, 200-212, 262-275, 356-362, 380-390, agree in this point with the pro-minority views in Robert W. Seton-Watson, *Racial Problems in Hungary* (London, 1908), 224-233, 331-351, 440.

⁷Emily Greene Balch, *Our Slavic Fellow-Citizens* (New York, 1911), 121-131, 141; Ivan L. Rudnytsky, "The Role of the Ukraine in Modern History," *The Slavic Review,* XXII (June 1963), 203-215; Dmytro Doroshenko, *History of the Ukraine* (tr. Hanna C. Keller; Edmonton, Alberta, 1939), 585-594; R. Smol-Stotsky, "Centers of Ukrainian Learning," *Slavic (and East European) Review,* II (March 1924), 556-558; and Henry Baerlein, *Over the Hills of Ruthenia* (London, 1923), 9-10, 21-23, 38, 61, 88-89, 98-109, reveal effects of this awakening.

⁸Balch, *Our Slavic Fellow Citizens,* 134-135, 138-140, 144-145.

⁹Mark Zborowski and Elizabeth Herzog, *Life is With People: The Jewish Little-Town of Eastern Europe* (New York, 1955).

¹⁰My student and colleague William Galush has examined at the Jagellonian University Library, Krakow, annual and other publications of *Towo Sakoty Ludowej* [The Society for Popular Education] and *Towo Oswiatowy Ludowej* [The Society for General Education], both of which organizations were based in Krakow and both of which had local units in Eastern Galicia.

¹¹Erich Prokopowitsch, *Die Rumanische Nationalbewegung in der Bukowina und der Dako-Romanismus (Studien zur Geschichte der Österreichisch-Ungarischen Monarchie,* III, Graz, 1965), 35-110. Vladimir Kaye, *Early Ukrainian Settlements in Canada, 1895-1900. Dr. Josef Oeskow's Role in the Settlement of the Canadian Northwest* (Toronto, 1964), deals chiefly with Galicians from Lvov and its environs.

¹²Mousset, *Les Villes de la Russie Subcarpatique,* 21-26, 67-69; Macartney, *Hungary and Her Successors,* 212.

¹³A. Tiszai Ag. Hitv. Ev. Egyházkerület Értesitoje Az 1900-1901. Iskolai Euröl [The Yearbook of the Evangelical College in Prešov, 1900-1901] (Prešov, 1901), 73-74.

¹⁴David Friedmann, *Geschichte der Juden in Humenné vom 13 Jahrhundert bis auf die Gegenwart* (Beregsas, 1933), 48-74.

¹⁵Jahresbericht der Eperieser Isr. Kultusgemeinde und der Eperieser "Chewra Kadischa," 1925 (Prešov, 1925), 6-7, 12, 22-23, reflects an urbanized Jewish community's effort to preserve Hebrew culture in a situation of long-standing pluralism.

¹⁶Fedor Ruppeldt, "The Lutheran Church in Slovakia," in R. W. Seton-Watson (ed.), *Slovakia Then and Now: A Political Survey* (London, 1931), 196-203, 208; A. Hlinka, "The Influence of Religion and Catholicism on States and Individuals," *ibid.,* 168; and M. Emma Hovozdovič, "History and Accomplishments of the Society of St. Adalbert, Trnava, Slovakia," *Slovak Studies,* V (Cleveland, 1965), 207-211, 221-222.

¹⁷See, for the Lutherans, *Almanach cirkvi evangelickej a.v. na slovensku z rokov, 1919-1928* (Sv. Martine, 1930), 200-203, for elementary schools using the German and Slovak languages in Szepes and Saros counties. On Lutheran teachers' associations see Marton Roth, *Lövy Mór: A szepesi tanitoegyesület natvan éves totonete [A Sixty-Year History of the Teachers' Association in Szepes]* (Iglo, 1896), 7-27, describing an association which down to 1868 was exclusively Lutheran. *Evangelische Glocken. Blätter für Kirche, Schue und Haus* (Bratislava, 1889-1900), a biweekly, served the German Lutherans of the Old Kingdom, while *Evangelikus Egyház és iskola* (Bratislava, 1883-1895) served Lutherans of Magyar speech.

[18]I talked with church officers at Bardejov in August 1968, and made photographs of the physical structures.

[19]Mark Stolarik's work in Prešov Roman Catholic marriage and death records for the years after 1894, and Oksana Dragan's in those of Byzantine Rite Rusins, will, when published, show a substantial and continuing migration into this town from both nearby and distant villages. My own cursory examination of marriage and death records of the Prešov Lutheran congregation showed that between 1895 and 1902, 14 of the 43 husbands married there were born outside the parish (which included the town itself and nine neighboring villages), as were 20 of the 38 communicants who died in the year 1896 at age 10 or over.

[20]The foregoing is based upon observation and conversations with pastors of several of these congregations. Many of the school buildings, including a large one attached to the town's largest synagogue, are still standing. The enrollment register of the Lutheran *Volkschule* in Košice, in the pastor's office, lists occupations of students' fathers. In the 1880's, merchants and craftsmen were predominant.

[21]Again, Macartney, *Hungary and Her Successors,* 383-389, 406-407, 414-416, is a convenient summary. An auto trip through the countryside was for me an enlightening experience.

[22]Balch, *Slavic Fellow Citizens,* 156-157, 441, 454; Macartney, *Hungary and Her Successors,* 356-361; Gunther E. Rothenberg, "The Croatian Military Border and the Rise of Yugoslav Nationalism," *Slavonic and East European Review,* XLIII (December 1964), 35-38, 42; Louis P. M. Leger, *La Save, le Danube, et le Balkan, Voyage chez les Slovenes, les Croates, les Serbes et les Bulgares* (Paris, 1884), 62-70.

[23]C. A. Macartney, *Hungary* (London, 1934), 152-154; cf. *ibid.,* 149-151, on Reformed Protestant identification with Magyar sentiment through the centuries.

[24]Almanacs published by the several communions before 1914 are exceedingly informative on all these points, as are the congregational *matriken* (records of baptisms, marriages, and deaths) for Spiš County which are in the Slovak State Archives at Levoca.

[25]Andrew J. Shipman, "Greek Catholics in America," *The Catholic Encyclopedia* (15 vols.; New York, 1907-1912), VI, 745; Douglas Ollila, "The Formative Period of the Finnish Evangelical Lutheran Church in America, or Suomi Synod" (unpub. Ph.D. Dissertation, Boston University, 1962 [Ann Arbor microfilms]), 166-187.

[26]Alex Simerenko, *Pilgrims, Colonists, and Frontiersmen: An Ethnic Community in Transition* (Minneapolis, 1964), 37-52; John Dzubay, *The Light of Orthodoxy, The Sixty-Sixth Anniversary of St. Mary's Russian Orthodox Greek Catholic Church* (Minneapolis, 1953), 1-20; Dimitry Gregorieff, "The Historical Background of Orthodoxy in America," *St. Vladimer's Seminary Quarterly,* V (1961), 9-12.

[27]Dzubay, *The Light of Orthodoxy, passim;* Simerenko, *Pilgrims, Colonists and Frontiersmen,* 52-53. The early records of the Minneapolis seminary are on deposit with other Russian Orthodox materials at the Immigrant Archives, The University of Minnesota, but they are not yet open for research.

[28]Louis A. Kalassy, "The Educational and Religious History of the Hungarian Reformed Church in the United States" (unpub. Ph.D. Dissertation, The University of Pittsburgh, 1939), 23.

[29]Christine A. Galitzi, *A Study of Assimilation Among the Romanians in the United States* (New York, 1929), 88-89, 94-95; Vasile Hategan, *Fifty Years of the Romanian Orthodox Church in America* (pamphlet; Jackson, Michigan, 1959), 15-16.

[30]Kalassy, "Educational and Religious History of Hungarian Reformed Church," 23-26; on the South Slavs and the Finns, see Timothy Smith, "Religious

Denominations as Ethnic Communities: A Regional Case Study," *Church History,* XXXV (June 1966), 207, 226. Cf. Saloutos, *Greeks in the U.S.,* 123-127, on Greeks; and, for a Polish land speculation which gave rise to a parish, Edward A. Masalewicz, *History of St. Hedwig's Congregation, Thoro, Wisconsin. Commemorating the Diamond Anniversary, 1891-1966* (Thoro, Wisconsin, 1966), 19.

[31] Bernard D. Weinrib, "Jewish Immigration and Accommodation to America," in Marshal Sklare (ed.), *The Jews: Social Patterns of an American Group* (Glencoe, Ill., 1958), 17-19. Cf., on the parallel forces at work in Zionism, Jacob Kabakoff, "The Role of Wolf Shur as Hebraist and Zionist," in Jacob R. Marcus (comp.), *Essays in American Jewish History to Commemorate the Tenth Anniversary of the Founding of the American Jewish Archives* (Cincinnati, 1958), 427, 443, 450-453.

[32] I am indebted to Yeshayahu Jelinek for photocopies of *The American Israelite,* Vol. 34 (September 26, 1887), 3, and *The Cleveland Plain Dealer,* September 5, 1887, 8, cols. 1-3, which recount the history of the congregation; and of *The Jewish Review and Observer,* 39, no. 43 (October 17, 1913), 5, and 39, no. 45 (October 31, 1913), 3, and *The Cleveland Plain Dealer,* September 8, 1880, 4, col. 4, on the history of the society. Cf., on Romanian Jewish congregations in Minneapolis, Albert I. Gordon, *Jews in Transition* (Minneapolis, 1949), 13-20.

[33] Peter Roberts, *Anthracite Coal Communities: A Study of the Demography, the Social, Educational, and Moral Life of the Anthracite Regions* (New York, 1904), 209-210.

[34] Peter Roberts, "The New Pittsburghers: Slavs and Kindred Immigrants in Pittsburgh," *Charities and the Commons,* XXI (January 2, 1909), 550-551. Cf. Peter Roberts, *The New Immigration* (New York, 1913), 200-201.

[35] George Dolak, *A History of the Slovak Evangelical Lutheran Church in the United States of America, 1902-1927* (St. Louis, Mo., 1955), 14-15, 24-26, 31, 33-43, 51-53.

[36] *Ibid.,* 53. 63-67; cf., on Old World background of lay prerogatives, esp. the office of inspector, Ruppeldt, "The Lutheran Church in Slovakia," 193.

[37] Kalassy, "Educational and Religious History of Hungarian Reformed Church," 23-26, 65-72, 132.

[38] See selection of historical documents reprinted in *Glasilo K.S.K.J.* (Chicago) for April 7, 1915; *Amerikanski Slovenec* (Tower, Minnesota), April 20, 1894, 2; Matija Savs, "Monsignor Fran Josef Buh," *Ave Maria Koedar,* X (1923).

[39] The paragraph is based on interviews with a dozen-odd Slovenian pioneer priests and laymen, and with local and national officers of K.S.K.J.

[40] Bak, *Life and Struggles,* 35-39; the newspaper quotation is on p. 39.

[41] *Ibid.,* 44-46. A microfilm edition of the weekly newspaper *Strasz,* organ of the Union, is at the Immigrant Archives, the University of Minnesota.

[42] Greek Catholic Union of the U.S.A., *Jubilee Almanac* (Munhall, Penna., 1967), 34-44, quotes extensively from the minute books. Files of the newspaper *Amerkansky Russky Viestnik,* which began publication in 1892, are on microfilm at the University of Pittsburgh Library. Cf. Ukrainian National Association, *Jubilee Book . . . In Commemoration of the Fortieth Anniversary of its Existence* (Jersey City, N.J., 1933), 194-198, and *passim.* Andrew J. Shipman, "Greek Catholics in America," *Catholic Encyclopedia,* VI, 745-749, is based on the almanacs of all parties.

[43] Shipman, "Greek Catholics in America," 749; Andrew J. Shipman, "Our Russian Catholics: The Greek Ruthenian Church in America," in *The* [Russian Orthodox] *Messenger.* XLII (November 1912), 664-667.

[44]Stephen E. Gulovich, *Windows Westward: Rome, Russia, Reunion* (New York, 1947), 124-135; Walter C. Warzeski, "Religion and National Consciousness in the History of the Rusins of Carpatho-Ruthenia and the Byzantine Rite Pittsburgh Exarchate" (unpub. Ph.D. Dissertation, The University of Pittsburgh, 1964), 118-139.

23

Judaism in America

Will Herberg

In an influential sociological essay, Protestant-Catholic-Jew *(1955-1960), Will Herberg advanced the thesis that three major religious communities in the United States have been transmuted through a historical process that blurred their traditional distinctive characteristics and united them as the three "religions of democracy." In the following selection from that work, Professor Herberg reviews the history of American Judaism in the perspective of this development. Professor Herberg teaches at Drew University.*

American Jewry first established itself in this country as an ethnic-immigrant group. In its earlier phases it seemed but little different from the other immigrant groups with whom it had made the overseas journey to the New World. But unlike the rest, it somehow did not lose its corporate identity with advancing Americanization; instead—largely within the last quarter of a century—it underwent a change of character and turned into an American religious community, retaining, even enhancing, its Jewishness in the process. It has thus in its own history exemplified with exceptional clarity the fundamental restructuring of American society which transformed the "land of immigrants" into the "triple melting pot." Nothing is more characteristically American than the historical evolution of American Jewry,[1] revealing, as it does, the inner patterns of American social development.

From *Protestant, Catholic, Jew* by Will Herberg. Copyright © 1955, 1960 by Will Herberg. Reprinted, with abridgements, by permission of Doubleday & Company, Inc.

I

Though in 1954 American Jewry celebrated its tercentenary, the American Jewish community of today is predominantly the product of the great wave of immigration from eastern Europe that set in some three quarters of a century ago. Yet the earlier history of American Jewry is not without its significance. The early Jews in this country, including the twenty-three who landed in New Amsterdam in 1654, were largely Sephardic, Spanish and Portuguese Jews seeking some place to settle after their expulsion from the Iberian peninsula and their wanderings through Europe and Latin America. With them came a few Ashkenazic Jews from central Europe and Poland. The immigration was slow—by 1776 there were perhaps 2,500 Jews in British America—but their acculturation was rapid. They settled along the coast—in New York, Newport, Philadelphia, the Carolinas, Georgia—and engaged in trade and finance, which sometimes reached considerable proportions. As quickly as possible they established their synagogues according to the Sephardic rite, and more slowly added the various auxiliary institutions. These Jews were, of course, orthodox, and it was their desire to re-establish the orthodox pattern as they knew it. Nevertheless, as they soon discovered, the old patterns could not be simply reproduced, and adaptation began with their first accommodations to American life.

These adaptations were at first imperceptible, but by 1825, when Jews in this country numbered some 5,000, the demand for readjustment became explicit. Partly under the influence of early German Reform, but largely under pressure of their own circumstances, a group of younger people in the Jewish community in Charleston that year organized themselves as the Reformed Society of Israelites. The year before they had petitioned the established congregation for certain reforms and modifications—greater decorum in the services, elimination of Spanish from the ritual, sermons in English—but their petition had been rejected, and so they seceded. They could not make their bold act good and were soon forced to return to the older congregation, but the future was obviously with them.

By the 1820s the handful of Jews in the United States, some 5,000 out of a population of 13,000,000, had established their way of life as Americans and as Jews, a way recognizably Jewish though also characteristically American. In that decade, however, began the wave of German immigration, which was to last half a century and was to remake Jewish life in America. From 1820 to 1870 between 200,000 and 400,000 Jews came to the United States, mostly from central Europe.[2] These "Germans" did not by any means immediately fuse with the native Jews, any more than the German Catholics who came in the same migration fused with the native Catholics they found in this country. The German Jews were foreigners, of different ways and cultural background; and they were Ashkenazim, whereas the native Jews, actually descended from immigrants of many different strains including East Europeans, regarded themselves as Sephardim and therefore superior. Decades were to pass before the social and institutional distinctions were overcome.

Americans tended to regard the newcomers as primarily Germans rather than Jews, one with the German Catholics and Lutherans who had migrated with them. On their part, the German Jews also identified themselves as Germans and joined cultural and mutual benefit societies set up by Germans without regard to religious lines. But their identification was actually double, and before long, where the German Jews were numerous enough, they established specifically Jewish institutions and movements, often existing side by side with their all-German counterparts. Only gradually, with increasing Americanization, did the German Jews cease to feel themselves part of the German community in the United States.[3]

The Jews who came in this German migration took up occupations that dispersed them throughout the land with the advancing frontier. They became peddlers, retail merchants, ultimately even bankers and large-scale businessmen. The high degree of dispersal and the relative prosperity which they achieved made their accommodation to American life remarkably easy. Before mid-century they were already busily erecting a network of community institutions that "were reflections of their conditions of settlement and not simply traditions carried over from the past or from abroad."[4] Synagogues were established, charitable and philanthropic efforts were launched, cultural activities were set going, and education became a serious concern. In the two decades before the Civil War, Hebrew Benevolent Societies made their appearance in New York, Philadelphia, and other cities; in Cincinnati, New York, and Chicago, Jewish hospitals were built. Literary and cultural societies prepared the way for the establishment of the first Young Men's Hebrew Association in 1854 in New York "for the purpose of cultivating and fostering a better knowledge of the history, literature, and doctrines of Judaism . . ." Attempts were made to set up full-time religious schools, but with the expansion of the public school system, the effort failed and was replaced by various schemes of supplementary education. By 1860, also, American Jews had already established five national orders of their own, including the B'nai B'rith (Sons of the Covenant), which then had some fifty lodges. Settlements of American Jews were to be found in all inhabited parts of the land.[5]

Reflecting the dispersal and the speed of acculturation of the German Jews under mid-nineteenth century conditions, intermarriage and defection from the Jewish community reached considerable proportions. "As the second generation grew to maturity, there was a strong likelihood that, eager to be Americanized, it would discard everything associated with the immigrant heritage of its fathers, including religion."[6] To stem the tide of dissolution, leaders of the German-Jewish community in America made strenuous efforts to hasten the adaptation of Jewish religious patterns to

American conditions. Unless the synagogue adjusted itself to the new way of life, warned the *American Israelite* in 1854, "we will have no Jews in this country in less than half a century."[7]

The new venture at reform was more directly influenced by the outlook and program of the German Reform movement, by this time some fifty years old. Yet the first attempts related not to theology but to synagogue procedures and forms of worship. Again there was a call for more decorum, for the revisions of the liturgy to permit shorter and more intelligible services, for the replacement of "German and Slavonic dialects" by English, for family pews to eliminate the segregation of women, for sermons in the American style, for mixed choirs and organs. Later, demands for the "simplification" of *kashrut* (dietary) and Sabbath prohibitions were heard. At Emanu-El in New York, Har Sinai in Baltimore, and other of the German synagogues, the reforms were introduced all at once; elsewhere, they came gradually. There was a great deal of conflict, but on the whole, at least so far as the synagogal reforms were concerned, the new order spread rapidly. . . .

In 1885 the rabbis of some dozen congregations, meeting in Pittsburgh, adopted what came to be known as the Pittsburgh Platform. It represented a drastic revision of traditional Jewish teaching along lines of German idealism and American Protestant liberalism. It substantially sanctioned the various Reform practices that had already established themselves and foreshadowed others. It relegated the Talmud and Talmudic tradition to the margin of Jewish life. It converted the messianic hope and expectation into an affirmation of the nineteenth century doctrine of progress, and eliminated Zion (Palestine) from the Jewish vision of fulfillment.[8] While many of the more conservative synagogues had been quite ready to go along with the reforms in practice, they rose against the radical theological innovations contained in the Pittsburgh Platform. A substantial group, primarily Sephardic, under the leadership of Sabato Morais, withdrew, and the Cincinnati institutions and movement very soon became the expressions of a "party" in American Judaism, Reform in the specific and narrower sense. Nevertheless, Reform continued to grow and seems unquestionably to have dominated American Jewish religious life before the new wave of immigration from eastern Europe.

The dissidents who rejected the Pittsburgh Platform regarded themselves as orthodox, but they were very far from being orthodox in the East European sense. Their differences with Reform were largely matters of temper and degree; they accepted almost wholly the emerging pattern of accommodation, though they shied away from some of its extreme manifestations (for example, replacing Saturday by Sunday for Sabbath worship) and objected to the radical theological revisionism of Reform. In defense of what they felt to be the enduring tradition of Judaism, to be made viable under American conditions, they proceeded to set up a parallel set of institutions under the banner of "historical Judaism," later to become the Conservative movement.[9] With Sabato Morais were such men as Benjamin Szold and Alexander Kohut; but the man who really made the new movement was Solomon Schechter. That, however, was the work of a new time.

The second epoch in the history of American Jewry, the "German" period roughly from 1820 to 1880, thus ended with two forms of an Americanized Judaism substantially similar in pattern though different in temper and ideology. Sporadic attempts had been made to unite the Jewish community in an over-all organization and to establish a central authority for American Jews, but they failed: American Jews remained loosely and autonomously organized, unwilling, or unable, not merely to transplant the traditional *kahal*-type of all-inclusive community, but equally reluctant to follow the British Jews in the establishment of an authoritative Board of Deputies. In this respect, too, they were American, following closely the Protestant-American pattern of decentralization and voluntarism.

II

Some East European Jews had come to America in colonial times, and by 1852 immigrants from Russia and Poland were sufficiently numerous to set up a congregation in New York. But the great deluge of East European immigration did not begin till the 1870s. Between 1870 and 1914 some 2,000,000 Jews migrated to America, 60 per cent from Russia and 20 per cent from the Austro-Hungarian Empire. During the years of World War I, some 100,000 more, and from 1920 to 1924, when immigration restrictions were finally clamped down, an additional 250,000 entered the country. All in all, therefore, nearly 2,500,000 Jews arrived in the five and a half decades after 1870.[10] The sudden mass deluge of East European Jews completely upset the settled pattern of American Judaism that had begun to emerge in the third quarter of the nineteenth century.

This time the Jews came not as part of a larger migration from their countries of birth; "in eastern Europe, the Jews were almost alone as emigrants, and were the first to take the move, peasants from that part of the continent . . . [arriving] in large numbers . . . not until after 1890."[11] This time, too, there was much less dispersal; the great bulk of the immigrants settled in a few large cities and established urban ghettos as areas of primary settlement. They came as petty merchants, artisans, or men without occupation, and went into small retailing and light manufacturing, particularly the garment trades. For the first time in the United States, and indeed in the Western world, there emerged a large Jewish proletariat, making a living by working for wages in industry. There is, indeed, reason to believe that at the turn of the century the Jews were the most industrialized ethnic group in the city of New York.[12] But side by side with the Jewish factory operative there soon appeared the Jewish businessman, the Jewish whitecollar worker, and somewhat later, the Jewish professional man. The "deproletarianization" of the Jewish immigrant began almost as soon as he became proletarianized; it proceeded apace with the second generation.[13]

Like the German Jews before them, many of the early East European Jewish immigrants were identified with the nation and culture from which they came, and some of them indeed so identified themselves.[14] But the fact that the great bulk of East European Jewry derived from Yiddish-speaking communities but little associated with the national culture of the land of their birth soon changed their context of identification. With the vast influx of East European Jews in the first years of the new century, a well-defined Yiddish-speaking Jewish ethnic group emerged, very different indeed in self-understanding and social conformation from the Jews of Sephardic and German origin who had preceded them.

At the opening of the new century, and for some two decades thereafter, the Jews in this country, and particularly in New York City (where, in 1909, half of the American Jews were to be found), constituted in effect two distinct communities, German and East European, each with its own characteristic outlook and pattern of behavior, each busily engaged in building and developing its own network of institutions. "These newcomers [from eastern Europe] were strangers . . . not much less strangers to the Jews already settled than to other Americans."[15] They felt themselves to be strangers and were treated as strangers, and they proceeded to make their own adjustment to American reality.

East European Jewry came in two ideological streams, thoroughly mingled in the migration. The great majority were religious Jews in the age-old tradition of the East European ghetto; a significant minority, however, had broken with Orthodoxy and with Jewish religion and were caught up in one or another of the secularist ideologies of the time, usually labor radicalism. This group was small at first but grew appreciably after 1905; it wielded a very considerable influence among American Jews in the decade before World War I. Both Orthodoxy and secular Judaism flourished in the first quarter of the century, each working to extend its institutions and to establish its ascendancy among the new arrivals.

Orthodoxy attempted persistently to transplant the old religious and community institutions, but without success; it, too, had to make its adjustments, though it frequently did not recognize how far-reaching they were.[16] The old unity of the *kahal* was gone; Jewish life was fragmented in many parts, under many and often conflicting authorities. In the crucial field of the education of the young the East European Jews tried to fall back on the *heder* and *yeshivah,* as these had functioned "at home," but of course they could hardly be made to serve the old purpose in the new environment. Part-time Hebrew and religious instruction in Talmud Torah schools unattached to synagogues in the area was attempted, with somewhat better success. But in 1908, Samuel Benderly, after an extensive survey, found that "only 28 per cent of the Jewish children in New York between the ages of six and sixteen received even the scantiest Jewish education."[17]

The record was better in the field of charitable and social organization. The newer immigrants did not, like the older and wealthier Jews, establish large-scale organized charities, but they did set up countless informal agencies of mutual aid and comfort, as well as a great variety of *lantsmanshaftn.* The Yiddish press and theater were vital expressions of the expanding community life of East European Jewry. All of these enterprises, it should be noted, were essentially American, however foreign their appearance. They were the normal forms of expression of the ethnic-immigrant group as that came into being in this country in the period of the great immigration.

The labor-radical element among the East European immigrants was ethnically and culturally identical with the Orthodox, but the ideological differences were so great that coexistence within the same community institutions was hardly possible. The Jewish labor movement, when it emerged toward the end of the nineteenth century, became, in effect, the core of a dual community within the East European immigration. It set up its own secular Yiddish schools, its own *lantsmanshaftn,* its own press, its own welfare agencies, even its own national fraternal order (Workmen's Circle).[18] Thus, in the half century from about 1870 to the end of World War I, there were not only two communities of American Jews in this country, different ethnically and culturally—the "Germans," with whom all the older elements were now identified, and the "Russians," as the Yiddish-speaking newcomers were known[19]—but the East European community was itself deeply divided between the religious Jews and the labor-radical secularists. It was a period of turmoil and conflict, dissension and disorder; but it was also a period of new creativity.

With the turn of the century, unitive forces and processes began to make themselves felt. As the newcomers advanced in Americanization, prospered, and improved their social status, the cultural divergence between the two communities was narrowed and ethnic amalgamation encouraged through intermarriage of "Germans" and "Russians." Common enterprises and concerns also helped to bridge the chasm. Mounting persecution of Jews abroad—the Dreyfus case, the Russian and Rumanian pogroms, the Beilis blood libel—roused American Jewry to united protest. Philanthropy at home and abroad established contacts that improved with time.[20] The European "minority" problems in the Versailles settlements as they affected the Jews called for united American Jewish intervention. "Defense" against manifestations of anti-Semitism at home also stimulated a "German-Russian" rapprochement. The labor-radical secession, however, was not to be overcome till almost the fourth decade of the new century. . . . By 1924 American Jewry, despite all internal divisions, already constituted a well-defined ethnic group.

By that time, however, all of the ethnic groups in America were entering upon a new phase of development that could only end with their dissolution, or radical transformation, into a new structure of American society.

III

Like the earlier Sephardic settlers, the German Jews of the nineteenth century, once they had become American and produced one, perhaps two, native-born generations, came increasingly to lose their sense of ethnic and cultural distinctiveness and to see themselves as essentially a religious grouping. By the end of the century the older community had stabilized itself as a community of Americans differing from other Americans in little but religion. They had ceased to be Spaniards, or Portuguese, or Germans, or whatever else their forebears had been at the time of migration; they were now Americans who remained Jews by virtue of their religious affiliation. Such as their understanding of their Jewishness.

Very different was the conception of the East European Jews who were arriving by the hundreds of thousands. They understood their Jewishness in terms of the religio-cultural complex that had developed in the East European Jewish communities through the previous centuries. Yiddish was both the vehicle and expression of this culture, and Yiddish they virtually identified with their Jewishness. Their predecessors, too, had tended to associate their religion with their immigrant native language and culture, but that language and culture—Spanish, German, or whatever it may have been— was something shared with a vastly larger number of non-Jews, and so could hardly be equated with Jewishness. But Yiddish was the peculiar possession of Jews, the cultural mark of their Jewishness; indeed, in the Yiddish language "Yiddish" meant "Jewish" and could not be distinguished from it. In the eyes of the immigrants they were substantially identical. Religion and the cultural matrix in which it happened to be embedded were fused into a single religio-cultural entity known as *Yiddishkait* (Jewishness). The secularists merely replaced the element of traditional religion in this complex with their particular radical gospel; for them, too, their Jewishness was *Yiddishkait,* virtually inconceivable apart from the Yiddish language and culture.

Both the religious and the secularist Jews in the new immigration were "cultural pluralists" insofar as they had any views on their future in their new home. They looked forward to the perpetuation of their Yiddish cultural community, with its language, literature, and ways of life, in the New World, and all their institutions were designed to achieve this end. This was not, in their minds at least, a rejection of America, but their way of adaptation to it without losing their Jewishness. When the Russian Jew undertook to teach Yiddish to the Turkish Jews on the East Side, he did so in order to make them both "real" Jews and better Americans.[21] How could one be a "real" Jew without knowing Yiddish?—while for a Jew to live on the East Side without knowing Yiddish was obviously to be some kind of foreigner.

Because religion and immigrant culture were so thoroughly fused as to seem almost indistinguishable, the East European immigrants came up against a shattering crisis as they confronted the second generation, their American sons and daughters. The second generation, desperately anxious to become unequivocally American, was resentful of the immigrant culture which the older generation seemed so eager to transmit to it. "The whole process of its upbringing had emphasized the contrast between 'American' and 'foreign'; for the children, Judaism was still associated with the foreign,"[22] because the Judaism they knew was indeed a foreign immigrant culture. Rejection of foreignness meant rejection of Jewishness and Judaism. The second generation, for the East European Jews even more than for their German and Sephardic predecessors, became indeed the "weakest link in the chain of Jewish continuity," an "inbetween layer . . . which [had] broken with the Jewish past and [had] lost faith in a Jewish future."[23]

... The characteristic response of the second generation was secularism. Yet it was secularism with a difference, for even in their secularism the young people of the second generation often showed the impress of the religion they were abandoning. Many of them became radicals and "internationalists," but their radicalism was usually quite different culturally from the radicalism of the immigrants, with whom they had little real contact. Others, in a reaction against devaluation, became Zionists; their "nationalism" was paradoxically also an effort to adjust themselves to America, where ethnic nationalism was a recognized feature of acculturation.[24] Both radicalism and Zionism were second-generation phenomena;[25] yet both were also somehow strangely "Jewish," for was not internationalist socialism a secularized version of the "universalist" aspect of Jewish messianism and Zionist nationalism a secularized version of the "particularist" aspect? Both grew in the 1920s and 1930s, strengthened by world developments; both began to wane in the next two decades, when the world situation changed and the third generation emerged.

IV

The emergence of the third generation changed the entire picture of American Jewry and Judaism in America. Each of the earlier immigrations, the Sephardic and the German, had had its third generation, but in both cases the emergence of the third generation had fallen in with a new and overwhelming wave of immigration, so that it was not this generation but the newcomers who came to define the character and structure of the Jewish community. Now, however, immigration was virtually at an end—the restrictive legislation of 1924 became the settled policy of the nation—and the third generation of East European stock that began to appear in the 1930s and 1940s became increasingly the decisive element. With the appearance of this generation, the whole aspect of American Jewry began to undergo a profound transformation, perhaps the most significant in its entire history on this continent.

The third generation played a role in American Jewry that was in many ways quite unique. Among other immigrant groups the emergence of the third generation regularly meant the approaching dissolution of the ethnic group, which the first generation had formed and the second generation had perforce been identified with. True, according to "Hansen's Law,"[26] the third generation, secure in its Americanness, was not unwilling to "remember" what the second generation had been so eager to "forget." But all that the third generation of the Italian or Polish group, for example, could, as Americans, remember was the religion of the grandfather; the immigrant language and culture and way of life were, of course, irretrievably gone. And so the emergence of the third generation meant the disappearance of the "Italianness" or the "Polishness" of the group, or rather its dissolution into the religious community. With the Jews, however, it was different. The first and second generations of Jews in America repeated the common immigrant pattern: immigrant foreignness followed by an anxious effort to overcome that foreignness and become American. But the third generation of

American Jews, instead of somehow finally getting rid of their Jewishness, as the Italians were getting rid of their "Italianness" and the Poles of their "Polishness," actually began to *reassert* their Jewish identification and to *return* to their Jewishness. They too were striving to "remember" what their parents had so often striven to "forget," but the content and consequences of their "remembering" were strikingly different.[27]

We can account for this anomaly by recalling that the Jews came to this country not merely as an immigrant group but also as a religious community; the name "Jewish" designated both without distinction. As the immigrant Jews developed their ethnic group in the United States, the same duality—and ambiguity—persisted: the Jewish community was both ethnic and religious, and was so understood by all except a few hard-bitten secularists, who tried to replace its religious character by a secular nationalism or culturalism. When the second generation rejected its Jewishness, it generally, though not universally, rejected both aspects at once. With the third generation, the foreign-immigrant basis of the ethnic group began to disappear and the ethnic group as such began to give way. Among the Jews, as among other immigrants, the advancing dissolution of the old ethnic group meant the returning identification of the third generation with the religious community of its forebears, but among the Jews alone this religious community bore the same name as the old ethnic group and was virtually coterminous with it. The young Jew for whom the Jewish immigrant-ethnic group had lost all meaning, because he was an American and not a foreigner, could still think of himself as a Jew, because to him being a Jew now meant identification with the Jewish religious community. What the Jewish third generation "returned" to was, of course, that which, as American, it could "remember" of the heritage of its forebears—in other words, their religion—but in returning to the religion it was also returning to Jewishness, in a sense in which the Italian or Polish third generation, in returning to Catholicism, was *not* returning to "Italianness" or "Polishness." The dual meaning of "Jewish" as covering both ethnic group and religion made the "return" movement of the third generation into a source of renewed strength and vigor for the American Jewish community.[28]

The American Jewish community, under the sign of the third generation, was in many ways significantly different from what it had been in earlier decades. Many of the earlier tendencies were being carried to completion. Ethnic amalgamation of the many stocks and strains that had gone into American Jewry was now virtually accomplished. The Jews who had come to this country neither spoke the same language nor felt particularly eager to mix with other Jews of different origins; intermarriage had often been "opposed not simply on religious grounds, but also because it disrupted the continuity of the particular group—Lithuanian Jews objected to a German or Galician or Syrian daughter-in-law almost as violently as to a gentile, and to the latter even were she converted."[29] These bars had already begun to crumble with the second generation; by the time the third appeared, they had ceased to have any meaning whatsoever. Intermarriage within the Jewish community was rapid and unhampered, and a new American type of Jew, a mixture of many strains with the East European predominant, came into being.[30] Wide ethnic amalgamation within the Jewish group was accompanied by a somewhat reduced rate of outside inter-marriage,[31] which now came to mean not ethnic but religious mixing.

In the same way, the earlier tendencies towards "bourgeoisification" were carried further with the third generation. "The evolving style of life of the group fell imperceptibly into the molds of American middle-class culture, although retaining distinctive features derived from the past."[32] The Jewish proletarian in the United States was, indeed, a man of one genera-tion; it was his ambition that neither his son nor his daughter should follow him into the factory, and to make sure that this would be so he strained every effort to give them an education. Proportionately three times as many Jewish young people were going to college in 1950 as young Americans of their age generally.[33] Jews were to be found increasingly in business, white-collar occupations, professions, government service, decreasingly in shops and factories. This trend was one characteristic of all immigrant groups as they became acculturated and acquired American goals and standards. "The difference between the Jew and the non-Jew in this area was one of degree rather than of kind. Both moved in the same direction; only the Jew moved at a faster pace. And for obvious reasons: the drift entailed a greater measure of urbanization and a higher education, and Jews had both."[34] With the new American and middle-class style of life came the dispersion of the older ethnic "ghettos" in the large cities. Jews had begun to move away from the areas of first settlement with the second generation or even earlier, but they still gathered in "Jewish" neighborhoods. Now they were leaving these "Jewish" neighborhoods and spreading out into the suburbs and other areas of third settlement, in line with the trend of the social and cultural strata to which they belonged. This change involved not merely an altera-tion in place of residence; it involved a certain transformation in the entire outlook and mode of life of the Jews making the shift.[35]

The third generation, as we have seen, felt secure in its Americanness and therefore no longer saw any reason for the attitude of rejection so characteristic of its predecessors. It therefore felt no reluctance about iden-tifying itself as Jewish and affirming its Jewishness; on the contrary, such identification became virtually compelling since it was the only way in which the American Jew could now locate himself in the larger community. Third-generation attitudes became prevalent among all but the most "old-fashioned" elements in American Jewry. . . .

As the third generation began to "remember" the religion of its ancestors, to the degree at least of affirming itself Jewish "in a religious sense," it also began to lose interest in the ideologies and "causes" which had been so characteristic of Jewish youth in earlier decades. Social radicalism virtually disappeared, and the passionate, militant Zionism es-poused by groups of American Jews until 1948 became diffused into a vague, though by no means insincere, friendliness to the State of Israel.[36] The retreat from radicalism and Zionism fell in with certain larger trends in American life and was reinforced by historical developments, but the sur-mounting of the anxieties and insecurities of the marginal second generation undoubtedly played a major part.

Over and above, and within, the general movement for religious identification, there could be discerned, in certain sections of the third generation, a deeper religious concern, motivated by a new need for self-
understanding and authenticity. Serious works dealing with Jewish faith and
destiny began to find interested readers precisely among the most American
segments of the Jewish community,[37] and the response of Jewish students on
the campuses and of the younger married people in their communities to the
new religious thinking was markedly different from what had been
customary in earlier decades.

What was the shape and form of the religion of the Jewish community
in mid-twentieth century America? It was characterized by a far-reaching
accommodation to the American pattern of religious life which affected all
"denominations" in the American synagogue. The institutional system was
virtually the same as in the major Protestant churches—the same corporate
structure, the same proliferation of men's clubs, sisterhoods, junior congregations, youth groups, "young marrieds," Sunday school classes, discussion circles, adult education projects, breakfasts, "brunches," dinners, and
suppers. With minor variations, "the arrangement of the synagogue, the
traditional appurtenances of worship, and the religious ceremonies showed
the effects of change wrought by the American environment."[38] The central
place of the sermon, congregational singing, mixed choirs, organs, responsive readings, abbreviated services, the concluding benediction, and many
other commonly accepted features obviously reflected the influence of
familiar Protestant practice.

The pattern of holidays and ceremonials had also undergone considerable modification. There was weekly worship on Friday night
(sometimes Saturday morning), usually poorly attended. There were the
High Holy Days—Rosh Hashanah (New Year) and Yom Kippur (Day of
Atonement)—at which attendance was at its maximum. Hanukkah,
traditionally of minor importance, was much emphasized because of its
seasonal coincidence with Christmas, and many "Christmas" customs
(Hanukkah cards, massive gift-giving, "Uncle Max the Hanukkah Man" as
the "Jewish Santa Claus") were associated with it. Passover, coming at
Easter time and made into the occasion of family reunions, retained its
traditional importance, though with changed significance. Novel, too, was
the extraordinary prominence given to the boy's Bar Mitzvah (religious
"coming of age" at thirteen); lavish Bar Mitzvah parties were the rule. For
girls, there was "confirmation," though often a parallel Bat Mitzvah was introduced. Weddings and funerals were almost always religious affairs, with
traditional procedures drastically modified along American lines.[39] Practices
relating to memorials for the dead—*kaddish, yortsait,* and *yizkor*—were
widespread and much stressed.

Of the elaborate and comprehensive system of ritual observance in
traditional Judaism what remained was primarily circumcision, universally
practiced, though not always in the proper ritual form; synagogue services,
lighting candles, and occasionally making *kiddush* on Sabbath eve (Friday
night); and a token *kashrut* (dietary law), primarily the avoidance of ham,
pork, and similar forbidden foods.[40] "The rituals which had special appeal,"

the Sklare report concludes, "were those which were joyous, which marked the transition from one stage of life to another, which did not require a high degree of isolation from non-Jews, which did not demand rigorous devotion and daily attention, which were capable of acceptance to the larger community, and which this larger community had itself reserved for the sacred order." In Orthodox and Conservative, even in some Reform communities, there developed a curious form of vicarious observance by the rabbi, who was expected to live up more or less to the traditional standards which were no longer operative among the members of his congregation. . . .

In general, the religious pattern that emerged with the new third-generation Jewish community was characteristically American, reflecting a far-reaching and systematic accommodation of the East European tradition to American reality.[41] The accommodation was not limited to one or another group in American Jewry; it was pervasive and affected all segments of the community, Orthodox as well as Conservative and Reform—whatever differences still remained were altogether secondary.[42] There was, in fact, under way a notable convergence between the three groups, or "denominations," in American Judaism, in everything at least except their institutional affiliations and loyalties. All were becoming American and therefore more and more like each other.

Reform Judaism had drastically modified the old Pittsburgh Platform at Columbus in 1937; the new Columbus Platform toned down much of the exuberant optimism of the earlier document, took a much more friendly attitude toward Zionism and Palestine, and placed a new emphasis on religious rituals and practices.[43] American Orthodoxy, as distinct from the immigrant Orthodoxy that still remained, adopted American ways and procedures which inevitably involved extensive changes in the traditional pattern. Thus, while Reform moved to the "right," American Orthodoxy moved substantially to the "left." In between stood Conservatism, particularly suited to the new temper and therefore apparently growing faster than either of its rivals. . . .

As the new religious pattern of American Jewry began to define itself, it became increasingly clear that, with certain qualifications (discarding of Sunday services, a more positive attitude to Zionism), what was emerging resembled very closely the original moderate Reform program. Samuel S. Cohon was quite justified in asserting: "The Conservative and Reconstructionist movements have been following in the footsteps of Reform";[44] indeed, he might almost have included American Orthodoxy as well. And yet, while the Reform program was thus triumphing, the Reform movement did not seem to be making any comparable headway. Reform, which in the 1870s seemed to be destined to carry everything before it, was overwhelmed by the deluge of East European immigration. To the East European Jew, whether religious or secular, the kind of Judaism championed by Reform appeared ridiculous, even abhorrent. Reform, therefore, was driven into retreat, and Orthodoxy became dominant. With advancing Americanization, however, the East European Jews themselves began to make their adaptations and adjustments to American life, in the field of religion as in every other field. Orthodoxy began to change, and Conservatism came to the fore as the characteristic expression of the acculturated East European Jew. What resulted was substantially similar to moderate Reform, but since it had not come about through direct Reform influence, but rather through the continuing pressure of the American environment, it was not recognized as having any relation to the older Reform idea. Not Reform but Conservatism thus became the prime beneficiary of the Americanization of Judaism in this country. But this was only a matter of degree; by the mid-century all three of the "denominations" were substantially similar expressions of the new American Jewish religious pattern, differing only in background, stage of development, and institutional affiliation. . . .

V

Whatever may be the institutional situation at the moment, it is incontrovertible that the Jewish community in the United States has become a religious community in its own understanding, as well as in the understanding of the non-Jew. Old-line secular Judaism is obsolescent. "The type of secular Jewish organizations which existed around the turn of the century, and for some years thereafter," the Sklare report finds, "are hardly a force today." But while Jewish community life has become more religious in this sense, it has also become more secularist in another. Virtually all Jewish children become Bar Mitzvah today,[45] as was not the case twenty, thirty, or forty years ago, but the Bar Mitzvah is usually nothing but a lavish and expensive party, with the religious aspect reduced to insignificance, if not altogether ignored.[46] Much of the institutional life of the synagogue has become thus secularized and drained of religious content precisely at the time when religion is becoming more and more acknowledged as the meaning of Jewishness.[47]

The Jewish community in the United States presents an anomalous picture in other ways as well. It has no over-all organization, and every attempt to give it one so as to eliminate "overlapping" and "conflict" has failed.[48] It has, therefore, all along given the appearance of hopeless chaos and confusion. And yet this community without central control is capable of great communal efforts;[49] without over-all organization, it yet embraces the vast majority of American Jews.[50] In the last analysis, it is, as we have had occasion to note, based on a voluntarism that is characteristically American.[51]

But perhaps it is not correct to say that the American Jewish community possesses no over-all organization. It does possess what comes close to being a single hierarchical structure embracing the entire community, and that is the machinery of fund raising and fund allocation.[52] Not the synagogal bodies but the fund-raising agencies, combined in the Council of Jewish Federations and Welfare Funds (1932), and operating mainly through the United Jewish Appeal (1940), reach into every nook and cranny of the land to establish connections with the tiniest of Jewish groups.[53] "Fund raising [among American Jews] has reached an exceptionally high level of efficiency. The Jews contribute considerably more per capita than any comparable group in the United States . . ." But fund raising is not simply a financial operation. "The initial efforts to establish welfare funds and federations soon disclosed that it was not possible to restrict the new organizations to problems connected with the collection of funds. Relatively early in the development of these welfare funds, it became clear that there was a close relationship—an inevitable one—between unified efforts at fund raising and unified control over allocations."[54] Since all Jewish institutions raise funds under centralized control and virtually all are in some way dependent on allocations, it is by no means far-fetched to think of the vast and complex machinery of fund raising and allocation as in fact the organizational armature of the American Jewish community.

From the very beginning, from the first settlements in New York, Newport, Philadelphia, and Charleston, the Jews in America strove to become American and establish themselves as an American community. Twice in the nineteenth century the measure of stability they had achieved was upset by new waves of immigration, which vastly increased their numbers and enriched their heritage, but also threw into confusion the patterns of accommodation they had developed in their adjustment to American life. Finally, as America approached mid-twentieth century, the confusion began to subside and the shape and form of Judaism in America, reflecting the rise of a secure and confident third generation, began to emerge. The American Jewish community became integrally part of American society; the American Jew was now in the position where he could establish his Jewishness not apart from, nor in spite of, his Americanness, but precisely through and by virtue of it. Judaism had achieved its status in the American Way of Life as one of the three "religions of democracy."

And yet among some American Jews there was perplexity and restlessness. Was this all there was to Judaism after all? Had it no higher purpose or destiny? What was it, in the last analysis, that made the Jew a Jew, and kept him a Jew? A young Jewish sociologist, at mid-century point, formulated his perplexity in a way that was bound to find an echo in many of the third generation: "A social group with clearly marked boundaries exists, but the source of the energies that hold [it] separate, and of the ties that bind it together, has become completely mysterious."[55]

NOTES

[1]No adequate history of American Jewry to the present day exists. Three studies, from very different standpoints, are: Oscar Handlin, *Adventure in Freedom: Three Hundred Years of Jewish Life in America* (McGraw-Hill, 1954), Rufus Learsi, *The Jews in America: A History* (World, 1954), and Nathan Glazer, *American Judaism* (Chicago, 1957). Moses Rischin, *An Inventory of American Jewish History* (Harvard, 1954) is very useful. Marshall Sklare, *Conservative Judaism: An American Religious Movement* (Free Press, 1955) is the first really adequate sociological study of Jewish religion in America.

[2]Oscar and Mary Handlin, "A Century of Jewish Immigration to the United States," *American Jewish Year Book,* Vol. 50 (American Jewish Committee, 1949), p. 11.

[3]See Rudolf Glanz, "Jews in Relation to the Cultural Milieu of the Germans in America up to the Eighteen Eighties" (in Yiddish), *Yivo Bleter,* Vol. XXV, Nos. 1 and 2.

[4]Handlin, *Adventure in Freedom,* pp. 71-72.

[5]A survey of Jewish communities in the United States in 1860 is to be found in Learsi, *The Jews in America,* pp. 66-75.

[6]Handlin, *Adventure in Freedom,* p. 76. Handlin adds: "To the well-established native American Jews, this was no danger. Judaism was not 'foreign' to their children, as it was to the children of Germans and Poles."

[7]Quoted by Handlin, *Adventure in Freedom,* p. 76.

[8]For the Pittsburgh Platform, see *Year Book of the Central Conference of American Rabbis,* Vol. I, pp. 120-23.

[9]"Historical Judaism," too, had its German inspiration. It derived from the position taken in Germany by Zecharias Frankel in his struggle against Reform. See Louis Ginzberg, *Students, Scholars, and Saints* (Jewish Publication Society, 1928), chap. viii, pp. 195-216.

[10]Handlin, *Adventure in Freedom,* pp. 84-85; also Handlin, "A Century of Jewish Immigration in the United States," *American Jewish Year Book,* Vol. 50 (1949), pp. 11-13.

[11]Handlin, *Adventure in Freedom,* p. 84.

[12]Sherman, "Jewish Economic Adjustment in the U.S.A.," *The Reconstructionist,* December 18, 1953.

[13]Sklare, *Conservative Judaism: An American Religious Movement,* pp. 26, 48; Glazer, "Social Characteristics of American Jews, 1654-1954," *American Jewish Year Book,* Vol. 56 (1955), p. 29.

[14]Handlin, *Adventure in Freedom,* p. 121.

[15]Handlin, *Adventure in Freedom,* p. 113.

[16]For an account of "Orthodoxy in Transition" in Chicago, see Sklare, *Conservative Judaism: An American Religious Movement,* chap. ii, pp. 43-65.

[17]Handlin, *Adventure in Freedom,* p. 119.

[18]See Will Herberg, "The Jewish Labor Movement in the United States," *American Jewish Year Book,* Vol. 53 (1952), esp. pp. 29-30. For a valuable study of the Jewish labor movement, see Melech Epstein, *Jewish Labor in the U.S.A.,* 2 vols. (Trade Union Sponsoring Committee, New York, 1950, 1953).

[19]Handlin, *Adventure in Freedom,* p. 142.

[20]Eli Ginzberg, *Agenda for American Jews* (King's Crown, 1950), p. 17.

[21]See Handlin, *Adventure in Freedom,* p. 162.

[22]Handlin, *Adventure in Freedom,* pp. 162-63.

[23]Sherman, "Three Generations," *Jewish Frontier,* Vol. XXI, No.7 (229), July 1954.

[24]See *Protestant-Catholic-Jew,* chap. ii, pp. 17-18.

[25]Handlin, *Adventure in Freedom,* p. 217. For the meaning of second-generation radicalism, see Sherman, "Three Generations," *Jewish Frontier,* Vol. XXI, No. 7 (229), July 1954.

[26]"Hansen's Law": "What the son wishes to forget, the grandson wishes to remember."

[27]For some comments on the Jewish third generation, see Herberg, "Religious Trends in American Jewry," *Judaism,* Vol. III, No. 3, Summer 1954; and Sherman, "Three Generations," *Jewish Frontier,* Vol. XXI, No. 7 (229), July 1954.

[28]Sherman, "Three Generations," *Jewish Frontier,* Vol. XXI, No. 7 (229), July 1954. In other words, thorough acculturation of American Jews has led not to assimilation but to a stronger affirmation of Jewishness.

[29]Handlin, *Adventure in Freedom,* p. 164.

[30]Abraham G. Duker, "Emerging Culture Patterns in American Jewish Life," *Publications of the American Jewish Historical Society,* No. XXXIX, part 4, June 1950.

[31]Milton L. Barron, *People Who Intermarry* (Syracuse, 1946), p. 341.

[32]Handlin, *Adventure in Freedom,* p. 254.

[33]See Robert Shosteck, "Jewish Students in American Universities," *American Jewish Year Book,* Vol. 50 (1949), pp. 767-74.

[34]Sherman, "Jewish Economic Adjustment in the U.S.A.," *The Reconstructionist,* December 18, 1953.

[35]For a very suggestive discussion of what is implied in the shift from areas of second to areas of third settlement, see Sklare, *Conservative Judaism: An American Religious Movement,* pp. 47-48, 67-72.

[36]Jacob B. Agus, *Guideposts in Modern Judaism: An Analysis of Current Trends* (Bloch, 1954), p. 13.

[37]Among recently published works in the new spirit may be mentioned: Ludwig Lewisohn, *The American Jew: Character and Destiny* (Farrar, Straus, 1950); Abraham J. Heschel, *Man Is Not Alone: A Philosophy of Religion* (Farrar, Straus, 1951); *Man's Quest for God* (Scribner's, 1954); *God in Search of Man: A Philosophy of Judaism* (Farrar, Straus, 1955); Herberg, *Judaism and Modern Man: An Interpretation of Jewish Religion* (Farrar, Straus, 1951). Translations and interpretations of Martin Buber's works, and *Franz Rosenzweig: His Life and Thought,* presented by Nahum N. Glatzer (Schocken, 1953), have exerted significant influence.

[38]Handlin, *Adventure in Freedom,* p. 255.

[39]For an interesting account, with many details, see Duker, "Emerging Culture Patterns in American Jewish Life," *Publications of the American Jewish Historical Society,* No. XXXIX, part 4, June 1950.

[40]Despite the relatively slight observance of *kashrut,* there has developed a very considerable "kosher" and "kosher-style" food industry, with an appeal by no means limited to observant Jews, or to Jews only. Use of these foods does not by any means imply observance of *kashrut.*

[41]An extensive syncretism of practice has developed among many Jews in which, for example, Christmas and Hanukkah are both celebrated, sometimes together.

[42]Duker, "On Religious Trends in American Jewish Life," *Yivo Annual of Jewish Social Science,* Vol. IV (1949), pp. 58-59, 60.

[43]See Samuel S. Cohon, "The Contemporary Mood in Reform Judaism," *The Journal of Bible and Religion,* Vol. XVIII, No. 3, July 1950. For the Columbus Platform, see *Yearbook of the Central Conference of American Rabbis,* Vol. LXVII, pp. 94-100.

[44]Cohon, "The Contemporary Mood in Reform Judaism," *The Journal of Bible and Religion*, Vol. XVIII, No. 3, July 1950.

[45]Even the secularist Workmen's Circle schools now conduct "special Bar Mitzvah classes."

[46]A typical Bar Mitzvah invitation announces a "Bar Mitzvah Reception" at a big hall in Brooklyn for six o'clock Saturday evening, and then adds in tiny type in the corner: "Religious Services at 10:30 A.M. . . ."

[47]See Herberg, "The Postwar Revival of the Synagogue," *Commentary*, Vol. IX, No. 4, April 1950, esp. pp. 321-25.

[48]For a brief survey of the American Jewish community as an institutional system, see Duker, "Structure of the Jewish Community," in Janowsky, ed., *The American Jew: A Composite Portrait*, pp. 134-60; also Samuel C. Kohs, "The Jewish Community," in Louis Finkelstein, ed., *The Jews: Their History, Culture, and Religion*, Vol. IV, pp. 1267-1324. For a list of national Jewish organizations, see *American Jewish Year Book*, Vol. 55 (1954), pp. 397-418.

[49]"In 1947 the [United Jewish] Appeal raised a total of about $170,000,000 about half of it being allotted to Palestine . . . In the five years that followed, the new State of Israel received $416,000,000 from American Jews, of which two thirds came from the proceeds of the United Jewish Appeal" (Learsi, *The Jews in America*, p.314 and note).

[50]Handlin, *Adventure in Freedom*, pp. 229-30.

[51]The same principle permeates Jewish religious life. Jewish religious polity is ultra-congregational, and this is equally true of all three "denominations." The various rabbinical and synagogal associations have no formal power over their constituents and can make no decisions binding on the individual congregations.

[52]Handlin, *Adventure in Freedom*, pp. 223-24.

[53]Duker, "Structure of the Jewish Community," in Janowsky, ed., *The American Jew: A Composite Portrait*, p. 153 note.

[54]Ginzberg, *Agenda for American Jews*, pp. 48, 50.

[55]Glazer, "What Sociology Knows About American Jews," *Commentary*, Vol. IX, No. 3, March 1950. For an account of the perplexed and disturbed reaction of many young people to the externalism and secularization of Jewish religious life in America today, see Herberg, "Religious Trends in American Jewry," *Judaism*, Vol. III, No. 3, Summer 1954. For divergent forecasts as to the future of American Jewry, see: Jacob R. Marcus and Oscar Handlin, "The Goals of Survival: What Will U.S. Jewry Be Like in 2000?—Two Views," *The National Jewish Monthly*, May 1957.

24

American Catholicism and American Religion

David O'Brien

David O'Brien, a historian at the College of the Holy Cross, asserts that Protestant historians have neglected the history of American Catholicism in their studies of American religion, while Catholic historians have focused too narrowly on the Catholic church. What is necessary, he suggests, is a broader understanding of American Catholicism as part of the history of American religion and culture.

All who profess history as a way of knowing and making a living are acutely aware that we live in an anti-historical age. Youthful radicals and their most vigorous opponents appear as opposite sides of a coin; both engage in historical myth making which manifests a common abhorrence for the uncertainty, ambiguity, and conflict which are the fruits of the historical consciousness. Worse, some of our most respectable scholars seek to correct the situation with a pseudo-historical realism which mocks human purpose and contemporary man's efforts to master his destiny. Americans have always rejected such fatalism and ignored the supposed demands of an impersonal and inexorable history. Instead, they have continually manufactured for themselves new and hopeful histories to underpin their truly religious faith in the nation, its ideals, and its mission.

This American aversion to a history which seeks to confine men's hopes to the obviously possible and to debunk their deepest yearnings and

Permission to reprint from *Journal of the American Academy of Religion*, XL (1972), pp. 36-53, granted by *JAAR* and the author.

aspirations has considerable significance for contemporary Christians. In *The Search for a Usable Future,* Martin Marty contends that men act in the light of futures which they envision or project, futures whose raw materials are things remembered, the usable past. If Marty is right, perhaps what American religion in general—American religious historiography in particular—needs is less a revision of the record than a rebirth of vision. A usable past makes sense only in relation to a desirable future; both require a rending of past and future, of what has been and what should be.[1] They require specifically a truly critical view of America; this, in turn, demands recognition of the extent to which many of the most cherished notions of American Christians rest on unexamined assumptions about America itself. Whatever the merit of these assumptions and of the American civil religion which they define, American Christians are going to have to deal with their problems within the American framework which continues to shape their awareness and response long after they believe they have "come of age."

"While the past itself has been almost entirely an old-world possession," Henry Steele Commager writes, "Americans have resolutely studied themselves as if they were an isolated chapter in history and exempt from the processes of history."[2] From the very beginning America was somehow beyond the history that men knew. The novelty of the new world infused thought about America long before the first settlers arrived. Once here, those same settlers needed an explanation of who they were and where they were headed. To unify a diverse, fluid, uneasy populace, to legitimize and pass on to the young a sense of corporate responsibility, the nation required a usable past, one which could both bind the people together and confirm their hopeful expectations. Americans thus looked to the past to learn that they were free of its burdens.

History became a major vehicle through which Americans learned what it was to be American. As the nation grew in space and numbers and complexity, its history had to be done over and over again, updated and invigorated, assuming new shapes and contours for a mobile and polyglot people. The story had to be woven around highly symbolic and abstract themes: Providence, Manifest Destiny, the American Way of Life, the American Dream, in order to suit these diverse peoples and subsume their very real economic, racial, ethnic and religious conflicts. While the central question was always Crevecour's, "What then is the American, this new man?" the answer changed to reflect the nation's changing needs and fears and hopes.

With a future of self-improvement and corporate greatness taken for granted, the historian's task was largely conservative. He helped preserve the American community by reminding its people of their origins and their shared objectives. Puritan clergymen who carried on "God's Controversy With New England," reminded men of their covenant with the Lord and their failure to abide by its terms. By the middle of the nineteenth century the covenant had been secularized, but George Bancroft could still recall his readers to the Lord's lofty expectations for them. Frederick Jackson Turner and Charles Beard used a more academic and scientific terminology but their message was equally clear: the meaning of America was to be found in its origins and its destiny remained unimpaired. Beneath the superficialities of the most dramatic changes, the national story was a tale of eternal changelessness.

History, then, was a major component of national self-consciousness, a source of common understanding of the meaning of the continual process of movement and settlement. Yet America's was a history oriented to the future rather than the past. Somehow the past was given; a new start had been made by man and had been ratified in the sacred covenant of the Puritans to which every immigrant adhered by his journey. The revolution and the constitution confirmed the transaction by binding men together in the new order America demanded. The past was notable for this gift to men of escape from the old way—it was closed. Only the future was open: to be sure, its ultimate goodness was guaranteed, but its shape and contours were in men's hands. Individually and collectively they had the responsibility to build and to grow, to become what they could in a land which made hope truly possible. American history was, then, America's theology of hope, recording the good news of man's resurrection from Europe and pointing to the future as the location of the completion of the quest for liberation and fulfillment.

Throughout most of their history, Americans have blended religious and national identities. Perry Miller demonstrated that Protestant Christianity provided the English settlers, even those whose explicit motives were far more secular than those of the Puritans, with the symbols which explained and justified what they were about. Thereafter, Christian and secular models and images interacted creatively to generate a national consciousness which was truly religious and religious attitudes which were distinctly American. As numerous historians have noted in recent years, categories of sacred and secular merge and blend in America, producing churches preoccupied with secular affairs and, on the other hand, "a nation with the soul of a church." In both cases the result was welcome for, unlike many Europeans nations, America experienced little polarization of church and state.[3] Rather the state praised the church as the agency of civic virtue and the church praised the state as the embodiment of the nation's highest aspirations.

Of course, to the outside observer, the situation was distressing. Was not Christianity a historical faith, bound to the past, to traditions? How could it adapt to a nation which exalted novelty, innocence, and nature? If the churches turned their back on Europe, and the past, how could they preserve the Christian heritage? Generations of churchmen and church historians rejected the dilemma. They promoted and defended the Americanization of Christianity, arguing, indeed, that the apparent chaos and disorder of America were marks of the approach of Christ's kingdom.

The dilemma of American Christianity should have been particularly acute for Roman Catholics. Indeed, many Protestant leaders long believed that the Catholic Church, with its strong institutional controls and its reactionary view of history, could never adapt to American conditions, and many a Catholic visitor from Europe agreed. The American religious scholar has been able to develop his work within an almost entirely Protestant framework, secure in the assurance that the possible contradictions which might be raised by the Catholic experience in America were confined to a small, insignificant portion of the population. "Doubtless Roman Catholicism had made important contributions to American life," H. Richard Niebuhr wrote, "yet both history and the religious census support the statement that Protestantism is America's 'only national religion and to ignore that fact is to view the country from a false angle.' "[4]

Non-Catholic historians invariably regarded the nation as Protestant; they took little interest in Catholicism, and when they did, they sought to fit it into their own biased view of the nation, which meant appending a description of the Catholic population as a deviant, still foreign, enclave outside the normal, natural area of American religion. As William Clebsch put it: "In a certain sense the history of Catholics and the history of Jews in America arise precisely as these people are viewed apart from their involvement in American society . . . ."[5]

Religious historians were not unique in this regard. Historical scholarship in America was characteristically a Protestant preserve. In the nineteenth century George Bancroft, James Ford Rhodes, Henry Adams, and John W. Burgess dominated the historical profession, and in varying ways presented an interpretation of the American past which reinforced the WASP's conviction that the United States was his country, destined to bring about the triumph of Protestant Christianity and Anglo-American democracy. Frederick Jackson Turner revolutionized historical writing at the turn of the century, but he was a nationalist who believed that the American frontier had blended diverse peoples together into a new breed of men. Turner's followers in religious history retained a Protestant focus, adding the traits of frontier Methodists and Baptists to the heretofore dominant Congregationalism and Presbyterianism. Turnerism additionally reinforced a growing intellectual hostility to the city, often seen as an artificial and parasitic growth permeated by European remnants and populated by alien Catholics and Jews, where the assimilating power of the American environment could be felt only indirectly if at all. Both Catholics and Lutherans, William W. Sweet wrote as late as 1939, "were to a large degree direct European transplantations, and neither was modified in any marked degree by frontier influences."[6] The more recent consensus historians similarly stressed the powerful attachment of all Americans to a common creed or faith. Whether its content was the tenets of liberal capitalism, Calvinist Protestantism or Lockean liberalism, it flourished to such a degree that alternative perspectives, conservatism or socialism, Catholicism or Judaism, were blotted out.

The Protestant and Americanist bias of church history comes through clearly in a volume of essays written by scholars at one time or another associated with the University of Chicago. Martin Marty, Jerald C. Brauer, Winthrop Hudson, and Sidney Mead all discuss the state of American religious history, but not one notes the lack of scholarship on American

Catholicism as a serious drawback to a comprehensive picture of American religious life. Hudson, for example, protests against the preoccupation with uniqueness prevalent among American church historians: "Church historians have tended to depict the European heritage in terms of the initial colonial settlements, and largely ignore the continuing interplay of influence, as though there were no larger Christian community to which we belonged."[7] Yet, in response, Hudson suggests that historians recognize the importance of contacts between American and English churches and religious movements. However useful this may be for many branches of the Protestant church, it has almost no relevance for American Jews and Catholics, whose attention must be focused on other sections of Europe.

Jerald C. Brauer comes closer to the point, but in the end still identifies American religion with Protestantism. After examining the historiography of American religion, almost all of which was written by and about Protestants, he concludes that church history must adopt the techniques and tools of the history of religion and comparative religion, a suggestion that could well lead to consideration of the entire spectrum of the religious experience of the American people.[8] Like Hudson and Brauer, Sidney Mead expressed his dissatisfaction with American church history, but unlike the others he insists on relating the subject more intimately to general American history. Here as in his other writings Mead emphasizes the need to see the institutional churches in relation to their ideals and aspirations and to see both in creative interplay with other features of American culture. The peculiar dynamics of this relationship are, in Mead's view, shaped by the ability of America to foster and encourage a critical discontent with the status quo, a discontent frequently embodied in churchmen, which "brings about continuous evolutionary change and periodically creates constructive revolution" in the life of the nation.[9] This in turn derives from the critical decision of the Founding Fathers to "deliberately" shape a form of government "to prevent an unimaginative orthodoxy from ever again gaining control over society."[10] America was thus "a nation with the soul of a church," with a real, although non-sectarian, religion of its own; a religion which, like that of the churches, always contained a tension between its expressed goals and values and their embodied political reality. Instead of a conflict between church and state, America witnessed competing theologies, the particular theologies of the sects versus "the common, universal theology" of the Republic.[11]

Mead's thesis, like the "civil religion" argument of Robert Bellah,[12] confirms the view that America is a religious nation, though its religion is fluid and but vaguely defined. Whatever the merits of this case, it rests like others on the unexpressed assumption that American Protestantism is both the lock and the key of American religion, that the denominational structure is natural and good for this country, and that it provides the framework to which alternative religious systems must conform themselves.

The Protestant preoccupation of American religious historiography has not been confined to self-consciously Protestant scholars. In 1964 Henry F. May wrote that American religious history, which was of little interest to secular historians twenty years before, had become one of the most fruitful and influential areas of scholarship, so that no serious student of American culture questioned the fact that religion had been a most essential component of American culture.[13] This recovery he attributed to several sources, among them the ecclesiology of H. Richard Niebuhr, whose sharp distinction between Protestantism as order and as movement had enabled scholars to deal both with the church and with the religious dimension of other aspects of American life and thought. Still it was clear that the recovery of American religious history was a Protestant phenomenon. Not that it was brought about by Protestant scholars; on the contrary it was led by secular scholars many of whom had no personal involvement in a Christian church. Rather the recovery was one of interest in American religion as American Protestantism. The articles and books cited by May almost invariably dealt with aspects of Protestantism, and the essay reflected the continuing conviction that American religion, American Christianity and American Protestantism were synonymous terms. May noted that Catholics, together with atheists, had made the least contribution to the recovery, not simply by not writing about themselves but, presumably, by not persuading others to write about them.

Invariably, then, American religious history has been Protestant history, resting on the unannounced assumption that Protestantism—particularly in its least authoritarian, least formal, expressions—has been the true religious expression of the American people. Sydney Ahlstrom recently confirmed this judgment when he spoke of the "synthesis of American church history," dominant until very recently, as an "uncritical Protestant celebrationism," written from a point of view that was "proud, nationalistic, stridently Protestant."[14] Similarly, William Clebsch writes of the newer historians of American religion: "They recognize American man as religious—primarily Christian and specifically Protestant man—just as clearly as Charles and Mary Beard have understood him as economic man."[15] This has resulted not from any deep conviction that Catholics and others were not religious, or not Christian, but that in some sense they were not really American. In the non-Catholic world, history and historiography united around the common ground of unexamined assumptions, even faith statements about the nation and its meaning.

The dilemmas of American Christian history have been a matter of concern for Protestant scholars in recent years, but they have seldom been part of the consciousness of the intellectual leaders of American Catholicism; even though in the case of their church the dichotomy of religious and national values was particularly severe, as non-Catholic scholars knew. Yet the historians of American Catholicism, and the leaders of the church, affirmed the central features of the American faith and refused to enter any significant Catholic dissent.

In regard to the church, they were "Americanists." Before the 1950s no prominent American Catholic historians admitted that there had been any significant failures in the record of his church or country. Frequently and with regret scholars noted the church's failures in other lands, but in

America they saw an unmarred record of growth, prosperity, and virtue. By every available criterion the church had been remarkably successful. Of course there had been difficulties but invariably they were the product of alien intrusions. The "scandal" of trusteeism resulted from the combination of "foreign" priests and congregations and "Protestant" notions of church law. The condemnation of Americanism at the end of the century similarly derived from the inability of outsiders to comprehend the genius of the American church. For the historian and his community both church and America were given, taken for granted, in little need of analysis or criticism.

In many ways the work of the major historians of American Catholicism drew strength from points of view common among general American historians. The uniqueness of the American experience, the spontaneity of American institutions, and the emphasis upon adaptation to the American situation constituted staple themes for Catholic scholars. Historians saw the experience of the church in this country as unique; they noted the spontaneous development of indigenous attitudes and institutions, and they regarded their church's policy of adapting to the given conditions of America as not only necessary but desirable. While less likely than their non-Catholic counterparts to ignore the European background, Catholic historians distinguished between the roots of the faith in Europe and the special qualities the church developed in America, qualities which gave it a distinctive character. Most articulate ecclesiastical leaders urged the church to become fully American, and the historians eased the process by demonstrating the compatability, even the identity, of American and Catholic values.

American Catholic history was essentially denominational history and seldom encompassed American religion as a whole, but it depended upon several unstated assumptions about the nature of American society and the conditions of religious life in the United States. For example, Catholic historians invariably referred to the anti-Catholic and nativist hostility which the church experienced as deviations from true Americanism rather than as expressions of any fundamental defect in the country. While denying without qualification that America was Protestant and insisting that a pluralism of faith and practice was natural in the American context, they continually insisted that this implied no diminution of their love of country or their loyalty to the nation's institutions and operative social values. These feelings they insisted they shared with right minded Americans of every faith, little recognizing how puzzling their claims were for outsiders informed about contemporary church teaching abroad.

Recent historians of American Catholics continue to utilize the long dominant motif of Americanization. Andrew Greeley, for example, argues that the church was forced in spite of itself to adapt to American conditions, with little insight into what it was about. Only the great liberal prelates of the late nineteenth century began to understand, and the condemnation of Americanism repressed their effort to deal with the realities of American life. The result of the unfortunate eclipse of their ideas and policies was not that Americanization ended or even slowed down, but that the church and

its leaders held fast to old ideals and attitudes while simultaneously struggling to keep pace with the on going acculturation of the Catholic people.
Intellectually the church remained entrenched in a ghetto largely of its own
creation while its people entered rapidly into the not-so-secular city. "The
Catholic population has become Americanized," Greeley writes. "The ecclesiastical structure has yet to follow suit. It missed the marvelous opportunities presented to it in its past, and Americanizers, whatever their
theoretical triumphs, were not always practically successful."[16]

Far more sophisticated and precise is Philip Gleason's description of
the church as a highly successful "institutional immigrant," itself caught in
the conflicting pressures to conform to American ways and uphold old
world traditions. Today, as in the past, Gleason argues, the Catholic
Church, like other institutions, is compelled to change to meet the new
needs of its members, while preserving enough of its traditional beliefs and
practices to retain its identity and sense of purpose. All institutions must
"accommodate to the changes in their clientele" while avoiding betrayal of
their heritage, Gleason argues, "for the preservation of the heritage is the
fundamental purpose of their existence and the surest ground of their appeal."[17] The church now, as in the past, must understand what is happening
and seek to "maintain identity without isolation and achieve relevance
without absorbtion" into the broader society.

The Americanization thesis has many advantages. It insists on close attention to the sociological dimensions of contemporary Catholic life, correcting the overly abstract speculations of the more theologically oriented.
Moreover, the concept of Americanization provides an indispensible key to
the past, for upward mobility and acceptance into American culture were indeed the objectives of immigrant Catholics and their leaders. The story was
one of adaptation to the demands of the American situation and debate over
the meaning of what it meant to be an American Catholic. Nothing was
scarcer than an admittedly un-American Catholic; nothing was more difficult to prove to Catholics than that any belief or practice of theirs was contrary to "true Americanism." This is one reason why, as one scholar notes,
Catholics "have been influenced by the American environment to a far
greater degree than they have influenced it."[18]

The weakness of the approach is its bias toward the descriptive, toward
what has been, rather than what should be; and its reliance upon relatively
uncritical tools for dealing with American society as a whole. It underrates
the impact of the urban-Catholic-ethnic component upon American culture
generally and thus tends to give a one sided view of the processes of assimilation. Additionally, its objective, social science approach to history
weakens its impact and obscures the extent to which the historian and those
he describes utilize America itself as the solid anchor of interpretation,
finding in the life of the church the values and style most admired in
American society. Today, for the first time, significant numbers of American
Catholics are seriously questioning the moral basis of American life. Unless
the contemporary crisis in America, a crisis already profoundly shaking the
professions, including history, is understood, the concept of Americaniza-

tion may continue to provide clues for understanding the past, but it may well confuse and misdirect efforts to shape the future.

In the 1950s widespread self-criticism reappeared in the American church for the first time since the 1890s. As Thomas T. McAvoy pointed out, vigorous demands for liturgical reforms and lay participation in church affairs anticipated the advent of John XXIII,[19] and the character of these demands reflected the continuing faith in American society which marked the liberal tradition, now provided with a mass base by the emergence of a new, educated Catholic middle class. Liturgical reform, for example, which in the 1930s had been advanced as a vehicle for promoting Christian social reconstruction, by the 1950s had been stripped of its social content. Rather it had become part of a broader movement for a stronger lay voice in church affairs.

The election of John F. Kennedy climaxed the long quest for respectability. A Catholic president eased remaining doubts about Catholic status. All that remained to the task of completing construction of a truly American Catholicism was the reform of the church along American lines. Michael Novak echoed an old cry when he proclaimed the advent of "a new generation—American and Catholic,"[20] while Daniel Callahan in *The Mind of the Catholic Layman* described in convincing detail the conflicts between the values of church and society which laymen had always felt but seldom expressed.[21] The Americanized Catholic, taught by his society to value individual initiative, personal liberty, and popular participation, was expected to be silent, docile and obedient in church. For men like Callahan, Novak, and Donald Thorman, the solution was clear: The church should officially confirm the validity of American church-state separation and religious liberty; it should validate the layman's positive response to secular activity, and it should recognize his personal freedom and dignity through liturgical reform, democratic structures, and an end to paternalism and authoritarianism.

The intellectual monument of these years was John Courtney Murray's *We Hold These Truths,* whose publication in 1960 earned its author a place on the cover of *Time* magazine.[22] Murray had, in fact, challenged many of the assumptions which had prevented accommodation of Americanism and Catholicism in essays published in the 1940s, but the controversy excited by those articles reached Rome, and Murray ceased publication for a decade until the changed intellectual climate under John XXIII encouraged him to present his thesis in book form. Catholics had long argued that, although the First Amendment was quite acceptable in the American context, it did not provide an ideal arrangement of church-state relations. Murray rejected the expediency of this position, but he wanted nothing to do with absolutist views of religious liberty and separation either. Instead, he sought to demonstrate that the political system of the United States accorded fully with Catholic doctrine. In particular he argued that the American Constitution clearly limited governmental power and provided broad exemptions from government's jurisdiction, allowing the church full freedom to be itself and do its work. The combination of limited government and a broad consensus on moral and procedural values eliminated the need for religious establishment, which was, indeed, positively harmful. Murray provided, then, the badly needed justification of religious liberty by approaching the problem not from traditional theological or ecclesiological perspectives but from the viewpoint of political theory, of "Western constitutionalism, classic and Christian." His success was measured by the adoption of his main arguments in the Vatican Council Declaration on Religious Liberty.

For Murray, the heart of the American system was a consensus, "an ensemble of substantive truths, a structure of basic knowledge, an order of elementary affirmations that reflect realities in the order of existence."[23] Without such a consensus, true dialogue or conversation, and thus true civil society, was not possible. America had begun with a statement of consensus: "We hold these truths to be self-evident" and its institutions, including its arrangements of church and state, had been based upon it. Unfortunately, Murray believed, the consensus was in danger, for it had been all but destroyed by the naturalist currents of modern thought, which had created "a climate of doubt and bewilderment in which clarity about the larger aims of life is dimmed and the self confidence of the people is destroyed."[24] The inability of America to respond to the post war crisis in the world positively, its reliance upon a sterile anticommunism as a substitute for a public philosophy, was evidence of the erosion of the American consensus.

Yet, Murray continued, the American creed did live in the hearts and minds of many Americans, most notably among American Catholics. Widespread intellectual defection from the American consensus had created the paradox that "the guardianship of the original American consensus, based on the western heritage, would have passed to the Catholic community."[25] Thus Murray turned things around. With scholarly precision he demonstrated that Catholics who drew upon their intellectual heritage of scholastic philosophy and political theory were not only capable of being good Americans; they were in fact the best and most convinced adherents of America's most cherished propositions. "Catholic participation in the American consensus," Murray argued, "has been full and free, unreserved and unembarrassed, because the contents of this consensus—the ethical and political principles drawn from the traditions of natural law—approve themselves to the Catholic intelligence and conscience."[26] The American *ralliement* had been motivated not by mere expediency, as anti-Catholics like Paul Blanshard charged, but by "the evident coincidence of the principles which inspired the American Republic with the principles that are structural to the Western Christian political tradition."[27]

Murray's work was the most successful effort ever made to reconcile the apparently conflicting demands of Catholicism and Americanism. It marked the ultimate intellectual expression of the liberal Catholic Americanism which had begun with the conversion of Isaac Hecker and Orestes Brownson more than a century earlier. Nevertheless, it is important to remember that Murray's interpretation of the church-state problem rested upon an interpretation of the American political process which was characteristic of the 1950s. Shocked by the war and its aftermath, American historians and political commentators turned away from the sharp class and sectional conflicts which Charles Beard and an earlier generation had seen as central to American history. In comparison with European political evolution, the American experience seemed to have been placid, with major issues centering on questions of technique. As one historian put it, Americans shared a set of values which were essentially those of liberal capitalism: respect for individual initiative and private property, insistence on limited government, and the pragmatic accommodation and compromise of pressure group politics. There had been no feudalism, no conservatism, no socialism; only a monolithic liberal consensus which obviated the necessity for positive government and made possible peaceful evolution through a selective government intervention which carefully respected traditional civil liberties.[28]

In the 1950s, the United States could make a virtue of its lack of ideology and discover its "genius" in its processes and institutions, as did historian Daniel Boorstin, whose work Murray cited.[29] Both men contributed to the school of thought which proclaimed "the end of ideology" for both saw America as nonideological society which traditionally had avoided sharp division by a common affirmation of consensus. For example, Murray argued that the civil war "was not an ideological conflict but simply...a conflict of interests."[30] That this historical outlook might itself be part of a conservative stance which inhibited radical criticism and efforts at fundamental reform seldom occurred to its exponents. Even Murray himself, while recognizing that America must ultimately stand under the judgment of Christianity, nonetheless found few political or social evils in American society and politics, though he did discover many intellectual aberrations.

In less sophisticated hands than Murray's, his argument easily blended in with opposition to secularism in government and education, for the consensus Murray saw as political and procedural was seen by others as religious, even sectarian. John Ireland had once said that America was "at heart a Christian country" and many who hoped to gain public support for parochial schools or who opposed Supreme Court rulings on religion in public education adapted Murray's thesis without difficulty to such a reading of American history. "All sorts of philosophical isms have dominated most of our institutions of learning and have seriously threatened to secularize our national culture," Father Joseph Costanzo wrote. Nevertheless, he concluded, "the religious tradition is the *original* and *prevailing* one; it is *authentic* in the very fiber of our body politic and as such constitutes the genuine American consensus."[31]

There was an air of complacency about this, one which could not withstand the shocks that lay ahead. But it reflected the long time feeling of Catholics that America, rightly understood, raised no real problem for Catholics and that Catholicism raised no real problem for the Americans. After Murray, Catholics could contend with renewed assurance that while they belonged to the true church, the rights of conscience were guaranteed by both church and state. The only dissent came from a number of conservative theologians at Catholic University, but their voices were gradually stilled as the church moved slowly to the left under John XXIII.[32]

Just as Murray's work marked the culmination of the intellectual reconciliation of church and nation, so the work of the younger laymen brought the drive to reform the church along American lines to a climax. In *The Emerging Layman* Donald Thorman caught the mood of the new breed of articulate, sophisticated Catholics dissatisfied with the church of their fathers.[33] Thorman contended that the laity, now safely established in the middle class, no longer needed or wanted the paternal guidance and direction of the clergy. Catholic Action, "the participation of the laity in the apostolate of the hierarchy" through official lay organizations under clerical control, did not represent a style suitable to a newly confident and responsible generation. The theology of Catholic Action was already under severe attack in Europe, and Thorman drew on this work to support his demand that laymen be granted autonomy in their organizational work, that they be encouraged to participate on equal terms in non-sectarian movements for social reform, and that they be given a voice in the operation of Catholic schools and other agencies conducted with their money. Too long had the laity been silent in the churches, Thorman argued. They needed to bring the democratic and participatory experience of their secular life into the church, and such voluntary service would free the clergy for the more energetic pursuit of their distinctive tasks of spiritual guidance, sacramental administration, and teaching. A new church, characterized by freedom, openness and cooperation, would be the outcome, a church better able to fulfill its responsibilities and to participate more effectively in the life of the nation.

The layman's newly found independence should manifest itself in the temporal sphere as well, Thorman argued. The widespread belief that the layman's work was inferior to that of the clergy was misguided and should be replaced by a positive conception of common Christian vocation shared by all, whatever their state of life. Rather than trying to organize the laity into a solid phalanx under the direction of the clergy, the church should encourage the layman in his creative work and sanction his participation with non-Catholics in social and political action aimed at eliminating social evils and constructing a more decent and humane society. The Christian impact on the world had to be made not simply by the organization—the church— but by men who were Christians. A new role for the layman in a new age, one no longer characterized by the presence of immigrant working class Catholics in an alien land but by educated, prosperous, Americanized business and professional men who knew America as their own: This was the setting for the emerging layman.

Thorman and Murray both wrote out of a solid liberal tradition in American Catholicism. Both accepted the major and minor dogmatic propositions of the faith. Neither questioned the basic structure of ecclesiastical authority, nor did they call for a reevaluation of episcopal centralization. The need for Catholic schools, the responsibility of all to remain loyal to the church, the traditional limitations on ecumenical exchange, the church's prohibitions of birth control and divorce; none of these were major concerns of the liberals in the years before the Vatican Council. The proposals they did make were not new either. As Father McAvoy asked of Thorman, from what was the layman emerging?[34] In the nineteenth century there had been many argumentative laymen who had not hesitated to engage their bishops in public controversy or to question official church policy. Nor had the church ever overtly placed any roadblocks in the way of the Catholic's political action or economic advancement. Catholic schools had taught civics to the immigrant and the bishops had repeatedly urged laymen to vote as independent minded men concerned solely with civic welfare. The schools had likewise inculcated the values of success; hard work, self discipline, sobriety, punctuality, reliability. The canons of the handbooks on how to succeed were as pervasive in Catholic as in public schools. Church related universities had not hesitated to depart from traditional structures of education to add programs in engineering and business administration and the church's leaders had honored successful laymen in business and the professions. Catholic learned societies supported by the episcopate were evidence that the church desired its members to value the intellectual life. Thorman advocated no basic changes, as Father McAvoy saw it, but only those reforms which would come naturally as the Catholic minority gained increased affluence and respectability.

The very moderation of the proposals of reformers may explain the remarkable degree to which the Council acted upon them. Murray's defense of religious liberty was incorporated into a conciliar decree; representative structures were established and national episcopal conferences gained real authority. A new theology of the church replaced clerical legalism with a more democratic imagery of the "people of God." The Council Fathers led the way in ecumenical contacts and a wave of self-criticism and reform swept over the universal church. Yet the changes were to prove incomplete and disappointing. Religious liberty for non-Catholics did not necessarily mean freedom of conscience for Catholics themselves. Liturgical reforms, which were to revitalize community life, found few communities and generated no great spiritual or social awakening. Democratic and national structures, when they were established, frequently expressed a point of view at variance with that of their exponents. Yet even these changes occasioned division and reaction. Frightened ecclesiastical bureaucrats and their lay counterparts retreated to the security of old ways and attitudes while disillusioned liberals often faced crises of faith and conscience more severe than they would have dreamed possible just a few short years before.

The problems inherent in moderate reform in an institution like the Catholic church were magnified for Americans by events at home. If faith in the possibility of a modernized Catholicism was severely challenged by events, faith in the secure assumptions of Americanism was for many all but destroyed. For the first time in the American Catholic experience America itself appeared to have not just "unfinished business," as President Kennedy had put it, but to be morally questionable in its most basic structures and beliefs. Brutal assassination of the nation's best leaders, a vicious and immoral war, the disaffection and hostility of the country's youth, the polarization of blacks and whites, all helped destroy the consensus view of American society as completely as they shattered the consensus politics of Lyndon Johnson. Adherence to the traditions of American democracy and liberty was increasingly replaced by an apocalyptic vision of America as a land of violence and oppression. A church remade in the American image, the goal of Catholic liberalism for over a century, now seemed to many the basest form of blasphemy.

While it is surely too early to argue that the mass of American Catholics seriously question the moral validity of the nation, it seems true that for many Catholics America can no longer simply be taken for granted. It is events, and the conflicts they occasion, which have brought this about— not the superior wisdom of scholars maturing amid the trials of the 1960s. It must be clear that the Americanist heritage, which seems so sordid today, was a humane and honorable stance which reflected the best aspirations of the Catholic community. Nevertheless it was a position which was confined in its vision and limited in its critical edge. Expressing as it did the self-consciousness of the Catholic community, it too frequently was shaped by the dialectic of argument with conservative Catholics and anti-Catholic Americans, with the result that it lacked a critical sense of the character of the religious situation in America and of the dynamics of American society itself.

The common element in American Catholic and American religious history lies in the Americanism of both. Each group found as its major exponents men determined to demonstrate the compatability of American culture and American religion on the one hand and American religion and world Christianity on the other. They did this in subtly different ways. The Protestant historian, with a few exceptions, accomplished his goal by endowing the nation with religious attributes. Faced with the multiplicity of sects and churches he professed to discern an underlying unity, an American Christianity which was often indistinguishable from the nation. "At the very time the denominations ceased to function as the church, the nation came more and more so to function," John E. Smylie has written.[35] Voluntaristic, respectful of individual conscience while claiming to rest on self evident truth; able to cut through superficial national, economic, racial, and national divisions among men and unite them on the ground of their common humanity; providentially guided to redeem men from the chains of history and sin, the nation became an American church.

While the Catholic historian and intellectual undoubtedly felt a similar impulse to make a church of the nation, and to make it a Catholic church, he was inhibited by several factors. His loyalty to an ecclesiastical authority located abroad raised the danger of heresy or schism. Moreover, his constituency held fast to many old world ties, which a too complete Americanism might erode. Most important he could not have the same sense of intimacy of his religion and the national culture that was felt by his evangelical Protestant counterparts. In Europe Catholic churchmen could and did endow the state with divine attributes in those countries where they had no need to regard the state as competing for the popular allegiance. In

England and Germany where the church was a minority, or in Republican France, Italy, or Spain, where the state was in hostile hands, the church was acutely conscious of the need to stress the temporal, limited character of the state's claims. In Franco's Spain the situation was different. In America, where Catholics were a minority and where their enemies, real or imagined, exercised great influence, the church would endorse national values while deploring national practice, exhort patriotism while debunking the claims of the state and its leaders. Thus until the social changes of the post World War II years destroyed minority consciousness, Americanism, as strident as it often was when directed at the Catholic community, had in the end a more pragmatic character than that of many Protestants. This was a stance which might have interacted creatively with Protestant scholarship, were it not for the general problems which inhibited the development of Catholic intellectual life and the additional burdens fostered by the Catholic scholar's training and conception of his role.

Recognition of the complexity and limitations of Americanism, evident in the work of Mead and Ahlstrom, is perhaps the beginning of a real possibility of a new ecumenical and critical approach to American religious studies. There are today several signs of a real vitality in American Catholic historical scholarship. The council, the controversies which it unleashed, the upheavals in the church in this country, and the effect of events at home have combined to open up all phases of Catholic intellectual life while exciting interest in the church on the part of non-Catholic scholars. The rigidity in Catholic ideas of the Church, which May cited as a major drawback to the development of American Catholic history, has been overthrown and new notions of the nature and function of the church contain a reservoir of possibilities for reinterpretation. To the older and still useful areas of diocesan history and episcopal biography are being added studies which place the history of American Catholicism within American history as a whole. . .[36] Immigration historians have turned their attention to the later immigration and in the process are dealing with the social history of the church in the immigrant community and in the Americanization process.[37] New sources are being utilized, new perspectives are emerging, and the possibility exists that the near future will see American Catholicism become an extremely important area of research in American studies, a possibility accentuated by growing interest in and financial support for research in urban history and in ethnic groups and their organizational life. . . .

If these promising developments are to contribute to a new approach to American religious history they will have to take place in a context open to the work of the newly self-critical scholars of American Protestantism and to the changing configurations in religious scholarship generally. Historians of American religion, Protestantism, Catholicism, Judaism, civil religion, the whole variegated religious experience of America, have to face some very serious questions, and they will need help to answer them. They will need the alternative perspectives offered by historians of other periods and other cultures and the challenge of involvement in the ideological controversies now agitating all the learned societies and their constituent departments. Most important they will need theology, general church history, scripture studies and the social sciences, all of which must contribute to the effort to grasp the meaning, significance, and implications of religious experience. Amidst the collapse of old assumptions about the church and American society, the historian of American religion is forced once again to ask himself the meaning of history for the Christian and the meaning of Christianity for the historian. American religious history must leave its terms open, relating creatively to American history, to religious studies and to historiographical debate. In the past dialogue between disciplines and denominations in religious studies has been limited at best. Now it must be full and free if scholarship in general and religious history in particular, is to contribute to the resolution of the crisis now wracking the churches and the nation.

NOTES

[1]Martin Marty, *The Search for a Usable Future* (New York: Harper & Row, 1969).

[2]Henry Steele Commager, *The Search for a Usable Past* (New York: Alfred A. Knopf, 1967), p.x. Much of the following draws on David Noble's *Historians Against History* (Minneapolis: University of Minnesota Press, 1965).

[3]Perry Miller, *Errand Into the Wilderness* (Cambridge: Harvard University Press, 1956), ch. IV.

[4]H. Richard Niebuhr, *The Kingdom of God in·America* (New York: Harper and Bros., 1937), p. 17.

[5]William Clebsch, "A New Historiography of American Religion," *Historical Magazine of the Protestant Episcopal Church*, XXXII (September, 1963), 225-258.

[6]William Warren Sweet, "The Frontier in American Christianity," *Environmental Factors in Christian History*, ed. John E. McNeill et al. (Chicago: University of Chicago Press, 1939), p. 391.

[7]Winthrop Hudson, "How American is Religion in America," *Reinterpretation in American Church History*, ed. Jerald C. Brauer (Chicago: University of Chicago Press, 1968), p. 155.

[8]Jerald C. Brauer, "Changing Perspectives on Religion in America," *Reinterpretation in American Church History*, ed. by Jerald C. Brauer (Chicago: University of Chicago Press, 1968), pp. 1-28.

[9]Sidney Mead, "Reinterpretation in American Church History," *Reinterpretation in American Church History*, ed. Jerald C. Brauer (Chicago: University of Chicago Press, 1968), p. 185.

[10]*Ibid.*, p. 187.

[11]Sidney E. Mead, "The Nation With the Soul of a Church," *Church History*, XXXVI (September, 1967), 262-283.

[12]Robert Bellah, "Civil Religion in America," *The Religious Situation: 1968*, ed. Martin Marty (Boston: Beacon Press, 1968), pp. 331-355.

[13]Henry F. May, "The Recovery of American Religious History," *American Historical Review,* LXX (October, 1964), 79-92.

[14]Sydney E. Ahlstrom, "The Problem of the History of Religion in America," *Church History,* XXXIX (June, 1970), 228-229.

[15]Clebsch, "A New Historiography of American Religion," p. 231.

[16]Andrew Greeley, *The Catholic Experience* (Garden City: Doubleday Co., 1967), p. 291. See also my review article, "Andrew Greeley and American Catholicism," *Catholic World,* CCVII (April 1968), 36-38.

[17]Philip Gleason, "The Crisis of Americanization", *Contemporary Catholicism in the United States,* ed. Philip Gleason (Notre Dame, 1969), pp. 3-32.

[18]*Ibid.,* "Introduction," p. xvii.

[19]"American Catholicism and the Aggiornamento," *Review of Politics,* XXX (July 1968), 275-291; revised in chapter 14 of McAvoy's posthumously published *A History of the Catholic Church in the United States* (Notre Dame: University of Notre Dame Press, 1969).

[20]Michael Novak, *A New Generation: American and Catholic* (New York: Herder and Herder, 1964).

[21]Daniel Callahan, *The Mind of the Catholic Layman* (New York: Herder and Herder, 1963).

[22]John Courtney Murray, *We Hold These Truths* (New York: Sheed and Ward, 1960).

[23]*Ibid.,* p. 9

[24]*Ibid.,* p. 12.

[25]*Ibid.,* p. 43.

[26]*Ibid.,* p. 41.

[27]*Ibid.,* p. 43.

[28]See, for example, Richard Hofstadter, *The American Political Tradition* (New York: Alfred A. Knopf, 1955), preface; and Louis Hartz, *The Liberal Tradition in America* (New York: Harcourt, Brace and World, 1958).

[29]Daniel Boorstin, *The Genius of American Politics* (Chicago: University of Chicago Press, 1953).

[30]Murray, *We Hold These Truths,* p. 73.

[31]Joseph F. Costanzo, S.J., "Religious Heritage of American Democracy," *Thought,* XXX (Winter 1955-1956), 488-489.

[32]The controversy is traced in Thomas T. Love, *John Courtney Murray: Contemporary Church-State Theory* (Garden City: Doubleday Co., 1965).

[33]Donald Thorman, *The Emerging Layman* (Garden City: Doubleday Co., 1962).

[34]"The Emerging Layman—Emerging From What?", *Davenport Messenger,* November 4, 1965.

[35]John E. Smylie, "National Ethos and the Church," *Theology Today,* XX (October 1963), 314.

[36]See, for example, Frank T. Reuter, *Catholic Influence on American Colonial Policies, 1898-1904* (Austin, Texas: University of Texas Press, 1967); Philip Gleason, *The Conservative Reformers: German American Catholics and the Social Order* (Notre Dame: University of Notre Dame Press, 1968); George Q. Flynn, *American*

Catholics and the Roosevelt Presidency, 1932-1936 (Lexington: University of Kentucky Press, 1968); Aaron I. Abell, editor, *American Catholic Thought on Social Questions* (Indianapolis: Bobbs-Merrill, 1968).

[37]Timothy L. Smith has led the way here. See his articles, "Religious Denominations as Ethnic Communities: A Regional Case Study," *Church History,* XXXV (June, 1966); "New Approaches to the History of Immigration in Twentieth Century America," *American Historical Review,* LXXI (July, 1966), 1265-1279. See also Rudolph J. Vecoli, "Prelates and Peasants: Italian Immigrants and the Catholic Church," *Journal of Social History,* (Spring 1969), 217-268. And Victor Greene, "For God and Country: The Emergence of Slavic Catholic Self Consciousness in America," *Church History,* XXXV (December 1966), 446-460.

25

The Origins
of Fundamentalism

Ernest R. Sandeen

Fundamentalism has frequently been described as the religious response of some American Protestants to the increasing complexity of an urbanized, industrial society. Ernest R. Sandeen questions this conclusion and maintains that the roots of fundamentalism were located within the millennial culture of nineteenth century British and American Protestantism. Professor Sandeen is a member of the faculty at Macalaster College.

The fate of Fundamentalism in historiography has been worse than its lot in history. The whirlwind of the twenties, after twisting through the denominations, ended by tearing even the name to shreds. Who were the Fundamentalists? Few today will use the name, and there seems to be no unity among those that do.

There have been only two book-length attempts to trace the history of this movement. Stewart G. Cole, who wrote his *History of Fundamentalism* in the middle of the controversy (1931), has remained the standard authority although he was writing too close to the events to put them in proper perspective. The late Norman F. Furniss published in 1954 a monograph limited to one decade of the controversy (1918-1931).[1] Both of these books are not so much discussions of Fundamentalism as investigations of one aspect of denominationalism during the twenties. Both Cole and Furniss

First published in *Church History*, XXXVI (1967), pp. 66-83 (abridged). Reprinted with permission of *Church History* and the author.

were interested in Fundamentalism primarily as a negative force, interested in it because it impinged upon denominational machinery. This approach shaped their understanding of the movement. Fundamentalism was described as a political controversy within denominationalism, which it was, of course; but in their accounts it never appears to have been a religious movement at all.

In addition to its treatment as a political controversy, Fundamentalism has been discussed as a psychological and sociological phenomenon. In fact, this is the context in which discussions of the origin and nature of the movement most commonly appear. Even when we exclude those who treat Fundamentalism as one among many "varieties of religious experience" and concentrate upon those who are specifically interested in the history of this one movement, sociological and psychological explanations still predominate. The factors that explain the Fundamentalists' brash behavior, most historians have argued, can be discovered in the economic and intellectual forces which alarmed and agitated the churches so terribly in the last decades of the nineteenth century and in the psychological states of those whose lot it was to live through those days.[2]

But no matter what tack scholars have taken in approaching Fundamentalism—political, sociological, psychological—they have all tacitly assumed or flatly asserted that theologically and dogmatically Fundamentalism was indistinguishable from nineteenth-century Christianity. The Fundamentalists themselves always proclaimed the same theme. As James M. Gray once wrote, ". . . there is nothing new in Fundamentalism except it may be its name. It is the same old 'offense of the cross'.[3]"

Thus, though historical interest in Fundamentalism has not diminished over the years, historians have not found it necessary to study this group within its religious and theological context.[4] The aura of intellectual disrepute surrounding the Scopes trial has discouraged serious consideration of the faith of the Fundamentalists. Most American historians have felt that the Fundamentalists were mistaken and seem to have concluded that they cannot have been serious—that their theology must have been only a cloak to hide their socio-economic or psychological nakedness. I will attempt to prove that it was these neglected theological affirmations which gave structure and identity to Fundamentalism and that only through the understanding of this aspect of American intellectual history can we lay the foundation for a historical interpretation of Fundamentalism. . . . My thesis is that Fundamentalism was comprised of an alliance between two newly-formulated nineteenth-century theologies, dispensationalism and the Princeton Theology which, though not wholly compatible, managed to maintain a united front against modernism until about 1918.

Dispensationalism stems principally from a small British sect, usually called Plymouth Brethren, which sprang up in Ireland and England during the 1820's and from one man in particular, John Nelson Darby. Dissatisfied with what they felt to be the dead hand of tradition and legalism in the Church of England, the Brethren admitted any professing Christian to their informal weekly communion services, refused to acknowledge or create any special caste of clergy, conducted their meetings without order of service in order to allow the Holy Spirit to lead their worship, and in everything attempted to recreate the New Testament pattern of church government and worship.[5]

Dispensationalism refers primarily to the division of history into periods of time, dispensations, seven of which are usually named. The *Scofield Reference Bible,* the most influential dispenser of dispensationalism in America, named them Innocence (the Garden of Eden), Conscience (Adam to Noah), Human Government (Noah to Abraham), Promise (Abraham to Moses), Law (Moses to Christ), Grace (Christ through the present to the judgment of the world), and the Kingdom or Millennium. Proponents argued that God judged man not on an absolute and unchanging standard but according to ground rules especially devised for each dispensation. For example, under the dispensation of Grace, men are required to repent and turn in faith to Christ, while under Moses they were commanded to obey the law.[6]

For the dispensationalist, the earthly people of Israel and the spiritual community of the Church must be sharply distinguished. The one is entered by natural birth, the other by conversion—the "new birth." Both have promises and prophecies given to them which must be distinguished and separated. In the millennium, the Church will reign as the "bride of Christ," while Israel will be restored to its ancestral land and inherit the earthly kingdom forecast by the prophets. This particular emphasis within dispensationalism accounts for the enthusiastic Zionism manifested by many Fundamentalists.[7]

The dispensationalist accepted an intensely pessimistic view of the world's future combined with a hope in God's imminent and direct intervention in his own life. God has established covenants which have always been broken by virtually all those involved in them. God has waited, restraining judgment, but eventually punished the disobedient while saving out of the destruction a little band, a remnant of just men such as Noah, Joshua, or Ezra. This pattern of past events was projected into the future through the interpretation of prophecy. Dispensationalists became prophets themselves, predicting the speedy end of their own era in an act of God's cataclysmic judgment. They looked for a literal, imminent second coming of Christ as the next event before God judged the world and brought in the next dispensation, the millennium, and, therefore, referred to their eschatology as premillennialism.[8] In their view the religious leadership has always been the chief center of apostasy (as in the case of Israel and the golden calf) while the righteous remnant has been neglected, overlooked and even despised. In nineteenth-century America as in Europe, the apostates were quickly identified as liberal theologians.

Thus a doctrine of the Church emerged from a philosophy of history: The church was made up of God's elect who were always only a handful, seldom if ever the possessors of power. The true church could not possibly be identified with any of the large denominations, which were riddled with heresy, but could only be formed by individual Christians who could expect to be saved from the impending destruction. It is impossible to overestimate the importance of this ecclesiology for the history of Fundamentalism. Most protest groups within American Protestantism turn into denominations themselves. Yet Fundamentalism has not so solidified, and one of the unappreciated factors in this anomalous situation is certainly the retarding influence of dispensationalism. According to their teaching, the true Church can never be an organization but must remain a spiritual fellowship of individual Christians.

As has been intimated, the interpretation of biblical prophecy played a large role in dispensationalism. A glance at the history of other nineteenth century religious groups—Millerites, Irvingites, Mormons, Campbellites, or Shakers—would show them to be concerned with prophetic interpretation as well. Millennial expectations are woven into the fabric of early nineteenth century life in both Europe and America.[9] One factor which differentiates the dispensationalists is their concern for biblical literalism. To speak of a concern for biblical literalism may seem redundant in the context of the evangelical tradition in which dependence upon scripture alone had become a shibboleth. But care must be taken to differentiate between the common evangelical belief in biblical inspiration, the effect of which was to distinguish the Bible from other books, and the principles of hermeneutics which guide the interpretation of the Bible itself. Literalism, in the early nineteenth century, usually refers quite specifically to the interpretation of prophecy and contrasts with the figurative or symbolic manner of interpretation. This literalistic approach puzzled many scholars although they themselves might not have any doubts concerning the inspiration of the scriptures. Writing in the *Princeton Review,* one American noted:

> Millenarianism has grown out of a new "school of Scripture interpretation" and its laws of interpretation are so different from the old, that the Bible may almost be said to wear a new visage and speak with a new tongue—a tongue not very intelligible, in many of its utterances, to the uninitiated. The central law by which millenarians profess always to be guided, is that of giving the literal sense.[10]

It is not difficult to see how some of the characteristic doctrines of dispensationalism arose from this hermeneutic. The second coming of Christ, the restoration of the Jews to the land of Israel, the Great Tribulation, and the 1000 years of peace and justice—dispensationalists believed these prophecies would be fulfilled quite as literally as Christ had fulfilled prophecy during his first advent. When the verbal inspiration of the Bible became a matter of theological dispute later in the century, the dispensationalists were able to win many converts to their cause by arguing that only dispensationalism really took the Bible seriously. Dispensational theology was based upon hermeneutical principles which required, in fact presupposed, a frozen biblical text in which every word was supported by the same weight of divine authority.[11]

Dispensationalism was being taught in the United States and Canada as early as the 1840's, and not the least important apostle of the new movement was John Nelson Darby himself, who travelled to North America on seven occasions from 1862 through 1877, frequently traveling around the continent for as long as a year. During this sixteen-year period (1862-1877), Darby resided in North America at least forty percent of the time. The great bulk of his time was spent working in large cities, mostly on the eastern seaboard. . . . Of course, Darby's was not the only voice preaching dispensationalism. Other advocates of these views visited North America, dispensational publications found their way to the U.S., and a few were published in the U.S. as well.

Many converts to dispensationalism were won during these years, but few of these would take the step of leaving their denominations. According to Darby, this was the main aim of his teaching. He once wrote, ". . . our real work . . . is to get Christians clear practically of a great corrupt baptized body. . . ."[12] But most converts to dispensational theology refused to abandon their denominations and pastoral posts. Darby complained in one of his letters,

> . . . There is a great effort to keep souls in the various systems while taking advantage of the light which brethren have and preaching their doctrines. They do not even conceal it. One of the most active who has visited Europe told ministers that they could not keep up with the brethren unless they read their books, but he was doing everthing he could to prevent souls leaving their various systems called churches.[13]

Thus the instrument of propagation for the dispensational system in the U.S. became the clergy and religious periodicals of American denominations and voluntary societies, who, without announcing their conversion to anything new or different, began to influence the evangelical churches.

To what kind of Christians did dispensationalism appeal?—particularly the Calvinists.[14] Most of the converts seem to be Presbyterians or Calvinistic Baptists. Very few Methodists were ever caught up in dispensationalism, nor were many U. S. Episcopalians, although many British and Canadian Anglicans became converts.[15] This alignment is significant for the later composition of Fundamentalism, for the Presbyterian and Baptist denominations were the two most racked by the Fundamentalist controversy in the 1920's.

After dispensationalism had become an American movement, the institution most influential in its spread was the summer Bible conference and the most significant of these was the Niagara Conference. From 1868 until 1900, a relatively small but stable group of pastors and laymen met for one or two weeks at a summer resort (during 1883-97 at Niagara Falls) for concentrated Bible study.[16] The men who led these conferences during the 1870's deserve to be known as the founding fathers of Fundamentalism: James H. Brookes, a Presbyterian and alumnus of Princeton Seminary, for many years pastor of the Walnut Street (now Memorial) Presbyterian Church in St. Louis and editor of his own periodical, *The Truth;* William J. Erdman, at various times pastor of Presbyterian and Congregational churches as well as Moody's Chicago Avenue Church, one of the founders of the Moody Bible Institute, an editor of the *Scofield Bible* and father of Charles R. Erdman, Professor of Practical Theology at Princeton Seminary; Adoniram Judson Gordon, a Baptist, pastor for most of his life of the Clarendon Street Church, Boston, founder of the Boston Missionary Training School (now Gordon College and Seminary), editor of the periodical *Watchword,* a close associate of Moody in the management of the Northfield Conferences; William G. Moorehead, a Presbyterian, Professor of New Testament and President of Xenia Seminary, and editor of the *Scofield Bible.*

The series of prophetic and premillennial conferences which began in 1878 were the direct outgrowth and offspring of this Niagara Group. But not only dispensationalists collaborated in the calling and direction of the First International Prophetic Conference in 1878. A group of conservative Calvinists closely related to Princeton Theological Seminary were drawn into this conference movement through their concern with the premillennial return of Christ and other prophetic themes. The 1878 Premillennial Conference marks the beginning of a long period of dispensationalist cooperation with Princeton-oriented Calvinists. The unstable and incomplete synthesis which is now known as Fundamentalism at this point first becomes visible to the historian.

The Princeton Theology was born with the founding of Princeton Seminary in 1812 and endured as a living force for about 100 years. Inspired by its first professor, Archibald Alexander, and given its most complete formulation by Charles Hodge in his *Systematic Theology,* the Princeton Theology was defended and modified throughout the nineteenth and early twentieth centuries by competent scholars such as A. A. Hodge, Benjamin B. Warfield and J. G. Machen.[17] Princeton Seminary was very inbred, but its outreach was extensive, passing far beyond the bounds of Presbyterians into Episcopal, Congregational, Baptist and other denominations. The Princeton faculty never admitted that they were teaching a unique theology, but staunchly insisted that they only intended to defend the system of John Calvin. In this belief they were deceived, both the methodology and the conclusions of their theology differing clearly from the work of Calvin himself and the standard of the Westminster Confession.[18]

The methodology of the Princeton Theology laid down by Archibald Alexander and Charles Hodge remains the most characteristic aspect of the school's teaching. Insisting that theology must be pursued scientifically, the Princeton professors, completely ignoring the criticism of Hume and Kant, constructed a rationalistic method which was compared by Charles Hodge himself to Newtonian physics.

> As natural science was a chaos until the principle of induction was admitted and faithfully carried out, so theology is a jumble of human speculations, not

worth a straw, when men refuse to apply the same principle to the study of the Word of God. . . . The Bible gives us not only the facts concerning God, and Christ, ourselves, and our relations to our Maker and Redeemer, but also records the legitimate effects of those truths on the minds of believers. So that we cannot appeal to our own feelings or inward experience, as a ground or guide, unless we can show that it agrees with the experience of holy men as recorded in the Scriptures.[19]

Princeton thus took the position of the scientist who observes, arranges, and systematizes but does not participate in his experiment. Furthermore, the world of epistemology for Princeton seemed to be divided between reason and mysticism, fact and inner light. Though they criticized their early deist rivals for mistreating right reason, they reserved their hardest words for mystics, hewing a rationalist line in their own theology. Their doctrine of inspiration, as it developed during the century, never wavered from this fundamental tenet—that if the Bible was to be proven to be God's inspired word, the demonstration must be made on the basis of reason through the use of external marks of authenticity—not inner convictions.[20]

Building upon this methodology, Charles Hodge, A. A. Hodge, and B. B. Warfield constructed what they considered a shock-proof doctrine of Biblical authority. Their fundamental assumption seems to have been that God would not reveal his truths through a fallible book. They tried to prove that God had so inspired the Biblical authors that their every word as recorded on the original autographs was inerrant—a term more specifically rationalistic than the word infallible. The frequency with which these aspects of the doctrine of inspiration occur in the Fundamentalist controversy seems largely due to the influence of the Princeton Theology. That the Bible was 1) verbally inspired, 2) inerrant in its every reference, statistic, and quotation, 3) when first written down on the original autographs—these phrases have become the shibboleth of the Fundamentalist doctrine of the Scriptures. This doctrine did not exist either in Europe or America prior to its formulation in the last half of the nineteenth century. It has become an essential ingredient in the theology of Fundamentalism.[21]

That dispensationalists and advocates of the Princeton Theology should find it possible to cooperate and accept each other as fellow Chrisitans (when they rejected so many others) should not seem strange. They agreed with one another in general mood and in the elaboration of their central theme of Biblical authority. Both groups insisted upon an inerrant scripture, and, whether by accident or design, began at about the same time to defend their views by recourse to the "original autographs."[22] Both groups thought in pre-Kantian, pre-Schliermacherian, rationalistic terms. Over against the new theologies of immanence and social gospel, both stressed God's transcendence and supra-historical power and expressed themselves in very pessimistic terms when discussing social problems. The two movements were by no means completely compatible, but the common Modernist foe kept them at peace with one another throughout the nineteenth and early twentieth centuries. Attacks upon the dispen-

sationalists were occasionally heard from such a man as B. B. Warfield, but
at the same time the books of the dispensationalists were being regularly
reviewed and recommended in the *Presbyterian and Reformed Review.*

Bible conferences seem to have provided the Niagara Group with a
good opportunity to widen its influence. This may have been their chief purpose in calling the first International Prophetic Conference in the Holy
Trinity Episcopal Church in New York City, October 30, 1878. The
religious press treated the conference in sceptical terms, labeling the participants Millerites and Adventists.[23] One rather complacent Baptist editor,
noting that pessimism about the future was a distinguishing mark of the premillennialists, prophesied that only Anglicans and Roman Catholics were
likely to be attracted to it.[24] But the conference itself proved impressive.
Whether by design or default, very little dispensationalism, as such, was
taught. Instead a considerable body of respected American and European
support was rallied behind pre-millennialist beliefs. Although not a dispensationalist, the able Samuel H. Kellogg, a Princeton Seminary graduate and
at that time Professor of Theology at Western Seminary, delivered a paper
in support of premillennialism at the conference and followed up his address with a long article in a respected American theological journal, in
which he defended premillennialism as an historic doctrine of the Church.
In the premillennial advent, the dispensationalists had apparently hit upon
a theme suitable for building an alliance with certain other Biblically-
oriented conservatives, particularly those following the path toward Biblical
inerrancy laid out by Princeton. No formal alliances were ever drawn up.
No official conferences were held in which the two groups publically
declared their intention to cooperate. But during the last two decades of the
nineteenth century, there were frequent occasions on which representatives
of these two groups were found speaking on the same platforms and
publishing their articles in the same books, all with an end to defeating the
Modernist heresies. . . .

Another important conference of this period was D. L. Moody's
Northfield Conference—important because of the size and continued duration of the series (from 1880 to 1902), and because of the importance that
Moody's presence lent to the proceedings. Few men in American
nineteenth-century Protestantism could equal Moody's influence. Comments about the broad, perhaps too inclusive nature of Moody's spirit have
frequently been made. No historian of Moody's amazing career has noted,
however, that his Northfield Conferences were virtually dominated by dispensationalists, particularly from 1880 through 1887 and again from 1894 to
1902.[25] Moody himself never appears to have become a convinced dispensationalist. But, whatever his own beliefs, he gave up control of the conference, when he himself was absent, to dispensationalist leaders such as A.
J. Gordon or A. T. Pierson and invited so many dispensationalist speakers
that they were referred to as "the usual war horses" in accounts of the
proceedings.[26] "Dispensational Truth" was the announced theme of the
conference in 1886, the same year that the Student Volunteer Movement

was initiated in Northfield. In that famous conference, in which the first 100 volunteers of the S.V.M. were recruited, the leadership was dispensationalist to a man.[27]

By 1900 Fundamentalism, though still unchristened, was already a significant force in American life. How influential is difficult to estimate, for, as has been indicated, the movement had not yet become divisive. The lines of battle were becoming clear by 1900, but (as was tragically true in Europe at just this time) no one could predict that a great war was imminent nor that this war would involve almost everyone in American Protestantism. The great majority of the pastors and laymen had not yet been forced—as they later would be—to choose sides between the Fundamentalists and the Modernists, and many Christians felt that they could live peaceably with both camps. It is clear that the Fundamentalists, though alarmed and dismayed by the teachings of the Modernists, were not ill-informed nor ignorant. Nor were they behaving like obscurantists or retreating from the world. Their movement at this time possessed great vigor, particularly in evangelism and world missions. The leadership was concentrated in urban centers, particularly in the Philadelphia-New York-Boston area with lesser centers in Chicago, St. Louis and Los Angeles. The South was almost unrepresented. Fundamentalist leaders were occasionally found in the pastorate, but more often held positions which allowed them wider influence—the editorship of a journal (Charles G. Trumbull or Arno C. Gaebelein), the deanship of a Bible school (James M. Gray or Reuben A. Torrey), a chair in a seminary (Wm. G. Moorehead or Melvin G. Kyle) or the calling of an evangelist (J. Wilbur Chapman or L. W. Munhall).

In the early twentieth century, the most commonly cited source of Fundamentalist teaching was the series of volumes entitled *The Fundamentals*. This series of twelve pamphlets was published and distributed free, in numbers ranging from 175,000 to 300,000 copies by two brothers who preferred to be known only as "Two Christian Laymen."[28] That these two were Lyman and Milton Stewart, founders and chief stockholders of the Union Oil Company of Los Angeles, has been common knowledge for many years. The Lyman Stewart correspondence reveals, however, that Lyman Stewart was the real sponsor of the series and Milton a silent partner, that Lyman Stewart spent a great deal of energy attempting to bolster the Christian faith particularly through the printed word, and, most significantly, that he was both a Presbyterian and a dispensationalist.[29] In the summer of 1909, Stewart met the Rev. Amzi C. Dixon, a dispensationalist Baptist minister at that time pastor of the Moody Memorial Church, and impressed by Dixon's militant defense of Christian truth, enlisted him as chairman of an editorial committee to supervise the publication of *The Fundamentals*. This committee, selected by Dixon, was comprised of several laymen who were members of Dixon's church and three clergymen—Reuben A. Torrey, a dispensationalist who was Dean of the Bible Institute of Los Angeles (another Lyman Stewart project), Elmore Harris, possibly a dispensationalist, President of the Toronto Bible Institute and an editor of the *Scofield Reference Bible,* and Louis Meyer, a Jewish convert to Christianity then working among Jews under the auspices of the Presbyterian Board of Home Missions.[30]

What kind of editorial matter did Stewart and his committee produce? The tone of the volumes is quite calm. Though the articles are polemical, they are almost never vituperative. This approach seems to have been intentional. Stewart explained the rejection of an article by saying that its language was not ". . . the chaste and moderate language which causes even the opponent to stop and read."[31] In content the volumes seem broader than the make-up of the editorial committee might indicate. Altogether 64 authors furnished a total of 90 articles to *The Fundamentals.* In articles defending specific Christian doctrines, the subject of Biblical authority certainly predominated, 29 separate articles being devoted to it, including five specifically on Biblical inspiration. It is significant that all five were written by dispensationalists, and that the two articles by James M. Gray and L. W. Munhall, which most clearly attempt to structure a theological argument for verbal inspiration, depend upon and quote directly from the works of the Princeton theologians. Dispensationalism as such was never made the subject of a separate article; when it did occur, it appeared only as the natural mode of expression of a dispensationalist author. Nineteen authors responsible for contributing 31 articles can be identified as dispensationalists. Only three members of the Princeton Seminary faculty contributed articles (David James Burrell, Charles R. Erdman, and B. B. Warfield), but a great many Calvinist-oriented clergy were recruited to write for *The Fundamentals.*

There apparently was no overall plan followed in the publication of *The Fundamentals*, although individual volumes do occasionally show a common theme—volume VII, for instance, was devoted almost entirely to biblical problems and volume XII to evangelism and missions. The volumes do tend toward a more popular level during the last half of the series, apparently intentionally, for Lyman Stewart wrote to his brother in 1911 when the series was about half published, ". . . thus far the articles have been more especially adapted to men of the highest culture, . . . and a series of articles adapted to the more ordinary preacher and teacher should follow."[32] Some historians have speculated that *The Fundamentals* were part of an elaborate plan or the first shot in the subsequent controversy. There is no evidence that this series had any other intent than its title implied—the reaffirmation of fundamental truths. That such a heavily dispensationally-dominated committee should produce such a balanced series would seem to demonstrate that these early Fundamentalists could still find some grounds for cooperation with other Christian leaders.

To this point I have refrained even from mentioning the "five points" of Fundamentalism. Historians, and contemporary Fundamentalists have commonly talked as though there was a kind of Fundamentalist creed of five articles which all defenders of Christianity accepted and defended, and which all Modernists and Liberals attacked and rejected.[33] The General Assembly of the Presbyterian Church in 1910 did adopt a five-point doctrinal deliverance—naming the inerrancy of the Scripture, virgin birth, substitutionary atonement, physical resurrection, and miracle-working power of Christ as essential Christian doctrines.[34] But this was the only occasion (relevant to early Fundamentalism) on which any denomination or group ever made a five-point statement. Stewart Cole was probably responsible for the confusion, for he carelessly stated that the Niagara Group had also adopted such a five-point declaration, but the only creedal statement ever produced by that group (in 1878) contained fourteen points.[35] What a career that simple mistake has made for itself. Through uncritical acceptance of Cole's mistake, generations of students have been taught to identify the Fundamentalist beast by its five points. That Fundamentalists defended many traditional doctrines is obvious. They did not define themselves in relation to any five particular points, however; and as has been pointed out, their innovations were more significant than their preservations.

In the climate of the 1920's, the calm, determined spirit of *The Fundamentals* quickly gave way to the clangor and strife that has turned Fundamentalism into a term of reproach. An analysis of the controversies of the 1920's is impossible in this paper, but it is essential to note the presence of dispensationalism and Princeton-Calvinism within the contending factions.

The Baptists did not split in the 1920's, but their denomination was as badly racked by controversy as any. Two organizations, The National Federation of Fundamentalists and the Baptist Bible Union, led the attack upon Modernism in the Northern Baptist Convention. The Federation was determined in its program, but refused to carry the issue to the point of schism. The Baptist Bible Union, however, carried on as if it had no real concern for the continuance of the denomination and did contribute eventually to several small schisms.[36] It has been common practice to ascribe only a difference in temperament to these two uncooperative Fundamentalist groups, whereas it is clear that the Baptist Bible Union was controlled largely by dispensationalists and the Federation by the other more Calvinistic wing of the movement. Many of the leaders of the militant Baptist Bible Union, such as A. C. Dixon, William B. Riley, T. T. Shields, and W. L. Pettingill, were dispensationalists. Whatever the source of the militancy of Union members, it is clear that their dispensational doctrine of the church would have made it very much easier for them to countenance schism.

The other denomination badly shaken by the Fundamentalist controversy was, of course, the Presbyterian. The 1920's do not mark the beginning of the Fundamentalist controversy within Presbyterianism, but the disputes in the General Assembly, seminaries and mission boards of the church became much more acrimonious, leading to the reorganization of Princeton Seminary (and simultaneous establishment of the Fundamentalist Westminster Seminary in Philadelphia), the creation of a Fundamentalist Presbyterian mission board to rival the official denominational board, and, finally in 1936, the withdrawal of about 100 ministers and many congregations to form the Orthodox Presbyterian Church.[37] Breathing a rhetorical sigh of relief, J. Gresham Machen, the leader of the new denomination, wrote, "On Thursday, June 11, 1936, the hopes of many long years were realized. We became members, at last, of a true Presbyterian Church. . . ."[38] But within a matter of months the members of the new Presbyterian denomination were fighting with each other more bitterly than they had with the Modernists. Another schism quickly ensued in which the two groups, which we have traced in the origins of the Fundamentalist movement, appeared as opponents. Machen's group, representing the Princeton element, separated from a group calling itself the Bible Presbyterian Synod which was heavily influenced by dispensationalists.[39] The Princeton faction, in an editorial in their periodical, apologized for not recognizing the dangers of dispensationalism earlier. "We cannot," they wrote, "offer a very good reason for a failure to raise the issue at an earlier time. Evidently the only reason is that we were absorbed in fighting that great enemy, Modernism."[40]

This kind of analysis should be pursued more widely in denominational studies and nearer to our own day. The skeleton of the thesis has been made plain, however—Fundamentalism of the late nineteenth and early twentieth centuries was comprised of an alliance between dispensationalists and Princeton-oriented Calvinists, who were not wholly compatible, but managed to maintain a united front against Modernism until about 1918. This is a working hypothesis, subject to criticism and correction. The implications of the thesis have been examined for only a few major denominations. Perhaps other historians will attempt to test the thesis within their own areas of special competence.

Whether or not this thesis can provide a new context for the historiography of Fundamentalism, historians ought to be able to agree that the old explanations cannot be defended. A critique of traditional Fundamentalist historiography can be phrased in four parts.

First, this study has demonstrated that the Fundamentalist considered himself a champion of certain religious truths and worked within the scope of definable beliefs. Each Fundamentalist spokesman ought to be examined in the light of his theological position. The sociologist, or historian equipped with tools of sociological analysis, is welcome to work in this field but let us hope that he will approach his subject with enough sophistication in theology to recognize the factors of religious belief that played a discriminating role in the controversy. Most previous studies of the sociology of Fundamentalism have proved nothing because they could never produce an adequate definition of the subject. Even those historians concerned only with a narrative explanation of the events of the 1920's ought to recognize the inadequacy of a purely denominational-political explanation of the struggle. Power blocks do confront each other within the denominations, but to explain the origin of these power blocks without treating theological questions has reduced much of this agonizing struggle to buffoonery and monkey shines.

Second, this study has shown that the Fundamentalist's assertion of his own orthodoxy and conservatism cannot be accepted uncritically. Both dispensationalism and the Princeton Theology were marked by doctrinal innovations and emphases which it is mistaken to confuse with apostolic belief, Reformation theology or nineteenth-century evangelism. It is almost incredible that a dispute over the nature of orthodox Christianity could be discussed by a generation of historians without any of them analyzing the validity of Fundamentalist claims. This is especially significant in view of the fact that the Fundamentalist arguments—before, during, and after the controversy of the 1920's—rested entirely upon their claim to be defending the truths of an historic faith. Some Fundamentalists were only attempting to conserve their traditional faith, that is true. But the assumption that only the Modernists reconstructed their theological position during the intellectual crisis of the late nineteenth century cannot be maintained.

Third, though my own attempt at the formulation of a definition of Fundamentalism will not satisfy everyone, the task of formulating a historical definition is not insuperable. Fundamentalism was a movement which people joined, not an amorphous entity or an abstract category. By discovering what Fundamentalists believed and taught, who they counted among their friends and confidants, and what they said about themselves, a representative, honest portrait of Fundamentalism can be drawn. Our earlier historiographic surrender to semantic confusion has been unnecessary and unfortunate.

Fourth, we ought to stop referring to Fundamentalism as an agrarian protest movement centered in the South. Only by uncritically accepting the setting and conduct of the Scopes trial as the model of all other Fundamentalist activity can such a parody of history be sustained. If one turns to Fundamentalist periodicals and conference platforms, he does not find them dominated by ill-taught stump preachers or demagogues. In the nineteenth century, especially, the proto-Fundamentalists were frequently men in high esteem in their own denominations and communities. Only in the later twentieth century (if then) did Fundamentalism become particularly a phenomenon of the South. Fundamentalism was not a sectional controversy but a national one, and most of its champions came from the same states as their Modernist opponents. Fundamentalism originated in the northeastern part of this continent in metropolitan areas and should not be explained as a part of the populist movement, agrarian protest or the Southern mentality.

NOTES

[1] Stewart G. Cole, *The History of Fundamentalism* (New York, 1931). Norman F. Furniss, *The Fundamentalist Controversy, 1918-1931* (New Haven, 1954).

[2] The most famous advocate of this position has been H. Richard Niebuhr. He has written,". . . fundamentalism was closely related to the conflict between rural and urban cultures in America. . . . Furthermore, fundamentalism in its aggressive forms was most prevalent in those isolated communities in which the traditions of pioneer society had been most effectively preserved and which were least subject to the influence of modern science and industrial civilization" (H. Richard Niebuhr, "Fundamentalism," *Encyclopaedia of Social Sciences,* V, 527).

[3]James M. Gray, "The Deadline of Doctrine Around the Church," *Moody Monthly* (November, 1922), p. 2

[4]Happily there are a few exceptions which ought not to be passed over in silence: Winthrop S. Hudson, *Religion in America* (New York: Scribner's, 1965), and H. Shelton Smith, Robert T. Handy, and Lefferts A Loetscher, *American Christianity* (New York: Scribner's, 1963), Vol. II.

[5]W. Blair Neatby, *The History of the Plymouth Brethren* (London, 1901); and W. G. Turner, *John Nelson Darby* (London, 1944).

[6]C. Norman Kraus, *Dispensationalism in America* (Richmond, 1958), p. 67-8.

[7]Charles C. Ryrie, *Dispensationalism Today* (Chicago: Moody Press, 1965), p. 44ff.

[8]Many historians have become quite familiar with references to premillennialism without ever becoming acquainted with the dispensational system of which it frequently formed a part. Not all premillennialists were dispensationalists, but every dispensationalist was a premillennialist. Some of the best-known works of dispensationalists have been tracts on the premillennial return of Christ. Three of the most influential were William E. Blackstone, *Jesus is Coming* (2d ed., New York, 1886), James H. Brookes, *Maranatha* (5th ed., New York, 1878), and Adoniram J. Gordon, *Ecce Venit* (New York, 1889).

[9]David E. Smith, "Millenarian Scholarship in America," *American Quarterly,* XVII (Fall, 1965), 535 ff.

[10]"Modern Millenarianism," *The Princeton Review,* XXV (January, 1853), 68.

[11]For an early reference to the connection between inspiration and literalism, see "Inspired Literality of Scripture," *Quarterly Journal of Prophecy,* II (1850), 297-307; and for a contemporary reference to the same point, see Ryrie, *op. cit.,* p. 86 ff.

[12]Darby, *Letters* (London: Stow Hill Tract Depot), II, 228.

[13]Darby, *Letters,* II, 304.

[14]Darby once wrote, ". . . one had to insist on the first principles of grace. No one will have it as a rule in the American churches. Old school Presbyterians, or some of them, have the most of it" (Darby, *Letters*, II, 193). Cf. also Kraus, *op. cit.,* pp. 57 ff.

[15]Two qualifications ought to be noted. German-speaking Methodists seem to have been attracted to dispensationalism in undue proportion to their numbers within Methodism, and the nineteenth century secession from the Protestant Episcopal Church, the Reformed Episcopal Church, also seems to have been especially susceptible to dispensationalist penetration.

[16]Sources for this conference are extremely varied. Addresses from the conferences were published occasionally (James H. Brookes, *Bible Reading on the Second Coming of Christ* [Springfield, Illinois, 1877]; *Lakeside Studies, Proceedings of the 1892 Niagara Conference* [Toronto, n.d.] and *The Second Coming of Our Lord, Papers Read at a Conference Held at Niagara, July 14-17, 1885* [Toronto, n.d.]). An account of the origin of the conference can be found in George C. Needham, *The Spiritual Life* (Philadelphia, 1895), pp. 18 ff. James H. Brookes edited a periodical which made cryptic references to the conference regularly from 1876 on, and it is in this source that the Niagara creed was first published (*The Truth,* IV [1878], 452-8). The best place to catch a glimpse of the workings of the conference is the July, 1897, number of *The Watchword,* where narrative statements concerning the progress of the conference are combined with virtually a complete list of the sessions and sermons.

[17]Charles Hodge, *Systematic Theology* (New York, 1874). The best general treatment of this subject is Lefferts A. Loetscher, *The Broadening Church* (Philadelphia, 1957).

[18]I have analyzed the accuracy of their assertion in my article, "The Princeton Theology," *Church History*, XXXI (September, 1962).

[19]Hodge, *Systematic Theology*, I, 14 ff.

[20]J. Gresham Machen, illustrating the state to which this kind of rationalism was finally carried, once wrote, "Christian doctrine, I hold, is not merely connected with the Gospel, but it is identical with the Gospel" (Ned. B. Stonehouse, *J. Gresham Machen* [Grand Rapids, 1957], p. 376).

[21]I am not ignoring the Lutheran and Reformed dogmatic tradition of the sixteenth and seventeenth centuries. I have shown in my article in *Church History*, XXXI, that Princeton began as the offspring of that tradition and developed from that point, in the course of the nineteenth century creating something unique. As will be illustrated when discussing *The Fundamentals* later in this paper, the Princeton doctrine of inspiration has become the common property of dispensationalists and Calvinists alike.

[22]The first reference to the original autographs in the Princeton Theology occurs in 1879 (A. A. Hodge, *Outlines of Theology* [New York, 1879], pp. 66 and 75).

[23]"We confess that we look with some anxiety upon the spread of the view represented at the so-called Prophetic Conference held in New York last week" (*Watchman*, [November 7, 1878], p. 356). See also the *Christian Advocate* (October 31, 1878) and the *Standard* (November 7, 1878).

[24]*Watchman* (November 14, 1878), p. 364.

[25]A. T. Pierson, "The Story of the Northfield Conferences," *Northfield Echoes*, I (June, 1894), 1-13.

[26]*Northfield Echoes*, I, 6.

[27]*Ibid.*

[28]*The Fundamentals: A Testimony to the Truth* (Chicago, [1910-1915]).

[29]Lyman Stewart to J. M. Critchlow, April 14, 1911, Lyman Stewart Papers, Bible Institute of Los Angeles; L. S. to C. I. Scofield July 21, 1908, Lyman Stewart Papers; L. S. to J. W. B., October 8, 1908, Lyman Stewart Papers.

[30]For Torrey, see W. G. McLoughlin, Jr., *Modern Revivalism* (New York, 1959), pp. 366 ff. For Harris, see W. S. Wallace, *The Macmillan Dictionary of Canadian Biography* (3rd ed., London, 1963). Louis Meyer is not known to me outside the Lyman Stewart Correspondence.

[31]Lyman Stewart to A. C. Gaebelein, December 5, 1911, Lyman Stewart Papers.

[32]L. S. to Milton Stewart, March 3, 1911, Lyman Stewart Papers.

[33]See for example, Furniss, *The Fundamentalist Controversy*, pp. 13, 16, 50, 72, 119, 121, 122, 130, and *passim*.

[34]Loetscher, *The Broadening Church*, p. 98.

[35]Cole, *History of Fundamentalism*, p. 34. For Niagara, see note 16 above. The World Conference on Christian Fundamentals affirmed nine points in a doctrinal statement in 1919 (*Sunday School Times*, June 14, 1919).

[36]Furniss, *op. cit.*, pp. 103 ff.

[37]Loetscher, *op. cit.*, especially chapter XV.

[38] *Presbyterian Guardian,* June 22, 1936.

[39] Carl McIntire, leader of the new schism, clearly aligned himself with dispensationalists in the *Presbyterian Guardian,* November 14, 1936.

[40] *Presbyterian Guardian,* March 13, 1937, p. 217.

26

The American Religious Depression, 1925-1935

Robert T. Handy

Historians have frequently analyzed the depression of the 1930s as a crisis in American political, economic, and social life. Robert T. Handy identifies a "religious depression" which began in the 1920s, and he argues that through the experience, American Protestantism turned from its "quest for a Christian America" to grappling with religious pluralism and new social forces. Professor Handy teaches American Church History at the Union Theological Seminary in New York City.

"It is too early to assess the impact of the Great Depression upon American Protestantism," wrote Robert Moats Miller in his study of American Protestantism and social issues in the period between the world wars.[1] No doubt it is too early for any overall assessment, yet it is becoming steadily clearer that American religion passes through an important transition in the depression period. If we are to gain a fuller understanding of developments in American Christianity since the 1930's, then serious attention needs to be given to that bleak period. Inasmuch as our understanding of times long past are significantly influenced by our definitions of the present situation, attempts to deal with that particular period of crisis in our recent past may help us more adequately to see the whole story of American religion in fairer perspective. Furthermore, a number of recent dissertations, articles and books have dealt in whole or in part with the period between the

First published in *Church History*, XXIX (1960), pp. 3-16. Reprinted with the permission of *Church History* and the author.

wars; they provide guidance for handling the vast array of sources relevant for an understanding of religion in the depression, supply material for at least preliminary interpretations, and point to the need for further analysis. This is one effort to suggest some interpretative guide lines for further exploration into an important topic.

I

In approaching the problem, I believe that it is important to distinguish between the economic depression of the 1930's and what may be called the religious depression. There was an intimate relationship between them, yet they are also distinguishable phenomena. William Kelley Wright, professor of philosophy at Dartmouth College, writing in the heart of the depression period, declared that "today we are passing through a period of religious depression not less severe than the concomitant moral and economic depression."[2] Some months before the stock market crash of October, 1929, William L. Sullivan, a Unitarian writer, prepared an article entitled, "Our Spiritual Destitution," in which he noted that the religion of his day was "timorous, unimaginative, quick with comment upon the contemporaneous, but unable in the authentic manner of its great tradition to judge the contemporaneous by categories that are eternal."[3] The effects of religious depression began to be felt by the middle 1920's within Protestantism, then the dominant and of course numerically the largest among the three overall religious groupings into which American religion is familiarly, though too simply, cast.

One sensitive indicator of a religion's vitality is its missionary program. By the middle of the third decade of the present century, Protestantism was becoming aware of a serious decline in missionary enthusiasm and conviction. At the 1926 meeting of the Foreign Missions Conference of North America, there was evident discouragement on the part of missionary leaders concerning the apathy of local churches toward the cause of missions.[4] Even after the disastrous effects of the economic depression had overtaken the missions boards, there was clear recognition that the problem was much more than financial, and that it had predated the economic crisis. "However, we all know that this is not a sufficient explanation of what was happening on the home base," Edmund B. Chafee reported in 1934. "Interest in missions was waning before the depression. All through the decade of the 1920's the foreign missionary enterprise was being questioned and it was failing to attract the vigorous support which it formerly enjoyed."[5] In his sociological study of religion in the economic depression, Samuel C. Kincheloe reported that "even before the depression, missionary funds had begun to decrease."[6] Examination of the income figures of the major mission boards for the later 1920's reveals an irregular pattern but with a generally declining trend—and this in a period of booming prosperity![7] In an article entitled "The Decline of American Protestantism," Charles Stelzle in 1930 reported that according to the United Stewardship Council, per capita gifts for benevolence fell from $5.57 in 1921 to $3.43 in 1929.[8]

There was also a decline in the missionary force in these same years. The number of foreign missionaries in 1929 was less by 4.7 percent than that for 1923.[9] The steadily waning interest of young people in responding to the missionary challenge was a source of concern at the 1929 meeting of the Foreign Missions Conference of North America, at which it was reported that though 2700 students had volunteered for foreign service in 1920, only 252 had offered themselves in 1928.[10] The decline of the missionary force for China was especially perplexing to missionary leaders, and led Albert W. Beaven to make a statement in 1928 that was in a strange way more prophetic than he could know. "What an absurdity if after one hundred years of service," he exclaimed, "after building up in China $90,000,000 of missionary investments in terms of helpfulness, we were to abandon it, withdrawing our Christian representatives, forsaking the whole enterprise, while at the very same time Russia with all the questionable principles she stands for is eager to offer the Orient men, counsel, money and moral backing."[11] It was the decline in missionary interest that led to the Laymen's Foreign Missions Inquiry in the early 1930's, which itself reflected a questioning of familiar missionary emphases within Protestantism.

The home missions movement also felt the pinch of declining interest and diminishing funds before 1929. Nearly two years before the crash, the executive secretary of the Home Missions Council said:

> Almost all major denominations are now in a period of financial stringency in the conduct of mission work. We are in the days of falling budgets. There has been more or less retrenchment all along the line, and new work has been for several years practically at a standstill.[12]

On the rural church scene there was clear evidence of decline before 1929, both in terms of benevolence contributions and the attendance at services of resident members.[13]

The problem of falling attendance was not limited to the rural scene, of course, for churches in all areas reported difficulties in maintaining attendance levels. A general trend toward the dropping of traditional Sunday evening services, especially in the cities, was observed.[14] Decline in Sunday school enrollment was also evident; C. Luther Fry found in 1930 that "the proportion of young people attending church schools is greater today than in 1906, but less than in 1916."[15] Attempts to plot an "evangelistic index line" for a number of major denominations point to a sharp downturn in the winning of converts and the reception of new members in the 1920's.[16] A somewhat less tangible evidence of Protestant decline was the lowered status of ministers. Paul A. Carter has pointed out that the ministry sank low in public esteem in this period; he quotes a minister of that time who declared that it was "a fairly safe generalization to say that no profession of men is so thoroughly empty of dignity and grace as that of the Protestant minister today."[17]

Many observers have called attention to the slump which overtook the social gospel in the later 1920's; it is referred to in the very title of Carter's book, *The Decline and Revival of the Social Gospel.* But in his examination of

the period, Robert Moats Miller has found that "social Christianity continued to burn bright enough to warrant future historians in using slightly
less somber hues in painting their pictures of the social attitudes of
American Protestantism in the Prosperity Decade."[18] I think the apparent
contradiction may be resolved by concluding that though proportionately
the social emphasis remained strong, the social gospel movement as a whole
was caught in Protestantism's overall decline.

Some of the keenest observers of the religious life of the late 1920's
recognized that they were in some kind of a religious depression. For example, the Episcopal Bishop of Central New York, Charles Fiske, was convinced in 1928 that he had "evidence of a sad disintegration of American
Protestantism."[19] And in his first book, published in 1927, Reinhold
Niebuhr remarked that "a psychology of defeat, of which both fundamentalism and modernism are symptoms, has gripped the forces of religion."[20]
At least part of the reason for the decline was the penetration into the
churches of the prevailing mood of the 1920's. For Protestantism was deeply
affected by the general disillusionment of the postwar decade. During the
war itself, the American people, with the vigorous support of most religious
leaders, maintained a spirit of high optimism.

But the tide turned swiftly. As Arthur S. Link has reminded us, "the
1920's were a period made almost unique by an extraordinary reaction
against idealism and reform."[21] The rapid subsidence of the war spirit, so
Walter M. Horton observed in a book written in 1929 but published the following year, led "to a wave of spiritual depression and religious skepticism,
widespread and devastating."[22] Protestantism felt the corrosive effects of
disillusionment at the very beginning of the decade, for the collapse of the
grandiose Interchurch World Movement in 1920 was at least in part caused
by the swift change in mood. Winthrop S. Hudson has summarized the swift
decline of Protestantism in a vivid way:

> Nothing is more striking than the astonishing reversal in the position occupied
> by the churches and the role played by religion in American life which took
> place before the new century was well under way. By the nineteen twenties, the
> contagious enthusiasm which had been poured into the Student Volunteer
> Movement, the Sunday School Movement, the Men and Religion Forward
> Movement, the Laymen's Missionary Movement, the Interchurch World
> Movement, and other organized activities of the churches had largely
> evaporated.[23]

As the decade wore on, scientism, behaviorism, and humanism became
more conspicuous in the thought of the time. Religion was often viewed
with a negative if not with a hostile eye. In his effort to state the case for "a
promethean religion for the modern world," William Pepperell Montague
declared in 1930 that "there is today a widespread and increasing belief that
the minimum essentials of Christian supernaturalism . . . have been
rendered antiquated, false, and absurd by our modern knowledge."[24] More
extreme was Joseph Wood Krutch's pessimistic statement of "the modern
temper" in 1929. Referring to such classic words as "Sin" and "Love,"

Krutch wrote that "all the capital letters in the composing-room cannot make the words more than that which they have become—shadows, as essentially unreal as some of the theological dogmas which have been completely forgotten."[25] Criticism of religion and the churches was expressed not only by men like Montague and Krutch, by H.L. Mencken and Sinclair Lewis, but also by many less well-known men. One opinion study showed that although about 78 per cent of the views about traditional Christianity published in 1905 were favorable and only 22 per cent were unfavorable, by 1930 the situation had almost reversed, so that 67 per cent of the opinions published were unfavorable.[26]

Protestantism was deeply penetrated by the disillusionment of the time in part at least because of a long-standing identification of Protestantism with American culture which left the churches quite exposed to cultural cross-currents. The roots of this identification go far back to the beginnings of American history. As André Siegfried stated the matter in 1927:

> If we wish to understand the real sources of American inspiration, we must go back to the English Puritanism of the seventeenth century, for the civilization of the United States is essentially Protestant. Those who prefer other systems, such as Catholicism, for example, are considered bad Americans and are sure to be frowned on by the purists. Protestantism is the only national religion, and to ignore that fact is to view the country from a false angle.

Siegfried was fully aware of the denominational nature of Protestantism, yet still insisted on his main point: "In order to appreciate the influence of Protestantism in this confusion of sects, we must not look at it as a group of organized churches, for its strength lies in the fact that its spirit is national."[27] Sidney E. Mead has recently shown that the fusion of Protestantism with Americanism was especially evident in the later nineteenth century. He has suggested that "during the second half of the nineteenth century there occurred a virtual identification of the outlook of this denominational Protestantism with 'Americanism' or 'the American way of life' and that we are still living with some of the results of this ideological amalgamation of evangelical Protestantism with Americanism."[28] During and just after the first World War there was an intensification of this synthesis through an emphasis on "Christian Americanization," by which was meant growth toward national democratic and spiritual ideals, of which the churches were the best custodians.[29] One feature of this identification was illustrated in the Lynds' comment following their 1925 study of "Middletown": "In theory, religious beliefs dominate all other activities in Middletown."[30]

The religious education movement, which was at the peak of its influence in the later 1920's, clearly illustrated the theme of the ideological amalgamation of religion and culture. Shailer Mathews pointed to its triumphs in 1927 by declaring that "it commands the same sort of enthusiastic following from idealistic young men and women as did sociology a generation ago. The most generally elected courses in theological seminaries, the greatest activity in churches are in its field." But

Mathews warned religious educators that they were tending to neglect the church in their concern for education, insisting that "it is our privilege to teach young people that religion has some other task than that of making good citizens and good neighbors."[31] As H. Shelton Smith was later to document, many religious educators "sought to blend the democratic theory of education and the democratic theory of the Kingdom of God."[32]

In view of this identification, it was inevitable that Protestantism would be deeply and directly influenced by trends within the culture, and that many of them would be accepted and even blessed by the churches. In 1929 the self-styled "puzzled parson," Charles Fiske, indicated that he was not quite as puzzled as he claimed to be when he said:

> America has become almost hopelessly enamoured of a religion that is little more than a sanctified commercialism; it is hard in this day and this land to differentiate between religious aspiration and business prosperity. Our conception of God is that he is a sort of Magnified Rotarian. Sometimes, indeed, one wonders whether the social movement and the uplift in general have not become, among Protestants, a substitute for devotion; worse than that, a substitute for real religion. Efficiency has become the greatest of Christian virtues. I hope I may be forgiven a note of exaggeration that is necessary to make my meaning clear when I say that Protestantism, in America, seems to be degenerating into a sort of Babsonian cult, which cannot distinguish between what is offered to God and what is accomplished for the glory of America and the furtherance of business enterprise.[33]

Edwin Lewis of Drew, reviewing in 1934 the course American Protestantism had taken during the previous twenty years, declared:

> We borrowed our criteria of evaluation from the world about us—a world gone mad in its worship of mere size, a world that had set itself to create bigger ships, bigger aeroplanes, bigger locomotives, bigger buildings, bigger universities, bigger corporations, bigger banks, bigger everything—except men! . . . And we were guilty of the incredible folly of supposing that "Christ's church was of this world," to be judged by the world's standards, to be modeled on the world's ways, to walk in the world's procession, and to keep step to the crashing discord of its brazen shawms.[34]

In the light of such identification with the culture, Protestantism could hardly avoid a share in the spiritual poverty of the time, or escape wholly from the spirit of disillusionment that swept American life in the 1920's. The American spiritual depression and the decline of Protestantism in the 1920's were intimately correlated.

It was on churches already seriously weakened, already in some decline, that the blow of economic depression fell. When the Lynds returned to Middletown ten years after their first study they found that "the city had been shaken for nearly six years by a catastrophe involving not only people's values but, in the case of many, their very existence. Unlike most socially generated catastrophes, in this case virtually nobody in the community had been cushioned against the blow; the great knife of the depression had cut down impartially through the entire population, cleaving open the lives and hopes of rich as well as poor."[35] The great knife of depression also cut deep into church life. "Outwardly the churches suffered along with the rest of the nation," wrote Robert M. Miller. "Memberships dropped, budgets were slashed, benevolent and missionary enterprises set adrift, ministers fired, and chapels closed. All this can be demonstrated statistically."[36] The evidence need not be summarized here, but a single illustration of the impact of depression may be in order. In 1927 Shailer Mathews had reported the triumph of religious education; less than ten years later, after depression had done its work, Adelaide Teague Case painted a dark picture.

> What shall we say to Christian Education today? Obviously it is in distress. The machinery has broken down. All the denominational boards of education have suffered great losses. The International Council of Religious Education is struggling on with a greatly reduced staff and budget. The Religious Education Association is in abeyance, trying to maintain itself with a handful of volunteers who are holding it together in spite of a staggering debt. Training schools and departments of religious education in universities and seminaries are severely reduced in size; some of them have reorganized or disappeared. The professional leadership is discouraged; directors of religious education are transferring to social work or public education or joining the ranks of the unemployed.[37]

This illustration could be matched by pointing to many other aspects of the churches' programs. Hidden in such a flat statement as "twenty out of thirty-five leading denominations compared in 1934 had reduced their total expenditures by from thirty to fifty per cent and five over fifty per cent" are countless stories of struggles, discouragement, and tragedy.[38]

I believe that this approach to religion in the depression, to distinguish between religious and economic depressions, throws light on many aspects of religious life in the 1930's, but on the following three in particular. First, one of the persistent questions of the depression period was "why no revival of religion?" Some religious leaders, reported Samuel Kincheloe, "actually hailed the depression with rejoicing since they had the idea that previous depressions had 'driven men to God' and felt that the time was overdue for men again to be reminded of the need to let the spiritual dominate the materialistic order."[39] At various times in the American past, depression and revival had been related, classically in 1857-1858. But when the distinction between religious and economic depression is made, it becomes clear that it was an already depressed Protestantism that was overtaken by the economic crisis. Without inner changes it was unable to deal with the needs of the time in a fresh and creative way. The changes that finally came did contribute to conspicuous currents of renewal, but only after the depression itself had passed.

Second, a significant aspect of the religious depression, perplexing to the major denominations, was the mushrooming of the newer and smaller religious groups, the sects. Detailed analyses of particular communities, such as Pope's study of Gastonia, the Lynds' probing of Middletown, and Boisen's samplings of several communities, all document the proliferation of the sects in the depression decade.[40] A number of observers have pointed out that many, probably a majority, of the supporters of sectarian movements were formerly adherents of the older and larger Protestant denominations. That the sects attracted many among the "disinherited" and economically depressed classes has been stated many times.[41] A significant but indirect factor in the rapid growth of the sects in the 1930's would seem to be the internal Protestant depression with its consequent lack of clarity and energy in the churches. Individuals won from older to newer religious bodies often indicated their dissatisfaction with the coldness and formality of the old-line churches.

Third, one of the major shifts of mood which was certainly speeded by the lash of depression was the somewhat precipitous decline of the evangelical liberal theology, which had been so conspicuous a part of Protestant life in the first quarter of the century. There were some signs of the internal disintegration of liberalism even before the first world war.[42] In 1925, Justin Wroe Nixon explained the liberal's dilemma in a forceful article in the *Atlantic*. While the liberals were fighting off the frontal attack of fundamentalism, he declared, they were inadvertently backing toward the humanist position; they were seriously embarrassed by the flank attack of the naturalists and humanists.[43] The latter claimed to speak for a scientifically and naturalistically-minded age far better than the liberals, who were accused of clinging to an unsatisfactory and unstable compromise, could. By the early 1930's, liberals were finding it increasingly difficult, in terms of their optimistic orientation and idealistic heritage, to deal satisfactorily with the realities of depression, the rise of totalitarianism, and the resurgence of barbarism on the world scene. In his famous article of 1933, "After Liberalism—What?" John C. Bennett said emphatically,

> The most important fact about contemporary American theology is the disintegration of liberalism. Disintegration may seem too strong a word, but I am using it quite literally. It means that as a structure with a high degree of unity theological liberalism is coming to pieces. The liberal preacher has had a coherent pattern of theological assumptions in the background of his message. He has often had the kind of self-confidence which goes with the preaching of an orthodoxy, for liberalism has been a new orthodoxy in many circles. It is that coherent pattern of assumptions, that self-confidence, which are going. Now many of us are left with a feeling of theological homelessness.[44]

Into the vacuum new theological currents immediately flowed, as interpreters of European dialectical theologies appeared.[45] Benson Y. Landis could report in 1933 that "the economic crisis seems to be breeding a theology of crisis."[46] But one must not press too hard the relationship between the depression and the decline of liberalism. It was not the depression alone, however, but the many crises of the 1930's which together weakened the liberal synthesis and made men receptive to new views. When the *Christian Century* published in 1939 its oft-quoted series of articles on

"How My Mind Has Changed in This Decade," many of America's leading theologians told how the fateful events of the decade had led them to shift their position to a neo-liberalism if not a neo-orthodoxy. A characteristic expression of the impact of the decade on the liberals was penned by E. G. Homrighausen. "I saw evidences of man's lostness: the depression, the constant threat of war, the return to brutality on so vast a scale, the loss of the spiritual substance of life that alone gives society structure, the uncertainty and insecurity of life."[47]

Somewhat paradoxically, for the rise of the social gospel had been intimately related to the earlier success of theological liberalism, there was clearly a resurgence of the social gospel in the 1930's, despite the decay of liberalism. The works of Paul A. Carter and Robert M. Miller document this resurgence of social concern abundantly; a hasty examination of denominational social pronouncements in the bleak decade provides convincing confirmation. Hornell Hart reported some years ago on this aspect of religion in the depression in these words:

> The most striking increase in religious discussion in magazines has been in the field of Christian ethics. *Readers' Guide* entries under this heading and under "Church and Social Problems," "Christian Socialism," and "Christian Sociology" increased from 17 per 100,000 in 1929 to 140 in 1932, and in 1941 they were still more than twice their 1929 level. The rise and recession of this curve is notably similar to the rise and decline in the amount of unemployment and to other indices of the economic depression.[48]

That there was something of a resurgence of the social gospel I do not doubt, but on the whole the resurgence of social interest in the 1930's is perhaps more to be seen as related to a permanent contribution which the social gospel in its creative days earlier in the century had made to the larger Protestant world: a sensitivity to social issues and an awareness of social need. A Protestantism which had been alerted by such a vigorous social movement could not easily be callous to serious social need. Not a few of those who took leadership in movements to the theological right were also conspicuous for their continued attention to social thought and action.

II

I have argued that Protestantism entered the period of religious and economic depression as the dominant American religous tradition, closely identified with the culture. But Protestantism emerged from depression no longer in such a position; it was challenged by forces outside the Protestant churches and questioned by some within. Siegfried, who identified Protestantism as the national religion as late as 1927, saw the trend of the times: "The worldliness of this Protestantism and its pretensions to be a national religion reserved for the privileged few have antagonized many of its followers as well as its adversaries. They feel that something is lacking, almost the spirit of religion itself; for the ultimate has been reduced until it embraces little more than ethics."[49] And though the Lynds had indicated that *in theory* religious beliefs dominated all other activities in Middletown, they hastened to add that "actually, large regions of Middletown's life appear uncontrolled by them."[50] In this period, the vast rural reservoirs of Protestant strength were rather rapidly being outmatched by the flooding cities. The Protestantism that threw itself so strongly behind prohibition in the 1920's was one in which the rural tradition was still very strong. Indeed, prohibition itself was in one sense part of the struggle of country against city. The legislative superintendent of the Anti-Saloon League recognized in 1917 that the Eighteenth Amendment had to pass before 1920, for with reapportionment would come, as he put it, "forty new wet Congressmen . . . from the great wet centers with their rapidly increasing population."[51] The final failure of prohibition made it clearer to many Protestants that the familiar American culture in which they had flourished and with which they had been so closely identified was going. The comfortable identification with American cultural patterns no longer seemed so relevant or so helpful.

The beginnings of Protestant renewal, which Herbert Wallace Schneider notes as arising in the "dark 30's" and continuing as an "offensive which has grown steadily since then,"[52] developed in part as religious leaders challenged the identification of Protestantism with American culture and summoned the church to recover its own independent standing-ground. In 1935, Harry Emerson Fosdick preached the famous sermon in which he appealed to Protestants to go "beyond modernism." He exclaimed,

> And in that new enterprise the watchword will be not, Accommodate yourself to the prevailing culture! but, Stand out from it and challenge it! For this inescapable fact, which again and again in Christian history has called modernism to its senses, we face: we cannot harmonize Christ himself with modern culture. What Christ does to modern culture is to challenge it.[53]

And in that same year, to cite another example, appeared a book with the revealing title, *The Church Against the World*. It vigorously protested the identification of the church with American culture. Francis P. Miller wrote, "The plain fact is that the domestication of the Protestant community in the United States within the framework of the national culture has progressed as far as in any western land. The degradation of the American Protestant church is as complete as the degradation of any other national Protestant church."[54] What the church should therefore do was stated by H. Richard Niebuhr in these words:

> We live, it is evident, in a time of hostility when the church is imperiled not only by an external worldliness but by one that has established itself within the Christian camp. Our position is inside a church which has been on the retreat and which has made compromises with the enemy in thought, in organization, and in discipline. Finally, our position is in the midst of that increasing group in the church which has heard the command to halt, to remind itself of its mission, and to await further orders.[55]

As James H. Smylie has analyzed the theological trend of a steadily enlarging group in American Protestantism, it was "a trend from an irrelevant attachment to society toward a relevant detachment to society without becoming irrelevantly detached from society."[56] The "Christ of culture" motif, which had long been of great significance in American Protestantism, was being challenged from within. From a widening circle of Protestants seeking to return again by one route or another to the independent sources of their faith, there came movements of renewal which marked the beginning of the end of the religious depression for Protestants. There were also other sources of renewal, but this one bears an especial relation to our theme.

I have entitled this paper the "American" religious depression because there was a nationally observable spiritual lethargy evident in the 1920's and 1930's, and because the then clearly dominant religious tradition of the country was in decline. Certainly both Judaism and Roman Catholicism were deeply affected by the economic depression; to what extent they were internally affected by spiritual depression the authorities on those bodies must say. Jewish congregations enjoyed a healthy growth in the 1926-36 decade, reporting a 13.7 per cent increase. Roman Catholicism also grew, but considerably more slowly than in the preceding ten year period. The church had then reported an 18.3 per cent growth, which dropped to 7 per cent for 1926-1936.[57] Perhaps this change was influenced both by the cutting off of immigration and by the generally unfriendly attitude toward religion. But neither Judaism nor Catholicism was embarrassed by too close identification with the surrounding culture, for both felt their minority situation rather keenly. When George N. Shuster wrote his widely-read work on the Catholic spirit in America in 1927, he began by noting that "twenty or thirty years ago ambition would have dictated silence about one's mere connection with what is termed the Roman Church. Today prudence still seems to suggest keeping this matter under cover as fully as possible."[58] But during the depression years a significant change took place; Protestantism declined and lost its sense of being the national religion, while Roman Catholicism, reflecting advances made during and after the war years, consolidated by the National Catholic Welfare Conference, rather quickly became more visible on the American scene. It was less than fifteen years from the time that Shuster wrote the words just quoted that the popular historian Theodore Maynard made this claim: "Protestantism—especially American Protestantism—is now so doctrinally decayed as to be incapable of offering any serious opposition to the sharp sword of the Spirit, as soon as we can make up our minds to use it. Except for isolated 'fundamentalists,'—and these are pretty thoroughly discredited and without intellectual leadership—Catholicism could cut through Protestantism as through so much butter."[59] The contrast between the two quotations dramatizes an important religious transition of the depression period. The upshot of that transition which focused in depression years, though it had been long in the making, was summarized by Will Herberg in his book, *Protestant-Catholic-Jew:*

> In net effect, Protestantism today no longer regards itself either as a religious movement sweeping the continent or as a national church representing the religious life of the people; Protestantism understands itself today primarily as one of the three religious communities in which twentieth century America has come to be divided.[60]

During the period of religious and economic depression, then, the "Protestant era" in America was brought to a close; Protestantism emerged no longer as the "national religion." The test of depression was a severe one; it laid bare certain weaknesses in American Protestantism. But the repudiation of the virtual identification of Protestantism with American culture by an able and growing group of religious leaders freed many Protestants to recover in a fresh way their own heritages and their original sources of inspiration. The depression stimulated many Protestants to seek new and deeper understandings of their own religious heritage, though this "positive" contribution of the depression to religion could probably be appreciated only later. The years of religious and economic depression were years of significant transition for the American churches, for in that period trends long in the making were dramatically revealed, and developments important to the future became visible.

NOTES

[1]*American Protestantism and Social Issues, 1919-1939* (Chapel Hill: University of North Carolina Press, 1958), p. 63.

[2]"The Recovery of the Religious Sentiment," in Vergilius Ferm, ed., *Contemporary American Theology: Theological Autobiographies* (2 vols., New York: Round Table Press, 1932-1933), II, 367.

[3]*Atlantic Monthly,* 143 (January-June, 1929), 378.

[4]Fennell P. Turner and Frank Knight Sanders, eds., *The Foreign Missions Conference of North America . . . 1926* (New York: Foreign Missions Conference, 1926), pp. 125-47.

[5]"Some Conditions in North America that Affect Foreign Missions," in Leslie B. Moss and Mabel H. Brown, eds., *The Foreign Missions Conference of North America . . . 1934* (New York: Foreign Missions Conference, 1934), p. 148.

[6]*Research Memorandum on Religion in the Depression* (New York: Social Science Research Council, Bulletin 33, 1937), p. 51.

[7]Based on a study of the figures by the Rev. Donald A. Crosby, whose assistance in the research for this paper I acknowledge with thanks.

[8]*Current History,* XXXIII (October, 1930), 25.

[9]C. Luther Fry, "Changes in Religious Organizations," *Recent Social Trends* (2 vols.; New York: McGraw-Hill, 1933), II, 1046.

[10]Stanley High, "The Need for Youth," in Leslie B. Moss, ed., *The Foreign Missions Conference of North America, 1929* (New York: Foreign Missions Conference, 1929), p. 152.

[11]"What the Church Has to Say to Business Men About Foreign Missions," in Leslie B. Moss, ed., *The Foreign Missions Conference of North America, 1928* (New York: Foreign Missions Conference, 1928), p. 85.

[12]*Home Missions Council Annual Report . . . 1928* (New York: Home Missions Council, 1928), p. 80.

[13]Kincheloe, *Research Memorandum,* pp. 133 f.

[14]*Ibid.*, p. 51; *Recent Social Trends,* II, 1055.

[15]*The U.S. Looks At Its Churches* (New York: Institute of Social and Religious Research, 1930), p. 58.

[16]H. C. Weber, *Evangelism: A Graphic Survey* (New York: Macmillan, 1929), pp. 181 f.

[17]*The Decline and Revival of the Social Gospel: Social and Political Liberalism in American Protestant Churches, 1920-1940* (Ithaca: Cornell University Press, 1954), p. 70.

[18]*American Protestantism and Social Issues,* p. 47.

[19]*The Confessions of a Puzzled Parson* (New York: Charles Scribner's Sons, 1928), p. 191.

[20]*Does Civilization Need Religion? A Study in the Social Resources and Limitations of Religion in Modern Life* (New York: Macmillan, 1927), p. 2.

[21]"What Happened to the Progressive Movement in the 1920's," *American Historical Review,* 64 (1959), 833. See also the perceptive article by Henry F. May, "Shifting Perspectives in the 1920's," *Mississippi Valley Historical Review,* 43 (1956), 405-27.

[22]*Theism and the Modern Mood* (New York: Harper and Bros., 1930), p. 6.

[23]*The Great Tradition of the American Churches* (New York: Harper and Bros., 1953), p. 196.

[24]*Belief Unbound: A Promethean Religion for the Modern World* (New Haven: Yale University Press, 1930), p. 20.

[25]*The Modern Temper: A Study and A Confession* (New York: Harcourt Brace and Co., 1929), pp. 191 f.

[26]Hornell Hart, "Changing Social Attitudes and Interests," *Recent Social Trends,* I, 403.

[27]*America Comes of Age* (New York: Harcourt, Brace and Co., 1927), trans. by H. H. Hemming and Doris Hemming, pp. 33, 38f.

[28]"American Protestantism Since the Civil War. I. From Denominationalism to Americanism," *Journal of Religion,* XXXVI (1956), 1.

[29]Cf. Chap. III, "Christian Americanization," of my *We Witness Together: A History of Cooperative Home Missions* (New York: Friendship Press, 1956) pp. 64-82.

[30]Robert S. Lynd and Helen Merrell Lynd, *Middletown: A Study in Contemporary American Culture* (New York: Harcourt, Brace and Co., 1929), p. 406.

[31]"Let Religious Education Beware!" *Christian Century,* 44 (1927), 362.

[32]*Faith and Nurture* (New York: Charles Scribner's Sons, 1941), p. 41.

[33]*Confessions of a Puzzled Parson,* p. 14.

[34]*A Christian Manifesto* (New York: Abingdon Press, 1934), p. 202.

[35]Robert S. Lynd and Helen Merrell Lynd, *Middletown in Transition: A Study in Cultural Conflicts* (New York: Harcourt, Brace and Co., 1937), p. 295.

[36]*American Protestantism and Social Issues,* p. 63.

[37]"Christian Education," in Samuel McCrea Cavert and Henry P. Van Dusen, eds., *The Church Through Half a Century: Essays in Honor of William Adams Brown* (New York: Charles Scribner's Sons, 1936), pp. 243 f.

[38]H. Paul Douglass and Edmund deS. Brunner, *The Protestant Church as a Social Institution* (New York: Harper and Bros., 1935), p. 208.

[39]*Research Memorandum*, p. 1.

[40]Liston Pope, *Millhands and Preachers: A Study of Gastonia* (New Haven: Yale University Press, 1942), pp. 126, 128; *Middletown in Transition*, p. 297; Anton T. Boisen, "Religion and Hard Times," *Social Action*, V (March 15, 1939), 8-35.

[41]E.g., cf. Boisen, *loc. cit.;* Elmer T. Clark, *The Small Sects in America* (rev. ed.; New York: Abingdon-Cokesbury Press, 1949), pp. 16-20, 218 f., 230.

[42]Walter Marshall Horton, *Realistic Theology* (New York: Harper and Bros., 1934), p. 35.

[43]"The Evangelicals' Dilemma," *Atlantic Monthly*, 136 (July-December, 1925), 368-74.

[44]*Christian Century*, 50 (1933), 1403.

[45]Cf. Sydney E. Ahlstrom, "Continental Influence on American Christian Thought Since World War I," *Church History*, XXVII (1958), 256-72.

[46]"Organized Religion," *American Journal of Sociology*, 38 (July, 1932-May, 1933), 907.

[47]"Calm After Storm," *Christian Century*, 56 (1939), 479.

[48]"Religion," *American Journal of Sociology*, 47 (July 1941-May, 1942), 894.

[49]*America Comes of Age*, p. 46.

[50]*Middletown*, p. 406.

[51]Wayne Wheeler, as quoted by Paul A. Carter, *The Decline and Revival of the Social Gospel*, p. 37.

[52]*Religion in 20th Century America* (Cambridge: Harvard University Press, 1952), p. 18.

[53]"Beyond Modernism: A Sermon," *Christian Century*, 52 (1935), 1552.

[54]H. Richard Niebuhr, Wilhelm Pauck, and Francis P. Miller, *The Church Against the World* (Chicago: Willett, Clark and Co., 1935), p. 102.

[55]*Ibid.*, pp. 1 f.

[56]"The American Protestant Churches and the Depression of the 1930's" (Th.M. Thesis, Princeton Theological Seminary, 1950), p. 125.

[57]Bureau of the Census, *Religious Bodies: 1936*, I (Washington: U.S. Government Printing Office, 1941), 51.

[58]*The Catholic Spirit in America* (New York: Lincoln Mac Veagh, The Dial Press, 1927), p. vii.

[59]*The Story of American Catholicism* (New York: Macmillan, 1941), p. 613.

[60]*Protestant-Catholic-Jew: An Essay in American Religious Sociology* (Garden City: Doubleday and Co., 1955), pp. 139 f.

27

The Radical Turn
in Theology and Ethics:
Why It Occurred in the
1960s

Sydney E. Ahlstrom

By contrast with the argument advanced by Robert T. Handy (reading 26), Sydney E. Ahlstrom identifies the tumultuous 1960s as the period in which American religious groups came to confront directly the reality of social disintegration and the forces which produced it. In this essay, he outlines the responses of the American churches and suggests how the 1960s changed Americans' understanding of their churches and their nation. Professor Ahlstrom teaches American Religious History and related subjects at Yale University.

Like many of its elegant, gay, or roaring predecessors, the decade of the 1960's will probably gain a name or two. Men will, of course, identify it with the "Great Society" (though not without irony) and with the Vietnam war, but adjectives like "secular" or "permissive" will probably commemorate other aspects of these ten eventful years. The decade may also be remembered for the "Death of God" or the "Great Moral Revolution." These terms, moreover, will rest on actualities far more pervasive than, say, the gaiety of the troubled 1890's or the elegance of the 1880's. New cosmic signs *were* being read in the 1960's. The decade *did* experience a fundamental shift in American moral and religious attitudes. It is no accident that phrases such as post-Puritan, post-Protestant, post-Christian, post-modern, and even post-historical were commonly used to describe the American

First published in the *Annals of the American Academy of Political and Social Science*, 387 (1970), pp. 1-13. Reprinted with abridgement by the permission of the American Academy of Political and Social Science and the author.

scene. The decade of the 1960's was a time, in short, when the old grounds of national confidence, patriotic idealism, moral traditionalism, and even of historic Judaeo-Christian theism, were awash. Presuppositions that had held firm for centuries—even millennia—were being widely questioned. Some sensational manifestations have come and gone (as fads and fashions will), but the existence of a basic shift of mood rooted in deep social and institutional dislocations was anything but ephemeral. The nation was confronting revolutionary circumstances whose effects were, in the nature of the case, irreversible.

Given this situation, I accept the traditional twofold task of historians, first to clarify the *explicandum* and second to attempt the *explicans*. What follows, therefore, is a description of the new elements in the moral, intellectual, and religious atmosphere which came to pervade America during this decade. Then will come certain suggestions which may help us to understand why this nation found itself in such revolutionary circumstances at this particular time. Much that will be said would, of course, apply, *mutatis mutandis,* to Western civilization generally or even to the whole world. This sense of global involvement is, indeed, a fundamental feature of the times. My chief focus, nevertheless, will be on the American scene, where the transition that succeeded the "postwar revival" seems to have been especially abrupt.

Lest the reader's expectations become too exorbitant, however, a *caveat* is in order. The truth is that phenomena of this scope could only be "explained" with a "God's-eye view" of the whole past and the whole future. Teilhard de Chardin rightly observed that "not a thing in our changing world is really understandable except in so far as it has reached its terminus." In the strict sense, our situation is historically inexplicable. We face the *mysterium tremendum.* How the 1960's would appear in some ultimate roll call of decades, therefore, is something about which we can only speculate.[1] Yet, we know that it has been turbulent—that it has brought excitement and liberation to some, bewilderment and pain to others. Nearly everyone has wondered at some time or other why this "almost chosen people" should have encountered so much unsettlement at just this juncture in history. In somewhat different terminology, I have, in fact, had the question put to me with equal seriousness by both student militants and members of parish church boards. (That I should state the extremes in just that way also reveals a crucial aspect of the times.) And it is my conviction that a telling of the many-stranded *histoire* that leads up to the criss-cross crisis of the 1960's can offer more assuagement to the curious than could the characteristic findings of more scientific disciplines.

The most widely publicized aspect of the decade's religious history was the emergence of a radical movement in theology which betokened, even if it did not cause, a major reappraisal of the most assured grounds of the historic Judaeo-Christian consensus. Familiar signposts can be cited. From beyond the grave, Dietrich Bonhoeffer's demand for a "secular interpretation" of biblical language was answered by a deluge of serious efforts to meet the needs of a "world come of age."[2] In America, it was H.

Richard Niebuhr who, at the age of sixty-six, delivered the crucial inaugural address to the 1960's, with his great essay on *Radical Monotheism* (1960); but it was Gabriel Vahanian who first brought Nietzche's famous phrase into public currency with his book on *The Death of God: The Culture of Our Post-Christian Era* (1961). Far more noticeable, however, were three startlingly popular best sellers: Bishop J. A. T. Robinson's *Honest to God* (1963) in Great Britain, Pierre Berton's *The Comfortable Pew* (1965) in Canada, and Harvey Cox's *The Secular City* (1965) in the United States. More provocative were the works of three or four rather diverse thinkers who either proclaimed the "death of God," or insisted on an entirely "secular" interpretation of the Gospel, or thoroughly "demythologized" the biblical message.[3] The major themes of these books were, in the meantime, being popularized in the mass media—and rendered more erudite in the treatises of a wide range of writers, both lay and clerical, and of all faiths. A critical, sometimes exceedingly hostile, literature of equal proportions soon arose; yet, the "movement" has won support both at the grass roots and in halls of learning. Specific theologians aside, the trend thus marked out would have long-lasting consequences.

Contemporaneous with this development, and closely related to it, was a veritable tidal wave of questioning of all the traditional structures of Christendom, above all, the so-called "parish" church. After Peter Berger's sounding of an early tocsin with his *The Noise of Solemn Assemblies* (1961), "morphological fundamentalism" became the key word of the new critics. In the meantime, the ministry and laity alike have shown an increasingly widespread tendency to regard local church structures as irrelevant, or as extremely unadaptable to the most urgent needs of the times, or even as an impediment to social action. With cities in crisis, men accepted Gibson Winters' diagnosis of *The Suburban Captivity of the Churches* (1961). Recognizing the moribund state of the old structures and traditions, Martin Marty wrote of *The Second Chance for American Protestants* (1963). This kind of critical self-examination was not being restricted to Protestants, moreover. Roman Catholics were soon involved in an equally drastic process of theological and institutional reformation.[4] In my own city, the most trenchant statement on the problem of involving religious congregations in urban problems came from a Jewish rabbi.[5] Concomitantly, both the old pietistic notions of the religious life and the "high-church" liturgical movements have been deeply eroded.[6] Traditional forms of evangelism, both at home and on "foreign mission fields," have been seriously questioned by all but the most culturally alienated religious groups.[7]

Meanwhile, in the realm of ethics and the moral life, an equally significant shift could be noted. Not only did the mass media devote much time and space to a "new morality," but even in doing so they often exploited a new permissiveness by dealing frankly with long-forbidden subjects. In schools, colleges, and universities, this "moral revolution" first took the form of opposition to the traditional doctrine that schools and colleges operate *in loco parentis*. Students demanded and received greater freedom, and then moved on, often with strong faculty support, to question the structures and value-priorities of higher education generally. Questions of loyalty and obedience to constituted authority, even to the national state itself, have also been reopened with new intensity. And, in all these cases, action has preceded or accompanied ethical reflection. Matching these popular trends, furthermore, was a distinct tendency among ethical thinkers to form less legalistic, more situational modes of guiding the moral life.[8] As a corollary of these developments, nearly every church-body in America (as well as many in Europe, including Pope Paul VI) decided—after two thousand years!—that the time had come to appoint a commission for the re-examination, not only of sexual ethics, but also of the theological and philosophical grounds for its making any kind of moral pronouncement.

No account of the decade's radicalism, especially at the ethical level, is complete, however, unless it also takes cognizance of the ways in which a vast, and long overdue, renewal was taking place. A revolt against the hypocrisies and superficiality of conventional moral codes by no means resulted in nihilism or libertinism. Much of the violence and organized protest of the 1960's arose, basically, from moral indignation, from a deep suspicion of established institutions, and from a demand for more exalted grounds of action than social success, business profits, and national self-interest.[9] In the realm of public affairs, indeed, it can be said that revulsion for long-accepted American priorities was most pronounced. America's patriotic "civil religion," which Will Herberg, in the mid-1950's, had quite rightly designated the basic faith of most Americans, was receiving the most searching criticism.[10] The old patriotic rhetoric seemed hollow and deceitful—even blasphemous. Nor was the death of this faith occurring only in youthful hearts, for superannuated congressmen were, at the same time, transforming the nation's calendar of national holy days into a convenient series of long weekends. Environmental pollution and widespread depredations of nature were undermining the power of "America the Beautiful," while the government's subordination of social and economic needs to those of war and military might was robbing "The Star-Spangled Banner" of its unifying power. Even flag-flying had become a divisive manifestation, with overtones of ironic debates on law-and-order versus social justice.

In summary, one may safely say that many ancient modes of thinking were being altered in the 1960's. For Protestants, the layer of dogmatic asphalt with which neo-orthodoxy, during the 1930's, sought to overlay the old claims of scientific and historical investigations was cracking up. For Roman Catholics, the same fate overcame the stern condemnations of liberalism and modernism contained in the constitutions of the Vatican Council of 1869-1870 and a long series of encyclicals extending from Pius IX's *Quanta Cura* (1864) to Pius XII's *Humani Generis* (1950). The need for deeper foundations was exposed. A credibility gap had opened up between the dominant forms of traditional theology and the secularized mind of a rapidly increasing number of educated Americans.

One must not exaggerate the depth and extent of change whenever the reference is made to a whole national population—or even to a nation's churchgoers. If common observation were not enough, there are surveys to prove that most adult Americans, though deeply troubled by the state of the nation, still hold to the religious convictions of earlier years.[11] Polls and questionnaires are admittedly very crude tools for measuring a thing so delicate and subjective as a human being's religious and moral commitments, but they tend to show considerable popular resistance to change. On the other hand, the declining growth rate of all the large denominations, plus their widespread budgetary problems, reveal a loss of vitality which is, in any case, affirmed in any meeting where parish clergy frankly discuss their problems. Parallel to these trends was a marked tendency among the clergy and religious (both Catholic and Protestant) to leave their churchly callings for work in the world. And among seminary students, the same tendency was noticeable. At the same time, youth of high school and college age were showing a strong sense of estrangement from traditional forms of Christian and Judaic nurture. The campus ministry, indeed, provided the earliest premonitory warnings of an institutional malaise which would mature during the course of the decade.

The three basic but closely intertwined elements that underlie this steady rise of religious antitraditionalism are profound matters of outlook; they seem to involve a deep shift in the presuppositional substructures of the American mind. One can designate them as metaphysical, moral, and social: (1) a growing attachment to a naturalism or "secularism" that makes people suspicious of doctrines that imply anything supernatural or which seem to involve magic, superstition, or divine interventions in the natural order: (2) a creeping (or galloping) awareness of vast contradictions in American life between profession and performance, the ideal and the actual; and (3) increasing doubt concerning the capacity of present-day ecclesiastical, political, social, and educational institutions to rectify these contradictions. Rich natural resources, technological marvels, vast productive power, great ideals, expanding universities, and flourishing churches seemed to result only in a country wracked by fear, violence, racism, war, and moral hypocrisy. Nor is this simply the characterization of a few black militants and campus radicals. Similar intimations of uneasiness are voiced by a gentle old lady reading the newspaper in a nursing home and the plumber who repairs my kitchen sink.

Yet, the question returns, Why now? Why so suddenly? Why should a moral and intellectual revolution that was centuries in the making have been precipitated in the 1960's? What happened to the religious revival? Why should the complacency of the Eisenhower years fade so swiftly? Why did shortcomings of American society that have aroused reformers ever since the eighteenth century suddenly become explosive in the 1960's? Why, in summary, have so many diverse processes dropped their bomb-load on the 1960's? It is to this complex question that the second part of this paper is addressed.

Radical theology is fundamentally an adjustment of religious thought to an ordered understanding of the natural world that has been gaining strength at an accelerating rate for over four hundred years. The most basic element in this process is the attitude toward the physical universe typified by Galileo's telescopic discovery of the moon's rocky surface in 1610. Three centuries later, Henry Adams reflected on the great intellectual revolution that separated the age of the Virgin of Chartres from the Age of the Dynamo. Struggling with the implications of Josiah Willard Gibbs' discoveries in physical chemistry, he became one of America's early death-of-God theologians. "The two-thousand-years' failure of Christianity roared upward from Broadway, and no Constantine the Great was in sight."[12]

Even more troubling was the steady advance of knowledge in the realm of "natural history," especially after the place of man in the over-all scheme became a subject of intensified investigation. Until the nineteenth century, the idea of providential design had easily turned man's knowledge of the animate, as well as the inanimate world to the uses of natural theology. With the rise of evolutionary theory, however, and especially after Darwin, this grand structure of apologetical theory began to crumble before the incoming tide of naturalism. A great resurgence of idealistic philosophy blunted the force of this new impulse for a time, but as the twentieth century wore on, the full force of still another long development began to be felt: the efforts of historians, anthropologists, sociologists, and psychologists to explain the behavior of man in scientific terms. Serious threats to the inerrancy of Scripture had been raised by the "Copernican revolution" which Isaac Newton had consolidated; other threats provoked the Genesis-and-Geology controversy. But these problems were mild compared to the impact of biblical criticism, the history of world religions, and developmental studies of religion and doctrine. In the churches of the United States, the crisis of relativism which these investigations portended was staved off by liberalism's roseate world view, by widespread convictions as to America's glorious destiny, and by the tendency of popular evangelical revivalism to ignore the problems.[13] Americans were even spared the devastating blows which the First World War brought down on the notion of Christendom's triumphant world role. And when the great economic collapse did finally bring this message home, the resurgent forces of fundamentalism and neo-orthodoxy—each in different ways, to separate constituencies— staved off the accounting for yet another generation. During the Eisenhower years, Norman Vincent Peale and Billy Graham could link hands, as it were, and preside over an Indian Summer of revivalism and confident living. Beneath the affluence and the surging religiosity, however, a vast range of unresolved issues remained. Inasmuch as these were the very years in which the mass media, notably television, were making an unprecedented impact on the popular awareness of social and intellectual change, and in which a college education was becoming an expected, or even necessary, stage in the life of every moderately ambitious American youth, the day was fast disappearing when traditional religious views would be accepted without serious questioning.

Almost as basic to the rise of radical theology as this broad development of the modern mind was the inexorable development of what is now being referred to as modern technocratic society. Max Weber performed a great office by turning men's attention to the ways in which the Judaeo-

Christian world view in general, and the Protestant Reformation in particular, accelerated the rationalization of social and economic life which underlies the rise of organized technology.[14] The United States, moreover, provided a living demonstration of the fact that if unhindered by medieval notions of class and status, if animated by sufficiently powerful beliefs in the virtues of work and exploitation, and if blessed with natural resources in sufficient abundance, a "nation of immigrants" can outstrip the world in achieving technocratic maturity. Yet, given the strongly agrarian terms in which the American idea of the good life has been couched and the relentless way in which industrialism fosters the growth of cities, American history—especially during the last century—has experienced many harsh confrontations of urban and rural values. In the sectional crisis of the 1860's, again in the 1890's, and yet again in the 1920's, these value-conflicts were exceedingly severe. . . . Since then, technological inroads on old ways of life have steadily advanced all over the world, from Arkansas to China. Regardless of governmental forms—fascistic, communistic, or democratic—this process destroys primordial social structures. Despite protest and violence, it proceeds to make "organization men" of the entire human race, with that portion of the race living in North America feeling every major transition first.

In addition to these two world-wide trends—one intellectual, the other social—there is another major transformatory process which the United States shares with few, if any, other countries, namely, the eclipse of the Protestant establishment which presided over its early colonial life, its war for independence, and its nineteenth-century expansion. In theory, the federal union has been, from its origins, a nation of minorities and a land of freedom and equality. But, in fact, it has never been so. Radical inequality and massive forms of oppression have been features—fundamental features—of the "American way of life." The election of the first American legislature and the first importation of African slaves took place in Virginia in 1619, and from that time forward, the rhetoric of American democracy has been falsified by the actualities of racism and bondage. Catholics were also subjected to disabilities, intolerance, and violence from the earliest times; and anti-Semitism began to grow virulent as soon as Jewish immigration began to assume large proportions in the 1880's. The American Indian has been excluded from American life from the start, and Spanish-speaking citizens, whether gained by annexation of territory or by immigration, have been consistently relegated to subordinate status. During the past century, however, the social structures, legal arrangements, values, and power relationships that supported the White, Anglo-Saxon, Protestant (WASP) establishment have been gradually undermined. Immigration contributed much to this denouement, but the largest single factor in effecting the changed relationships has been the urban explosion of the twentieth century.

A final long-term factor stems from the very dominance of Puritanism in the American religious heritage. One can imagine a different turn of affairs, for example, if English authorities, in the manner of the French,

Spanish, and Dutch, had kept their dissenters at home and peopled the New World colonies only with orthodox conformists. But it was not so, and the future United States was settled, and to a large degree shaped, by those who brought with them a very special form of radical Protestantism which combined a strenuous moral precisionism, a deep commitment to evangelical experientialism, and a determination to make the state responsible for the support of these moral and religious ideas. The United States became, therefore, the land *par excellence* of revivalism and "puritanic legalism." It came to have a popular religious tradition that tended to be oblivious to the intellectual revolutions of the modern world. In its church life, as in its forms of popular democracy, intellectualism was deprecated and repressed. Since higher education was under the control of these same forces, many of the most powerful sources of modern thinking lagged far behind those of continental Europe. And as a result of the strength of these ideas in over-represented rural constituencies, they had a kind of illicit hold on the national life even after their actual strength had waned. The "Land of the Free," therefore, has contributed relatively little to the Western concept of academic freedom, By the mid-twentieth century, the circumstances were such that a genuinely post-Puritan situation could rapidly develop.

Yet, I can hear the reader protest that these several long-term developments do nothing to explain why the 1960's should have experienced anything more than the same gradual adjustments that befell each preceding decade. Processes that are centuries old hardly constitute a sufficient explanation for the outbreak of a revolution. And it is this objection that leads me directly to the crucial question. What precipitated so violent and sudden a moral and theological transformation in this particular decade? To satisfy such questioning, one must point to special contingencies and partly accidental convergences which together might plausibly be designated as catalytic in their effects. And this can, I think, be done.

What happened, I believe, is that each of the long-term processes already discussed was brought to a critical stage by the years of enormous economic expansion and rapid social change that the United States experienced, and, for the most part, thoughtlessly enjoyed, during the affluent years that followed the close of World War II. And here again the phenomenon can be subdivided for clarity's sake—by reference to five diverse but very familiar sequences.

> (1) The long-developing problems of rampant, unregulated urban growth began to create environmental problems with which American political and fiscal practices could not cope. Problems of management, crime, medical care, education, sanitation, communication, housing, pollution, and transportation made American cities barely capable of sustaining the levels of existence and popular acceptance that are necessary to their viability. This situation had a timetable of its own, moreover, and crises were developing even in cities where race conflict was almost nonexistent.
> (2) Technological developments in agriculture and industry produced migrations of people that led the national electorate to repudiate many of those arrangements that had long maintained the Protestant establishment

and the WASP ascendancy in American life. And what voters did not do, the Supreme Court accomplished. In 1961 a Roman Catholic entered the White House, while Pope John XXIII almost simultaneously began a revolution in the Roman Catholic church which brought the Counter-Reformation to an end and led to a drastic alteration of old interfaith relationships. In 1962 and 1963, respectively, the Court called for reapportionment of legislative districts on a one man-one vote principle and ended the privileged place of Christian religious ceremonies in the public schools. And, most important by far, black America, first in the context of the civil rights movement and then, after 1966, under the banner of Black Power, began to seek rectification of the historic inequalities that had featured its American circumstances.[15] For the first time in American history, in other words, the traumatic implications of true pluralism began to be realized. As a result of these traumas, radical discontent, militancy, and violence became, as never before, everyday features of American life. John Kennedy, Martin Luther King, and Robert Kennedy—all of them men on whom so many pinned their hopes for a better world—were assassinated. For obvious reasons, moreover, the cities were the main focus of attention.

(3) Rapid technological development and widely publicized advancements in science contributed another vital dimension to the national mood. Their impact was enormously increased, moreover, by sensational accomplishments that aroused the popular imagination. The successful trip to the moon, for example, capped a decade of technical triumphs, while heart-transplants dramatized progress in the study of human life. In this way, the cumulative educative effects of television and of vastly expanded enrollments at the college level were suddenly magnified. Man's technical capabilities seemed to have no conceivable bounds. Transcendant reality faded from view.

(4) Less benign achievements, on the other hand, mitigated this essentially humanistic optimism. The Cuban missile crisis, continued nuclear testing, an indecisive series of attempts to achieve international control of nuclear armaments, and the proposal to construct an Anti-Ballistic Missile (ABM) defense system seemed to underline the tentativity of mankind's earthly existence. Nazi extermination camps and American atomic bombs on Japan, writes Robert Jay Lifton, inaugurated a new era in human history—a time in which man is devoid of assurance of living on as a species. His "self-destructive potential" seemed to be without limit. And, in the 1960's, not only was the memory of Auschwitz and Hiroshima renewed, but their implications were interiorized. A "new history" was being shaped.[16]

(5) And, finally, as the supreme catalyst, President Lyndon Johnson began a drastic escalation of the war in Vietnam. This not only prevented an effective assault on the nation's problems of poverty and urban dislocation, but also exposed the terrible inequities of the United States system of military conscription. When coupled with other signs that military considerations were determining American priorities, these policies activated the student movement of dissent and led to an unprecedented loss of confidence in American institutions. With practice so far removed from principle, the entire "system" became suspect.

In the area of religion and morals, the catalytic power of these converging developments has proved to be enormous. The sharp crescendo of social strife seemed to demonstrate that the time-honored structures of

American church life were "irrelevant" to the country's actual condition. To many critical observers, moreover, churchgoing America—both black and white—came to be seen, not as a moral leaven in the land, but as an obstacle to change. Those who believed that the church's mission is to "save souls," and not to save society, were less disturbed by its social irrelevance; but to the mainstream of Kingdom-building, co-operative Protestantism, with its strong social-gospel orientation, the times brought profound and widespread disillusion. Yet, equally grave problems were visited on those who sought only to preach a gospel of salvation to a world of sin. Not only did the universe seem unmindful of man's plight, but man's very achievements—even the educative measures on which so much effort and money were lavished—rather suddenly began to produce an intellectual atmosphere in which traditional belief did not flourish. There seemed to be no place under the sun, or beyond the sun, for a "God who acts."

As the decade of the 1960's draws to a close, dissension rends the country. Where one kind of moral outrage ends, another begins. The profound depths of racism are exposed. Doubts, despair, and moral confusion are endemic. One great portion of the population wonders if a just society can ever be achieved; another portion feels that law-and-order are being needlessly and foolishly sacrificed. Among those "under thirty" and their many allies, a counterculture struggles to be born, with the accent on spontaneity and freedom from dogma—whether theological or social. Yet, militancy in the student movement and among the oppressed threatens to become counterproductive.

Americans, whether conservative, liberal, or radical, find it difficult or impossible to believe that the United States is any longer a beacon and blessing to the world. Even less are they prepared to understand themselves as "chosen" to suffering and servanthood. Amidst fears of genocide and the coming of a police state, a new kind of secular apocalypticism gains strength. In this context, the inducements to nihilism are powerful. Because the national scene looks hopeless, and with so many hopeful leaders prematurely in their graves, the tendency to irrational destructiveness or withdrawn communalism is very strong. In any event, the yearnings that underlie these responses and these temptations provide the ground in which radical theology sends down its roots and draws its nourishment, seeking to bring a measure of transcendence, hope, and community to those who are alienated from technocratic society generally, from the American nation-state in its present orientation, and from outworn forms of religious life and practice. The future of this theology, however, is unknown.

NOTES

[1]Pierre Teilhard de Chardin, *Pantheisme et Christianisme* (Paris, 1923), p. 8.

[2]Dietrich Bonhoeffer, *Letters and Papers from Prison* (New York: The Macmillan Company, 1953), especially the later letters.

[3]See, for example, Schubert M. Ogden, *Christ Without Myth* (New York: Harper & Row, 1961); Paul Van Buren, *The Secular Meaning of the Gospel* (New York: The Macmillan Company, 1963); Thomas J. Altizer and William Hamilton, *Radical Theology and the Death of God* (Indianapolis: Bobbs-Merrill, 1966); Van A. Harvey, *The Historian and the Believer* (New York: The Macmillan Company, 1966); William A. Beardslee, ed., *America and the Future of Theology* (Philadelphia: Westminster Press, 1967); and, as indicative of related matters, William Braden, *The Private Sea: LSD and the Search for God* (New York: Quadrangle Books, 1968). A general essay on American church history which reflects this mood is William A. Clebsch, *From Sacred to Profane America: The Role of Religion in American History* (New York: Harper & Row, 1968).

[4]See E. E. Y. Hales, *Pope John and His Revolution* (Garden City, N.Y.: Doubleday, Image Books, 1966); Edward Wakin and Joseph F. Scheuer, *The De-Romanization of the American Catholic Church* (New York: The Macmillan Company, 1966); Leslie Dewart, *The Future of Belief: Theism in a World Come of Age* (New York: Herder & Herder, 1966).

[5]See Richard Israel's article and the responses printed in *Religion and Community Action* (November-December 1967), published by Community Progress Inc., New Haven, Connecticut. See also Richard Rubenstein, *After Auschwitz* (Indianapolis: Bobbs-Merrill, 1966).

[6]See Edward Farley, *Requiem for a Lost Piety* (Philadelphia: Westminster Press, 1966).

[7]Foreign missions are being prosecuted most vigorously by Jehovah's Witnesses, Pentacostalists, and Fundamentalists—groups that show very limited concern for contemporary intellectual dilemmas and domestic social problems. See William G. McLoughlin, "Is There a Third Force in Christendom," *Daedalus,* vol. 96, no. 1 (Winter 1967), pp. 43-68.

[8]See Joseph Fletcher, *Situation Ethics: The New Morality* (Philadelphia: Westminster Press, 1966); Paul Lehmann, *Ethics in a Christian Context* (New York: Harper & Row, 1963); and Harvey Cox, ed., *The Situation Ethics Debate* (Philadelphia: Westminster Press, 1968). James M. Gustafson provides a masterful statement of the contemporary situation in Christian ethics in *Christ and the Moral Life* (New York: Harper & Row, 1968).

[9]See Theodore Roszak, *The Making of a Counter Culture: Reflections on the Technocratic Society and Its Youthful Opposition* (Garden City, N.Y.: Doubleday, Anchor Books, 1969).

[10]Will Herberg, *Protestant-Catholic-Jew* (Garden City, N.Y.: Doubleday, 1955).

[11]See Andrew M. Greeley, *et al., What Do We Believe?: The Stance of Religion in America* (New York: Meredith Press, 1968).

[12]*The Education of Henry Adams* (Boston: Houghton Mifflin, 1918), p. 500.

[13]See A. C. McGiffert's once-controversial volume, *The Rise of Modern Religious Ideas* (1915), but also Jerry W. Brown, *The Rise of Biblical Criticism in America, 1800-1870* (Middletown, Conn.: Wesleyan University Press, 1969), and Sydney E. Ahlstrom, *The American Protestant Encounter with World Religions* (Beloit, Wis.: Beloit College, 1962).

[14]See Benjamin Nelson, "Conscience, Revolutions, and Weber," *Journal for the Scientific Study of Religion,* 7 (Fall 1968), pp. 157-177, which cites much of the recent literature.

[15]See Francis Broderick and August Meier, eds., *Negro Protest Thought in the Twentieth Century* (Indianapolis: Bobbs-Merrill, 1965); and Stokely Carmichael and Charles V. Hamilton, *Black Power: The Politics of Liberation in America* (New York: Random House, 1967).

[16]Jay Robert Lifton, "Notes on a New History," *The New Journal,* vol. 3, no. 1, September 28, 1969, pp. 5-9.

Related Materials

There are numerous bibliographies concerned with religion in American history as a whole or with one or another aspect of the subject. Nelson R. Burr, *A Critical Bibliography of Religion in America*, 2 vols. (1961) is the most comprehensive. See also Burr's abridged version, available in paperback, *Religion in American Life* (1971). Moses Rischin, *An Inventory of American Jewish History* (1954) and Edward R. Vollmar, *The Catholic Church in America: An Historical Bibliography* (1963) should be consulted as supplementary to it for Jewish and Catholic materials. As a readily available guide to the field, see Edwin S. Gaustad, *Religion in America: History and Historiography* (1973). A comprehensive annotated bibliography of *Blacks in America* (1972) was edited by James M. McPherson et al.

The Introduction to this volume has called attention to the most recent and comprehensive synoptic history of American religion, *A Religious History of the American People* by Sydney E. Ahlstrom (1972, 2 volume paperback ed., 1975). Other broad-gauged treatments are: Edwin S. Gaustad, *A Religious History of America* (1966); Winthrop S. Hudson, *Religion in America* (1965, 1973); and Clifton E. Olmstead, *History of Religion in the United States* (1960). In addition, James W. Smith and A. Leland Jamison (eds.), *The Shaping of American Religion* (1961) is a series of essays which, taken together, constitute a wide-ranging interpretation of American religious history. A contemporary "map" of American religion is offered by Martin E. Marty, *A Nation of Behavers* (1976).

Numerous recent studies have been devoted to major and self-conscious traditions within the religious life of American society. Protestantism in America, the most internally diverse, has been interpreted in a variety of perspectives. The following are prominent among the more widely

457

used studies: Jerald C. Brauer, *Protestantism in America* (1953, 1965); Robert T. Handy, *A Christian America: Protestant Hopes and Historical Realities* (1971); Winthrop S. Hudson, *American Protestantism* (1961); Martin E. Marty, *Righteous Empire: The Protestant Experience in America* (1970); and influential sets of essays by Sidney E. Mead, *The Lively Experiment: The Shaping of Christianity in America* (1963) and *The Nation with the Soul of a Church* (1975). Discussions of American Catholic experience have been offered by John Cogley, *Catholic America* (1973); John Tracy Ellis, *American Catholicism* (1956, 1969); Andrew M. Greeley, *The Catholic Experience: An Interpretation of American Catholicism* (1967); Philip Gleason (ed.), *The Catholic Church in America* (1970); Theodore M. Maynard, *The Story of American Catholicism* (1941); and Thomas T. McAvoy, *A History of the Catholic Church in the United States* (1969). For Judaism in America, the following interpretations have been widely utilized: Joseph Blau, *Judaism in America* (1976); Nathan Glazer, *American Judaism* (1957, 1972); Oscar Handlin, *Adventure in Freedom* (1954); and Jacob Neusner, *American Judaism: Adventure in Modernity* (1972). Religion among Black Americans has been studied in E. Franklin Frazier and C. Eric Lincoln, *The Negro Church/The Black Church since Frazier* (1974); Benjamin E. Mays, *The Negro's God, as Reflected in his Literature* (1938); Benjamin E. Mays and Joseph W. Nicolson, *The Negro's Church* (1933); and Carter G. Woodson, *The History of the Negro Church* (second edition, 1921).

Additional long-term interpretations of one or more aspects of religion in America may be found in William A. Clebsch, *From Sacred to Profane America: The Role of Religion in American History* (1968) and *American Religious Thought: A History* (1973); Edwin S. Gaustad, *Dissent in American Religion* (1973); H. Richard Niebuhr, *The Social Sources of Denominationalism* (1929) and *The Kingdom of God in America* (1935); Russell E. Richey and Donald G. Jones, *American Civil Religion* (1974); Elwyn A. Smith, *The Religion of the Republic* (1971); Ernest Lee Tuveson, *Redeemer Nation* (1968). Hal Bridges, *American Mysticism: From William James to Zen* (1970), and Donald E. Meyer, *The Positive Thinkers* (1965) are also useful.

Collections of source readings which may be useful, many with extensive introductions and headnotes, include the following: Aaron I. Abell, *American Catholic Thought on Social Questions* (1968); Sydney E. Ahlstrom, *Theology in America: The Major Protestant Voices from Puritanism to Neo-Orthodoxy* (1967); Conrad Cherry, *God's New Israel: Religious Interpretations of American Destiny* (1971); Robert D. Cross, *The Church and the City, 1865-1910* (1967); John Tracy Ellis, *Documents of American Catholic History* (1962); Robert T. Handy, *Religion in the American Experience: The Pluralistic Style* (1972); Alan Heimert and Perry Miller, *The Great Awakening* (1967); William R. Hutchinson, *American Protestant Thought: The Liberal Era* (1968); William G. McLoughlin, *The American Evangelicals, 1800-1900* (1968); Perry Miller and Thomas H. Johnson, *The Puritans: A Sourcebook of their Writings* (1963 2nd ed.); Edmund S. Morgan, *Puritan Political Ideas* (1965); Darrett B. Rutman, *The Great Awakening: Event and*

Exegesis (1070); H. Shelton Smith, Robert T. Handy, and Lefferts A. Loetscher, *American Christianity*, 2 vols. (1960-63); John F. Wilson, *Church and State in American History* (1965); and Alden T. Vaughan, *The Puritan Tradition in American, 1620-1730* (1972).

An especially useful research tool is Edwin S. Gaustad, *Historical Atlas of Religion in America* (1962, 1976) which has been supplemented by Douglas W. Johnson, Paul R. Picard, and Bernard Quinn, *Churches and Church Membership in the United States* (1974).